CONTENTS

Foreword by Mary Robinson   v

Preface   vii

Acknowledgments   ix

1 The Government and the Taoiseach   1

2 Ministers and their Departments   35

3 The Dáil and the Seanad   67

4 The Constitution of Ireland   114

5 The President of Ireland   136

6 The Civil Service   158

7 The Judiciary, Courts and Legal Officers   200

8 Local Government   227

9 State Agencies and Bodies   259

10 The Health Services   290

11 Appeals and Inquiries   333

12 The Impact of the European Union   390

13 The Management of Government   434

References   487

Index   513

FOREWORD

The system of government operating in a country is of fundamental importance in that it facilitates the achievement by a people of their aims and aspirations at local, regional, national and international levels. Article 21 of the Universal Declaration of Human Rights recognises that:

(1) Everyone has the right to take part in the government of his country, directly or through freely chosen representatives.
(2) Everyone has the right of equal access to public service in his country.
(3) The will of the people shall be the basis of the authority of government; this will shall be expressed in periodic and genuine elections which shall be by universal and equal suffrage and shall be held by secret vote or by equivalent free voting procedures.

As we mark the sixtieth anniversary of the Universal Declaration, I welcome the publication of the third edition of *Irish Government Today*.

The strength and capacity of the architecture of the system of government is essential to the proper functioning of a democracy. Ireland's membership of the European Union and of the United Nations has exposed the machinery of government to a range of direct and indirect interactions with counterpart organisations in other European countries and more widely across the globe. It has encouraged Ireland to become outward looking and extrovert and to play a constructive role among the nations of the world. In a rapidly changing and complex world, with vast flows of instantaneous information, there is a strong need for citizenship education to promote understanding of the system of government, to facilitate access to public services, to encourage voter participation, to highlight civic rights and responsibilities, to encourage participation in local government and community activities, to understand the decision-making process and to sustain our democratic system.

This third edition sets out in clear and straightforward terms how the machinery of government operates in Ireland. There has been a sea-change in the way in which our public services have been organised, structured and delivered in the past twenty years. The book charts the transformation in the operation of the government at central level, the review and amendment of the Constitution, the impact of information technology, developments in the civil service, the growth of agencies, the changes in local government and the emphasis on greater efficiency and effectiveness.

This text provides a clear picture of the various arms of government and makes a serious contribution to citizenship education. It is a useful reference book for anyone interested in or trying to understand Irish government today.

Mary Robinson
President, Realizing Rights: The Ethical Globalization Initiative
Former United Nations High Commissioner for Human Rights
Former President of Ireland

PREFACE

The world is changing rapidly as a result of the new international division of work, the development of new economic powers, the continuing turbulence in financial markets and the global economic downturn. In Ireland, globalisation, major demographic changes including an ageing population, concerns about international competitiveness, the need for sustainable development, and rapid technological advances all impact on the work of the public service. Diversity is both a challenge and an opportunity facing the public service in terms of professional equality between the genders, the inclusion and integration of people of foreign origin and the access of disabled persons to employment and services. To keep pace with these changing realities, the Irish public service must continue to be flexible and responsive to change. All levels of government face these challenges.

This thoroughly revised and updated edition reflects the extensive changes that have taken place in recent years in the Irish system of government. The task of the government is to run the country and the public service plays a central role alongside ministers in that task. This book provides information on the institutions of government, the central departments, local authorities, state bodies and health services. It describes the operation of government in practice and includes a great deal of information not hitherto published about cabinet procedures, the appointment and responsibilities of ministers, private offices, political advisers, the election and work of TDs, the whips' offices, the work of the Dáil and the Seanad, and what civil servants do. It sets out the provisions of the Constitution and discusses the functions of the President. There is a description of the informal and formal means by which people may seek redress from the actions of public bodies, which gives insights into the 'representations' system and the use of parliamentary questions. The influence of EU membership on the work of government and the public service is also examined, and the book concludes by exploring a number of current issues including management practices and techniques as well as public service reform. Issues such as strategic management, parliamentary procedures, the management of EU business, freedom of information and developments in information technology are addressed throughout.

The book is aimed primarily at third-level students in a number of faculties, especially those studying politics, public administration and management, law, commerce, social science, journalism, marketing and business studies. It will, of course, be of interest and use to a wide variety of other general readers, such as public servants and those working with the public service; trade union officials, politicians, journalists and other commentators on public affairs; persons in agriculture, business and the professions who have dealings with the public service; and those working in international organisations who want reliable and up-to-date information on government in Ireland.

Any views expressed are entirely personal and do not reflect the views of any organisation. The author can be contacted by e-mail at the following address: johnotoole@europe.com.

ACKNOWLEDGMENTS

This book is dedicated to the memory of Sean Dooney, who was the co-author with me of the first and second editions. Sean was a colleague, a good friend and a mentor. He was born in Charlestown, County Mayo in 1924 and educated at St Nathy's College, Ballaghaderreen and Trinity College, Dublin from which he graduated with the degrees of MA and MLitt. He joined the civil service in 1942 and spent his entire career in the Department of Agriculture, retiring from the position of assistant secretary in 1989. He was vice-chairperson of the Institute of Public Administration (IPA), chairperson of its education committee and for many years lectured part-time in the IPA to students taking various courses. The IPA published his first book, *The Irish Civil Service*, in 1976 and he went on to author numerous articles and papers on the public service in Ireland. Married with four children, he pursued interests in music, sport, theatre and, in retirement, politics. He died in July 2004. I would like to thank and acknowledge the support of Sean's wife, Clodagh, for this third edition.

I would like to thank former President Mary Robinson, who wrote the foreword in recognition of the fact that, sixty years after the Universal Declaration of Human Rights, there is still much to be done to make rights an everyday reality for millions around the globe. I would like to thank Joseph O'Connor for permission to reproduce his *Clientelism Rap*, which was originally broadcast on RTÉ Radio One's *Drivetime* programme on 17 September 2008. I would also like to thank Frances Lawlor of the Institute of Public Administration, who was instrumental in providing the inspiration to bring forward this third edition.

I gratefully acknowledge the immense amount of encouragement, advice and information received from many friends and colleagues in the civil and public service who read chapters and made suggestions, and who, in accordance with the best traditions of the public service, remain anonymous. I wish to thank the information officers, librarians and receptionists who are the first line of contact with many public service agencies and who provide such excellent help and assistance to all those seeking practical assistance and information about the machinery of government.

I would like to thank the team at Gill & Macmillan for their professionalism at every stage. Marion O'Brien, Emma Farrell and Aoife

O'Kelly were excellent and great to work with. Special thanks are given to the editor Jennifer Armstrong, whose skill contributed enormously to the finished work.

Thanks also to Barbara, who read many of the chapters. Above all, I appreciate the support of Patricia, who so agreeably accorded 'the book' the priority it warranted.

John O'Toole
May 2009

1

THE GOVERNMENT AND THE TAOISEACH

Structure and Scope of the Government

The Constitution acknowledges that all powers of government derive, under God, from the people, whose right it is to designate the rulers of the state; that the state is to be governed in accordance with the provisions of the Constitution; that the executive power of the state is exercised by or on the authority of the government; and that the government is responsible to the Dáil. The government consists of not less than seven and not more than fifteen members. It is frequently referred to as the cabinet, though this term does not appear in the Constitution. The members are selected by the Taoiseach, and in the case of a coalition government by agreement between the leaders of the parties involved, and appointed by the President. No specific qualifications, beyond membership of the Oireachtas, are prescribed for membership of the government, but it is generally accepted that, in the selection of ministers, considerations of general ability, suitability for particular portfolios, personal popularity, service to or standing in the party and geographical location are matters taken into account. The Taoiseach may request a minister to resign, and if he or she refuses to do so, the President, on the advice of the Taoiseach, must terminate the minister's appointment.

The government meets and acts as a collective authority and is collectively responsible for the departments of state. The Constitution contains no specification regarding the number of departments (this depends largely on the preferences of individual Taoisigh), and if there are more than fifteen at any time, individual ministers are assigned responsibility for more than one department. The Taoiseach and the Tánaiste, as well as the Minister for Finance, must be members of the Dáil; the other members of the government must be members of the Dáil or the Seanad, but not more than two may be members of the latter body. (Since the foundation of the state there have, in fact, been only three appointments of senators to the government: Joseph Connolly in 1932, Seán Moylan in 1957 and James Dooge in 1981.) Every member of the government has the right to attend and be heard in each House of the Oireachtas. On the dissolution of the Dáil, ministers continue to carry on their duties and hold office until their successors are appointed.

In addition to its general provision that the government is the chief executive organ of the state, the Constitution contains express provisions relating to the powers, duties and functions of the government in certain matters. For example, in relation to the public finances, the Minister for Finance presents the estimates to the Dáil after detailed consultation with the other members of the government, and it is the government that has final control over the form and amounts of the estimates, as well as the responsibility for them. The Dáil may not authorise the spending of money for any purpose unless such spending has first been authorised by the government and recommended to the Dáil by the Taoiseach.

The distribution of business between the government departments and the designation of members of the government to be the ministers in charge of particular departments are matters governed by law. The law is contained in the various Ministers and Secretaries Acts, the earliest of which was passed in 1924 and the most recent in 2007, which increased from seventeen to twenty the number of ministers of state that may be appointed by the government. The 1924 act designated the eleven departments then set up and indicated the work allocated to each. It provided that the minister in charge of each department would be a *corporation sole*, i.e. that the minister could sue and be sued as a corporate entity rather than as an individual. Subsequent acts provide for the setting up of new departments and outline their work. Under the Public Service Management Act 1997 managerial responsibility for the department is assigned to the secretary general, while the minister remains responsible for the administration of the department.

The harp is used as the emblem of the state by the government, its agencies and its representatives at home and abroad. It is the principal element of the seals of the office of President and of all government ministers. The harp is also found on the obverse of euro coins minted in Ireland. It has been used as a national symbol for over five hundred years.

The Work of the Government

In addition to the Ministers and Secretaries Acts, there are various acts that confer functions and powers on the government. For example, the government appoints the Data Protection Commissioner, members of the Review Body on Higher Remuneration in the Public Sector, the chairpersons of some state-sponsored bodies, senior officers of An Garda Síochána and the members of the Higher Education Authority and it decides on applications by barristers to become members of the inner bar and to be designated senior counsel. As the chief executive organ of the state, the government also has a considerable amount of work to do besides that which is specifically conferred on it either by the Constitution or by statute. This work includes such diverse duties as considering applications for increases in air fares, allocating emergency aid to groups affected by natural disaster, appointing army officers, approving cultural agreements with countries abroad, refurbishing government buildings and considering visits to Ireland by foreign heads of state.

A major task, which impinges on every citizen, is the consideration of the advice and recommendations of the officials in the Department of Finance and the Office of the Revenue Commissioners relating to the total tax revenue for the year ahead. Within this total, the government decides on the changes to be made in the rates and scope of individual taxes and also on the introduction of new taxes or the abolition of existing ones. Factors that the government takes into account include the estimated expenditure on what are called goods and services for the year ahead, the level of Exchequer borrowing and the desirability of reducing this, the estimates of tax revenue based on existing rates, the effects on the economy and the individual sectors thereof of increasing or decreasing individual rates, the need for equity between the various groups in the community, EU requirements in regard to reduction in rates of value added tax and of excise duties, and political commitments made by the parties in government before an election or as part of a post-election government programme in regard to taxation matters. Such matters are considered by the government over a number of meetings, and the final decisions are announced by the Minister for Finance during the budget speech.

The government is the centre of the administrative system in Ireland. In a sense it is Ireland's board of directors: formulating policies, promoting legislation and directing the operations of the various departments of state. Farrell (1988b: 42) describes the cabinet as a 'closed group . . . bound together by shared experience . . . indisputably in charge of the executive organs of the state and usually able to push through its own legislative programme'.

The Public Services Organisation Review Group elaborated on the role of government in its 1969 report (known as the Devlin report):

> In addition to the basic functions of defence of the nation against outside aggression and maintenance of law and order, the role of government now embraces the provision of adequate health, education and welfare services. It also embraces the provision of environmental services and assistance of cultural activities. Government must exercise some regulatory function in regard to individual enterprise and ensure that the rights of the individual are exercised with due regard to the general good. It encourages economic activity in the private sector, and there are certain activities which it has undertaken itself.
>
> The government has two main tasks. First, it has to run the country, under the Constitution in accordance with the rules laid down by the Oireachtas and

with the resources granted by, and accounted for to, the Oireachtas each year. Secondly, it deals in the Oireachtas with changes affecting the community . . . Through its legislative programme (including financial measures) the government exercises its main influence over the future development of the country; thereby it influences the economy and the structure of society. Acting collectively, the ministers decide what is needed and how it should be achieved; their decisions depend on the quality of the information available to them and on their assessment of the requirements. They will, of course, become aware of these requirements in several ways – through their political machine, through the press and through the representations of the interests concerned – but, primarily, they will need to know the emerging needs of the community through the public service which operates existing programmes.

When Dr Garret FitzGerald formed his first coalition government in 1981 he announced the appointment of Mr Alexis Fitzgerald as special adviser to the government, with the right to attend government meetings. In 1994 Taoiseach John Bruton allowed one minister of state (Pat Rabbitte) to attend cabinet meetings. This post became known as the 'super junior' minister of state. The Taoiseach outlined this role to the Dáil as follows:

The Minister of State to the Government attends Government meetings in the same way as the Government Chief Whip. He receives all Government papers and participates in discussions at Cabinet. Like the Government Chief Whip and the Attorney General, he is not entitled to vote should an occasion arise where that would be necessary. However, as this Government is committed to conducting its business on the basis of consensus, the fact that the Minister of State does not have a vote at Cabinet does not have any real significance (*Dáil Debates*, 25 January 1995, vol. 448).

In the Fianna Fáil/Progressive Democrats coalition government formed in 1997, then Minister of State at the Department of the Environment, Robert Molloy, was given similar treatment in order to give the Progressive Democrats a second presence at cabinet meetings. In 2005 Brian Lenihan assumed the role of 'super junior' Minister for Children, Brendan Smith was appointed to a similar position in 2007, as was Barry Andrews in 2008. The post of minister of state was created in 1977 to replace an older post of parliamentary secretary. There were ten minister of state posts in 1977; this number increased to fifteen in 1980, seventeen in 1995, twenty in 2007; it was reduced to fifteen in 2009.

Legislation

Ministerial proposals that call for new or amending legislation must always be submitted to the government. If approval is given, the papers are sent to the Attorney General's office, where a bill is drafted by the office of the parliamentary counsel. The bill (at this stage known as a 'white print') is submitted to the government to approve the text and to authorise the minister concerned to present it to the Dáil (or Seanad) and have it circulated to members.

Before the government brings forward any legislation, it may publish a green paper (a document setting out its proposals and inviting suggestions thereon) or a white paper (a statement of decisions taken). Any such papers are prepared in the promoting department. Bills (other than those dealing with budgetary matters or estimates) are usually, when published, accompanied by an explanatory statement outlining the existing law and how the new bill proposes to change it.

The government has great power and influence in the system. Mitchell (2003: 241) notes:

> Irish governments (at least majority governments) have not been heavily constrained or monitored by other institutions and agencies, least of all by Parliament. It is tempting to conclude that the Irish political system has been strong on delegation and weak on accountability. While the system generally appears to have been quite successful, the recent and ongoing attempts at reform need to constrain agents and hold them accountable for their actions in government.

Other Business

The government agenda also includes matters that ministers consider it advisable to bring to their colleagues' notice. For example, the Minister for Foreign Affairs will communicate information on political developments abroad and their consequences; or the Minister for Justice will inform colleagues about criminal matters. Among the many items regularly laid before the government for scrutiny are the annual reports and accounts of state-sponsored bodies before their presentation to the Oireachtas.

Farrell (1988b: 76) comments:

> The available evidence . . . suggests a considerable degree of overload in the Irish cabinet system. The complex, the controversial and the insoluble compete with the current, the commonplace and the critical for scarce time and attention on the government agenda. The internal problems of Northern Ireland, the latest transport strike, the painful disciplines of controlling public expenditure, the dismissal of a postman, the effects of technical developments in the EC policies, the appointment of a Supreme Court judge, the timing of a by-election, the detailed discussion of major legislation and a myriad of other things crowd out considerations of longer-term strategic planning.

There are also what are loosely termed 'twelve o'clock' or informal items. The phrase derives from an arrangement whereby the government sets aside time for consideration of matters that are not on the formal agenda which a minister wishes to raise informally and which may be dealt with quickly, for example any matters of current topical interest. Ministers also use this procedure to consult their colleagues informally as to the attitude they should take in relation to matters that come to them for decision on a day-to-day basis in the management of their departments but which might not be regarded as suitable for submission to the government in the normal manner. Ministers may also wish to signal in advance problems that have arisen in their respective areas and in relation to which they may be submitting formal proposals at a later date. Matters thus mentioned might include strikes or pay disputes, petrol prices, proposals for visits abroad on St Patrick's Day, meetings with deputations or the attitude to be taken on a private member's bill. Business initiated in this way is rarely the subject of a formal government decision, but any informal decisions are conveyed by the government secretariat to the relevant ministerial offices, usually by telephone.

Government Meetings

Cabinet meetings are usually held weekly on Tuesday mornings but sometimes take place on Wednesday when the Dáil is not sitting. They last for about two and a half hours in Government Buildings, Upper Merrion Street, Dublin. Attendance is confined to the members of the government, the Government Chief Whip (see page 26), the Attorney General and the Secretary General to the Government. On occasion, however, other persons such as ministers of state or civil servants may be called in to assist in the discussion of specific matters. FitzGerald (2003: 50) notes that the Attorney General at cabinet will, where appropriate, express a view on the constitutionality or otherwise of amendments, and few governments will take the risk of ignoring such advice.

The unique aspect of the cabinet is that it acts as a forum for ministers to meet weekly in person to discharge their collective responsibility. There is no quorum for meetings, and in any case voting is not common. The government secretariat co-ordinates all the proposed business and prepares the agenda for each meeting. Meetings take place in the cabinet room. The original cabinet room (known as the council chamber from the days of the Executive Council of the Irish Free State) has been refurbished so that ministers and officials can avail of a full range of communications equipment to obtain any up-to-date or additional information they need during the meeting.

> The procedure at Cabinet meetings is that the Secretary of the Government carefully rea   the minutes of the previous Cabinet meeting. The normal

practice in any Government of which I was a member is that Ministers listen at least to the minutes that refer to their Departments and are conscious of what is said about any decisions in that regard so that they can pick up on anything that may be wrong in the minutes. They may wish to comment on a decision or it might jog their minds to do something if they had not done it (Deputy Bertie Ahern, *Dáil Debates*, 21 November 1996, vol. 471).

Because of the volume of business with which the government has to deal, the agenda for its meetings is always heavy. Sometimes there may be up to thirty items for consideration. To enable the members of the government to assimilate material quickly and thoroughly, a detailed procedure is laid down for the submission by departments of issues for decision. This procedure is set out in a booklet entitled the 'Cabinet Handbook', which is prepared in the Department of the Taoiseach.

The Cabinet Handbook is primarily concerned with the procedures for the conduct of business at cabinet meetings. It is effectively the standing orders of the cabinet. It replaces the earlier 'Government Procedure Instructions' and is available on the website of the Department of the Taoiseach. The Cabinet Handbook was first produced in October 1998 and has been amended subsequently as required. An Irish language version was produced in May 2001. The handbook sets out the guidelines for appropriate behaviour for office-holders. It contains detailed and clear guidelines on ethical matters under the Ethics in Public Office Act 1995. Some of the guidelines are incorporated in law, others are on a more informal basis. All cabinet members are bound by the rules, which are internal to the cabinet. The handbook sets out the general guidelines for ministers on areas including collective responsibility, access to records, ethical and related matters, visits outside the state, delegation of functions, transfer of functions, personal staff and staffing of private and constituency offices.

In relation to collective responsibility, it provides that, in order not to prejudice government discussions, ministers and ministers of state should avoid making public statements or commenting on specific policy proposals that are to be brought to government or that are under consideration by government. For example, only in exceptional circumstances would it be appropriate to disclose the fact that a particular matter is due for consideration at a specific government meeting. Similarly the details of what is recommended to government should not be divulged. In both instances, prior disclosure may limit the government's options to have consideration of a matter postponed or withdrawn or to amend the proposal.

The government is concerned with strategy and policy – not necessarily with operational detail. The handbook sets out detailed instructions for the preparation and submission of memoranda for government, including the layout and content requirements for memoranda concerning international agreements, annual reports and accounts. The handbook requires that a regulatory impact analysis (RIA) must accompany any proposal seeking approval for a change to the regulatory framework, including the transposition of EU directives and regulations. The steps to be conducted in carrying out an RIA are set out in the handbook. RIA was formally introduced in June 2005. It applies to all proposals for primary legislation involving changes to the regulatory framework, significant statutory instruments and proposals for EU directives. A review of RIA (Goggin and Lauder 2008) found that good progress had been made but that the process needs to be embedded earlier in the policy development process. For many legislative proposals, no specific, significant implications have been identified under RIA guidelines.

Every item of business must be the subject of a memorandum from the minister concerned. Its format is rigidly prescribed. The first paragraph should outline what is being requested of the government. This may be the authority to initiate legislation; to establish, modify or abolish some programme; to bring forward for consideration an entirely new policy option; to note developments in some areas of national importance; or to make a statutory instrument. Then comes the background information, and, in cases requiring substantive action, an account of the problem, the solution being put forward and the arguments for and against. The costs and staffing implications are then indicated, as well as the views of other ministers concerned, together with any counterviews of the promoting minister. The rule is that memoranda should be as brief as possible and not discursive, and that detailed material should be supplied in appendices. The aim is that memoranda should not exceed ten pages, and, where they do, they should be accompanied by a brief self-contained summary of the proposals, with the arguments for and against.

Thirty copies of each memorandum are sent by the private secretary of the promoting minister to the Secretary General to the Government. These must reach the latter not less than three days before the meetings at which they are to be considered. At the same time, a copy is sent to the offices of the ministers consulted during the drafting. The need for consultation with ministers directly concerned and the requirement for consultation with the Department of the Taoiseach, the Department of Finance and the Attorney General's office are clearly outlined in the Cabinet Handbook. If a draft memorandum is likely to be of interest to ministers generally – apart from their purely departmental responsibilities – all other members of the government may be furnished with the memorandum. Except in the case of complex issues, departments are reasonably requested to provide their obser-vations on draft memoranda within two weeks (ten working days) of receipt. Departments are not asked to provide observations within a shorter time limit unless it is absolutely essential and, even then, the maximum time possible should be allowed. If, for any reason, the minister has not been able to approve departmental views, the views should be clearly identified as being those of the department.

In order to avoid wasting the government's time in seeking to reconcile differences, departments aim to evaluate arguments as comprehensively as possible and the maximum degree of agreement between ministers and between departments is established prior to the submission of memoranda. Ministers and secretaries general are asked to involve themselves personally in sorting out, as far as possible, not only policy differences, but differences relating to administration, staffing, legal and constitutional implications, before memoranda are submitted to the government. In the cases of differences of opinion between departments after the submission of a memorandum to the government, the Secretary General to the Government is informed at once with a view to consulting the Taoiseach.

Where there is disagreement on the merits of a proposal, the minister concerned is asked to consider its modification. Where ministers disagree, the matter may be referred to a sub-committee of the government for resolution. If disagreement persists, it may be necessary to have a decision reached by vote. No record of any such vote is kept other than its outcome. Gemma Hussey (1990: 12), a former Minister for Education, said that the Department of Finance 'rarely agreed to any spending proposal and fought the battles at full cabinet'. Cabinet proceedings are strictly confidential, and the principle of collective responsibility applies to decisions taken. In this connection, an amendment to the Constitution was enacted in 1997 providing that the confidentiality of discussions at government should be preserved except where the High Court rules that disclosure should be made either (a) in the administration of justice or (b) on foot of an application by a tribunal of inquiry.

On occasion, a minister may wish to have a matter considered at a particular government meeting but it may not be possible to have the memorandum finalised in time to meet the specified deadline. In such circumstances a certificate of urgency is signed by a senior official stating why the matter is urgent and why the memorandum could not be ready by the prescribed time. The reasons must be good if they are to result in such an item being accepted, ultimately by the Taoiseach, as urgent.

If a minister is unable to attend a government meeting, his or her private secretary is obliged to inform the government secretariat as soon as possible and to state whether any other minister is to be briefed to deal with any item on the agenda that is of relevance to the absent minister's department.

Immediately after meetings the Secretary General to the Government transmits the decisions relating to particular departments to the private secretaries of the ministers concerned so that they may be acted on depart-mentally. Departments are advised of cabinet decisions by the Department of the Taoiseach through the distribution of pink slips by army motorcyclists. It is the responsibility of individual ministers to ensure that such decisions are implemented at the earliest practicable date. In this connection, the government secretariat prepares at regular intervals a schedule of outstanding decisions, indicating the current position in each case. This schedule enables the Taoiseach to monitor progress and to raise any major deviations from targets with colleagues.

The normal practice is that ministers are personally involved in any follow-up after government meetings. They brief the secretary general and senior officials on their return to the department, or give instructions for action to be taken on the decisions made. Following the controversy sur-rounding the implementation of a government decision on the de-listing of Judge Dominic Lynch from the Special Criminal Court in 1996, detailed arrangements were put in place to monitor the implementation of cabinet decisions. These arrangements require weekly reporting between the secretaries general and the assistant secretaries of departments to ensure that decisions taken by the government are acted upon immediately and that implementation difficulties, if any, are promptly identified.

The role of the cabinet and the way it structures its business is centrally important in the effective management of the political and administrative system. Whelan *et al.* (2003: 128) comment that 'there is a need for clear lines of responsibility from cabinet to ministers, ministers of state and officials'. In relation to cabinet meetings Dunlop (2004: 88–9) states:

> There was then, and perhaps still is, a certain mystique about what happens at cabinet meetings, and politicians love to give the impression that momentous discussions take place before decisions are arrived at. The theory is that they read the voluminous material that is circulated by the cabinet secretariat and then have an informed debate. In my experience, for the simple reason that there just aren't enough hours in the day to read everything, most of this material was ignored. When a particular issue was raised at cabinet, everybody looked to the relevant minister for his or her view – or more accurately, the views of his or her department – and voted accordingly. The cabinet merely gives its imprimatur to decisions that have already been taken elsewhere, mainly in the line departments, after consultation with the relevant minister, who then brings them as *faits accomplis* to his or her colleagues. Rarely does it happen that a minister would find himself or herself in a position where the cabinet would overturn a decision already approved. Rarely are there major rows. Everything is usually smoothed out in advance between the departmental secretaries, and any compromises are signalled well in advance.

Dunlop (2004: 87) recalls looking at his first cabinet agenda:

. . . in amazement. It contained nothing more than requests to authorize the publication of various Annual Reports of state and semi-state bodies and attached these huge wordy reports as addenda. There was nothing relating to government policy on anything, no matter how innocuous. When I brought this to his [Secretary to the Government's] attention, he merely laughed and said that I would learn in due course that the most important matters were never put on the agenda and that in some instances the most important issues of all were never recorded.

I did indeed learn that there was absolutely nothing on an agenda to indicate what might happen at a cabinet meeting. The items listed would be dealt with in a very short time, and it was then that the real business of government took place.

As explained above, cabinet minutes record only the decisions taken. In 1976 Taoiseach Liam Cosgrave instituted a policy of releasing, for inspection by the public, cabinet minutes and supporting records that were more than thirty years old. With the passing of the Archives Act 1985, there is now a statutory obligation to make such minutes available for public inspection in the National Archives, the body which replaced the State Paper Office and Public Record Office. The Freedom of Information Act 1997, section 19, as amended by the 2003 act, section 14, provides that government records (for example memoranda for government, ministerial briefing papers and advisory papers, but not discussions at cabinet) be withheld from access for ten years. These papers are released after ten years. This came into operational effect on 21 April 2008. Information concerning actual discussions (as distinct from decisions) at government meetings is constitutionally exempt from disclosure under the acts.

In recent years the government has adopted a practice of allocating some of its time to theme discussions, concentrating on particular policy areas for more in-depth analysis and discussion of possible policy solutions. This allows a more serious and reflective consideration of a policy area, taking it out of the restrictive framework of the public financial estimates cycle and facilitating a 'whole-of-government' approach. The government has also held cabinet meetings on a regional basis from time to time. Speaking in the Dáil on 5 December 2001 Taoiseach Bertie Ahern stated, 'I do not agree that cabinet meetings held outside Dublin are public relations initiatives. There is no harm in having meetings outside Dublin. In many ways it is good for members of a cabinet to see what is outside the Pale.'

Cabinet Sub-committees

Cabinet sub-committees comprise small groups of key ministers who specifically discuss priority policy areas of significant national importance.

Cabinet sub-committees are an increasingly important part of the modern machinery of government and have been established on science and technology; justice; health; social inclusion; and climate change. The committees meet a number of times each year.

E-cabinet

Significant progress has been made on implementing the e-cabinet system, which has been in operation for all departments since June 2004. There are four aspects to this initiative:

- Electronic distribution and management of cabinet papers.
- Use of technologies to improve presentation of complex issues at cabinet.
- Use of technologies in direct support of cabinet meetings.
- Creation of new information resources.

Initially consultants were engaged between 2000 and 2002 on an e-cabinet feasibility study to identify opportunities to apply technologies to the cabinet process in consultation with key stakeholders. Working closely with the cabinet secretariat, the consultants set out a model for an electronic cabinet system and identified considerable associated benefits. The report of the consultants (PricewaterhouseCoopers 2001) drew on the experiences of key stakeholders, including ministers and secretaries general. It placed particular emphasis on the scope for electronic management of cabinet papers. For example, it proposed that memoranda for government, the cabinet agenda and government decisions would be disseminated electronically. The adoption of this proposal has resulted in greater speed and efficiency in the process. Another important aspect of the initiative was that document structures were examined so that complex proposals might be presented more effectively at cabinet. This involved changes in the structure of memoranda for government to present key data up front, the use of embedded audio-visual material where that is helpful and enhancements of a similar type.

The e-cabinet initiative deploys modern technologies to assist departments in the preparation of memoranda for government and related matters. The new system involves built-in screens, which are fitted neatly into the cabinet table using recessed and slanted screens. Among the benefits of the system are a secure network for electronic transmission of these documents, improved facilities for inter-departmental consultation on proposals for cabinet, and electronic transmission of cabinet decisions. Ministers are able to monitor decisions coming before cabinet. Departments are able to manage documents more quickly and efficiently in a secure electronic environment to improve cross-departmental co-ordination of policy proposals. McCarthy (2005: 15) states that the e-cabinet project 'has fundamentally improved the efficiency of the process by which memoranda are prepared, circulated and submitted to cabinet'.

Documents were redesigned to make them more accessible on screen. This impacted on all users but especially on ministers, who have the option of dispensing with some or all of the existing paper-based memoranda in favour of screen-based ones. The consultants found that large volumes of paper (in excess of 1.2 million A4 sheets) were being processed every year, with ministers bringing on average 4.75 kilograms of paper to a typical cabinet meeting. The challenge was not just to make documents available electronically at cabinet meetings, but to present them in a way that over-comes the difficulties normally associated with reading lengthy documents on screen. The report envisaged the use of web-enabled documents to address this. Additionally, the technology deployed at the cabinet table supported functions other than accessing cabinet documents. For example, ministers can send and receive e-mail during meetings, and departmental briefing is also provided online for each minister. The introduction of technologies to the cabinet table was carried out in a way that respects the culture within which those meetings take place, specifically that they do not dominate the human interactions, which are fundamental to the process.

There are 5,400 civil servants registered to use the e-cabinet system across the civil service, with access rights appropriate to their responsibilities. In the twelve-month period from November 2004 approximately 25,000 draft electronic documents were securely circulated using the system. Previously each of these transactions would have involved a printed copy of each document being delivered by hand either within a department or between departments. The system applies to all departments and virtually all govern-ment memoranda, with just a few that may come in late falling outside the process. The system provides instant secure transmission within departments.

Incorporeal Meetings

Apart from the formal meetings, there are, on occasion, what are termed incorporeal meetings. These meetings relate to the conduct of unforeseen business that is so urgent as to require a decision before the next ordinary government meeting. It is business of a type that does not require substantive discussion and is extremely unlikely to provoke disagreement. An incor-poreal meeting could be held if it were necessary, for example, to clear some routine report with a publication deadline, to finalise a decision on a matter discussed earlier or to approve the urgent departure from the country of the President to attend, say, a funeral abroad.

The procedure in such cases is that the minister concerned prepares a brief note on the matter at issue, which is circulated by the government secretariat to all ministers available, together with a notification that an incorporeal meeting will be held to discuss the matter at a specified time. In practice, what then happens is that the Secretary General to the Government telephones all the ministers available at that time to get their agreement to what is proposed. The meeting is formally recorded as having taken place with the Taoiseach, Tánaiste or most senior government member available as chairperson. A high-profile incorporeal meeting was held on 30 September 2008 to introduce the bank guarantee scheme in response to the global financial crisis. Minister for Defence Willie O'Dea (2008) wrote:

> There are few commonplace sounds more likely to bring a chill to the heart than the unexpected sound of a phone ringing in the small hours of the morning. So it was around 1am last Tuesday morning when I woke to hear my phone ringing. Though it had stopped ringing by the time I reached it, no sooner had I located the source of the missed call than it started ringing again. Within seconds of answering I was in touch with the Cabinet secretariat and my Cabinet colleagues.

Collective Responsibility

Collective cabinet responsibility is a fundamental principle underlying the operation of Irish government, as referred to in Article 28.4.2° of the Constitution. It results in all ministers being obliged to support government actions and policies regardless of their personal opinions or private feelings. Thus, the cabinet is collectively responsible for public policy, and the policy programmes of individual ministers must complement it. Once a cabinet decision is taken, it reflects the decision of all the ministers.

Cabinet responsibility is achieved through a combination of three principles:

1. *The confidence principle:* a cabinet will continue in office so long as it maintains the confidence of a majority in the Dáil.
2. *The unanimity principle:* because confidence rests in a cabinet, that is to say a collective body, the decisions of the cabinet must be presented as unanimous ones – the only way to record dissent from a government decision is to resign.
3. *The confidentiality principle:* discussions in cabinet about government decisions are absolutely confidential. Cabinet confidentiality supports the unanimity principle and in turn supports the confidence principle and is a feature of European cabinet government.

In practice, a minister may, on occasion, be fundamentally opposed to a decision but may not wish to make that opposition public. If a minister is unable to accept a decision, wishes to be distanced from it in public or feels obliged to explain his or her point of view in public, then the question of resignation must be seriously considered. Occasions have arisen when ministers have expressed fundamental opposition in public and have not resigned. James Gibbons, Minister for Agriculture, made his opposition to the Family Planning Bill 1979 public, but did not resign. Nor did then Taoiseach Liam Cosgrave or Minister for Education Richard Burke resign after voting against the Control of Importation, Sale and Manufacture of Contraceptives Bill 1974, introduced in the Dáil by the Minister for Justice in the cabinet of which they were all members. On the other hand, Frank Cluskey, Minister for Trade, Commerce and Tourism, did resign in December 1983 in opposition to government proposals in regard to the Dublin Gas Company.

Considerable efforts are made to achieve consensus at cabinet. Then Taoiseach Seán Lemass, in an interview in the *Irish Press* (3–4 February 1960), said it is 'the job of the Taoiseach to keep a team of ministers who are all individuals with their own personal characteristics working in harmony and ultimately emerging with agreement upon every matter put before them'. In 1972 the Review Body on Higher Remuneration in the Public Sector, in its consideration of the role and functions of various office-holders, commented, 'We regard as of paramount importance the collective responsibility of ministers, as members of the government, for the business of the government, i.e. the formulation of national policy and its execution subject to the approval of the Oireachtas. No greater or more complex task and no more important task for the well-being of the people faces any other body or group in the country.'

Murphy (2005) comments, 'I suspect that the Constitutional concept of collective responsibility has been diminished by the Office of Taoiseach becoming more akin to an executive Head of State. The original concept of collective responsibility was developed at a time when a Prime Minister was seen as *primus inter pares* and when, as I recall it, there was much more robust debate between individual Ministers.' Undoubtedly, the Taoiseach plays a central role in the system, with a supporting role for the cabinet.

Ministers' Obligations

Should an occasion arise where a minister or a member of a minister's family has an interest in a matter before the government for decision, there is an obligation on that minister to bring this to notice before the matter comes up for discussion. Unless the government decides otherwise, the minister concerned may not take part in the discussion or vote on the issue, or seek to influence the attitude of other members of the government.

In so far as business interests or membership of other organisations is concerned, the basic rule is that a minister should not engage in any activity that could reasonably be regarded as interfering or being incompatible with the proper discharge of the duties of his or her office. Ministers may not hold company directorships carrying remuneration. Even if remuneration is not paid, it is regarded as undesirable for a government minister to hold a directorship. A resigning director may, however, enter into an agreement with a company to be reappointed as a director on the termination of his or her public office. Similarly ministers are not permitted to carry on a professional practice while holding office, but there is no objection to making arrangements for the maintenance of a practice during the period of tenure of office.

It was long regarded as undesirable that ministers should retain membership of subordinate public bodies, such as county councils, while in government. Nevertheless, this was a practice tolerated by successive governments. The Local Government Act 1991 provided that ministers and ministers of state are excluded from election to or membership of local authorities. The Local Government Act 2003 abolished the dual mandate under which serving TDs and senators could also be members of local authorities.

Members of the government proposing visits or receiving invitations to travel abroad that will involve government-to-government contacts or public attendance, as distinct from attendance at meetings of bodies such as the European Union (EU) or the Organisation for Economic Co-operation and Development (OECD), are obliged to consult the Minister for Foreign Affairs and the Taoiseach. They must have the approval of the latter before entering into commitments. Ministers who intend to visit Northern Ireland must advise the Minister for Foreign Affairs. In the case of private travel abroad by a minister, it is normal practice that Irish diplomatic missions and the authorities of the countries concerned are advised of the minister's travel plans.

Ethics and Standards

There is a substantial body of legislation in place to regulate the ethical standards of people in public office. This includes the Ethics in Public Office Act 1995 and the Standards in Public Office Act 2001, as well as the Electoral Act 1997. There is also a statutory code of conduct for office-holders, and the Dáil and Seanad have adopted codes of conduct, drawn up by the Select Committee on Members' Interests of each House, for their non-office-holding members.

The Ethics in Public Office Act 1995 provides for the disclosure of interests by holders of certain public offices, including ministers and members of the Houses of the Oireachtas, and deals with gifts to holders of public office. It established a Public Offices Commission and a Select Committee on Members' Interests in each House of the Oireachtas. The fundamental principle is that office-holders should not accept an offer of gifts, hospitality or services where this would, or might appear to, place them under an obligation. The commission has issued guidelines to office-holders. Broadly, these require that office-holders should disclose certain gifts and that they should surrender valuable gifts to the state where these are given by virtue of office. There are guidelines also for gifts that cannot readily be surrendered to the state, such as property, below-cost loans, free services and so on. In sum, the guidelines provide information on the steps office-holders need to take in order to comply with the requirements of the act.

The Standards in Public Office Commission is an independent body established in December 2001 by the Standards in Public Office Act 2001. It replaced the Public Offices Commission established in November 1995 by the Ethics in Public Office Act 1995. The 2001 act required the government to develop codes of conduct that would provide guidelines for ethical behaviour as well as 'professional accountability' for those in public life. The legislation limits donations to political parties in Ireland; defines prohibited donations and sets out annual reporting procedures. For example, an individual or group in receipt of a contribution in excess of €126.97 in value in a particular calendar year for the purposes of campaigning on the 2008 Lisbon Treaty referendum was required to register with the Standards in Public Office Commission as a third party. Such individuals or groups cannot accept a donation or donations from the same person exceeding an aggregate value of €6,348.69 in any one year. They were required to supply a bank statement to the commission by 31 March 2009. The contributors and the bank statement are not made public. Similarly, a registered political party may not accept a donation that exceeds €6,348.69 in value from the same person in the same calendar year. In 2008 the government increased the thresholds on gifts and shareholdings before office-holders and members of the Oireachtas have to declare them from €650 to €2,000 for gifts, and for a shareholding or interest in land from €13,000 to €20,000.

The Standards in Public Office Commission is also responsible for codes of conduct for politicians, office-holders and civil servants. A code is designed to indicate 'the standards of conduct and integrity for the persons to whom it relates in the performance of their duties'. The commission has drawn up a code that applies to office-holders, namely the Taoiseach, the Tánaiste, ministers, ministers of state, an Attorney General who is a member of Dáil Éireann or Seanad Éireann, the chairperson and deputy chairperson of Dáil Éireann, the chairperson and deputy chairperson of Seanad Éireann, the chairpersons of committees of either House of the Oireachtas and the chairpersons of joint committees of both Houses of the Oireachtas. Paragraph 1.5 of the code provides that 'office holders should at all times observe the highest standards of behaviour and act in good faith with transparency, fairness and impartiality to promote the common good in the performance of their official functions' and 'act only by reference to and dedicate the resources of their offices in furtherance of the public interest'. For example, a serving office-holder should not be directly associated with the endorsement of a particular product unless such is required in the performance by that office-holder of his or her official functions. Byrne (2008) comments, 'In the last 10 years we have travelled from one extreme of self-regulation to that of over-regulation. We have now legislated for our moral behaviour. In doing so we have abandoned our personal ethical responsibilities solely to legislation.'

The Taoiseach: Office, Duties and Powers

The Taoiseach is appointed head of the government, or prime minister, by the President on the nomination of the Dáil. The Taoiseach may resign at any time by tendering his or her resignation to the President. If the Taoiseach resigns, the other ministers are deemed to have resigned also. A list of Taoisigh and their terms of office is included as Appendix I to this Chapter.

In addition to the responsibilities of being head of the government, the Taoiseach has certain constitutional and statutory powers and duties. The Taoiseach:

- May, in effect, compel any minister to resign for any reason he or she deems sufficient.
- Nominates the Attorney General for appointment by the President.
- Nominates the ministers of state for appointment by the government.
- Appoints eleven members of the Seanad.
- Appoints the clerks (chief officers) and clerks assistant of the Dáil and Seanad, as well as the Superintendent and Captain of the Guard in the Houses of the Oireachtas, after consultation with the chairpersons of the Houses and the Minister for Finance.
- Initiates the process for the selection by interview board of candidates for the office of Director of Public Prosecutions and proposes the candidate selected to the government for appointment.
- Keeps the President informed on matters of domestic and international policy.
- Is an ex officio member of the Council of State.
- Presents the bills passed by the Dáil and Seanad to the President, who signs them into law.

- Notifies the President in the event of both Houses passing resolutions for the removal of the Comptroller and Auditor General, or of a judge.

On the advice of the Taoiseach, Dáil Éireann is summoned and dissolved by the President, but the President has absolute discretion to refuse a dissolution to a Taoiseach who has ceased to retain the support of a majority in the Dáil. In fact no President has yet refused a dissolution. Thus, the practice in Ireland differs from that in several European countries where the head of state frequently calls upon another member of the parliament to form a government in such a situation.

The Taoiseach must resign upon ceasing to retain the support of a majority in the Dáil, unless the President dissolves the Dáil on the Taoiseach's advice and the Taoiseach then secures the support of a majority in the new Dáil. A unique situation arising from these provisions occurred in 1989. The twenty-sixth Dáil, on convening after the general election in June, failed to elect outgoing Taoiseach Charles Haughey. Relying on the constitutional provision just cited, the opposition parties pressed the view that the Taoiseach should resign. Haughey did not accept the opposition view, on the basis of advice received by him from the Attorney General, and proposed instead that the Dáil adjourn to enable consultations between the parties with a view to forming a government. He acceded, however, to the political pressure and resigned, with his ministers. They remained in office, in an acting capacity, pending the outcome of the inter-party negotiations, which eventually led to Haughey becoming Taoiseach of a coalition government. These events evoked considerable discussion on the interpretation of the provision in the Constitution. FitzGerald comments in this regard (2003: 53), 'I believe that attention also needs to be given to the method of selection of the Taoiseach under the Constitution. Our constitutional practice here is out of line with that of most other democracies, in which the head of state plays a role in relation to selection of the person whose name is to be submitted to parliament.'

The decision by the government initially to accept, and then later to defer, a pay increase in late 2007 led to salary comparisons and showed that the Taoiseach is very well paid, receiving a larger salary than the President of the United States, the President of France, the Chancellor of Germany or the Prime Ministers of Britain, France, Canada and Australia. In his budget 2009 speech Minister of Finance Brian Lenihan informed the Dáil that members of the government and ministers of state would surrender 10 per cent of their total pay and that officers at secretary general level in government departments had volunteered to make a corresponding surrender in respect of their pay.

Leadership: Style and Influence

The Taoiseach's position as head of the government has been described by a former government secretary (Ó Muimhneacháin 1969) as 'captain of the team':

> In this capacity, he is the central co-ordinating figure, who takes an interest in the work of all departments, the figure to whom ministers naturally turn for advice and guidance when faced with problems involving large questions of policy or otherwise of special difficulty, whose leadership is essential to the successful working of the government as a collective authority, collectively responsible to Dáil Éireann, but acting through members each of whom is charged with specific departmental tasks. He may often have to inform himself in considerable detail of particular matters with which other members of the government are primarily concerned. He may have to make public statements on such matters, as well as on general matters of broad policy, internal and external.

The Taoiseach presides over all government meetings and has considerable influence in relation to the business transacted. In the first place, the agenda is prepared under the Taoiseach's direction. If there are items of business that he or she does or does not want to be taken at a particular meeting, this can usually be arranged. Second, as chairperson, the Taoiseach can structure the discussion and so determine the manner in which the various items on the agenda, as well as other matters which ministers may wish to raise, are dealt with. Third, and perhaps most importantly, the Taoiseach may put forward a proposal to government by way of memorandum or otherwise on any item of major policy. The length of meetings is also influenced by the personal style of the Taoiseach. Farrell (1993: 176) notes, 'The Taoiseach is extremely influential in determining the outcome of cabinet discussions. Votes are taken infrequently, usually on less important issues, and not recorded. Nor is there a quorum for cabinet meetings. Typically decisions are consensual in character and dissent is not minuted. A minister whose proposals are being resisted will usually require the Taoiseach's support to be successful.'

The introduction of leaders' questions on a weekly basis in October 2002 has given the Taoiseach a much more important role in the Dáil. MacCarthaigh (2005: 124) notes, 'The introduction of leaders' questions has been the most significant development in the parliamentary timetable in terms of increasing the opposition's opportunities to raise matters of immediate concern in the Dáil.' The Taoiseach regularly answers questions every week when the Dáil is in session. This has given the Taoiseach a highly visible role in the Dáil.

Elgie and Stapleton (2003) found an overall increase in the parliamentary activity of Taoisigh since the foundation of the state. There has been a sharp increase from the beginning of the 1960s in activities such as the presentation of the daily order of business, question answering and statement making. The introduction of leaders' questions and Taoiseach's questions has served to reinforce this pre-eminent role.

Ultimately, the Taoiseach carries the responsibility for the achievement or lack of achievement of the government. It is sometimes said that the office of Taoiseach is what the holder wishes to make of it. Speaking in the Dáil in May 1976 Deputy Charles Haughey commented:

> In every democracy every Prime Minister, in ours every Taoiseach, has his own approach to the high office which he holds. He puts his own stamp on the office while he holds it. Deputy Cosgrave is no exception to that. In his own way, by his personality, his approach, his political philosophy, the Taoiseach has put his own impression on the office of Taoiseach and has made his own particular contribution to the development of that office.

The Taoiseach's authority has been described as 'a function not merely of the office but of the multiplicity of roles thrust upon him – simultaneously chief executive, government chairman, party leader, national spokesman, principal legislator, electoral champion and media focus' (Farrell 1988b: 44). Taoiseach Bertie Ahern in a 2005 speech noted, 'Brian Farrell famously posed the question as to whether the job I have is that of *"Chairman or Chief"*? I am still not sure how to answer that one except to say that it often feels like both at once – with maybe a few more roles thrown in for good measure.' As Taoiseach, Ahern held several rounds of regular policy discussions with the minister and secretary general of each department.

In formulating public policy on all major issues, the Taoiseach plays a leading part in bringing together various strands of opinion around the cabinet table and in achieving consensus on the lines of major policy to be adopted. The Review Body on Higher Remuneration in the Public Sector (1972) has commented on the implications of the Taoiseach's overall authority:

> He has a special responsibility and a particularly onerous one. Apart from his constitutional position and responsibilities . . . he is in growing degree personally identified with – and regarded by the public as answerable for – the totality of government policy. He must concern himself with all departments of state, in particular on all major matters. He must co-ordinate the efforts of his colleagues in the development and implementation of national policy. The achievement or lack of achievement of the government is laid primarily at his door.

Ireland has moved from having a predominantly single party government (between 1932 and 1982) to a situation where multi-party government is the norm. Coalition formation is a fundamental part of the process of democratic government in Ireland. Therefore, an essential requirement for a Taoiseach is to have empathy and to be sensitive to coalition partners. Successful coalition governments have been characterised by mutual trust and confidence, the avoidance of suspicions and recriminations. The Taoiseach has to manage the politics of coalition at the heart of multi-party government by providing the mutual trust and respect that acts as the glue to hold different political parties with different policies and perspectives together in a spirit of co-operation and consultation based on genuine partnership. This trust is essential in a coalition government. The Taoiseach, as head of government, has to manage this political partnership skilfully to maintain the unity of the political parties in government. Equally, several Taoisigh have maintained good relations and lines of communication with independent (non-party) members in the Dáil, given their importance over the years.

While the Taoiseach is pre-eminent among the members of the government, Chubb (1974: 13) notes that the 'precise degree of this pre-eminence, however, may well vary from Taoiseach to Taoiseach'. Chubb (1982: 201) sees the pre-eminence of the Taoiseach as stemming from four facts. Firstly, the Taoiseach is usually the party leader. Second, elections often take the form of gladiatorial contests between two designated party leaders, thus emphasising the personal leadership of the victor, and television and modern campaign practices have increased the propensity to focus on the leader. Third, except in the case of coalition governments, the Taoiseach has chosen all the other members of the government. Fourth, the position of Taoiseach carries a special responsibility to take the lead or speak when an authoritative intervention is needed. Research carried out by Marsh *et al.* (2008) and based on six years of detailed and comprehensive surveys of Irish voters found 'that leaders had a limited impact on their party's fortunes. Most had a positive impact, but there is little to suggest that Irish elections are a presidential-style battle between likely leaders of government'. Clearly, however, the confidence of the electorate in the leadership capability of the candidates for the post of Taoiseach is crucial. As the Taoiseach can personify the country in terms of the perception of Ireland at home and overseas, issues such as media profile and image are also vital.

The role of the Taoiseach has altered from being first among equals under the 1922 Constitution to one of effective authority under the 1937 Constitution. W.T. Cosgrave, President of the Executive Council from 1922 to 1932, reflecting the older approach, said that it was not open to the head of the government to ask for and to compel the resignation of a minister (*Dáil Debates*, 14 June 1937, cols. 347–8). Seán Lemass (1968: 3) set out succinctly the role of the Taoiseach:

A minister is supposed to know everything about the affairs of his department; the Taoiseach is supposed to know something about the affairs of every department. The Taoiseach's primary task, apart from acting as spokesman for the government on major issues of policy, is to ensure that departmental plans are fully co-ordinated, that the inevitable conflicts between departments are resolved, that cabinet decisions are facilitated and that the implications of government policy are fully understood by all cabinet colleagues and influence the shaping of their departmental plans.

Under the 1937 Constitution successive Taoisigh have moved ministers from department to department or dismissed them. The power to remove members of the government by requiring their resignation enables the Taoiseach to hold considerable dominance over ministers. Many commentators today speculate on a transition from cabinet to prime ministerial government.

Taoiseach Jack Lynch dismissed Charles Haughey and Neil Blaney in 1970 on the occasion of what was known as the 'arms crisis'. In 1986 the government, on the recommendation of Taoiseach Garret FitzGerald, dismissed four ministers of state – Joseph Bermingham, Donal Creed, Michael Darcy and Edward Collins, the last for alleged conflict of interest and the others for differences over government policy. In 1990 Taoiseach Charles Haughey dismissed Tánaiste and Minister for Defence Brian Lenihan because of conflicting statements he had made about the making of telephone calls to the office of the President on the occasion of the defeat of the government in a Dáil vote in 1982. In November 1991 Haughey dismissed the Ministers for Finance and for the Environment, Albert Reynolds and Pádraig Flynn, for publicly expressing lack of confidence in him as leader of the Fianna Fáil party. In 1995 Taoiseach John Bruton effectively dismissed Minister for Defence Hugh Coveney for a breach of the ethical standards appropriate to members of the government, although Coveney in fact tendered his resignation. Coveney was subsequently appointed a minister of state. In 1996 Bruton effectively dismissed Michael Lowry, Minister for Transport, Energy and Communications, for conduct unbecoming to a minister, although again, Lowry in fact resigned.

In sum, it is difficult to define the office of the Taoiseach. It can only be described in terms of the use to which it is put by different individuals of varying personalities who face different problems and deal with different colleagues. A Taoiseach may, to quote Farrell (1971) again, operate as either 'chairman or chief', encouraging, co-ordinating and monitoring the work of other ministers, or exercising a very positive leadership role and virtually dictating policy for the cabinet as a whole. Lee (1998: 555) comments, 'Clear vision, and firm political leadership, may not suffice to attain national goals. Without them, however, paralysis prevails.' Elgie and Fitzgerald (2004: 325) offer a succinct summary: 'So while the chairman or chief distinction provides a useful way of categorising different leadership styles, Taoisigh are likely to have to exhibit both styles at some stage during their term of office as they react to the problems caused by differing circumstances.'

The Tánaiste

The Constitution provides that the Taoiseach shall nominate a member of the government to be Tánaiste under Article 28.6.1°. The Tánaiste, who must be a member of Dáil Éireann, acts in the place of the Taoiseach during the latter's temporary absence or, where the latter dies or becomes permanently incapacitated, pending the appointment of a new Taoiseach. Article 31 of the Constitution grants the Tánaiste ex officio membership of the Council of State. In 1998 the Supreme Court noted:

> The powers and duties of the Tánaiste are not fully described in the Constitution. But neither are the powers and duties of the Taoiseach. It is quite clear that the system of government referred to in the Constitution is a cabinet system of government. This is a system of government by committee. It is a flexible system of government and not all of its attributes are described in law. Suffice it to say that the Tánaiste is the Taoiseach's deputy. Within the limits of the Constitution and the law the manner in which the Taoiseach and the Tánaiste share the burdens of office is a matter for arrangement among themselves (Barrington J. in *Riordan v An Taoiseach* 381/97, 19 November 1998).

In a coalition government, the Tánaiste is often the leader of the smaller (or second largest) party. The Programme for Government 1993, agreed between Fianna Fáil and the Labour Party, boosted the role and status of the Tánaiste. Then Labour leader, Dick Spring, took on the office in addition to his post as Minister for Foreign Affairs. He was provided with office space in Government Buildings, close to the Taoiseach, and a staff separate and distinct from that in the Department of Foreign Affairs. These arrangements continued until the government was replaced in 1997 by the Fianna Fáil/Progressive Democrats coalition, in which then leader of the Progressive Democrats, Mary Harney, became the first woman to hold the office of Tánaiste. Elgie and Fitzgerald (2004: 322) note, 'Overall, what power the Tánaiste has tends to be derived from his or her position as a minister and coalition party leader rather than from anything inherent in the position itself.'

The Supreme Court held in 1997 that there was no constitutional obligation on the Taoiseach and the Tánaiste to be in the country at the same time, 'except in the circumstances that a duty or function falls to be performed by the Taoiseach in a particular circumstance' (*Riordan v An Tánaiste* [1997] 3 IR 502).

A list of Tánaistí and their terms of office is included as Appendix II to this Chapter.

Department of the Taoiseach: Functions

The Department of the Taoiseach has two overall strategic objectives: supporting the government and supporting the Taoiseach; and six strategic priorities: Northern Ireland, EU and international affairs, economic and social policy, social partnership, public service modernisation, and knowledge society and e-government. It has a total staff of about 220 and is headed by a secretary general who also acts as Secretary General to the Government. The 2007 Review Body on Higher Remuneration in the Public Sector recognised the significant demands of this post.

The mission statement of the Department of the Taoiseach is 'To provide the Government, Taoiseach and Ministers of State with the support, policy advice and information necessary for the effective conduct of Government and for the dynamic leadership, co-ordination and strategic direction of Government policy.' The responsibilities of the department include:

1. Organisation, co-ordination, preparation and processing of government business in the Dáil and Seanad.
2. Formulation of policy and overseeing of the implementation of settled policy in respect of matters of major national import in which the Taoiseach needs to be involved from time to time, for example international and Northern Ireland affairs.
3. Preparation of replies to parliamentary questions addressed to the Taoiseach.
4. Maintenance of liaison with the office of the President.
5. Major state protocol.
6. Processing of correspondence addressed to the Taoiseach.
7. Government press relations and the government information services.
8. Provision of the secretariat to the government and to government committees.
9. Administration of specific functions of government discharged from time to time under the aegis of the Taoiseach, for example the work of the Central Statistics Office.

In reply to a parliamentary question to the Taoiseach in February 2008, it was revealed that the Department of the Taoiseach is represented on fifty-two different inter-departmental teams and committees, indicating its central role in the machinery of government. The department limits its interventions to areas where it can add value to the work of other departments.

In recent years the Taoiseach has been increasingly active in the foreign relations of the state, mainly as a result of Ireland's membership of the EU. Heads of state and government meet several times a year as the European Council, which requires 'a more active and interventionist role for the Taoiseach' (Scott 1983: 173). In this regard, Taoiseach Bertie Ahern commented, 'It does bug me that nobody in this country, unlike all other countries, takes any notice of the international work that a Taoiseach does. Nobody cares' (Hannon 2004: 249).

The focal point in the European context is the European Council, which normally meets at least twice a year. Many of the major issues in the EU now come to the European Council for discussion, for guidance and for decisions. While the Department of Foreign Affairs has overall responsibility for the co-ordination of EU business, and while the Department of the Taoiseach relies heavily on the departments primarily concerned to keep it informed about important and sensitive issues in this and other international areas, all Taoisigh since Ireland's accession have found it desirable to maintain an advisory unit within the Department of the Taoiseach that was sensitive to their personal approach and preoccupations. 'The atmosphere of the Taoiseach's Department is affected by the personality of who's in power, and has become increasingly so, as the Department expands and accumulates advisers' (Delaney 2001: 53).

Department of the Taoiseach and Dáil Business

Government Chief Whip

Every Taoiseach assigns a minister of state to the Department of the Taoiseach to act as chief whip of the government party. The Government Chief Whip's role relates essentially to (a) the progression of government business that is placed before the Dáil for discussion and determination, and (b) the attendance of deputies from the government side. His or her primary responsibility is to ensure that the government always has enough bodies in the Dáil chamber when the division bells ring for a vote. The Government Chief Whip attends cabinet on an administrative basis and maintains close liaison with the whip of any other party in government and also with the whips of the opposition parties. The relationship between the whips of all parties is one of friendly trust.

Before each Dáil session, through circulars addressed to all ministers, the Government Chief Whip finds out what legislation (or other business) their departments expect to place before the Dáil in the coming session and its state of preparation. During Dáil sessions, he or she prepares weekly reports for the Taoiseach on the progress of legislation in the pipeline. Although Government Chief Whips are automatically made ministers of state, with the associated privileges, Hannon (2004: 133) comments that 'few do it for the money. The post is prized because the potential for networking and advancement is immense'.

The officials in the Government Chief Whip's office keep in touch with ministers' private secretaries about business that ministers might wish to have dealt with in the week ahead, for example approval of a supplementary estimate or the introduction of a bill that has become urgent. Arising from these contacts, and having regard to the items that may be already on the order paper (agenda) of the Dáil – there being nearly always a backlog of items awaiting discussion, the Government Chief Whip prepares an agenda and a timetable for each sitting day of the following week. By convention, this is discussed with the opposition whips each Wednesday. While the business to be dealt with is primarily a matter for the government, the opposition may on occasion seek to have time allocated by the government to discuss a matter that it considers to be of particular current importance. In such an event the Government Chief Whip will consult the minister responsible; sometimes it may be necessary to consult the Taoiseach or even the government. On these occasions the length of the debate as well as the length of the contributions to be made by the minister responsible, the opposition spokesperson and other deputies are normally determined by precedent. No minutes of whips' meetings are kept.

When agreement has been reached on the business for the week ahead, the Government Chief Whip sends to each deputy on the government side a notice of the times during which the Dáil will meet in that week, the business to be transacted, the times at which the various items will be taken and when voting is most likely to take place. The notice indicates the varying degrees of importance attached to the business and to deputies' attendance. Deputies are advised to be in the House at all times. This weekly notice is commonly called the whip. Deputies who cannot be present are obliged to notify their whip and explain their absence.

On each day that the Dáil is in session the Taoiseach announces the business for that day. Each item on the order paper (already circulated) is numbered, and the Taoiseach's announcement indicates the order of their discussion. Sometimes the order of business is disputed by the opposition parties, for example when it does not provide for discussion of some business considered urgent by them, when it provides for the taking of all stages of a bill on that day, or when no explanation is given as to why items are to be discussed in a particular order. Farrell (1983: 256) notes that governments and oppositions have 'remained committed to a traditional, and largely artificial, parliamentary mock battle in which the real prize is less the issues of politics than the opportunity to retain or gain governmental power'.

Deputies wishing to contribute to a debate normally notify their party whip. In general they determine the nature and length of their contributions themselves. The rule under which government deputies may not be absent save with the permission of the whip is necessary to ensure the carrying of any measure put forward by the government in the event of its being challenged to a vote by the opposition. If a member is unavoidably absent or (in the case of a minister) on government business elsewhere, the Government Chief Whip approaches the whip of the main opposition party for a pairing – a request that, in the event of a vote, one opposition deputy abstains from voting for each government deputy absent. The practices in this regard are largely governed by convention. Informal arrangements between deputies of opposing parties are frowned upon by the whips on both sides; all pairing arrangements are expected to be made through the whips' offices. The Government Chief Whip has an important role in maintaining party discipline. Following a narrow government victory in the Dáil in May 2008, the Government Chief Whip, Pat Carey, wrote to Fianna Fáil deputies that it was vital that they:

> . . . never miss a vote without full permission from my office. Under no circumstances are informal pairing arrangements to be entered into with Opposition members. Following discussions with the Taoiseach, I will be keeping record of any votes that may be missed by members. In the event of any missed votes, I will, on a systematic basis, be informing the Taoiseach of these. Both the Taoiseach and I will be dealing with these missed votes together if they happen to arise.

Government Backbenchers

Party discipline is very strong in Ireland and it is rare that one hears of a 'backbench rebellion'. Where serious misgivings arise on a measure, government backbenchers force the withdrawal or amendment of a bill behind closed doors in the parliamentary party. The partial privatisation of Aer Rianta was deferred in 2000 due to political opposition. Similarly, due to the opposition of many government backbenchers and a strong campaign by the vintners' associations, Minister for Justice Michael McDowell dropped his café bar license proposal in June 2005. Loyalty, team spirit, tradition and ambition for advancement are factors in maintaining a strong sense of party discipline. Strong party loyalty and the whip system ensure that a government majority will normally last throughout an entire Dáil term, with little or no likelihood of a backbench revolt. However, the hostile public reaction to budget 2009 in October 2008 created a crisis for the government with one Fianna Fáil TD, Joe Behan, resigning from the party and others expressing grave concern about the proposed means testing of the medical card for people aged over seventy, the application of a 1 per cent income levy and cuts in planned education and health spending. As a result the government dramatically increased the medical card income thresholds for the over-seventies, axed the income levy for those outside the tax net and reversed a decision to stop paying disabled teenagers the disability allowance.

Parliamentary Questions to the Taoiseach

A period of time is set aside every Tuesday and Wednesday for Dáil questions to the Taoiseach. In general, the questions relate directly to government policy and to the activities of the Department of the Taoiseach on issues such as Northern Ireland; public service reform; the social partnership programme; the President; the European Council; and the Government Press Service. Questions relating to other departmental matters, such as the Central Statistics Office, are generally answered by the minister of state at the Department of Taoiseach. The Taoiseach also answers questions about statements he or she has made in the course of speeches outside the Dáil.

Some deputies prefer to address their questions to the Taoiseach if the subject is even remotely relevant to the department; some do as the result of a misunderstanding on their part. In the vast majority of such cases the question is transferred to the appropriate minister. This practice frequently arouses the ire of the opposition, who accuse the Taoiseach of seeking to avoid responsibilities that they regard as proper to the head of government.

Parliamentary questions are not allowable about the discussions that take place at meetings of the government; nor are questions about government sub-committees, on the grounds that the work of such committees is a direct extension of the work of the government itself. In addition, questions may not be asked about matters for which the Taoiseach is not responsible to the Dáil, such as legal advice given by the Attorney General; bodies that are independent of the government; or meetings with private individuals.

Department of the Taoiseach: Other Areas of Responsibility

The Taoiseach has a leadership role, and a corresponding involvement, in all major policy areas. In addition, the Taoiseach may take responsibility for a second government department (for example the Department of the Gaeltacht in 1987 and 1989).

Northern Ireland

Successive Taoisigh have reserved to themselves responsibility for Northern Ireland affairs. It is the Taoiseach who makes significant policy statements in this area and who answers parliamentary questions. It is the practice for the Taoiseach and the British Prime Minister to avail themselves of the opportunity provided by meetings of the European Council to meet in the margins thereof and discuss matters of common concern. However, in so far as Northern Ireland policy affects relations with the British government, such policy is also the concern of the Minister for Foreign Affairs.

Liaison with the President

The constitutional requirement that the Taoiseach keep the President informed on domestic and international policy is fulfilled by the Taoiseach's visits to Áras an Uachtaráin. There is regular contact between both offices at senior official level. Apart from the constitutional requirement, there are a number of matters on which consultation between the Department of the Taoiseach and the office of the President is necessary. These include the arrangements to be made for visits abroad by the President, such as the drawing up of programmes and the preparation of speeches; the provision of advice on invitations received by the President to extend his or her patronage to events or to attend functions; messages to and from other heads of state; and matters relating directly to the work of other departments, including the presentation of credentials by incoming ambassadors, the signing of commissions for officers of the Defence Forces and the appointment of judges.

Protocol

On the occasion of visits to Ireland by heads of state, prime ministers or other persons in high office (such as the President of the European Commission), the protocol arrangements are made in consultation with the Department of Foreign Affairs. Major state protocol is the responsibility of the Department of the Taoiseach, for example the ceremonial activities surrounding the inauguration of the President, the national day of commem - oration and state funerals.

Correspondence

As might be expected, the Taoiseach receives a large volume of representations, correspondence and requests for meetings. Almost all of the correspondence is about issues for which the Taoiseach has no direct responsibility. The procedure generally adopted in dealing with such correspondence is that material for reply thereto is sought from the department concerned, if it is not already available in the Department of the Taoiseach. The reply itself is signed by the Taoiseach, by his or her private secretary or by a departmental official. Alternatively, the correspondence is merely acknowledged and referred to the department responsible for direct reply. Replies to constituents are usually signed by the Taoiseach.

Requests from individuals or groups for meetings are normally directed to the appropriate minister. In general, the Taoiseach meets only those groups that are representative of what are loosely termed the social partners (representatives of employers, unions, churches etc.) in connection with issues of major national policy.

Government Press and Information Services

Within the Department of the Taoiseach, the Government Press Secretary and the Assistant Government Press Secretary/Head of Government Information Services (GIS) brief political and other correspondents on issues relating to government policy. The Government Press Secretary does not attend government meetings, but is briefed after each meeting by a minister designated to do so. He or she normally accompanies the Taoiseach on official visits abroad and, in collaboration with the Irish ambassadorial staff in the country concerned, briefs the media from the Irish point of view. As former Government Press Secretary Mandy Johnson (2008) explained, 'my role wasn't to make me popular, I was there to make a politician popular, or to help explain a politician's policy. That's all I was there for. I had no interest in endearing myself to journalists and I'm not afraid of the media, and so I just told the truth, did what I had to do for my political masters and I couldn't make any apologies for it, everybody can't be popular, sometimes, yes, you had to be the tough person.'

The press office supplies news and official documents to the press, radio and television and provides them with information and facilities, arranges press conferences for ministers, briefs correspondents on the background to official statements and interprets public feeling to departments. It advises on the co-ordination of departmental publicity and information and collaborates with the Department of Foreign Affairs in relation to the dissemination abroad of information about Ireland.

Government press secretaries in recent years remain in office only for the duration of a government's term of office. The press office includes a number of press officers, who are permanent civil servants and who deal with general media queries. Since 1997 there is a also a Media Monitoring Unit, which acts as an 'early warning system' for the government and departments. It monitors radio, television and newspaper coverage of daily events and developments and provides the information to the various ministers. The unit works an eighteen-hour day based on a flexible rota of three working shifts and is staffed by six established civil servants, five of whom are seconded from other departments. The work of the unit means that departments have greatly reduced their use of external companies and ensures that they no longer duplicate transcripts and tapes. It provides a clippings and transcript service for government and normally covers *The Irish Times*, *Irish Independent* and *Irish Examiner*. As the media has developed its oversight and investigative roles in recent years, so too has the desire of politicians to be able to use the media effectively to get their message across.

Farmleigh House

Farmleigh, an estate of seventy-eight acres situated in Dublin's Phoenix Park, was purchased from the Guinness family by the state in 1999 for €29.2 million. The house was carefully refurbished by the Office of Public Works as the premier accommodation for visiting dignitaries and guests of the nation and as a venue for high-level government meetings and public enjoyment. Visiting dignitaries who have stayed there include the Emperor and Empress of Japan, the Governor General of New Zealand, the King of Norway, the President of the Republic of Poland and the President of the European Parliament. Farmleigh hosts high-level government events such as international meetings and has a very active public access programme. In 2007 almost 177,000 visitors attended the various open days, guided tours and free public events held from March through to December.

The state has refurbished a house, the Steward's Lodge, in the grounds of the Farmleigh estate with the aim of providing a suitable residence for the Taoiseach. Previously Ireland had not followed the practice common in other countries of having a state-provided residence for the prime minister of the day. However, modern security requirements, coupled with the practical operational advantages of having a house in which the Taoiseach can work and receive visitors on official business, has led to the earmarking of this house for the use of Taoisigh. The four-bedroom house is highly suitable as a Taoiseach's residence. A high-specification security system has been installed for the house and grounds. In addition to the renovation work done by the building maintenance division of the Office of Public Works, external contracts directly associated with the renovation work amounted to €568,076 inclusive of VAT and direct landscaping contracts came to €30,748 inclusive of VAT (reply to a parliamentary question, 5 February 2008).

Conclusion

Although the term 'cabinet' has no formal basis in the Constitution, it is frequently used to describe formal meetings of the government and to distinguish them from more general activities of government. The cabinet is at the heart of government, setting strategic priorities for the decades ahead. The efficient operation of the cabinet and clear lines of communication from cabinet to ministers, ministers of state and civil servants are essential to the smooth functioning of the machinery of government.

The dynamics of the cabinet process are unique and surrounded by a certain mystique. They are designed to ensure that all cabinet members share a strong sense of collective responsibility and duty, and they are effective in achieving that aim. The e-cabinet initiative has put information and communications technologies at the centre of government, the business of which is now more complex and challenging than ever before. It also shows a commitment to ensuring that government remains to the fore in the development of the global information society.

Web Resources

Cabinet Handbook online at www.taoiseach.gov.ie (under publications)

Department of the Taoiseach and Government Press Office at www.taoiseach.gov.ie

Farmleigh House at www.farmleigh.ie

Government of Ireland at www.irlgov.ie

Government press and information officers at www.dcenr.gov.ie/Corporate+Units/Virtual+Press+Room/Government+Press+and+Information+Officers.htm

Review Body on Higher Remuneration in the Public Sector at www.reviewbody.gov.ie

APPENDIX I: TAOISIGH OF IRELAND

29 December 1937 to 18 February 1948	Eamon de Valera*
18 February 1948 to 13 June 1951	John A. Costello
13 June 1951 to 2 June 1954	Eamon de Valera
2 June 1954 to 20 March 1957	John A. Costello
20 March 1957 to 23 June 1959	Eamon de Valera
23 June 1959 to 10 November 1966	Seán Lemass
10 November 1966 to 14 March 1973	Jack Lynch
14 March 1973 to 5 July 1977	Liam Cosgrave
5 July 1977 to 11 December 1979	Jack Lynch
11 December 1979 to 30 June 1981	Charles J. Haughey

30 June 1981 to 9 March 1982	Garret FitzGerald
9 March 1982 to 14 December 1982	Charles J. Haughey
14 December 1982 to 10 March 1987	Garret FitzGerald
10 March 1987 to 11 February 1992	Charles J. Haughey
11 February 1992 to 15 December 1994	Albert Reynolds
15 December 1994 to 26 June 1997	John Bruton
26 June 1997 to 7 May 2008	Bertie Ahern
7 May 2008 to date	Brian Cowen

* The 1937 Constitution created the office of Taoiseach, which replaced the office of President of the Executive Council, a position held by Eamon de Valera since 9 March 1932.

APPENDIX II: TÁNAISTÍ OF IRELAND

29 December 1937 to 14 June 1945	Seán T. Ó Ceallaigh*
14 June 1945 to 18 February 1948	Seán Lemass
18 February 1948 to 13 June 1951	William Norton
13 June 1951 to 2 June 1954	Seán Lemass
2 June 1954 to 20 March 1957	William Norton
20 March 1957 to 23 June 1959	Seán Lemass
23 June 1959 to 21 April 1965	Seán MacEntee
21 April 1965 to 2 July 1969	Frank Aiken
2 July 1969 to 14 March 1973	Erskine Childers
14 March 1973 to 5 July 1977	Brendan Corish
5 July 1977 to 30 June 1981	George Colley
30 June 1981 to 9 March 1982	Michael O'Leary
9 March 1982 to 14 December 1982	Ray MacSharry
14 December 1982 to 20 January 1987	Dick Spring
20 January 1987 to 10 March 1987	Peter Barry
10 March 1987 to 31 October 1990	Brian Lenihan Snr
13 November 1990 to 12 January 1993	John Wilson
12 January 1993 to 17 November 1994	Dick Spring
19 November 1994 to 15 December 1994	Bertie Ahern
15 December 1994 to 26 June 1997	Dick Spring
26 June 1997 to 13 September 2006	Mary Harney
13 September 2006 to 14 June 2007	Michael McDowell
14 June 2007 to 7 May 2008	Brian Cowen
7 May 2008 to date	Mary Coughlan

* The 1937 Constitution created the office of Tánaiste, which replaced the office of Vice-President of the Executive Council, a position held by Seán T. Ó Ceallaigh since 9 March 1932.

2

MINISTERS AND THEIR DEPARTMENTS

The principal legislative provisions relating to the powers of ministers and their departments are the Ministers and Secretaries Acts 1924 to 2007 and the Public Service Management Act 1997. Section 2(1) of the Ministers and Secretaries Act 1924 provides that each minister, as head of a department of state, shall be a corporation sole and shall have perpetual succession, an official seal, may sue and be sued and may acquire, hold and dispose of land for the purposes of the functions, powers or duties of the department of state of which he or she is head or of any branch thereof. By virtue of the fact that the minister is a corporation sole, contracts or other legal rights or liabilities are entered into and accepted, explicitly or implicitly, in the name of the minister or on the minister's behalf. Under section 3 of the Public Service Management Act 1997 ministers are responsible for the performance of functions that are assigned to their department pursuant to the Ministers and Secretaries Acts.

The Public Service Management Act 1997 also requires the preparation of strategy statements by secretaries general, in which they specify the key objectives, outputs and related strategies (including the use of resources) to be pursued by the department. The strategy statement must be approved by the relevant minister, who arranges for it to be laid before the Oireachtas. There is also a requirement to prepare progress (annual) reports on its implementation. According to the Working Group on the Accountability of Secretaries General and Accounting Officers (Mullarkey report 2002), 'The objective in building the concept of outputs into the departmental strategy statement and in making them subject to consideration by Oireachtas Committees was to broaden the scope of accountability beyond the focus on inputs to include a greater emphasis on the outputs and performance of public services'. This was taken a step further with the production by ministers of the annual output statements from 2007.

Murphy (2005) distinguishes between the two separate and distinct types of ministerial responsibility: legal responsibility and political responsibility. Individual ministers are legally responsible for the performance of the functions of their department. The minister is legally responsible for the actions of each and every employee, even though he or she may not have been aware of those actions. Politically, Article 28.4.2° of the Constitution provides for collective cabinet responsibility. Ministers have a duty to inform and explain actions to the Oireachtas through speeches and parliamentary questions. Thus, they retain the prime democratic accountability for actions in areas under their supervision.

Selection and Appointment

Ministers do not attain their positions by accident. Personal ambition and public service combine to reinforce a TD's desire to be a minister. As membership of the Dáil is increasingly becoming a full-time career, more and more TDs are likely to aspire to ministerial status. To this end a TD must make considerable efforts to be well thought of in the party, in the Dáil, by the media and, above all, by the party leader.

It is the Taoiseach who has absolute discretion, subject to the provisions of the Constitution, to nominate ministers for appointment by the President (except in a multi-party coalition government, where portfolio and policy pay-offs reflect the outcome of the bargaining process and negotiations between the political parties). Casey (2000: 155) notes that 'even if his choice of personnel is somewhat restricted, he may enjoy greater liberty in the actual allocation of ministerial responsibilities'. No formal selection criteria are prescribed, and Taoisigh do not indicate why they appoint a particular person to be a minister. At the same time, various 'qualifications' may be identified. These include such considerations as seniority, loyalty, popularity and length of service within the party. Taoisigh are keen to achieve balance and fairness, and do not want to favour only their strongest political supporters. Hussey (1993: 41) comments, 'There are many criteria which an Irish prime minister must consider when appointing a Cabinet: rewards for the loyal, appeasement of powerful party groups, attractiveness to the electorate, a geographical balance and fitness for the post'. In June 2002 it was widely reported that Taoiseach Bertie Ahern changed his mind about dropping Joe Walsh and Michael Smith from his new cabinet following strong lobbying on their behalf by prominent businessmen and politicians.

O'Malley (2006) notes that, comparatively, Taoisigh have one of the most restricted pools from which to select ministers. He comments that the small and stable political elite in Ireland cause personal relationships and loyalty to be important and as a result Taoisigh tend to be conservative when selecting ministers and select only those TDs with experience, or who are well known, to be ministers. Ability to perform properly all of the tasks expected of a member of the government is increasingly seen as an over-riding consideration, though occasionally a newly elected deputy has been appointed a minister on first election to the Dáil (for example Niamh

Bhreathnach, Noel Browne, Kevin Boland, Martin O'Donoghue and Alan Dukes). Former Health Minister Barry Desmond (2000: 120) comments, 'From my 20 years' experience in the Dáil, half of which was in government, I have concluded that the Taoiseach or party leader in coalition who appoints a newly elected deputy to the government, is for the most part, storing up a great deal of unpredictable trouble.'

Whether it is desirable that ministers should have detailed expert knowledge of their portfolios is a widely debated question, i.e. whether the Minister for Health should be a medical doctor, or the Minister for Education a teacher. On the one hand, there are those who argue that it is entirely logical that this should be the case. On the other, many say that ministers have sufficient advisers both inside and outside their departments to provide them with all the expert information they need. They say that it is better if ministers are reasonably objective and able to make decisions based on an intelligent appraisal of the advice proffered to them and in light of government policy and any other relevant political considerations.

On a personal level, a Taoiseach is likely to take into account a prospective choice's compatibility with the rest of the ministerial team, including its leader. Individuals may be considered for inclusion in the cabinet because they might provide a focus for party disaffection if left on the backbenches. Although constitutionally the selection of ministers is a matter for the Taoiseach alone, there can be little doubt that he or she will discuss the subject with close advisers in the party. Not in doubt either is that those selected will be informed before the Taoiseach makes the formal announcement in the Dáil, following his or her own appointment by the President at Áras an Uachtaráin. At that stage the Taoiseach also announces the assignment of departments. A debate on the nominations for membership of the government follows the announcement, to which only the main spokespersons of the political parties contribute. When the Dáil approves the names, it adjourns for a few hours to enable the new ministers to go to Áras an Uachtaráin and receive from the President the boxes with their seals of office. Former Finance Minister Ruairí Quinn (2005: 210) notes, 'The seal of office was in a small green leather case that opened to reveal a metal medallion. The seals had to be returned when the photographs had been taken.' The first meeting of the new government, lasting for fifteen or twenty minutes, takes place in the Áras and then there are photographs and a drink with the President.

Disposition of Portfolios; Inter-departmental Relations

The Taoiseach decides what the departmental structure of the government is going to be and assigns ministers to particular departments. The order in which ministers' names are presented to the Dáil for its approval is determined by the Taoiseach and becomes the order of precedence. Although the hierarchical principle has no basis in the Constitution, it is generally perceived by the electorate that some departments are of more importance than others. Some reasons for the perception would be the size of the department and its budget, its accepted importance in the life of the nation and its day-to-day impact on the ordinary citizen. It is obvious that the ministers in charge of the Departments of Finance and Foreign Affairs have a higher political profile than, say, the Ministers for Defence or the Marine.

If a minister is absent for a period of time, or is ill, his or her ministerial responsibilities are usually assigned to another minister, or indeed to the Taoiseach, during the period of absence. (The Finance and Justice portfolios are those generally assigned to the Taoiseach.)

In recent years there have been several changes in the titles and in the functions assigned to the various departments. Changes of personnel, i.e. cabinet reshuffles, are rare, but do occasionally occur. Such changes may be made in order to improve the technical or administrative efficiency of a government, to signal a new priority or to change an existing priority, to give the impression of dynamism and reform or to alter the balance of power within a government.

Every minister, in addition to being a minister responsible to the Dáil, has two commitments. The first is as an individual heading a department; and the second is as a member of the government collectively responsible for what other ministers do. Because of the second of these, there is a need to resolve conflicts between individual ministers to the satisfaction of ministers collectively. Issues where individual departments and ministers do not see eye to eye arise all the time as the programmes of different departments get entangled with one another. For example, in the international negotiations on the World Trade Organization, the Departments of Foreign Affairs, Agriculture and Enterprise may not always adopt the same line (the last two departments tend to see a continuing need to protect the interests of farming and industry, while the Department of Foreign Affairs is liable to take a broader view and see particular issues as part of a global problem). Differences arise frequently between the Department of Finance and other departments in relation to various financial matters, for example the estimates campaign can be adversarial in nature (NESC 2002) and disputes may have to be resolved at cabinet. There is no fixed procedure for dealing with such issues other than a spirit of give and take between officials in the first place and between ministers eventually. The ultimate arbiter is, of course, the government. However, the Taoiseach and ministers themselves do not take kindly to government business being clogged with issues that could (and should) be settled between the departments involved. Quinn (2005: 322–3) notes the importance of 'a positive and clear relationship' between the Taoiseach and the Minister for Finance.

Taking up Office

New ministers, on their first full day in office, are conducted by the secretary general of their department to the office in the department vacated by their predecessor. All documentary material will have been removed from that office – emphasising that the new incumbent is starting from scratch. One of their first tasks is, therefore, to discuss with their secretary general the question of the staffing of their private office, who their private secretary is to be and how many support staff they need. The private secretary is a key post as the holder runs the minister's office and is the channel of communication between the minister and the department. The private secretary is generally in the grade of higher executive officer, which is the highest grade that ministers are, under Department of Finance regulations, permitted to have. Only the Taoiseach has a private secretary of a higher grade, usually an assistant principal. It is not unusual for new ministers to appoint the private secretary of their predecessor, thus displaying confidence in the apolitical nature of the civil service. More often, however, they appoint a new officer to the post and in such cases ministers are guided by their secretary general in conjunction with the personnel section of their department. That section provides the names of four or five persons whom it considers suitable for the post, the minister normally interviews these candidates before making a selection. The other staff assigned are usually those who have worked in the private office up to the date on which the previous minister left office.

On their first day in the office new ministers normally meets their senior officers – the assistant secretaries and the technical officers of equivalent rank, and perhaps principals and others as well. At such meetings ministers may outline their plans, priorities and aspirations for their period in office and seek the co-operation of all present in advancing these. The next task is incoming correspondence, much of it from various pressure and interest groups seeking early meetings. In acknowledging such correspondence new ministers will generally plead for time to familiarise themselves with their portfolio and promise action as soon as possible.

During their early days in office new ministers spend much of their time with the secretary general of their department, upon whom they realise they must depend greatly. They will be briefed on the major issues facing the department and on the timescale for action on these. They will discuss, in particular, those matters relating to their department that were highlighted in the government's pre-election programme and will endeavour to implement them as a matter of priority. They seek information on the various groups with which the department deals. (Dooney [1989] describes thirty-seven bodies that played a substantial part in the work of the Department of Agriculture and lists 138 others that played a lesser part.) They learn of the sensitive areas of the work and, in particular, of those where there is the potential for public controversy. They find out what legislation is pending and the background to this, as well as the attitude of the opposition parties and outside individuals or groups who are concerned. They enquire about the progress of any state-sponsored bodies under their aegis, the relationships between the department and them, and the appointments to the boards thereof that fall to be made during their period of office. They learn of the meetings abroad that they will have to attend, whether of the European Union or of other international bodies or for the promotion of the department's work. They ask what money is available to carry out their plans. Above all, they are advised of any impending crisis and how best this might be dealt with.

Barry Desmond (2000: 179) notes:

> One of the most traumatic losses of innocence on the part of all new ministers is the extraordinary process of implementing a legislative reform. As soon as the minister is once again reminded of his party's promise, he asks his departmental secretary to allocate a senior official to the work. This official, often burdened with other pressing tasks, must research how the issue is dealt with in other jurisdictions; he or she must discuss the issue with other staff in the department; they may contact pressure groups and outside experts for their views; they may conclude that the minister's promises were 'off the wall'. But he is not to know yet. A draft memorandum is then prepared indicating why the legislation is urgently necessary; the cost to the exchequer or the consumer is estimated; the positives and negatives of the legislative scheme are stated, and the parties affected are listed. Eventually he is presented with the memorandum. But he is bluntly informed by the secretary of his department that first of all it must go to all other government departments for their observations prior to submission to government.

Internal Department Work

The route to ministerial office is always more political than administrative. Ministers are not some kind of superior civil servant. In many cases, the responsibilities that they assume on taking ministerial office are ones that they are facing for the first time. The organisation and management of their departments is an aspect of their work for which ministers have not been trained and for which they may have little experience. As it is an area in which the officials have long experience, ministers are generally happy to leave the day-to-day running of the department to the secretary general. As a general rule, ministers do not see their job as motivating their officials, improving the organisation of the department or monitoring the performance of routine tasks. The secretary general of the department is happy to accept the responsibility, since he or she is familiar with the ethos of the department and its needs, and also knows the staff and their needs, and is thus in a position to prevent any of the upheavals that might otherwise arise following a change of minister. Zimmerman (1997: 540), following interviews with former ministers and civil servants, concludes that interviewees believed that ministers did not play a 'direct role in the internal management of their departments' and that the civil servants did this.

One function where the minister must be personally involved is the promotion of staff. As explained in Chapter 6, the minister is the employer of all of the staff in his or her department and is responsible for their promotion. In practice, however, ministers do not interfere in the actual promotion arrangements made by the Department of Finance for intra- or inter-departmental promotions but accept the recommendations in this respect submitted for approval by the secretary general. Nor, by convention, do ministers intervene in staff matters, unless they are absolutely forced to do so. They see no profit for themselves in interfering and are thus very willing for such matters to be dealt with by the personnel section and the secretary general.

The main task of a minister is to ensure that his or her department advances the national interest and, in particular, the interest of that sector of the community or of national life for which it was established. Success in this task calls for the correct policies and for their effective implementation. Policies are, in the main, outlined in the pre-election programme. If the minister has ideas for a new policy, he or she simply describes it in broad terms and then leaves it to the officials to indicate what might be done. Quinn (2005: 222) notes that 'Because the next general election seems to be at least four years away does not mean that a minister has four years to complete a project . . . There are proposals that are on the minister's desk when he or she takes office, or else are part of a programme for government. By contrast, a minister's own initiatives can be difficult to introduce'.

The sources of policy include: the election manifesto commitments of the party or parties in government; the policy initiatives of ministers; recommendations from senior civil servants; public consultations; European Union and international developments; recommendations from government advisory committees and parliamentary committees; national and European court judgments; aspects of the social partnership process; the views of interest groups; new technologies; and reform programmes. Clearly the vision, drive and determination of an individual minister can have a significant impact on a particular policy area. Noel Browne with the campaign to eradicate tuberculosis, Micheál Martin with the introduction of smoke-free workplaces and Mary Harney with smoke-free coal are examples of this. Hardiman (2005: 17) comments:

The civil service is deeply imbued with the ethos established by the Ministers and Secretaries Act, 1924, whereby policy initiatives come from the Minister. Developing policy alternatives is a core element of their job, but the direction is set by the Minister in charge of each Department. A senior civil servant comments that 'There needs to be a strong policy focus. A Minister with a clear agenda can make a big difference. A Minister can unlock the process.' Ministers, like other politicians, 'have an ear to the ground', understand electoral preferences, and above all, are accountable to the electorate on the doorsteps and through the ballot box.

On the decisive influence of a minister, former Minister for Finance Charlie McCreevy was very clear, 'I made a vow that if I ever got the chance I was going to do what I wanted to do. That's why I'd be very critical of other ministers in my own party and in other parties. You're in a very rare position. You can change things. So go about doing it. I've had to listen to ministers proclaiming about what they can't do. I say to them: "funnily enough, we are in the government. We can change the law"' (Hannon 2004: 164).

Ministers and Civil Servants

There is a close, but hierarchical, relationship between ministers and their senior civil servants. In the course of their collaboration, care is taken by both the minister and the departmental secretary general to avoid any issues of a purely party political nature. In particular, neither touches on, even by implication, the personality or performance of the previous minister. Secretaries general maintain the traditional attitude of the civil service: that it is there to serve successive ministers with equal commitment and loyalty. Likewise, ministers are conscious of the unwritten rules of the political club to which they belong, one of which is that members do not criticise each other in front of officials. Officials seeking to ingratiate themselves with their minister by passing a critical comment on the minister's predecessor can be assured of an icy response or none at all.

At the same time, neither ministers nor civil servants allow themselves to forget the obligation of officials to involve themselves in, and be committed to, the policies and political preferences of the government of the day. Civil servants' tasks include support for ministers in promoting the interests of the government against those of the opposition. For example, in writing speeches for the Dáil, in preparing replies and accompanying notes for parliamentary questions and in assembling briefs for other occasions, civil servants present their minister's case in the best light possible, without reference to the positive aspects of the opposition's case. At all times the aim is not so much to denigrate the opposition as to enable the minister's light to shine as brightly as possible. This applies equally when the opposition is the former minister. Thus, in addition to technical or expert advice that is intellectually rigorous and does not avoid inconvenient questions, ministers get support of a positive nature.

The roles of ministers and their civil servants are complementary. Ministers are the link between their department and the representative aspects of government and politics, and the deference that it is customary to pay to their office is, in a certain sense, a deference to the democratic process itself. Civil servants like to see their minister display certain attributes. They want their minister to project what they regard, in almost a proprietary way, as their department in the best possible light, i.e. as a dynamic organisation with a competent and enthusiastic staff concerned at all times with the national interest. They want their minister to advance or defend, as occasion demands, the department at cabinet meetings, in the Dáil and elsewhere. This aspect of the relationship has been succinctly and humorously described by a former diplomat: 'It also helps if the Minister is seen to protect the Department and 'bat' for them at the Cabinet table' (Delaney 2001: 21).

Civil servants greatly value ministers who are decisive in dealing with the department's work and who know and communicate what they want. Above all, when officials put forward proposals to the minister for decision, they want to have decisions taken. Indecisiveness in a minister is the characteristic that most frustrates them. Official proposals are never lightly put forward. They are always the outcome of intensive and extensive examination of the subject at issue and are presented in such a way as to lend themselves to decision taking. Civil servants do not generally mind what the nature of the decision is. What does upset them, though fully recognising the minister's prerogative and responsibilities, is the non-return of the papers because the minister is unable or unwilling to make up his or her mind. They do not want to be continually approaching the private secretary to place the papers on the top of the minister's pile and otherwise to nudge the minister towards a decision. Equally upsetting are changes of mind on the part of the minister. It goes without saying that courtesy and appreciation are always valued by officials, especially a minister's willingness to back them when they are under attack by the media, pressure groups or others.

Different ministers have different practices in dealing with their officials. Some discuss the work only with the secretary general, the assistant secretaries and the heads of the technical branches. Some prefer to go deeper into the hierarchy and discuss issues with the officials actually dealing with them. The more restrictive style of consultation is undoubtedly more convenient for ministers, but it has two disadvantages. The first is that it cuts them off from those who are closest to the ground, so to speak. The second disadvantage, as noted in the Devlin report (Public Services Organisation Review Group 1969) and commented upon frequently by civil servants, is the forcing of unnecessary detail on senior officers at the expense of time that could be more usefully devoted to organisation, planning and more policy-oriented initiatives. Hence, matters which in a well-run business organisation would be dealt with at middle or lower level are in a government department often dealt with at the top.

A 2001 Ombudsman's report on nursing home charges argued that the increased tendency of ministers not to put their views explicitly in writing undermines accountability within departments and leads to uncertainty concerning responsibility. The Joint Committee on Health and Children (2005), following an examination of responsibility for nursing home charges in the Department of Health, said that the responsibility of ministers needs to be clarified urgently. It also suggested the establishment of cabinet systems in ministers' offices to administer departments and noted that there should be clarification of the roles of advisers and ministers of state. Connaughton (2006) notes that recent legislative reforms seeking to clarify political/managerial roles have not had the anticipated and desired impact and that the growth in ministerial advisers also seems to complicate interpretations of accountability.

Discussions with their officials take up part of every day that ministers spend in their office. Even if they do not have matters that they want to discuss with their officials, their officials will have matters that they want to discuss with their minister, so as to get a guideline or a decision, and will have informed the minister's private secretary accordingly. Nevertheless, the vast majority of officials, especially in larger departments, never meet the minister; indeed, a large number of them may only ever see the minister on television.

Dunlop (2004: 85) suggests that 'The reality is far nearer to *Yes Minister*, the classic BBC comedy depicting the relationship between a bumbling politician and his scheming civil servants than most democrats would like to think'. During an exchange in the Dáil in June 2008 Deputy Richard Bruton commented that 'The Minister could put Sir Humphrey of *Yes Minister* to shame in his capacity to defend the status quo in long, rambling replies without seeking to reform anything that makes his department more transparent or accountable to this House' (*Dáil Debates*, 4 June 2008, vol. 656, no. 2). Delaney (2001: 3) overstates the case considerably when he comments that 'the civil service is the real and permanent government and that the politicians are only puppets, time-serving mannequins who, if they are clever, will work to the strengths of their scriptwriting masters'.

SIR HUMPHREY [civil servant]: Minister I have something to say to you which you may not like to hear.

JIM [minister]: Why should today be any different?

SIR HUMPHREY: Minister, the traditional allocation of executive responsibilities has always been so determined as to liberate the Ministerial incumbent from the administrative minutiae by devolving the managerial functions to those whose experience and qualifications have better formed them for the performance of such humble offices, thereby releasing their political overlords for the more onerous duties and profound deliberations which are the inevitable concomitant of their exalted position.

JIM: Now, whatever made you think I wouldn't want to hear that?

SIR HUMPHREY: Well I thought it might upset you.

JIM: How could it, I didn't understand a single word. Humphrey for God's sake, for once in your life put it into plain English.

SIR HUMPHREY: If you insist. You are not here to run this Department.

Files

The work of officials is carried out on a file, the first page of which may be a note from the minister, the minister's private secretary or the secretary general of the department saying that 'The minister wishes to have . . . examined'. The civil servants concerned take the matter on from there. In due course the file containing all the details of the examination, including accounts of the discussions carried out with concerned parties, supported by the relevant e-mails, is presented to the minister. The minister is not expected to read all of these details, but may wish to do so. The last page of the file contains a very brief summary of what has gone before and a recommendation to the minister as to what action seems desirable. In the normal course the recommendation is that of the secretary general, who may or may not concur in the recommendation made by the officials who carried out the examination.

For example, a Minister for Agriculture who is under pressure from small farmers wanting to increase the size of their holdings or from landless people wishing to enter farming might ask his or her officials to examine how such people could be facilitated in achieving their aims. Policies might include controls on the sale of land, or the provision of low-interest loans or grants. Any social and economic advantages of the course proposed would be pointed out, as would any likely objections from all possible quarters. When the matter has been examined the minister must decide whether to accept the recommendations arising from the examination, either fully or in part, or to reject them.

Ministers have different ways of dealing with files. Some read the file from cover to cover. This, however, is rare, since time does not normally permit such attention to detail. Most ministers read the final page only and draw up a mental or written list of questions (usually the former) to ask the secretary general. Others may not read any of the papers but may invite the secretary general to tell them what they contain. Some ministers are more disposed to discussion than to reading. One way or the other, ministers arrive at some decision – even if it is a decision to put the file away among their papers for further consideration at a later date. When a positive decision is taken – and such a decision may be not to proceed further – this is communicated. Again, ministers differ in their manner of communication. Rarely do they write at length on a file. More generally, they merely note 'I agree' or 'Go ahead' over their initials, or will communicate their wishes orally to their private secretary or to the secretary general of the department, who will then briefly note the minister's decision on the file. Some commentators suggest that Freedom of Information legislation has resulted in less records being put on file.

The file is returned through the assistant secretary to the official directly involved, who then arranges for whatever action is required, for example the putting in train of new legislation, the drafting of a scheme or the writing of a letter. Ministers do not normally get involved in the details of the implementation of their decisions, though this depends on the importance of the issue. If there is a need for a publicity campaign, ministers will wish to be very much involved.

A wide variety of other files is also submitted to a minister. These include files on which the minister's wishes are sought, on who should be appointed to a particular board or committee, or on whether he or she will attend a certain function or meet some deputation. It is not unusual that a recommendation is made in each of these situations. They include also files where the minister's signature is required on statutory instruments or on warrants of appointment.

All files and all requests by officials to see the minister are channelled through the private secretary. The latter uses discretion in presenting the files and requests, choosing the most opportune moment for doing so. On those occasions when it is vital to have some matter cleared quickly, the private secretary can usually find a way to help departmental colleagues, using his or her own experience of when and how it is best to get the minister's consent.

The report of the Joint Committee on Health and Children (2005) and the Travers report (2005) concerned the whereabouts of a file in the Department of Health and Children and their recommendations on file management are dealt with in Chapter 6.

Meetings, Communications and Public Relations

Meeting people is an essential part of ministers' daily work. The meetings they attend range from formal assemblies such as Dáil sessions and cabinet meetings to private interviews with individuals or small groups. Ministers and their staff must make special preparations for each type of meeting. For many of these occasions ministers are provided with a brief, which (in the case of meetings that will be conducted by the minister) explains the background and purpose of the visit and suggests what action might be appropriate. In addition, ministers have contact with a much wider circle of people by means of correspondence; they also devote considerable care to maintaining a high profile and projecting their image in the most favourable light among the public in general.

Dáil

Ministers must attend the Dáil for all business relating to their department. By convention, they also attend for the announcement of each day's business. They normally assemble for these occasions in the office of the Government Chief Whip in Leinster House and enter the chamber in file behind the Taoiseach, usually occupying the same seats each time. When presenting their own legislation ministers are accompanied in the chamber by the officials who have prepared it. Thorough briefing is provided, and ministers ensure that they are familiar with its every detail. The same level of briefing is not required when ministers are replying to a motion, whether one being debated in private members' time or on the adjournment of the Dáil, since on these occasions they deliver a prepared speech and the opposition has little opportunity to raise detailed questions of an ad hoc nature.

Under Dáil Standing Order 21(3), TDs may raise issues that relate to a particular minister's department through a 'Motion on the Adjournment of the House'. This takes place after the normal business of the House on Tuesdays, Wednesdays or Thursdays. Only four matters can be raised on any one day and the discussion lasts for ten minutes per issue: five minutes for the TD who raises the matter and five for the minister who replies. No vote is taken as the issue is purely for debate. No supplementary questions are allowed. Items will be disallowed if they are too broad for one individual minister or if they were already treated in the previous four months.

Government Meetings

Ministers are expected to attend all government meetings. The agenda always contains one or more items that have been placed there at each minister's request, seeking authority to proceed with some piece of legislation, to introduce some new programme or merely to bring to the notice of the government some matter such as the accounts of a state-sponsored body. Ministers argue forcibly for measures that they want to introduce and must be in a position to counter arguments put forward by other ministers, particularly by the Minister for Finance, who is always fully briefed on every proposal. Ministers are often judged on their success in achieving what they seek at government meetings, where, however good their briefing, they must also exhibit considerable personal skills.

A second role that ministers have at government meetings is to contribute to the collective deliberations and decisions of the cabinet as a whole on matters that are intrinsically important or sensitive. A minister's officials do not, because they are not so equipped, advise on matters that do not concern their own department, and for such briefing the minister relies greatly on the counsel provided by his or her political adviser. The skills required by ministers in cabinet include succinctness and persuasiveness as well as analytic ability and a general understanding of issues that are not obviously inter-connected. Also helpful is 'political weight' and a past record of good judgment.

Party Meetings

All the political parties hold weekly meetings of TDs, senators and members of the European Parliament in Leinster House when the Dáil is in session. Meetings of the party in office are attended by ministers, who advise the backbenchers of legislation and other projects under consideration in their departments. The ministers, for their part, receive grass-roots views on how the public is reacting to the government's policies and on the issues that are of most immediate public concern. From these reactions the ministers quickly gauge how they themselves are performing.

Government Backbenchers

Government backbenchers may meet a minister individually or as a group. Individual interviews are much more frequent because government parties have few backbench committees. The minister is not accompanied by officials when meeting backbenchers. Ministers take particular care to be helpful to their backbenchers and many deputations are met at their request. Any information that is likely to be helpful to them in their constituencies is made available, and if a minister is going to visit a constituency, the first to know about the visit, and be invited to take part, are his or her local backbench colleagues.

Constituents

Ministers are keenly aware that without their constituents they would not be in office in the first place and therefore the needs of constituents are very high on a minister's list of priorities. Being a high-profile cabinet minister is no guarantee of re-election, as illustrated by Brian Lenihan Snr in 1973, by Justin Keating, Patrick Cooney and Conor Cruise O'Brien in 1977, by Niamh Bhreathnach in 1997 and by Michael McDowell in 2007. In 1987 Labour Party leader Dick Spring held his Dáil seat for Kerry North by just four votes after a total recount and in 2002 he narrowly lost this seat. Then Minister Mary Coughlan comments, 'It's an awful, awful way to live your life: to think that you could burst yourself for five years and because of one thing or another you lose your seat. I've been very lucky; I have never lost. There are others who have lost and come back and I very much admire their willpower' (Banotti 2008).

Constituents' needs tend not to take up much of a minister's departmental office time, since such matters are comprehensively dealt with by the staff of the minister's private office. Constituents do, however, take up a considerable amount of time at weekends. It is not unusual for a minister to spend Friday evening, all of Saturday and even part of Sunday in meeting constituents. Constituents expect this level of attention. At these meetings, or 'clinics' as they are called, the minister listens, notes and promises to do all he or she can about the problems presented. It is then for the staff of the minister's private office to follow up these matters. Barry Desmond (2000: 43–4) states that he held clinics every Saturday morning and afternoon and every Sunday morning:

> Our four sons saw me in between these clinics and our family social life at weekends was minimal. Apart from a social drink with close friends on Saturday nights, my clinic routine continued unrelentingly for twenty years. The only respites were the month of August and bank holiday weekends. Sitting in cold and damp rooms in the middle of winter, jaded from a hectic week in the Dáil, carefully recording all the details of multiple constituents' problems, was an exercise in sheer endurance. Without this grind and the voluntary assistance at every clinic of dedicated party activists, I would never have been returned to the Dáil . . . It all added up to an eighty-hour week, thirty hours in the Dáil, thirty in the constituency and twenty at party meetings.

Deputations

In the case of deputations, which are usually seeking some specific action or favour, ministers are presented with a detailed brief informing them of all they should know about the group, what further information they should seek from them and how far they can accommodate their demands. Ministers generally have considerable skill in using their briefs during these meetings and in being able to send groups away impressed with their reception. Ministers are invariably accompanied by officials on these occasions, who can assist should unanticipated matters arise in the course of the meeting. This arrangement clearly suits the minister, but it also suits the officials, since it keeps them in the picture. It has been cynically observed that the civil servants are there to ensure that the minister does not give anything away; civil servants might not altogether disagree with this, but are more likely to say they are there to ensure a productive outcome.

Members of opposition parties normally visit a minister's office only as part of a joint deputation on some constituency issue. This applies even to former ministers or current shadow ministers.

Courtesy Visits

In the case of visitors who have no specific business and whose visits are more in the nature of a courtesy call (for example foreign dignitaries or ambassadors or the heads of international organisations), the minister's brief contains personal information about the visitor, the current state of relations between the visitor's organisation and the department and suggestions as to matters that the minister might raise in the course of their meeting. Officials do not generally attend on these occasions.

Journeys Abroad

Overseas journeys fall into four broad categories: to attend meetings of international bodies; to promote the image of Ireland abroad and to encourage investment both in Ireland and in Irish exports; to study particular developments that might be relevant to planned initiatives at home; and to support members of the Defence Forces engaged on foreign duty. Meetings in the first category include those of the European Union, mainly held in Brussels and Luxembourg, and of bodies such as the World Health Organization, the International Labour Organization, the World Trade Organization, the United Nations and the Organisation for Economic Co-operation and Development.

The meetings of the Council of Ministers of the EU are the most numerous and regular. The ministers most in demand are those for Foreign Affairs, Agriculture and Finance, who are generally involved in at least one meeting a month. Meetings demanding the attendance of other ministers are held less frequently and at irregular intervals. The minister attending is provided with a brief on each item on the agenda and also with a speaking note (a short speech) on those items in which Ireland has a specific interest. Before each meeting the minister and the minister's officials generally discuss the brief with Ireland's Permanent Representative to the EU and his or her staff to ensure that they have the latest information on the subject at issue, including the stances likely to be adopted by the other member states, and to reach agreement on the line to be taken at the meeting.

Attendance at meetings of the Council of Ministers generally involves bilateral contacts with other ministers or with members of the European Commission. These meetings, held on the margins of the council meetings, are also attended by officials.

In addition to the formal meetings of the Council of Ministers, it is sometimes necessary for a minister or even a group of ministers to go specially to Brussels to make representations on behalf of Ireland or to explain more fully the Irish position in certain cases, for example in the case of Ireland's application for structural funds.

When ministers travel abroad on official business the practical arrangements in terms of transport and accommodation are normally made by the embassy in line with local practice. Meetings to promote investment at home or marketing abroad are generally arranged by the state-sponsored bodies concerned, such as IDA Ireland (Industrial Development Agency), An Bord Bia (Food Board) or Fáilte Ireland (Irish Tourist Board), or by the co-operative An Bord Bainne (Milk Board). Potential investors or purchasers are invited to meet the visiting minister, while appearances on local television and at other social functions are also arranged. The detailed programme is put in place by the state-sponsored body concerned, some of whose officials accompany the minister, as does one departmental official. Sometimes the party is accompanied by exporters and by journalists. In reply to a parliamentary question on 28 February 2008 it was revealed that the number of ministerial-led trade missions was twenty-three in 2006 and fourteen in 2007.

As regards the use of the Ministerial Air Transport Service, the Cabinet Handbook requires that applications should be submitted to the Taoiseach in respect of every mission, including the destination, route, timings, passenger details and purpose of travel. The justifying need to use the service should be set out in every application. The relative cost of the Ministerial Air Transport Service over possible alternatives is always borne in mind in preparing travel plans. The service is primarily provided by the Gulfstream IV and Learjet 45 aircraft, which were specifically acquired for that purpose. The average total cost per hour of the Gulfstream is €7,100 and of the Learjet is €2,100 (reply to a parliamentary question on 10 July 2008). The Beech Super Kingair 200 turboprop aircraft, which is now used primarily in a training role, is made available for ministerial air transport from time to time, mainly for internal flights and a limited number of flights to European destinations (*Dáil Debates*, 4 October 2007, vol. 638, no. 5). The aircraft are housed at the main Air Corps base at Casement Aerodrome, Baldonnel, County Dublin, and flights are considered as military flights.

Visits by the Minister for Defence to the forces on duty abroad under the auspices of the United Nations are largely for reasons of morale but also to see at first hand the situation in which they operate and to acquire information that may be of use in advising on government policy. On such occasions the minister is accompanied by the Chief of Staff of the Defence Forces and by a departmental official.

Another regular occasion of visits abroad is the celebration, by parades, concerts and other social occasions, of St Patrick's Day, particularly in the United States and Australia. Irish ministers are often the central figures in such celebrations, which are a global marketing opportunity and a truly unique framework to showcase modern Ireland on the world stage. In a valued, decades-old tradition, the Taoiseach travels to Washington to present a bowl of shamrock to the US President at the White House. The Taoiseach takes advantage of this unique opportunity to exchange views on a number of international issues.

Correspondence

All letters addressed to the minister are processed in the first instance by his or her private secretary, who reserves by far the greater proportion to be dealt with by the staff of the private office and the department. Ministers see very little of the routine correspondence and are entirely dependent on their private secretary's judgment as to what they should see. The private secretary is also responsible for determining which replies should be signed by the minister and those which require careful scrutiny. The general guidelines are that ministers sign letters to other ministers, to government backbenchers, senators and local councillors, to previous ministers of any party, to shadow ministers, to people who are considered 'important' and, perhaps most frequent of all, to the minister's constituents.

The Media/Public Relations

One of the central pillars in democratic society is the mass media. In recent years the media has taken a significantly increased interest in all aspects of the activities of government departments and the wider public service. It has played an important role in providing a forum for debate and dialogue, both among politicians and more widely. Feeney (2003: 75–6) comments:

Political communication is facilitated through the mass media. Politicians and aspirant politicians use newspapers, radio and television to communicate with the electorate. The battle for political influence and support takes place in print and on the airwaves. The era of political communication through mass meetings has disappeared. Other means of communication, through clinics and door-to-door canvassing, are still important, but they only reach a small fraction of the electorate. So, there is a heavy dependency on access to and use of mass media. It is therefore clearly very important that the media fulfil two functions. Firstly, that it is a means of communication. This means that it is successful in reaching all the population. Secondly, that it provides an objective and fair vehicle for the transmission of information, debate and opinion. This latter function is at the heart of the role of the media in a democratic society. If the mass media is biased towards government or other vested interests it cannot fulfil this role properly.

However, there is a delicate balance here. Callanan (2006: 11), referring to a popular radio programme, notes that one 'effect can be "Government by *Liveline*" a firefighting exercise where it is necessary to respond to the latest "crisis". This may have the virtue of being a highly responsive approach, but it tends to result in short term "quick fixes", which taken together can often work at cross-purposes from one another.'

Another particularly noticeable development in recent years is the constant and increasing search for publicity by ministers of all governments. All ministers are now very concerned with their public image and take considerable care to ensure that their activities are projected to the public as frequently and as favourably as possible. This projection is effected in a number of ways.

Nearly every department has an information section headed by a press or information officer, with whom the minister is in constant touch. This section is the point of contact for journalists and others seeking information about the department's activities. Civil servants do not speak to the press themselves, but are expected to supply promptly all requested material through the information section.

A significant part of the work of an information section is the issue of press releases about departmental developments to the daily and provincial newspapers, to the radio and television stations and to relevant journals. These may be announcements about projects being introduced or being discontinued; exhortations to the public about health issues or safety measures; statements about EU moneys procured by the minister, or about the minister's attendance at meetings at home or abroad.

The addresses given by ministers on purely party political occasions are not circulated by the information section, even though they touch on the work of the minister's department. Instead, they are circulated as appropriate by the minister's private office, with the phrase 'as requested' as a heading.

The same degree of propriety is exercised in regard to material sought by ministers for use either by themselves or by other ministers at national party conferences or during general election campaigns. This is a delicate area, and one in which each side appreciates the sensibilities of the other. It is generally dealt with by tactful requests on the part of the minister's private office and by the provision of purely factual information on the part of the civil service. The minister or his or her special adviser then injects the desired political slant into the material provided. On major political occasions, however, such as regional party conferences or by-election conventions, the Government Press Secretary usually gives copies of the speeches to the political correspondents.

Ministers prepare carefully for their appearances on television and radio programmes or at press conferences. In recent years their preparation includes coaching by public relations and media consultants. Most ministers and their information officers seek to establish a close relationship with the specialist journalists covering the work areas of their department and, indeed, with journalists generally. Journalist contacts are used to get publicity for ministers' legislative and policy plans, for their stance in cabinet, for their victories over colleagues, or to publicise cuts by the Department of Finance affecting their projects. This publicity is achieved through telephone calls from the minister, interviews, press releases, entertainment and invitations to accompany the minister on official visits and other public appearances.

Ministers of State

Ministers of state are commonly referred to as junior ministers. They are not members of the government and have no right of attendance at government meetings. They may attend when invited to present information on subjects with which they are particularly familiar. Their responsibilities are assigned to them either by special orders (known as delegation of functions orders) made by the government and vesting ministerial powers in named ministers of state, or by specific delegation by the minister in charge of the department. Delegation of ministerial functions orders are made under section 2 of the Ministers and Secretaries (Amendment) (No. 2) Act 1977. There must be a request from the relevant cabinet minister for such an order; the delegation lasts only as long as the cabinet minister and minister of state are in the relevant department, the delegation is 'subject to the general superintendence and control of the minister of the government' (section 2.2(d)), the cabinet minister remains concurrently vested with the powers (section 2.2(e)) and the cabinet minister remains responsible to the Dáil (section 2.2(f)).

It is the ministers of state who initiate legislation in their areas of responsibility, but they may not submit any proposals themselves to government. Such proposals must first be approved by the minister in charge. If the minister does not approve of them, the proposals do not emerge publicly and must be abandoned by the minister of state. If they are approved by the minister and reach government, the minister of state may, depending on the attitude of the minister, present them there. If they are approved it is normally the minister of state who presents them to the Oireachtas subsequently and pilots them through the various stages. Parliamentary questions related to their area of work are also taken by ministers of state.

In general, the work of ministers of state is largely the same as that of ministers – in relation to their Dáil and constituency responsibilities, meeting deputations and attending to the needs of backbenchers and party members. In all of this work they have available to them the services of officials, including a private office almost identical in staffing and structure to that of the minister.

Ministers of state carry out their responsibilities under the watchful eye of their superior, who does not want to be upstaged and who wishes to be kept informed about everything that is going on. Indeed, it is not unusual to have a certain rivalry between minister and minister of state in the carrying out of the work of the department. Generally the minister retains all the high-profile work, such as that relating to the European Union and the announcement of new projects that are likely to be publicly well received.

The role and status of a minister of state, therefore, to some extent depend on the attitude of the senior minister. Those to whom little of the department's work has been delegated must console themselves by devoting their time to their constituencies. Nevertheless, frustration occasionally leads them to approach the Taoiseach. Depending on the personality of the minister concerned, the complaint can sometimes be redressed. If it cannot, the Taoiseach can usually find a means of utilising the services of the minister of state by assigning him or her some work of benefit to the party, such as reviving party organisation in a constituency where it is flagging. In departments where rivalry exists between a minister and a minister of state, the officials, by a judicious exercise of their traditional discretion, not to say caution, are generally able to maintain the balance to the satisfaction of all concerned.

Taoiseach Bertie Ahern announced in June 2007 that he had decided to expand the number of ministers of state from seventeen to twenty because of the increasing pressures they faced, among them the increasing complexity of policy issues and the need for accountability to Oireachtas committees. Taoiseach Brian Cowen justified this number in his reply to a parliamentary question on 1 July 2008:

> I am absolutely satisfied that, in order to discharge political accountability, two or three democratically elected politicians – a Minister and one or two

Ministers of State – should be asked to run a Department which may have many hundreds of thousands of people working for it. I do not see what could be more respectful of our democratic institutions than to give political responsibility for running Departments to politicians. We do not live in a technocracy – we live in a democracy. People elect us to this House. This House elects Governments. We have a broad range of domestic and international responsibilities in terms of how we serve the people and the country. I assure the Deputy that those who hold positions in this Administration have extensive and responsible jobs to do.

The Taoiseach reduced the number of Ministers of State to fifteen in April 2009.

The Minister's Private Office

Guidelines as to the staffing of ministers' offices are laid down by the Minister for Finance. The guidelines refer to their private and constituency offices, though in practice no such separate offices are discernible. The staff in the private office, headed by the private secretary, carry out whatever tasks the minister requires, making no distinction between departmental and constituency tasks. The guidelines specify the number of staff in a private office and in a constituency office, and that there should be only one personal secretary, one personal assistant and one special adviser per minister. Either the personal assistant or the personal adviser may be located in a minister's constituency office.

The purpose of the private office is threefold: to provide a secretariat for the minister, to co-ordinate the minister's activities and to act as a liaison between the minister and the department. The office communicates ministerial instructions to the sections of the department and also acts as a filter between them and the minister. The private secretary must be prepared to work long and irregular hours. These arise particularly when the Dáil is in session. Ministers may be required to be in Leinster House until the Dáil adjourns and often some time after that. These late hours are a favourite time for backbenchers to seek out a minister. They are often accompanied by outsiders whom they want to introduce to the minister. The private secretary usually meets such persons in the first instance, advises them of the minister's availability and notes their requirements in order to pass them on, if necessary, to the department on the following day.

A major part of a private secretary's job is to get to know how the minister thinks so that he or she may confidently advise departmental officials what view the minister would take in a particular situation, or make a decision in the absence of the minister. A private secretary must know which letters should be seen by the minister personally and which he or she may sign on the minister's behalf, which telephone calls should or should not be put through, and what firm appointments can be made. Thus, a new private secretary or a private secretary who gets a new minister requires some months before he or she is at ease in this aspect of the job.

The private secretary must normally deal with all of the correspondence addressed to the minister. A large proportion of this relates to constituency matters, from the minister's own constituents and from other ministers and backbenchers about their constituents' affairs. The balance is not of such an overtly political nature and deals, indirectly or directly, with the subject matter of the minister's portfolio, making suggestions, drawing attention to developments and extending invitations. Nearly all the correspondence will be sent to the heads of the various divisions for reply. The replies fall into different categories. Some are for signature by the minister (a minister's signature always appears on letters to constituents), some by the private secretary, and some (mainly those with no political element) by the officials as part of the normal departmental correspondence. The private secretary usually signs the letters to politicians not belonging to the government party and also such other letters that the minister would be content to have him or her sign.

A certain amount of confidential or sensitive material is also received in a minister's office. This may relate to national security, political, financial or other such matters. This correspondence does not leave the minister's office. Examples are the British–Irish Intergovernmental Conference's reports received in the Departments of Foreign Affairs and Justice or those from diplomatic missions received in the Department of Foreign Affairs, and the budgetary and financial data received in the Department of Finance.

A diary of all the minister's engagements for each week is circulated to the offices of the minister(s) of state and the secretary general. Liaison is maintained with the Dáil staff, with the government secretariat, and with the Government Chief Whip's office in regard to the minister's attendance at government meetings and in the Dáil and Seanad. The private secretary is also responsible for ensuring that the minister has a firm 'pairing' arrangement if official functions will prevent him or her from being available for a critical vote in the Dáil. The private secretary also ensures that the minister has: all the necessary papers for meetings of the government; the replies to be made to oral parliamentary questions in good time; copies of the speeches to be made on the various occasions in good time; the briefs for meetings well in advance; and whatever other service the minister requires. If there is slippage, the minister complains to the secretary general of the department, who then 'reminds' the entire staff of what is expected of them through the issue of an appropriate notice over his or her own name.

The private secretary presides over a busy suite of offices with the most up-to-date equipment, including secure telephones, controlled by An Garda Síochána, with frequent changing of codes. The private secretary's office is immediately adjacent to that of the minister, and the two are in constant liaison. The degree of formality between the minister and the private secretary varies greatly, and it is not unusual for those ministers with a less formal disposition to find time to chat with the staff in their office. All the staff in the private office develop a special loyalty to the minister of the day, different in some indefinable way from their loyalty to the department.

Ministerial Cars and Drivers

Each minister is provided with a state car and ministerial cars are driven by members of An Garda Síochána who have completed special advanced driving courses. The garda authorities are responsible for the maintenance and operation of the cars. There are twenty-six vehicles in the state car fleet (reply to a parliamentary question on 10 July 2008). Vehicles used by members of An Garda Síochána in the performance of their duties are specifically excepted by regulation from the speed limits prescribed under section 46 of the Road Traffic Act 1961 and are also exempt from road tolls under section 62 of the Roads Act 1993. Hannon (2004: 147) notes, 'A gig as a ministerial driver is a much-coveted position within the gardaí and, as each appointment is entirely at each minister's discretion, the more likely candidates for preferment are subjected to intense lobbying in the run-up to the cabinet announcement. Gardaí who drive the new ministers to the Phoenix Park hope that they will click with the elated minister and be kept on.'

Special Advisers

The demands on ministers and ministers of state have grown. In the past, ministers were a group of full-time politicians served by their civil servants. They were expected to be absolute repositories of all knowledge and wisdom in the areas covered by their briefs, with the doctrine of corporation sole making ministers legally answerable for the acts of every civil servant in their department. Ministers can no longer carry this burden alone and therefore share the load with special advisers, who 'help keep the minister in touch with party political opinions, with other ministers and with outside interests' (Collins and Cradden 1989: 56).

The practice of appointing special advisers to ministers dates back to the inter-party government of 1954 to 1957, when two appointments were made. The next such appointment was not made until 1970, when Dr Martin O'Donoghue (on the staff of Trinity College, Dublin) became personal adviser to Taoiseach Jack Lynch. The governments that took office in 1973 and 1977 had four and six advisers respectively. Since the early 1980s almost every minister has an adviser (variously designated as special, political, economic, social or policy adviser). The Taoiseach usually has more than one.

The role of the special adviser is set out in section 11 of the Public Services Management Act 1997 as being to monitor the Programme for Government and assist with its implementation. They are also tasked with giving ministers advice and keeping them informed on a wide range of issues, including business, financial, economic, political, administrative and media matters. They perform other functions, such as speechwriting, as may be directed by the minister. They have access to departmental files and may see all submissions to the minister. Special advisers generally meet on the afternoon before a cabinet meeting, with the Taoiseach's programme manager as chairperson.

Special advisers cease to hold their position when the relevant minister ceases to hold office as outlined in the 1997 act, and their terms and conditions are determined by the Minister for Finance. The appointments are determined by the Civil Service Regulations Acts 1956 to 1996 and any other act in force relating to the civil service. They are generally paid at the level of principal in the civil service. The code of conduct for office-holders produced by the Standards in Public Office Commission in July 2003 provides in paragraph 1.5 that 'Ministers also have a responsibility to ensure that special advisers are accountable to them for the performance of their functions in accordance with the provisions of the Public Service Management Act, 1997'.

Advisers are not normally civil servants. Some are former political activists, others are career civil servants who have established a good working relationship with a particular minister, and still others have worked as journalists or broadcasters. The selection is made by the minister, but the appointment must be approved by the Taoiseach. The job is not advertised. Ministers appoint someone they know personally, generally a party supporter in whom they have complete trust, with qualifications and contacts that the minister considers useful, and total commitment to advancing the minister's policies and career. The qualifications need not be those of an expert. Advisers frequently accompany a minister from one portfolio to another. They are usually fiercely loyal to their minister, on whose career they themselves depend, and sensitive to what they perceive as disloyal criticism. The British Cabinet Secretary (Britain's most senior civil servant), Sir Richard Wilson (2002: 10) said, 'I believe it is right that ministers should be able to have special advisors to act as their political eyes and ears, help the Department understand the mind of the Minister, work alongside officials on the Minister's behalf and handle party-political aspects of government business. They can help protect the civil service against politicisation.'

In considering the role of advisers, it is necessary to bear in mind that while civil servants are conscious of political realities generally in furnishing advice to ministers and in recommending courses of action, they see their role as that of serving successive ministers and not as one of taking overtly political matters into account in framing policies, even if they were competent to do so. It is necessary to remember also that officials' experience is such as to enable them to provide information and advice only on the subject matter of the minister's portfolio and not on the wider issues with which, as a politician and as a member of the government, a minister must be concerned. The adviser, on the other hand, regards the minister as a politician, as a deputy, as a member of the government and as a person. Thus, the service which an adviser provides for a minister is essentially different from that provided by officials. It includes the following elements:

1. Discussing with the minister the political and electoral implications of the advice coming from the civil service, including its likely reception by the media, especially in the case of delicate measures such as the withdrawal of a benefit or the imposition of a charge, for example a fee for a fishing licence.
2. Discussing organisational changes suggested by the secretary general of the department, or changes which the minister is thinking of proposing, for example in regard to the location of staff away from headquarters.
3. Examining matters in breadth as well as in depth by consulting outside sources and taking soundings on (1) and (2), and drawing attention to aspects that the civil servants may not have referred to.
4. Researching those matters to be raised by other ministers at government meetings and providing briefing to enable the minister to take part in the discussion and put forward a point of view. As implied earlier, this is a service that the minister's departmental officials cannot provide.
5. Dealing with constituency matters in a broader framework than the normal constituency correspondence handled by the private secretary demands. This entails keeping in touch with government, local authority or other public service developments in the constituency and with commercial and business interests there.
6. Examining formal speeches and informal addresses from a presentational point of view, having regard to the minister's personality and style of delivery, and thus turning information from within the department into politically usable material.
7. Writing speeches of a specifically political nature for the minister.
8. Acting as a replication of the minister in many respects, as an extension of his or her political personality, as an extra pair of eyes and ears, doing what the minister would do personally if the time was available.

The arrangement bears some, though only a very limited, resemblance to the so-called 'cabinet' system that obtains in many European countries and in the European Union. Under that system a minister (or a member of the European Commission) has a group of eight to ten people, known as a 'cabinet', whose work is broadly that described above, though on a more elaborate scale. There have been casual references from time to time to the establishment of a 'cabinet' system in Ireland, but the matter has not been considered in any detail. Its introduction would necessitate radical changes affecting the patterns, traditions and values of Ireland's political culture, to an extent that would probably be unacceptable.

The current system of advisers has found general favour. In support, three broad arguments have been advanced. The first is that it prepares ministers for discussions at government level on areas outside their department's responsibilities, thus enabling them to make a constructive contribution to the collective decision-making process of any government. Second, it supplies specialised advice to ministers on certain policy areas, providing a different perspective (and thus a valuable alternative) to the expert advice available within the department. Third, it gives advice on the political implications of policy or other measures, including the maintenance of a high public profile, thus enabling the civil service to keep out of party politics. Ministers and advisers often say that officials can be hidebound by their narrow specialist approach to issues and that they do not sense, and are not interested in, the political angle.

The role of the adviser was described in detail by two political advisers to the Joint Committee on Health and Children on 27 April 2005. All policy documents submitted to the minister were copied to the relevant advisers, and the relevant advisers were made aware of any key meetings concerning either a policy change or any high-profile topic or incident. Relevant documents were circulated to advisers who participated at management committee meetings. As a general rule it was a matter for each principal to decide on which issues should involve the advisers. Alternatively, advisers could ask to be involved in a particular topic or issue in the department. In practice, the working relationships developed on an informal and constructive basis. Direct contact occurred between the minister and members of staff of the department in accordance with normal practice. The advisers did not see themselves as part of the management team. They reported to the minister and worked very closely with the secretary general and other officials on implementing policy. There was a two-pronged approach. The minister and the secretary general were the bosses, so to speak, of the department, but the adviser reported to the minister. The MAC (management advisory committee) of the department held meetings, on

Monday mornings, which did not include the minister, advisers or anybody else. That is where officials did the work that was relevant for the running of the department. The MAC meetings that the minister and political advisers did attend were normally issue driven, with items on the agenda for discussion on the day. 'Politicians and ministers, in particular, cannot do without the civil servants and civil servants cannot do without the ministers or the government. There must be intertwining and respect for both positions' (D. Gillane, political adviser, evidence to Joint Committee on Health and Children, 27 April 2005). The 2005 Travers report said that special advisers should avoid becoming involved to a great extent in the day-to-day operation of the administration of the department. It commented (2005: 85):

> Be clear that special advisors to the minister, appointed to the department for no longer than the minister's term of office in the department, are *not* part of the line management system of the department. The briefing of special advisors by department officials and the fact that special advisors attend particular meetings should not be considered, and should not be accepted as, an alternative to the direct briefing of the minister on important areas of policy and operation.

In general, civil servants live happily with advisers, especially now that an adviser's appointment terminates when the minister leaves office. (Up to 1981 those advisers who wished to remain were often appointed established civil servants 'in the public interest', as provided for in the Civil Service Commissioners Act 1956 – since revoked. Needless to say, this practice interfered with promotion arrangements and consequently did not find favour with existing civil servants.) Strains can arise, however, as when advisers reword letters, speeches or replies to parliamentary questions prepared by officials to make them overtly political or to include material discarded as unsuitable by the civil servants; or when advisers intrude into routine departmental work or departmental contacts, creating confusion as to who actually speaks for the minister. Nevertheless, a spirit of altruism generally prevails. Civil servants recognise that ministers and advisers tend to live for the present, whereas departments take the long-term view and have seen ministers come and go; they recognise the minister's prerogative in making such appointments and understand their political desirability. The advisers, for their part, though impatient at the outset at what they sometimes refer to scathingly as 'bureaucracy', come in time to see at least some of its advantages. Both sides know the rules of the game, and each is conscious of the need to keep off the other's territory. However, Murphy (2005) observes that the role of the civil service in providing non-political objective advice, and acting as a buttress for ministers against the demands of sectional and constituency interests, seems to him to be weakening.

In 2008 two junior ministers had special advisers appointed to them by virtue of their special status in government. These are the Government Chief Whip and the 'super junior' Minister for Children, who are entitled to attend cabinet meetings. Requests more widely from ministers of state for the assignment of special advisers to them have not, in general, been successful.

In 2008 Taoiseach Brian Cowen told his ministers that special advisers were no longer allowed to attend meetings of cabinet sub-committees. A practice had grown where ministers and ministers of state attending cabinet sub-committee meetings were accompanied by their special and political advisers. Instead, ministers can only be joined at sub-committee meetings by the secretary general of their department. No politically appointed special advisers are allowed to attend.

Programme Managers

A new development introduced by the 1993–1994 Fianna Fáil/Labour government was the appointment of programme managers. Programme managers are there to monitor that the government party leaders' wishes and decisions are executed and that the agreed Programme for Government is implemented. They operate 'along the blurred borders between politics and administration' (O'Halpin 1996). Some of them were civil servants and some were appointed from outside the service. The practice was continued by the succeeding Fine Gael/Labour/Democratic Left government but was discontinued by the Fianna Fáil/Progressive Democrats government that took office in 1997, save for the Taoiseach and the Tánaiste. The outgoing government in 2007 and its Fianna Fáil/Green/Progressive Democrats successor in 2007 continued this practice.

In reply to a parliamentary question on 20 April 2005 Taoiseach Bertie Ahern stated:

> The role of the programme managers is to assist in dealing with the complexities and volume of Government business. Their primary function is to ensure effective co-ordination in the implementation of the Government's programme. The terms of reference and the job description of my programme manager are no different than those of his predecessor in the rainbow government led by former Deputy John Bruton. My programme manager advises me on a wide range of matters including administrative, business, social, financial and economic issues. My programme manager meets other ministerial advisers on a weekly basis and reviews the papers for the Government meeting of that week. With his colleagues, he monitors and reports to me on the implementation of the Programme for Government.

The managers meet formally each week, when they monitor the implementation of legislative and other commitments in the Programme for Government. They also meet bilaterally, where they seek solutions to inter-departmental disagreements and so save ministers' time. The atmosphere between appointees of different coalition parties is businesslike and professional.

FitzGerald (2003: 99) comments, 'it is, however, most important that such appointees to posts as Special Advisers or Programme Managers be genuine experts, well qualified to undertake this kind of work, and not just pals of a minister brought in to give moral support, or to promote his or her public image – both of which have clearly happened in quite a number of instances in recent years'.

Press Officers

Since the government must be able to communicate, it makes sense for its statements to be co-ordinated, and issued efficiently. Although all information may have political consequences, it is not all necessarily political in content. Vincent Browne (2005) comments:

> RTÉ news and its news feature programmes fix the national agenda. It influences whether crime (people's criminality) shall dominate public debate (always does), whether tax reductions are the major issue (again), indeed how we perceive taxation (RTÉ repeatedly refers to exchequer monies as 'taxpayer's money', thereby giving a twist to public understanding of taxation – the alternative way of looking at this is to regard public finances as properly belonging to the public at large) . . . Next to RTÉ, *The Irish Times* is the most influential media organ in Ireland. It is the 'opinion former'.

Every government has sought to present its policies, and its results, in the best light. In recent years there has been a growing trend towards the appointment of press advisers by ministers. The press advisers meet on the same morning as the cabinet to discuss the coming events of the week and what their respective ministers are doing; this meeting is chaired by the Government Press Secretary. Press officers are generally paid at principal or assistant principal officer level.

Aileen O'Meara (2007: 165), formerly RTÉ's Chief Health Correspondent, notes:

> To get a story radio needs sound and voices; television needs pictures. Micheál Martin [then Health Minister] was happy to provide both. He made himself readily available, held numerous press conferences, facilitated tight deadlines, and did live interviews at the drop of a hat. The Minister and his team 'fed' the stories, and the media responded.

As well as the Department's own media office, staffed by civil servants from other parts of the service with little or no media training, the Minister also had his own personal media adviser. Catriona Meehan's job was to be on round-the-clock call for the health correspondents, news editors, and programme editors looking for a 'spin' or the presence of the Minister in the studio or on television that evening. The starting point for every communications adviser is to make sure everyone had a press release; going beyond this straightforward task is essential if the client is to keep on top of the media's demands. Meehan facilitated the tight deadlines that broadcast journalists worked to; she complained if she felt the story did not reflect what the Minister said; she phoned journalists before press events to ensure their attendance, especially the television cameras. In contrast, it was difficult, if not impossible, to get to talk to a policy maker. From the top down, officials were suspicious, or feared the media, especially, the broadcast media.

An important element is that the public sector does not enjoy favourable treatment in the media in Ireland, which tends to focus on negative stories. Callanan (2007: 27) notes, 'While the media does play some role in debating and discussing public policy choices as well as prompting analysis and highlighting problem areas, much media reporting is devoted to incidents of policy failure and ultimately finding people to throw stones at. Most achievements or successes go unnoticed.'

The timing of news releases is important. A British special adviser and press officer famously circulated a memorandum on 11 September 2001 suggesting to ministers that it would be a 'good day to bury bad news', which ultimately led to the resignation of the special adviser and the minister. Finlay (1998: 28) comments in relation to the reduction of food subsidies in August 1984 that 'The cabinet decided instead to instruct the Government Information Service to release the decision through civil service channels, apparently hoping that the fact that it was a holiday weekend would mean that no-one would notice'. The government was criticised in May 2008 for the publication of the sixth report of the Morris Tribunal into the conduct of some gardaí in Donegal on the day that the new government was formed, thereby overshadowing the report.

The wealth of information from public service organisations available on the Internet, together with instantaneous information, detailed discussions on blogs and commentaries on policy matters is unprecedented. Brandenburg and Zalinski (2007) note that the 2007 general election was 'the first time in Irish politics when the internet and the new media played such an important role both for the media and for the parties and the candidates'. Certainly RTÉ did excellent work in bringing this content online, and this was picked up by Internet users.

Conclusion

The business of government is now more complex and demanding than ever before. Ministers have been personally involved in a range of policy initiatives, including the promotion of the Irish language, the plastic shopping bag levy, the ban on smoking in workplaces and a proposed ban on incandescent light bulbs. They face a growing range of challenges posed by factors such as economic uncertainty, integration, changes in the labour market, reducing carbon emissions, multi-drug use, the incessant demand for electricity and energy generally, developments at EU level and the need to achieve consensus on the major issues facing the country, which impose enormous demands on ministers. Ruairí Quinn reflects (2005: 305) on his time as a minister:

> Reading back over my journals for that period, I had forgotten just how intense and time-consuming the life of a government minister can be. The range of issues, combined with the speed at which they arrive on your desk, is enormous. I suspect that part of the satisfaction of being in power is the constant challenge of decision-making, but the other side is the fear of defeat, of public reproach and intense opposition within your own ranks.

The demands on ministers are likely to increase, rather than decrease, as we face into the future.

Web Resources

Iris Oifigiúil (Irish official state gazette) at www.irisoifigiuil.ie
Standards in Public Office Commission (including codes of conduct for office-holders and non-office-holders) at www.sipo.gov.ie

3

THE DÁIL AND THE SEANAD

The Oireachtas

The Constitution provides that the national parliament be known as the Oireachtas and it consists of the President and two Houses, namely Dáil Éireann and Seanad Éireann. The Oireachtas has the sole power of making laws, but any law repugnant to the Constitution may be annulled by the Supreme Court. It may not declare acts to be infringements of the law that were not so at the time of their commission. The Dáil and the Seanad must hold at least one session each year (the Houses sit for three terms each year punctuated by Christmas, Easter and summer recesses) and sittings must be public. In an emergency, however, either House may decide, with the agreement of two-thirds of the members present, to sit in private. Each House elects its own chairperson, designated Ceann Comhairle of the Dáil and Cathaoirleach of the Seanad, and deputy chairperson (Leas-Cheann Comhairle and Leas-Chathaoirleach) and determines its own rules and standing orders. Each House also determines its own quorum – twenty for the Dáil and twelve for the Seanad. Members have the privilege of immunity from arrest in going to and coming from either House, and are not answerable to any court or authority other than the House itself for any remark they make within either House. No person may be at the same time a member of both Houses.

The Constitution sets out the powers of the Oireachtas. In *Haughey v Moriarty* [1999] 3 IR 1 the Supreme Court, invoking the concept of the implied powers of the Oireachtas, per Hamilton CJ, noted, 'The powers of the Houses of the Oireachtas are not limited to those specifically set forth in Article 15 of the Constitution but must include such powers as are normally and necessarily exercised by a legislature in a democratic state. These powers and the exercise thereof may of course be limited by the provisions of this Constitution.'

The central role that Dáil Éireann plays in the process of Irish government cannot be overstated. However, the notion that the Oireachtas sets policy, makes the laws and then leaves it to the executive to implement the laws does not fit with how government operates in practice. The reality, as attested by many political scientists and commentators, is that the government once elected controls the Houses of the Oireachtas with a resulting diminution in the capacity of the Houses to supervise the executive. For all practical purposes, it is the government that decides policy, proposes legislation and ensures its passage through the Oireachtas and, subsequently, in its executive capacity, ensures that the laws are implemented. The only weapon available to the Dáil is a constitutional blunderbuss, a vote of 'no confidence' and the subsequent resignation of the entire government. The All-Party Oireachtas Committee on the Constitution (2002: 9–10) commented:

> . . . there is a widespread and powerful sense that the two Houses are not fulfilling their functions as effectively as they should, and that their standing and relevance are in decline. There is also a view that within the institutions of the state the role of the legislature has declined vis-à-vis those of both the executive and the judicial branches: some commentators refer to 'the executive state' to describe a system in which the government controls and regulates the life of the people to an excessive and unchecked extent. Moreover, the control of the executive usually extends, including through use of the whip system, to domination of the proceedings of parliament itself.

Hogan and Morgan (1998) describe the Irish governmental system as a 'fused executive-legislature' rather than one in which the executive and the legislature are separate. They write:

> . . . all the Dáil's powers over the Government are conditioned by the basic fact of political life which is that a Government can almost always command the support of a majority of deputies, because deputies are elected principally on the basis of the party which they have pledged themselves to support in the Dáil. Such is the strength of the whip-system that the legislature cannot be regarded as speaking with a voice independent of the executive and, so, it is realistic to characterise the central element in the Irish governmental system as a fused executive-legislature.

Writing almost thirty years earlier, the same issue was addressed by Chubb (1970) in somewhat starker terms:

> A division of functions and powers along the lines suggested by the literal meaning of the words of the Constitution does not obtain in Ireland. It would be absurd to think of the Government as having only 'executive' functions . . . Again, it would be misleading to envisage the Oireachtas as 'making laws' in the literal sense or to the extent that American congressmen, for example, are 'legislators'. The Oireachtas has the authority to declare law and thus to legitimize it. Although it makes some contribution to its content by way of criticism and amendment, the initiative in preparing and proposing bills rests

almost wholly with the government, and the origins and formulation of legislation owe little to the Oireachtas as such.

Roles of the Oireachtas

The Oireachtas:

- Provides the government (executive) from among its members.
- Debates, refines and passes all laws.
- Examines and scrutinises the work of the government.
- Seeks to ensure that the government is accountable to the people.
- Controls finances and enables the government to raise taxes.
- Protects the public and safeguards the rights of individuals.
- Examines European Union proposals before they become law.
- Debates the major political, social, economic and international issues of the day.
- Oversees the operation of the machinery of government.
- Articulates interests and mediates solutions in the political system.
- Represents the people in the democratic process.
- Legitimises the actions of government through granting or withholding support.
- Determines the life of the government through providing or withholding support.
- Provides a public forum in which opposition parties demonstrate whether they could form a good alternative government.
- Meets the needs of constituents through highlighting grievances and seeking remedies.
- Facilitates the recruitment of new politicians.
- Trains aspiring ministers and candidates for high political office.

These parliamentary functions are performed within a constitutional framework that includes the doctrine of the separation of powers.

Leinster House

Leinster House, the building that now houses the Dáil and Seanad, was commissioned by James Fitzgerald to be built in 1745. He set out to create the stateliest of Dublin's Georgian mansions, to reflect his eminent position in Irish society. On his becoming the Duke of Leinster in 1776 the house became known as Leinster House. The architect was Richard Castle, who was born in Germany about 1690. It has been claimed that it formed a model for the design of the White House, the residence of the President of the

United States. This claim may have its origins in the career of James Hoban, who was born in County Kilkenny, studied architecture in Dublin, and in 1792 won the competition for the design of the White House. The inscription on the foundation stone, when translated from the original Latin, reads:

> The house, of which this stone is the foundation, James, twentieth Earl of Kildare, caused to be erected in Molesworth's field, in the year of our Lord 1747. Hence learn, whenever, in some unhappy day, you light on the ruins of so great a mansion, of what worth he was who built it, and how frail all things are, when such memorials of such men cannot outlive misfortune.
>
> By Richard Castle, Architect

Significant repairs, engineering and conservation works are planned for Leinster House, including the possible temporary relocation of the Seanad.

Edmund Burke, whose statue at Trinity College, Dublin looks towards the former parliament building, now the Bank of Ireland in College Green, in his famous 1774 speech on 'The Duties of a Representative' said, 'Parliament is a deliberative assembly of one nation, with one interest – that of the whole – where not local purposes, not local prejudices, ought to guide, but the general good, resulting from the general reason of the whole.'

THE DÁIL

Membership

Membership of the Dáil is open to citizens over the age of twenty-one. Members of the judiciary, civil service, Defence Forces and An Garda Síochána are ineligible, as are persons undergoing prison sentences, persons of unsound mind and undischarged bankrupts. The total number of deputies is fixed by law, though the Constitution specifies that this number may not be less than one for every 30,000 of the population or more than one for every 20,000. The thirtieth Dáil (elected in 2007) has 166 members, known as Teachtaí Dála or TDs.

A survey by John O'Keeffe in the *Sunday Independent* in January 2008 showed that 'almost three quarters of the Dáil attended some form of third-level college and this pathway would appear to be a prerequisite to becoming a member of government. All ministers can boast such an achievement'.

Constituencies

Deputies represent constituencies, which are also fixed by law. The constituencies must be revised at least every twelve years to take account of

Dáil Éireann

population changes. The Constitution provides that the ratio between the numbers to be elected for each constituency and the population of each constituency is to be, as far as practicable, the same throughout the country. In practice, constituencies are revised on the publication of the results of each census of population (normally every fifth year).

Proposals for constituency revision are the business of the Constituency Commission. The commission must be established by ministerial order, under the Electoral Act 1997, whenever the Central Statistics Office (CSO) publishes a census report. It invites submissions from members of the public. The practice is for the commission, presided over by a judge of the High Court, to recommend a revised scheme of constituencies, which may or may not be accepted by the Dáil when submitted to it. Casey (2000: 108) notes, 'The 1997 Act does not – and perhaps could not – oblige the Oireachtas to implement the report; nonetheless it will be implemented without amend - ment or variation. Precedent – established since the creation of the first (non-statutory) commission in 1979 – so requires, and that precedent was fully honoured when the Commission's 1998 Report was implemented by the Electoral (Amendment) (No. 2) Act 1998.' The 2007 Constituency Commission comprised a High Court judge, the Clerk of the Dáil, the Clerk of the Seanad, the Secretary General of the Department of the Environment, Heritage and Local Government and the Ombudsman.

In May 2007 High Court Judge Frank Clarke dismissed arguments that the Oireachtas had breached the Constitution in how the constituencies were revised. However, he also stressed the need for the Oireachtas to move speedily to address 'impermissible variations' existing in several constituencies relating to the number of TDs per capita of population. The Electoral (Amendment) Bill 2008 revises the procedures to be followed by the Constituency Commission. While most of the existing law in this area is being retained, the main change is that, in future, commissions will be established on publication by the CSO, following a census of population, of the census report setting out the preliminary result of the census in respect of the total population of the state; the commission will have to report as soon as may be after the CSO publishes the census report setting out the final result of the census in respect of the total population of the state and, in any event, not later than three months after such publication. Previously, commissions had to await final results before starting work.

Elections and Convening

The Ceann Comhairle of the previous Dáil is returned automatically as a member. The other members are elected under a system of proportional representation (PR) by means of a single transferable vote, and no constituency may have fewer than three members. Gallagher (1987), based on the 1922–1987 period as a whole, finds no coherent case against the single transferable vote electoral system and that it cannot be faulted for failing to produce proportional representation or for creating unstable government. O'Connor (2007: 20) notes that the electoral system has given equitable results with a broad correlation between the percentage of votes and the seats obtained by the competing political parties.

The Constitution provides that no Dáil may continue for more than seven years and that a shorter period may be fixed by law. Such a shorter period has, in fact, been fixed (under section 33 of the Electoral Act 1992) at five years.

The Minister for the Environment determines the date of the poll when the President has dissolved the Dáil. A general election must take place not later than thirty days after a dissolution, and the new Dáil must meet within thirty days of polling day. Under Article 16.4.1° of the Constitution, polling 'shall as far as practicable take place on the same day throughout the country'. Traditionally voters on the islands off the west coast cast their vote before the rest of the country because of the possibility that bad weather might cut the islands off and ballot boxes would not reach the count centre in time to be counted with the rest of their constituency's votes. After islanders have cast their votes the ballot boxes are securely stored on the mainland until the count begins.

Turnout at general elections gradually declined in the period 1969 to 2002, from 76.9 per cent to 62.6 per cent. In 2007 it rose to 67 per cent. Mair (1998) asks, 'If coalition politics in the coming decades becomes a matter of musical chairs – or musical beds – how should voters go about choosing between the parties? More to the point, why should voters even bother to try to choose between the parties?'

The Electoral (Amendment) Act 2001 provided for the inclusion of photographs of the candidates and political party emblems on the ballot paper for local, national and European elections. The aim was to facilitate greater engagement and voter participation and to assist people with literacy problems. Buckley *et al.* (2007) note that the advent of ballot paper photographs could allow candidates to be evaluated on the basis of appearance and could possibly introduce a new level of superficiality into the voters' decision-making process.

The people of Ireland tend to elect a significant number of independent TDs, which is unusual for Western Europe (Gallagher and Mitchell 2005). Weeks (2004) notes that independent (non-party) members have participated a great deal in Irish governments, with 30 per cent of all administrations dependent on them. He comments, 'When independents are treated like a coalition partner rather than as a prop, they can be like partners in government . . . The effect on government stability of dependence on independents is not necessarily negative; it rests entirely on the attitude of the government. If they ignore the independents they are likely to lose their support as they would if they ignored the wishes of a coalition partner.'

When the votes have been counted at a general election, the person responsible for the conduct of the election in each constituency (who is called the returning officer and is normally the county registrar) notifies the Clerk of the Dáil of those who have been elected. The Clerk of the Dáil then notifies each member to attend at Leinster House to sign the Roll of Members in his or her presence. Members are not entitled to take their seat nor to be paid any allowance until they have signed the Roll.

The first business at the first meeting of the Dáil after the election is the reading by the Clerk of the Dáil of the proclamations of dissolution and convening, and then the names and constituencies of all the members elected. The Clerk acts as chairperson until the Ceann Comhairle is elected.

Electronic Voting

Electronic voting is said to improve the efficiency, accuracy and user-friendliness of election procedures. It aims to improve the efficiency of the electoral administration, create minimum maintenance for the pre-election,

election and post-election periods and support the positive image of electronic information in the country.

The Local Elections (Disclosure of Donations and Expenditure) Act 1999 gave authority to the Department of the Environment to obtain ballot papers used at the local elections for the purpose of research relating to the introduction of electronic voting and counting. The Electoral (Amendment) Act 2001 provided for the application of the new system to elections to the Dáil, the European Parliament, the presidency and the local authorities and to referenda. The government's aim was to use electronic voting at the 2002 general election and nationwide at the European and local elections of 2004. Electronic voting was first piloted in the May 2002 Dáil election in three constituencies (Meath, Dublin North and Dublin West). For the second referendum on the Nice Treaty, held in October 2002, a further pilot was carried out in seven constituencies (Dublin Mid-West, Dublin North, Dublin South, Dublin South-West, Dublin West, Dún Laoghaire and Meath).

The government believed that electronic voting and counting provided the Irish people with a more modern, user-friendly and efficient system of voting (*Dáil Debates*, 4 March 2004). In the development of electronic voting the security and integrity of the system were of paramount importance. The system incorporated security and audit features at all stages from initial set-up of the poll to the production of the count result. The system was said to be benchmarked with the five objectives of integrity, confidentiality, enfranchisement, availability and verifiability.

The system was purchased in 2003 and paid for by the Exchequer. The company that won the government's €50 million contract to supply electronic voting machines subsequently went into liquidation. There was strong opposition, little consultation and little consensus on the proposal in the political system. The government was unable to sell off its voting machines when experts proved that voter preferences could be tampered with. There was much negative publicity, with concerns about the costs and contracts for the storage of the machines around the country, and demands that any voting system implemented must include a voter-verified audit trail. The total cost incurred in the development and roll-out of the system was €51.3 million, including some €2.6 million in respect of awareness and education initiatives. Responsibility for the security and safe storage of manual electoral voting materials (such as ballot boxes, stamping instruments and stationery) is a matter for the returning officers, who are statutorily responsible for conducting the polls. Accordingly, returning officers have similar responsibility for the storage of electronic voting equipment. A reply to a parliamentary question on 22 April 2008 stated that the total annual storage cost for the equipment was €489,000 in 2007. Over half of the machines are stored at the Gormanstown Aerodrome, County Meath. The Independent Commission on Electronic Voting and Counting at Elections was established by the government in March 2004, and was dissolved in September 2006. The 2007 Programme for Government agreed by Fianna Fáil, the Progressive Democrats and the Green Party agreed to establish an Electoral Commission, charged with delivering 'modern and efficient electoral practices', which include electronic voting.

Advocates of the traditional manual paper ballot highlighted its positive features, including stability, a detailed legislative framework, established case law, vast experience, security, familiarity, reliability and public ownership of the process. As the All-Party Oireachtas Committee on the Constitution (2002: 25) noted, 'Continuity is an important virtue of any electoral system. It can be argued that electorates trust what is familiar, and, as has certainly been the case in Ireland, understand how to make effective use of their system's various features.' The people have developed a strong degree of confidence in the existing manual system, built up over the years. If anything was to happen to undermine this confidence (arising from, for example, alleged tampering with the software, a distortion of the results or a court challenge to the electronic voting results), then the already weakening support for representative democracy could be dealt a serious blow. Environment Minister John Gormley announced that the electronic voting system was to be abandoned in April 2009.

Procedures

The Ceann Comhairle

The duties of the Ceann Comhairle (chairperson of Dáil Éireann) are set out in elaborate detail in the 171 standing orders of the Dáil. Broadly speaking, these duties are to preside over the sittings, to keep order, to call members to speak, to put questions to a vote if called for at the end of the debate, to enforce the rules of the debate, and generally to exercise supervision over the conduct of business. The Ceann Comhairle is strictly non-partisan. Upon election, he or she makes a declaration to act in an impartial and fair manner. Under Article 15.9.1° of the Constitution TDs also elect a Leas-Cheann Comhairle (deputy chairperson of Dáil Éireann), who deputises in the absence of the Ceann Comhairle. In the event that neither the Ceann Comhairle nor the Leas-Cheann Comhairle is able to preside, there are a number of TDs on a panel of chairpersons, appointed by the Ceann Comhairle, who may perform this role on a temporary basis; they receive no extra remuneration.

The Ceann Comhairle, or the presiding chairperson, has no vote except where there is equality of voting. In such cases the Ceann Comhairle must under Article 15.11.2° of the Constitution exercise a casting vote. The basis on which the casting vote is given is the usual one, namely maintenance of the status quo, thus providing an opportunity for review of the question at issue. In effect, this involves the Ceann Comhairle voting with the government of the day.

Standing Orders and Conventions

Standing orders set out the procedures for the conduct of the day-to-day business in the Dáil. These provide for the conduct of proceedings, the passage of bills, the rules of debate, the rules of financial procedures, the preservation of order, and the operation of committees. The Ceann Comhairle's rulings on the interpretation and application of these orders may not be questioned in the House, though members may bring complaints to the attention of the Committee on Procedure and Privileges. To ensure consistency in interpretation, a book containing rulings of the chair, i.e. a book of precedents, is kept, showing all rulings made by chairpersons since the foundation of the state. This book is updated as new situations arise.

The standing orders are supplemented by conventions and practices. Many of these relate to the behaviour of members. For example, when the Ceann Comhairle rises to speak, any member then speaking must sit down; members must bow to the chair when passing to or from their seats in the chamber; they must address the chair; they are called on to speak at the discretion of the Ceann Comhairle; it is the practice that members are called upon in turn by party, with a preference for ministers and for leaders of the opposition parties. In general, members may speak once only in a debate, though interventions not exceeding thirty seconds may be permitted in certain circumstances by the Ceann Comhairle. Words which may be deemed offensive or disorderly may not be used; imputations of improper motives and personal reflections on members are regarded as disorderly. Members who persist in irrelevance or repetition may be ordered by the chair to stop speaking, though ruling deputies out of order is extremely rare.

There is a long-standing parliamentary practice that members do not comment on, criticise or make charges against a person outside the House or an official, either by name or in such a way as to make the person identifiable. Other conventions are that matters sub judice may be discussed in certain circumstances only, and that a member making a maiden speech is heard without interruption.

Dáil business can be suspended, for example for periods of five, ten or thirty minutes due to 'disregarding the authority of the chair' or 'grossly disorderly conduct'. In the case of great disorder the Ceann Comhairle can adjourn the House. A member who behaves in a disorderly fashion may be suspended on a motion by the Ceann Comhairle. The duration of the suspension is determined by the frequency of the offence.

The courts have refused to become involved in a dispute between a member of the Dáil and the Ceann Comhairle. The Supreme Court has several times declined to interfere in 'the internal machinery of debate of the House' because this is 'within the competence of Dáil Éireann to deal with exclusively, having regard to Article 15.10 of the Constitution' (*O'Malley v Ceann Comhairle* [1997] 1 IR 427, per O'Flaherty J.). In that case the High Court and the Supreme Court declined to permit judicial review to challenge a decision of the Ceann Comhairle, that a parliamentary question was repetition, in respect of Standing Order 33 of the Dáil, which provides, 'The Ceann Comhairle, or the Clerk under his authority, may amend any question, after consultation with the member responsible for the Question, to secure its compliance with Standing Orders.'

Non-aligned TDs have no speaking rights in the Dáil and rely on the generosity of other parties to express their views. Seven or more TDs can form a technical group, which has certain speaking rights under the Dáil standing orders.

Debates

The Dáil has three sessions a year, from about the third week in January to Easter, from after Easter to about the end of June, and from early October to Christmas. It meets on Tuesday at 2.30 p.m. and on Wednesday and Thursday at 10.30 a.m. By convention, a minister or minister of state (not necessarily the minister whose business is being discussed) is present in the chamber throughout each debate. The minister is accompanied by officials who assist with matters that arise during the debate and take notes of points raised by speakers for the use of the minister in the course of his or her reply. The disposition of members is shown overleaf. Delaney (2001: 31) comments, 'In the chamber, the officials sit near the Minister inside a rail near the wall. On the TV, it appears as the section just beyond the Taoiseach – a sort of non-elected cage. Whereas most people look at the TV to see what politician is speaking, civil servants look to see which officials are pulling the strings'. The press gallery is situated behind the Ceann Comhairle, and the public galleries are behind the members. The business under discussion is shown on the indicator board in the chamber by reference to the number of the item on the order paper, and on closed-circuit television in all the principal areas of Leinster House, with the name of the member speaking, and in the case of a bill, the stage it has reached.

Layout of the 30th Dáil Chamber for the purposes of electronic voting

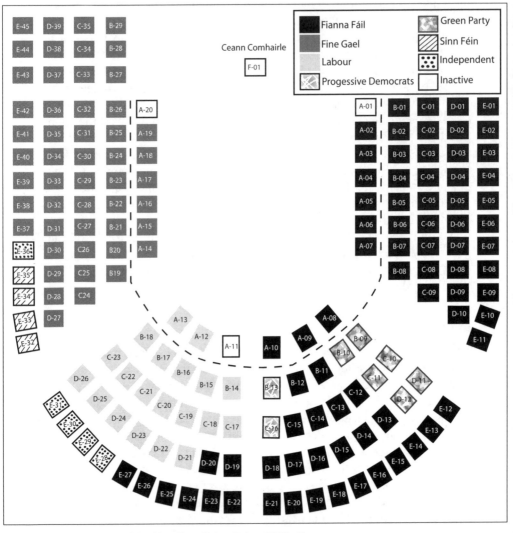

Source: Houses of the Oireachtas Commission (2008: 7)

At the end of each day's sitting members may bring forward matters that they wish to have discussed, by way of a five-minute speech. Four matters may be discussed under this arrangement and in each case a minister has five minutes to reply. The matters selected must, of course, relate to public affairs connected with government departments or to matters of administration for which a minister is responsible.

When a vote is to take place, electric bells are rung in Leinster House and also in the offices of those ministers in the immediate vicinity, for example in Merrion Street and Kildare Street. The doors to the chamber are locked and only those present may vote. Members may vote electronically or by passing though the lobbies. Non-electronic votes are often used for legislation. In this method, having gone up the steps, those voting for the government turn left and those opposing turn right into what are usually referred to as the Tá and Níl lobbies. Tellers are appointed by the government side and by the opposition, two for each, and they count the numbers entering each lobby. The result of the vote is brought to the Ceann Comhairle by the tellers for the lobby in which there was a higher vote. The Ceann Comhairle formally announces the result and then proceeds to the next business. The introduction of electronic voting (described below) in the Dáil chamber in 2002 replaced this traditional lobby process for most votes.

An official report of the debates of each House is published under the supervision of the Ceann Comhairle. These are periodically revised, collated, indexed, bound and published in volumes and are on sale at the Government Publications Sales Office. Minutes of the daily proceedings of each House are made by the Clerk. These include times of sittings, business transacted and related matters. Signed by the Ceann Comhairle, they are the permanent official record of the work of the Dáil and are referred to as the *journal of proceedings*. The translation section of the Houses of the Oireachtas, Rannóg an Aistriúcháin, is responsible for translating the Acts of the Oireachtas, documents and terminology into Irish.

Speaking in the Dáil on 1 July 2008 Taoiseach Brian Cowen noted:

> The Parliament must do its business according to the priorities it sets itself, which must include policy formulation and dealing with issues that will develop over a certain timeframe. We must not accept the idea that we are only relevant if we discuss issues that happen to be topical or are mentioned on morning radio programmes. Parliament must find a balance between taking up issues of urgent public importance and maintaining its role as the main legislative and debating forum in the democratic life of the country.

Work of the Dáil

The Dáil sat for 92 days in 2005, for 96 in 2006, for 76 in 2007 and for 96 in 2008. The Dáil is the only forum in which the Taoiseach and the other government ministers can be held to account on a regular basis. Given the power of the executive, this is particularly important. The Dáil also plays an invaluable function in reviewing and improving government legislation and in presenting alternative views on how society might operate. The work of the Dáil falls into four broad categories. The Dáil considers proposals for legislation initiated by ministers or by private members; it considers expenditure proposals presented by ministers; it debates motions; and it is a forum in which questions may be addressed to ministers.

Legislation

Proposals for legislation are initiated as bills. Bills fall into various categories: public bills (including private members' bills), private bills, consolidation bills, money bills and bills to amend the Constitution. The Dáil passed 34 acts in 2005, 42 in 2006, 42 in 2007 and 25 in 2008. Legislation that is enacted by the Oireachtas is known as *primary legislation*. Speaking in the Dáil on 3 October 2007 Taoiseach Bertie Ahern said that government departments should publish the outline proposed structure of legislation (the heads of bills) following cabinet approval as more discussion ultimately leads to better legislation and more agreement.

Secondary legislation means legislation for which responsibility has been delegated by the Oireachtas to some other party. It is also referred to as delegated legislation or subordinate legislation. In practice, responsibility has usually been delegated to a government minister and secondary legislation usually takes the form of statutory instruments. A statutory instrument can be defined as any order, regulation, rule, scheme or bye-law made in exercise of a power conferred by statute. Byrne and McCutcheon (2001) give three reasons for secondary legislation: the time constraint on parliament; the technical and administrative nature of legislation; and the need for a flexible and timely response to changing social and technical circumstances. Secondary legislation has the disadvantage of less parliamentary scrutiny and due to the sheer volume of statutory instruments there may be less knowledge or publicity about the changes being made.

There is increasing usage of statutory instruments: in 1970 there were 315 statutory instruments made and in 2008 there were 607. Different types of statutory instrument include: an order, which is a single exercise of delegated power; a regulation, which is a set of detailed provisions; a scheme, generally dealing with pay and pensions; rules, generally setting out court practices and procedures; and bye-laws, for minor matters.

The largest number of bills are *public bills*, i.e. bills for the benefit of the public as a whole, such as a bill to deal with broadcasting. Public bills may be initiated by either a minister or a private member. The majority of bills that become law are those initiated by ministers. Bills other than money bills or bills to amend the Constitution can be introduced in either House. Each bill has five stages, or readings, in the House in which it was initiated, i.e. it is considered on five separate occasions.

The first of these stages is when the House is made aware that the bill is on the way. The title of the bill and a short description of its purpose appears on the order paper. This stage is normally a formality and evokes no debate. It leads to the fixing of a date for the second reading, when the minister deals with the general principles of the bill. The minister indicates why it is necessary and explains the reasons for each of its provisions. These explanations lead to a debate on what is proposed, including suggestions for improved or alternative means of achieving the ends sought. (Those seeking to know the background to any act should study the minister's speech introducing the second reading.) Opposition to the proposals in a bill is expressed by voting against it. Amendments are not permitted at this stage.

At the third (committee) stage the bill is considered in detail – section by section, even word by word – by one of the specialised committees of the House. This stage is one of relative informality and members may speak more than once on the same aspect. Amendments may be made, to add, delete or substitute words, but these may not be in conflict with the principle of the bill as approved at the previous stage. Amendments to government bills are rarely accepted by ministers. If a bill is going to result in increased public expenditure, a special money resolution authorising such expenditure must be put forward by a minister and passed before the committee stage. This is to show that the proposed expenditure has the authority of the government as provided for in the Constitution. The bill is then 'reported' to the House as its fourth stage. Only amendments arising out of committee stage are in order. If no amendments are offered, there is no debate on the report stage.

The fifth stage is usually a formality, unless a bill is contentious. In that event there may be a debate similar to that which took place on the second reading. The stage is normally taken immediately after the report stage, and the question put to the Dáil is 'that the bill do now pass'. This means that in the case of a bill that originated in the Dáil it goes to the Seanad for its consideration, or in the case of a bill that has originated in the Seanad it goes to the Dáil.

Another form of public bill is a *private member's bill*, which is a bill initiated by a member who is not a minister, usually a member of an opposition party, with the approval of his or her party. The party must have at least seven members. The title of the bill and its purpose appear on the order paper, in the same way as a government bill, as its first stage. If introduction is opposed (in practice, this would be by the government), the member moving the bill has five minutes in which to explain its purpose and the member designated to oppose has five minutes in which to outline objections to it. After that there is a vote to determine whether the bill goes on to a second reading. If a bill is not opposed, the second reading is taken in private members' time, i.e. in the time set aside for business other than government-initiated business. Private members' business is usually dealt with between 7.00 p.m. and 8.30 p.m. on Tuesdays and Wednesdays. The time normally allowed for debate on the second reading is six hours. If it passes this reading, it is referred for its third reading to a special committee of the House in which it has been introduced. As mentioned earlier, a bill involving expenditure (as most bills do) cannot proceed beyond the second stage without a positive money resolution from the government, i.e. a resolution to provide the public funds, for example salaries or cost of equipment, needed to give effect to whatever the bill provides for. Thus, if the money message or financial resolution is not put forward, a bill can, in effect, be made to lapse at this stage. If, however, the bill proceeds, the fourth and fifth stages are taken in government time.

Relatively few private members' bills are passed (although in recent times the number of successful bills has increased) because even if the government accepts the principle of the bill, it usually asks the member to withdraw it on an assurance that the government will itself introduce a measure, officially drafted, to meet the situation. The Judicial Separation and Family Law Reform Act, passed in December 1989, was the first successful private member's bill for thirty years.

When a public bill has been passed in the Dáil, it is sent to the Seanad, where it is regarded as having passed its first stage but is debated at the other stages in the same way as in the Dáil. If the Seanad makes amendments, or recommendations in the case of money bills, these are considered by the Dáil. If the Dáil does not agree with the amendments, the matter is reconsidered by the Seanad, which may decide to insist on them. If so, the Dáil may, after a period of ninety days from the date on which the bill was first sent to the Seanad, pass a resolution deeming the bill to have been passed.

Private bills are bills dealing with special interests, such as those of a particular body or locality, as distinct from the public interest as a whole. An example of a private bill is the Limerick Marts Bill 1989, which was deposited in the Private Bill Office in December 1989 and subsequently referred to a select committee of the Dáil and Seanad. (The main purpose of this bill was to increase the number of commodities that may be sold in the Limerick market place and to give the trustees certain powers in relation to tolls, rents and disposal of premises.) Another example of a private bill is the Royal College of Surgeons in Ireland (Charters Amendment) Act 2003, which amended the charter under which the college is incorporated.

The persons who wish to have a private bill passed, known as the pro - moters of the bill, engage a parliamentary agent (a practising solicitor) to undertake on their behalf the formalities prescribed under standing orders relating to the presentation of such a bill. These include the extensive adver - tising of its contents, as well as the notification of parties likely to be interested. A private bill is lodged with the Examiner of Private Bills – the Clerk of the Seanad. The bill is introduced in the Seanad at second stage, after which it is referred to a committee of both Houses, consisting of three TDs and three senators, none of whom may have a personal interest in the bill and, in the case of the deputies, none of whose constituents has a personal interest. The committee consults government departments, takes evidence from interested parties and hears counsel on behalf of the promoters and any objectors. The committee makes a report on the bill to both Houses and then sends it to the Seanad for consideration at fourth and fifth stages. After that it goes to the Dáil, also for fourth and fifth stages. It is then enacted in the same way as a public bill, i.e. it is signed by the President and becomes law. Fees must be paid to the state by both promoters and opponents of private bills.

Consolidation bills are bills designed to tidy up the law, i.e. they consolidate existing law. Where, for example, there have been a number of acts passed through the years, each amending and/or adding something to the law relating to a particular subject, it may be considered desirable, for ease of reference, to get all of the up-to-date provisions into one act. A consolidation bill does not contain any new legislative provision. After its second reading it is referred for examination to a joint committee of both Houses. The bill is then considered for fourth and fifth stages in the initiating House, after which it is sent to the other House, where the first, second and third stages are waived and it is considered on fourth and fifth stages only. Such bills are rare because neither ministers nor officials are enthusiastic about devoting scarce time to them unless there is a very obvious need and supporting pressure. A recent consolidation act was the Social Welfare (Consolidation) Act 2005.

Money bills may be initiated in the Dáil only. They are bills concerning taxation, public debt, loans and such matters and are dealt with in the same way as public bills. When they go to the Seanad for consideration, that body has only twenty-one days to consider them, and it may make recommendations only; it cannot amend them. If a money bill is not returned within twenty-one days, or is returned with recommendations that the Dáil does not accept, it is deemed to have been passed by the Dáil at the end of that time.

Any proposal to amend the Constitution must first be passed in the form of a *bill to amend the Constitution*, which may not contain any other proposal. Such a bill may be initiated in the Dáil only. When passed there, it is considered in the Seanad in the same way as a public bill.

Financial Procedures

Article 28.4.3° of the Constitution obliges the government to prepare estimates of receipts and of expenditure for each year and to present these to the Dáil. The White Paper on Receipts and Expenditure, which contains these estimates, is usually published by the Department of Finance on the weekend before the annual budget, which is usually in November each year. Due to the rapidly deteriorating economic and public financial situation, budget 2009 was introduced early in October 2008, with a supplementary budget in

April 2009. The Minister for Finance's annual budget statement outlines, among other things, his or her taxation proposals for the years ahead. As it is desirable that some of these, such as excise duties on petrol or tobacco, come into operation on the day they are made public, the proposals are voted upon on budget day. They are put forward in the form of budget resolutions that, under the Provisional Collection of Taxes Act 1927, have immediate effect and continue in operation for up to four months from the date of passing. The main debate on the budget proposals continues over a number of weeks. When it is concluded, the Finance Bill is introduced by the Minister for Finance. Its enactment gives final legislative effect to the taxation measures in the budget.

The Dáil, through a number of select committees, then considers the estimate for each individual department, which is presented by its minister. The minister's speech reviews the work of the department in the previous year, outlines its programme for the year ahead and explains the need for the money it is seeking to raise. The estimates are presented in the form of a number of spending items called subheads, which enumerate clearly the various items of expenditure. Thus, in all departments the A subheads represent the administrative costs, i.e. pay, travel, equipment, postal and telephone expenses etc. The other letters of the alphabet are used for the specific needs of individual departments. When the Dáil has approved the expenditure of the total sum, the estimate then becomes known as the vote for the relevant department.

Under the terms of the Central Fund (Permanent Provisions) Act 1965, the Minister for Finance is empowered to make available to a department four-fifths of the sum that it had in the year before, to enable it to carry out its work, i.e. to enable public services to be carried on during that part of the year when the estimates for these services are being considered. When the estimates for all departments have been agreed by the Dáil, normally by May or June of each year, the Minister for Finance introduces the Appropriation Bill to give statutory effect to the individual estimates for each department and to transfer moneys voted for them.

If a minister finds in the course of a year that for some unforeseen reason more money is required to run his or her department than the Dáil has allowed under the procedures described above, that minister must seek the Dáil's approval of a supplementary estimate. The debate on this occasion is confined to a discussion of the particular items for which the extra money is being sought.

Motions

A motion is a proposal made by a member (a minister or an ordinary TD) to do something, order something to be done or express an opinion with regard to some matter. It must be phrased in such a way that, if passed, it will be seen to express the judgment or will of the House. Motions may be conveniently classified into *substantive motions*, which are self-contained proposals drafted in such a way as to be capable of expressing the will of the House; and *subsidiary motions*, which are purely procedural in character, such as 'that the debate be adjourned'. Under Dáil Standing Order 32 there is provision for debate on a matter of 'urgent public importance' during a sitting day. It allows a TD to seek permission from the Ceann Comhairle to move a motion on the adjournment, which is to do with 'a specific and important matter of public interest requiring urgent consideration'. Before the order of business, the proposer reads out the proposal, the reason for and the need for the debate. The Ceann Comhairle then informs the TD whether or not the debate will occur. TDs use this device to focus publicity on the issue. The debate can last up to ninety minutes. If it is permitted by the Ceann Comhairle, the issue must have the support of twelve TDs.

Parliamentary Questions

The principal method by which TDs attempt to hold the government to account is through parliamentary questions (PQs). There are two types of parliamentary question: oral and written. There are five types of oral question: questions to the Taoiseach; ordinary questions; priority questions; private notice questions; and leaders' questions. The number of parliamentary questions was 39,236 in 2005, 42,538 in 2006, 33,753 in 2007 and almost 45,000 in 2008.

Taoiseach's questions are arguably the highlight of the Dáil timetable as the leaders of the opposition parties question the head of government on a range of issues. In Taoiseach's questions any TD can ask the Taoiseach a question during a period of forty-five minutes on a Tuesday and on a Wednesday. As of 2001, in leaders' questions only, opposition party leaders are entitled to ask a question or a supplementary question relevant to the business of the day of the Taoiseach. Under Dáil Standing Order 27(b) of 2007 the total time allocated to leaders' questions may not exceed twenty-one minutes on any given day and the Taoiseach may nominate another member of the government in his or her absence.

Deputies may address questions to ministers about matters connected with their department or about public affairs for which they are officially responsible. There is no formal obligation on ministers to answer such questions, but, in practice, they do so. One hour and three-quarters is set aside during each sitting on Tuesday and on Wednesday and one hour and twenty minutes on Thursday for parliamentary questions.

The procedure is that TDs submits their questions in writing to the general office in the Dáil before 11.00 a.m. on the fourth preceding day for questions seeking an oral reply and on the third preceding day for questions nominated for priority and for written replies. Each question is examined in the office (and ultimately by the Ceann Comhairle) to ensure that its purpose is genuinely to seek information or clarification on matters of fact or policy; that such information has not been provided within the preceding four months; that it contains no argument or personal imputation; that it does not deal with a matter that is sub judice; and that it does not seek to anticipate a matter of which the Dáil has been given notice and on which the Ceann Comhairle is satisfied a debate will take place within a reasonable time.

Priority questions are confined to groups in opposition (parties of not less than seven members), and no more than five such questions may be tabled to any minister. The party decides what questions may be tabled in any one day, what questions are to be designated as priority and the members in whose names they are to be asked. Only the members in whose names the questions are tabled may ask supplementary questions seeking elaboration of the information provided in the answer to the question. Although a member of the government may group questions put down for oral answer and questions put down for written answer for the purposes of reply, the minister is not permitted to group priority questions with other oral questions.

Private notice questions must relate to matters of urgent public importance that have arisen suddenly. They may be tabled up to 2.30 p.m. and, given the time constraints, do not appear on the order paper.

Oral questions are answered by ministers on a rota system. Under this system, ministers present themselves in the Dáil in sequence to answer the questions addressed to them. This means that each minister answers oral questions about once in every five weeks. Where a question put down for oral answer is of such a nature as to require a lengthy reply, or a reply in the form of a tabular statement, the minister may not wish to answer it orally. In such a situation the Ceann Comhairle must accept a request from the minister that the answer be provided in the official report for that day. The deputy gets a copy of the reply in advance of publication. In addition to the questions to which deputies seek an oral reply (so that they may ask a supplementary question to press for additional information if not satisfied with the reply), deputies also ask questions for written reply. The vast majority of these written questions relate to constituents' problems, such as when payments are expected to be made under social welfare and grant schemes of various kinds.

Presentation of Documents

Many kinds of documents are presented to the Dáil under the provisions of legislation, for example the annual reports and accounts of state-sponsored bodies and statutory regulations made by ministers. Rarely are these documents debated. Statutory regulations may, however, be revoked by the passage of a resolution to that effect, but such a resolution is also rare. The purpose of presenting these documents is to make their existence known and to make them available in the library for interested members of the Oireachtas. An e-Chamber pilot has been successfully introduced involving the use of laptops in the Dáil chamber.

Dáil Reform

In recent years there has been considerable efforts to reform the practices and procedures under which the Dáil conducts its business. The government published a discussion document, *A Dáil for the New Millennium*, in 2000, which it described as 'the most radical reappraisal of the workings of the Dáil parliamentary system since the foundation of the State'. These proposals were designed to 'increase the relevance and effectiveness of the Oireachtas by way of reform of some of its undoubtedly outmoded procedures and practices'. A comprehensive and historic package of reforms of the workings of the Dáil parliamentary system, designed to increase the relevance and effectiveness of the Oireachtas, was announced in February 2002, but was not fully implemented. In the Dáil in February 2008 Government Chief Whip Tom Kitt explained that the slow progress was due to the agreement between the parties that 'nothing is agreed until everything is agreed'.

These wide-ranging reforms were the culmination of more than two years of deliberations, debate and research by the Dáil Reform Committee, chaired by then Government Chief Whip Seamus Brennan. They included the introduction of electronic voting in the Dáil chamber in 2002. This computer-based system (see below) replaced for most votes the traditional lobby process that has been in use since 1922. When a question is put to the House by the Ceann Comhairle, responses are first given orally by those present. If the result is not clear or a deputy challenges the result, a division is called. A minimum of ten TDs is necessary to force a division or vote. Voting is done electronically in both Houses but whips may call for a manual 'walk through' vote. Divisions can take place electronically or manually. The division bells are rung calling TDs to vote. Normally, the bells ring for ten minutes and after the first six of those minutes the door is locked. In the case of lobby voting, tellers count the number of votes and record the final result.

During the negotiations a number of significant Dáil reform measures were agreed and implemented, including:

• Increased monitoring of proposed European Union legislation to allow for more sustained, systematic and rigorous investigation and assessment. The system for monitoring proposed EU legislation by the Dáil and Dáil committees, which was agreed by government, addressed two key stages in the legislative process: the initiation of a proposal for legislation and the eventual consideration by the EU Council of Ministers with a view to a decision. It is envisaged that within four weeks of the initial receipt of fresh legislation the responsible department will provide the relevant committee with a short paper indicating the nature and purpose of the proposal and an initial indication of possible implications for Ireland. The proposals would be defined by the department as falling within one of three categories of importance, with the highest being 'proposals of major potential significance'. The committee could decide to hold hearings; seek the views of interested parties, including ministers; and forward its findings to either or both Houses of the Oireachtas. The government would be required to take serious account of the views presented by the committee when formulating its negotiating position on the legislation. The EU Scrutiny Committee and EU Affairs Committees have been put in place. The EU monitoring systems are examined in Chapter 12.

- Electronic voting commenced in the Dáil in February 2002. This has considerably reduced the length of time it takes to complete a vote. A vote takes on average eighteen to twenty minutes under the traditional lobby system, however, using electronic voting reduces this to an average of eleven minutes. The new computer-based network allows members to vote from their seats by selecting the Tá or Níl button on a personal panel beside them. As members vote the corresponding seat lights up in green or red on a large display panel, designed in a horseshoe pattern to reflect the layout of the chamber and set into the wall above the seat of the Ceann Comhairle. The 'rising vote' is displayed and a countdown clock informs members of the time remaining within which they may vote. The Ceann Comhairle, party whips, appointed tellers or twenty or more members may request that a vote be taken again, either electronically or in the traditional way.

- The introduction of a time limit of six minutes on all parliamentary questions to encourage a more focused and concentrated debate and to increase considerably the number of questions that are answered. In addition, written questions will be answered throughout the year, including during Dáil recess.

- A major breakthrough was the introduction of leaders' questions, which has proved to be of growing importance in increasing the relevance of the Dáil.

- Priority questions extended to allow for more questions.

- Reform of the committees so that they shadow government departments, rather than the previous subject-based system.

- Additional powers to committees to send for documents and to require witnesses to attend.

- Oireachtas Broadcasting Committee was assigned the additional duties of disseminating information on the workings of the parliament to schools, organisations and individuals. Then Labour Party leader Pat Rabbitte famously described the audience of RTÉ's *Oireachtas Report* as being made up of 'drunks and insomniacs'. He was, however, making an important point about the late night and anti-social slot on the television schedule that a programme that provides such a valuable public service function as *Oireachtas Report* occupies. A feasibility study was commissioned by the Houses of the Oireachtas on the establishment of a parliamentary television channel and work is proceeding on the introduction of a Dáil channel.
- The establishment in 2003 of an independent Oireachtas Commission with responsibility for funding, staffing and organisation of the Houses of the Oireachtas.
- The post of Clerk of the Dáil was re-titled secretary general to reflect a modern administration.

Other reform measures proposed, but not yet implemented, were:

- The traditional format of the order of business to be replaced by two new procedures, a new 'House Business Group' and a half-hour 'Current Issues Time'.
- 'Current Issues Time' will allow for the raising without notice of issues of current national importance, to be answered by the minister responsible and not just the Taoiseach, as at present. It would replace the unsatisfactory system under which matters of national relevance raised on the order of business are often tenuously linked to a piece of legislation.
- The House Business Group, chaired by the Government Chief Whip, will meet each week to plan and propose to the Dáil the following week's sittings and business.
- The Dáil to sit for three weeks in the month and the fourth week, from Monday to Friday, to be set aside as committee week. This would allow members to participate in committee sittings without interruption to attend in the Dáil, and would also strengthen the role and heighten the profile of the work of the committees. By sitting for ten extra hours per week, the Dáil will be in session for ninety-three hours over three weeks compared to the existing arrangement of ninety-two hours over four weeks. In addition to these hours, the committees would sit throughout the fourth week, totalling some forty hours of committee time per week.
- The membership of joint committees to be reduced from fourteen to ten, thus ensuring that no member is on more than two committees.
- A weekly individual members' discussion hour to debate a national or international public policy issue.

- A new commencement debate will replace the adjournment debate. The debate on Tuesday (12.00 p.m. to 1.00 p.m.) and Wednesday and Thursday (9.30 a.m. to 10.30 a.m.) will allow for six separate issues to be raised.
- To facilitate more comprehensive and appealing coverage of the House on television and radio a dedicated Oireachtas channel should be inaugurated as a matter of urgency.
- To increase emphasis on the role and functioning of the Dáil, there will be an annual ceremony for the opening of the House each September.
- A scroll, listing the name and term of service of each member elected to parliament since the foundation of the state, will be placed in a prominent location on a corridor in Leinster House.
- To note the legislation enacted with all-party agreement in the ethics area, which has considerably strengthened the ethical framework for the conduct of public business.
- Committees may meet outside Dublin once a year.

The 2007 Programme for Government drawn up by Fianna Fáil, the Green Party and the Progressive Democrats agreed to 'pursue the issue of reform of Oireachtas sitting times, Oireachtas procedures and strengthening the role of committees'. The truth is that most TDs (on both sides of the House) do not want the Dáil to sit longer because, if it did, they would have less time for the constituency work that makes up the bulk of what a TD does. Martin (2008: 11) notes that 'focusing on constituency service leaves little time for legislators to perform non-parochial legislative roles such as active involvement in committee work'.

Oireachtas and Executive

The Dáil and Seanad find it very difficult to exercise any legislative or supervisory role other than what is permitted by the government of the day. In June 2005 former Ombudsman Kevin Murphy made one of the most forthright interventions by a previous holder of office. He said, 'the Oireachtas has neither the capacity nor the willingness to hold the government responsible to it as provided for in Article 28.4.1° of the Constitution. There are many reasons for this, not least the greater loyalty TDs have to their party than to the Dáil.'

In considering what changes should be made, all commentators are conscious of individual deputies' perception of their role. In general, TDs do not see this as helping to formulate policy by contributing to debates on legislation, as monitoring the performance of ministers and public bodies and as giving leadership to the community. They regard themselves mainly as welfare officers for their constituents, and as having a need to preserve their image with a view to protecting their seats. They spend a large amount of time processing representations on behalf of constituents and attending clinics in their constituencies, as well as functions and funerals. TDs are forced into this situation largely because of the multi-seat proportional representation system, which generates competition not only between deputies of different parties but between deputies of the same party.

Deputy Micheál Martin wrote in the *Sunday Tribune* in 1991 that 'you will never have Dáil reform without fundamental electoral reform . . . the system is woefully wasteful and creates a bureaucratic monstrosity'. FitzGerald (2008a) argues strongly in favour of a reform to the system of proportional representation, claiming that the electoral system 'has a seriously distorting effect on our political system because it makes the electoral survival of our parliamentary representatives much more dependent on close involvement with their constituents than is normal in most other states. This is because the multi-seat constituency system places about three-quarters of TDs in a competitive situation vis-à-vis members of their own parties at each election.' He points out that 'of the 57 Fianna Fáil TDs who lost their seats in the last six general elections, 19 were defeated by opposition deputies, but almost twice as many – 35 – lost to rivals within their own party!' The All-Party Oireachtas Committee on the Constitution considered this matter in detail and found that 'no change to the provisions regarding Dáil elections is necessary or desirable' (2002: 29).

Opposition Proposals for Reform

The Dáil sub-committee on Dáil reform meets infrequently, there are no minutes of its meetings and its last report was in 1997 (MacCarthaigh 2006). Frustrated with lack of change and participation, Fine Gael and the Labour Party have unveiled a short programme of reforms to 'make the Dáil more effective'. Both Fine Gael and Labour have long traditions of publishing proposals for parliamentary reform – the Labour Party did so in 1968, 1975 and 2003, and Fine Gael in 1980, 1990 and 2000 – reflecting the fact that, as the parties most frequently in opposition, they have the most to gain from reforming parliamentary procedures, which currently give the government strong control of the agenda in the Dáil. In 2000 Fine Gael published *A Democratic Revolution – A Thorough Overhaul of the Institutions of the State*, which was a proposal for a radical reform of state institutions, including the Dáil. It suggested independent control over the adequacy of ministerial replies to questions and said that 'the nub of the matter is that the Houses of the Oireachtas have failed to assert their proper role in the governance of our society'. The Labour Party document on Dáil reform,

Putting Our House in Order (2003), referred to the establishment of a committee of investigations, oversight and petitions in the section dealing with parliamentary inquiries.

The key features of further Fine Gael proposals made in 2003 for Dáil reform (Kenny 2003) were:

- The overall number of hours in which the Dáil sits in plenary session should be increased by up to 30 per cent through a combination of shorter recesses and more and longer sitting days.
- Oireachtas committees should have an opportunity to question ministers on draft departmental estimates and make recommendations for reallocation of resources within departmental budgets before estimates are finalised. Ministers should also present their legislative proposals before the relevant committee for discussion before the start of each session.
- Appointments to state boards and top-level civil service posts should be approved by the relevant Oireachtas committee.
- All major government policy changes, initiatives or announcements should be made first in the Dáil. The relevant minister should make the announcement and provision should be made for a response from the opposition.
- TDs should be able to raise topical issues at the start of proceedings, with replies given by ministers, and supplementary questions asked, no later than mid-afternoon. The Ceann Comhairle should insist that the government response comes from the senior or junior minister at the relevant department.
- The Ceann Comhairle should be diligent in requiring ministers to be accountable to the House, and should ensure that replies to questions and motions are according to a code of practice to be drawn up. Specifically, the Ceann Comhairle should be given explicit power to refer a reply to a parliamentary question back to a minister if he or she feels that it does not adequately answer the question asked.

In January 2006 Fine Gael and the Labour Party launched an agreed ten-point programme for Dáil reform. Among the key proposals contained in the programme were an extension of the Dáil sitting week, which, together with shorter recesses, would lead to an increase of close to 50 per cent in the number of sitting days each year. The Green Party has also consistently advocated longer sitting times for the Dáil.

Murphy (2006) notes that while the reforms that have been introduced have streamlined the operation of the Dáil they have not responded to the central criticisms, particularly the executive–parliament balance of power. This is a fundamental aspect of the Irish machinery of government.

Support Services

A report compiled by consultants Deloitte & Touche in 2002 found that the Dáil and the Seanad were badly under-resourced in their levels of research, secretarial and general support services in comparison with parliaments in several other countries. The countries involved in the comparison were New Zealand, Scotland, Wales, Germany, Northern Ireland and England. As a result, TDs and senators were given the assistance of a special research unit in the Oireachtas to provide independent, non-partisan research. Oireachtas members will also benefit from the services of nearly two hundred new parliamentary assistants and committee staff. According to the report, the assistants will perform tasks such as speech-writing and public relations. Each TD will get one assistant.

A new one-stop-shop to process the allowances paid to TDs and senators is also proposed, as is a dedicated courier service for members of the Oireachtas. The hiring of parliamentary assistants is considered a key measure to assist TDs and improve the workings of the Dáil and its committees. This Deloitte & Touche report found the existing secretaries spent over half their time dealing with constituency queries. The rest of their time was taken up with normal secretarial duties and with more political tasks – from speech-writing and public relations to attending funerals, which is a function specifically mentioned in the report. Deloitte & Touche also conducted a survey among TDs in 2002, which found that 68 per cent of them rated the secretarial support to be 'poor' or 'fair'. The survey also found some dissatisfaction with a range of other services in Leinster House. Some members wanted the complex to be open twenty-four hours a day, seven days a week; others suggested six-day opening but said the car park should be open at all times.

The reforms are being overseen by the Houses of the Oireachtas Commission, the body responsible for financing and running the Oireachtas. It was set up by the Houses of the Oireachtas Commission Act 2003. It provides parliament with financial independence and the power to decide how it spends its budget. It is composed of eleven members: the Ceann Comhairle of the Dáil (who is Chairperson of the Commission), the Cathaoirleach of the Seanad, the Clerk of Dáil Éireann (as Secretary General of the Commission), a member appointed by the Minister for Finance, four TDs and three senators. The Oireachtas Commission is chaired by the Ceann Comhairle and became operational in 2004, following the Public Accounts Committee's first report on the DIRT Inquiry, which recommended the creation of a 'Parliamentary House Commission' (1999: Chapter 17). In response to the 2002 Deloitte & Touche international benchmarking report, funding was significantly increased on a three-year budgetary cycle, with the result that there has been significant additional expenditure in this area.

THE SEANAD

The theoretical case for having a bicameral legislature is that the upper House (Seanad Éireann) provides (1) a system of checks and balances on the main legislative chamber; (2) representation for particular areas or interest groups; and (3) an additional input of expertise into policy formation and legislation. The Constitution of 1937 introduced a new concept, that of a vocational Seanad, to draw on the knowledge of persons from a wide range of vocations. The concept has remained merely a concept, since, in practice, the emphasis in the election of members is on political affiliation rather than on professional knowledge.

The Seanad has no independent life. The Constitution confines the Seanad to a strictly subsidiary legislative role. An election for the Seanad must take place not later than ninety days after dissolution of the Dáil, and the first meeting of the new Seanad takes place on a day fixed by the President on the advice of the Taoiseach. Outgoing senators hold their seats until the day before polling day for the new Seanad. The Seanad normally meets on Tuesdays, Wednesdays and Thursdays and its main business is the reviewing of legislation sent to it by the Dáil. The government can also initiate legislation in the Seanad and this is increasingly becoming the case. The Seanad has brought fresh perspectives and made a significant contribution to the quality of legislation passed by the Oireachtas.

Membership

The Seanad is provided for in Articles 18 and 19 of the Constitution. The same conditions apply in relation to eligibility for membership as in the case of the Dáil. The Seanad consists of sixty members, of whom forty-nine are elected and eleven are nominated by the Taoiseach. Of the forty-nine elected members, forty-three are selected from vocational panels of candidates; three are elected to represent the National University of Ireland; and three are elected to represent the University of Dublin.

The five vocational panels contain the names of persons having knowledge and practical experience of: (1) the national language and culture, literature, art, education, law and medicine; (2) agriculture, fisheries and allied interests; (3) labour matters; (4) industry and commerce; (5) public administration and social services. Each panel is divided into two sub-panels. One of these (the Oireachtas sub-panel) contains the names of candidates nominated by not less than four members of the Houses of the Oireachtas. The other (the nominating bodies' sub-panel) contains the names of those nominated by bodies on the register of nominating bodies. The method of

Seanad Éireann

compilation and revision of the register, and the provisions relating to eligibility, are laid down in the Seanad Electoral (Panel Members) Acts 1947 to 1960. The register is the responsibility of the Clerk of the Seanad.

The electorate for the forty-three members from the panels consists of the members of the Dáil, Seanad and county and city councils, a total of approximately one thousand practising politicians. Election is by proportional representation and by secret ballot. The six university representatives are elected by the graduates of the two universities indicated. This provision has frequently been criticised as being curiously out of date in the present day. Apart from its overtones of elitism, there is a considerable imbalance in the two electorates. The National University of Ireland, with four constituent colleges, has an electorate of about 102,000 while the University of Dublin has one constituent college only (Trinity College) and an electorate of 39,000. Furthermore, the two new universities established in 1989, Dublin City University and the University of Limerick, do not have representation in the Seanad.

The nomination of eleven members by the Taoiseach under Article 18.3 of the Constitution enables persons of special calibre to reach parliament without going through the electoral process. Casey (2000: 122) notes, 'There is no constitutional or legal bar to the Taoiseach appointing someone a senator in order to qualify that person to be a member of the Government; and in 1981 Dr FitzGerald as Taoiseach used this device to appoint Professor James Dooge as Minister for Foreign Affairs.' The Taoiseach, however, tends to nominate party candidates who failed to get elected in the preceding Dáil election, those who seem to stand a good chance of being elected at the next Dáil election or persons who have worked well for the party over the years. As well as rewarding the worthy, this helps to strengthen the voting power of the government party (or parties) in the Seanad. The arrangements for election of members, and the appointment of eleven of them by the Taoiseach, as well as the standing orders of both houses, ensure that the Seanad is largely the creature of the government and the Dáil.

In its *Second Progress Report: Seanad Éireann* in 1997, the All-Party Oireachtas Committee on the Constitution recommended that six seats should continue to be allocated to representatives of third-level education, including all Irish graduates of third-level institutions. It suggested arrangements for a broader, more direct election of the Seanad and the retention of the right of the Taoiseach to appoint eleven senators, subject to conditions on the various traditions in Northern Ireland and gender balance. No action has been taken on these proposals, although the government has indicated its intention to proceed with an overall Seanad reform plan.

Functions

While the Seanad does have a role in initiating legislation, relatively few bills (though the number is increasing) begin their life in the upper House. Traditionally, the main function of the Seanad has been to review legislation passed by the Dáil. In practice, however, the Seanad exerts no significant control on the business of the Dáil. Bills passed by the Dáil are normally passed by the Seanad and it is only occasionally that it suggests any significant amendment. This is because the manner of electing senators results in the Seanad having the same political complexion as the Dáil. While those elected by the universities are seldom members of any political party, and are therefore independent, the vast majority of the remainder are, inevitably, members of one or other of the political parties.

The low level of Seanad activity has sometimes been adversely commented upon. The number of days on which the Seanad was in session in each of the years 1989 to 2008 is as follows: 42 in 1989; 61 in 1990; 68 in 1991; 68 in 1992; 64 in 1993; 52 in 1994; 75 in 1995; 73 in 1996; 61 in 1997; 82 in 1998; 73 in 1999; 74 in 2000; 79 in 2001; 49 in 2002; 83 in 2003; 88 in 2004; 83 in 2005; 81 in 2006; 64 in 2007, and 92 in 2008. The average number of sitting days each year over the period 1999 to 2008 was seventy-seven. Clearly, the upper House is neither overused nor overworked, and this has led to a questioning of the need for such a body, almost since the beginning of the state. Some argue that the Seanad is redundant; FitzGerald (2003: 55), however, does not share that view:

> There are many bills which are far more fully and effectively debated in the Seanad than the Dáil . . . The reasons for the better legislative performance by the Seanad in relation to some bills are complex. But, one reason is that, despite its largely political composition, the atmosphere in the Seanad is less partisan than the Dáil, and perhaps senators, just because they have less work to do than members of the Dáil, are sometimes inclined to do that work more thoroughly.

The main contribution of the Seanad has been to bring forward new ideas, new thinking and fresh perspectives, particularly through university representatives who have made an enormous contribution to political life, especially in the area of social reforms. Political parties have used the Seanad for those Dáil members who lost their seats and as a training ground for aspiring TDs. As a forum for introducing new perspectives and ideas to the political system and for debating social partnership issues, for considering the challenges in Ireland's developing multi-cultural society and for scrutinising European Union legislation, it has a significant potential contribution.

Calls for Reform

Speaking in the Dáil in 1928, Deputy Seán Lemass expressed his party's belief that the Seanad should be abolished, and declared that, failing this, it should be 'a group of individuals who dare not let a squeak out of them except when we [the Dáil] lift our fingers to give them the breath to do it'; he also concurred with the description of the ideal Seanad as 'a penny-in-the-slot machine' (*Dáil Debates*, 14 June 1928, col. 614). Subsequently, in the 1930s, there was a long-drawn-out feud between Eamon de Valera's government and the Seanad, culminating in its abolition in 1936. It is clear that in the formulation of the 1937 Constitution de Valera had serious doubts about the desirability of having an upper House at all, or at least of giving it any effective role in legislation. Garvin (2004: 220) notes that 'like so many of de Valera's constitutional devices, Seanad Éireann was an ideological red herring, and clearly intended to be so'.

In 1966 a committee of nine TDs and three senators was set up to review the constitutional, legislative and institutional bases of government. It reported in 1967 and in regard to the Seanad it recommended, in essence, no change in the status quo.

In more recent years there have been calls to make changes in the manner of electing the Seanad and to find ways to make it more effective. Indeed, one of the parties in the government formed in 1997, the Progressive Democrats, openly supported the abolition of the Seanad. These calls, however, receive very little support from politicians generally.

In April 1995 the government established a Constitution Review Group under the chairmanship of Dr T.K. Whitaker. Its 1996 report recommended 'a separate, comprehensive, independent examination of all issues relating to Seanad Éireann'. For this reason, it made no substantive or technical recommendations relating to the Seanad. The government established an All-Party Oireachtas Committee on the Constitution to consider the review group's report. The all-party committee commissioned a report, 'Options for the Future of Seanad Éireann', from John Coakley, Department of Political Science, University College Dublin, and Michael Laver, Department of Political Science, Trinity College, Dublin. This 1996 report observed that 'There is a case for looking carefully at the capacity of the Seanad to act as a voice for special groups that might otherwise be kept at a distance from Irish political life, such as representatives of the Irish abroad, and of marginal groups within Irish society'. Laver (2002) suggests a potential future role for the Seanad if it were directly elected and given important jobs to do such as the oversight of European Union legislation.

The all-party committee's own report on the Seanad, published in 1997 when the committee was chaired by Deputy Jim O'Keeffe, commented (1997b: 6), 'The Committee is persuaded by the argument in Coakley/Laver that the Seanad does make a useful contribution to the democratic life of the state. The Committee also agrees with Coakley/Laver that the Seanad is a resource that could be deployed for greater effect if it were reformed.' It concluded that (1997: 5) 'The function of the upper house in providing calm deliberation and deep analysis of national issues is an important one', and that, on balance, the Seanad should continue to exist but that a fresh innovative approach needed to be taken to what the Seanad should do and who the senators should be. It also concluded that the proper function of the Seanad is to act as a consultative body where people with knowledge, experience and judgment over the whole spectrum of public affairs should be available in a broadly non-partisan way to help the Dáil to carry out its functions more effectively and efficiently. It went on to identify a number of tasks that the Seanad could undertake to increase the productivity of the legislative process. For example, it could carry out special reviews of government programmes, debate policy reports and maintain a focus on Northern Ireland relationships, thus enriching the political system by helping the Dáil. The all-party committee also made recommendations in regard to the composition of the Seanad: that membership should remain at sixty, that there should be directly and non-directly elected members, that some should be elected by the incoming Dáil and some by county councils, that there should be provision for gender balance and that the Taoiseach should retain the power of appointing eleven senators.

In 2002 the Seanad Committee on Procedure and Privileges established a sub-committee on Seanad reform. It proposed an increase in the membership of the Seanad to sixty-five, new methods of electing senators, and that the Seanad be allowed to review the activities of government departments, state agencies and social partnership arrangements, as well as scrutinising senior public appointments. Some 158 groups responded to the public advertisement relating to the work of the committee and there was a significant volume of public interest.

The All-Party Oireachtas Committee on the Constitution in 2002 (then chaired by Deputy Brian Lenihan) was broadly in agreement with its predecessor:

> It agrees that the Seanad has played a useful role in our national political life. It has a number of distinctive characteristics, including its relatively non-partisan atmosphere and its capacity to take a long-term view, which make it, as a second chamber, complementary to the Dáil, the primacy of which is not contested . . . We would endorse the O'Keeffe committee's recommendations in relation to:
> - The scrutiny of EU legislation or, more broadly, of EU business generally
> - The scrutiny of secondary legislation through statutory instruments
> - Detailed consideration of policy reports by commissions, expert groups etc, in particular those with a medium-to-long-term focus.

In summary, therefore, three recent reports have urged fundamental reform of the functions and composition of the Seanad and its election processes. These reports followed the 1979 referendum that provided for changes in the electoral base for the six university seats. No changes were made. Russell and Sandford (2002), based on the experience of second chambers in Canada, Australia, Italy and Ireland, suggest that an ineffective chamber can be of value to the government and that second chamber reform comes a long way down the list of a government's priorities. In July 2007 Minister for the Environment and Green Party leader, John Gormley, reopened the issue following concerns in relation to the management of the electoral registers and the difficulties of working with these registers in election campaigns. He told the Seanad in November 2007 that he would proceed with plans to replace the two Seanad university constituencies with one new six-week constituency in which all graduates would be eligible to vote. He said that he intended to reform the Seanad with the co-operation of the opposition parties, but would not be deterred from pressing ahead with the university changes if that co-operation did not materialise.

Reformers have approached the issue of the Seanad on the basis that it should be made more relevant and democratic. Even Seanad members took as their starting point the premise that it should be abolished if a viable and credible role could not be found for it. On that basis, a Seanad group led by Mary O'Rourke put forward in 2004 many proposals that will be considered by the Minister for the Environment and another all-party committee.

THE INFRASTRUCTURE

Oireachtas Committees

The Oireachtas has established a number of committees to deal with aspects of its work. Some of these are joint committees of both Houses; others contain members of the Dáil or Seanad only. Party representation on committees is determined by reference to their relative strengths in the Houses. Generally, committees are set up to do work for which either House, as a large assembly, would not be suited, for example detailed inquiry or examination of witnesses. They may engage any legal, economic or financial consultants they require to assist them in their work. Committees do not have the power to make decisions in their own right. They prepare reports on the matters they have examined for presentation to the Oireachtas and for publication. Committees refrain from inquiring into the merits of a policy or policies of the government or a minister of the government or the merits of the objectives of such policies (Dáil Standing Order 158). One of the original purposes of the parliamentary committee system was to consider the heads of bills – the draft structure and titles of a legislative proposal. In March 2008 Taoiseach Bertie Ahern indicated his willingness to publish these, saying that 'legislation which may seem uninteresting to us in here will be of interest to groups outside the House and the political system. The best way to allow them to have an input is to publish the Heads of the Bill'.

The development of the committee system provides greater opportunities for TDs and senators to become involved in all aspects of the parliamentary process. The committees are formed early in the lifetime of each new Dáil and Seanad. The number and range of committees have expanded greatly in

Joint Committee of the Houses of the Oireachtas

recent years, enabling the Houses to deal in a detailed manner with an ever-increasing range and complexity of business. Most committees meet in public session throughout the year, save for August. Each House has power under its standing orders (rules) to form committees for specific purposes. There are four types of committee – standing, select, joint and special (rare). Standing orders provide for the automatic creation of *standing committees* in a new Dáil or Seanad, for example the Committee of Public Accounts and the Joint Committee on Consolidation Bills.

Select committees comprise membership of one House only, whether Dáil or Seanad. Select committees are set up at the discretion of the House and vary as to number and type. In general they are investigatory or legislative and deal either with a specialised subject that is referred to them by the Dáil or with the committee stages of bills. The terms of reference of some select committees may give them powers to send for persons, papers or records under the provisions of the Committees of the Houses of the Oireachtas (Compellability, Privileges and Immunities of Witnesses) Act 1997. This act provides a substantial increase in committee powers to require witnesses to attend hearings and to respond to questions. Section 15 of the act precludes public servants from expressing an opinion on the merits or objectives of any policy of the government or a government minister. As a corollary of this increase in powers, there are concepts of privilege and immunity. Accordingly, committees are able to grant witnesses who are compelled to give evidence before them the equivalent of High Court privilege.

Joint committees comprise select committees from both Houses sitting and voting together under common orders of reference. They are set up for specific purposes, for example to oversee the administration and provision of services to both Houses. A joint committee may also function as a specialised committee of experts, for example the Joint Committee on European Affairs. The joint committees of the thirtieth Dáil are:

- Joint Committee on Agriculture, Fisheries and Food
- Joint Committee on Arts, Sport, Tourism, Community, Rural and Gaeltacht Affairs
- Joint Committee on Communications, Energy and Natural Resources
- Joint Committee on the Constitution
- Joint Committee on Education and Science
- Joint Committee on Enterprise, Trade and Employment
- Joint Committee on the Environment, Heritage and Local Government
- Joint Committee on European Affairs
- Joint Committee on European Scrutiny
- Joint Committee on Finance and the Public Service
- Joint Committee on Foreign Affairs
- Joint Committee on the Implementation of the Good Friday Agreement
- Joint Committee on Health and Children
- Joint Committee on Justice, Equality, Defence and Women's Rights
- Joint Committee on Social and Family Affairs
- Joint Committee on Transport
- Joint Committee on Climate Change and Energy Security
- Joint Committee on the Constitutional Amendment on Children
- Joint Committee on Economic Regulatory Affairs.

In the case of the Joint Committee on Foreign Affairs and the Joint Committee on European Affairs, Irish MEPs (including Northern Ireland MEPs) and members of the Irish delegation to the Parliamentary Assembly of the Council of Europe can attend and participate at their meetings but they do not have voting rights. These committees can also invite MEPs of other EU member states to attend under similar conditions.

Special committees are set up to consider a particular bill at its third, or committee, stage. These committees cease to exist when their work has been completed and a report has been made to the Dáil. In recent years, however, the practice is to refer bills to select committees responsible for a particular area of government activity.

Most committees meet in public session and their proceedings are televised. Representatives of the media and members of the public may attend. The advantages of committees are that they allow the work of the

Oireachtas to proceed more efficiently, they allow backbenchers, experts and senators to contribute in areas of specialist interest, and they allow committees to acquire detailed interest in complex technical areas such as the Constitution or climate change. The powers of committees depend on their orders of reference and include the power to:

- Send for persons, papers and records.
- Receive submissions and hear evidence from interested parties or groups.
- Discuss and draft proposals for legislative change.
- Print and publish minutes of evidence and related documents.
- Require attendance of ministers to discuss current policies.
- Require attendance of ministers to discuss proposals for legislation.
- Require attendance of principal office-holders in bodies in the state that are wholly or partly funded by the state.

All committees have a secretariat and each has a clerk. Where necessary, committees are provided with a budget to engage specialist or technical assistance. Some committee chairpersons are members of the opposition and it is not the practice for ministers or ministers of state to be chairpersons. There is provision for the payment of an allowance to the chairperson (€19,058), vice-chairperson (€9,747) and whip of an Oireachtas committee, and to the chairperson of a sub-committee. There have been calls for the rotation of Oireachtas committee chairpersons on a yearly or two-yearly basis and that committee chairs should not be doled out as perks for government backbenchers and disappointed aspirants to ministerial office.

The committee system is a feature of parliamentary life in many countries, including the United States and several EU member states. The system has, however, come late to Ireland, and increasingly members of the Oireachtas view participation in the work of parliamentary committees as an integral part of their work. The number of committee meetings was 531 in 2005, 524 in 2006, 235 in 2007 and 593 in 2008. Hannon (2004: 132) notes that 'the first thing an ambitious TD must do is get well in with the whip and the party leader to ensure that they bag a seat on one of the more high profile Oireachtas Committees . . . Some of these offer more opportunities for sound bites and foreign travel than others so they must be targeted with care'.

The expansion in the number and range of committees in recent years has enabled the Houses of the Oireachtas to deal with an ever-increasing volume of parliamentary business while providing members with additional opportunities to participate in all aspects of the work of the Dáil and Seanad. The decision of Taoiseach Bertie Ahern to increase the number of committees after the 2007 election to twenty-three indicates that committees play an increasingly important part in the Oireachtas. No formal evaluation of the cost or worth of the committee system has yet been made public. Advantages generally put forward are that it provides a more relaxed atmosphere with more give and take than obtains in the House itself, where contributions are largely adversarial in nature, and that it enables members to acquire a detailed knowledge of the subject at issue and to discuss it in a minute way.

Compellability and Privilege

There are two mechanisms that hold the government accountable to the Dáil: question time and the committee system. The Committees of the Houses of the Oireachtas (Compellability, Privileges and Immunities of Witnesses) Act 1997 strengthened the committee system and significantly increased transparency and accountability. Committees are not automatically entitled to the powers of compellability and must apply for them from a sub-committee of the Committee on Procedure and Privileges, known as the 'Compellability Committee', which is chaired by the Government Chief Whip.

The act confers on those Oireachtas committees whose terms of reference include provision for the calling of persons and papers, statutory powers to compel the attendance and co-operation of witnesses and the furnishing of documents. It confers High Court privilege and immunities, virtually identical with the absolute privilege of members of the Houses of the Oireachtas, on all witnesses giving evidence or, on direction, sending documents to such committees. Both elements of the act are, of necessity, intertwined. Clearly, it would be arbitrary to compel witnesses to answer questions without according to them the safeguards essential to protect them from what might otherwise be the legal consequences of full and frank responses to the questions put to them. Under Article 15.13 of the Constitution members of the Houses of the Oireachtas have absolute privilege in respect of utterances in either House. In 1976 this was extended by legislation to cover them at meetings of committees. On the other hand, witnesses appearing before such committees enjoyed only 'qualified privilege'. This did not prevent legal action being taken against a witness for anything he or she said before a committee but it did provide a defence against libel or slander unless it could be proved that he or she was actuated by a motive not connected with the privilege, for example ill will, spite or any other improper motive. The possibility of legal action with the attendant costs of representation, even where a good defence existed, constituted a serious hazard for any witness. In addition, however, the privilege that witnesses enjoyed did not extend to other legal actions, for example for breaches of confidentiality and of duty of care, which could have resulted in their having to pay damages. One of the two major aims of the act was to correct this situation.

The other aim of this measure was in relation to compellability. Certain Oireachtas committees include in their terms of reference provision for the calling of persons and papers. While these requests to attend were in general honoured, there were well-publicised incidents that showed that committees had no statutory power to enforce such provisions. Under the terms of the act virtually anyone a committee believes can provide information relevant to its mandate can be compelled to appear before it or provide evidence. This applies to individual members of the general public. The Taoiseach, the Tánaiste, ministers, ministers of state and their officials are all compellable. In the case of civil servants, only one restriction applies – they are debarred in giving evidence from expressing opinions in relation to the merits of policy. This does not preclude them from explaining particular policies. This restriction extends to An Garda Síochána and members of the Permanent Defence Forces. In keeping with convention, the President and members of the judiciary are exempt from the application of the legislation. The Attorney General and the Director of Public Prosecutions, because of their independent roles as defenders of the public interest, are exempted also. Compellability does not in any instance apply to:

• Discussions at meetings of the government.
• Discussions at meetings of committees appointed by the government.
• Matters which are the subject of proceedings currently before the courts (sub judice).
• Matters that would affect adversely the security of the state.
• Matters related to law enforcement.
• Tax assessment information.

The act provides that non-attendance in response to an Oireachtas committee's direction shall be an offence, and also contains the provision that false evidence shall constitute perjury.

The power of compellability and the subsequent protection of witnesses' rights has assisted the operation of the Oireachtas committee system. It has enhanced the conditions for accountability and transparency in this regard. Committees are obliged to report to a plenary session of the Dáil on the work they have completed, the work on hand, attendance at meetings and their voting records. A full debate on that information takes place, thereby completing the cycle of transparency and accountability. The supreme principle of this act is that parliament, through its elected representatives, must have the power to ensure that everybody in the public service is accountable to it. The act provides improved means for democratically elected public representatives to elicit information, and increases the accountability of office-holders and public administration to parliament.

Gender Equality

The number of female representatives in the Houses of the Oireachtas is low by international standards. Minister for Health Mary Harney comments (Banotti 2008: 72):

> There are still relatively few women in the Oireachtas. I feel that we still live in an environment where people think that if they have one woman or two women they have covered the women. There was a lot of progress made in the 1980's, the kind of women who came into politics as much as the numbers. Garrett FitzGerald deserves a lot of credit because he brought a lot of new women into politics, not just in Fine Gael. He encouraged them.

Studies have isolated family responsibilities and lack of finance as significant barriers for Irish women wishing to enter, and stay in, political life. Galligan (2004: 297) notes 'no significant bias among the electorate against women candidates'. Knight *et al.* (2004) highlight the broad consensus among women politicians, irrespective of party, self-interest or length of service, favouring certain positive action initiatives that would assist in increasing women's legislative presence.

Remuneration; Expenses; Pensions

The remuneration paid to each deputy, senator and office-holder is referred to in the relevant legislation – the Oireachtas (Allowances to Members) and the Ministerial and Parliamentary Offices Acts – as an 'allowance'. The allowances are subject to review from time to time by the Review Body on Higher Remuneration in the Public Sector, which makes recommendations to the government about their appropriate level. The pay rounds, applied on a general basis to the civil service, are normally applied to members of the Oireachtas. TDs are paid their salaries up until the day of the dissolution of the Dáil, and then receive an allowance to cover the period between then and polling day. TDs who lose their seats receive a portion of their salaries on a sliding scale lasting over a year after they lose their seat.

Each member is entitled to travel and overnight allowances. If they live within fifteen miles of Leinster House they are entitled to a flat-rate daily allowance. Those living more than fifteen miles away can claim a flat allowance or overnight allowance plus mileage. The overnight allowance can be claimed for the nights before the Dáil or Seanad sits or a committee meeting takes place, as well as for the sitting day itself. The allowance can be claimed for a meeting of two or more members on days when the chamber is not in session, up to a maximum of five times per annum. In addition, up to twenty-five overnights can be claimed by members using House of the Oireachtas facilities when it is not in session. TDs are entitled to a constituency travel allowance, dependent on the size of their constituency, to travel to meet their constituents. Members are also entitled to allowances for their constituency telephone lines and mobile telephones. Party whips and committee chairpersons are entitled to additional telephone allowances. Members are entitled to send telemessages from Leinster House. TDs are entitled to a once-off grant to set up a constituency office and an annual allowance to maintain that office. All members are entitled to secretarial allowances both in Leinster House and in their constituency offices. There is also a miscellaneous allowance for TDs to cover the costs of running their clinics and advertising. The expenses claimed by individual TDs and senators have been published annually since 1999. The 2007 report of the Houses of the Oireachtas Commission indicated that a report by A & L Goodbody Consultants on making the expenses system for politicians fairer and more transparent is under consideration.

Official cars with drivers (members of An Garda Síochána) are supplied to the President, Taoiseach, ministers, Chief Whip, Chief Justice, Director of Public Prosecutions, Attorney General and Ceann Comhairle. Former Taoisigh are supplied with state cars. The cars are available for private use as if they were the office-holders' own cars, but may be used only with their official drivers. The benefit deriving from the private use of these cars is taken into account by the review body in determining remuneration. Ministers of state, the Leas-Cheann Comhairle and the Cathaoirleach provide their own cars and are paid mileage allowances for official travel in these cars. In these cases, civilian drivers are engaged by the office-holders themselves; the drivers are paid by the state.

Pension schemes apply to members of both Houses, depending on age and length of service.

Declaration of Interests

Under the Ethics in Public Office Acts 1995 and 2001, ministers and members of the Dáil and Seanad are required to make an annual declaration of their interests and ministers are further obliged to declare any conflict of interest in fulfilling the functions of their office. The key requirements on members under the act are: firstly, an annual statement of members' interests, which will be entered into the register and laid before the House; and second, an ad hoc statement by the member when speaking or voting in the House or one of its committees on a matter in which the member or a connected person has a material interest. The Dáil Select Committee on Members' Interests assists members to meet these requirements. The committee discharges its functions in three ways: firstly, providing guidelines to members on compliance with the act; second, issuing advice in individual cases where appropriate; and third, undertaking investigations of possible breaches of the act and, where necessary, reporting to the House on such matters.

Most of the TDs and senators listed their employment status in the declaration of interests for the Dáil and Seanad in 2007. The most popular previous occupation for members of the Oireachtas is teachers. Teachers elected to the Oireachtas are currently entitled to take paid leave of absence.

Allowances to Parties

Political parties are not mentioned in the Constitution; the right to form and join parties is a normal aspect of the right of association. The Electoral Acts provide for a 'Register of Political Parties', which lists political parties that fulfil three conditions: firstly, the party must be organised in the state to contest Dáil, European, local or Údarás na Gaeltachta elections; second, either it has not less than three hundred members over eighteen years of age, half of whom are on the register of electors, or one member who is a member of the Dáil or the European Parliament and who certifies in writing his or her membership of the party; third, the organisation of the party is governed by written rules that provide for a periodic conference and the conduct of the business by an executive committee or similar body. The Clerk of Dáil Éireann is the Registrar of Political Parties.

Under the Ministerial and Parliamentary Offices Act 1938, as amended in 1996, and the Oireachtas (Allowances to Members) Act 1962, as amended in 2001, allowances for party expenses are paid to the leaders of political parties that contested the previous general election as organised political parties. Under the 1996 amendment act the amount paid to the leader of each parliamentary party is dependent on the number of Dáil deputies elected as members of that party in the preceding general election. The 2001 amendment act deals with three aspects of the payments made to leaders of parliamentary parties: how they are computed, how they are audited and how they are adjusted following a merger of parliamentary parties. The allowance is specified as being for parliamentary purposes (including research) and, following the Supreme Court McKenna judgment of 1995, is prohibited for use for electoral purposes. The allowance is used to provide back-up services to the leader and the parliamentary party and is more a 'parliamentary allowance' than a 'leader's allowance'. Under the party leaders' allowance legislation, independent TDs received an annual allowance of €41,152 and independent senators received €23,383 in 2008. Such members are not required to furnish the Standards in Public Office Commission with a statement of expenditure in relation to the allowance. Funding received under the party leaders' allowance is not subject to income tax.

Political Expenditure and Funding

The Electoral Acts prohibit the use of public funds for election purposes. Elections can only be financed through donations. Part V of the Electoral Act 1997 introduced a new and complex system that limits the amount that candidates may spend, or which their parties may spend on their behalf. The Electoral (Amendment) Act 1998 extensively amended this system. Each candidate must have an election agent, who alone may incur election expenses on the candidate's behalf. The agent is obliged, within fifty-six days of polling day, to furnish the Standards in Public Office Commission with an itemised written account of all election expenses incurred, together with the relevant vouchers. Under section 37(1) of the 1997 act, the commission must cause a copy of each such statement to be laid before each House of the Oireachtas. In advance of each Dáil election, each political party must appoint a national agent, who alone may incur election expenses on that party's behalf. The national agent is obliged to furnish the commission with an itemised written statement of all the election expenses incurred, together with all relevant vouchers. This statement must include all details of the central party funding made available to each of the party's candidates. The commission likewise causes a copy of each such statement to be laid before each House of the Oireachtas.

The Electoral Acts provide for the reimbursement – out of public funds – of a proportion of the election expenses of certain Dáil candidates. To qualify, the candidate must either secure election or obtain a vote in excess of one-quarter of the quota. There is a maximum limit for reimbursement and this is conditional on the Standards in Public Office Commission certifying details of actual expenses incurred to the Minister for Finance.

Under the Electoral Acts there is not a prescribed amount that a political party may spend on a Dáil or European election. The spending limits prescribed in the legislation are for candidates only. Under section 31 of the Electoral Act 1997, as amended by section 10 of the Electoral Act 1998 and section 50(k) of the Electoral Act 2001, only election expenses incurred on goods, property or services (for example posters, leaflets, mobile display advertisements) used during the election period are subject to the expenditure limits applying at a Dáil general election and must be accounted for in an election expenses statement furnished to the Standards in Public Office Commission after the election. The election period for a Dáil general election is from the date of dissolution of the Dáil until polling day.

The Standards in Public Office Commission has suggested a review of the transparency of political party funding in the light of its finding that only a fraction of the €11.8 million spent by political parties in 2007 was publicly disclosed. The fourteen political parties spent in excess of €10 million during the three-week general election campaign in 2007, yet only disclosed €1.122 million. Its 2008 report on political donations commented that 'in terms of transparency there is a large gap between the amount of disclosable donations and reported expenditure'. As the €10 million was spent entirely during the three-week election campaign, the commission notes that the actual gap is even wider, as some parties spent heavily in early 2007 before the campaign got under way.

Excluding subscriptions from the salaries of elected representatives to their parties, the donations disclosed by political parties in 2007 amounted to just €43,693. The commission says that it is obvious that political parties are soliciting donations that are below the disclosure threshold, which is set at €5,078 for a party. 'The commission does not consider that there is anything wrong with this', states the 2008 report. 'However, if the purpose of the [legislation] is to demonstrate transparency in how political parties are funded, and in particular how political parties and their candidates fund election campaigns, then this part of the legislation is not achieving that purpose.' The commission reiterates its recommendation for a new approach to the general funding of political parties. Because of the revelations at recent tribunals of inquiry, those who donate to political parties are stigmatised by unfair assumptions of attempts to gain improper influence. The perception that political donations have been diverted for personal use may also promote reluctance to donate. Following the commission's report, the government announced plans in June 2008 to set up an independent electoral commission with responsibility for drawing up constituency boundaries, maintaining the electoral register and acting as the state's watchdog for political funding. Political scientist Professor Richard Sinnott of University College Dublin was commissioned to conduct a study into the current arrangements in Ireland and the models used in other countries. This follows a commitment in the 2007 Programme for Government to make progress in this area.

Secretarial Assistance

Ministers have offices in their departments and in Leinster House. They are assisted in all of their work – parliamentary, departmental, constituency and social – by the civil service. Some deputies choose to have their secretaries located in Oireachtas premises, while others prefer to locate them in their constituency offices. Under Statutory Instrument No. 36 of 2008 government parties reduced the number of their Oireachtas secretaries in an effort to 'level the playing field'. Secretaries were redistributed among the bigger opposition parties according to the numbers of TDs and senators they have. The Houses of the Oireachtas Commission said the plan was designed to help opposition parties to hold the government to account. In addition to the above secretarial assistance, the new system allocated one secretary to every two non-office-holding TDs and one to every four non-office-holding senators.

Every TD is entitled to employ one secretarial assistant and one parliamentary assistant; senators have a 'half share' of each. The position of parliamentary assistant was introduced in 2005 to help TDs in writing speeches and researching issues and legislation. In addition to the library, there has been a marked increase in the research facilities available to members. Some members of the Oireachtas employ family members as secretarial assistants and parliamentary assistants.

Each deputy and senator is allowed a number of ordinary prepaid envelopes each month, which they may post in Leinster House. They also enjoy free telephone facilities, including a constituency telephone allowance. Some American students spend time working in the Dáil as interns to TDs.

Staff

The staff in the Houses of the Oireachtas are civil servants, but with a legal distinction from the civil servants who serve ministers in government departments. Because they are under the control of the chairpersons of the Dáil and Seanad, rather than under that of ministers as other civil servants are, they are properly referred to as civil servants of the state under the Staff of the Houses of the Oireachtas Act 1959 and the Houses of the Oireachtas Commission Acts 2003 and 2006. The total number of staff was about 435 in 2008.

The most senior official in each House is called the clerk of that House, and his or her deputy is called the clerk assistant. These officials are appointed by the Taoiseach on the nomination of the appropriate chairperson and the Minister for Finance. The Secretary General of the Office of the Houses of the Oireachtas is the Clerk of the Dáil. Other senior staff are also designated clerks, for example principal clerk, committee clerk; they are interchangeable and known as the joint staff of the Houses of the Oireachtas.

The staff includes a Superintendent of the Houses and a Captain of the Guard. Their duties are not prescribed, but, broadly speaking, the former is responsible for members' accommodation and security; and the latter is a uniformed officer who can remove disorderly members at the request of the Ceann Comhairle or Cathaoirleach. It rarely comes to this, however, since such offenders usually leave voluntarily when called upon to do so.

Also on the staff is an editor of debates and a number of reporters. As it is stipulated that all acts of the Oireachtas, the daily order paper, the journal of proceedings and other official documents must be published in both Irish and English, the staff also includes several translators. The Public Relations Office provides a service for the Houses of the Oireachtas as a whole, including information for interest groups, schools and members of the public.

The Houses of the Oireachtas have an excellent website and Dáil, Seanad and committee debates are freely available to anyone with access to the Internet. Work is ongoing on making all parliamentary records from the foundation of the state available on this website.

A Members' Informal Feedback Forum started in September 2006. It consists of a small cross-party group of members from both Houses that meets with the secretary general (Clerk of the Dáil) every six weeks to discuss service delivery to members informally in the forum.

Accommodation

Most of the business of the Oireachtas is carried out in Leinster House. In recent years, however, because of the increased use of committees, and the increase in the numbers of secretarial staff, some of the work is now done in adjacent buildings – in the former College of Science in Merrion Street and in the former College of Art in Kildare Street.

Members of the public may gain access to Leinster House only on introduction by a member of either House. This necessitates asking a member to make arrangements for access. This having been done, the person may enter in the company of the member, or, more frequently, the member authorises the issue of an admission ticket to the public gallery that is available from the usher's office. A special gallery is reserved for the press, and another for distinguished visitors.

Conclusion

The importance of the functions of the two Houses of the Oireachtas is manifest. The number of sitting days of both Houses is low. Parliamentary wrangles about the length of the Dáil recess have become a standard feature of end-of-term political exchanges. A bemused public has come to regard this annual ritual as little more than a sham fight between government and opposition. Governments insist that they have been fully accountable to the Dáil, having attended for ninety days in plenary session in an average parliamentary calendar. However, strong party loyalty and the use of the whip system allows government to dominate the proceedings of parliament itself. Depauw and Martin (2008), in cross-national research in sixteen European democracies, show that party voting unity tends to be highest in Ireland. In addition, real decision making is perceived to take place away from traditional structures and in direct dialogue with the social partners and other interest groups. The media plays an important role in providing a forum for debate, discussion and dialogue among politicians and the wider public. Finally, the growing volume of legislation emerging from the institutions of the European Union is also a relevant factor in the work of the Dáil and Seanad.

The Dáil and Seanad play a central role in Ireland's representative democracy and their efficiency and effectiveness are central to a healthy democratic system. Norris (2009) notes that 'Seanad Éireann has consistently proved itself to be a seed bed of ideas which are subsequently taken up by the Dáil'. The Houses of the Oireachtas have introduced an education outreach programme, in conjunction with the second-level Civic, Social and Political Education syllabus, to increase understanding of the parliamentary system in a classroom environment. It produces a volume of information material, and open days in Leinster House have been well attended. However, public cynicism about politics and politicians has increased due to a decade of tribunal hearings that have eroded trust. Other factors – such as the pay, performance and productivity of Oireachtas members – have contributed too. TDs are now better paid than their counterparts in most European assemblies. The parliamentary year is shorter in Ireland than in most other countries and the TD's role as a legislator is a good deal less demanding. Given the scale of contemporary challenges, more sitting days and a fundamental reform of Dáil procedures are urgently needed.

Web Resources

Ceann Comhairle at www.ceanncomhairle.oireachtas.ie
Dáil reform at websites of main political parties [www.fiannafail.ie; www.finegael.com; www.greenparty.ie; www.labour.ie; www.sinnfein.ie]
Houses of the Oireachtas and Oireachtas Committees at www.oireachtas.ie
Parliamentary debates (current) at http://debates.oireachtas.ie
Parliamentary debates (historical) at http://historical-debates.oireachtas.ie
Parliamentary questions to the Health Service Executive at www.hse.ie/ eng/Access_to_Information_PQs/Parliamentary_Questions
Public financial procedures at www.finance.gov.ie

4

THE CONSTITUTION OF IRELAND

The Constitution of Ireland (Bunreacht na hÉireann) is the basic law of the state (bun-reacht – basic-law). It is a fundamental document that establishes the state, expresses legal norms and reflects the aspirations, aims and political theories of the people. It is necessarily concerned with guiding principles and guarantees certain basic rights of the people in general terms and imposes limitations on those rights in almost equally general terms.

The Constitution regulates the government and the distribution of the powers of government and, more importantly, limits the power of government and imposes obligations upon those exercising that power; as such, it has been defined as 'a selection of the legal rules which govern the government of that country and which have been embodied in a document' (Wheare 1966: 2). It is a body of rules that specifies how all other legal rules are to be produced, applied and interpreted. It has a higher legal status and authority than other laws and cannot be changed in the manner of ordinary legislation. In combination with an independent judiciary that has the power to review, it comprises an essential framework to protect the welfare of a liberal democratic country. The Constitution, which is written in the present tense, is a current living document that adapts with the times and society.

The Constitution was adopted by referendum in 1937. Its Preamble envisages a system of fundamental law that can absorb or be adapted to changes as society changes and develops. It can therefore be fully appreciated only in conjunction with the legal traditions and precedents and the body of constitutional cases that have evolved since 1937.

Earlier Constitutions of Ireland

The current Constitution should also be considered against the background of the two constitutions that preceded it in 1919 and 1922. Denham J. gives a succinct insight in her Supreme Court judgment in *Maguire v Ardagh* ([2002] IESC 21, 11 April 2002):

> The Constitution of the Irish Free State, 1922 was a step on a different road, which journey was continued by the Constitution of Ireland, 1937. These Irish

constitutional instruments were, in many respects, different from those of England and other colonies and dominions. Another line of thought developed in Ireland. While retaining the Common Law System, Ireland wished to establish an Irish legal order. There was no reality in returning to the ancient Irish Brehon Law. A modern constitution was required. Thus in 1937 principles and theories such as the principle of the separation of powers, fundamental rights, including the right to a good name and fair procedures, were continued, and expanded, powers were given to the executive and the legislature and the courts, which were given the duty of guarding the Constitution. A new constitutional basis for the State was laid. The constitutional government established was not a mirror image of that in London or Washington.

These steps of 1922 and 1937 were taken on a journey on a road then less travelled by other countries with a common law legal system. Ireland took the road

'less travelled by,
And that has made all the difference.' (Robert Frost)

Ireland took the road less travelled in 1937. It was a decision in advance of its time. It presaged a move toward modern constitutions. The Constitution of Ireland, 1937 was prescient of European Constitutions and international instruments to follow. In 1937 the Constitution of Ireland protected fundamental rights, fair procedures and gave to the Supreme Court a role as guardian of the Constitution. A decade later, after World War II, the United Nations Charter and the Universal Declaration of Human Rights were brought into being and in Europe the European Convention on Human Rights followed. Over the succeeding decades of the twentieth century, courts, through judicial review, have sought to protect human rights.

The Constitution of Dáil Éireann, 1919

This was the first Irish Constitution. The definitive text is in Irish and is published in the minutes of the first Dáil. It is a short document with five articles, covering the appointment of a chairman, the competence of the Dáil, the appointment of a prime minister and a government and their powers, the provision of funds, the audit of expenditure and provision for amendment. It is written in a clear and straightforward manner.

The system of government adopted by the 1919 Constitution was parliamentary democracy based on the Westminster model then in operation in Britain. 'The founders of the new state were constitutionalists within a strongly developed parliamentary tradition' (Farrell 1969: 135). The Sinn Féin candidates elected at the general election of December 1918 were in rebellion against British rule in Ireland. They did not have the means, the time or the inclination to draw up a detailed constitution. The members of the first Dáil saw themselves as completing the work of 1916 by ratifying and establishing the Republic of the 1916 Proclamation. By drawing up a constitution that set out the machinery of government, together with an economic and social programme, the Dáil sought to give practical effect to the declaration of independence and establish the legitimacy of the independence movement.

The Constitution of the Irish Free State, 1922

The Constitution of the new Irish Free State (Saorstát Éireann) was enacted by Dáil Éireann sitting as a constituent (i.e. constitution-making) assembly in the autumn of 1922 and was included as the first schedule to the Constitution of the Irish Free State Act 1922. The Treaty (Articles of Agreement) signed in London on 6 December 1921 between Britain and the Irish delegation was included as a second schedule to this act. Section 2 of the constituent act stated, 'If any provision of the said Constitution or of any amendment thereof or of any law made thereunder is in any respect repugnant to any of the provisions of the Scheduled Treaty, it shall, to the extent only of such repugnancy, be made absolutely void and inoperative.'

The 1922 Constitution acknowledged, in its Preamble, that all lawful authority 'comes from God'. Article 1 declared, 'The Irish Free State is a co-equal member of the Community of Nations forming the British Commonwealth of Nations.' Article 2 declared, 'All powers of government and all authority, legislative, executive and judicial, in Ireland, are derived from the people of Ireland, and the same shall be exercised in the Irish Free State through the organisations established by or under, and in accord with, this Constitution.'

Among the innovative features of the 1922 Constitution was that it provided for the protection of certain fundamental rights and vested the courts with express powers to invalidate legislation adjudged to infringe such rights. It guaranteed the liberty of the person, the inviolability of the dwelling of each citizen, freedom of conscience and the free profession and practice of religion, the right of free expression of opinion, the right to assemble peaceably and the right to free elementary education.

The legislature of the new state was the Oireachtas, which was to consist of the British monarch and two Houses: the Dáil and the Seanad. The sole and exclusive power of making laws for the Irish Free State was vested in the Oireachtas, with the Dáil as the dominant partner. It was to be elected by all adult citizens, voting by proportional representation. Each of the two universities was to elect two members, and there was to be one Teachta Dála (TD) for every 20,000 people. The Dáil was empowered to elect the President of the Executive Council (replaced by the office of the Taoiseach in the 1937 Constitution) and to approve his or her ministers; it could also, in theory, dismiss the president and select a successor.

The Seanad had sixty members, of whom one-quarter were to be elected every three years by popular vote. It could delay bills for 270 days, but could not stop them. Membership of the Seanad was 'composed of citizens who shall be proposed on the grounds that they have done honour to the Nation by reason of useful public service or that, because of special qualifications or attainments, they represent important aspects of the Nation's life' (Article 30). As a result of the very active part played by the Seanad, which frequently brought it into conflict with the government – especially after 1932 when the first Fianna Fáil government came into office – it was abolished in May 1936.

The 1922 Constitution could be amended by referendum and also by the Oireachtas without reference to the people (both provisions of Article 50), so it imposed no effective limitations on the power of the legislature. Article 47 did, however, provide for the reference of bills to the people, but this article was removed by the Constitution (Amendment No. 10) Act 1928, when the Fianna Fáil party sought to have a referendum on the oath of allegiance to the British monarch, provided for in the Constitution. No referendum on a constitutional amendment was held under the 1922 Constitution. It was initially intended that all amendments would require a referendum, but during the Dáil debate this was changed to allow for parliamentary amendment of defects that might become obvious during its first eight years. This period of flexible amendment was subsequently extended to sixteen years. 'So, during the whole of its life, the Irish Free State Constitution could be changed as easily as any other law, without direct reference to the people. Both the Cosgrave and de Valera governments took full advantage of the latitude, and between 1923 and 1936 twenty-five bills were passed amending many provisions of the original text' (Farrell 1988a: 29).

The 1922 Constitution reflected some of the major features of the unwritten British Constitution, such as the institution of cabinet government led by a prime minister, accountable to and ultimately controlled by the legislature, and an independent judiciary. It formally defined the separation of legislative, executive and judicial powers. It also sought to qualify the doctrine of ministerial responsibility by creating an additional tier of 'extern ministers' outside the executive council. These ministers were placed in charge of departments of a technical or non-controversial nature (for example Agriculture, Fisheries, Posts and Telegraphs). This interesting constitutional experiment in enhancing individual responsibility at the expense of collective cabinet responsibility failed and was abandoned in 1927, when the Constitution was amended in such a way that no extern ministers were ever appointed again.

The 1922 Constitution contained an inherent conflict between the British monarchical system and Irish republicanism, which caused Mansergh (1952:

296) to describe it as 'an essay in frustration'. Examples of the influence of the British monarchy were the oath of allegiance to the British crown to be taken by members of the Oireachtas under Article 17; the monarch's assent to legislation was necessitated; and there was provision for appeal to the British Privy Council, which was a usual feature of Commonwealth constitutions. Ó Briain (1929: 71) described the 1922 Constitution as 'monarchical in external form, republican in substance and, withal, essentially democratic'. However, Keogh and McCarthy (2007) note, 'Having been conceived under duress and enacted through a series of threats, de Valera considered the Free State constitution an imposition rather than a document worthy of a free and proud people.'

Main Provisions

The basic elements of the Constitution of Ireland, 1937 can be broadly stated as follows. All powers derive, under God, from the people. For the purpose of enacting laws and taking other major decisions, the people periodically elect representatives to sit in the principal house of the Oireachtas, the Dáil, which is free to take whatever decisions it thinks proper within the limits set by the Constitution. Every person over eighteen years of age has the right to vote in these elections, and every person over twenty-one years to seek a seat in the Dáil. In addition to the Dáil, the Oireachtas consists of a President elected directly by the people, and an indirectly elected Seanad. The President, who is the head of state, has prescribed functions in relation to the protection of the Constitution. The day-to-day administration of the nation's affairs is entrusted to the executive body known as the government, which is chosen by the Dáil and is responsible to that House only; the government goes out of office on losing support in the Dáil. The interpretation and application of the laws is entrusted to the courts, which are independent and subject only to the Constitution and the laws; these courts also have the function of determining whether any law is repugnant to the Constitution; and trial by jury for ordinary offences is guaranteed.

The Constitution guarantees certain fundamental rights of the individual, such as personal liberty; equality before the law; freedom of expression, including criticism of the government; freedom of assembly and association; rights relating to the family, education, dwelling and property; and religious freedom.

Retrospective legislation may not declare any action to be an offence. Broad principles of social policy are set out for the guidance of the Oireachtas. Certain provisions of the Constitution may be suspended in times of emergency, in accordance with procedures set out in the Constitution; but actual amendments to the Constitution may be effected only by vote of the people in a referendum. As Taoiseach Eamon de Valera put it during the Dáil debate on the draft Constitution, 'If there is one thing more than another that is clear and shining through this whole Constitution, it is the fact that the people are the masters.' There is no doubt that the Constitution embodies that principle to a unique degree.

Article 1 refers to the nation's 'sovereign right . . . to determine its relations with other small nations'. In the original 1937 version Article 2 stated that the national territory consisted of the whole island of Ireland, its islands and territorial seas; and Article 3 conferred reality on the situation by providing that, 'pending the reintegration of the national territory', the laws enacted by the Irish parliament 'shall have the like area and extent of application as the laws of Saorstát Éireann and the like extra-territorial effect'. By referendum in 1998 a 94.4 per cent majority voted to replace Articles 2 and 3 of the Constitution as follows:

Article 2
It is the entitlement and birthright of every person born in the island of Ireland, which includes its islands and seas, to be part of the Irish nation. That is also the entitlement of all persons otherwise qualified in accordance with law to be citizens of Ireland. Furthermore, the Irish nation cherishes its special affinity with people of Irish ancestry living abroad who share its cultural identity and heritage.

Article 3
1. It is the firm will of the Irish nation, in harmony and friendship, to unite all the people who share the territory of the island of Ireland, in all the diversity of their identities and traditions, recognising that a united Ireland shall be brought about only by peaceful means with the consent of a majority of the people, democratically expressed, in both jurisdictions in the island. Until then, the laws enacted by the Parliament established by this Constitution shall have the like area and extent of application as the laws enacted by the Parliament that existed immediately before the coming into operation of this Constitution.
2. Institutions with executive powers and functions that are shared between those jurisdictions may be established by their respective responsible authorities for stated purposes and may exercise powers and functions in respect of all or any part of the island.

Article 4 provides that the name of the state is Éire, or in the English language, Ireland. Article 5 declares that Ireland is a sovereign, independent, democratic state.

Article 6 provides for a tripartite division of powers between the three powers of government: legislative, executive and judicial, which are the cornerstone of the Irish system of government. It acknowledges that these powers derive, under God, from the people. The President acts as head of state and the guardian of the people's rights under the Constitution. The national parliament is referred to as the Oireachtas and consists, as already indicated, of the President, together with the Dáil and Seanad, with the Dáil holding the dominant position. Article 15.2.1° vests the exclusive power of making laws for the state in the Oireachtas. The same article forbids the Oireachtas from enacting any law repugnant to the Constitution.

The status and powers of the government and the Taoiseach (see Chapter 1) are defined in Article 28; and other articles set out procedures for the passage of legislation, for example presentation to the Dáil and Seanad, signing and promulgation, and reference to the Supreme Court.

The constitutional text in both official languages is authentic. Article 25 provides that in case of conflict between the enrolled texts, the Irish language text prevails. Ó Cearúil (1999 and 2002) conducted a comprehensive analysis of the Constitution in the Irish language and found that almost every section contains slight divergences of some degree between the Irish and the English texts. However, the courts have rarely found a discrepancy and they have sought to harmonise the text. Both texts, therefore, have served to illustrate each other.

Article 27 provides that a bill, other than a bill to amend the Constitution, may be recommended to the President for referral to the people by a majority of the Seanad and not less than one-third of the members of the Dáil. This article has never been invoked.

Article 28.4.2° states that the government shall meet and act as a collective responsibility, and shall be collectively responsible for the departments of state administered by the members of the government.

The Constitution provides for the offices of Attorney General, who advises the government on legal matters, and Comptroller and Auditor General, who audits all moneys administered by the Oireachtas. Under the Constitution, the financial powers of the Dáil are limited. It may not pass any vote or resolution or enact any law for the spending of public moneys unless it has been recommended to the Dáil by a message from the government, signed by the Taoiseach.

Under Article 34 justice is to be administered in courts established by law, and by judges appointed under the Constitution. The courts comprise courts of first instance, including courts of local and limited jurisdiction and the High Court, as well as a court of final appeal, the Supreme Court. Judges of the High Court and the Supreme Court are appointed by the President on the recommendation of the government. All other judges are appointed by the government. The independence of the judiciary in the exercise of judicial functions is provided for.

Article 50.1 carries into force laws enacted before the Constitution came into operation, provided that they are not inconsistent with it.

Political parties are not mentioned in the text. They are neither presumed nor protected by the Constitution.

Fundamental Rights

The Constitution firmly establishes the natural law as the basis of many of the rights guaranteed as fundamental rights. It puts outside the reach of the executive or of the legislature the power to act contrary to these rights or to endeavour to suppress them or deny them. One of the most fundamental political rights that the citizen is guaranteed is the right of access to the courts. Another essential civil liberty is the right to vote and to have an electoral system, and 'no voter may exercise more than one vote at an election for Dáil Éireann'(Article 16.1.4°).

Under the heading 'Personal Rights' it is declared, 'All citizens shall, as human persons, be held equally before the law.' This is qualified by the statement: 'This shall not be held to mean that the State shall not in its enactments have due regard to differences of capacity, physical and moral, and of social function.' Persons may not be deprived of rights to their liberty save in accordance with law, to express convictions and opinions, to associate with fellow citizens and to assemble. The rights of association, of assembly and of freedom of speech are all subject to the overriding consideration of public order and public morality.

Under Article 40 the state also guarantees in its laws to respect and, as far as practicable, to defend and vindicate the personal rights of the citizen; in particular, to protect the citizen as best it may from unjust attack and, in the case of injustice done, to vindicate the life, person, good name and property rights of every citizen. Article 40.3.1° states, 'The State guarantees in its laws to respect, and, as far as practicable, by its laws to defend and vindicate the personal rights of the citizen' and has emerged as the 'due process' clause of the Irish Constitution. Ó Dálaigh CJ said *In re Haughey* (1971 IR 217, p. 263) that 'Article 40.3 of the Constitution is a guarantee to the citizen of basic fairness of procedures. The Constitution guarantees such fairness, and it is the duty of the Court to underline that the words of Article 40.3 are not political shibboleths but provide a positive protection for the citizen and his good name'.

Article 41 recognises the family as the natural, primary and fundamental unit of society and as a moral institution possessing inalienable and imprescriptible rights. Inalienable means that which cannot be transferred or given away, while imprescriptible means that which cannot be lost by the passage of time or abandoned by non-exercise.

The family is also dealt with in Article 42, where it is recognised as the primary and natural educator of the child. Article 42 guarantees to protect the right and the duty of parents to provide, according to their means, for the education of their children. In this context, education is referred to as including religious, moral, intellectual, physical and social training. In the provision dealing with the state's right, as guardian of the common good, to require certain minimum levels of education for all children, the reference is to the moral, intellectual and social elements of education.

Article 43 declares the right to private ownership of external goods. The state accordingly guarantees to pass no law attempting to abolish the right to private ownership or the general right to transfer, bequeath and inherit property. It goes on to recognise that in civil society the exercise of these rights should be regulated by the principles of social justice, and that the state accordingly, as the occasion requires, may delimit by law the exercise of these rights with a view to reconciling their exercise with the exigencies of the common good.

The guarantee of freedom of conscience and the free profession and practice of religion in Article 44 is made subject to public order and public morality. This consideration is not referred to in Articles 41, 42 or 43.

Supremacy of the Constitution

The supreme status of the Constitution is reflected in its adoption by the people; in the declaration of its own supremacy in Article 15.4, which states that any laws that are repugnant to its provisions are null and void; in the process of judicial review, which makes independent adjudication possible; and in the process of amendment under Article 46, which states that a proposal to amend must be passed by both Houses of the Oireachtas and then submitted to the people in a referendum.

Constitutional supremacy is, however, qualified in two ways. Firstly, under Article 28.3.3°, nothing may invalidate any law enacted by the Oireachtas that is expressed to be for the purpose of securing the public safety and the preservation of the state in a time of war or armed rebellion. Second, following a referendum in 1972, membership of the European Union imposes limitations which provide that laws enacted or measures adopted by the state that are necessitated by EU membership may not be invalidated by the Constitution. The Supreme Court in the 1987 Crotty case (*Crotty v An Taoiseach* [1987] IESC 4; [1987] IR 713, 9 April 1987) held that a referendum was required wherever the 'essential scope of objectives' of the existing structures of European integration was altered. Casey (2000: 215) describes this case as 'arguably the most significant, and certainly one of the most controversial, of its decisions'.

Constitutional Amendments

The Constitution is rigid but can be amended. Between 1937 and 2008 it was amended twenty-three times.

Article 51 of the 'Transitory Provisions' of the original 1937 Constitution permitted amendments to be made by the Oireachtas without reference to the people. The first two amendments to the Constitution were made by this method. These transitional arrangements were superseded in 1941, and all subsequent amendments have required the approval of the people in a referendum. Gallagher (2003) notes that the referendum is exceptionally important in Ireland. The following amendments have been made to the 1937 Constitution:

- The first two amendments were passed by the Oireachtas without a referendum in 1939 and 1941 respectively, both made changes to take account of the emergency created by the outbreak of war in Europe.
- May 1972: allowed Ireland's membership of the European Community (3rd amendment; Article 29.4.3°).
- December 1972: lowered the voting age from twenty-one to eighteen (4th amendment; Article 16).
- December 1972: removed the reference to the 'special position' of the Roman Catholic Church and the recognition of other Churches and religious denominations (5th amendment; Article 44).
- July 1979: rendered adoption orders made by the Adoption Board immune from the requirement that justice must be administered by a court (6th amendment; Article 37).
- July 1979: allowed the redistribution of university seats in the Seanad (7th amendment; Article 18).
- September 1983: added the right to life of the unborn to the Constitution (8th amendment; Article 40).
- June 1984: extended the franchise in Dáil elections to non-citizens (9th amendment; Article 16).
- May 1987: enabled the state to ratify the Single European Act 1986 (10th amendment; Article 29).
- June 1992: enabled the state to ratify the Treaty on European Union signed at Maastricht (11th amendment; Article 29).
- November 1992: confirmed the freedom to travel to use an abortion service lawfully operating elsewhere (13th amendment; Article 40).
- November 1992: confirmed the freedom to obtain or make available information relating to abortion services, subject to conditions laid down by the law (14th amendment; Article 40).
- November 1995: allowed the introduction of divorce in Ireland (15th amendment; Article 41).

- November 1996: changed the constitutional provisions on the right to bail (16th amendment; Article 40).
- October 1997: changed the constitutional provisions on the right to cabinet confidentiality (17th amendment; Article 28).
- May 1998: enabled the state to ratify the Treaty of Amsterdam 1997 (18th amendment; Article 29).
- May 1998: allowed the state to be bound by the British–Irish (Good Friday) Agreement of 1998 and amended Article 2 and Article 3 (19th amendment; Articles 2 and 3).
- June 1999: recognised the role of local government in providing a forum for the democratic representation of local communities (20th amendment; Article 28a).
- June 2001: prohibited the death penalty (21st amendment; Articles 13.6 and 15.5).
- June 2001: enabled the state to ratify the 1998 Rome Statute of the International Criminal Court (23rd amendment; Article 29).
- October 2002: enabled the state to ratify the Treaty of Nice 2001 (26th amendment; Article 29).
- June 2004: removed the automatic right to Irish citizenship from children born on the island of Ireland (27th amendment; Article 9).

There have been eight unsuccessful attempts to amend the Constitution. Proposals were defeated for electoral reform in 1959 and 1968, both including the replacement of proportional representation by the 'straight vote' system; to change the formation of Dáil constituencies in 1968; to legalise divorce in 1986; on the right to life in 1992; to ratify the Nice Treaty in 2001; to protect human life in pregnancy in 2002; and to ratify the Lisbon Treaty in 2008.

In November 1995 the Supreme Court held in the McKenna judgment (*McKenna v An Taoiseach* (No. 2) [1995] IESC 11; [1995] 2 IR 10, 17 November 1995) that popular sovereignty, not government preference, is the cardinal principle of constitutional change. The court ruled that the government 'had not held the scales equally' (Hamilton CJ) and declared it unconstitutional for the government to spend public money advocating a particular result in any such context. The McKenna judgment prevents governments from spending public money in support of just one side of the case. It does not prevent government members from campaigning as actively as they wish, nor does it prevent government parties from spending their own money.

A Referendum Commission to prepare and disseminate information and to foster, promote and facilitate debate in a fair manner was announced in January 1998. Under the Referendum Act 2001 the Referendum Commission is expected to prepare statements containing a general explanation of the subject matter of the referendum and to publish and distribute these statements, including by print and broadcast media. The 2001 act supersedes the Referendum Act 1998, under which the commission had the role of setting out the arguments for and against referendum proposals. The commission no longer has to carry out this function. The commission is under the remit of the Minister for the Environment. Staff are seconded from different sections of the civil service to the commission, which is dissolved after each referendum.

A senior Labour Party adviser Fergus Finlay noted (1998: 297):

> Sooner or later, people are going to realise that there is something deeply undemocratic about a government being unable to promote its own legitimate policies, and being forced to pay for the promotion of policies to which it is opposed – and which, by definition, it cannot see as being in the public interest. No real public interest, and no democratic value, is ever going to be served by the crazy McKenna judgment. Instead, the judgment paves the way for absurdities, like tax revenue being spent to encourage people to vote against the Peace Agreement.

Directive Principles of Social Policy

Article 45 consists of a number of principles 'for the general guidance of the Oireachtas', presenting a comprehensive vision of society and social policy founded on Catholic social teaching. In the early years this article was largely ignored by the courts, as exemplified by the judgment of Kingsmill Moore J. in the case of *Comyn v Attorney General* (1950 IR 142), when he said that Article 45 'puts the state under certain duties, but they are duties of imperfect obligation since they cannot be enforced or regarded by any court of law, and are only directions for the guidance of the Oireachtas'.

In more recent years Article 45 has become an increasingly important influence, as exemplified by the decision of Finlay J. in *Landers v Attorney General* (109 ILTR 1), in which he held that he was entitled to be guided by these directive principles of social policy, which impose upon the state the obligation of endeavouring to meet the common good. However, Henchy J. in the Supreme Court in *The People (Director of Public Prosecutions) v O'Shea* (1982 IR 384) stated, 'If any person were to institute proceedings in the High Court seeking to compel the state to give effect to any of the specified directives, the High Court would be bound to strike out those proceedings for want of jurisdiction.' The 1937 observations of the Department of Finance on the first draft of the Constitution noted that these articles were:

. . . not of a kind usually enshrined in a Constitution. They will not be helpful to Ministers in the future but will provide a breeding ground for discontent, and so create instability and insecurity. Their provisions are too vague to be of positive assistance to any Government and are yet sufficiently definite to afford grounds for disaffection to sections of the community, who might claim that the Government were not living up to the Constitution (quoted in Fanning 1978: 268).

The 1996 Constitution Review Group was divided as to whether Article 45 should be deleted or retained in an amended form. A majority considered that if it is to be retained it should be amended so as to indicate that the principles are for the guidance of the government as well as the Oireachtas and relate to executive action as well as to the making of laws. It recommended that, Article 45, if retained, should be amended to reflect modern concerns in regard to socio-economic rights. In relation to this article, FitzGerald (2003: 53) comments, 'It should, I believe, either be scrapped, or, in so far as it contains provisions that might have a genuine impact of a positive kind in the social area, should be made justiciable to whatever extent might be thought appropriate. The present halfway house of an article that is not binding but can be used for interpretative purposes carries dangers of increasing the uncertainty as to how the courts will interpret legislation.' Keane (2004: 16) agrees with the directive stating that the 'view of the framers of the Constitution that the enforcement of what has come to be called "socio-economic rights" is the function of the parliament not the courts'. Keane continues that the courts will not usurp what they regard as the role of the legislature and the executive in determining priorities in the allocation of national resources or in supervising the expenditure of money for specific needs.

Judicial Review

Judicial review includes the power to invalidate on constitutional grounds acts of any administrative agency and to decide whether any law is in keeping with the provisions of the Constitution. It is an important aspect of the organic process of review and interpretation of the Constitution and ensures that constitutional provisions are observed and that the various political institutions act within their proper sphere of authority. This power is conferred on the High Court and Supreme Court (under Articles 26, 34.3 and 34.4). The process can be used before a bill becomes law if the President, under Article 26, decides to refer it to the Supreme Court for a decision (except for a money bill or a proposal to amend the Constitution). As Walsh (1988: 193) points out, the 'Supreme Court is the ultimate interpreter of the law. It is also the ultimate interpreter of the Constitution.' The more common practice, however, is to have laws tested in the High Court or Supreme Court in the course of ordinary legislation.

The Irish judiciary became, from the mid-1960s, increasingly innovative in interpreting the Constitution. This approach included, for example, considerations relating to the Preamble, Article 45 on the directive principles of social policy, the nature of Irish society, and 'concepts of prudence, justice and charity which gradually change or develop as society changes and develops and which fall to be interpreted from time to time in accordance with prevailing ideas' (O'Higgins CJ in *The State (Healy) v Donoghue* 1976 IR 325, p. 347). In *Tormey v Ireland* (1985 IR 289) Henchy J. said, 'The Constitution must be read as a whole, and its several provisions must not be looked at in isolation, but be treated as interlocking parts of the general constitutional scheme.' The entire body of judicial decisions on constitutional law is regarded as part of the living aspect of the Constitution. The courts are the ultimate guardians of the Constitution, but they cannot move until their powers are invoked. By virtue of the Attorney General's constitutional office, the Attorney General has, in the appropriate case, the duty of defending the Constitution.

In 1972 Ó Dálaigh CJ, speaking for the majority in the Supreme Court in *McMahon v Attorney General* (IR 69), a case about the electoral system, said, 'Constitutional rights are declared not alone because of bitter memories of the past, but not least because of the improbable, but not-to-be overlooked, perils of the future'.

In a wide range of cases the courts have made explicit certain rights and entitlements of citizens that they have found to be implicit in the 1937 Constitution. For example, in the case of *Ryan v Attorney General* (1964 IR 294), which is related to the fluoridation of water, the court held that there are many personal rights of the citizen that follow from the Christian and democratic nature of the state but which are not mentioned in Article 40 at all. It instanced as examples of such personal rights the right to bodily integrity, the right to free movement within the state and the right to marry. Speaking fifteen years after his Ryan judgment, Mr Justice Kenny acknowledged the significance of the epoch that he inaugurated, when he said, in connection with Article 40.3: 'Judges have become legislators, and have the advantage that they do not have to face an opposition' (1979 NILQ 189, p. 196). Ó Dálaigh CJ, in delivering the Supreme Court's judgment in this case, said, 'The Court agrees with Mr Justice Kenny that "personal rights" mentioned in section 3.1 are not exhausted by the enumeration of "life, person, good name, and property rights" in section 3.2 as is shown by the use of the words "in particular", nor by the more detached treatment of specific rights in the subsequent sections of the article' (pp. 344–5).

In a further case, relating to a law prohibiting the importation or sale of contraceptives (*McGee v Attorney General* 1974 IR 284), Walsh J. stated, 'Articles 41, 42 and 43 emphatically reject the theory that there are no rights without laws, no rights contrary to the law and no rights anterior to the law. They indicate that justice is placed above the law and acknowledge that natural rights, or human rights, are not created by law but that the Constitution confirms their existence and gives them protection.'

Since the decision in the Ryan case the courts have defined many other rights that the state is pledged to defend and vindicate even though they are not specifically enumerated in the Constitution. These include the right not to be unconstitutionally restrained from earning one's livelihood (*Murtagh Properties v Cleary* 1972 IR 330); the right to litigate claims, found to be a personal right of the citizen within Article 40 in *O'Brien v Keogh* (1972 IR 144); the right to work (*Murphy v Stewart* 1973 IR 97); the right to marital privacy (*McGee v Attorney General* 1974 IR 284); the right of access to the courts (*Macauley v Minister for Posts and Telegraphs* 1966 IR 345); the right to avail of such facilities as the state has obtained for its citizens to travel abroad (*The State (M) v Attorney General* 1979 IR 73); the right to fair procedures (*The State (Healy) v Donoghue* 1976 IR 325); the right to communicate (*AG v Paperlink* 1984 ILRM 74); and the right to privacy in one's communications with others (*Kennedy v Ireland* unreported, 12 January 1987).

Not all these rights are equal and the Supreme Court has distinguished between a hierarchy of rights. Freedom of expression must be balanced against the right to a fair trial, for example. The constitutional position of the applicant's right to a fair trial was considered to be superior to the right of freedom of expression by Denham J. in *D v The DPP* (1994 2 IR 465), 'The applicant's right to a fair trial is one of the most fundamental constitutional rights afforded to persons. On a hierarchy of rights it is a superior right.'

However, there have been concerns about unrestrained judicial activism in this area. The Constitution Review Group (1996: 263) recommended the relocation of unenumerated rights by amending the Constitution to mention them within other suitable provisions. In recent years the Supreme Court has taken a more conservative approach in this area. Keane CJ (2004: 9) notes the 'serious jurisprudential problems' encountered by such 'judicial creativity'. In a 1998 judgment (prior to his appointment as Chief Justice) Keane alluded to problems encountered in developing a coherent, principled jurisprudence in this area of implied rights and commented (*I.O'T v B* (1998) 2 IR 321: 370), 'It is sufficient to say that save where such an unenumerated right has been unequivocally established by precedent as for example in the case of a right to travel, the right to privacy, some degree of judicial restraint is called for in identifying new rights of this nature.'

Kelly (1967: 360) highlights that uncertainty in the law is 'repugnant to the central value of the law itself' and that 'the result of the judgement in *Ryan v. AG* is to place the Oireachtas in a position of not knowing just what personal rights it must respect and how far it can go in delimiting them or abridging them'. Hogan (1995: 114) refers to the 'loose language of Article 40.3.1' and the 'unprincipled expansion of the power of judicial review'. Morgan (1998: 107) is also critical and notes that dubious reasoning and inconsistent reasoning pervade the jurisprudence on unenumerated rights.

The courts have on numerous occasions referred to the separation of powers as being a fundamental principle in the Constitution. Thus, the Supreme Court in *Attorney General v Hamilton* (1993 ILRM 81 at 96) stated, 'The doctrine of the separation of powers under the Constitution has been identified by the Court as being both fundamental and far-reaching, and has been set out in various decisions of this Court in very considerable detail.'

There have been concerns regarding this judicial activism in terms of the separation of powers. In the case of *TD v Minister for Education and Others* (2001 4 IR 259), the Supreme Court held that in order to comply with the Constitution the plaintiff's claims should be advanced in Leinster House rather than in the Four Courts. In the case of *Sinnott v Minister for Education, Ireland and the Attorney General* (2001 2 IR 545), the Supreme Court held that free primary education for Jamie Sinnott was an issue for the legislative and executive arms of government and that the High Court was precluded by virtue of Article 6 of the Constitution and the doctrine of the separation of powers from making an order in the case. In her dissenting judgment in *TD v Minister for Education and Others* (3 IR at 289), Denham J. comments (2000), 'The separation of powers is an important aspect of the Constitution. However in addition to that doctrine there is the jurisdiction of the courts to protect fundamental rights. This is not only a jurisdiction but a duty and obligation of the courts under the Constitution.' Whyte (2002) comments that the judiciary's constitutional duty to vindicate personal rights should inform judges' understanding of the doctrine of the separation of powers, rather than, as appears to be the case at present, the doctrine informing judges' under - standing of their power to protect constitutional rights. The Supreme Court held in July 2008 that 'For the Court to determine that community rating had the meaning argued for by the respondents and the notice party simply because such an interpretation is thought necessary from a policy point of view for the effective implementation of a risk equalisation scheme would be to usurp the function of the Oireachtas' (BUPA 16 July 2008, Murray CJ).

A number of decisions reaffirmed that it is for the Oireachtas to determine issues relating to the allocation of resources. The judgments on social and economic matters must be made by legislators in the Oireachtas and not litigated in the courts. The Supreme Court has developed this view in recent years because one individual social problem examined from an administrative and legislative viewpoint can also be tackled from a societal public policy perspective. However, a case litigated in the Four Courts may reach a good solution for one individual, but is not always litigated to a correct conclusion in terms of the broader interest of the people as a whole.

The Republic of Ireland

The Constitution provides (Article 4) that the name of the state is Éire, or in the English language, Ireland. The normal practice was to use the name 'Éire' in texts in the Irish language and to use 'Ireland' in all English-language texts. James J. McElligott, Secretary [General] of the Department of Finance commented in 1937 that while Éire might 'be quite justifiable from the traditional and scholarly point of view, . . . from a realistic point of view it seems a mistake. This land is generally known internationally as Ireland or some derivative of that name, and so there will probably be a long period of confusion and misunderstanding before the unaccustomed name conveys a definite meaning to educated people throughout the world' (quoted in Fanning 1978: 267). The Republic of Ireland Act 1948 provides for the description of the state as 'the Republic of Ireland', but this provision has not changed the usage 'Ireland' as the name of the state in the English language. Since January 2007 the formal title used on all official nameplates at EU meetings is 'Éire Ireland'. (This title is not used at other international meetings such as United Nations conferences.) The move followed the designation of Irish as the twenty-first official and working EU language. Due to the prevalence of the English language within the EU, the state continues to be identified as Ireland for practical purposes.

Article 5 of the Constitution declares that Ireland is a sovereign, independent, democratic state. It does not, however, proclaim that Ireland is a republic, nor does any other article of the Constitution, despite the fact that many of its provisions have a distinctly republican stamp. The omission was deliberate. Taoiseach Eamon de Valera stated in the Dáil on 14 June 1937 that if the Northern Ireland problem was not there, 'in all probability, there would be a flat, downright proclamation of the Republic'. The Republic of Ireland Act 1948 repealed the Executive Authority (External Relations) Act 1936, which had retained the crown for the purposes of diplomatic representation and international agreements (in the hope that such an arrangement might, as de Valera put it, facilitate the construction of a bridge 'over which the Northern Unionists might walk'), and provided instead for the declaration of a republic. In accordance with this act, on Easter Day 1949, Ireland became a republic.

The Irish Language

Article 8 of the Constitution states, 'The Irish language as the national language is the first official language.' The Official Languages Act 2003 was signed into law on 14 July 2003. The act is the first piece of legislation to provide a statutory framework for the delivery of services through the Irish language. The primary objective of the act is to ensure better availability and a higher standard of public services through Irish. It placed a statutory obligation on all public bodies to make specific provision for delivery of such services in a coherent fashion through a statutory planning framework, known as a 'scheme', to be agreed on a three-year renewable basis between the body concerned and the Minister for Community, Rural and Gaeltacht Affairs. Under section II public bodies have a duty to prepare a statutory scheme detailing the services they provide through Irish, English and bilingually, and the measures to be adopted to ensure that any service not provided through the medium of Irish would be so provided. The act provided for the preparation of guidelines by the minister in relation to the preparation of draft schemes. The three-year renewal process aims to secure a significant improvement in the level of public services available through Irish over time. The act also specifies some basic general provisions of universal applicability, for example correspondence to be replied to in the language in which it was written, providing information to the public in the Irish language or in the Irish and English languages, bilingual publications of certain key documents and the use of Irish in the courts. Many public bodies were already meeting these bilingual requirements in areas such as signage and stationery prior to the 2003 act. The High Court held in 2004 that there was a constitutional responsibility to publish statutory instruments simultaneously in Irish and English. A 2008 High Court case decided that health warnings on cigarette packets will have to be bilingual. Section 68 of the Local Government Act 2001 enables a local authority to take steps to encourage the use of the Irish language in the performance of its functions. This development reflected initiatives taken by individual local authorities, particularly those with Gaeltacht areas, to promote the everyday use of the Irish language.

Constitutional Review

The desirability of revising the Constitution has been discussed from time to time. It is recorded that, as early as 1947, Taoiseach Eamon de Valera expressed a wish to change the provisions relating to proportional repre - sentation, Seanad representation and property rights (Rau 1960: 130). In 1966 an informal all-party committee of TDs and senators was set up to consider possible changes to the Constitution. Its report (Government of Ireland 1967) discussed twenty-seven aspects of the Constitution, leaving it to the government of the day to decide the items that should be selected for inclusion in any legislative proposals that might emerge. It made the unanimous recommendation that Article 44.1.2°–3° (on the special position of the Roman Catholic Church and recognition of the other Churches) should be deleted; this was given effect by the fifth amendment in 1972. It also made recommendations for the rewording of Article 3 (on the extent of the application of the laws of the state) and of Article 41 (on marriage). The report commented that the all-party committee was not aware of any public demand for a change in the basic structure of the Constitution and concluded, 'As a general proposition, therefore, it might be said that our inclination was to adhere to the constitutional provisions which have worked so well in practice, and to consider changes only in the case of those provisions which, from experience, might be regarded as not adequately fulfilling their purpose.'

In April 1995 the government set up a Constitution Review Group, composed of fifteen experts under the chairmanship of Dr T.K. Whitaker, 'to review the Constitution and to establish those areas where constitutional change may be desirable or necessary'. The review group produced a 700-page report in May 1996, setting forth in a clear and concise manner, with a summary of the relevant arguments, the areas where it considered constitutional change was appropriate. It found that the Constitution has stood the test of time quite well and, as interpreted by many judicial decisions, has shown a considerable degree of adaptability to new circumstances and norms.

Among the recommendations of the review group were amendments relating to: the name of the state; making the Irish language and the English language the two official languages; describing the President as head of state; the nomination and election of the President; providing for a time limit within which a Dáil by-election should be held; the one-judgment rule where the validity of a law is in question; including a time limit for a law enacting a state of emergency and specifying the fundamental rights and freedoms retained; the nomination of a senior minister where the Taoiseach and Tánaiste are unavailable to act; clarifying that Article 29.3 covers public international law; permitting delegation of the Attorney General's functions to another senior lawyer; providing for accountability of the Attorney General to the Dáil through the Taoiseach; giving the Oireachtas greater flexibility to develop different court structures; allowing for regulation by judges themselves of judicial conduct; providing for an impeachment process for judges and other constitutional officers; giving explicit constitutional recognition of, and protection for, enumerated rights in the trial of offences; providing that special courts may be established only for a prescribed period; and regulating the establishment of military tribunals.

The review group recommended a separate, comprehensive, independent examination of all issues relating to the Seanad. New provisions recommended by the group for inclusion in the Constitution relate to the placing of all family rights in Article 41; the right of every child to free primary education; new articles on the Ombudsman, local government and the environment; and the establishment of a human rights commission.

Following publication of the Constitution Review Group's report in 1996, the government established an All-Party Oireachtas Committee on the Constitution in 1997. Its terms of reference were to provide focus to the place and relevance of the Constitution and to establish those areas where constitutional change may be desirable or necessary. The all-party committee undertook a full review of the Constitution and issued several comprehensive reports into various aspects of the Constitution.

In October 2007 the government announced the formal establishment of the Joint Committee on the Constitution to complete a full review of the Constitution in order to provide focus to the place and relevance of the Constitution and to establish those areas where constitutional change may be desirable or necessary.

Conclusion

'Nowhere in the world is the right to personal liberty more fully protected than under the Irish Constitution', so wrote Mr Justice Brian Walsh of the Supreme Court in *The Irish Times* in 1987 on the occasion of the fiftieth anniversary of the Constitution. He continued:

> The Constitution is a living law. As a document it dates from 1937, as a law from today. It is written in the present tense. It has always been interpreted in the light of the circumstances of the contemporary epoch. Therefore it is designed in general principles to look after the future as well as the present. In practice the Constitution of Ireland has worked very well. In many ways the civil service has shown a greater awareness and appreciation of its provisions than has been the case among many politicians.

Dr Tom Garvin noted in his contribution to the same edition of the newspaper:

> The great achievement of 1937 was that an arena was established in which the issues of individual versus collective interest could be contested. This was the first time such an arena or basic framework had ever been provided in Irish history and was a major step forward in the provision of political order in Ireland. We have come to take that political order so much for granted that we sometimes forget what a formidable achievement it was.

The Constitution gives an incomplete picture of the mechanics of Irish government. What the Constitution says and what actually happens may be quite different things. Indeed, as the All-Party Oireachtas Committee on the Constitution (2002: 10) noted, 'The Constitution is sufficiently broadly phrased to allow for a wide range of alternative approaches.' While the sole power of making laws is vested in the Oireachtas, in practice it is the government that makes the laws, which are then passed by the Oireachtas. Farrell (1987: 162) notes:

> The Constitution provides not merely an incomplete, but in a number of important respects a misleading, account of the nature, functions and operations of basic political institutions. It enshrines mythologies that bear little relation to the actualities of power. It ignores some real sources of influence, elevates some marginal authorities, distances some relationships and misrepresents the balance of forces that maintain the Irish political system. Political parties are not even mentioned. The role of both Dáil and Seanad in the actual making of legislation is exaggerated. The real dominance of the government is obscured by a pedantic emphasis on parliamentary accountability. The Constitution is a rulebook that has only a tangential connection with the Irish political and governmental game.

Ireland is not unique in having a gap between political practice and constitutional theory. The most important aspect of this is the decline in the power of the legislature. Farrell (1987: 163) notes that the government controls the Dáil rather than the declaration in Article 15.2.1° that 'The sole and exclusive power of making laws for the State is hereby vested in the Oireachtas'. The reasons for this, he suggests, include party politics, the clientelist role of deputies, the electoral system of multi-seat proportional representation constituencies, and the government's control over public expenditure.

Ferriter (2007: 197) notes that 'De Valera's Constitution of 1937 has stood the test of time'. On the same theme, Murphy (2005) asks the question:

> So how has the Constitution stood the test of time? Pretty well in relation to civil and political rights and in adapting to changes in society by changes in the provisions on religion, divorce, the right to travel and, of course, Northern Ireland. Changes in relation to bail and citizenship may be viewed by many as indicating a more inward looking and conservative society. The jury is still out on our willingness as a society to face up to the challenges which face us in the context of a multi-cultural, multi-ethnic society as well as in relation to the economic and social rights of disadvantaged and vulnerable groups. I have publicly expressed the view that the first of the three great organs of State – the Oireachtas – has neither the capacity nor the willingness to hold the Government responsible to it as provided for in Article 28.4.1 of the Constitution. There are many reasons for this, not least the greater loyalty TD's have to their party than to the Dáil despite the great privilege of their being elected to it.

In his foreword to O'Reilly and Redmond (1980), Mr Justice Brian Walsh observed, 'For so long as the Constitution reflects the politics and social culture of the majority of the people, and there is little real evidence that it does not, it is difficult to justify claims that a drastic overhaul is needed.' FitzGerald (2003: 58) comments, 'Our constitutional system has come to incorporate a series of checks and balances that in practical terms is almost unique.' He concludes (2003: 59) that:

> . . . without any illusions as to its defects, it must be added that that our Constitution, enacted under different circumstances well over a half century ago, has proved to be a remarkably firm bastion of human rights, proving a healthy restraint on the Executive and Legislature in matters of legislation . . . the great bulk of its provisions, many of them dating back to the first Constitution of 1922, should certainly, by general agreement, be retained, as serving the public interest well.

In a similar vein, Hogan (2007) comments that:

> De Valera's achievement was to find a drafting team who transcended the limitations of their age, to have the courage to put the Constitution to the people for our first ever referendum in July 1937, where the end product was a Constitution which brought much needed stability after the hectic constitutional changes of 1922–1937, a Constitution which, on the whole, has operated as a salutary check on the other branches of government and which has promoted the protection of individual rights and which has proved to be sufficiently durable and adaptable that it has not only survived, but which is also thriving.

Web Resources

An Coimisinéir Teanga, who monitors the compliance of public bodies with the Official Languages Act 2003 at www.coimisineir.ie
Constitution of Ireland (1937)/Bunreacht na hÉireann at www.constitution.ie
Constitution of Dáil Éireann (1919) at www.difp.ie/viewdoc.asp?DocID=6
Constitution of the Irish Free State (1922) at http://acts.oireachtas.ie/zza1y1922.1.html
Referendum Commission at www.refcom.ie

5

THE PRESIDENT OF IRELAND

The President of Ireland (Uachtarán na hÉireann) is the only officer of state who can be directly elected by all the citizens of the country. The President is elected for a period of seven years and can be re-elected only once. The main functions of the President include acting as ceremonial head of state; formalising a number of appointments; summoning and dissolving Dáil Éireann in certain circumstances; signing into law and promulgating bills that have been passed by the Dáil and Seanad; and operating as a check but not as a veto on legislation. The office of President of Ireland, the executive head of the state, was established by the Constitution of 1937, Articles 12, 13 and 14 of which define the status, election, powers and functions of the position.

By virtue of being elected by the direct vote of the people, being head of state and taking precedence over all other people, the President represents all the people of Ireland. The Constitution underlines the non-political, non-partisan nature of the office. The President is always described as being 'above politics', in the sense of abstaining from any public statement that could be judged to be politically biased or inconsistent with the fundamental principle that there can be only one executive authority. The symbolic value of the office derives from the detachment of the holder from partisan politics.

The role of the President is defined in the Constitution of 1937, and the limitations on that role have been determined not only by the articles of the Constitution but more emphatically by convention. Among the relevant provisions of the Constitution are Article 12.1, which provides for the office of the President of Ireland, 'who shall take precedence over all other persons in the State', and Article 15.1.2°, which provides that the Oireachtas shall consist of the President and two Houses. The President is the head of state and, although formally a part of the Oireachtas, his or her primary function is to act as a check on the Houses of parliament. Frank Aiken TD summed up clearly and succinctly the role of the new head of state as 'A person who will guard against any attempt to set up a dictatorship by either the Executive Council or the two Houses of the Oireachtas (*Dáil Debates*, 13 May 1937, vol. 67, col. 326). Under Article 13.8.1° the President is not 'answerable to either House of the Oireachtas or to any Court for the exercise and performance of the powers and functions of his office'. While the President is expected to be above and apart from politics, under Article 28.5.2° the Taoiseach is obliged to keep the President generally informed on matters of domestic and international policy. (In practice, the Taoiseach briefs the President every eight weeks. According to the annual reports of the Department of the Taoiseach, this was done formally on eight occasions in 2004, five in 2005 and six in 2006. The Taoiseach briefed the President six times in 2007 and 2008.)

Presidents of Ireland

The first President of Ireland was Douglas Hyde, a Gaelic scholar who was appointed in 1938 following all-party agreement. Seán T. Ó Ceallaigh became President in 1945 after an election and served a second term when he was re-elected unopposed in 1952. Eamon de Valera served two terms following election in 1959 and in 1966. Erskine Childers was elected to the office in 1973. Cearbhall Ó Dálaigh was appointed in 1974 following all-party agreement; as was Patrick Hillery in 1976 and 1983. Mary Robinson became the first woman to hold the office of President when she was elected in 1990. In 1997 Mary McAleese was elected the eighth President of Ireland and she was re-elected unopposed in 2004. A list of Presidents and their terms of office is included as an Appendix to this Chapter.

Eligibility

Every Irish citizen over thirty-five years of age is eligible for the office. The All-Party Oireachtas Committee on the Constitution (1998) recommended the reduction of the minimum age of eligibility for election to the office of President to eighteen years; however, in the Dáil on 8 December 1998, Taoiseach Bertie Ahern repeated that he did not see a requirement for this change. A candidate must be nominated by at least twenty members of the Dáil or Seanad or by four county or city councils. In practice, this confines nominations to the main political parties. Critics of this system suggest that there should be wider democratic procedures for nominating candidates. The Constitution Review Group (1996) reached the unambiguous conclusion that 'the constitutional requirements for nominating a presidential candidate are too restrictive and in need of democratisation'. The All-Party Oireachtas Committee on the Constitution (1998) agreed with this point. During the 1997 presidential election campaign, two candidates: Dana, Rosemary Scallon and Derek Nally, each successfully secured nominations by the required four local authorities. A former or retiring President may become a candidate on his or her own nomination.

A President may not be a member of either House of the Oireachtas or hold any other office or position for which he or she receives payment. On election to office the President must vacate any such seat or position.

The electorate is the same as that for Dáil elections. If only one candidate is put forward, there is no election and the candidate becomes President on the declaration of the returning officer. Elections have in fact been avoided by the nomination of a single agreed candidate on six out of twelve occasions since the office was first filled in 1938.

Remuneration; Residence; Support Services

The emoluments of the President are fixed by statute from the Central Fund and cannot be reduced during a term of office. The President is provided with an official residence, Áras an Uachtaráin in the Phoenix Park, Dublin, which is maintained by the Office of Public Works. There are a large number and a wide range of events hosted at Áras an Uachtaráin by the President each year. Visits of heads of state and other dignitaries, public tours and other events held at the Áras resulted in 15,559 visitors in total being catered for in 2006.

The President is assisted by a number of staff, including the Secretary General to the President. Under section 27 of the Civil Service Regulation (Amendment) Act 2005 the office established by the Presidential Establishment Act 1938 and previously known as Secretary to the President is now known as Secretary General to the President. This officer is a civil servant of the state, who is appointed by the government following consultation with the President and who does not retire from office with the President. The Secretary General to the President is Clerk to the Council of State and ex officio Secretary to the Presidential Commission. The President also has the assistance of an aide-de-camp, who is normally a colonel in the Army.

The President has a seal of office, which is referred to in Articles 27, 31, 33 and 35 of the Constitution. The Presidential Seal Act 1937 provides that the President shall have custody and control of this seal, which is affixed to documents issued by the President and which must be authenticated by his or her signature.

The presidential Rolls-Royce, which has been used by seven Irish heads of state, was manufactured in 1948. The vehicle is used for ceremonial occasions such as the inauguration of presidents and the National Day of Commemoration. It is maintained by the barrack master at An Garda Síochána headquarters, close to Áras an Uachtaráin in the Phoenix Park. President Eamon de Valera used the stately Rolls-Royce almost on a daily basis in the 1960s, and it featured in events marking the fiftieth anniversary of the 1916 Rising. It has been used by Presidents since then. On state occasions, the vehicle is usually escorted by twenty-nine motorcycles drawn from the Second Cavalry Squadron, based in Dublin's Cathal Brugha Barracks. The motorcycles must convey the Rolls-Royce with 'dignity and bearing' according to Defence Forces regulations.

Representing the People

The President has a symbolic capacity as the representative of the nation. The President must reside in or near Dublin. During inauguration ceremonies, which are held in St Patrick's Hall, Dublin Castle, the President takes an oath as provided in the Constitution. The President is 'above politics' and represents all of the people in a variety of ways, for example when receiving foreign heads of state on visits to Ireland or when making state visits abroad. Visits abroad provide valuable opportunities to promote Ireland's interests in the international arena and to strengthen links with the Irish diaspora. Public and private enterprises frequently organise promotional events to coincide with presidential visits abroad.

At home, the President undertakes a wide range of activities and engagements with particular emphasis on valuing the contribution of local community and self-help groups and in promoting peace and reconciliation throughout the island of Ireland. Whether participating in formal ceremonial events or meeting people in a wide range of informal settings, the President is giving expression to the undertaking in the oath of office to 'dedicate my abilities to the service and welfare of the people of Ireland'.

The office of the President has a very well-developed website – www.president.ie – which includes sections on news, the President's role, speeches, biographies, engagements and a virtual tour.

Functions and Limitations of the President

The President normally acts on the advice and authority of the government. The Constitution emphasises in several places that the President requires the approval of the government before taking action. Article 13.9 declares that the powers and functions conferred on the President by the Constitution are exercisable and performable by the President only on the advice of the government, except where it is provided by the Constitution that the President acts in his or her absolute discretion or after consultation with or in relation to the Council of State, or on the advice of any other person or body. In addition, Article 13.11 provides that 'No power or function conferred on the President by law shall be exercisable or performable by him save only on the advice of the Government'. In the case of appointments and decisions, the President acts only on the binding advice of the government. For example, members of the judiciary or Irish ambassadors cannot be appointed except on that advice. There are also important provisions in the Constitution that specifically require the initiative of some other person or body before action can be taken by the President. For example, the Attorney General is appointed by the President on the nomination of the Taoiseach (Article 30), and the Comptroller and Auditor General is appointed by the President on the nomination of the Dáil (Article 33). In the case of the removal of persons from these offices, the Constitution obliges the President to act as requested by the appropriate authorities. The President must terminate the appointment of the Attorney General and of ministers on the advice of the Taoiseach, and terminate that of the Comptroller and Auditor General and of judges on a resolution of the Dáil and Seanad.

The primacy of the government is manifest from the provision of Article 12.9, under which the President cannot leave the state during his or her term of office without the consent of the government, as a visit abroad may have political implications. Thus, for example, the government was reported as deciding that, because of the Northern Ireland situation at that time, it would be inappropriate for President Patrick Hillery to attend the wedding of the heir to the British throne (*The Irish Times*, 8 July 1981). Under Article 13.1 the President appoints the Taoiseach on the nomination of the Dáil, and other members of the government 'on the nomination of the Taoiseach with the previous approval of the Dáil' (Article 13.1.2°); however, the President is required to terminate ministerial appointments on the advice of the Taoiseach only. The Dáil is summoned and dissolved by the President on the advice of the Taoiseach under Article 13.2.1°.

The President is required by the provisions of Articles 13.3 and 25.2.1° to sign bills passed by both Houses of the Oireachtas, thereby giving them the force of law; in addition, the President must, under Article 25.4.2° (except in cases where reference to the people or the Supreme Court is involved), promulgate each new legislative measure by publishing in *Iris Oifigiúil* (the official gazette) a notice stating that the bill has become law.

The President may, after consultation with the Council of State, communicate with the Houses of the Oireachtas and address a message to the nation on any matter of national or public importance. Article 13.7.3° states that every such message or address must have received the approval of the government. This power has been used several times, for example, by:

- President Eamon de Valera on 21 January 1969 to a simultaneous sitting of both Houses of the Oireachtas on the fiftieth anniversary of the first meeting of the first Dáil Éireann.
- President Mary Robinson on 8 July 1992 to a joint sitting of the Houses of the Oireachtas on the Irish identity in Europe.

- President Mary Robinson on 2 February 1995 to a joint sitting of the Houses of the Oireachtas on cherishing the Irish diaspora.
- President Mary McAleese on 16 December 1999 to a joint sitting of the Houses of the Oireachtas as a millennium address on Ireland's lifting shadows.

The Constitution is silent on whether the President can make a statement of a political nature without the consent of the government. Successive governments have tended to believe that the President could not speak publicly on any issue without their approval. While it is not appropriate for the President to be involved in confrontation with the government on legislative or policy matters, Kelly (1984: 65–6) holds that the President retains the ordinary rights of a citizen in regard to freedom in expressing personal opinions or, in particular, replying to criticism. In 1991 the government asked President Mary Robinson not to deliver the BBC Dimbleby Lecture in London and in 1993 it asked her to decline a Ford Foundation Committee on the future of the United Nations. On each occasion the President accepted this advice (O'Leary and Burke 1998). President Robinson in a newspaper interview in February 1997 spoke about the fact that the President must work through government, even for rudimentary matters such as clearing speeches in advance. She said:

> It was something that required getting used to, probably on both sides. I think the process of adjustment has worked well because the constitutional framework is very clear in providing that the executive and legislative and judicial power rests elsewhere and that to do this job well you must be in tune with the role of government. I think it has been challenging to develop the role of the Presidency in a way that is compatible with and complements the role of government.

President Patrick Hillery, in an interview after he had left office, said, 'Your respect for the office keeps you silent. You don't want to get into a squabble because you're no longer Head of State if you're squabbling' (*The Irish Times*, 28 November 1990).

Under Article 13.6 the President has the right to commute the sentences of criminal offenders, but by virtue of Article 13.9 this power can only be exercised on the advice of the government. Very few cases of the receipt of a pardon are reported and three of these occurred during the period in office of Ireland's first President, Dr Douglas Hyde. The power was used more recently in the case of the Sallins train robbery when in 1992 Nicky Kelly was invited to Áras an Uachtaráin to receive a presidential pardon from President Mary Robinson, one of the lawyers who unsuccessfully attempted to take his case to the European Court of Human Rights.

The supreme command of the Defence Forces is vested in the President by Article 13.4, but this is followed by a provision requiring that the exercise of this command is to be regulated by law. Section 17 of the Defence Act 1954 provides that the military command of and all executive and administrative powers in relation to the Defence Forces shall 'under the direction of the President' be exercisable by the government through the Minister for Defence. Acting under the Defence Act 1954 and on the advice of the government, the President makes appointments to the following offices in the Permanent Defence Forces: Chief of Staff, Adjutant General, Quartermaster General, Inspector General and Judge Advocate General. Under Article 13.5.2° of the Constitution, all commissioned officers of the Defence Forces hold their commissions from the President.

While Article 13.10 permits the conferring by law of additional powers and functions on the President, this is qualified by the provision of Article 13.11 referred to above. The Republic of Ireland Act 1948 provides that 'The President on the advice of the government may exercise the executive functions of the State in or in connection with its external relations'. For this reason, it is to the President that foreign ambassadors present their credentials, and it is the President who, on the advice of the government, accredits Irish diplomatic representatives abroad. The President represents Ireland abroad. Finally, in the declaration of war or emergency no function is allotted by the Constitution to the President under Article 28.3.

Among the additional powers which have been conferred on the President by law under Article 13.10 are formal powers of appointment. These include the appointment of council members and senior professors of the Dublin Institute for Advanced Studies (under sections 8 and 9 of the Institute for Advanced Studies Act 1940); of the Governor of the Central Bank (under section 19 of the Central Bank Act 1942); and of the Ombudsman (under section 2 of the Ombudsman Act 1980). The Red Cross Act 1944 provides that the President of Ireland shall, by virtue of this office, be President of the Irish Red Cross Society. These additional powers are exercised by the President either on the advice of the government or pursuant to a resolution of the Oireachtas. The President also presents the centenarian's bounty, a once-off payment (€2,540) made to Irish citizens living in Ireland who have reached the age of one hundred years. For those who turn 101, and on subsequent birthdays, the President presents a centenarian's medal, the design of which changes each year.

The provisions of the Constitution relating to the impeachment of the President effectively establish the supremacy of the legislature over a President whom it deems to be unfit for office. Article 12.10 provides for the impeachment of the President for 'stated misbehaviour' after a charge made against him or her by either House of the Oireachtas is sustained by the prescribed two-thirds majority. When such a charge has been preferred, the other House will investigate it or cause it to be investigated. The relevant constitutional provisions are designed to ensure that this serious step will be undertaken only on a matter of widespread public concern. The Constitution does not define or specify 'stated misbehaviour' or in any way limit the nature of the charge to be brought against the President. It provides, however, that, in addition to proving the charge, the House responsible for the investigation must pass a resolution that the misbehaviour that was the subject of the charge was such as to render the President unfit to continue in office. This elasticity leaves it to the wisdom of that House to decide whether the particular charge, if proved, is or is not, in the special circumstances of the case, such as to render the President unfit to continue in office (McDunphy 1945: 23).

The Constitution provides at Article 12.3.1° for the removal from office of a President whose permanent incapacity has been 'established to the satisfaction of the Supreme Court consisting of not less than five judges'.

Although there is no vice-president of Ireland, the Constitution ensures that there is no gap in continuity as regards the powers, duties and functions of the office. A Presidential Commission discharges the powers and functions of the President in the event of the President's absence, temporary or permanent incapacity, death, resignation, removal from office or failure to exercise and perform the powers and functions of the office. This commission consists of the Chief Justice, the Ceann Comhairle of the Dáil and the Cathaoirleach of the Seanad. The commission may act by any two of its number. In the event of the removal from office or death, resignation or permanent incapacity of the President, an election for a successor must take place within sixty days (Article 12.3.3°).

The All-Party Oireachtas Committee on the Constitution (1998) endorsed the conclusion of the Constitution Review Group (1996) that the President should not be given further discretionary powers. However, the all-party committee commented (1998):

> Express provision should be made in Article 13, which deals with the powers and functions of the President, to allow the President, in consultation with the Council of State, to confer titles of honour, which would be non-hereditary and – to assert their honorary character – non-remunerative, on both citizens and non-citizens.
>
> As with most of the other discretionary powers of the President, this proposed additional power should be exercised only after consultation with the Council of State, with an additional two members of the Dáil who belong to parties other than the party or parties that form the government for the life of that government.

Elgie and Fitzgerald note (2004: 308), 'In all of these ways, then, the President's room for manoeuvre is not just limited; it is altogether absent'.

Discretionary Powers of the President

While the President acts on the advice of the government and has limited discretion in the making of certain appointments and decisions, there are six independent powers which the President may exercise on his or her own initiative, independent of the government. These are:

1. Article 26 of the Constitution enables the President, after consultation with the Council of State, to refer any bill (with certain exceptions) to the Supreme Court for a decision as to its constitutionality. Eamon de Valera referred to this when he explained that the President 'in exercising these powers . . . is acting on behalf of the people who have put him there for that special purpose. He is there to guard the people's rights and mainly to guard the Constitution' and is invested with certain functions and powers to do this (*Dáil Debates*, 11 May 1937, col. 51). This power is politically sensitive and has involved one incumbent in controversy that led to a constitutional crisis. The exercise of the power and the crisis of 1976 are examined in detail below.

2. The second, and arguably most important, independent power is the very wide power under Article 13 that enables the President, in his or her absolute discretion, to refuse to dissolve the Dáil on the advice of a Taoiseach who has ceased to retain the support of a majority in the Dáil. Since this power must be exercised by the President's 'absolute discretion' according to the English language version of the Constitution (or under the Irish language wording of the Constitution *as a chomhairle féin*, which is usually translated as 'under his own counsel'), it is considered inappropriate for the President to be contacted by the leaders of any political parties in an effort to influence this decision. Where the President does so refuse, it is presumed the Taoiseach concerned would have to resign, and the Dáil would then have an opportunity of nominating a successor. De Valera explained that the wise exercise of this power 'by the President may mean that he is maintaining the supremacy of the people at a time when it is vital that the people's supremacy should be maintained' (*Dáil Debates*, 11 May 1937, col. 45). Three occasions have arisen when this crucially important power could have been used. Having considered all the options, however, the President on each occasion granted the dissolution (in 1944, in January 1982 and in November 1982). Casey (2000: 85) points out:

The view generally held is that a dissolution can be refused only if an alternative government is feasible, can be assured of a working majority and can be expected to carry on for a reasonable period of time. Similar considerations must apply to the President's power under 13.2.2°; and the difficulty of predicting whether these conditions will be fulfilled need hardly be stressed. Consequently, to allow a dissolution will normally be the wiser and less controversial course.

Michael McDunphy (1945: 47, 52), who was secretary to the first President of Ireland, Dr Douglas Hyde, and as such whose views must carry considerable weight, comments:

Here we find the President endowed with the authority entirely his own, independent of the Taoiseach, independent of the Government, independent of the Oireachtas, not answerable even to the Supreme Court, which is the final authority on matters of constitutional validity. The President's power in the matter is absolute; in its exercise he is governed only by his personal judgement of what is best for the people, and his decision, when made, is final and unchallengeable . . . This power is unique in the Irish Constitution. It is the only case in which the President has an absolute and unquestionable right to act in direct opposition to a constitutional request from the Head of the Government, to reject an advice which in other matters is equivalent to a direction, which must be complied with as a matter of course.

There is no evidence that, as regards the dissolution of the Dáil, the President has declined to act on the advice of the Taoiseach on an occasion in which the support of a majority in the Dáil was lost. The President cannot dissolve the Dáil without the request of the Taoiseach. A President who refused such a request from the Taoiseach would invite controversy, yet in McDunphy's words (1945: 51), 'The Constitution gives no indication as to the evidence which would entitle the President to decide that a Taoiseach has in fact ceased to retain the support of a majority in Dáil Éireann.' Clarification of this point might have had a decisive effect in reducing the uncertainty generated by three general elections in rapid succession in 1981 and 1982.

This discretionary power of the President was at the centre of a political controversy that erupted during the presidential campaign of 1990. Following the collapse of the Fine Gael/Labour coalition government in January 1982 (after its defeat in the Dáil on a budgetary provision), Fianna Fáil issued a public statement that it was available for consultation with President Patrick Hillery if he was going to exercise his absolute right of not dissolving the Dáil, and it was widely reported that efforts were made by senior members of the party to contact the President. Such an attempt to contact the President after the collapse of the government was not necessarily improper, and the President's discretion might be better exercised with full information and advice on the situation. It would, however, be wrong if *advice* became *pressure*; and it was subsequently alleged that telephone calls were made to Áras an Uachtaráin in January 1982 in an attempt to persuade the President to secure a transfer of power without an election. This claim appeared to receive substance from the admission made by Brian Lenihan Snr, a presidential candidate, in the course of an interview in 1990, that he had telephoned Áras an Uachtaráin on the night in question. Lenihan later retracted this statement and requested a meeting with Hillery to obtain his confirmation that the telephone call had not been made. On the following day, however, he withdrew his request in order to avoid drawing the President into the election campaign.

3. Article 13 enables the President at any time, after consultation with the Council of State, to convene a meeting of either or both Houses of the Oireachtas. In this situation the President has the freedom to ignore the advice of the government. This power could become important if, for example, an unpopular government tried to avoid criticism by not calling a meeting of the Dáil. The power has never been exercised in the circumstances envisaged by the Constitution (although President Eamon de Valera summoned a joint meeting of the Dáil and Seanad on 21 January 1969 to commemorate the fiftieth anniversary of the first meeting of Dáil Éireann).

   In an interview with the *Cork Examiner* on 8 October 1991 President Mary Robinson envisaged the possibility of using this power, while acknowledging that it had to be a matter of timing and circumstance and that it could not be done at a time of political sensitivity.

4. Under Article 27 a petition may be addressed to the President by a majority of senators and at least one-third of the members of the Dáil, requesting him or her not to sign a bill until it has been approved by the people either at a referendum or at a general election. The President then decides whether the bill 'contains a proposal of such national importance that the will of the people thereon ought to be ascertained'. This provision is designed for a situation in which a matter of fundamental national importance is passed in the Dáil but is almost unanimously rejected in the Seanad. It applies to bills in respect of which the Seanad has been overruled by the Dáil in exercise of the powers given by Article 23. The President can act only after consultation with the Council of State. Where the President accepts a petition, the bill cannot become law until it has been approved by the people at a referendum or by resolution of the Dáil passed after a dissolution and re-assembly. No bill has so far been referred to the people under these provisions.

5. Article 22 enables the President, at the request of the Seanad, to refer the question as to whether or not a bill is a money bill (a bill relating to the finances of the state) to a Committee of Privileges, a committee consisting of an equal number of members of the Dáil and of the Seanad with a judge of the Supreme Court as chairperson. For the discussion of money bills, the Seanad has only twenty-one days, although it has three months for the discussion of an ordinary measure. De Valera explained:

> To prevent any fraud upon the Seanad by compelling them to discuss within twenty-one days and practically not to interfere with the bill which they would have a perfect right to discuss if it came in the guise of an ordinary measure, and to prevent the possibility of mistakes by the Chairman of the Dáil, there is an appeal to the President against a certificate of the Ceann Comhairle. There can be an appeal made by the House affected, that is the Seanad (*Dáil Debates*, 11 May 1937, col. 49).

The Seanad may complain to the President that the bill was certified a money bill in error and may accordingly ask the President to set up a Committee of Privileges to determine whether the bill was or was not a money bill. This function has not been exercised.

6. The final independent power of the President relates to the need to get legislation passed quickly during a state of emergency. Under Article 24, when a bill is 'urgent and immediately necessary for the preservation of the public peace and security, or by reason of the existence of a public emergency whether domestic or international', the time for its consideration by the Seanad may be shortened. There may be occasions in which the very safety of the state may depend upon making a quick decision. The President has to agree with the government's view that a bill is in this category before this procedure can be adopted. The Dáil can then compel the Seanad to reach a decision within a very limited period; and if the Dáil does not accept this decision, the law can be enacted without the approval of the Seanad.

It is in order to diminish the chances of a misuse of this power that the President's consent has to be obtained. The President has to agree with the Dáil before the power of the Seanad can be curtailed. He or she is put in a very responsible position to act as umpire to see that the Dáil acts in accordance with the spirit of the Constitution. It would have to be a clear and an obvious abuse of power before the President would interfere. No attempts appear to have been made to avail of the powers given by this article.

The Constitution Review Group (1996) considered the question of whether the powers of the President should be expanded. It recommended against such an extension, as likely to embroil the President in party politics and to reduce accountability, since the President, unlike the government, is not answerable to the Oireachtas and the courts. The All-Party Oireachtas Committee on the Constitution (1998) endorsed this conclusion with the possible addition of the President having the power to administer a national honours system. FitzGerald (2003: 55) comments:

> . . . now that the monarch has been exorcised from our Constitution for over half a century, we might revert to the more normal international practice under which the name (or possible successive names), coming before Dáil Éireann for nomination [as Taoiseach] would, as in most other democracies be proposed by the Head of State . . . The President would also by this process be given an enhanced role, which I think would be helpful in increasing the respect for the office. On this issue, I disagree with the Constitution Review Group which rejected any increase in the powers of the President in the government formation process and, indeed, proposed the removal of the President's discretionary powers in relation to the dissolution of the Dáil, on the grounds of avoiding his or her involvement in party political issues.

The Council of State

The Council of State aids and counsels the President. It plays a vital role when the President opts to use the discretionary powers listed under (1), (3) and (4) above. De Valera spelt out the role of the Council of State, 'They will, therefore, be in a position to explain or try to make clear any point of view that they may have on it before the President makes up his mind. So that he certainly is provided with a body competent to advise and warn him of any dangers and of all the facts of the situation. He is supposed then to judge for himself, having heard that advice' (*Dáil Debates*, 11 May 1937).

The Council of State is composed of:

- Ex officio members: the Taoiseach, the Tánaiste, the Chief Justice, the President of the High Court, the Ceann Comhairle of the Dáil, the Cathaoirleach of the Seanad and the Attorney General.
- Every able and willing person who has held office as President, Taoiseach or Chief Justice
- A maximum of seven other persons whom the President may appoint at his or her discretion. Members in this category serve only during the term(s) of the President who appoints them, and the President has the power to remove them for any reason he or she deems sufficient. Their appointment enables the President to make the Council of State 'as representative as possible' (*Dáil Debates*, 13 May 1937, col. 430).

The term of office of the Council of State is the same as that of the President who appointed it.

Members of the Council of State take an oath to 'conscientiously fulfil duties' as members and meet only when summoned by the President. The meetings are held in camera, and the President is not bound to follow the advice given; the final decision on the matter in question is the President's alone – Article 32 of the Constitution states that 'The president shall not exercise or perform any of the powers or functions which are by this Constitution expressed to be exercisable or performable by him after consultation with the Council of State unless, and on every occasion before so doing, he shall have convened a meeting of the Council of State and the members present at such meeting shall have been heard by him'.

Article 14 provides for the establishment of a Presidential Commission, consisting of the Chief Justice, the Ceann Comhairle and the Cathaoirleach, to exercise the powers and functions of the President in the event of his or her absence, temporary incapacity or at any time when the office of the president may be vacant. In any contingency not provided for in the situation envisaged by Article 14, the Council of State may exercise its sole power to make such provisions as it may seem necessary for the exercise and performance of the President's powers and functions.

Barry Desmond (2000: 190), who served on the Council of State from 1973 to 1991, comments:

> The Council meetings were very formal. The secretary to the President circulated before the meeting a copy of the Bill forwarded to him for signature and copies of the relevant Dáil and Seanad debates. The Taoiseach and the Attorney General were invariably the first to respond to the President's invitation to advise him on the constitutionality of the Bill. The rest of us spoke once giving our personal opinions. The presidents always indicated that they would give full consideration to our advice but gave no indication at the meetings of their ultimate decision which, under the Constitution, was theirs and theirs alone.

Independent TD Finian McGrath requested President Mary McAleese to call a meeting of the Council of State in 2008 to discuss the Lisbon Treaty. The President was barred constitutionally from even considering this request let alone acceding to it. This is because the power granted to the President under Article 26 to refer legislation to the Supreme Court does not apply to 'a Money Bill or a Bill expressed to be a Bill containing a proposal to amend the Constitution'.

Reference of Bills to the Supreme Court

Under Article 26 (discussed above), the President is given the special function of highlighting the fact that a particular bill, or section of a bill, may be against the Constitution and of stopping it before it becomes law. If the President is of the opinion that the measure, if passed, might be invalid by being contrary to the Constitution, he or she has the power of referring that measure for decision to the Supreme Court. It is not the President who decides whether it is against the Constitution or not; his or her function is simply one of referral to the Supreme Court, which makes the ultimate decision. It is an important power, because if the President did sign the bill into law, some of its consequences might well be irreversible.

Every reference of a bill to the Supreme Court by the President must be made not later than the seventh day after the date on which the bill is presented to him or her by the Taoiseach for signature. 'Thus the President has only one week in which to meditate on the Bill, assemble the Council of State and reflect on the views expressed, and make a decision' (Casey 2000: 90). The President is not permitted to refer money bills, bills to amend the Constitution or bills whose time for consideration by the Seanad had been abridged under Article 24.

The Supreme Court must deliver a single decision, with no dissenting or separate judgments, not later than sixty days after the date of reference. Hamilton CJ in *Re Article 26 and the Employment Equality Bill 1996* [1997] 2 IR 321 comments:

> When one considers that the Bill consists of 74 sections and either amends or refers to 33 other statutes one can see that the task confronting the Court is a formidable one. The task is not made any lighter by the fact that the Court is constitutionally obliged to give its decision on the Bill within 60 days of which the Bill was referred to the Court by the President. Within this time the Court must assign counsel, give them time to prepare their written submissions, hold an oral hearing at which the issues are debated in open court, make its decision and deliver its judgement.

The advantages of the Article 26 procedure are that it allows the President to take action in good time to prevent legislation that is unconstitutional from getting onto the statute book and affecting rights. The procedure plays an important preventative role in the protection of rights in that some problems may be anticipated before they arise and can be resolved at this early stage. Hogan and Whyte (2003: 412) note that 'There are clearly cases for which the Article 26 procedure is especially suited. These are cases presenting net points of law and in respect of which certainty is particularly important'. Article 26 is particularly useful in the defence of rights and principles that might otherwise not come before the court because affected parties would not have sufficient opportunity to take such a case under normal circumstances. Use of Article 26 avoids the consequences of a later pronouncement of unconstitutionality. It allows the Supreme Court to take a dispassionate view of the constitutional issue. It saves citizens from the trouble and expense of contesting the legislation later in the courts. It has the further advantage of deterring governments from introducing legislative proposals that might be repugnant to the Constitution.

The disadvantages are: firstly, that the procedure is hypothetical in nature and is based on abstract adjudication. Testing at this stage may be unsatisfactory, as there is no experience of operating the legislation. Arguments are put forward solely on the 'creation and imagination of the lawyers involved' (Ryan 2001: 29). Furthermore, Article 34.3.3° provides that 'no court whatever shall have jurisdiction to question the validity of a law' that has been cleared through the Article 26 procedure. This means that although the act may have disclosed highly objectionable aspects in its operation, which were unforeseen at the time of the Article 26 reference, or if unanticipated situations arise, it cannot subsequently be challenged. This permanent immunity is termed by Byrne and McCutcheon (2001: 554) as 'a judicial death sentence'. Casey (2000: 338) sees this as 'the most serious disadvantage of the Article 26 procedure'. In addition, commentators have noted that the leading constitutional court decisions have been taken in the course of ordinary proceedings brought in the courts. It is also argued that the Supreme Court is the ultimate arbiter and, as such, is the real guardian of the people's rights in the Constitution. 'Another disadvantage is that should the Supreme Court decide that even a minor provision of a Bill is invalid, the entire measure falls and the President must refuse to sign it' (Casey 2000: 335). On this point, the Constitution Review Group (1996: 78) noted:

> As the number of Article 26 references increases and with on-going constitutional development, there is a real risk that this rule will operate to protect the validity of law in circumstances where, if the Supreme Court could later consider the matter afresh in the light of new circumstances, it would probably take a different view. The law should never be frozen. It should be free to flow with the needs of the people.

In the case of a reference of a bill under Article 26, the Attorney General (or counsel on his or her behalf) argues the case in favour of the constitutionality of the bill, and counsel assigned by the court argues the case that the bill is repugnant to the Constitution, largely by drawing attention to hypothetical results of its enactment. Such hypothetical argument is often difficult because it is not always possible to envisage the consequences of the bills if enacted.

Fifteen bills have been referred by the President to the Supreme Court under Article 26. These were:

1. Offences Against the State (Amendment) Bill 1940   Valid
2. School Attendance Bill 1942   Invalid
3. Electoral (Amendment) Bill 1961   Valid
4. Criminal Law (Jurisdiction) Bill 1975   Valid
5. Emergency Powers Bill 1976   Valid
6. Housing (Private Rented Dwellings) Bill 1981   Invalid
7. Electoral (Amendment) Bill 1983   Invalid
8. Adoption (No. 2) Bill 1987   Valid
9. Matrimonial Home Bill 1993   Invalid
10. Regulation of Information Services Outside the State for
    Termination of Pregnancies Bill 1995   Valid
11. Employment Equality Bill 1996   Invalid
12. Equal Status Bill 1997   Invalid
13. Planning and Development Bill 1999 (Part V on affordable
    housing)   Valid
14. Illegal Immigrants (Trafficking) Bill 1999   Valid
15. Health (Amendment) (No. 2) Bill 2004 (on long-term
    institutional charges)   Invalid

Thus, Hogan and Whyte (2003: 400) note, 'There seems to be an increase in the Article 26 procedure'. Provisions of seven of these bills were declared to be repugnant to the Constitution. The School Attendance Bill 1942, in the opinion of the court, infringed the rights of parents to decide how their children should be educated. The Housing Bill 1981 was deemed to interfere with the property rights of owners of particular dwellings. The Electoral (Amendment) Bill 1983, in extending voting rights, was deemed to conflict with other basic provisions of the Constitution. The Matrimonial Home Bill 1993; the Employment Equality Bill 1996; and the Equal Status Bill 1997 were also deemed invalid. In the Health (Amendment) (No. 2) Bill 2004, on the method of charging medical card holders for long-term institutional care, the Supreme Court clearly indicated those aspects that were repugnant to the Constitution, which were those that purported retrospectively to validate illegal charges made over thirty years. Equally, it noted that the prospective provisions that proposed the future levying of charges were not repugnant.

The bills of 1940 and 1961 were amendments of legislation that had already been declared unconstitutional. The 1967 report of the Committee on the Constitution stated in relation to Article 26, 'We feel that, on the whole, this kind of provision is useful in the Constitution, and we are unable to agree, therefore, that it should be deleted. While we are unanimous in this opinion that Article 26 should be retained, we feel that some changes are necessary, but we have been unable to agree on the best approach to the problem.'

The Constitution Review Group (1996) favoured the retention of the reference procedure of Article 26, but considered that, on balance, the 'unchallengeability' provision under Article 34.3.3° should be deleted in its entirety. The All-Party Oireachtas Committee on the Constitution (1997c) agreed with this. Jaconelli (1983: 327) notes in this regard 'that a catalogue of human rights should ideally be a flexible instrument, ever responsive to the changing needs of society'. Hamilton (1996: 545) recommended the removal of the permanent immunity rule in the hope that Article 26 would be invoked more frequently and utilised to the fullest extent.

The Emergency Powers Bill 1976

In September 1976 President Cearbhall Ó Dálaigh referred the Emergency Powers Bill 1976, which conferred great powers on the authorities, to the Supreme Court under Article 26 for a decision as to its constitutionality. The government's view was that the exemption provided by Article 28.3.3° meant that the bill could not be declared unconstitutional because the Supreme Court did not have jurisdiction to review the bill as it was for the purpose of securing the public safety of the state. The Supreme Court found that the bill was not repugnant to the Constitution, but stated, 'As to the right of the President to refer the bill to this Court, it is clear that he has power to do so notwithstanding that the bill is one passed by both Houses of the Oireachtas by reference to the provisions of subsection 3.3 of Article 28. The power of the President to do so has not been questioned in these proceedings.'

The exercise of this independent power under Article 26 involved the President in political controversy. Then Minister for Defence, Patrick Donegan, publicly criticised the President 'in a clearly improper manner' (Chubb 1982: 200) in a speech delivered at Columb Military Barracks, Mullingar on 18 October 1976 during which he referred to the President as 'a thundering disgrace', adding, 'The fact is that the army must stand behind the state.' President Ó Dálaigh, in a letter to Donegan dated 19 October 1976, asked the question, 'Can this sequence be construed by ordinary people otherwise than as an insinuation that the President does not stand behind the state?' In addition, it was widely suggested at the time that the actual language used was stronger. However, the only journalist present on the occasion – Don Lavery, then a correspondent with the local *Westmeath Examiner* newspaper – insists that the words used were 'thundering disgrace' and nothing else (personal interview and Lavery 2007).

Taoiseach Liam Cosgrave referred to Donegan's outburst as no more than 'excessive verbal exuberance', and a Dáil motion calling on the minister to resign was defeated by 63 votes to 58 on 21 October. On the following day, moved by the government's failure to take action against the minister, Ó Dálaigh resigned as President. He took this course of action to assert publicly his personal dignity and independence as President of Ireland and – a matter of much greater importance for every citizen – to endeavour to protect the dignity and independence of the presidency as an institution. Donegan had apologised by letter for what he had said, telling Ó Dálaigh that he deeply regretted the use of the words 'thundering disgrace'. Immediately after resigning, Ó Dálaigh published the correspondence exchanged between himself and the minister, in the course of which he had written, 'The President's role in relation to the Defence Forces is honorary in character; nevertheless, a special relationship exists between the President and the Minister for Defence. That relationship has been irreparably breached not only by what you said yesterday, but also because of the place where, and the persons before whom, you chose to make your outrageous criticism.'

Referring to this event and the Ó Dálaigh presidential papers, former Supreme Court Judge Donal Barrington (2006) notes:

> However, it also appears from these papers that the main cause of the constitutional crisis was the failure of the Taoiseach to take the President into his confidence. It would appear that relations between the two men were perfectly cordial, but the Taoiseach simply did not discuss matters of state with the President. This appears to be contrary to Article 28 Section 5, Sub-section 2 of the Constitution, which provides that the Taoiseach 'shall keep the President generally informed on matters of domestic and international policy'. Certainly it appears that the President deeply resented this failure on the Taoiseach's part, going so far as to describe it, in one of his notes, as 'an act of constitutional defiance'. The British Prime Minister did not help matters by publicly referring to Cearbhall Ó Dálaigh as 'a menace to civilisation'. This insult, coming from a man who had presided over the British government at the time of Bloody Sunday, should not have rattled Cearbhall Ó Dálaigh, but it did. It was an extraordinary insult directed at the President of Ireland for exercising one of his legitimate constitutional powers. But there was no one to defend the President. Instead, the Minister for Defence, addressing a group of army officers, referred to their commander in chief as a 'thundering disgrace'. This crude insult precipitated the President's resignation, but it was clear that it was not the real cause.

Thus, the combination of the roles of guardian of the people's rights under the Constitution and of ceremonial head of state can involve the President in political controversy in the exercise of the independent powers bestowed on the office by the Constitution, particularly in so far as they have been designed and fall to be exercised at times of crisis and where a conflict of opinion may emerge.

Conclusion

The President of Ireland is head of state with very few powers or functions that may be exercised independently of government control. This accords with constitutional practice in most other countries where the government is led by a prime minister; it differs radically from the United States, where the powers usually found in the hands of the nominal head of state are vested in the President together with the real executive power of government. In Ireland the Taoiseach is the head of the government and the President is the ceremonial head of state. The President, freed from executive functions and the divisiveness of party politics, serves as a personification of the state. From the President the people seek a reflection of their higher values and aspirations. In return, the President takes precedence over all persons in the state.

The Constitution spells out the President's powers in detail so that conflict over spheres of authority between the cabinet and the President should not arise. The President's powers are directly circumscribed, and he or she normally acts on the advice and authority of the government. Any appointments that the President makes under the Constitution (with the exception of the seven appointees to the Council of State, a purely consultative body) are made following the advice of a third party. Such independent powers as the President possesses are intended for use only in emergencies, and to date only two of these independent powers have been exercised. The constitutional crisis of October 1976, which led to the resignation of President Cearbhall Ó Dálaigh resulted from the exercise by him of one of his independent powers under the Constitution.

From time to time there has been discussion as to how far it is possible or desirable to develop, within the existing constitutional controls, a new and more open style of presidency in which each individual incumbent can make a distinctively personal contribution. In this connection, Erskine Childers, on the announcement of his candidature for the office of President in 1973, declared, 'I have learned by experience that outside the party political field, some leaders should give guidance to the people, some leaders should reflect the most reasonable aspirations of the people on matters where discussion and debate will not create fundamental national division, but will encourage enlightened examination.' President Childers did not follow this strategy with much vigour, partly because of the generally unfavourable reaction among politicians of all parties to this suggestion, and partly because of his untimely death. Clearly, it would be extremely difficult for a President to combine the diverse roles of titular head of state, guardian of people's rights under the Constitution and advocate of enlightened examination of social issues without falling foul of political controversy, criticism and misunderstanding. Casey (2000: 92) wisely notes, 'Some commentators seem to envisage an ill-defined leadership role for the President. Whatever the merits of such an idea it is abundantly clear that no such role is conceived of, or can be exercised under, the Constitution as it stands. Making policy is a matter for the Taoiseach and the Government.'

In her inauguration speech on 3 December 1990 President Mary Robinson described her aim for a presidency of 'justice, peace and love'. Horgan (1997: 185) notes, 'In all her trips abroad, President Robinson made a special point of arranging meetings with groups representing the Irish diaspora.' President Mary McAleese, at her inauguration on 11 November 1997, said, 'I am honoured and humbled to be successor to seven exemplary presidents. Their differing religious, political, geographical and social origins speak loudly of a presidency which has always been wide open and all-embracing. Among them were presidents from Connacht, Leinster and Munster, to say nothing of America and London. It is my special privilege and delight to be the first president from Ulster.'

The 1967 report of the Committee on the Constitution considered a proposal that the separate office of President should be abolished and set out the arguments advanced for and against. The committee was divided on the question. The arguments put forward in favour of abolition included: (1) that the President is largely a figurehead; (2) that the President's formal duties as head of state could without difficulty be discharged by the Taoiseach, who could act as both head of government and head of state; (3) that the abolition of the separate office of President would give rise to substantial financial savings. However, it can be reasonably argued that it would be neither desirable (in view of the President's function as guardian of the Constitution) nor practicable to combine the offices of Taoiseach and President; nor would it result in any significant financial saving. The Constitution Review Group (1996) considered that there was no public demand or good reason for the abolition of the office, 'A State requires a Head of State; the President's function as guardian of the Constitution requires that the office be separate from the executive.' The All-Party Oireachtas Committee on the Constitution (1998) agreed with this finding. The 1996 report considered that the Constitution should be amended to describe the President as head of state, however, the 1998 report felt that the popular election of the President elevates the President and forms a bond between the people and President and that 'The term "Head of State" – a literally statist one – would tend to relate the people to an abstraction rather than a person'.

The President is in constitutional theory elected by the people to safeguard their rights under the Constitution and is an important part of the system of checks and balances on the power of the legislature. While the President has very few independent powers under the Constitution, it is clear that these independent powers are potentially very important because they are designed to act as a check in circumstances of conflict or crisis. The fact that these powers have not often or never been exercised does not diminish their potential importance.

Clarke (2008) notes succinctly, 'Having never really understood what the President's job is about, I suddenly got it. She is a role model, not a ruler. She is a person who embodies grace and compassion and forgiveness and true mobility, and in doing so inspires the rest of us to think about abandoning envy and greed and small-mindedness and snobbery and resentment and whatever other evils we have within our consciousness. She is a true leader.'

Web Resources

President of Ireland at www.president.ie

APPENDIX: PRESIDENTS OF IRELAND

25 June 1938 to 25 June 1945	Douglas Hyde
25 June 1945 to 25 June 1959	Seán T. Ó Ceallaigh
25 June 1959 to 25 June 1973	Eamon de Valera
25 June 1973 to 17 November 1974	Erskine Childers
19 December 1974 to 22 October 1976	Cearbhall Ó Dálaigh
3 December 1976 to 3 December 1990	Patrick Hillery
3 December 1990 to 12 September 1997	Mary Robinson
11 November 1997 to date	Mary McAleese

6

THE CIVIL SERVICE

The civil service comprises those persons who have been selected by the Public Appointments Service to serve the organs of state defined by the Constitution, namely the President, the Houses of the Oireachtas, the judiciary, the Taoiseach, government ministers, the Attorney General and the Comptroller and Auditor General. The term finds no mention in the 1937 Constitution and can be used roughly to describe those who work in government departments. The legal basis for the civil service is provided in the Ministers and Secretaries Act 1924. That act authorises ministers to appoint the civil servants in their department (except the secretary general) in such numbers and grades as the Minister for Finance approves. The secretary general of each department is appointed by the government on the recommendation of the minister concerned. The procedure by which appointments are made is described below.

Technically, there are two categories of civil servants. Those employed in parts of the civil service not under the direct control of ministers are *civil servants of the state*, for example the staff in the Houses of the Oireachtas (who are employed under the Staff of the Houses of the Oireachtas Act 1959 and are independent of whatever government may be in power). All other civil servants – the vast majority – who are employed in the government departments are *civil servants of the government*.

There were 38, 700 civil servants at the end of March 2009. Although this is less than the number of persons employed in the local authorities, the health services or the state-sponsored bodies, the civil service occupies a key position in the public service in that it is the part of that service which is closest to ministers and government and, therefore, more immediately involved in the making of policy. Moreover, its supervisory influence extends to the various other parts of the public service, on whose activities it impinges in one way or another, whether in matters of policy, finance, organisation, pay or personnel management. It is at the hub of the wheel of government, so to speak.

The mission of the civil service is the achievement of an excellent service for government and the other institutions of state as well as for the public as citizens and users of public services, based on principles of integrity, impartiality, effectiveness, equity and accountability. The prime purpose of the civil service as a whole is, of course, to serve the public, and the first duty of individual civil servants is to help their minister meet his or her responsibilities to the Oireachtas. Civil servants work continuously for, with and under politicians in a system that responds to a complex series of demands emerging in various ways: from political parties, organisations, groups and the media; from administrators themselves through their perception of needs, their appreciation of the problems hindering development and their concern to get these resolved; from decisions of the courts and other appellate bodies; from Ireland's membership of international organisations such as the European Union; and from developments abroad generally such as economic recession or war.

An interesting aspect of the Irish civil service is that although politicians and ministers change, the civil service is permanent. There is something of a paradox in this, in that the civil service is at one and the same time the permanent servant of the state and the servant of the administration that is for the time being in power. The Ombudsman, Emily O'Reilly (2005), has described this feature:

> Well, the civil service is not called the permanent government for nothing. Ministers come and go. The vision thing can be a short term vision thing, complicated by political expediency, internal party politicking and other issues. Senior civil servants are in for the long haul, they don't have to play the short game, they can note and analyse societal problems in the round and assess those problems into the future, long after any particular Minister has gone. The public would, I believe, therefore benefit from that long term, macro vision, be it in relation to waste management, energy policy, immigration, the Boston Berlin debate, the who should pay for what debate in relation to education and other costs. Senior civil servants are, almost by definition, among the brightest, best educated and best informed people in the State; all of that should not be lost simply in fulfilling the shorter term needs of their political masters.

Recruitment

Civil servants (with some exceptions noted below) are recruited as a result of competitions held by the Public Appointments Service. In 2004 the Civil Service Commission and the Local Appointments Commission were dissolved and two new bodies were established: the Public Appointments Service and the Commission for Public Service Appointments. The Public Appointments Service acts as the centralised recruitment, assessment and selection body for government departments. The role of the Commission for Public Service Appointments is to regulate recruitment in the public service bodies. It publishes recruitment and selection codes of practice, which outline the standards to which all public service bodies must conform. It can license public service bodies, such as government departments, to recruit on their own behalf or with the assistance of private sector recruitment agencies specifically approved by the commission. This change gave the civil service new opportunities to modernise its recruitment practices. The commission's membership consists of the Ceann Comhairle, the Secretary General of the Department of the Taoiseach, the Secretary General for Public Service Management and Development at the Department of Finance, the Ombudsman, and the Chairperson of the Standards in Public Office Commission.

The competitions can be of different kinds and may consist of one or more of the following: a written, oral or practical examination, an interview, or any other test considered appropriate. Candidates fall into two broad categories. The first category is that of persons seeking admission on the basis of the school certificate examinations or specially set tests. In addition to an examination, such candidates are usually obliged to undergo an interview before being appointed, as, for example, potential administrative officers. The second category comprises persons who have technical qualifications usually acquired after some form of third-level education or who have certain prescribed experience. Generally persons in this category (for example engineers) are selected after interview. These competitions are described as open competitions, i.e. they are open to persons outside the civil service who fulfil the conditions laid down. For each competition by interview, a special interview board is set up, normally consisting of three members. The services of interviewers drawn from all sections of the community are used. A detailed scheme of marking is provided for each board so as to give it a framework within which it may make its assessments.

Canvassing on behalf of competition candidates is prohibited, and this rule is rigidly enforced. As the minister in charge of each department is legally the employer of all the staff in that department, the names of those selected are submitted to departments to get ministers' approval to their appointment. No alternative names are provided, and invariably those recommended are appointed.

Certain exceptional appointments, which are not the result of competitions held by the Public Appointments Service, relate to persons appointed in the public interest, to those in the broad category of skilled worker, porter and cleaner, and to short-term or contract appointments such as temporary seasonal staff for the Passport Office. Those appointed in the public interest are usually persons who have particular skills or talents that the civil service lacks, for example a geologist with special experience or an expert in nuclear energy. Where such appointments are made, the Public Appointments

Service has no function to perform. The procedure is that the minister to whose department the person is to be appointed obtains first the consent of the government, after which a notice must be published in *Iris Oifigiúil*, the official gazette. If any questions are raised in the Dáil, or elsewhere, the minister and the government must be prepared to defend the appointment. For other types of non-competitive appointment specified above, the manner of recruitment is left to individual departments. The usual procedure is for the jobs to be advertised and then filled by interview.

Open recruitment was launched for certain management jobs in the civil service in 2007. Greater use of open recruitment was seen as necessary to allow the civil service to attract staff with the wide range of skills and experience needed in a modern public administration. A major recruitment campaign was launched for management positions within the civil service. For example, the Revenue Commissioners sought to attract applications from solicitors, accountants, barristers, tax experts and those with experience in taxation, accountancy, law, business or a financial discipline. Equally, other opportunities were advertised across the entire civil service, with many of the positions located outside Dublin.

Successful candidates for positions within the civil service are likely to have a track record in quality customer service, experience at management level including leading and managing large teams, satisfactory management experience of projects and budgets and most likely a third-level qualification.

Career Structures

The civil service may be divided into three main career structures: general, departmental and technical. Within these categories are the grades described below.

General Service

The general service grades consist of a central core of general service officers who are recruited to perform the general duties of departments from the routine clerical operations to the higher policy, advisory and managerial work.

Departmental

Departmental grades are confined to a few departments or offices, such as the Department of Foreign Affairs, the Houses of the Oireachtas and the Office of the Comptroller and Auditor General.

Technical

There are technical officers employed in nearly all departments. They are recruited to the civil service for the performance of specialised work and already possess a qualification related to the work to be performed. The qualification is usually a formally recognised degree, diploma or certificate. In so far as it is possible to generalise, their role is to bring expert knowledge, skill and experience in specialist fields to bear on the determination and execution of government policy, for example in advising on the interpretation of the law, on health schemes, on environmental issues or on the development of natural resources. Examples include the solicitors in the Office of the Chief State Solicitor, doctors in the Department of Health, and engineers in the Department of the Environment.

Grades

The civil service is divided into several hundred grades, i.e. within the three categories outlined above there are several hundred job titles. A great number of these are one-person grades and relate specifically to specialised jobs, for example the Director of the Meteorological Service or the Registrar of the Supreme Court. There are large numbers in a relatively small number of grades and an enormous number of grades that contain one or two persons. There are not, however, that many pay scales, since many grades have the same scales.

GRADE GROUPING CATEGORIES AND DESCRIPTION OF GRADES

Grouping	Description
Senior management	Secretary general, deputy secretary, assistant secretary
Management	Principal officer, assistant principal
Executive	Higher executive officer, administrative officer, executive officer
Administrative support	Staff officer, clerical officer
Non-clerical support	Services officer, services attendant
Technical/professional	Technical and professional grades

Source: Mercer Human Resource Consulting (May 2004)

There is no legal definition of a grade. Persons are appointed to what are called 'positions' in the civil service. Positions requiring broadly the same level of qualifications and with comparable levels of work, responsibility, pay and conditions of service are then grouped by the Department of Finance into grades. Examples of grades are the executive, engineering, librarian and draftsman grades. The general service is made up of grades that are common to two or more departments; these are described below. A reply to a parliamentary question in 1986 revealed that there were some 700 civil service grades. Discussions are ongoing on the rationalisation of grade structures.

The work of the general service grades has been more closely defined, with the result that the lines of demarcation between grades are clear. Job descriptions are now standard in the civil service. Persons moving from one job to another within a grade, or moving to a higher grade on promotion, get a statement listing their new duties. Those in the various general service grades are expected to be able to perform efficiently any work assigned to them. This arrangement has enabled the civil service to take in its stride, more or less, the challenges and changes that it has faced.

Clerical Officers

The work of clerical officers includes filing, operating machines, recording information, checking accounts, making payments, less difficult analysis and presentation of findings, and drafting letters and memoranda that follow established practice and seek or give factual information. In general they deal with work that requires substantial dependence on acquired knowledge and experience. The receptionists in public offices are generally clerical officers.

Executive and Higher Executive Officers

The executive grades, which are often referred to as the middle management grades, could be regarded as the most central to the smooth working of every government department. The executive officer grade has traditionally been the entry level to junior management in the civil service. A high proportion of the most senior civil servants entered the service at this level. At one time executive officer recruitment was aimed at school leavers but an increasing number of graduates have been entering the civil service as executive officers in recent times. The work of executive officers includes presenting all the important aspects of complicated cases in a logical and readable sequence; summarising accurately the particular issues; recommending a course of action where there are a number of options; preparing briefs for, and reports of, meetings; analysing statistical material; and accounting for unusual developments.

The work of higher executive officers is an extension, at a higher level, of the work of the basic grade. Higher executive officers have to make more difficult decisions and give directions where there are exceptions to standard procedures. They and their staff perform a wide range of tasks. Some are charged with large areas of responsibility, such as the payment of salaries in the Departments of Education (teachers), Justice (gardaí) or Defence (soldiers); travelling expenses of the inspectors employed by the Department of Agriculture; and social welfare allowances. Many are engaged in what is known as case work; for example, examining proposals and making suggestions about the provision of a new school or health clinic; the introduction of a youth help scheme; or a new measure to deal with an environmental problem. Some are engaged in monitoring the progress of ongoing measures such as fisheries protection, energy conservation or projects to attract tourists. Many, such as those in the transport and aviation divisions of the Department of Transport, oversee the operations of state-sponsored bodies. Very many are involved in European Union work and some are engaged in the work of the other international organisations of which Ireland is a member, for example the World Health Organization, the World Trade Organization or the Organisation for Economic Co-operation and Development, and regularly attend meetings of these bodies abroad. Very many also are engaged in the operation, maintenance and enhancement of computerised systems, as, for example, those who are responsible for the processing and payment of social welfare claims. They implement the provisions of legislation (such as the collection of taxes) and assemble information for new legislation, consulting the legal officers as required on this and on the taking of prosecutions under existing legislation. Officers in the Department of Justice ensure the smooth operation of the judicial system. Nearly all officers in all departments at one time or another have to prepare replies to parliamentary questions. The above examples are only a small and random selection of the varied work undertaken by higher executive officers.

Administrative Officers

Prior to the introduction of open recruitment the administrative officer grade was the highest level to which staff members were regularly recruited to the civil service. The selection process for administrative officers seeks graduates who show the potential to undertake the most demanding duties at the highest level of the service. The objective is to recruit the next generation of senior managers. For this reason, a high level of academic attainment is required, and candidates are also expected to show a wide range of skills and abilities in the course of the selection process. Administrative officers are usually engaged on critical analysis and research over a wide range of government activities. In their initial assignments they work closely with experienced officials. As they gain experience they are assigned to a broader range of duties involving, for example, the drafting of briefing and other documents for ministers, the government and contacts with other departments, professional bodies or international organisations. A lot of time is spent on policy analysis and statistical work. Administrative officers are employed in most departments and are assigned to a wide variety of responsibilities, for example the development of policies in the areas of transport, education, environmental protection or industrial development. The greatest number are assigned to the Department of Finance and work on matters such as short-term management of the economy, budgetary policy, the allocation of financial resources or the development of human resource policies in the public service.

The Higher Civil Service

Those in the general service grades from assistant principal upwards, sometimes referred to as the administrative grades, constitute the higher civil service. Their work is broadly concerned with formulating policy, pursuing and examining proposals for change, offering alternative lines to ministers, preparing legislation, organising projects or schemes and the general management of large blocks of executive work. They are responsible for the administration of the state and for the execution of policy and are expected, on a continuous basis, to devise ways of improving efficiency. In general, as officers move up the administrative grades, their policy role grows and widens, while their executive role is correspondingly diminished. These grades also supply the advisers who accompany ministers when meeting deputations or attending meetings abroad.

Principals and Assistant Principals

The grade of principal is a central one in the sense that principals are in charge of large blocks, known as units, of a department's work. Each department has a finance and a human resource unit. Other examples of units are those dealing with old-age benefits, national school buildings or petroleum products in the relevant departments. Where a principal is engaged on policy work relating to broad national issues, the work is typically divided into sub-areas with an assistant principal in each, putting forward proposals for dealing with the issues in his or her sub-area. Where the work involves national schemes, it could be divided on a geographical basis. Each principal has, in the normal course, the help of at least two assistant principals. The area of work controlled by an assistant principal is normally called a *branch*. The officials who accompany ministers on their appearances in the Dáil in connection with routine parliamentary business are usually in the grades of assistant principal or principal.

Assistant Secretaries

The duties of assistant secretaries are rather similar to those of principals, but on a higher level of responsibility and usually in a broader field. A main feature of the assistant secretaries' role is their access to the minister; the terms and frequency of this access depend on the attitudes of individual ministers and secretaries general. On major parliamentary occasions, such as the presentation of the budget or of departmental estimates, or when the issues being debated are otherwise politically important or sensitive, the official accompanying the minister in the Dáil is usually an assistant secretary. The majority of Ireland's ambassadors are civil servants serving in the grade of assistant secretary.

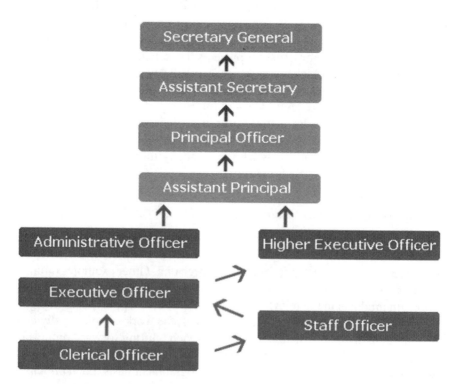

Civil Service Grade Structure

Secretaries General

The secretary general is the chief adviser to the minister and is the apex of the pyramid. He or she is, in effect, the managing director of the department. All policy proposals formulated within the department, and all matters on which the minister's views or directions are sought (or which it is considered desirable to bring to the minister's notice) are submitted to the secretary general for presentation to the minister. The secretary general is personally responsible to the minister for the overall management of the department, including the regularity and propriety of all transactions and the efficiency and economy of administration in the department. The secretary general carries a range of significant responsibilities in a complex environment involving high-level policy planning, political, legal and financial elements. The term 'secretary general' originates from section 4(4) of the Public Service Management Act 1997 and replaced the term 'secretary'. Former Minister for Finance Ruairí Quinn (2005: 324) gives the background to this change and describes an official visit to Japan where the translators described the secretary of his department as the 'everlasting typist in the Department of Enterprise and Employment'.

The British Haldane report of 1918 saw an ever-present, indissoluble symbiosis between ministers and their top civil servants as the ideal. Indeed, in Britain in 1988 Sir Brian Cubbon, a permanent secretary, described his role mathematically as 'the reciprocal' of the minister (Hennessy 1989: 508). The product of any number and its reciprocal equals one. Padraig O hUiginn (2008), who was Secretary General of the Department of the Taoiseach for eleven years, serving under three Taoisigh, describes the role, 'you had the ability directly to influence the Taoiseach in regard to policy . . . you have a position of influence rather than a position of power . . . if your advice is sensible he [the Taoiseach] is very likely to accept it'.

The classic BBC series *Yes Minister* illustrated this situation:

> BETTY OLDHAM: Look, Sir Humphrey, whatever we ask the minister, he says is an administrative question for you, and whatever we ask you, you say is a policy question for the minister. How do you suggest we find out what is going on?
>
> SIR HUMPHREY [CIVIL SERVANT]: Yes, yes, yes, I do see that there is a real dilemma here. In that, while it has been government policy to regard policy as a responsibility of ministers and administration as a responsibility of officials, the questions of administrative policy can cause confusion between the policy of administration and the administration of policy, especially when responsibility for the administration of the policy of administration conflicts, or overlaps with, responsibility for the policy of the administration of policy.

Zimmerman (1997) concludes that the policy advice role has declined; the secretary general is primarily a co-ordinator of the activities of the various divisions within the department, and a co-operation model explains the relationship between a minister and a secretary general. In addition, the minister has the services of dedicated political advisers.

The secretary general is also the accounting officer for the department's vote. What this means is that he or she has primary responsibility for the administration of the money voted each year by the Dáil for the department. This is an important exception to the principle of ministerial responsibility. At the end of each year the secretary general must prepare an account, called the appropriation account, showing how the money voted by the Dáil for the department has been spent – in effect to show that it has been properly spent in the manner approved by the Dáil. The secretary general must be satisfied that adequate arrangements exist to ensure the correctness of all payments from the vote under his or her control and the bringing to account of all receipts connected with the vote. This account is presented to the Comptroller and Auditor General and subsequently to the Public Accounts Committee. When the committee is examining the report, the secretary general is the principal witness, who answers the committee's questions and otherwise explains matters as requested.

A significant change has been made to the way in which the personal accountability of secretaries general for their department has been reinforced and made more explicit. The publication of the report of the Working Group on the Accountability of Secretaries General and Accounting Officers (Mullarkey report 2002) put renewed emphasis on the responsibilities of secretaries general as accounting officers and assigned to them a number of specific additional obligations in terms of certifying that robust systems of internal financial control, internal audit, the adoption of risk management strategies, governance arrangements for state bodies reporting to departments and improved management information systems are all put in place. The Mullarkey report (2002: para. 13) notes:

> The working relationship between the secretary general and the minister who is in charge of the department is a key factor in the effective administration of government departments. The constitutional, legislative and administrative framework within which departments operate necessitate that civil servants operating under the authority of the minister implement government policy set by the minister. Within the statutory framework, secretaries general have considerable authority within departments of state subject to the overriding authority of the minister. They have a pivotal role in providing independent advice to the minister and in managing the interface between the department and the minister. In their capacity as managers of departments they have a responsibility to ensure that the systems and procedures are in place to enable

it to perform its functions within the resources available and to enable the minister to answer for the performance of those functions to the Dáil. This requires the minister to place trust and confidence in the secretary general. The distinctive relationship of trust and confidence between the minister and the secretary general is crucial to the effective administration of departments of state and places the secretary general in a different position to other civil servants. The relationship extends beyond the minister and requires the government as a whole to place confidence in the secretary general.

Secretaries general have faced major challenges in recent years, arising from the change programme. New legislation, for example the Public Service Management (Recruitment and Appointments) Act 2004 and the Civil Service Regulation (Amendment) Act 2005, has changed the recruitment processes in the civil service and has led to a more devolved and flexible structure, giving secretaries general managerial responsibility for all matters relating to appointments, performance, discipline and dismissal of civil servants below principal officer level. The Civil Service Regulation (Amendment) Act 2005 introduces significant changes to human resource management procedures in the civil service, particularly in relation to dealing with under-performance.

The Public Service Management Act 1997 requires the preparation of strategy statements by secretaries general in which they specify the key objectives, outputs and related strategies (including the use of resources) to be pursued by their department. The strategy statement must be approved by the relevant minister, who arranges for it to be laid before the Oireachtas. There is also a requirement to prepare progress (annual) reports on its implementation. Since 2007 ministers are required to produce annual output statements:

> The objective in building the concept of outputs into the departmental Strategy Statement and in making them subject to consideration by Oireachtas Committees was to broaden the scope of accountability beyond the focus on inputs to include a greater emphasis on the outputs and performance of public services (Mullarkey report 2002: 28).

As heads of government departments, secretaries general have authority for:

- Managing the department to implement and monitor policy, while achieving agreed outputs.
- Accountability in terms of the financial management of the department.
- Advising on policy.
- Ensuring that arrangements are in place to deal with cross-departmental issues.
- Appointments and discipline.

Secretaries general are accountable to:

- The government.
- Ministers and ministers of state.
- The Public Accounts Committee on voted expenditure.
- Oireachtas committees for policy implementation and value for money.
- The public through strategy statements and customer service standards.

Secretaries general are not immune from being removed from office. In reply to a parliamentary question in 1951 Taoiseach John A. Costello explained that the Secretary [General] of the Department of Social Welfare, D.J. O'Donovan, was removed from office by the government

> . . . for persistent failure to obey instructions properly given to him. These instructions were given to him by the Minister for Social Welfare twice on the 11th January, 1951, and again on the 6th February. They were given to him by me on the 3rd February and again on the 10th February. Finally, the directions were given by the Government as a whole and conveyed to Mr O'Donovan by me on the 12th February. It was not until Mr O'Donovan had made his persistence in his attitude clear, in his reply to the directions from the Government as a whole, that the Government decided, later on the 12th February, that his removal from office was unavoidable (*Dáil Debates*, 21 February 1951, vol. 124).

Former Secretary General of the Department of Health and Children Michael Kelly (2007: 23) recalls his appointment:

> There are few events in life which can match the tsunami of feelings and emotion that goes with such an appointment. There is a sense of pride and achievement, a feeling of honour, an anxiety to succeed, an awesome sense of responsibility, a sense of confidence and optimism about the future and a real sense of urgency about getting on with it and making a start. I interpreted it as a role which required strong leadership, an ability to think through to the future while remaining agile in responding to day to day pressures, an ability to work intensively with and through people and overall, an ability to project a strong sense of direction.

Kelly (2007: 25) notes from personal experience that 'The relationship between a Minister and a Secretary General can be a delicate organism. It thrives on mutual respect, mutual trust and open communication. The absence of any of these attributes on the part of either party to the relationship makes for difficulty. Where none of the prerequisites are present, in either direction, the relationship fails'. The 2005 Travers report on the nursing home charges issue sent shockwaves through the civil service and the Department of Health and Children, with the news that its secretary general, Michael Kelly, was to step down in the wake of the report. Kelly, who had been secretary general for the previous five years, was replaced following criticism in the report of the way the illegal charges issue was handled by the department. A highly respected and talented civil servant, Kelly played a major role in the drawing up of the health strategy and the health reform process. He had a background in human resources and personnel development and was closely associated with the government's modernisation programme, particularly in the area of performance management and in the development of the civil service performance management and development systems.

Work of the Civil Service

The Principle of Accountability

Under the Ministers and Secretaries Act 1924 ministers are responsible for administering their departments and for exercising the powers, duties and functions thereof. The act confers also on the minister, as head of the department, the status of corporation sole, that is perpetual succession enabling the minister, as an office, to sue and be sued, and acquire, hold and dispose of land for the purpose of the powers, duties and functions of the department. These two provisions, taken together, have had the effect that the acts of a department are seen to be the acts of its minister, for which he or she alone is responsible; and that, legally speaking, unless there is an exception provided by law (which there is, for example, in the case of civil servants determining tax liabilities in the Office of the Revenue Commissioners), no civil servant can in law give a decision. In effect, the minister is the department, and his or her civil servants have no separate existence. Every decision made by a government department comes, strictly speaking, from the minister. As it is obvious that ministers cannot personally make all decisions, owing to the demands on their time and the lack of the necessary detailed knowledge, the vast majority of the decisions are in fact made by civil servants. How the system works in practice is that the civil servants' decisions are regarded as being those that the minister would have made had the issues been brought to his or her personal notice. The work is carried on through a system of implicit delegation from the minister to the secretary general of the department and on down through the various grades. Hence the conventional opening phrase in letters from government depart - ments: 'I am directed by the Minister for X to state . . .'.

The system has had a major impact on the way in which the civil service does its work. It is the minister who is answerable to the Dáil and ultimately to the electorate for all the activities of the department; and as the minister may be questioned in the Dáil about them, the discretion and freedom of action of civil servants is limited. As a result, they are often regarded as being over-cautious. This caution arises from their anxiety to ensure that none of their actions/decisions is such as to cause the minister any embarrassment, which could in turn reflect on the individual official. There is, in particular, a need for consistency in dealing with individual cases; and this in turn leads to a reliance on precedents, which may not be quite apt in every instance. The overriding emphasis on equity and impartiality is marked in all aspects of civil service work.

Following a review of the Ministers and Secretaries Act, in the context of a programme of change for the civil service designed to bring about a greater focus on service delivery, performance and the achievement of results, the Public Service Management Act 1997 was enacted. Though this act is founded on the principle of ministerial accountability to the Dáil, it also provides for the formal assignment to the secretary general of authority, responsibility and accountability for carrying out specified functions and duties on behalf of the minister. In turn, there is provision for the secretary general to assign responsibility and accountability for functions to civil servants at other levels within the department. The act also provides for civil servants to appear before parliamentary committees duly authorised to examine the exercise of any such function. These provisions are significant additions to the arrangements in the Ministers and Secretaries Act, which did not provide for the formal assignment of statutory responsibility to secretaries or their subordinates for the exercise of functions on behalf of the minister.

The accountability of the minister to the Dáil and to the public is an integral concern of the daily work of many civil servants. This entails keeping detailed records, taking decisions at a higher level than may appear necessary, documenting discussions and negotiations leading to decisions, carefully drawing up and meticulously observing the rules relating to the making and receipt of payments, and having more centralised arrangements for financial control than are found in the private sector. Commenting on this aspect of the work, FitzGerald (1991: 54) notes, 'I came to appreciate also the commitment to thoroughness which, while sometimes frustrating in the slow tempo it imposes on change, protects the system against egregious error.'

The Department of Finance

Article 17.2 of the Constitution provides that there shall be no public moneys spent unless it has been recommended to the Dáil by a message from the government signed by the Taoiseach. Under the Ministers and Secretaries Act 1924 the role of the Department of Finance is 'the administration and business generally of the public finance of Ireland and all powers, duties and functions connected with the same, including in particular, the collection and expenditure of the revenues of Ireland from whatever source arising'. The department's 2008–10 strategy statement says that its mission is 'To support the achievement of the Government's economic and social objectives by promoting a sound, sustainable economic and budgetary environment, continuing improvements in the efficiency of public services, and an effective framework for financial services.'

The Department of Finance enjoys a prominent position among govern - ment departments. However, each department has a great deal of autonomy, and the Department of Finance, although it can cajole and persuade, cannot order. Policy disagreements between departments have to be resolved at cabinet level. The main divisions in the Department of Finance are: taxation and financial services; budget, economic and pensions; sectoral policy; personnel and remuneration; organisation, management and training; and corporate services. Each year, usually in December, the Minister for Finance presents his or her budget to the Dáil. This sets out the economic prospects for the year ahead and the tax and expenditure changes decided by government.

A large part of the work of the civil service has no commercial counter-part. Drafting and applying legislation, taking measures to protect the environment and making social welfare payments are typical civil service tasks. Government departments are judged not on their profitability but on their social, political, cultural and economic achievements, subject to some overall limitation upon the total demands for taxation. The level of taxation is judged in general terms; it is seldom linked to specific outputs. Increasingly, the efficiency and effectiveness with which departments conduct their business have become important factors in influencing the flow of funds towards them. Departments have found benefit in deploying the kinds of management systems common in the private sector, for example business planning and strategy development. This area is examined in Chapter 13.

In this context, the role of the Department of Finance is crucial in approving the funding for a particular project, initiative or development. Former Finance Minister Alan Dukes (2008) comments:

> There is a room in the Department of Finance on Merrion Street which I called the 'torture chamber' when I was minister for finance during the grim days of the 1980s. This was where we used to bring other ministers and senior officials in order to – literally – sweat down the financial allocations that they felt were due to them. That same room was what other ministers call the 'rogues gallery': pictures on the wall of all ministers for finance up to the present. During my period in the finance hot seat (December 1982 until February 1986) discussions in that room were always difficult and frequently tetchy. I

recall one of my officials questioning what seemed to be a large allocation in the Department of Defence estimate for the purchase of linoleum. The sharp reply came back from the other side of the table: 'Soldiers wear heavy boots'. There was silence for a moment, followed by laughter. But the allocation was then reduced.

Each year, I would produce a list of proposals for expenditure reductions putting the most objectionable ones first in the (mostly vain) hope that colleagues would finally opt for those with which they felt the least discomfort. For a couple of years, that was known as the 'sell the Asgard' list, for the obvious reason. One year, I changed tack and put a proposal to sell the Government jet at the top (tongue firmly in cheek, as I was a frequent user of it myself). Pat Cooney, then minister for defence, neatly snookered me by immediately agreeing, knowing that the Taoiseach and other colleagues would not permit it for perfectly good reasons of efficiency.

Former Finance Minister Ruairí Quinn (2005: 7–8) describes 'An elaborate process of bargaining, begun initially at departmental level but which, ultimately, became face-to-face encounters between the line minister and the Minister for Finance – encounters which always took place in the Department of Finance. It was, from a psychological and negotiating point of view, important for the Minister for Finance to be in control of the venue.' Kelly (2007: 24) notes, 'the annual estimates cycle was a very poor mechanism for achieving strategic change, although it had considerable strengths in copperfastening the role of the Department of Finance in controlling the volume of public spending'. Lee (1989: 345) notes that 'The Finance perspective was even more myopic than that of the politicians, who at least often looked as far ahead as the next election. Finance gave the impression that it rarely looked beyond the next budget'. In relation to the attitude of the Department of Finance, Fanning (1978: 595) observes:

> A fine disregard for the Department's image, a willingness to court unpopularity – these are among the hallmarks of the Department of Finance and we can hardly improve, in ending our discussion of Finance's relations with other departments, upon that quotation from an ex-secretary of the Treasury with which Dr Whitaker concluded his study of 'The Finance Attitude': 'if at any moment it should become popular the fact itself would be conclusive proof that it was not properly fulfilling the task for which it exists'.

Basic Functions

The civil service has two main tasks: to assist ministers in the making of policy, and to carry out policy decisions. Policy formulation means analysing the problems that exist, defining the issues they present and finding out how they should be dealt with. Among the range of major issues to which civil servants have addressed themselves in recent years are: keeping beaches free from pollution; amendment of the criminal justice laws; the welfare of children; neutrality; and changes in secondary education.

Having thoroughly examined all aspects of the problems laid before them, civil servants then inform their ministers of the various alternatives open to them, making a recommendation as to which should be selected. Thus, the decision of the minister is considerably influenced by what has gone on before. The calibre of mind that civil servants bring to their appraisal of the facts of a specific problem influences, and often determines, the character of the minister's decision. The nature and importance of the policy-making process illustrate the necessity for civil servants to have ability, professional knowledge, integrity and independence of thought. Generally ministers have a relationship with their advisers in which no one feels restrained from freely expressing their views. FitzGerald (1991: 301) notes:

> . . . civil servants rightly consider it to be their duty to advise ministers fully of the possible adverse consequences of proposed political decisions; they would be failing in their duty were they to do otherwise. It is also humanly understandable that they should often tend to feel that the status quo, the product largely of their own and their predecessors' efforts, has a certain merit and deserves to be preserved unless very cogent arguments are put forward for altering it. Some resistance to change is thus to be expected from the civil service, each department of which tends to have its own attachment to policies developed in the past.

When decisions are taken, civil servants at all levels seek faithfully to implement them, irrespective of whether they accord with the advice given. The situation is neatly expressed in the well-worn phrase 'minister on top, civil servant on tap'. The relationship between a civil servant and a minister is one in which the former is publicly silent and the latter generally has little to say. Ruairí Quinn (2005: 192) mentions an example, in relation to the restoration of the Custom House, of how 'the permanent staff could harness the enthusiasm of a temporary office-holder to achieve success with projects that had been stalled'. In the course of civil servants' work in advising ministers and in seeing that decisions are implemented, the types of task are many and varied.

Civil servants are almost always invariably present when ministers meet to do official business. They are there when ministers meet outsiders officially. They accompany ministers to take a note at outside meetings and debrief those who need to know. There are good practical reasons for this. In a long, busy day it is not always easy to remember who said what to whom and what ministers wanted done. There are always people ready to put an unattractive gloss on a conversation, and a note written at the time can be used to refute this robustly. The minister's office controls the minister's diary and expects to know – with discretion – where a minister is and how to contact him or her at any time. A smoothly functioning minister's office is a great asset to any minister and is, in many ways, the nerve centre of the department, through which a huge amount of information flows between the minister and the department. The constituency/private office deals with the queries and requests that inevitably arise as ministers are approached by all sorts of people in their political and personal lives.

The Travers report (2005) analysed the way that charges for long-term care in institutions was managed within the Department of Health and made the following recommendations on civil service practices and procedures:

1. *Legal Basis.* Get the legal basis for decisions right.
2. *Analytical Capability.* Ensure that the analytical input into important decisions taken at the level of department, minister and government is commensurate with the policy and operational importance of the decisions being taken.
3. *Transparency.* Ensure that briefings for ministers on important issues of policy or operation are comprehensive, fully inclusive of all relevant facts and adequately recorded.
4. *Records.* Ensure at least a *de minimis* recording of decisions at official level and ministerial level within the department
5. *Risk Assessment.* Ensure a practical and effective system of risk assessment covering operational, legal and financial issues in relation to all areas of activity in the department.
6. *Decision Making.* Ensure that decisions are taken and recorded in a clear, transparent and timely way. Avoid the temptation to put important issues where decisions are required into an 'in process' mode. Bring reviews of policy and operational issues to a clear conclusion and record decisions taken and their rationale.
7. *Issues of Singular Importance.* Isolate issues of singular importance that have significant operational, legal, financial or wider social and economic (including political) implications and deal decisively with them.
8. *Issues of Political Sensitivity.* Be aware of issues of political sensitivity. Be responsive in dealing with them but do not allow issues of political sensitivity to compromise the integrity of the analysis undertaken and brought forward, the options for any associated decisions that require to be taken or the full articulation of the likely consequences of alternative decisions.
9. *Internal Organisation.* Rebuild the MAC (the department's top management group – the management advisory committee) as a cohesive, effective

and positive force of operational management, policy development and organisational leadership in the department. The MAC should also be the pivot of internal and external communication in relation to the management and operational activities of a department, which have an immense influence on the quality of life of many citizens and their perception of the public service.

10. *Logging/Recording of File Movements.* Put in place an effective and easily accessible logging system for recording the establishment and movement of all files (electronic and paper) and the periodic and timely review of 'files in process' until they are brought to appropriate conclusion.

11. *Ministerial Input.* Ministers should seek assurance that the management and administration of the department encompasses the fairly minimalist procedures and practices set out in the points listed above. They should probe, in an insightful and effective way, areas of policy implementation, operations and administrative difficulty – using an external source of review if considered necessary. Ministers should insist on full and periodic briefings on key issues of policy and operational performance.

Legislation

When legislation is needed to implement some new policy or to change an existing policy, one of the senior officials in the field of work where the new measures are to be taken usually has the task of preparing a background memorandum setting out why the legislation is necessary; why the present position in regard to the matter at issue is regarded as unsatisfactory; what benefits will accrue from passing the legislation (and what disadvantages, if any); what parties or activities are likely to be affected and in what respects; what changes will be required in existing cognate activities as a result of the new legislation; what the cost will be, and so on.

When the proposals have been approved by the minister and by the government, the civil servant then attends on the Attorney General during their drafting into the form of a bill for presentation to the government and subsequently to the Dáil or Seanad. The civil servant prepares the speeches that the minister delivers during the various stages of the bill, and waits on the minister during all stages of the debates. He or she takes notes on the points made by members, arranges for the inclusion in the bill of any amendments accepted, and prepares the minister's concluding speech, which deals with the various points raised.

When legislation has been passed by the Oireachtas (or otherwise when decisions have been taken by the government) requiring the introduction of new schemes or changes to existing schemes, a number of consequential matters have to be considered. These might include staffing, publicity, forms and procedures, discussions with bodies and groups who will be affected, and systems to provide management information.

Meetings Abroad

Over the last forty years or so civil servants have increasingly taken part in the work of numerous international organisations, most notably the European Union. Attendance at meetings abroad is now a feature of the work of many civil servants, mainly those at middle and senior levels. As far as possible, attendance is shared evenly among those engaged on a particular aspect of their department's work, and staff transfers take account of the desirability of providing this type of experience for as many persons as possible. The EU process involves the representatives of national governments in the preparatory and decision-making functions of the Council of Ministers. Officials from the Departments of Foreign Affairs, Finance, Agriculture, Enterprise and Environment frequently attend meetings in Brussels (and officials of the other departments less regularly). There they advance the views and interests of their departments and respond to initiatives from others.

In a typical instance the European Commission initially invites member countries, in effect officials from the departments concerned, to bilateral discussions on some proposal it hopes to put forward for the ultimate approval of the Council of Ministers. Examples of such proposals include the revision of the Common Agricultural Policy or the provision for EU-wide recognition of architects. After the bilateral discussions a draft regulation or directive is examined, first by a working group consisting of officials of the member states, and then by higher level committees – the Special Committee on Agriculture if it is of an agricultural nature, and the Committee of Permanent Representatives (COREPER) when it relates to any other issue – which seek to resolve any conflicts. This involvement in a wide range of issues for debate at EU level, as well as the scope for 'package deals', calls for co-ordination and agreement at national level. Overall co-ordination is achieved through a committee of senior officials from the departments concerned, meeting frequently in Dublin.

During the period of the Irish presidency of the EU in 2004 Irish officials served as chairpersons of over three thousand working groups. The work calls for a thorough knowledge of the subject matter and for the negotiating and diplomatic experience necessary to know when to stand firm, when to concede and when to support an alternative viewpoint.

Changes in the Work of the Civil Service

Consultants

There has been a significant increase in the number of external consultancies used by the civil service. Government departments engage the services of external consultants because of a lack of in-house skills or expertise or because there are insufficient in-house resources to complete a task in the time available. In other cases, external consultants are used because of a need for an independent or objective view or because external bodies require their use. In a 1978 letter to Taoiseach Jack Lynch concerning Dublin Corporation's plans to build on the Viking site at Wood Quay, T. K. Whitaker noted, 'In a matter of such significance, I would not rely on internal advice alone even in Finance, you will remember we always consulted outside experts before taking major decisions.' In reply to a parliamentary question on consultancies in the civil service on 30 November 2005, Taoiseach Bertie Ahern agreed that there is a trend across departments of using more consultancies and explained:

> The procurement of consultancy services in my Department is subject to the public procurement guidelines of the Department of Finance and they are set out in the Guidelines for Engagement of Consultants in the Civil Service of 1999. Procurement of outside expertise in the public relations field is also subject to public procurement guidelines as set out in the 2004 Department of Finance publication and the Public Procurement Guidelines Competitive Process, which replaced the previous Department of Finance guidelines entitled Public Procurement 1994 Edition – Green Book. That is the basis by which all contracts are governed. Any contract must fulfil those regulations, and the section, the Accounting Officer and the financial people in each Department must satisfy the arrangements as set out in those documents.
>
> In addition, the procurement of these services is also subject to the applicable EU procurement rules and guidelines. Since early this year additional guidelines have been specifically put in place for communications consultancies and that is now incorporated into the Cabinet handbook. Most recently a number of new measures were announced which will contribute to improving the management and value for money aspects of consultancies. On the Department of Finance guidelines for engagement of consultants, the way we operate these in my Department is we try to avoid needing consultants in the first place. These are the two circumstances in which we would get outside consultants: where we do not have the relevant specialists in the Department and where we think the work concerned requires an independent evaluation of the way we are doing it, or where it is questioned and we believe, for internal audit or other purposes, that maybe there is another way.
>
> My Department is relatively sparing in this regard. We use consultancies where the expertise is not available within the Department; where something additional is involved, as was the case with the EU Presidency, the change

management agenda where someone is brought in to advise, or where an independent assessment is needed, as has happened in only a few cases. On the Deputy's question as to whether there are more consultancies, with regard to the level, scale and examination of decisions made, whether by the House, Oireachtas committees or the outside world, increasingly, public servants, including those in my Department will consider getting the assessments and the analysis of would-be experts. The Deputy and I might often argue whether they are experts. I detect that people are becoming more protective and are watching what they do to a greater extent than was the case some years ago. Whether that is good is open to debate, but it is happening. It is not that the money is wasted, but the nature of decisions and the fact that we have an increasing number of regulators with whom Departments find themselves in debate mean that Departments must be armed with more sophisticated replies than they believe they can produce. The complexity of our work and its sheer size with the complexity of its examination have led to a different position than has previously been the case.

A value for money report by the Comptroller and Auditor General in 1998 found that 'While the use of external consultancies by government departments had increased significantly, the amount of information available about the nature and cost of consultancies and the reasons why they were commissioned was limited'. The report presents the findings of an examination that set out to gather information about consultancies undertaken by all government departments in the period 1994 to 1996. In this three-year period almost one thousand consultancies were commissioned by government departments, and at a cost of €80 million. In his report to the Dáil, the Comptroller and Auditor General said that 60 per cent of consultancies were commissioned due to a lack of in-house skills in departments and state offices. 'Departments and offices should assess the impact of consultancies on their operations after a suitable lapse of time. This was rarely done in a meaningful way, with the result that the effectiveness of spending on most consultancies was not established.' The Comptroller and Auditor General did not find, in any of thirty-four consultancies examined in detail, a formal written business case setting out the objectives, expected benefits and estimated cost of the consultancy. 'The examination found very little documentary evidence that departments gave due consideration to the likely cost-effectiveness of the use of consultants.'

The Quigley report of an inquiry into procurement (Government of Ireland 2005) found no evidence of inappropriate actions regarding the matter. The report to the Taoiseach made recommendations for improvements in the procurement procedures, and additional procedures were approved by the government for incorporation into the Cabinet Handbook. These procedures gave the Secretary General to the Government and the government secretariat a role in examining certain procurements. The report said that special care is needed where a contract provides for services to both a minister and a department. It recommended that the Department of Finance review the guidelines dating from 1999 with regard to the engagement of consultants, especially in the context of single tendering arrangements where 'urgency' is stated as the ground for proceeding.

FitzGerald (2003: 101) notes that 'Whilst it will, of course, always be necessary for the Civil Service to draw on outside talent for some very specialised tasks, the extent to which almost all departmental economic analysis, even of a relatively straightforward character, is now shipped out to enormously expensive consultants is very disturbing, and adds hugely to the cost of administration, as well as slowing down the decision-making process'.

In reply to a series of parliamentary questions in July 2008, ten government departments revealed that the total spending on external consultants was €20 million in 2007.

Cross-Departmental Working

The structure of the Irish administrative system is not well suited to the management of issues that cross the remits of single government departments or offices. Responsibility and accountability, politically and administratively, are rooted in departmental focus. Lee (1989: 635) notes that 'government departments are fragmented within and between themselves'. Des O'Malley commented that, as Minister for Industry and Commerce, although his department was 'only across the street from the Department of Agriculture in Dublin, they might as well be a thousand miles apart because of the very little coordination that goes on between them' (*The Irish Times*, 10 March 1986). The purpose of section 12 of the Public Service Management Act 1997 is to provide, as necessary, for the assignment by ministers or ministers of state of responsibility to civil servants for cross-departmental issues and the associated accountability arrangements. The act also requires, under section 4, that the heads of departments and offices ensure that appropriate arrangements are put in place to facilitate an effective response to these issues. Issues of policy, of course, cross departmental boundaries and there is a need to identify new ways of managing such issues more effectively in the future. The departmental strategy statements approved by ministers and laid before the Dáil have identified a number of cross-departmental issues arising. The Strategic Management Initiative (SMI) Implementation Group was asked by the Taoiseach to consider appropriate action in relation to cross-departmental issues.

The Irish system has made some efforts to adapt to the changing requirements of cross-cutting issues, for instance, in relation to the care of children, a minister of state has been appointed with a remit across a number of departments. After the 2002 general election Brian Lenihan Jnr was appointed minister of state with special responsibility for children's issues across three government departments (Health, Justice and Education). In December 2005 the government created the new Office of the Minister for Children (OMC) under Lenihan's direction as Minister for Children. This means that all those in government whose job it is to look after the interests of children are now working under one roof in a co-ordinated and integrated effort to deliver the best possible services for children. The Minister for Children, as a super-junior minister, attends cabinet meetings, thereby ensuring that the interests of children are taken into account in an unprecedented manner across all areas of government.

The OMC is an integral part of the Department of Health and Children. The OMC units that are part of the department include the Childcare Directorate (formerly part of the Department of Justice) and the National Children and Young People's Strategy Unit (formerly the National Children's Office). Two other units are co-located with the OMC, but continue to report to and be part of their parent departments: Irish Youth Justice Service (Department of Justice) and the Early Years Education Policy Unit (Department of Education). This co-location allows people to work side by side and provide an integrated government approach to the development of policy and delivery of services for children. It brings a cohesive approach to the delivery of services based on the recognition that they are fundamentally inter-linked and must be responded to on this basis to secure the best outcomes for children and young people.

The Minister for Children is at the cabinet table, and there is a cabinet committee on social inclusion and children. The Director General of the OMC attends the management advisory committee meetings of three departments (Health, Education and Justice). In addition, there is a senior officials group on social inclusion. As part of the *Towards 2016* social partnership agreement there is a national implementation group, chaired by the OMC, involving representatives of the relevant departments, the Health Service Executive (HSE), local authorities, the education sector and other key agencies as required, which will link with an expert advisory group on children being established by the HSE. The national implementation group has asked that a cross-departmental business plan be developed.

The result has been joined-up and better delivery of services. At local level multi-agency children's committees are being established within each of the city/county development boards. These mirror the composition of the national implementation group. County-level plans are being developed. These committees will be chaired by the HSE, which is best placed to drive this initiative to achieve co-ordinated and integrated services. The establishment of effective systems and strategies to enable the OMC to meet commitments under the National Children's Strategy is a key challenge in the initial strategic timeframe, which is set to conclude in 2010.

Another example is the proposal to move Galway port to Rossaveal in south Connemara as part of an integrated city development approach, where assistant secretaries of the five departments involved (Transport, Agriculture, Environment, Finance, and Community, Rural and Gaeltacht Affairs) are investigating the options.

One of the reasons for poor cross-departmental co-ordination 'may be the fact that there are no rewards for working across traditional departmental boundaries, e.g. working in inter-departmental working groups is seen as an additional responsibility without commensurate rewards' (Timonen *et al.* 2003: 54). In order to facilitate the examination of cross-departmental policy issues by Oireachtas committees, the government announced that responsibility would be assigned to a committee to take on an issue with a procedure to allow other relevant committees to contribute.

Speaking at the Institute of Public Administration's national conference in 2008, Taoiseach Brian Cowen said the government had begun to:

> . . . find new ways of working, coordinating, influencing within and beyond the public system. We have already begun to do this – many of my Ministers of State now have responsibility for cross-cutting issues such as Integration, Children and Youth Affairs, Older People and Lifelong Learning. In allocating responsibilities, I have ensured that key policy areas can be afforded the necessary level of attention that they require. I intend that these appointments should be seen as important signals to the public service system.

Social Partnership

Social partnership arrangements have created a new dynamic in the system of government. Social partnership describes an approach to government where interest groups outside of elected representatives play an active role in decision taking and policy making. It is a responsive and evolving process, an important aspect of which is ensuring wide and appropriate involvement. This form of participative democracy enables the social partners to enter discussions with government on a range of social and economic issues and to reach a consensus on policy. The Department of the Taoiseach is respon - sible for the overall negotiations and implementation of the social partnership agreements, of which the seventh is *Towards 2016, Ten-Year Framework Social Partnership Agreement 2006–2015*, and is pivotal to the co-ordination of the social partnership agreements. Secretaries general of that department have combined the role of Secretary to the Government with that of Chairperson of the National Economic and Social Council (NESC), throughout successive changes of government. Social partnership is, in this sense, embedded in the core of the governmental process. Indeed, Hardiman (2005: 21) notes, 'Moreover, there have been a number of occasions on which governments have made exceptional efforts to rescue social partnership agreements when they seemed to be in trouble, or indeed to get them off the ground when the negotiation of a new agreement has stalled. The encouraging appearance of the Taoiseach at a timely moment has more than once proved helpful in overcoming difficulties.'

Each of the social partnership agreements – which are focused principally on incomes, fiscal, social, economic and competitiveness policies – have been negotiated between the government and the social partners. The latter are organised into four pillars: a trade union pillar; a business and employer pillar; a farming pillar; and a community and voluntary pillar (included for first time in negotiations on *Partnership 2000*). The negotiations on each of the social partnership agreements were preceded by the production of frameworks agreed under the auspices of the NESC, which in 2005 noted a shift towards 'a more devolved participative and inclusive system of government'. The implementation of the agreements is achieved primarily through the production of quarterly progress reports.

Since 1987, partnerships helped Ireland escape from the economic crisis of the 1980s by delivering agreement on the need for fiscal correction and modest wage growth. The success of the first partnership programme prompted the government and the social partners to enter further agreements. The partnership approach delivered and reflected a shared understanding of the key mechanisms in the economy. Whelan and Masterson (1998: 62) note:

> The partnership approach quickly had a knock-on effect throughout the government. Ministers who were not inside the cabinet loop on social consensus soon realised that their individual ministerial priorities accounted for nothing unless they were within the parameters of the national programme. Finance Ministers hoping to make their mark also quickly discovered that their style was cramped with up to 90 per cent of their annual budgets written up through measures agreed in the partnership process.

One senior civil servant remarked that the social partners 'are now a more powerful influence in the policy process, to the extent that some politicians feel that trade unionists, for example, have more power than backbenchers. It would be unthinkable to set up a task force or policy committee of any seriousness or weight without social partner representation' (quoted in O'Donnell and Thomas 1998: 126). In December 2008 the government presented its renewal plan to the social partners before either House of the Oireachtas was informed of its contents.

NATIONAL PAY DEALS

1. Programme for National Recovery, 1987
2. Programme for Economic and Social Progress, 1991–1993
3. Programme for Competitiveness and Work, 1994–1996
4. Partnership 2000, 1997–2000
5. Programme for Prosperity and Fairness, 2000–2002
6. Sustaining Progress, 2003–2005
7. Towards 2016, 2006–2008
8. New pay deal negotiated in September 2008

Partnership works when the partners focus on their long-term interests and the wider national interest. Co-ordinated bargaining provides business, government, employees and others with a degree of certainty to pursue these interests. When conducted with skill, deliberation, interaction and negotiation it can help to create the climate and conditions to achieve significant economic progress.

The significant increase in the number of agencies and other bodies involved in public administration requires a greater emphasis on the civil service working together with other organisations in a system of mutual interdependence and joint problem solving. O'Donnell (2001: 14) comments:

> The proliferation of partnership bodies is identified as a problem by almost all participants. Another difficulty identified by many commentators has been the democratic deficit: social partnership, at times, seemed to replace the Dáil as the focal point for decision-making. Perhaps the most important problem identified is the inadequacy of monitoring arrangements in the partnership system. Although the partners pressed for the creation of monitoring arrangements, in private they admit the limitations of a system in which they interrogate civil servants on the progress of a wide range of initiatives.

Code of Conduct

Integrity

The Ethics in Public Office Act 1995 and the Standards in Public Office Act 2001 introduced measures in the areas of disclosure of interests and conduct of public officials. Under the Prevention of Corruption (Amendment) Act 2001 corruption is presumed where there is proof that certain persons in public office have received money or other benefits from a person who has an interest in the outcome of decisions, including planning decisions.

Civil servants are bound by the Prevention of Corruption Act 2001, which updated the old Corruption Acts 1889 to 1916. These provide penalties for corrupt acceptance of any gift, consideration or advantage as rewards or inducements for doing or not doing some act or for showing favour or disfavour in relation to the business of the department. The use of official information for private gain is also regarded as a corrupt practice. In addition to their statutory obligations, civil servants are expected to preserve a proper sense of integrity in all their work, whether in relation to their advisory or their executive role. Section 5 of the Standards in Public Office Act 2001 provides for immunity for whistle blowing where a person makes a complaint in good faith to the Standards in Public Office Commission.

The Ethics in Public Office Act 1995 requires senior civil servants to make written statements on an annual basis in respect of personal interests that could materially influence them in the performance of their official duties.

A code of standards and behaviour for the civil service was published by the Standards in Public Office Commission in 2004. The code applies to all staff (i.e. established and unestablished civil servants) whether full-time or employed on an atypical basis (i.e. temporary or part-time). The civil service differentiates between 'established' and 'unestablished' staff. Under the Civil Service Regulation Act 1956 an established civil servant means a civil servant who is rendering established service. A temporary appointment cannot be made to an established post, and the two categories have separate pay and pension schemes.

The main features of the 2004 code of standards and behaviour can be summarised as:

- Civil servants must be impartial in the performance of their duties.
- Civil servants are not permitted to stand for general or European elections. However, civil servants in the craft and state industrial-related grades are free to engage in political activity and stand for local elections.
- Civil servants must respect the constraints of the law.
- Under the Freedom of Information Acts 1997 to 2003 members of the public have a legal right to information held by government departments and other public bodies. However, the requirement under the Official Secrets Act 1963 that civil servants avoid improper disclosure of information gained in the course of their work still applies.
- Civil servants must maintain high standards of service in all of their dealings with the public.
- Civil servants who are convicted of criminal offences, or given the benefit of the Probation Act when tried for a criminal offence, must report that fact to their personnel officer.

- Civil servants are required to attend at work as required and to comply with the terms of sick leave regulations.
- Civil servants are required to have due regard for state resources to ensure proper, effective and efficient use of public money.
- Civil servants should show due respect to their colleagues, including their beliefs and values.
- The use of their official positions by civil servants to benefit themselves or others with whom they have personal or business ties is not allowed.
- Civil servants are forbidden to seek to influence decisions on matters pertaining to their official positions other than through established procedures.
- Civil servants may not engage in outside business or activities that would in any way conflict with the interests of their departments/offices.
- Civil servants who occupy 'designated positions' for the purposes of the ethics acts have certain statutory obligations in relation to disclosure of interests, which are additional to the code's obligations.
- Civil servants should not receive benefits of any kind from a third party that might reasonably be seen to compromise their personal judgment or integrity. Departments are required to apply the rules contained in the code on the receipt of gifts or to make local rules deriving from them.
- The same principle applies to any acceptance of hospitality. Within the general framework of guidelines set out in the code, every care must be taken to ensure that (a) any acceptance of hospitality does not influence, or be seen to influence, the discharging of official functions and (b) that there are clear and appropriate standards in place, which have been notified to all staff, in relation to payment for work on behalf of outside bodies.
- Civil servants must not seek contracts with government departments or offices for supply of goods or services whether for their own benefit or for the benefit of any company with which they may have an involvement in a private capacity.
- Civil servants shall not accept an appointment, or particular consultancy project, where the civil servant concerned believes that the nature and terms of such appointment could lead to a conflict of interest or the perception of such, without first obtaining the approval of the Outside Appointments Board, or secretary general/head of office, as appropriate.
- Additionally, civil servants who hold positions which are 'designated positions' for the purposes of the ethics acts must, within twelve months of resigning or retiring, obtain the approval of the Outside Appointments Board or the secretary general/head of office, as appropriate, before taking up any outside appointment.

It must be noted, however, that the fundamental concept of public service has for some years been in a state of change, reflecting the general atmosphere of change prevalent throughout Irish society as a whole. The old conventional practices such as the unquestioning acceptance of rules and regulations and the instinctive obedience to authority are now being challenged in a way unthinkable to previous generations of civil servants. Former certainties now seem less well established and increasingly irrelevant, and changing values and priorities are giving rise to new and less restrictive attitudes regarding what is right, important and acceptable in the conduct of public affairs.

Confidentiality

Obligations in respect of confidentiality derive from the Official Secrets Act 1963, which prohibits civil servants from communicating official information unless authorised to do so. Such information includes not only documentary material such as papers, minutes, briefs, letters and so on, but views, comments and advice acquired or transmitted verbally. The prohibition also applies to those who have retired, in relation to information to which they had access before retirement. Further, a civil servant may not publish without the agreement of the head of the department any material touching on the business of that or any other department. To a certain extent, no doubt, this accounts for the paucity of written information generally available on the workings of government departments, although this situation has improved in recent years. It also largely accounts for the fact that serving civil servants are very rarely heard on radio or television programmes discussing matters for which their departments are responsible.

Party Politics

Civil servants have a duty to provide recommendations and policy advice. The decision on what to do remains the minister's or the cabinet's, depending upon the degree of importance. To enhance that advice, civil servants have to be independent of party politics. As Kevin O'Higgins put it in the 1920s, 'Those who take the pay and wear the uniform of the state, be they soldiers or police, must be the non-political servants of the state' (De Vere White 1948: 165).

The rules on this subject are of very long standing. Their purpose is, generally speaking, to prohibit civil servants from participating in party politics. They originally applied to every civil servant but were modified in the 1970s along the lines indicated below, following representations from some staff associations. Essentially, the argument of the associations was that all civil servants, because of their experience of the administrative machine, are particularly well qualified for service in parliament; and that it is inconsistent with the natural rights of civil servants as citizens, and harmful to the public interest, if they are not allowed to offer themselves for this other form of public service and to serve the community in another capacity, without being expected to sacrifice their career, security of employment and pension rights. They pointed to the practice in a number of other member states of the European Union, where even senior civil servants are allowed to pursue political activities, including standing for parliament, and where civil servants there may resume their posts if unsuccessful in an election or when they wish to retire from parliament.

Successive governments and the Department of Finance, on the other hand, have long been apprehensive of the results of civil servants playing an active role in party politics. They point out that it is in the public interest that civil servants should be politically impartial and that confidence in their impartiality is an essential part of the structure of government in Ireland.

The modification referred to above permits clerical staff, analogous grades in the technical area and industrial workers to engage in politics (though not to stand for election to the Oireachtas), subject to the proviso that the permission could be revoked in the case of officers engaged in a particular category of work. Civil servants engaged in the framing of policy proposals remain completely barred from political activity. In practice, this means the executive, middle and senior grades. Civil servants in these grades seem, in general, happy with the present position, and there are no apparent moves to change it. They rarely discuss party politics, and the vast majority of civil servants do not know how their colleagues vote at elections. They tend to be very critical of the occasional colleague who may be seen to be overtly political. Civil servants in Ireland display a total loyalty to the minister of the day, no matter what party he or she belongs to.

Outside Occupations

Those in technical grades such as engineer, doctor or solicitor are prohibited from engaging in private practice or from having connections with outside business. In other cases, civil servants are not actually prohibited from taking on other work for remuneration outside office hours, for example teaching or taking part in a business. They are, however, obliged to ensure that any outside business activities do not conflict with their official duties and are not of such a nature as to hinder the proper performance of such duties. (Thus, a civil servant would probably be debarred from doing any work for a firm with which his or her department did business.) Where there is any doubt, an officer is obliged to reveal the position to the secretary general of the department and to abide by the latter's decision on the matter. In reply to a parliamentary question in May 2008, Taoiseach Brian Cowen said he favoured a buffer zone of 'some months' before civil servants can take up employment in related areas in the private sector.

Employment Arrangements

Pay

Following a decision by the government on the implementation of recommendations in the report of the Review Body on Higher Remuneration in the Public Sector in 2000, a revised scheme of performance-related awards was introduced for assistant secretaries and deputy secretaries in the civil service. The role of the review body is to make recommendations on appropriate rates of pay for those posts that come within its terms of reference. It has no role in relation to the assessment of the performance of individuals. The Committee for Performance Awards was established in November 2001 to oversee the performance-related award scheme. It comprises the Secretaries General of the Departments of Finance and the Taoiseach and three other members who are not civil servants. It ensures that overall guidelines are adhered to, objectives are clear and the approach is consistent across departments.

Civil servants generally have pay scales that provide for a number of annual increments. There are long scales for the basic recruitment grades (with up to fourteen points in some cases); medium-length scales for those in the middle grades (about seven points); and short scales for lower grades and for grades at the higher levels (three in the case of paper-keepers and assistant secretaries). Level three comprises the other secretaries general. The system of increments is designed to provide incentives, and before an increment is granted the head of the department or someone on his or her behalf (usually the head of the personnel section) must certify that the officer has worked satisfactorily during the preceding year.

Secretaries general have flat salaries. The salary rates for secretaries general are divided into three levels of salary to reflect differences in job weights and responsibilities. The Secretary General of the Department of Finance and the Secretary General of the Department of the Taoiseach/ Secretary General to the Government are paid at level one. The Secretaries General of the Departments of Agriculture, Communications, Education, Enterprise, Environment, Foreign Affairs, Health, Justice, Social Affairs and Transport and the Chairperson of the Revenue Commissioners are all paid at level two.

The civil service is divided into broad groups for the purpose of determining pay. The first and largest group is that comprehended within the conciliation scheme for the civil service. This scheme embraces those having salary scales up to the maximum of principal. The arbitrator is normally a lawyer and is appointed by the Minister for Finance after consultation with the staff associations. The second largest group is that of the industrial workers, whose rates are dealt with by a joint industrial council under the aegis of the Labour Court. The smallest group contains those with salaries higher than principal. Recommendations on the pay of this group are made to the government by the Review Body on Higher Remuneration in the Public Sector. The ultimate decision on matters of pay rests with the government, but in practice the rates are fixed by the Minister for Finance.

The pay structure in the civil service is much less flexible than the pay arrangements in ordinary commercial employment. The Public Service Benchmarking Body, established under the *Programme for Prosperity and Fairness*, was asked to undertake a fundamental examination of the pay of public service employees vis-à-vis the private sector. The benchmarking process was developed as an alternative to the previous system for determining public sector pay, which was based on individual claims and relativities. The report of the body was published in July 2002 and recommended varying levels of pay increases for the grades examined. It covered all the major groups in the public service (apart from top posts dealt with by the Review Body on Higher Remuneration in the Public Sector), including administrative and clerical grades, the gardaí, teachers, nurses, other health professionals and members of the Defence Forces. Public servants received an average increase of over 8 per cent in addition to pay rises under the national agreements. The pay of approximately 230,000 public servants was affected by the report. A subsequent report of the Public Service Benchmarking Body was published on 21 December 2007. It recommended pay increases for just fifteen out of the 109 grades that it examined. To the anger of public service unions, the report found that most teachers, nurses, gardaí and health workers did not merit pay increases.

In reply to a parliamentary question on 30 January 2008 Tánaiste and Minister for Finance Brian Cowen succinctly stated public service pay policy as follows, 'Public service pay must develop in a manner that is consistent with competitiveness, price stability and budgetary policy. Government policy on public service pay is that the public service should be in a position to attract and retain its fair share of good quality staff at all levels. It should neither lead the market nor trail it.'

Promotion

Promotions are technically regarded as appointments and are, therefore, governed by the Ministers and Secretaries Act 1924 and, as already indicated, made by the minister in charge of the department concerned. Promotions to the more senior posts also require the concurrence of the Minister for Finance. Where promotions are not done in the customary way, i.e. in the normal grade-to-grade progression, the approval of the Public Appointments Service must be obtained; such promotions are very rare.

The principle is accepted that those seeking promotion should be selected on merit. Before an officer is promoted, the head of the department must certify not only that the person is fully qualified for the vacant position but that he or she is the best qualified of all those eligible. Until recent years it had been left to the head of each department to select the most meritorious persons for promotion to vacancies occurring in that department. Increasingly, however, particularly in the general service grades, the net is being cast wider than the officers serving in the department where the vacancy exists. Thus, for promotion to the clerical officer grade about one-quarter of the vacancies arising are filled from inter-departmental competition; and for the executive, higher executive, assistant principal and principal grades nearly one-half of the vacancies are so filled.

The modernisation programme outlined in the *Sustaining Progress* partnership agreement contained a number of important measures designed to improve promotion procedures. In particular, the agreement commits the civil service to 'greater use of competitive, merit-based promotions within Departments'. In 2003 a cross-departmental group of assistant secretaries examined the area of competitive promotions within departments in light of best practice in Ireland and elsewhere, and considered the steps that should be taken by departments to meet the commitments in this regard. The group recommended that the personnel officers' network, in consultation with the Public Appointments Service, should draw up detailed guidelines on appropriate competitive processes to strengthen the internal promotions systems in operation in departments. Under *Towards 2016* two in nine vacancies at principal level and one in five at assistant principal level must be filled by open recruitment. Eligible civil servants may apply for open competitions in the same way as other applicants. The promotion procedures used within the civil service are in line with international best practice.

In December 2003 the equality officer upheld a claim of discrimination on the grounds of age and directed the Department of Health to ensure that internal interview boards have formal interview training, apply strict promotion criteria with adequate marking schemes and keep comprehensive interview notes. The equality officer further directed the department to cease its policy of promotion by consistory and introduce an objective and transparent mechanism that allows all applicants to be considered on their own merits. The consistory, which takes its name from the process of cardinals gathering to select a pope, involves the management team coming together to decide on promotions rather than having an open competition. Previously, promotion conferences were held in private and the head of each unit recommended staff members for promotion to the management committee, which is chaired by the secretary general of the department. In a landmark ruling in *An Employee v A Government Department* (DEC – E2008–04) in February 2008 the Equality Tribunal found the civil service system of promotion was 'discriminatory' and 'lacking transparency'. It said that the method of management choosing candidates behind closed doors has created 'an environment where discrimination can exist'. The tribunal's ruling obliged authorities to adopt a more transparent process and to make changes to the 'consistory method of promotion which has existed in the civil service since the year dot'. The ruling said that 'adequate records must be retained in order to demonstrate that the selection process is free from bias'. The remarks were made in a ruling that found that the Office of the Revenue Commissioners discriminated on the ground of age against a worker in a consistory process under section 6 of the Employment Equality Act 1998.

A new appointments system was introduced in 1984 for the highest posts in the civil service. Since then, appointments to posts at the level of secretary general and of assistant secretary (including technical posts at the same level) are made by the government (in the case of secretaries general) or by the appropriate minister with the approval of the Minister for Finance (in the case of other grades). These appointments are made on the basis of reports from the Top Level Appointments Committee (TLAC), established in 1984. Secretaries general may serve for a period of not more than seven years; if, on appointment as secretary general, a person is between fifty-six and sixty years of age, the government may, at its discretion, (a) waive that person's obligation to retire at sixty; and (b) permit the person to serve as secretary general for a period not exceeding four years in any case. There are normally five members of TLAC: Secretary General, Public Service Management and Development, Department of Finance (ex officio); Secretary General to the Government, Department of the Taoiseach (ex officio); a private sector member appointed for a three-year term; two other secretaries general, appointed for a three-year term; and additionally the secretary general in whose department the vacancy is being filled. TLAC does not deal with the following posts: Secretary General to the Government and of the Department of the Taoiseach; Second Secretary General of the Department of the Taoiseach; Secretary General of the Department of Finance; Secretary General for Public Service Management and Development, Department of

Finance; Secretary General of the Department of Foreign Affairs; and Chairperson of the Office of the Revenue Commissioners. These appointments are made directly by the government.

Central Statistics Office figures show that in the civil service, whereas 81 per cent of staff in clerical grades are women, only 10 per cent of those at assistant secretary or secretary general level are women. While women account for 64 per cent of all staff employed in the civil service, they continue to be seriously under-represented in senior management positions. The government decided in June 2000 that a target of one-third of posts at assistant principal level should be filled by women within five years. In September 2003 the Taoiseach launched a new gender equality policy for the civil service designed to improve equality of opportunity for both men and women in government departments. It was particularly designed to end the serious gender imbalance at senior management levels in departments. It stressed that government departments have a legal and moral obligation to treat their staff fairly and to make certain that discriminatory practices are not allowed.

The OECD 2008 review of the Irish public service recommended the creation of a Senior Public Service to strengthen a system-wide perspective at leadership level, to reinforce core values, and to reinforce and develop skills among the senior cohort of the public service.

Conditions

The Civil Service (Regulation) Act 1956 makes provision for the regulation, control and management of the civil service and empowers the Minister for Finance to make such arrangements to this end as he or she sees fit. The act provides under section 5 that 'every established civil servant holds office at the will and pleasure of the government'. (Section 7 of the 2005 Amendment Act reiterates this.) What this meant (until modified by recent legislation, discussed below) was that only the government could dismiss such a civil servant. In practice, however, this power is used very rarely and then only for a grave reason involving serious misconduct. Civil servants are rarely dismissed because of poor work performance, partly because of the difficulties of assessment, partly because job descriptions do not exist and partly because of a tendency to make generous allowances for incapacity. It is sometimes said that an Irish civil servant's tenure is, legally, the most insecure in the world, but that in practice it is the most secure. Among the other provisions of the act are that civil servants must retire at the age of sixty-five years, but that they may be required to retire at the age of sixty; that they may be suspended without pay for grave misconduct; and that they may be reduced in pay or in grade.

The Civil Service Regulation (Amendment) Act 2005 gives powers of dismissal to ministers for grades of principal and up, and to heads of office for other grades, and clarifies disciplinary arrangements, particularly in relation to performance and under-performance. Disciplinary action may be taken on the grounds of misconduct, irregularity, neglect, unsatisfactory behaviour or under-performance. The act introduced a framework of modern management and human resource practices into the civil service. It brought significant changes to the terms and conditions of employment of all civil servants in Ireland. The act provides for application of the Unfair Dismissals Act 1977 to certain civil servants and for the application of the Minimum Notice and Terms of Employment Act 1977 to civil servants. It gives human resource managers in the civil service new responsibilities and more options for the effective management of human resource and performance issues. The act also gives individual civil servants new rights and protections against unfair dismissal. Replies to a series of parliamentary questions to all government departments in February 2008 revealed that sixteen civil servants had been dismissed under the provisions of the 2005 act. The dismissals involved a mixture of full-time officers and those on contractual probationary periods.

Flexible Working Patterns

The civil service offers a variety of working patterns and arrangements that are designed to allow staff with parenting responsibilities to remain at work and to balance work and non-work responsibilities. Civil service staff can avail of flexitime in certain grades. Flexitime is an arrangement whereby staff are at work during defined core times but have flexibility to vary their starting and finishing times. Each department/office has its own detailed flexitime arrangements. Typically, staff must be in work during the core times of 10.00 a.m. to 12.30 p.m. and 2.30 p.m. to 4.00 p.m. A person may start work between 8.30 a.m. and 10.00 a.m. and finish between 4.00 p.m. and 6.30 p.m. A person may build up hours during a four-week flexi period, which can be taken as leave in a later period.

Increasingly, working from home is becoming an option for civil servants under teleworking or e-working arrangements. Staff can work from a local hub or from their own home. The schemes are mainly in the pilot stages at the moment but it is likely that such options will become more widely available in the future as technology improves.

A scheme to facilitate the sharing of jobs was introduced in 1984. The job-sharing scheme, whereby two people share one job, usually week on/week off, was replaced in 2001 with worksharing. What is different about worksharing is that two people do not have to share a job. Worksharing allows staff to opt for a part-time attendance pattern. The actual pattern of attendance adopted will depend on individual requirements and the needs of the department or office. Very many work patterns have evolved in response to employees' circumstances. Over the years of operation of job-sharing and more recently worksharing, management in departments and offices have exercised considerable flexibility in meeting the needs of staff. The most common arrangements involve staff working a 50 per cent attendance pattern, after that four-day weeks are most popular.

Career breaks (in addition to those granted for domestic or educational reasons) of between six months and five years are available where the demands of the work permit it, excluding grades with specialist skills. Those returning to the civil service after a career break have a guarantee of re-employment in a relevant grade (but not necessarily in their original department) within a period of twelve months of the date on which they planned to return to work. Members of staff may take two career breaks during their career. These arrangements bring a measure of flexibility and opportunity and facilitate work–life balance.

Term-time arrangements allow staff to take either ten or thirteen weeks' unpaid leave from June until the end of August, enabling parents to match their working arrangements to their children's summer holidays. To be eligible a member of staff must have a child or children (up to eighteen years of age) or be acting in *loco parentis* or be the primary carer for a person with a disability who needs care on a continuing or frequent basis. Kennedy (2008) noted that 'One in ten staff at the Revenue Commissioners is taking unpaid leave this summer, as part of family-friendly work initiatives'. These staff are replaced by temporary contract staff, who gain work experience and may be retained in these posts. Term time was replaced by the Shorter Working Year Scheme in April 2009.

Decentralisation

In December 2003 Minister for Finance Charlie McCreevy announced that eight government departments and the Office of Public Works would move their headquarters out of Dublin and that more than ten thousand civil and public servants would be relocated to fifty-three centres in twenty-five counties. Decentralisation of government agencies had been signalled since 2000 and many centres outside Dublin expressed great interest in hosting government agencies. 'I believe that over time decentralisation will lead to a radical change of culture in terms of policy formation in this country,' said Minister McCreevy. A number of 'early mover' departments were identified and the tender and construction process for these offices moved forward swiftly.

Civil service unions believed decentralisation would result in a poorer, more expensive and less efficient service to the public. Few civil servants were against the principle of decentralisation per se – just the manner of its speedy and enforced implementation and the overt politicisation of the process. Walsh (2004) stated:

> International experience provides convincing evidence that only free-standing public organisations and agencies not directly involved in central government policy making and strategy should be considered for relocation outside the administrative capital. Informal networking, nationally and internationally, is an important part of the policy-making process of central government and those involved should best be located in a compact area where close collaboration and formal and informal networking and easy international travel is facilitated.

In October 2007 Tánaiste and Minister for Finance Brian Cowen published the report of the Decentralisation Implementation Group (DIG). The recommendations in the report were accepted by the government. The Tánaiste noted the group's view that progress is well advanced in relation to the civil service aspects of the programme, and stated, 'the success of the programme can be judged from the fact that decentralisation is now a reality in 29 new locations and that over 2,000 civil and public servants will have relocated to 33 locations by the end of 2007'. He added, 'In the *Programme for Government* we committed to the implementation of the decentralisation programme. While I am satisfied with the progress reported so far, I am anxious to ensure that the momentum of the programme is maintained and developed' (Department of Finance 2007). In 2007 the Labour Court ruled that the state agency FÁS should not make promotions conditional on staff being prepared to relocate from Dublin to Birr.

The government acknowledged the remaining challenges identified by the DIG in its July 2008 report and confirmed that the Department of Finance and the wider management of the public service were continuing to work closely with staff representatives to seek appropriate solutions to address the concerns of the professional and technical staff and those employed in state agencies, while also ensuring the delivery of the government's programme. It also confirmed its determination to make significant progress towards advancing the state agency elements of the programme during the lifetime of that administration.

The OECD 2008 report on the public service in Ireland warned that the plan, which it termed 'administrative relocation', could lead to further fragmentation of the public service. Speaking on the report in leaders' questions in the Dáil in May 2008, Taoiseach Brian Cowen defended decentralisation. He said that 'the report makes the point that the ambitious and voluntary decentralisation programme is challenging and the government accepts that is the case'. He said the project was an 'unmitigated success' and indicated that approximately 2,200 posts had been relocated and decentralising organisations had established a presence in thirty-four locations; a further 1,200 civil service staff had been assigned to decentralising posts. He said that more than 11,000 civil and public servants had applied to decentralise, of whom more than 6,000 or 55 per cent were based in Dublin.

In July 2008, speaking at the opening of new Department of Justice offices in Tipperary town, Minister of State Martin Mansergh said, 'At the risk of shocking some of our metropolitan commentators, who are quite determined not to find a good word to say about it, decentralisation is part of the process of redistributing wealth within this country, and ensuring that the entire resources of this country are not swallowed up meeting the needs of an overcrowded greater Dublin area.' However, also in July 2008, the government decided, given the precarious Exchequer position, that further expenditure for the acquisition of accommodation for decentralisation would await detailed consideration of DIG reports. Budget 2009 announced the deferral of some fifty decentralisation projects involving 5,140 posts, pending a review in 2011. A series of parliamentary questions in November 2008 revealed that more than 2,500 public service posts had been moved to new locations outside Dublin, at a cost of €230 million, of which over €220 million was spent on property costs.

Redeployment

The important concept and practice of redeployment, which had hitherto proved virtually impossible, has been a feature of civil service human resource policy since 1982 for all grades and in all work categories. Persons in grades such as those of executive officer, customs and excise officer and building inspector, who were found to be surplus in certain work areas of their own departments were transferred to priority work relating to, for example, the collection of revenue and the making of social welfare payments.

Disabled Persons

The employment target set by the government is that at least 3 per cent of positions should be filled by persons with a disability. A survey published in 2002 showed that 7 per cent of civil service staff have a disability. Staff are recruited through the Public Appointments Service, which does not make a distinction between the qualification criteria for persons with disabilities and those with none. Under the Disability Act 2005 public bodies are required to ensure that public buildings, services and information are accessible to all people with a disability.

Conclusion

The Government decided in the April 2009 Supplementary Budget on a range of initiatives which were intended to lead to savings in the public service pay bill. The first of these initiatives was that no public service post, however arising, may be filled by recruitment, promotion or payment of an allowance for the performance of duties at a higher grade, and any limited exceptions to this principle require the prior sanction of the Minister for Finance. A special incentive scheme of early retirement in the public service and a special incentive career break scheme in the public service were announced. In addition, there were hints that lump sums may be taxed from 2010. Circulars were issued from the Department of Finance in regard to the operation of these schemes in the civil service and these are being extended through the public service. The practical effects of these measures on the actual delivery of civil and public services remain to be seen. The estimated payroll savings of these measures is of the order of €300 million annually, but these figures depend on the level of take up of the schemes.

The civil service is at the heart of daily political and administrative life. The work of the civil service is both challenging and fulfilling, given its central role in the machinery of government and the importance of the services it provides to the people. The civil service changed dramatically and rapidly during the 1980s and 1990s. The old hierarchical structures have been broken down through a series of radical reforms. While maintaining its political neutrality, the work of the civil service has become more multi-dimensional, more complex and more challenging than ever before. The civil service is required to ensure a flexible approach and innovative responses in meeting the increasingly complex demands made upon it.

Web Resources

Commission for Public Service Appointments at www.cpsa-online.ie
Decentralisation programme at www.decentralisation.gov.ie
Department of Finance at www.finance.gov.ie
Public Appointments Service at www.publicjobs.ie

7

THE JUDICIARY, COURTS AND LEGAL OFFICERS

The Judiciary

The doctrine of the separation of powers has highlighted the necessity of having an independent judiciary. The reason for the separation of the judiciary from the legislative and executive powers was provided by Montesquieu, 'Again, there is no liberty, if the judiciary be not separated from the legislative and executive. Were it joined with the legislative, the life and liberty of the subject would be exposed to arbitrary control; for the judge would then be legislator. Were it joined to the executive power, the judge might behave with violence and oppression.'

The rule of law is that characteristic of a civilised society that is created by the application of the law to every individual in an equal manner. The rule of law is therefore a pillar of civilised society and an independent judiciary ensures the rule of law.

Judges are appointed through a three-stage process. The first stage is establishing their eligibility. To be eligible for appointment as a judge one must be a member of the legal profession, either a solicitor or a barrister. The Courts and Court Officers Act 1995 provides that to be eligible for appointment as a judge to the Circuit Court and District Court one must be a practising barrister or solicitor of not less than ten years' standing. Only practising barristers of not less than twelve years' standing are eligible for appointment to the superior courts, i.e. the High Court and Supreme Court. The act also provides for the promotion of a Circuit Court judge to the Supreme Court or the High Court bench after four years' service in the Circuit Court.

The second stage is shortlisting. Under the 1995 act a Judicial Appointments Advisory Board was established to recommend persons for judicial positions. This board was established in the wake of the controversial appointment of Harry Whelehan as President of the High Court, which brought down Albert Reynolds' Fianna Fáil/Labour coalition government in 1994. The board consists of the Chief Justice; the Presidents of the High Court, Circuit Court and District Court; the Attorney General; a practising barrister nominated by the Chairperson of the Bar Council; a practising solicitor nominated by the

President of the Law Society; and not more than three persons appointed by the Minister for Justice, who have knowledge of commerce, finance or administration, or experience as users of the courts. The role of the board is to identify persons, through their own application or the board's invitation, who are suitably qualified for judicial office. Shortlisting is on the basis of merit and not political affiliation. The remit of the board excludes the offices of Chief Justice and presidents of the other courts. The board, on a request from the Minister for Justice, submits to him or her the names of all the applicants. In general the board is required to recommend at least seven names (if the numbers are sufficient) from the list it submits.

This procedure superseded the previous 'informal process pursued by successive governments who were seen to appoint, almost invariably, their own supporters to judicial office. There is no evidence, it should be noted, that such appointees displayed favouritism to the party that appointed them' (All-Party Oireachtas Committee on the Constitution 1999: 7).

The third and final stage is that all judges are appointed by the President on the advice of the government under the Constitution. The government has available to it a list of suitably qualified persons. Under section 16(6) of the 1995 act, 'In advising the President in relation to the appointment of a person to a judicial office the Government shall firstly consider for appointment those persons whose names have been recommended to the Minister pursuant to this section.' However, the government is encouraged to choose only persons recommended by the board by section 16(8) of this act, which provides that appointments must be published in *Iris Oifigiúil* – the official gazette – and the notice must include a statement that the person was recommended by the board, if that was the case. Under the act the government has total discretion in the appointment of the Chief Justice and the presidents of each of the other courts. The act opens the way, albeit indirectly, for solicitors to be appointed as judges of any court; as solicitors can now be (and have been) appointed as Circuit Court judges, they can be appointed to the superior courts.

Article 35.2 of the Constitution asserts the independence of the judiciary, 'All judges shall be independent in the exercise of their judicial functions and subject only to this Constitution and the law.' As the judiciary is an independent organ of state, it must be held accountable to the people. In an exploration of the interaction of law and politics in sixteen of the world's leading courts (Sturgess and Chubb 1988: 413–14), Finlay CJ commented for Ireland:

> At the end of the day somebody must be accountable for the standard and type of judiciary that is appointed. There is a significant amount to be said for making politicians accountable for the standard and type of judiciary that is

appointed. They are the ones to whom people in general can turn if bad judicial appointments are being made. If appointments are being made by some body of people who are relatively anonymous then there is no-one to turn to and blame.

A judge may only be removed from office for 'stated misbehaviour or incapacity' and if a joint resolution is adopted by both Houses of the Oireachtas. After such a resolution is approved, the judge is dismissed by the President. The procedure for removing a judge of the Supreme Court or High Court from office is specified in the Constitution, but by law the same mechanism applies to judges of the lower courts. The remuneration of a judge may not be diminished while they remain in office. No judge, since the foundation of the state, has been removed from office. In 1999 a report by Hamilton CJ on the interventions of two judges in the early release of Philip Sheedy, who had been convicted of causing death by dangerous driving, described their actions as inappropriate and unwise. Following strong political reaction, facing an Oireachtas debate on the report and a request by the executive to resign, the judges – Hugh O'Flaherty of the Supreme Court and Cyril Kelly of the High Court – resigned. In their resignation statements they said they had done nothing wrong, but were resigning 'to restore faith in the judicial system'.

In 2004 a motion to impeach Circuit Court Judge Brian Curtin was launched in the Dáil, the first time such a move was taken. This followed strong public reaction to his acquittal on charges of possession of child pornography due to evidence seized by gardaí being inadmissible and Judge Curtin's refusal of a government request to resign. The Dáil established a joint committee to consider the evidence and report to the Dáil, a process which was upheld by the Supreme Court following a challenge by the judge. In November 2006, facing questioning by the committee, Curtin resigned on health grounds, ending the impeachment process.

Court Registrars

The court registrar usually sits on a slightly raised platform below the judge, facing the court. Sometimes in the High Court, if the registrar happens to also be a barrister, he or she may wear barrister's robes, otherwise court registrars do not wear any special clothes in court. They are public servants and they are recruited directly from the civil service. Their main function is to assist the judge:

* The registrar has a list of all the cases before the court for the day and calls out each case in turn so that the parties can identify themselves to the court.

- When a witness is called in a case, it is the registrar who hands the witness the Bible and reads out the oath for the witness to repeat.
- The registrar keeps the court documents (writs etc.) for each case and hands them to the judge as each case is called.
- When the court makes an order, the registrar keeps a note of the order.
- After the day in court, the registrar drafts the orders that the judge has made that day and keeps a record of those orders.
- The registrar generally deals with the administration necessary for the smooth running of the courts.

Tipstaffs

Each judge in Ireland has a personal assistant in court called a tipstaff, who wears a black gown, carries a staff and when in court usually sits on a chair to one side of the judge. While carrying a staff is part ceremonial and the continuation of a long tradition, it is also recognised by those who work in the Four Courts and helps to allow easy passage through the crowded Round Hall and corridors. On reaching the court the tipstaff will request order in the courtroom as the judge takes his or her place on the bench. Tipstaffs have worked in the Four Courts since it opened in 1796. Their main function is to provide general assistance to the judge:

- Tipstaffs accompany judges while they carry out their duties. In the High Court and the Supreme Court, the tipstaff holds a long wooden staff when bringing the judge from chambers to the court and back.
- They communicate with the other tipstaffs to keep the judge informed about what is happening in the other courts on a day-to-day basis.
- If a judge wishes to communicate a message to another court, needs a book or needs another errand to be carried out, he or she may ask the tipstaff for assistance.

In reply to a parliamentary question on 28 February 2008 it was revealed that 'Tipstaffs – more usually referred to as Ushers and Criers – are available to judges of the High Court and Supreme Court (Ushers) and judges of the Circuit Court (Criers). At present, there are 46 ushers and 38 criers. The expenditure in 2007 for ushers and criers was €3.228m.'

The Courts

The Constitution outlines the structure of the court system in Ireland by expressly establishing the Supreme Court, a court of final appeal; and the High Court, a court of first instance, with full jurisdiction in all criminal and civil matters. Provision is also made in Article 34.3.4° for the establishment of courts of local and limited jurisdiction, on the basis of which the Circuit Court and the District Court, which are organised on a regional basis, were established by statute.

The courts consist of the Supreme Court, the Court of Criminal Appeal, the High Court, the Circuit Court and the District Court, which is the lowest court of the land. Ireland is a common law jurisdiction and trials for serious offences must usually occur before a jury. The High Court and the Supreme Court have authority, by means of judicial review, to determine the compatibility of laws and activities of other institutions of the state with the Constitution and the law. The current system of courts is provided for in Article 34 of the Constitution. Articles 34 to 37 of the Constitution deal with the administration of justice generally.

Unless there are exceptional circumstances, court hearings must occur in public. The 1937 Constitution removed any judicial discretion to have proceedings heard other than in public save where expressly conferred by statute. In *Re R Ltd* [1989] IR 126 at 134 Walsh J. said:

> The actual presence of the public is never necessary but the administration of justice in public does require that the doors of the courts must be open so that members of the general public may come and see for themselves that justice is done. It is in no way necessary that the members of the public, to whom the courts are open should themselves have had any business in the courts. Justice is administered in public on behalf of all the inhabitants of the State.

Addressing the annual Law Society Justice Media Awards on 21 November 2008 Mr Justice Hardiman, one of Ireland's most senior judges, stated:

> The Courts are the only one of the three branches of government, the Legislative, the Executive and the Judicial, which is able to perform its functions almost entirely in public. Moreover, the Superior Courts do nothing of significance without providing a written statement of the reasons for doing it. These aspects of the judiciary might be thought to commend themselves to journalists whose concern it is to inform the public. But most unfortunately, as I see it, they have not led to any significant improvement in media coverage of the Courts. It is, of course, absolutely essential that justice should be done and should be seen to be done. This involves a clear, accessible, intellectually rigorous and consistent administration of justice. A jurisdiction without constant, rational and clear exposition of the principles upon which it is based is a jurisdiction which would become opaque in its working, inaccessible to the man in the street and will therefore acquire a reputation for being unpredictable and hardly subjective. The responsibility for ensuring that the administration of justice possesses these qualities is a shared one. Certainly, judgments of the Courts must be clear, accessible, intellectually rigorous and

consistent. But that is not enough in itself. They must be properly presented to the public by the judges but also by commentators in the media who will be the sole source of information for 90% or more of the citizens. If this is not done, the result will be distortion.

Mr Justice Hardiman criticised the media for an unwillingness to come to grips with detail and for rarely providing any sense of the process that led to the result. He confessed his great disappointment that the media no longer sees its job as showing the system of administration of justice as a 'logical, rigorous, developing and humane one'. Responding to this speech, Dearbhail McDonald, legal editor of the *Irish Independent* and winner of the national newspaper award in 2007, defended the media, saying they do a very good job of reporting court cases in difficult and pressurised circumstances and claiming that the judge was overlooking the very good work done by the media in informing the public. Highlighting judges' use of arcane and often impenetrable language, she said members of the judiciary could do more to make their rulings more accessible and comprehensible to the public (O'Brien 2008). Speaking from the bench in the Supreme Court a week later on 28 November 2008 Mrs Justice Denham remarked, 'I'm delighted to see the exceptionally high standard of reporting we normally have in this court'.

From 1995 to 1998 Mrs Justice Denham of the Supreme Court chaired the Working Group on a Courts Commission established by the government to review the management of the courts. The commission published six reports and two working papers, advocating the establishment of an independent courts service, the introduction of a drugs court into Ireland and addressing the issues of case management and of information and the courts.

The Courts Service

The Courts Service Act 1998 created the Courts Service of Ireland. The service was established to manage the courts and its associated property and to provide assistance and facilities to its users, including judges. The service also provides information to the public. Judges of the courts are independent of the service in their judicial functions and are in that capacity paid by the state and not the service – the service is not accountable or responsible for the actual administration of justice. This act was at pains to emphasise the continuing independence of the exercise of judicial functions.

Superior Courts

The Supreme Court and the High Court are established by the Constitution. The Supreme Court is defined as the 'court of final appeal' but usually only hears appeals on points of law. Its decision as to the interpretation of the Constitution and the law is final. The Supreme Court has full original jurisdiction in only two situations: (1) where the President of Ireland, following consultation with the Council of State, refers a bill of the Oireachtas to the Supreme Court for a conclusive determination as to its constitutionality under Article 26 of the Constitution; and (2) where the question of the permanent incapacity of the President is in issue. There are not more than seven judges of the Supreme Court.

The High Court also has authority to interpret the Constitution. It also tries the most serious criminal and civil cases and hears certain appeals from lower courts. The High Court has full original jurisdiction in all matters, civil and criminal. In civil matters, there is no upper limit on the amount of damages that may be awarded. When exercising its criminal jurisdiction, the High Court is known as the Central Criminal Court and, in this capacity, has jurisdiction to try the most serious of offences such as murder, manslaughter, rape, aggravated sexual assault, treason, genocide and piracy. Criminal trials are held before a judge sitting with a jury. The President of the High Court may, in some circumstances, direct that the court sits with two or more judges. In these circumstances, it is referred to as a Divisional High Court. The High Court also hears appeals from the Circuit Court in civil matters.

Ireland's first commercial court began work in January 2004. The court is a division of the High Court, but operates under different rules. Cases are managed by the judges, who lay down a timetable for the production of relevant documents and draw up a programme of meetings between the parties. The High Court Commercial List was set up with the specific remit of providing fast-track decisions on business disputes valued at over €1 million. The court also deals with areas of judicial review and intellectual property disputes. This focused approach means that business disputes that once lasted up to several years are now completed in months, avoiding potentially catastrophic commercial consequences. The purpose-built court, in its own premises on Bow Street in Dublin, is five minutes' walk from the Four Courts. The courtroom utilises modern technologies and provides computer facilities for everyone, including clients, counsel and solicitors; electronic filing and exchange of documents; electronic presentation of evidence; video conferencing; and real-time stenography. There is also a large screen for members of the public, and consultation facilities for the parties and their lawyers. Unjustified delays are not tolerated; the court can award costs against any party that fails to meet set deadlines. Its caseload doubled between 2005 and 2008, reflecting the economic downturn.

In addition to its jurisdiction in civil, commercial and criminal matters, the High Court exercises a supervisory jurisdiction, in cases of judicial review, in which it has the authority to determine the validity of any law having regard to the provisions of the Constitution. Judicial review of any law in the High Court is governed by Articles 34 or 50 of the Constitution, depending on the vintage of the impugned law. A law passed by the Oireachtas since the enactment of the Constitution of 1937, to which the presumption of constitutionality applies, is challenged under Article 34. Laws passed prior to enactment of the Constitution of 1937, to which no such presumption of constitutionality applies, are challenged under Article 50.

There are not more than twenty-five judges of the High Court. The increase in the number of High Court judges in recent years and the refurbishment of courthouses around the country has meant that it is possible to hear High Court cases in provincial towns and county capitals as well as in Dublin. This facilitates the more expeditious hearing of cases on the list. High Court sittings have taken place in Trim, Castlebar, Cork, Dundalk, Galway and Tullamore for debt recovery, contract disputes and non-jury cases.

The Courts Service has advertised for highly qualified lawyers to work as judicial fellows, to assist High Court judges in research, collaboration of materials and the preparation of judgments.

The Special Criminal Court was established under the terms of the Offences Against the State Act 1939 and deals with two categories of offence: those which are known as 'scheduled offences' and those in respect of which the Director of Public Prosecutions has certified that the ordinary courts are inadequate to secure the effective administration of justice. The Special Criminal Court 'is an exceptional tribunal that can be set up in extraordinary circumstances' (Forde 1987: 162) and sits with three judges and no jury. The three judges invariably comprise judges of the High Court, of the Circuit Court and of the District Court. The Special Criminal Court functions subject to the Constitution and the ordinary law, its only substantive distinguishing feature being that there is no jury.

The Court of Criminal Appeal has no original jurisdiction, being solely an appellate court. Sitting with three judges (one Supreme Court and two High Court judges) and no jury, the Court of Criminal Appeal hears and determines appeals from the Circuit Court, the Central Criminal Court and the Special Criminal Court. The appeals may be against conviction or against either the severity or leniency of a sentence.

Lower Courts

The Supreme Court and the High Court are the only courts specifically required by the Constitution. Other courts are established by law. Beneath the superior courts are the Circuit Court and the District Court.

The Circuit Court deals with matters that must be tried before a jury. It is a court of local and limited jurisdiction, with appellate jurisdiction of all matters arising in the District Court. The Circuit Court has jurisdiction in civil matters where the claim exceeds the jurisdiction of the District Court but where it is not in excess of €38,092.14. In family law matters, the Circuit Court may grant orders of divorce, judicial separation and nullity as well as any ancillary orders. In criminal matters, the Circuit Court has jurisdiction to deal with all offences except those over which the Central Criminal Court has jurisdiction. Criminal trials in the Circuit Court are heard by a judge sitting with a jury. There are not more than twenty-five judges of the Circuit Court.

The District Court deals only with minor matters that may be tried summarily. The District Court is a court of local and limited jurisdiction, having the authority to deal only with certain matters arising within its functional area. The District Court's jurisdictional powers are conferred upon it by statute and it may not, therefore, deal with any matters that fall outside its statutory remit. In civil matters, the District Court has jurisdiction to deal with claims that are not in excess of €6,348.69. In family law matters, the District Court has jurisdiction in cases concerning maintenance and custody of, and access to, children and may make orders pertaining to domestic violence. In criminal matters, the District Court is a court of summary jurisdiction and deals with the non-jury trial of persons charged with minor offences. The District Court also has jurisdiction to grant bail in most cases and deals with the issue of sending an accused forward for trial in cases involving criminal offences outside its jurisdiction. In addition to the President of the District Court, there are not more than fifty judges of the District Court.

The aim of the Small Claims Court procedure is to provide an inexpensive, fast and easy way for consumers to resolve disputes without the need to employ a solicitor. This service is provided in the local District Court office. The District Court Rules give the Small Claims Court the right and power to apply and interpret the law. This process allows parties to a dispute to resolve the issues between them by mediation through a District Court clerk known as the small claims registrar. The Courts Service website contains the application forms to the small claims registrar. In addition to consumer complaints, certain other types of disputes are eligible. However, the claim cannot exceed €2,000 and the procedure is not available for use by one business person against another.

Other Courts

The Constitution provides for only two fora in which a serious crime may be tried in the absence of a jury. A trial before a military tribunal may occur without a jury, and the Constitution also grants the Oireachtas broad authority to establish 'special courts' that may try serious offences in the absence of a jury, whenever it considers this to be in the interests of justice

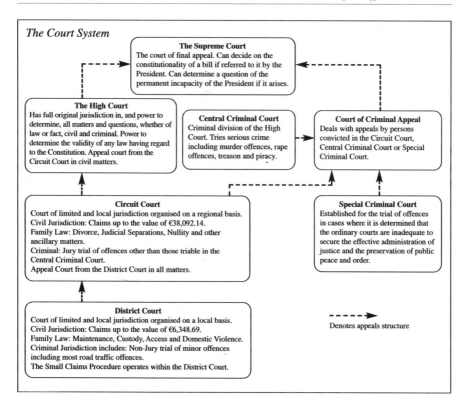

The Court System

The Supreme Court
The court of final appeal. Can decide on the constitutionality of a bill if referred to it by the President. Can determine a question of the permanent incapacity of the President if it arises.

The High Court
Has full original jurisdiction in, and power to determine, all matters and questions, whether of law or fact, civil and criminal. Power to determine the validity of any law having regard to the Constitution. Appeal court from the Circuit Court in civil matters.

Central Criminal Court
Criminal division of the High Court. Tries serious crime including murder offences, rape offences, treason and piracy.

Court of Criminal Appeal
Deals with appeals by persons convicted in the Circuit Court, Central Criminal Court or Special Criminal Court.

Circuit Court
Court of limited and local jurisdiction organised on a regional basis.
Civil Jurisdiction: Claims up to the value of €38,092.14.
Family Law: Divorce, Judicial Separations, Nullity and other ancillary matters.
Criminal: Jury trial of offences other than those triable in the Central Criminal Court.
Appeal Court from the District Court in all matters.

Special Criminal Court
Established for the trial of offences in cases where it is determined that the ordinary courts are inadequate to secure the effective administration of justice and the preservation of public peace and order.

District Court
Court of limited and local jurisdiction organised on a local basis.
Civil Jurisdiction: Claims up to the value of €6,348.69.
Family Law: Maintenance, Custody, Access and Domestic Violence.
Criminal Jurisdiction includes: Non-Jury trial of minor offences including most road traffic offences.
The Small Claims Procedure operates within the District Court.

Denotes appeals structure

or public order. Such a court has been established in the form of the Special Criminal Court, which has been used to try those accused of being members of paramilitary organisations or of leading organised crime.

Recent Developments

Court Statistics

The Courts Service's annual report for 2007 shows that more than 23,000 prison sentences and 4,000 community service orders were handed down by judges in 2007. There was a 13 per cent increase in Supreme Court appeals, new High Court cases were up 26 per cent and cases in the Commercial Court increased by 73 per cent. The report showed a 15 per cent increase in criminal cases coming before the courts, with a rise of 18 per cent in murder cases and of 26 per cent in rape cases. The courts recorded one of the busiest years on record with road traffic offences accounting for over half of all District Court offences. Over half of all new civil cases coming before the courts related to breach of contract and debt collection. There was a 70 per cent increase in medical negligence cases. There was also a 25 per cent increase in the number of claims lodged with the Small Claims Court. The Courts Service believes the increase is partly due to the fact that 41 per cent of such claims are made online. The largest numbers of cases involved complaints about holidays, followed by electrical goods. On average it takes six months for claims to be dealt with and more than three-quarters of small claims cases are settled or awarded in the public's favour.

Technological Change

The courts system has, over many years, provided exemplary service to the population. However, people are demanding an ever-increasing level of service and the courts system has not remained immune to the technological advances occurring in society, particularly the advent of the Internet. New systems that have been introduced or that are in development include: criminal and civil case management and tracking systems; accounting and funds management systems; financial management systems and a range of electronic commerce services. Some commentators suggest televising trials to give more people access to what is happening in the courts.

Conduct of Judges and Officials

In 2000 the Committee on Judicial Conduct and Ethics, under the chairman-ship of Ronan Keane CJ recommended that a judicial council representing all the members of the judiciary be established to deal with judicial conduct and ethics, judicial studies and the working conditions of judges. The committee made detailed proposals as to how instances of judicial misconduct should be dealt with. A working group with representatives of the Minister for Justice and the Chief Justice is progressing this issue.

Following controversy over a television series featuring the State Pathologist in 2007, it was announced that senior state officials were barred from featuring in such documentaries.

Victims of Crime

The government has taken steps to ensure that the victim has a central place in the criminal justice system. In 2005 the Commission for the Support of Victims of Crime was established with a remit to devise an appropriate support framework for victims of crime and to disburse funding for victim support measures. In its first three years of operation the commission provided funding to over forty groups engaged in the support of victims of crime. One of the most important services funded by the commission has been for the purpose of court accompaniment, where victims of crime are assisted by trained voluntary personnel in getting to understand the criminal court procedures, and where victims or their families have a friendly face to accompany them throughout any trial.

In September 1999 a new and comprehensive victims charter and guide to the criminal justice system was published, which set out the rights and entitlements to services and the levels and standards of treatment that crime victims could reasonably expect. The charter operated from the time of publication with clear complaint procedures whereby, if the victim's expectations were not met or where the level of service was not as set out in the charter, complaints could be lodged.

Victim impact statements are among the most effective mechanisms available to ensure that the interests and concerns of victims of crime are brought to bear on the criminal justice process. They are a controversial aspect of the law, with critics holding that they emotionalise the legal process. Proponents argue that they are valuable in aiding the emotional recovery of victims. Section 5 of the Criminal Justice Act 1993 provides that a court, before passing sentence, is required to take into account any effect, whether long term or otherwise, of the offence on the person in respect of whom the offence was committed. This is one of the rare instances where the court is specifically directed as to a matter to be taken into account at the sentencing stage. Otherwise, courts – other than in murder cases – have a large measure of discretion as to the matters to be considered in the context of determining the appropriate sentence. As a result of the procedure under section 5 of the act, victims can expect to have a level of involvement beyond that of a mere witness. The Court of Criminal Appeal made a statement on the law in relation to victim impact statements, and issued guidelines in relation to their use in criminal cases. A practice has developed by which a sentencing judge has discretion to permit a victim statement to be made in such circumstances. The court held that such a statement should only be permitted on strict conditions: it should be submitted both to the sentencing judge and to the legal representatives of the accused in advance of the reading or making of the statement. The person who proposes making the statement should be warned by the sentencing judge that if in the course of the statement in court they should depart in any material way from the content of the statement as submitted, they may be liable to be found to have been in contempt of court. If such a departure occurs and involves unfounded or scurrilous allegations against the accused, the fact may be considered by the sentencing judge to be a matter to be taken into account in mitigation of the sentence to be imposed. Every effort must also be made to ensure that the statement is not used to undermine the proper role of the prosecution in the trial, or to seek to place in the public domain unfounded allegations against a convicted person who is awaiting sentence.

A certain amount of attention has been given to the role of victim impact statements in recent times, prompted by the 2006 victim impact statement made by Majella Holohan following the killing of her eleven-year-old son, Robert. Ireland's senior criminal court judge, Mr Justice Kearney, adjunct Professor of Law at University College Cork (UCC), who presided at the trial, spoke about the role of the victim impact statement in an address to the UCC Law Society in October 2007. The Minister for Justice indicated that, following reflection on this complex issue, he may, if considered necessary and appropriate, bring forward proposals to address any defect in the current arrangements and that may enhance further the role of the victim. In that context, account will have to be taken not only of public debate on the matter, but it will also include consideration of the need for balance highlighted by the Balance in the Criminal Law Review Group, chaired by Dr Gerard Hogan SC, in its 2007 report for the Department of Justice. There are moves to extend the right to make a victim impact statement to the next of kin in homicide cases before sentence is handed down, thereby placing the victim at the heart of the criminal justice system. President of the Law Reform Commission Mrs Justice McGuinness noted in 2008 that victim impact statements may be helpful in giving a voice to victims, but they fit very awkwardly into the normal traditional criminal trial. She asked, 'From the point of view of victims, does the ability to submit a victim impact statement or give oral evidence of their suffering really assist in healing their wounds, in diminishing their sorrow and loss?' (Coulter 2008b).

Restorative Justice

The National Commission on Restorative Justice was established in 2007 to examine both national and international practices in restorative justice, to consider the recommendations of the Oireachtas joint committee's report on restorative justice, and to consider what model or models of restorative justice might be appropriate to Irish circumstances. The commission's interim report was published in May 2008. Restorative justice is a victim- and community-oriented approach requiring the perpetrator to face up to the harm he or she has caused and repair or make good the damage done. Restorative justice puts the victim at the centre of the process. Two restorative justice projects are currently funded in Ireland, one in Nenagh, County Tipperary and one in Tallaght, Dublin 24.

Defence of Honest Belief

Few judicial decisions in recent years generated as much controversy as those of the Supreme Court and High Court when section 1 of the Criminal

Law (Amendment) Act 1935, which made it an offence to have sex with a girl under the age of fifteen, whether or not she consented, was struck down. During the time that this controversy raged, a form of moral panic and legislative hysteria gripped virtually all the organs of the state – the executive, the legislature and the judiciary, reflecting the public concern. The section had been criticised as far back as 1989, when the Law Reform Commission's consultation paper on child sexual abuse said, 'The absence of any defence to any of the relevant offences of reasonable mistake as to the age of the girl is capable of producing serious injustice.' In its final report the commission (1990) recommended, 'The defence of reasonable mistake as to the age of the girl, not available at present under our law, should be introduced and this, if implemented, will reduce the possibility of serious injustice.'

In the C case, a man aged eighteen was charged with having sexual intercourse with a girl under sixteen (unlawful carnal knowledge under section 1(1) of the Criminal Amendment Act 1935). He claimed he had believed the girl was sixteen and that she had told him she was sixteen and he challenged the constitutionality of the law, which seemed to preclude the defence of 'honest mistake'. The Supreme Court held in May 2006 that, because under the act this claim was not available to him as a defence, the act was unconstitutional. Following this decision, another man, known as Mr A, brought proceedings in the High Court challenging his conviction. The High Court ordered his release and a number of other men sought to bring similar challenges to their convictions. There were sixteen persons in custody who had been convicted of an offence under section 1 of the 1935 act. In addition, there were forty-two persons on charges before the courts under section 1 of the 1935 act. As convicted child molesters moved to overturn their convictions, the public outrage and clamour for political action and scapegoats became deafening. Coulter (2007) comments:

> The airwaves were jammed with furious callers to radio stations. A demonstration was called by one such caller outside the Dáil, to which hundreds of people responded. Politicians were urged to act. Meanwhile, Mr A was rearrested and the State appealed the High Court decision. That case was heard by a five-judge Supreme Court, which found that his claim was ill-founded. The Chief Justice, Mr Justice Murray, said that a distinction could be made between a declaration of invalidity of a law and retrospectively annulling all decisions under that law.

On 2 June 2006 the Supreme Court issued a warrant for the arrest and imprisonment of Mr A. The Supreme Court ensured that Mr A returned to prison to serve his sentence. The response of the government to the understandable widespread concern was swift. Firstly, the Criminal Law (Sexual Offences) Act 2006 was enacted on 2 June 2006. It complied with the Supreme Court judgment by providing for a defence of honest belief as to the age of a child. Second, a Joint Committee on Child Protection was established by resolutions of both Houses of the Oireachtas to engage in a process of consultation and reflection on the issues involved. That committee reported on 30 November 2006. It recommended, *inter alia*, an amendment to the Constitution to permit the Oireachtas to enact laws providing for absolute criminal liability in respect of sexual activity with children. It also recommended that the defence of mistake as to age should not be available to a person accused of an offence involving sexual activity with a child under sixteen years of age. It did not address the question of the appropriate age of consent to sexual activity, believing that this is more properly a matter for the Oireachtas to decide in the context of the preparation of legislation arising from its recommendations. The then Minister for Children asked two leading experts on child protection, Professor Finbar McAuley of University College Dublin and Geoffrey Shannon of the Law Society, to provide reports to the Oireachtas on how to move forward including a framework of options to consider in this area.

Irish Language

The Legal Practitioners (Irish Language) Act 2008 replaced the existing statutory provisions for Irish language competence for barristers and solicitors in the Legal Practitioners (Qualification) Act 1929 and the Solicitors Act 1954. The 2008 act promotes the better provision of legal services through the Irish language. It required that the King's Inns and the Law Society:

- Provide Irish courses as part of their professional training courses.
- Establish registers of practitioners who are fully competent to provide legal services through the Irish language.
- Have regard to the status of the Irish language as the first official language of the state and take reasonable steps to ensure that an adequate number of barristers and solicitors are able to practise law through Irish.
- Hold courses on Irish legal terminology and the understanding of legal texts in the Irish language to enable practitioners to identify the nature of the service being sought and, where appropriate, to facilitate a referral to a practitioner competent to provide a service through Irish.

The Attorney General

Article 30 of the Constitution gives the Attorney General a special position as 'the adviser of the government in matters of law and legal opinion'. The

Attorney General is appointed by the President on the nomination of the Taoiseach, and cannot be a member of the government. The Taoiseach may request the resignation of the Attorney General; failure to comply with this request can result in the termination of the appointment of the Attorney General by the President if the Taoiseach so advises. The Attorney General retires from office upon the resignation of the Taoiseach, but may carry on his or her duties until the Taoiseach's successor is appointed. The remuneration to be paid to the Attorney General is regulated by law.

The Attorney General is not a member of the government but does participate in cabinet meetings. In a coalition government this appointment is a very significant one in terms of an extra presence at the cabinet table (Finlay 1998: 30). No specific qualifications for the post are required but the Attorney General is normally a senior counsel. Once appointed, the Attorney General performs his or her duties in an independent manner; he or she is not the servant of the Taoiseach or of the executive and does not take directions from them. The Attorney General may be a TD or a senator and may vote with the government in the Dáil or Seanad. In practice, very few Attorneys General have been members of the Oireachtas – only six since the foundation of the state, the last being J.M. Kelly in 1977. There were twenty-eight Attorneys General in the period 1922 to 2009, none of whom were female.

At meetings of the government the Attorney General advises on all the constitutional and legal issues that arise prior to, or at, the government meetings, including acts and treaties of the European Union and other international treaties. The Attorney General also presents the government's case if the President refers a bill to the Supreme Court for a decision on its constitutionality.

The Attorney General has an important role as guardian of the public interest in the protection of the Constitution and in the vindication of constitutional rights. However, the Constitution does not formally declare the Attorney General to be the representative of the public for the assertion of the public interest other than in the context of criminal prosecutions. Section 6(1) of the Ministers and Secretaries Act 1924 vests in the Attorney General responsibility for 'the assertion or protection of public rights and all powers, duties and functions connected with the same'. Hogan and Whyte (2003: 595) note, 'this aspect of the office, of great importance, has always been recognised'.

As a political appointee, the Attorney General is in an interesting position with two potentially conflicting roles, as legal adviser to the government and guardian of the public interest. A number of legal cases have noted that 'The public interests are committed to the care of the Attorney General' (Hamilton P. in *Attorney General (Society for the Protection of Unborn Children (Ireland) Ltd v Open-Door Counselling Ltd* [1988] IR 593, [1987]

ILRM 477). 'It is also clear that the Attorney General by virtue of his constitutional role also has cast upon him in the appropriate case the duty of defending the Constitution and vindicating the rights conferred or guaranteed by it' (Walsh J. in *Society for the Protection of Unborn Children (Ireland) Ltd v Coogan* [1989] IR 734 at 743). 'It has long been recognised that, in addition to the specific role assigned to him by the Constitution as legal advisor to the Government, the Attorney General is also guardian of the rights of the public and the courts will enable him to perform that role by the granting of injunctions or other appropriate relief where the other remedies available for ensuring that the law is observed are plainly inadequate' (Keane CJ in *Attorney General v Lee* [2000] 4 IR 298 at 303). The Constitution Review Group (1996) found that the function of guardian of the public interest requires at most 5 per cent of the time of the Attorney General. On this basis, it did not see the need for the creation of a separate office to look after this function and concluded there were political advantages in combining the two roles. The All-Party Oireachtas Committee on the Constitution (2003) in its eighth progress report on government agreed.

The remuneration of the Attorney General is the same as that of a minister. That remuneration is recommended to the government by the Review Body on Higher Remuneration in the Public Sector, the standing body whose primary function is to advise the government every four years on the general levels of remuneration appropriate to members of the Houses of the Oireachtas, members of the government (including the Attorney General), the judiciary and senior public servants. It is for the government to take the decisions on payment.

There is no legal objection to the Attorney General engaging in private practice. Some do and some do not; some regard the office as full-time and some do not. 'It is not uncommon for a government to nominate the Attorney General for appointment as a judge of the superior courts. It has also been known for a government to insist that the Attorney General should not engage in private practice while holding office' (Casey 2000: 305).

Responsibility for the office of the Attorney General rests with the Taoiseach and it is the Taoiseach who answers parliamentary questions about its activities. The Attorney General is independent in the exercise of the role of guardian of the Constitution and protector of the public interest. The basic function of the Attorney General is to act as law adviser to the government with which he has a lawyer–client relationship. The Constitution Review Group (1996), which comprised eminent experts of all political views and persuasions, states, 'that should entail no accountability to the Houses of the Oireachtas'. It further states, 'The Taoiseach should decide how much or how little he or she reveals of the advice as in any other lawyer-client relationship'. There should be no pressure to reveal confidential advice given by a lawyer to a client, in this instance, by the Attorney General to the government. There is a long-standing precedent that the advice of the Attorney General is not published. On the question of a possible conflict of interest between the function of the Attorney General to act as law adviser to the government, on the one hand, and guardian of the public interest, on the other, the report states, 'The Review Group considers that discretion as to whether a conflict arises should be left with the Attorney General who will have to act in the full glare of publicity and under the closest of scrutiny by the courts and under the legal system'. It is envisaged that the Attorney General will go to court as guardian of the public interest on important constitutional issues, as happened in the X case, where the Supreme Court allowed a minor to travel to Britain in 1992 for an abortion on the basis that her life and health were at risk.

Apart from advising the government, the Attorney General is also the adviser of ministers and departments. While the Attorney General is the central source of legal advice to government departments, many departments have their own legal advisers. The division of labour between these persons and the Attorney General's office follows a practical working arrangement. The primary recourse of such departments is to their own legal advisers but the Attorney General's office is consulted in certain situations, for example in connection with litigation or in relation to matters that involve the Constitution or that may have to be submitted to the government. In addition to these in-house legal advisers in government departments, Sullivan (2006: 7) notes that 'a scheme was recently initiated whereby Advisory Counsel from the Office of the Attorney General will be seconded to certain Departments to give legal advice and assistance'. Overall, FitzGerald (2003: 50) comments on the role of the Attorney General, 'as his task is to ensure that the government is not embarrassed by unintended breaches of the Constitution, in effect much of the Attorney General's work is de facto directed towards protecting citizens' rights vis-à-vis the Executive'.

Because of the doctrine of separation of powers, the Attorney General does not furnish legal advice to the other branches of government, that is to say the President and the legislative and judicial branches. The Attorney General does not furnish advice to individual members of the public.

The Attorney General is ex officio a member of the Council of State. He or she is also leader of the bar and takes precedence, for example, in court appearances. This leadership does not give the Attorney General any regulatory or disciplinary functions. The former are exercised by the Bar Council (of which the Attorney General is an ex officio member), the latter by the Benchers of the King's Inns (of which body the Attorney General is normally a member). The Attorney General is covered by the annual registration of interests under the Ethics in Public Office Act 1995.

Office of the Attorney General

The Office of the Attorney General is composed of four parts:

- The Advisory Counsel to the Attorney General (providing legal advice).
- The Office of the Parliamentary Counsel (drafting legislation).
- The Chief State Solicitor's Office (providing litigation, conveyancing and other transactional services).
- The Statute Law Revision Unit (simplifying and improving the body of statute law). In a reply to a parliamentary question in the Dáil in December 2007, Taoiseach Bertie Ahern indicated that the Statute Law Revision Act 2007 'provided for the repeal of 3,225 obsolete Acts which predated Irish independence'. He had previously noted that 'It would probably be the largest statute law revision Act ever enacted anywhere in the world' (*Dáil Debates*, 3 October 2007, vol. 638, no. 4). The act follows on from the Statute Law Revision Act 2005 under which over 200 obsolete acts were repealed.

On the legal advisory side, activities include representing the state in all legal proceedings involving the state, defending the constitutionality of bills referred to the Supreme Court and making decisions in regard to extradition. The range is broad, including constitutional and administrative law, commercial law, public international law and criminal law.

Requests for advice by the government or ministers are usually made directly to the Attorney General. Most requests for advice, however, come from civil servants in departments or offices, either directly to the office or via the Chief State Solicitor's Office. Advice is frequently provided under extreme pressure of time. Both the Travers report and the Joint Committee on Health and Children (2005) referred to the need for increased legal services in the Attorney General's office, and also in government departments and offices generally.

The Attorney General's office is not generally involved in criminal matters, which, instead, are dealt with by the Director of Public Prosecutions (DPP). The responsibility for criminal prosecution work previously undertaken by the office has been transferred to the Chief Prosecution Solicitor within the DPP's office.

The Office of the Attorney General has assigned an advisory counsel as legal attaché to the Permanent Representation of Ireland to the European Union in Brussels since 1996. This attaché provides legal advice to the representatives of all government departments who are stationed in the permanent representation on a wide range of legal issues which arise on a day-to-day basis during negotiations and often on an urgent basis.

The Office of the Parliamentary Counsel has a team of specialist lawyers, trained to a high level in the discipline of legal drafting. The principal players in the Attorney General's office in relation to the drafting of legislation are the draftsmen, with the legal assistants having an auxiliary role. Essentially, the tasks of the office are to provide the highest standard of professional legislative drafting to draft government bills and statutory instruments and various other types of ancillary documents. It is responsible also for drafting government amendments to bills, as each bill proceeds through the Dáil and Seanad. In addition, it prepares the indexes to the statutes and to the statutory instruments. There is a legal team of about twenty-five people, supported by the usual executive and clerical staff. Both the parliamentary counsel and the legal assistants are involved in the work of the Legislation Committee, which co-ordinates and monitors progress in the drafting of legislation approved by the government. This committee is chaired by the Government Chief Whip.

The government has launched an ambitious programme to repeal all the legislation remaining on the statute book that was enacted prior to Irish independence in 1922, leading ultimately to the codification of the Irish statute book. The electronic Irish Statute Book (eISB) published by the Office of the Attorney General includes the full text of the acts, statutory instruments and at present includes the Legislation Directory (Chronological Tables) from 1922. Alongside the searchable Irish Statute Book, the website (www.irishstatutebook.ie) includes the text of current statutory instruments in the eSIS (electronic Statutory Instrument System) to standardise electronic publication of statutory instruments. Additional statutory instruments produced through the eSIS will be included on the site as they become available.

In June 2007 the government agreed to introduce a new electronic system for the making of statutory instruments and to place it under the management of the Government Supplies Agency. This new system is now the sole process by which statutory instruments can be made. It ensures that all statutory instruments are produced in a standard electronic format, which departments then place on their websites as soon as the notice of their making appears in *Iris Oifigiúil*. This facilitates the faster and more accurate provision of statutory instruments and enables their placing on the online statute book more quickly.

The Statute Law (Restatement) Act 2002 enables the Attorney General to make available and certify updated versions of acts in a readable form. A restatement contains all the amendments that have been made to an act since it came into force. The certified version is presented in a single text. This is an innovative and modern method of displaying acts that may have been amended many times over a considerable number of years. Variations on this concept already operate very effectively in other common law jurisdictions such as Canada and Australia, and the Irish model most closely resembles procedures implemented in New South Wales in 1972. These restatements do not alter the law in any way. They combine acts and their amendments in a reader-friendly up-to-date version. They can, however, be cited in court as prima facie evidence of the law set out in them.

At the Attorney General's request, and following a government decision in May 2006, the Law Reform Commission agreed to take over responsibility for this function from the Office of the Attorney General. The Law Reform Commission is an independent statutory body established by the Law Reform Commission Act 1975. Its mandate was also expanded to include the Legislation Directory (formerly known as the Chronological Tables of the Statutes). The Legislation Directory consists of a searchable online database providing information on legislative amendments made by acts and statutory instruments since 1922. The Law Reform Commission has produced a comprehensive range of excellent consultation papers on every aspect of the reform of the law. It published a comprehensive consultation paper on the issue of statute law restatement in July 2007. The rights and responsibilities of fathers, gender recognition and the law relating to juries and victims' rights in the criminal justice system are among the areas to be examined by the commission. Its work has been very influential.

Office of the Chief State Solicitor

This office has been in existence since the foundation of the state, when it replaced the Crown Solicitor's Office. As indicated above, it is one of law offices within the remit of the Attorney General, however, possibly because it was once located separately in Dublin Castle, the Chief State Solicitor's Office (CSSO) tends to be regarded as a separate entity.

In general terms, the litigation functions that are the responsibility of the Attorney General are provided by the CSSO, which is divided into five legal divisions: advisory; justice and common law; asylum and legal services; public law; and state property. This organisation takes account of the principal demands of clients. The work of the CSSO includes the following tasks, set out in broad, and very brief, terms:

- Providing legal advice to government departments as well as any necessary accompanying legal documents.
- Conveyancing of state property.
- The preparation of all prosecutions initiated by ministers/government departments.
- Acting as agent of the government before the European Court of Justice.
- Providing a solicitor service in all civil courts in which departments/state authorities are involved.

• Advising and representing the state parties in asylum and refugee law cases.

The work includes dealing with personal injury claims taken by individuals against government departments, compensation claims by gardaí and soldiers for injuries sustained in the course of their duties, appeals to higher courts and applications for judicial review of decisions made by government departments. The foregoing provides a short summary only; to describe the work in detail would be tedious. A flavour may be obtained by mentioning landlord and tenant law, competition law, company law, labour law, merchant shipping law and so on, the type of work which comes within the ambit of any large legal practice.

Solicitors from the office appear in all of the courts and their functions embrace all of the varied types of case with which the courts deal. For example, up to 9,000 new District Court files are opened each year in the office, while about 850 new Dublin Circuit Criminal Court cases arise. Factors affecting the work include increases in the number of judges, new legislation and the lengthening of the court calendar.

Director of Public Prosecutions

The role of the Director of Public Prosecutions (DPP) is to enforce the criminal law on behalf of the people of Ireland. The DPP decides whether to prosecute people for committing crimes and if so what the charges should be. Once the prosecution starts, the DPP's office is in charge of the prosecution case. The DPP has an independent status as provided for in section 2 of the Prosecution of Offences Act 1974. Recent statute law has emphasised and reinforced the DPP's statutory independence, in particular the Committee of the Houses of the Oireachtas (Compellability, Privileges and Immunities of Witnesses) Act 1997, the Ethics in Public Office Act 1995, the Freedom of Information Act 1997 and the Public Service Management Act 1997.

The DPP, who is a civil servant of the state and must have been a practising barrister or solicitor, is appointed following a selection interview by a board consisting of the Chief Justice, the Chairperson of the Bar Council, the President of the Incorporated Law Society, the Secretary General to the Government and the Senior Legal Assistant in the Attorney General's office. The salary of the DPP is equivalent to that of a secretary general of a government department.

The main function of the DPP's office is to examine files, almost always submitted by or on behalf of An Garda Síochána, and, on occasion, by other agencies, such as the Revenue Solicitor, to see if a case is a proper one for prosecution. When gardaí complete their investigation of a case, they send a file to the DPP. The staff in the DPP's office dealing with the files are professional civil servants, barristers or solicitors, with civil servants in various other grades dealing with administrative matters. The prosecutor must read the file carefully and decide whether there is enough evidence to put before a court.

The Chief Prosecution Solicitor acts as solicitor to the DPP and is head of the solicitors' division of the DPP's office. The staff of this division represent the DPP in all courts in Dublin. Responsibility for the provision and management of the local state solicitor service transferred from the Chief State Solicitor's Office to the DPP's office in May 2007. State solicitors are solicitors in private practice in each county who are appointed by the state on a part-time basis to conduct cases which, if occurring in the Dublin metropolitan area, would be undertaken by the Chief Prosecution Solicitor's Office.

There would appear from public comment to be some uncertainty about the role of the DPP and the narrowness of the DPP's remit under the 1974 act is not well understood. The DPP does not investigate crimes, this is a function of An Garda Síochána, which investigates crime to establish if a crime or crimes have occurred and to identify a suspect or suspects. The DPP does not have a direct relationship with An Garda Síochána; gardaí do not answer to the DPP directly concerning their investigations and the DPP does not direct these investigations. If gardaí consider there is any chance of a prima facie case they put their evidence before the DPP in the form of a file and the DPP decides what charges, if any, to bring.

The decision on whether to prosecute a criminal action is one of major importance. Even if a person is eventually acquitted, the initiation of a prosecution may have significant adverse consequences for that person, leading to substantial expense, loss of reputation and/or loss of employment. Certain issues may be prosecuted in the District Courts by An Garda Síochána but decisions as to the initiation of cases involving murder and sexual, subversive and other serious crimes are taken centrally by the DPP, who nominates counsel for court appearance on behalf of the state. From 1922 to 1974 these functions in relation to the prosecution of offences were exercised by the Attorney General.

The DPP is independent when carrying out his or her job. This means that neither the government nor An Garda Síochána can influence the DPP's decision on whether or not to prosecute a particular case. The DPP has no general duty to assist the victims of crime, other than to make a decision, based on the information properly supplied, to prosecute or not to prosecute a suspect or suspects. This decision is made on the basis of the strength of the case against the suspect. The DPP is not an agent of the Courts Service or of the Minister for Justice. In some cases where the DPP decides not to prosecute, there are demands from the public, and even from politicians, for the reasons for such decisions to be made public.

Lack of evidence is the most common reason for decisions not to prosecute. If there is not enough evidence to convince the court that a person is guilty, the prosecution will not go ahead. Even where the prosecutor believes the victim's story, the evidence may simply not be strong enough to convince a jury beyond a reasonable doubt. In a small number of cases, even though the evidence may be strong, the DPP may decide not to prosecute for other reasons. For example, where:

- The offender is under eighteen and the case could be dealt with by the Juvenile Diversion Programme.
- An adult is cautioned under the Adult Caution Scheme for minor offences rather than prosecuted.
- In the public interest, it may be better not to prosecute, for example if the offender is elderly or ill.

The DPP's office has prepared detailed guidelines for prosecutors in this regard. Each case is different and receives careful consideration. The DPP generally makes a decision within two weeks for straightforward cases. Other cases may take longer because of complexity, the volume of material to consider, the number of people accused or the need to obtain more information. The DPP prosecutes cases on behalf of the people of Ireland, not on behalf of any one individual. For this reason, the views and interests of the victim cannot be the only consideration when deciding whether to prosecute. However, the DPP always takes into account the consequences for the victim of the decision to prosecute or not. The DPP also considers the views of the victim or the victim's family.

Until October 2008 the DPP did not give reasons for his or her decisions. When the DPP decides not to prosecute in a particular case, An Garda Síochána, or other investigating agency, is informed of the reasons for this decision. These reasons are kept confidential. This policy has been upheld in recent years by a number of High Court and Supreme Court decisions.

In 2008 the DPP, James Hamilton, published a consultation paper on the giving of reasons for making decisions not to prosecute. Submissions were sought and the DPP indicated to the Annual Prosecutors Conference in 2008 that a final report was likely to conclude that reasons should be given to victims and to their family members. However, he was convinced 'of the argument that any change should be made very carefully and gradually'. 'The reality is that in the vast majority of cases the decision not to prosecute is based on the fact that the Office has decided that the available evidence is not such that a case could be properly proved to the very high standard required in criminal cases, namely, proof beyond a reasonable doubt,' the DPP said. 'The decision is based on the professional assessment of the lawyer dealing with the case on the admissibility of evidence and the weight to be attached to particular evidence.' However, the Law Society (2008) expressed deep reservations about the proposal that the DPP might consider giving reasons for decisions to prosecute or not. It pointed out that the DPP 'occupies a highly specialised and sensitive position' and that much of the 'public interest' in matters relating to criminal justice relate:

> . . . not to justifiable public interest in the operation of the criminal justice system itself, but is directed at prurient, all-too-frequently media-driven issues relating to individual cases . . . The DPP must be able to retain total objectivity and be able to make unpopular decisions, either to prosecute or not to prosecute, without having to provide reasons, no doubt a first step to having to justify those decisions . . . The reputation of any suspect – and this is linked closely to the presumption of innocence, which is a cornerstone of the Irish system of criminal justice and is a constitutional entitlement – is all too easily put at hazard by publicity.

Following this consultation process the DPP (2008) announced his decision to introduce changes to the policy of the office in relation to giving reasons for decisions not to prosecute. The office will henceforth give reasons for decisions not to prosecute in cases involving deaths. Where possible, reasons will be given in writing and on request to members of a deceased person's family or household. These reasons will not be made available to the public at large.

'A fair and public hearing by a competent, independent and impartial tribunal established by law' is the exacting standard required by the European Convention on Human Rights and Fundamental Freedoms for the trial of every case, criminal or civil. In 2003 the European Court on Human Rights ruled, in a case involving the Northern Ireland DPP, that in the specific circumstances of a death caused by lethal force on the part of the state, if the prosecution arm of the state decides not to prosecute, reasons should be given to the family of the citizen.

Information from prosecution files on individual criminal cases cannot be obtained by making an application under the Freedom of Information Act 1997. Under section 46(1)(b) of this act, only records concerning the general administration of the DPP's office can be made public.

Under the Criminal Justice Act 1993 the DPP has the right to appeal a sentence that he or she considers to be 'unduly lenient'. This has happened in a number of high-profile cases in recent years. The three-judge Court of Criminal Appeal can then either quash the sentence and impose what it considers to be an appropriate sentence, or refuse the application.

Office of the Parliamentary Legal Adviser

The post of Parliamentary Legal Adviser, which is a post in the Office of the Houses of the Oireachtas, was created in 2000 and delivers a range of legal advice relating to the running of the Houses of the Oireachtas, its committees and the Houses of the Oireachtas Commission. The Parliamentary Legal Adviser has overall responsibility for the provision of all relevant legal advice. The main duties are to:

- Provide legal advice in relation to services administered by the Oireachtas.
- Provide legal advice to committees of the Houses in relation to the application of compellability legislation and other relevant legislation.
- Provide written and oral legal opinions in relation to issues of administrative legal liability, which arise from time to time.
- Advise on relevant legal issues as applicable to the parliamentary context.
- Prepare statutory instruments for the Houses of the Oireachtas Commission.
- Advise as necessary on legal aspects of the administrative implementation of relevant legislation in the Houses of the Oireachtas.
- Manage the conduct of any relevant legal proceedings.
- Attend and advise at relevant meetings of committees in circumstances where legal advice is required.

Office of the Revenue Solicitor

The Office of the Revenue Solicitor was established by a royal warrant of 12 March 1685 appointing the 'Commissioners and Governors of all Revenues . . . arising in Ireland' and which goes on to say that in order 'that the Commissioners may in no ways be diverted or hindered from giving their daily attendance upon this service', one John Thompson was appointed to be the commissioners' 'agent and solicitor in all causes and matters'. Until 1841 there were at various times one and two solicitors dealing with issues relating to customs and excise. In 1841 the office was expanded and became, as the Law Department, a separate department in the Office of the Revenue of Excise. In 1849, when the offices of the Commissioners of Excise, Stamps and Taxes were merged in the Board of Inland Revenue, the Law Department remained a discrete entity within that office, with the solicitor also being a special commissioner for income tax.

A separate Law Department has obtained up to the present day, with various changes in the nature of the duties performed by the solicitor. Today the office is known as the Office of the Revenue Solicitor. The tasks of the office are to provide a professional, comprehensive, efficient and cost-effective legal service to the Revenue Commissioners. In practice, it supports and advises virtually all areas of the Office of the Revenue Commissioners on issues ranging from court actions for breaches of tax and customs and excise legislation to recommendations on employment-related issues for Revenue staff. In very broad terms, the work of the office falls into two broad categories: litigation and advice. Court actions are taken and defended on behalf of all the Revenue divisions but mainly for debt collection and cases of insolvency, for tax appeals and compliance procedures, to deal with smuggled and prohibited goods, and for duties and licences. Three persons received prison sentences for tax evasion offences between 2002 and 2008 and €2.5 billion was recovered from defaulters over the same period. Over the six-year period, thirty-five people were convicted of tax evasion, with fines, community service and suspended sentences as the most favoured sanctions.

Conclusion

The judiciary, courts and legal officers provide an essential element in the machinery of government, clearly founded on the principle of the separation of powers. Following the reasoning of John Locke, the individual can do anything but that which is forbidden by law, and the state may do nothing but that which is authorised by law.

Web Resources

Attorney General at www.attorneygeneral.ie
Chief State Solicitor at www.csso.gov.ie
Courts Service at www.courts.ie
Director of Public Prosecutions at www.dppireland.ie
An Garda Síochána at www.garda.ie
Honorable Society of King's Inns at www.kingsinns.ie
Irish Statute Book at www.irishstatutebook.ie
Law Reform Commission at www.lawreform.ie
Law Society of Ireland at www.lawsociety.ie
Revenue Commissioners at www.revenue.ie

8

LOCAL GOVERNMENT

Ireland has had local government since the Middle Ages. The original authorities charged with its administration were the county sheriffs, assisted by the grand juries. In later years these were supplemented by a number of ad hoc bodies established to meet the needs created by various social and economic changes (town commissioners, poor law guardians, sanitary authorities, boards of governors of hospitals and asylums, harbour authorities and so on). The old system was essentially judicial in its mode of operation and thoroughly unrepresentative in character. It survived until 1898, when the Local Government (Ireland) Act inaugurated a comprehensive reform based on the principles of efficiency and democracy. It put county government on a representative basis, set up a number of multi-purpose authorities and extended the franchise to householders; these provisions, with subsequent modifications, form the basis of today's local government system.

The democratic system has played a strong role in shaping local democracy. Ireland is a small state with a higher ratio of national parliamentarians per head of population than most other European countries. Given that Ireland also has a strong executive system of government and an election system based on proportional representation with multi-seat constituencies, national politicians take great interest in local as well as national issues. This political environment has not been conducive to giving local government full scope to shape local destinies. Ireland has one of the most centralised systems of governance in the European Union. As the state developed its services, it tended to create them as central services. Of course, as a small state, it is clear that certain services such as education and policing should be delivered in this way, though this is not a universal approach among small states.

The Constitution as originally enacted in 1937 contained only indirect references to local government. This was increasingly difficult to defend in a modern European context, given that most countries provide for some constitutional commitment to local government. Hogan and Whyte (2003: 486) note, 'This failure appeared to leave the local government system increasingly prey to legislative control and executive encroachment of which the practice of frequently postponing local elections was merely the most remarkable example.' The Constitution Review Group (1996) and the

All-Party Oireachtas Committee on the Constitution (1997) both recommended that the Constitution should contain explicit recognition of the role of local government.

Article 28A of the Constitution was inserted by way of national referendum held in 1999 and provides for local authorities, elected every five years, to provide a forum for the democratic representation of local communities, to exercise certain functions at local level and to promote through its initiatives the interests of local communities. Article 28A.1 recognises 'the role of local government in providing a forum for the democratic representation of local communities'. Article 28A.2 requires that local authorities be directly elected. It requires that the powers and functions of local authorities are to be determined in accordance with law. Article 28A.3 provides that elections for local authorities shall be held not later than the end of the fifth year after the year in which they were last held. Article 28A.4 provides that every Irish and EU citizen has the right to vote in the area in which they are resident. Article 28A.5 provides that casual vacancies in the membership of local authorities shall be filled in accordance with law.

Following the 1999 constitutional amendment, a Local Government Act 2001 was enacted. It is the basic legislation governing local government structures, operations and functions. The act provided for the reconstitution of local authorities – as corporate bodies known as city councils, county councils, borough councils or town councils. Under the 2001 act each local authority has an elected council with a cathaoirleach (chairperson) and leas-chathaoirleach (vice-chairperson). It also provides for the holding of local elections and for the filling of casual vacancies, and sets out a statement of local authority functions, including a representational role and the promotion of the interests of the local community.

Types of Local Authority

Under the Local Government Act 2001 the state is divided into thirty-four areas (twenty-nine counties and five cities) for the purpose of local government. Together these cover the entire land area and the total population of the state. Each of the thirty-four cities and counties has its own local authority elected by the local community and known as the city council or the county council respectively. These thirty-four authorities are the primary units of local government with responsibility for the entire range of local government functions.

The twenty-six counties that constitute the Republic of Ireland convert into twenty-nine local government counties because County Tipperary has two county councils (North Tipperary and South Tipperary) and County Dublin has three county councils (Fingal, South Dublin and Dún Laoghaire-Rathdown).

The five cities are Dublin, Cork, Galway, Limerick and Waterford, each of which, since 2002, has a city council. City councils have equal status with county councils and have a similar range of functions and a similar right of representation on regional or other authorities. The city council operates independently from the county council, each having its own council and manager. Each of the five cities is divided into local electoral areas for election purposes. Membership of the city councils is 52 in Dublin, 31 in Cork, 17 in Limerick and 15 each in Waterford and Galway. The total number of members of each city council is set out in schedule 7 to the Local Government Act 2001. Under section 22 of that act a city council, following public consultation, may apply to the minister for an alteration in the number of members. The minister must obtain a report and recommendation from a local government commission before deciding on the application.

There are eighty local government towns, which elect their own local authority known as a town or borough council. There are seventy-five town councils and five large towns – Clonmel, Drogheda, Kilkenny, Sligo and Wexford – are titled borough councils. The residents of local government towns vote in two separate elections, which are held simultaneously, for the town council and for the county council. Under the 2001 act all the previous town-based local authorities (borough corporations, urban district councils, town commissioners) became known as town councils. Town councils exercise functions within the towns concerned. The county council has responsibility for some functions within the entire county, including the towns, for example library services, motor taxation, national roads, fire and environmental services.

The county and city councils exercise the full range of local government functions. The town and borough councils have limited responsibilities. Each local authority has two arms: the elected council, which makes policy, within limits prescribed by legislation; and the executive, which carries out the policy.

Councillors

Under the 2001 act all local authority members are known as councillors. Local authorities annually elect a chairperson, cathaoirleach or mayor (lord mayor in the case of two city councils) from among their members, who presides at all meetings of the council. The lord mayors and the mayors are elected on an annual basis by the city council members and act as chairperson of the city council. Dublin and Cork have lord mayors, while Limerick, Waterford and Galway have mayors. The 2001 act provided that from 2004 the mayor would be directly elected by the population of the locality for a five-year term, but this provision was repealed in 2003.

Councillors' expenses have been consolidated with representation payments, allowances, gratuities and training being provided for councillors in recognition of the significant public service provided by local representatives and to support them in their work. The representation payment was introduced with effect from 1 January 2002 and is specifically related to the basic amount of a senator's salary; in 2008 it was €17,175 per annum. In addition, the chairperson may, and usually does, receive an allowance for his or her term of office. The workload in being a councillor and the timing of committee meetings during the day in Dublin local authorities has made it difficult for those in full-time paid employment to perform their duties and as a consequence there have been several resignations of councillors in recent years.

Powers

Local authorities receive their powers through legislation. That legislation specifies what they can, or must, do and in some cases how they must do it. It also specifies whether, and to what extent, they are responsible to central government or, more specifically, to particular ministers. Irish local government is similar in design to the British system, where a local authority may do only what the law empowers it to do. Irish local authorities are, in carrying out their functions, enjoined to have regard to policies and objectives of the government or any minister of the government in so far as they may affect or relate to their functions. Limited financial resources have tended to restrict local authority functions to the traditional ones.

Elections

The President, the Dáil and the local authorities are the only directly elected entities in Ireland. There are 114 local authorities in Ireland with 1,627 elected members in all. These are elected by twenty-nine county councils with 753 members in total; five city councils with 130 members in total; five borough councils with 60 members in total; and seventy-five town councils with 684 members in total. All county, city, borough and town councils are divided into electoral areas under orders made by the Minister for the Environment, Heritage and Local Government. The thirty-eight larger local authorities are also divided into two or more local electoral areas and an election is held in respect of each local electoral area for the number of council members assigned to that area. In total, elections are held in respect of 268 areas. Persons who live in urban areas administered by borough councils and town councils are entitled to vote at elections for both the county council and the borough/town council concerned.

Local elections take place every five years. The system of voting, as for national elections, is by proportional representation. Polling day must, by law, be in June; the actual date is fixed by the minister. As for Dáil elections, political party af ations may be shown on the ballot paper. There are over three million local government electors. Those over eighteen years of age on the date the electoral register comes into force (15 April each year) are entitled to vote in the electoral area where they normally reside. Citizenship is not a requirement for voting at a local election.

Certain persons are disqualified from being elected, including European commissioners, members of the European Parliament, judges and advocates in the European Court of Justice, a member of the Court of Auditors of the European Communities; a minister or minister of state; the Ceann Comhairle of the Dáil and the Cathaoirleach of the Seanad; a judge or the Comptroller and Auditor General appointed under the Constitution; a member of An Garda Síochána or a whole-time member of the Defence Forces; those who have served, or are serving, prison sentences; and those guilty of misconduct while members of local authorities. In addition, certain officials of local authorities – generally those above the grade of clerical officer – may not retain their employment if they are elected to and wish to serve on their own or a neighbouring local authority. Restrictions also apply to civil servants: those in the executive grades and upwards may not put themselves forward.

There is no prescribed councillor:population ratio; in practice, the ratio varies considerably, even within one class of local authority. Research in 2008 indicated significant disparities in the ratios between county councillors and the population in different parts of the country: the area with the lowest ratio was Ballinamore in County Leitrim, where there was one councillor for 1,122 people, while the highest was in Mulhuddart in Dublin (Fingal), with one councillor for 13,327 people. The study by Joan Burton TD indicated a national ratio of one councillor to 4,802 people.

Gender balance within local authorities is also an issue as women's participation remains low and limited. Women are significantly under-represented across all senior decision-making posts in the sector.

Meetings

A local authority may make its own standing orders to regulate its meetings. Members of the public have no legal right to attend; it is a matter for each local authority to decide whether to admit them. The press is not entitled as a matter of right to attend meetings of the borough councils; in the case of other elected local authorities, the press may not be excluded from council meetings unless the Minister for the Environment, Heritage and Local Government so authorises. As in the case of the Dáil, there is usually a control mechanism to restrict numbers, especially at times of heightened tension, for example rezoning decisions affecting local areas.

Council meetings are presided over by the cathaoirleach or, in the case of a city, the (lord) mayor. These officers are elected annually by the council; a leas-chathaoirleach may also be elected. They have no executive role and are not responsible for administration, which is the responsibility of the manager. The cathaoirleach has, however, special power to obtain information from the manager – a right which no other individual councillor has – and the manager normally meets the cathaoirleach regularly to keep him or her informed.

The Management System

The city and county management system owes its origin to the United States. There, in the early part of the twentieth century, the idea of running municipal affairs in the same manner as business affairs took hold. This was the idea that, instead of elected members being in charge of activities, they and a manager should operate in the same way for a city as a board of directors and a general manager for a business. This idea spread rapidly in the United States and reached Ireland in the early 1920s. Thus, when the Dublin and Cork Corporations, which had been dissolved in 1924 and replaced by commissioners, came to be reconstituted in 1929, legislation provided for a city manager in each case to run the city with the elected members. Roche (1982: 101) notes that the original dissolution in Dublin was received with equanimity by the citizens, who seemed to share the accepted view of the corporation as a combination of corruption and inefficiency. Subsequently, Limerick and Waterford got city managers, and the counties got county managers.

The functions of local authorities are, under the management system, divided into *reserved functions*, discharged by the elected members, and *executive functions*, performed by the manager. The law provides for an exact division of the functions so that responsibility may be defined, however, in practice they are complementary; managers and councillors do not act independently of each other. Any function of a local authority that is not specifically designated in law as a reserved function (i.e. the responsibility of the elected members) is deemed to be an executive function (i.e. the responsibility of the manager). The powers and functions reserved for the direct performance of the elected members have grown in importance since 1929 and now include an impressive range of tasks. The manager is the experienced whole-time administrator responsible for the efficient discharge of day-to-day business without making an undue demand on the time of the elected members, who are part-time.

Managers

City and county managers are appointed by the local authority on the recommendation of the Public Appointments Service, which was set up in 2004 to select and recommend to local authorities persons for appointment to the principal posts. Internal promotions to the post of manager are not permitted. Nearly all managers have had previous service with local authorities, and it is exceptional when a person outside the local authority service succeeds in being recommended. In the current banding system there are five levels of salary for local authority managers based on differences in the scale of operation of the authorities, with, for example, the Dublin City Manager in level one and the Cork County Manager in level two.

The same person acts as manager for the county council and all boroughs and towns in the county. Managers appointed since 1991 have a maximum term of office of seven years, under the 2000 Local Government (Tenure of Office) Order. There was some concern that this situation led to a number of managers moving to different local authorities where a new seven-year term would commence. The 1997 Programme for Government recognised this issue and suggested that the seven-year term might be increased to ten years and that a loyalty bonus might be paid. The Local Government Act 2000 allows managers in their fifth year to opt to extend their seven-year term of office by a further three years, to a total of ten years (subject to an upper age limit of sixty-five years). Section 147 of the Local Government Act 2001 confirms this extension. Under the act a manager's tenure is automatically extended once he or she notifies the cathaoirleach of the local authority. A manager whose tenure period has been extended cannot apply for appointment to any office of manager (with the exception of county and city manager offices in Dublin and Cork) during the period between notification and six months before the end of the extended tenure period.

Reserved Functions

The reserved functions of the elected members are defined by law. They are specified across a whole range of enactments and include important matters of policy and finance. The elected members have an oversight role and responsibility for the general direction of the affairs of the local authority. The main functions that are reserved to elected members are those which set the policy parameters and include the adoption of the annual budget and the estimate of expenses, the fixing of the annual rate to be levied to meet these and the amount to be borrowed, the making of development plans and bye-laws, house-building programmes, and assisting other local bodies in providing services and amenities. The various functions can be exercised only on the passing of a resolution. The manager may not, save with the consent of the members, exceed the amount provided for any particular purpose.

The list of reserved powers granted to elected members has increased over the years in line with the growth of local government functions and new local government legislation. The booklet 'Local Government and the Elected Member' lists 142 separate powers reserved to councillors. However, the powers of councillors have also been curtailed in some of the more important areas of decision making (for example in relation to waste management).

A key feature of the system is the default provision that grants the manager power to act unless powers are specifically assigned to elected members. The basic formulation in local government legislation, stating that 'unless a function is explicitly reserved to the members it is a matter for the manager', has remained largely unchanged since 1929. However, the Local Government Act 2001 also states explicitly that policy of the local authority is a matter for the elected council and that it is a matter for the manager to exercise the executive powers of the council.

The area of planning has been of critical importance. The City and County Management (Amendment) Act 1955, under section 4, gave the elected members the power to direct the manager as to how to perform any of his or her executive functions. It provided that a local authority could 'by resolution require any particular act, matter or thing specifically mentioned in the resolution and which the local authority or the manager can lawfully do or effect to be done or effected in the performance of the executive functions of the local authority'. This reserved power has been used by elected members over the years to require managers to decide planning permissions in a particular way. Usually, section 4 motions required the manager to grant the permission sought, contrary to the official advice of the council planners. Grist (2003: 234) comments in relation to section 4 resolutions that:

> The frequency and ease with which such resolutions were passed, the spuriousness of some of the grounds advanced by members proposing such resolutions and allegations of payments to political parties and to individual councillors had, by the late 1980s, brought the planning process into disrepute. Most section 4 resolutions were viewed with disfavour by all the local residents except the beneficiaries. Consequently, controversial section 4 resolutions were usually proposed by councillors from outside the electoral areas in question, who might thus expect to escape retribution at the polls.

The Local Government Act 1991 tightened up on section 4 motions in respect of planning permission, requiring such resolutions to be signed by at least three-quarters of the members for the electoral area where the site is located, rather than by any three members; and to be passed by three-quarters of the total members of the authority, instead of by one-third. These provisions were incorporated in section 140 of the Local Government Act 2001. In reply to a parliamentary question on 25 October 2005 Minister for the Environment, Heritage and Local Government Dick Roche noted:

The application of section 140 of the Local Government Act 2001 is wholly a matter for local authorities, and my Department does not compile comprehensive data in relation to resolutions by authorities under this section of the Act. However, information is obtained from planning authorities regarding the use of section 140 procedures in relation to planning applications and this information is included in the annual planning statistics published by my Department. In 2002, 27 resolutions were tabled under this procedure and the related section 4 provisions of the City and County Management (Amendment) Act 1955, of which 23 were passed. In 2003, 130 section 140 resolutions were tabled of which 101 were passed.

It is essential that section 140 motions, directing the manager to grant planning permission, are valid directions. In order for a direction to be valid, it is necessary for the elected members to act strictly within the terms of section 34 of the Planning and Development Act 2000, which means that they are confined to a consideration of the proper planning and development of the area of the proposed development. In doing that, the elected members must consider any advice that may be given to them by officials of the council. They must also consider the arguments that have been put forward by the applicant in support of the application; the planning history of the site and any applications that may have been refused or any permission that may have been granted in the area; and the provisions of the relevant development plan. Managers have clashed publicly with councillors regarding the implementation of section 140 motions passed by councillors that materially contravene development plans by allowing for the building of one-off houses. The Irish Planning Institute (2004) has termed this an abuse of the planning system, which brings it into disrepute and which needs to be tackled by legislation.

Section 19 of the Local Government Act 2001 gives local authorities the power to co-opt replacements without a by-election. It provides that the person nominated to replace the resigning councillor must be nominated by the same party that nominated that councillor for election. Where the vacancy is cause by the resignation of a non-party councillor, or one who belongs to a group that is not a registered political party, the act provides that the local authority may fill the vacancy 'in accordance with such requirements and procedures as may be set out in its standing orders'. This has become an increasingly contentious area and the standing orders that apply in the local authority decide the issue. In May 2008 a High Court challenge was launched regarding the constitutionality of section 19 of the Local Government Act 2001.

Executive Functions

Executive functions are in practice all of those not reserved. The day-to-day management of the local authority, including staffing matters, is vested in the manager. The manager discharges executive functions within the framework laid down by the policies set by the elected members. The elected members are also empowered to direct the manager, subject to certain limitations, as to the manner in which an executive function is to be exercised in any particular case. The executive functions include arrangements made by the manager in relation to staff, acceptance of tenders, making contracts, fixing rents, making lettings, and deciding on applications for planning permissions. Councils are generally precluded from involving themselves in staff matters, other than the appointment of managers and, if necessary, their suspension or removal with the minister's consent. The elected members may remove from office the manager if two-thirds of the members vote for a resolution for removal. Removal is only effected with the sanction of the minister and has never happened.

The introduction of county and city development boards has involved a significant new role for managers. These boards are responsible for drawing up and overseeing the implementation of strategies for the economic, social and cultural development of the city or county.

The National Development Plans have also had a major impact on the work of local authorities and managers. Managers have a key role in the efficient and effective delivery of greatly expanded infrastructure investment programmes in the areas of roads, housing, water and waste management. In addition, there has been a closer integration of local government and local development systems, a new emphasis on service indicators and significant changes in planning and development arising from new legislation.

The personal responsibility and accountability of managers have also been affected by the public service Strategic Management Initiative (SMI) programme, public–private partnership structures and the development of market-tested benchmarks for the provision of public services. Government policy on local authorities entails a programme-based system of management and administration and a strengthening of the management and staff structures to improve the capabilities of local authorities to fulfil their responsibilities and to meet the demands of their communities. This programme-based management system involved the creation of a new tier of directors of services (generally at assistant manager level).

Manager/Council Relations

The sharp legal distinction made between the reserved and the executive functions does not, however, quite reflect the way in which business is actually carried out. Managers and councillors work in close co-operation, and the manager attends and participates in council meetings as if he or she were a member (though without the right to vote). Marshall (1967) notes,

'The undeniable fact is that Ireland having sought for an answer to the problem of reconciling ultimate democratic control with prompt discharge of duties, has found a solution which under Irish conditions is working well.'

The councillors appreciate that the manager is the expert in administration, having normally spent a career in local government. Indeed, the manager has often been described as the powerhouse of local government. Even in policy areas, therefore, which are their prerogative, councillors rely on the manager for guidance as to what can and cannot be done. The manager has a greater knowledge than they have because of his or her wider experience of the forming and execution of policy.

Collins (1987: 59) writes of the advantage enjoyed by the manager:

> . . . because he is the centre of a wide communications network involving the central government, other managers, his staff, the public and other politicians. A manager is liable to be in contact with the local business community, state agencies for economic development and a range of social institutions. Such a network keeps the manager abreast of possible sources of advantage or difficulty for his own plans. He is also able to use his administrative and technical staff to store and assess the information available to him.

Managers usually go beyond their legal obligation to keep the councillors informed about the business of the council, about new works or about the way in which he or she proposes to carry out any particular executive function. Because they now hold the power formerly vested in the council, managers generally are careful to retain the goodwill of members, and they like to keep them informed about matters affecting their constituents. Managers recognise the brokerage role expected of the individual councillor, and recognise also that their own overall policy responsibilities are not compromised by the occasional marginal adjustment to facilitate individual citizens.

Council policy is articulated by the manager. In doing so he or she is normally careful to be circumspect about appearing influential and freely refers to the assistance of the individual councillors in helping the council to arrive at decisions. Such a line of action reflects the manager's recognition of the councillors' wealth of local knowledge and collective wisdom. Real conflict is rare, though there may frequently be a semblance of conflict when councillors at meetings may wish to be seen as championing the interests of those who elected them against the tyranny of the bureaucracy. Certainly the conflict anticipated at the introduction of the management system is not in evidence today: both sides have learned to live in harmony with the system. Managers have a high level of responsibility and visibility in the system. Asquith and O'Halpin (1998: 71) note that 'Managers have always been public figures to some extent. This is due to both their statutory functions, and to the fact that they attend council meetings and speak on the record, sometimes in the face of very vigorous comments from councillors, and so are in the public eye in a way that civil servants are not'.

The manager has absolute authority in regard to control and suspension of staff, and this is an authority which the councillors are happy to do without. However, if the number of staff or their remuneration is to be changed, the council must agree. There has been a shift in the role of the manager away from passive municipal administration to a stronger managerial and leadership function. Positive results come from articulating a clear vision and building the necessary political support and administrative capability to implement this. Sheehy (2003: 137) notes:

> The manager is the chief executive officer for the local authorities in his or her bailiwick. He or she organises, controls and if necessary disciplines the staff; enters into contracts; gives or withholds planning permissions, allots house tenancies, and makes a host of other decisions as part of the day-to-day business of the local authorities. A major preoccupation is the budgetary process, in which the manager has a central role – preparing the annual budget (formerly known as the estimates) and seeing it through the council. Even where an estimates committee was appointed, the responsibility and burden of the work were often shouldered by the manager. Obviously, it would not be possible for the manager to personally perform all of these functions and in practice many are formally delegated to directors of service and other senior staff.

The balance of power between the manager and the elected representatives has been a recurring theme in local government reform over the years. For example, the reports *Local Government Reorganisation and Reform* (Barrington report 1991) and *Better Local Government* (Department of the Environment, Heritage and Local Government 1996) both looked at this issue and made recommendations on how the role of councillors could be enhanced within the system. The 1991 Barrington report looked at the manager/councillors balance and reported that 'we are of the view that this framework is essentially correct but that certain modifications in the actual operation of the system are needed'. The modifications that the Barrington report recommended included involving councillors more in assessing policy options and annual estimates; relaxing the ultra vires rule, which was a significant constraint on local government initiative; greater discretion in decision making; and more devolution of powers from central level, as reserved functions, to local authorities. The report also suggested more consultation by managers on the exercise of executive functions and better channels of communication.

Many of the Barrington report's recommendations were provided for in the Local Government Acts of 1991 and 1994. *Better Local Government* in 1996 noted that the general allocation of roles in the reserved–executive framework was considered to be 'essentially correct' and set out instead to improve the policy-making role for councillors within the framework of the reserved–executive divide. It focused on strengthening the policy-making function of councils with the establishment of the new structures of corporate policy groups and strategic policy committees (SPCs). Councillors' sphere of influence in public service delivery at local level was also to be recognised through their leadership of county and city development boards.

Since 1996 a new partnership-style decision-making structure has been introduced to local government. These SPCs involve representatives of business, unions and communities, through a series of committees, in making recommendations to the local authority in relation to specific issues. This approach has altered the way in which local authorities and managers operate. As well as overseeing the servicing and operation of the SPCs, managers have the specific task of servicing the corporate policy group, which is made up of SPC chairpersons and deals with overall policy issues.

The express intention of these reforms was to enhance councillor policy input. In addition to those policy-making functions, the local government reform legislation of the 1990s, culminating in the 2001 act, also gave legal recognition to important 'softer' roles of the elected representative, for example the recognition of civic leadership, the representational role of councillors and the role of local government in community development.

A further significant initiative was the end of the dual mandate under the Local Government Act 2003 as an effort to ensure a clear division in role between national parliament and local government. The abolition of the dual mandate sought to focus the work of national politicians on national and international issues and to allow local politicians to concentrate on local issues. This move has not been without its own problems. A significant part of the Irish public still expects the local TD to respond to local issues. TDs can feel frustrated that their access to local government is more restricted, notwithstanding information-sharing systems that were introduced at the time of the abolition. The local government system may itself feel that political leadership has weakened in some authorities due to the loss of the political skills and experience of full-time national politicians.

The managerial system works well. There will always be a need for a full-time professional chief executive, and modern management structures, to deliver quality local government services. The question for the local government reform process is to identify the optimum relationship between manager and elected representatives so that local authorities meet their democratic mandate and ensure impartial and effective service delivery. In reality, the division of power is not as black and white as the legal distinction suggests: councillors and managers work in co-operation with each other in a way that transcends the legal distinctions in order to achieve mutual goals. Such informal working is a natural feature of any democratic system.

The local government management system has provided impartial and professional management of local administration. Arguably, however, this professional management system has contributed to a weaker local political system. Managers do not have a political role or the mandate to represent the local community, while local politicians do not have the responsibilities or structures to optimise a strong local leadership role. This local democratic weakness in turn reinforces the tendency for local communities and politicians alike to turn to central government to deal with issues which could be dealt with locally. An examination of issues raised on adjournment in the Dáil as having significant 'national' importance shows a very heavy bias towards matters of primarily local significance.

Staff

The local authorities offer a diverse number of careers in the areas of local development, infrastructure, environmental protection and other regulatory functions. Over 35,000 people are employed in local authorities in areas such as professional, clerical and administration, technical, library service, craft, fire service, IT and finance as well as in sectors such as community, arts and leisure. In many ways the local authority service is a single service with a standard pattern of grades and uniformity in methods of recruitment, pay and conditions of service. The officials in these grades, in general, have permanent tenure of office.

The standard county administrative organisation is:

- County or city manager.
- Director of services, head of finance, assistant manager, principal officer.
- Senior executive officer, town clerk (for a town with a population of 15,000 or more), financial and management accountant, city and county librarian, head of information systems, county secretary, finance officer.
- Grade 7: administrative officer.
- Grade 6: senior staff officer, executive librarian, town clerk (for a town with a population less than 5,000), senior legal assistant, clerk of works – building inspector.
- Grade 5: staff officer, assistant librarian, legal assistant.
- Grade 4: assistant staff officer, senior library assistant.
- Grade 3: clerical officer, library assistant, branch librarian.

On the technical side, the grades include engineers, architects, planners, solicitors, technicians and fire officers. About 20,000 people are employed in the skilled, semi-skilled and manual grades. These have, in general, the same conditions as people in equivalent jobs outside the public service.

Functions of Local Government

Almost all the functions of local authorities derive from legislation emanating from the Department of the Environment, Heritage and Local Government, whether acts of the Oireachtas or statutory instruments made by the minister. There are, however, some tasks carried out on behalf of other departments, such as the dipping of sheep against scab, vocational education, grants for higher education, and certain traffic control measures.

In their day-to-day work managers and other staff of the local authorities have constant contact with the officials in the department. Managers and departmental staff meet frequently. Information is exchanged, plans are discussed and new proposals are sounded out. Managers themselves hold monthly meetings to compare experiences and discuss common business. The minister occasionally addresses managers collectively on policy issues.

Recent reforms of local government have focused on strengthening the administrative abilities of local authorities, streamlining service delivery, and efforts to give greater meaning to the policy formulation powers of councillors within the framework of the managerial system. Over the past twenty years or so, some specialist or national strategic functions have been taken from local authorities. The Environmental Protection Agency and the National Roads Authority were set up in the 1990s to bring a strategic focus and consistent national approach to major environmental functions and national roads developments respectively. However, the growing body of environmental law and the additional resources that have been assigned to non-national roads means that local authorities are doing significantly more in these key areas today than they were previously. In addition, there has been a significant movement towards partnership at all institutional levels, requiring a multi-player approach to problem solving.

The impact of local government on the social and economic life of the country, both as providers of services and as purchasers of goods and services, is very substantial. For example, local authorities spent some €10 billion in 2007, about 45 per cent of which consisted of current expenditure and 55 per cent of capital expenditure. Local authorities deliver and manage investment under the National Development Plan (NDP) in roads, water services, housing, waste management and urban and village renewal in their area. NDP investment has seen the roll-out of numerous schemes and projects throughout the country. The government actively promotes the use of public–private partnerships (PPP) for the provision of infrastructure and services within the local government sector. The State Authorities (Public

Private Partnership Arrangements) Act 2002 empowers state authorities to enter into PPPs. The 2007 annual report of the Department of the Environment, Heritage and Local Government noted that 147 PPP projects were under way with a further seventy-eight potential projects being investigated.

The services provided by local authorities may be classified under eight broad headings: (1) housing and building; (2) roads and transportation; (3) water supply and sewerage; (4) planning and development; (5) environmental protection; (6) recreation and amenity; (7) agriculture, education, health and welfare; and (8) miscellaneous. The impact of local government on the daily lives of citizens is very significant through, for example, traffic densities, waste management, incineration, the quality of drinking and bathing water, refuse collection, the development on floodplains, flooding, parking, homelessness, planning, the register of electors and the library service. Given the range and importance of these functions, it is essential that they perform efficiently.

1. Housing and building: National housing policy is that, as far as resources permit, every family should have a house of a good standard in an acceptable environment at a price or rent the family can afford. One-third of the housing stock was built between 1996 and 2006 and the per capita housing output in 2006 was twenty per 1,000 population – four times the European Union average. The home ownership rate in Ireland is very high at 81 per cent.

There are, of course, many bodies, as well as local authorities, involved in housing. These include building societies, the associated banks, assurance companies, and the Housing Finance Agency (a specialised agency through which local authorities fund house purchase loans). The role of the local authorities is to provide access to housing for those who cannot afford to get their own houses or who have difficulty in qualifying for loans from the recognised lending agencies.

Local authorities also manage and maintain their housing stock to enable the provision of social housing by other agencies. Local authorities are responsible for addressing problems of homelessness, the provision of housing for the Traveller community and the enforcement of housing standards at local level. Local authorities may assist in providing houses by administering loans financed by the Housing Finance Agency; by building houses for letting and possible subsequent sale to the tenants; by providing serviced sites for individuals or co-operatives who wish to build their own houses; by supporting the work of voluntary housing associations with grant and loan assistance; and by providing, in addition to what might be termed normal housing, special-category accommodation such as sheltered housing for the elderly and serviced halting sites for Travellers. Local authorities are required to produce five-year Traveller accommodation strategies. A significant number of social housing units have been completed. The main element of the current housing programme is the provision of social, affordable, voluntary and co-operative accommodation to households experiencing housing need.

The housing function was traditionally a fairly straightforward service of building houses. Nowadays, a much more complex response is required in building new communities, and in regenerating areas that have suffered from past challenges: the regeneration of Ballymun in Dublin and the redevelopment initiatives in Limerick are examples of the multi-task and multi-agency response that can be required. There has been a recognition that housing provision needs to be integrated with wider policies that address the social, economic, cultural and environmental aspects of everyday life. In this context, the advent of public–private partnerships with a multiplicity of stakeholders has increased this complexity.

2. Roads and transportation: There is a record number of vehicles on Irish roads. Under the NDP, significant resources are committed to continue the upgrade of the roads network. Local authorities have responsibility for non-national roads. Non-national roads, which comprise regional and local roads and equal 94 per cent of the country's roads, carry around 60 per cent of all road traffic. County and city councils have responsibility for regional roads in their administrative counties, including those in any borough or town; county councils have responsibility for local roads in their administrative counties excluding any city, borough or town; and all other road authorities have responsibility for local roads in their administrative areas. It is a matter for individual local authorities to carry out maintenance and improvement works on these roads, financed from their own resources, supplemented by state grants.

Developments have included the introduction of tolls to finance road construction and the establishment of the National Roads Authority. The legal basis for the former type of venture is contained in the Roads Act 1993, which allows road authorities to enter agreements with private interests for the construction, maintenance and management of toll roads and bridges. A formal toll scheme must be made (this is a reserved function of the elected members), and if there are objections, a public local inquiry must be conducted by a person appointed by the minister, after which the minister may confirm or refuse to confirm the scheme. The Roads Act 2007 facilitates the implementation of 'barrier-free' tolling. The tasks of the National Roads Authority are (1) to plan the roads of the future, to recommend how they should be paid for and then to make the payments; and (2) to arrange for the design of road improvement projects, the placing of construction contracts and the promotion of private investment in roads. The Local Government (Roads Functions) Act 2007 transferred functions in relation to non-national roads and the national vehicle drivers file from local authorities to the Minister for Transport.

Traffic congestion has reached crisis proportions in Ireland with commuter times increasing by almost 75 per cent between 2003 and 2008. A survey by the Irish Small and Medium Enterprises Association in August 2008 found that the average journey to work in Dublin takes forty-nine minutes, while commuters in the north-west of the country face the shortest trips to work at twenty-four minutes.

Responsibility for road traffic matters generally, and the preparation of 'rules of the road', rests largely with the Department of the Environment, Heritage and Local Government in consultation with the Department of Justice and An Garda Síochána. Local authority responsibilities include the provision of traffic signs and road markings, the preparation of traffic studies and the application of traffic management techniques, the employment of road safety officers and co-operation in road safety campaigns, the operation of meter-parking schemes and the employment of traffic and school wardens. Regulations have devolved other significant traffic management and parking functions on local authorities from both the Minister for the Environment, Heritage and Local Government and An Garda Síochána.

Motor taxation and the licensing of drivers provide a vital source of income for local authorities. These activities are carried out by the local authorities as agents of central government. The moneys collected are paid to a central Local Government Fund after the deduction of administrative costs. Operational costs represent approximately 5.8 per cent of income collected. This central fund is supplemented by an Exchequer contribution. The fund is used primarily to finance two significant grants to local authorities: non-national road grants and general purpose grants, which are discretionary grants used by local authorities to fund current expenditure on a wide range of services.

Public lighting is provided by the county councils and the urban authorities, through arrangements made with the Electricity Supply Board. Dublin City Council has its own public lighting department. Grants are available from the Department of the Environment, Heritage and Local Government towards the provision of new and improved lighting on main roads in built-up areas but not towards maintenance or operating costs.

3. Water supply and sewerage: Local authorities are designated sanitary authorities with an obligation to provide adequate supplies of water for domestic, agricultural and industrial use, and systems for the safe and environmentally acceptable disposal of sewage and other water-borne wastes. Responsibility for sanitation is one of local government's oldest functions. From 2004 town councils ceased to be sanitary authorities and the water services function was consolidated to county and city level. Technical advice and other assistance (for example access to a public mains supply) is provided to groups who organise their own supply of water through group schemes. The NDP provides for investment in water and sewerage facilities each year. This money is divided among the various authorities, in accordance with proposals on hand and the needs of each area, into: waste water; water supply; rehabilitation and management of infrastructure; and infrastructural support for economic activity. The European Union has a significant regulatory and financial impact through the relevant EU legislation, particularly the drinking water regulations and the urban waste water treatment directive.

Local authorities have charged for water supplies for many years, mainly to commercial users and to those domestic users connected to a public water supply. However, up to 1983 the charges did not apply to domestic users in urban areas. (Since the vast majority of houses in urban areas had a water supply, they were regarded as paying for this through their ordinary rates.) With the abolition of rates on private dwellings in 1978, the position changed, and subsequently in 1983 the powers of local authorities were extended to enable them to charge for services generally. A decision to levy charges is a function reserved to the elected members. In 1997 the government abolished charges to domestic consumers for water supply and sewage disposal. New contractual arrangements (design-build-operate) have been introduced to improve the efficiency and effectiveness of water treatment plants operated throughout the country.

Residents in parts of Galway city and county were hit by outbreaks of the cryptosporidium parasite in recent years. The presence of cryptosporidium in the water supply indicated a failure of the water treatment process to screen it out and remove it. The local authorities instructed residents in the affected areas to boil tap water before using it for drinking, brushing teeth or food preparation. In September 2008, following the discovery of excessive lead levels in the water supply in Galway city, the Environmental Protection Agency (EPA) sent a notice to all local authorities advising them of the need to inform the agency if lead levels were higher than 25 microgrammes per litre in the public water supply. Several local authorities including Clare, Cork city, Cork county, Dublin city, Kilkenny, Limerick county and Louth reported excessive lead levels following the EPA announcement.

4. Planning and development: The Local Government (Planning and Development) Act 1963 gave local authorities mandatory functions of physical planning. It constituted local authorities as planning authorities and obliged them to prepare a development plan within three years of the passing of the act and to review the plan at five-yearly intervals. A development plan is a statement of development objectives, supported by maps. The objectives must include the zoning of land for different uses, the development of roads and public utilities such as water and sewerage, the preservation and extension of amenities, and urban renewal. It may include a wide range of additional objectives to assist local interest groups, for example provisions for community and recreational development and measures to encourage the local economy.

The planning system has become more and more central to economic and social development. The retail planning guidelines, for example, impose limits on the size of grocery outlets. In the greater Dublin area, stores cannot be bigger than 3,500m² in floor size, in the rest of the country the limit is 3,000m². A discount chain cannot open a store that is greater than 1,500m² anywhere in the state.

The plan is the framework within which development, both public and private, is to take place. Its adoption is a reserved function of the elected council. Before adoption it must be prepared in draft form and displayed publicly for three months in order to give the public the opportunity to make representations. These representations must be considered (but not neces - sarily accepted) by the local authority before it formally adopts the plan.

While development plans are not subject to the approval of a central authority, the Minister for the Environment, Heritage and Local Government nevertheless has power to take whatever measures are necessary to co-ordinate the development plan objectives of the separate planning authorities and to resolve any conflicts that may arise between them. For example, the minister may require a number of authorities to work together, or may direct that the provisions of a plan be varied. Under section 28 of the Planning and Development Act 2000, the minister may at any time issue guidelines to planning authorities regarding any of their functions under the act. Section 29 gave the minister new powers to issue compulsory policy initiatives to local authorities to amend their development plans. It is important that development plans fully support national policies so that all local authorities play their full part in achieving national objectives. The minister may use powers under section 31 of the act to direct planning authorities to amend their plans accordingly. Control of development is ensured through the operation of a system of planning permissions and refusals. Most develop-ments may not proceed without permission from the authority or, on appeal, from An Bord Pleanála (the body set up by statute in 1976 to deal with appeals). Certain classes of development are exempt from the requirement of planning permission, for example small extensions to domestic dwellings, and agricultural and forestry development. Decisions on planning applications are a matter for the city or county manager, but the council may intervene in very restrictive circumstances to alter managers' decisions. Planning permissions lapse after a period of five years if the development is not undertaken.

An area of growing importance for local authorities in recent years is urban renewal. They can require works to be carried out to remove the appearance of dereliction, or, in extreme cases, acquire the property compulsorily. The minister may designate urban areas for the application of tax incentives to encourage development. Part IV of the Planning and Development Act 2000 provides for the protection of Ireland's architectural heritage and requires planning authorities to create a record of protected structures in their functional areas. These records include every structure of special architectural, historical, cultural, scientific, social or technical interest. Following controversy in the early 1990s over the construction by the Office of Public Works of interpretive centres, development by government departments, which up to then had been considered to be outside planning control, became subject to such control as a result of a court decision. Legislation subsequently regulated the application of the planning code to developments by state authorities.

The Planning and Development (Strategic Infrastructure) Act 2006 puts in place a more streamlined planning permission process for major infrastructure projects. This act applies to projects (including onshore gas or petrol extraction installations; crude oil refineries and oil pipelines; hydroelectric and windpower energy installations; railway, airport, harbour or port installations; waste water treatment plants; and incinerators) that are of strategic economic or social importance to the state or region within which they would be situated; or that would contribute substantially to the fulfilment of any of the objectives of the National Spatial Strategy or of any relevant regional guidelines. The act also applies where the development would have a significant effect on the area of more than one planning authority. The project goes straight to An Bord Pleanála for permission, bypassing the normal local authority planning stage. Under this process An Bord Pleanála can order applicants to fund community gain projects as a condition to granting permission. The act speeds up the planning process for relevant infrastructural developments in Ireland. However, there are mounting concerns from community groups about the decreased level of public consultation and the limiting of the persons entitled to judicially review a decision of An Bord Pleanála. A €500 million liquefied natural gas terminal near Tarbert in Kerry, which was the first project to be fast-tracked under this legislation, was challenged on safety, environmental and procedural grounds in the High Court in 2008.

According to the Chairperson of An Bord Pleanála, John O'Connor, the planning system lacks coherence at local, regional and national level. In a speech in September 2008 he noted that the system saw authorities regularly deviating from plans and urged a reduction in the ninety local authorities tasked with deciding planning applications. In November 2008 he reported a backlog in the planning system due to the volume of applications and criticised the inefficient use of land and infrastructure. He highlighted the board's concerns about the frequency with which decisions on individual developments 'do not reflect the policies in the Development Plan or the Local Area Plan. The board can often be seen as a stronger defender of the Development Plan than the local authority who adopted it. This has serious implications for the credibility of the whole system . . . if councils are not seen to respect their own plans, developers and the general public are less likely to do so.'

5. Environmental protection: The role of local authorities in environmental protection has been changing significantly since the 1980s as demands for protection – driven largely by EU legislation – intensify and become more complex. The emergence of the Environmental Protection Agency as a specialised agency taking over some of the functions of the local authorities was a significant feature of the 1990s. Nevertheless, local authorities retain a large number of functions in regard to, for example, air and water pollution, flood relief and the provision of notices and erection of fencing at dangerous places such as quarries, rivers and cliffs. They must collect refuse and clean streets, or arrange for this to be done. Litter wardens may be appointed and offenders prosecuted; one in every four people brought to court in 2007 on litter offences was convicted. They provide a recycling service for Christmas trees each January. Expenditure on fire brigades and fire services is included under this heading. As is the issuing of licences to ice cream vans under the Casual Trading Act 1995. Other responsibilities include the inspection of buildings to prevent fire hazards, Civil Defence arrangements (under the guidance of the Department of Defence) and the control of dogs, including their licensing.

6. Recreation and amenity: Services under this heading include the provision of archives, arts, heritage centres and museums and the giving of assistance to local festivals and exhibitions. Few state services provide greater customer satisfaction than the public library: some 14 million people visited one in 2007, a rise of one-sixth in five years according to a national survey commissioned by the Library Council (2008). Section 68 of the Local Government Act 2001 enables a local authority to take steps to encourage the use of the Irish language in the performance of its functions. Facilities for sport and for community development include the provision of parks and open spaces and of land free or at reduced prices for sports grounds or community halls. Some local authorities provide direct amenities such as golf courses, tennis courts and swimming pools, and some also provide caravan and camping sites. Local authorities are involved in the annual tidy towns, *entente florale* and blue flag for beaches competitions. Increasingly, local authorities are supporting local arts initiatives, and many employ a full-time arts officer.

7. Agriculture, education, health and welfare: The role of local authorities in this area is extremely diverse. Before 1970 this was one of the most significant areas of activity for local authorities. Today, however, responsibilities under this heading are mainly residual, as the bulk of the activities have been transferred elsewhere. Health functions, for example, were transferred to the regional health boards in 1970 (now the Health Service Executive). The main role here for the local authorities is in making nominations to the vocational education committees. Higher education grants are processed by the local authorities but under a scheme designed by the Department of Education. Local authority veterinary services at abattoirs are included here. Local authorities are responsible for the control of dogs and horses. Local authorities are also responsible for land drainage, piers and harbours and coastal development works. County and city councils employ coroners to carry out post-mortems and inquiries into sudden and unexplained deaths in their areas.

8. Miscellaneous: Activities under this heading include administration, publication, purchase of plant and maintenance of major emergency plans. In law, the preparation of the register of electors is a matter for each local registration authority. It is their duty to ensure, as far as possible and with the co-operation of the public, the accuracy and comprehensiveness of the register. Local authority fieldworkers have a prompt card in fourteen languages to help them explain the registration process.

Finance

The adoption of the annual budget is a key function of the elected council. Local authority expenditure is divided into current and capital. Each local authority's current expenditure covers the day-to-day running of the local authority (including, for example, staff salaries, housing maintenance and operational costs of treatment plants). Current expenditure is raised through a variety of mechanisms: state grants, charges for certain services, commercial rates and the Local Government Fund.

Capital expenditure, generally speaking, represents expenditure on fixed assets such as housing, including loans to house purchasers; water and sewerage schemes; libraries and swimming pools. Among the items in the government's public capital programme each year are sums to meet the needs of local authorities. The Minister for the Environment, Heritage and Local Government allocates these sums between the individual authorities, on the basis of proposals from them, the level of need in each area, and the state of ongoing works. The manager is required to submit each year to the elected council a report on the proposed programme of capital projects for the following three years, which is considered by the elected members at the budget meeting (section 135 of the Local Government Act 2001). This report usually takes the form of a multi-annual capital programme for the various local authority services such as roads and water services. Capital expenditure is funded by state grants, development levies, local authority internal capital receipts (sale of property, development levies) and local authority borrowing. Such borrowing must be approved by the elected council and both a scheme of development levies and proposals for property disposal must come before the council for consideration. The manager is required to bring proposals for new works to the attention of the members.

The budget, as adopted by the council, fixes the current income and expenditure of a local authority for the forthcoming year. The manager cannot exceed the total expenditure provided for in the budget for any particular purpose save with the authorisation by resolution of the elected members (section 104 of the Local Government Act 2001). The council may, if it so wishes, adopt a scheme permitting the manager to incur additional expenditure without authorisation in circumstances specified by them but subject to remaining within the overall budget level. In exceptional circumstances only (emergencies or receipt of additional funding at short notice) the manager can incur additional expenditure beyond that provided for in the budget; and in this situation the cathaoirleach must be informed and the matter brought to attention of the members at the next practicable meeting of the council.

The borrowing of money by a local authority, subject to the sanction of the Minister for the Environment, Heritage and Local Government, and the lending of money to another local authority are reserved functions (i.e. subject to approval by the members) under section 106 of the Local Government Act 2001.

Sources

The establishment of the Local Government Fund has improved the financial position of all local authorities. The main features of the system are the termination of the rate support grant, the abolition of domestic water and sewerage charges and the assignment of motor tax revenues to local authorities. In general local authorities had been entitled to retain 80 per cent of motor tax income, the balance being paid into a local government equalisation fund designed to ensure that local authorities did not lose out due to the new arrangements and to help weaker authorities to provide an acceptable level of service. *Better Local Government* (1996: 46) notes, 'A locally available, independent and buoyant source of finance is vital in the renewal process for local authorities . . . new sources of funding are urgently required by the local authority system but there is general political and community agreement that the provision of new funding should not involve an increase in the overall burden of taxation'.

A new funding system for local government was introduced under the Local Government Act 1998 and launched in 1999. It involved the introduction of a Local Government Fund to replace the local government equalisation fund. The new fund was financed from two sources: an Exchequer contribution and the full proceeds of motor taxation. The initial Exchequer contribution was specified in legislation, ring-fenced and future proofed. It involved significant additional resources for local authorities, which continue to have full discretion over how to spend existing income sources such as the income from goods and services (house loan repayments, rents, refuse collection charges, water charges to non-domestic consumers, planning application fees, employees' pension contributions and so on), rates and the Exchequer contribution. There is less discretion in the spending of motor tax revenues – since they have to be spent mainly on roads – and grants such as for higher education scholarships and FÁS schemes.

Rates are levied on the basis of valuations placed annually on all immovable property by the Commissioner for Valuation. The Valuation Act 2001 provided for a review of the law in relation to the valuation of property, including making the system more transparent to both ratepayers and local authorities. Rates are levied on immovable property in industrial and commercial use, including factories, shops, offices, power stations and mines. Certain places are exempt from valuation, such as places of religious worship, or from rating, such as second-level schools, domestic dwellings or land. The remaining buildings that attract rates are primarily those used for industrial or commercial purposes. The aggregate property valuation in each local authority area forms the basis for the levy of rates. The procedure is that each local authority is required to prepare and adopt an estimate of expenses for the year ahead. The estimate shows projected gross expenditure and the anticipated receipts available to meet that expenditure. The gap is bridged (on each of the programmes outlined) by dividing the residual amount by the aggregate valuation, thus producing a rate in the pound. Town commissioners are not rating authorities. They prepare an estimate, and the cost of their services is sought from the county council. The county council then levies 'town charges' on the county rate and applies that higher rate in the town only.

Audit

Accounts of receipts and expenditure are audited by auditors from the Department of the Environment, Heritage and Local Government. The auditors have the power to disallow payments made without authority and to surcharge those responsible for making them. On occasion, councillors, generally for political reasons, vote against the advice of the manager for some project that is not lawful or not approved. Surcharges may, and usually are, appealed to the minister, who has the power to remit them and often does so. Managers are obliged to warn elected members about the loss of money through decisions arising from the use of their reserved powers, which lack legal authority.

As part of the 1996 reform programme, the minister proposed to revise and modernise the existing accounting system for local authorities, broadly in line with commercial accounting practices. The aim was to shift the emphasis from that of an accounting system to a financial management system to facilitate the application of a public management approach to local government finances.

Regional Authorities and Assemblies

Eight regional authorities were established under the Local Government Act 1991. The eight authorities are: Border, Dublin, Mid-East, Midland, Mid-West, South-East, South-West and West. They do not provide services. The main functions of the authorities are to:

- Promote co-ordination, co-operation and joint action among the public services and local authorities.
- Prepare regional planning guidelines (Planning and Development Act 2000).
- Review the overall needs and development requirements of the region.
- Review local authorities' development plans.
- Monitor spending and progress of the NDP and EU funds.

A second regional tier, consisting of two regional assemblies, was established in 1999. The two assemblies – Border, Midland and Western (BMW) Regional Assembly and Southern and Eastern (SAE) Regional Assembly – were tasked with specific management responsibilities, including the reporting, evaluation, financial control and monitoring of EU spending under the NDP's two regional operational programmes.

Dublin

Ireland is increasingly beccoming an urban society. The National Economic and Social Council's report on the Irish economy (NESC 2008: 193) shows that Dublin is second only to Copenhagen among European capital cities in terms of its share of the national population, which is 39.2 per cent. Dublin ranked as the fastest-growing metropolitan region in the OECD countries (OECD 2006: 48); the OECD noted that 'it would be hard to imagine a strong national economy for Ireland without a thriving and innovative Dublin'. The NESC report identified the major inter-related challenges facing Dublin, many of which fall under the local authorities: to increase housing densities, to improve public transport, to bring the new Dublin Airport on stream, and to address water services and infrastructure. It said (2008: 195), 'Arguably, the single most important challenge in protecting the Greater Dublin Area's dynamism and attractiveness will be a step improvement in the integration of transport planning and land use.' The 2007 Programme for Government states that Dublin will have a directly elected mayor with executive powers by 2011.

As then Dublin City Manager John Fitzgerald (2004) points out:

> I am very aware that talking about Dublin and Dublin City Council can irritate local officials in other counties. Having worked previously in Cork Corporation and South Dublin County Council, I know how talks by or about Dublin City Council can rub our colleagues up the wrong way. The City Council, in their eyes, has incredible financial and staff resources, gets more than its fair share of political and media attention yet drags its heels on national initiatives such as waste charges. The council, like the citizens we represent, is accused of arrogance and ignorance about what is going on elsewhere in the country.

However, Fitzgerald also notes, 'If Dublin City Council was a private organisation we would be among the top four or five companies in the state. Even our council chamber with fifty-two representatives can resemble the legislative chamber of a small country.' Yet, when differences of scale are set aside, it works under the same legislative and political framework as every other local authority and it carries out the same range of functions.

Dublin City Council has demonstrated its innovative nature in a number of areas. For example, in December 2004, it was victorious at the inaugural 'Excellence in Local Government Awards' for its work in the waste management category, in introducing 'round the clock' street cleaning shifts to improve the quality of the city's environment.

Local Government Reform

Fundamental Considerations

Any consideration of the local government system must be influenced by two basic determinants. On the one hand, local authorities are providers of services involving very substantial public expenditure (€10 billion in 2007, some 5.5 per cent of GDP, counting current and capital). It is necessary, therefore, that local authority structures should be such as to ensure the efficient and effective operation of the local government system. This implies fairly large authorities having the necessary resources to meet this requirement.

On the other hand, the local government system is not merely a provider of services, but is one of the essential elements that go to make up the democratic nature of the state. In Irish terms, local democracy connotes small units, which may, however, be so small as to be unable to perform effectively and efficiently in the major services areas, but which must nevertheless be financed from public funds.

Reform of local government has been on the political agenda since about 1971 when a McKinsey report entitled *Strengthening the Local Government Service* recommended management posts under the county manager for each of the services, thus integrating technical and administrative responsibility, and functional officers in each county responsible for personnel and finance.

The Barrington report (1991: 14–15) identified the following local government deficiencies:

- Little integration of public services at the different levels of government, particularly local and regional.
- Lack of a coherent and comprehensive delivery mechanism below city/county level and the relatively narrow range of functions assigned to local government.
- Low number of councillors and authorities in European terms.
- Lack of a structured regional level and a poorly developed municipal level.
- Poor relationship between local government and the community sector.

The publication of *Better Local Government* in 1996 represented the most radical reform programme for the local government system in the twentieth century. The foreword to the report said, 'Reform of local government has been on the political agenda for 25 years, although real progress and meaningful change has been limited to date. It is now time for action.' The programme advocated change because:

- Local authority functions were too narrow, inhibiting comprehensive and integrated responses to problems.
- The system as it was operating had not allowed councillors to realise fully the policy role that was always envisaged for them.
- Local authorities had tended to be bypassed by new approaches to local development that had been pursued through the creation of a wide range of disparate organisations (enterprise boards, partnership companies, LEADER groups, tourism committees and strategy committees). (In reply to a parliamentary question on 17 December 2008 it was revealed that a total of ninety-four development bodies and 184 community development projects received funding through the Department of Community, Rural and Gaeltacht Affairs or through Pobal for local delivery of community and rural development measures. Arising from the cohesion process involving the merger of overlapping LEADER and partnership groups, the number of local development bodies was reduced to fifty-four.)
- There were too many central controls on local authorities, stifling local initiative and self-reliance.
- Scarce resources had adversely affected performance of the traditional local government functions and prevented proper use of discretionary powers to act in new areas of endeavour for the benefit of the local community.

The four principles underlying the reform programme were: enhancing local democracy and widening participation; serving the customer better; developing and maximising efficiency; and providing better resources to local government. In March 1996 local authorities were asked by the Department of the Environment, Heritage and Local Government to develop strategy statements, in the context of government policy generally and of the department's own strategy statement.

Other significant developments since the publication of *Better Local Government* include:

- Local authorities benefited from an increase in construction activity, which, together with legislative reforms, significantly increased capital receipts for the provision of new infrastructure.

- Local authorities put in place modern, financial management, accounting and audit systems, service indicators and corporate plans, a series of one-stop-shops, shared services locations and modern information and communications technology systems.
- A greater emphasis has been placed on sharing services, staff and structures between town councils and county councils.
- The ending of the dual mandate facilitated a dedicated corps of councillors, who are free to focus on local authority business without the constraints of parliamentary schedules.
- Victorian-era local government law was repealed and replaced with an updated consolidated code in the Local Government Act 2001.
- Strategic policy committees (SPCs) and corporate policy groups were put in place in 1998 to allow elected members to develop a central role in policy development in partnership with relevant sectoral interests and with proper support. SPCs mirror the functions of the local authority and replaced internal committees. One-third of members are drawn from sectors relevant to the committee's work, and the others are sitting councillors. The chair of each SPC is an elected representative.
- County and city development boards were established in 1999 to bring together, under the local government umbrella, the wide range of state agencies operating locally, with the social partners and local development bodies. These boards provide an opportunity to maximise the combined impact of state agencies at local level. They are independent bodies funded and supported by the local authority. They promote co-operation and co-ordination between all agencies and development groups in their geographical area. Members are drawn from four sectors: local government; state agencies; local development; and the social partners. They were designed to concentrate the collective energies of all local partners on devising ten-year strategies for economic, social and cultural development tailored to the needs of the county or city concerned. The aim was to integrate public services in the interests of the common good and, crucially, under the democratic leadership of local government.

Minister for the Environment, Heritage and Local Government John Gormley launched the government's Green Paper on local government reform, 'Stronger Local Democracy – Options for Change', in April 2008. The aim of this Green Paper, which was part of the commitment to reform local government in the Programme for Government, is to generate wide-ranging debate on the future of the sector. Its central theme is to strengthen local democracy, making it more transparent and more responsive to its customers. It argues that local government can deliver more if equipped to do so, and that this will help create a 'more dynamic and less dependent local government system'. Its key proposals are:

* A mayor for the Dublin region.
* Directly elected mayors in other cities and counties.
* Greater devolution of decision making to town councils.
* Improved customer service.
* Possible new political structures in other key gateways.
* Need for greater local decision making.
* Local government financing.
* An improved ethics regime.

The department has undertaken wide-ranging consultation on the Green Paper proposals with a view to producing a government White Paper.

Ethics

The Flood/Mahon Tribunal reports and proceedings and associated allegations of impropriety at local authority level have highlighted potential vulnerabilities of certain aspects and players in the local authority system in the past. The accountability and control framework is not as vigorous at local level as its national counterpart.

Under the Electoral Act 1997, section 72, it was originally provided that the Minister for the Environment, Heritage and Local Government would make regulations to limit spending at local elections. This provision was superseded by the Local Elections Act 1999 and the Electoral (Amendment) Act 2001. Part 15 of the Local Government Act 2001 subsequently introduced a separate ethical framework for local government. Consequently, disclosures of political donations and expenditure by local authority members and candidates at local authority elections are made to the relevant local authority. The ethics registrar in each local authority is responsible for the maintenance of the register of interests. In general, these registers of interests for locally elected representatives are not accessible on the websites of individual local authorities. It is not clear where these are available. The register of interests for national representatives is publicly accessible on the website of the Houses of the Oireachtas. In its 2006 annual report the Standards in Public Office Commission called for the publication of these registers on the Internet. Disclosures of expenditure and political donations for TDS, senators, members of the European Parliament and presidential candidates are available on the commission's website, but this is not the case for local authority candidates. The 2008 Green Paper proposes a clearer oversight role for the Commission in local government. It advocates local electoral expenditure limits, which will be overseen by the Commission, as is the case in national and European elections.

Conclusion

Local authorities play a vital role in the daily lives of citizens in their localities. The design and delivery of local authority services in communities, villages, towns and cities across Ireland affect the daily quality of life of individuals and also the actions and voting patterns of TDs in the Dáil. 'All politics is local.' Local government is likely to be renewed and reinvigorated by the May 2009 announcement by Environment Minister John Gormley that Dublin will have its first directly-elected mayor in 2010. The mayor will have responsibility for transport, planning and waste management across the four Dublin local authorities and will have the salary of a Minister. It is at the local level that people need to be empowered to engage with the machinery of government in their locality. The NESC (2008: 166) comments:

> The Council believes it is more in keeping with the evidence to acknowledge a significant heterogeneity in the quality of Ireland's public services, with some branches performing strongly and others poorly, than to subscribe to either pessimism or complacency overall. This observation applies across local authorities too where a wide variation in performance suggests there is excep-tional scope for learning from best practice through appropriately structured and resourced networks and mechanisms for benchmarking and co-operation.
>
> Local authorities have important functions at town, city and county level. Local authorities provide good opportunities for young candidates interested in public service to gain valuable experience and to improve their local communities.

Web Resources

Association of County and City Councils at www.councillors.ie
Association of Municipal Authorities of Ireland at www.amai.ie
An Bord Pleanála at www.pleanala.ie
Department of the Environment, Heritage and Local Government at
    www.environ.ie
Environmental Protection Agency at www.epa.ie
National Economic and Social Council at www.nesc.ie
National Economic and Social Forum at www.nesf.ie
Public–private partnership (PPP) at www.ppp.gov.ie
Public service modernisation at www.bettergov.ie

9

STATE AGENCIES AND BODIES

There are five broad categories of organisation working in the public sector in Ireland: state agencies; state-sponsored bodies of which there are commercial and non-commercial bodies; statutory/independent bodies; regulatory agencies; and north/south institutions. These state agencies and bodies cover an increasingly wide variety of functions, including many of the areas previously regarded as the 'core' functions of government provided by the civil service. They look after the schooling of children (National Educational Welfare Board), pay for people to avail of health services overseas (National Treatment Purchase Fund), collect health information (Health Information and Quality Authority), license radio stations (Broadcasting Commission of Ireland), decide the curriculum for schools (National Council for Curriculum and Assessment), build roads (National Roads Authority), manage the national debt (National Treasury Management Agency), lead innovation in the workplace (National Centre for Partnership and Performance), run the healthcare system (Health Service Executive – the biggest state agency) and develop sport (Irish Sports Council). A National Consumer Agency, a National Assets Management Agency, a National Sports Campus Development Authority, a National Building Agency, a National Development Finance Agency – the list seems endless. The Department of Enterprise, Trade and Employment alone has ten agencies acting under its aegis, which take up 90 per cent of its budget.

In 1927 there were just three such bodies operating in Ireland: the Electricity Supply Board (ESB), the Dairy Disposal Company (DCC) and the Agricultural Credit Corporation (ACC). These followed the traditional state-sponsored body model and operated in areas that were seen by the government as essential to the economic development of the country. By 1979 the number of state agencies was put at eighty and by 2008 the figure was in excess of six hundred. McGauran *et al.* (2005) report that almost 60 per cent of the 601 agencies in operation in 2005 had been set up since 1990, with over half being 'duplicate function agencies', i.e. with the same functions as carried out by other agencies. They found that three-quarters of agencies were non-commercial. In the process of the outsourcing of government, ministers have increasingly hived off their responsibilities to these agencies and bodies, which are not democratically elected and for which there is limited accountability.

With such a large number of diverse and different agencies, conducting business becomes extremely complicated and there is potential for duplication, overlap and gaps, particularly with so many fragmented state agencies. The expenditure of these bodies accounts for a large amount of public money. Clancy and Murphy (2006) comment:

> It seems self-evident that a state committed to openness and transparency, should at the very least provide a clear statement of who these bodies are, what their functions are, their form of accountability to the Oireachtas and the reasons for their existence, a statement which is updated regularly and made widely available to the public . . . the unplanned and ad hoc mushrooming of Public Bodies combined with the lack of good information about them is bad for democracy.

In addition, governments have also displayed an enthusiasm for 'task forces' – temporary groups set up to advise ministers on particular policy issues. Many commentators refer to agencies as 'quangos'. This is an acronym for 'quasi-autonomous non-governmental organisations'. The term originated in the United States and connotes a body that is not a government department but that is involved in the activities of governance, with a greater or lesser degree of independence.

Types of State-Sponsored Body

State agencies and bodies include:

- Commercial state-sponsored bodies such as Bord Gáis, Electricity Supply Board (ESB), Dublin Airport Authority, Dublin Bus, Bus Éireann, Iarnród Éireann and Radio Telefís Éireann (RTÉ).
- Non-commercial state-sponsored developmental bodies such as Enterprise Ireland, IDA Ireland, Fáilte Ireland, Bord Iascaigh Mhara (BIM) and Shannon Development.
- Health agencies such as the Health Service Executive (HSE), hospital boards, Health Research Board, Medical Council, An Bord Altranais, National Treatment Purchase Fund and Health Information and Quality Authority.
- Advisory bodies such as the National Economic and Social Development Office and the Economic and Social Research Institute (ESRI).
- Regulatory bodies such as the Veterinary Council, Commission for Aviation Regulation, Commission for Energy Regulation and Commission for Communications Regulation.

- Statutory/independent bodies such as the Office of the Chief Science Adviser to the Government and the Director of Public Prosecutions.

The Institute of Public Administration's *Administration Yearbook & Diary* provides a comprehensive annual listing of state agencies and bodies. In total there are several hundred state agencies of various types.

Definition of State Agencies and State-Sponsored Bodies

A state agency can be described as 'an organisation that stands at arm's length from its parent ministry or ministries and carries out public functions' (Pollitt *et al.* 2001: 271). There is no widely accepted definition of an agency and they tend to be all things to all people. A Committee for Public Management Research (CPMR) report (McGauran *et al.* 2005) defined an agency as a public sector organisation with the following characteristics:

- Structurally differentiated from other organisations.
- Has some capacity for autonomous decision making.
- Has some expectation of continuity over time.
- Performs some public functions.
- Has some personnel.
- Has some financial resources.

The term agency includes not just commercial and non-commercial semi-state bodies, but also bodies that have some autonomy from their parent department yet are nevertheless staffed by civil servants, and bodies that may be purely advisory, albeit permanent in character – these are organisations usually excluded from the definition of state-sponsored bodies (McGauran *et al.* 2005: 32).

State-sponsored bodies are the more traditional bodies with powers and duties set by either statutes or ministerial authority, whose staff are not civil servants and to whose governing boards or councils the relevant minister, with the approval and/or consent of the Minister for Finance, appoints all of the members. The description of state-sponsored bodies provided by FitzGerald (1963: 5) remains perhaps the most succinct. He defined them as autonomous public bodies, neither temporary in character nor purely advisory in their functions, whose staff is not drawn from the civil service but to whose board or council the government or ministers in the government appoint directors etc. They exclude bodies that (1) have some autonomy vis-à-vis government departments and that are staffed by civil servants, such as the Adoption Board; (2) are mainly advisory in function and permanent in character, such as the Animal Remedies Consultative Committee; (3) are advisory and temporary in character, such as the Constitution Review Group; and (4) are local authorities. Each body operates under the general control of a minister, who is responsible for ensuring that the body carries out the tasks for which it is set up, but who does not intervene in the day-to-day carrying out of those tasks. Regulatory bodies can be defined as external organisations that have been empowered by legislation to oversee, control and ensure compliance with the provisions of the establishing act.

Under the terms of the Good Friday Agreement of April 1998 the British and Irish governments set up a number of north/south implementation bodies on 2 December 1999. These bodies implement policies agreed at the North/South Ministerial Council and include *safe*food (food safety promotion), Inter*Trade*Ireland (trade and business development), the North/South Language Body (comprising Foras na Gaeilge and the Ulster-Scots Agency), the Special EU Programmes Body, Waterways Ireland and the Loughs Agency. In addition, a publicly owned limited company, Tourism Ireland, was established to market the island of Ireland.

State agencies and state-sponsored bodies are a growing part of the system of government, and the government is ultimately responsible for their performance. This situation underlines the fundamental difference between private sector companies, which are responsible to shareholders, and state agencies and state-sponsored bodies, whose shareholder is ultimately the Minister for Finance, and it leads to endless debate on the degrees of freedom and control appropriate in the case of these bodies.

The state-sponsored bodies form a large part of the public sector. They may be divided into two broad categories according to their basic purpose: the commercial (trading) bodies and the non-commercial. There is no standard framework for the setting up of state agencies and state-sponsored bodies; their legal status, terms of reference and mode of operation tend to be determined empirically as the need arises. Each is established by means of a constituent document (act, statutory instrument or some other form of written directive), which deals with such matters as functions, board membership, staff, funding, and the relationship between the minister and the board. It is possible to distinguish broadly six different methods of incorporation, which are briefly outlined below.

Reasons for Establishment

The corporation sole concept introduced in the Ministers and Secretaries Act 1924 meant that civil servants would be the employees of ministers and would carry out all the functions of government in the name of ministers. After only three years, however, it became clear that if certain tasks that were desirable in the national interest were to be undertaken, and if the only body in a position to undertake these was the state, it would become necessary to loosen the control of ministers. The rigidity of the civil service system was considered unsuitable for the running of the commercial operations that were becoming necessary. Thus, in order to cut through the red tape that often constrains speedy direct action by government, the first of the commercial bodies (the Electricity Supply Board and the Agricultural Credit Corporation) were established in 1927. Ministers were placed at one remove, so to speak, from these bodies; they were responsible for what the bodies were set up to do (i.e. for their functional area) but not for the details of the way in which they did their work.

From the beginning these bodies have been established for practical reasons. Something needed to be done, and the best, or sometimes the only, way of having it done was through direct public intervention. As former Taoiseach Seán Lemass (1959) put it, 'State financed industries have been set up only where considerations of national policy were involved or where the projects were beyond the scope of or unlikely to be undertaken by, private enterprise.' Thus, the system of state agencies and state-sponsored bodies emerged in a haphazard fashion in order to perform certain specific tasks that could not readily or appropriately be undertaken within the structure of government departments or local authorities. There has been little of the ideological motivation common elsewhere, as, for example, in Britain. O'Hagan (1984: 101) notes that the reason for the creation of state-sponsored bodies in Ireland has mainly been the result of 'individual responses to specific situations, intentions being primarily pragmatic'. The CPMR report identified five reasons for the establishment of these bodies (McGauran *et al.* 2005): economic/efficiency reasons; changing societal expectations; political reasons; specialisation; and the fashion or fad explanations.

Regulatory offices are responsible for overseeing competition in market areas dominated by one player. Another important reason for their establishment is to regulate a sensitive national area of economic activity such as aviation, taxis, telecommunications, competition and financial services. Regulatory activity resulting from the European Union is an important reason for the establishment of these agencies, for example the Environmental Protection Agency. EU regulations have a general scope, and are obligatory in all their elements and directly applicable in all EU member states. Any local laws contrary to the regulation are overruled, as EU law has supremacy over the laws of the member states. New legislation enacted by member states must be consistent with the requirements of EU regulations. For these reasons EU regulations constitute the most powerful or influential of the EU legislative acts. At national level, regulation of service quality and delivery within the public sector itself is also an important aspect, for example prison, social, health and psychiatric services. At local level there has been a proliferation of agencies, many with overlapping functions, including local area partnerships, new rural development groups, village renewal and heritage conservation initiatives, LEADER groups, development boards, enterprise boards and fisheries boards.

Thus, there are a myriad of reasons for the establishment of state agencies. They are set up to implement policy, to regulate, to advise and develop policy, to provide information, to conduct research, to supply representation, to promote economic development, to register professional groups, to investigate politically sensitive issues and to encourage the development of all-island relations. There are a total of sixty-five different tasks carried out by agencies. These are categorised in ten types of function: communication; co-ordination; monitoring and control; networking; programme design and management; registration and licensing; research; scientific and technical advice; service provision; and training. Certain agencies carry out a mix of these roles.

An OECD report identified the following reasons, implicit and explicit, for the creation of agencies in Ireland (2008b: 298): signalling and embodying new policy priorities; involving stakeholders; providing executive bodies with managerial flexibility, bringing in specialised skills and allowing more performance focus; co-ordinating government policies at local level; and responding to EU requirements related to the independence of regulators.

Ireland is not unique in this situation. The OECD previously noted that a key observation in many countries was the 'lack of clarity about the differences between the various types of agencies and their strengths and weaknesses' (2002: 24).

The management of state agencies and bodies in Ireland is also determined by practical considerations. In contrast to the civil service (the structure of which is designed essentially for the purpose of assisting ministers), agencies have freedom to adopt the structures most suitable for the efficient performance of the duties assigned to them. They also have greater freedom in matters such as recruitment. A further advantage is that the system enables the state to assemble boards of directors who have experience in the private sector.

The tendency has been to set up a new body or agency to meet each new need or opportunity as it arose. In many cases, these new bodies engaged in tasks that were formerly carried out by government departments. In the past, however, following close financial scrutiny, some state agencies and state-sponsored bodies have been abolished and their work assigned to government departments (as in the case of Bord na gCapall, the Health Education Bureau and An Foras Forbartha). In other cases, tasks have been amalgamated, as in the instance of Teagasc (merger of the Agricultural Research Institute and the National Agricultural Advisory and Training Service). The Health Research

Board was established in 1986 from the amalgamation of the Medico-Social Research Board and the Medical Research Council. The Employment Equality Agency was abolished and replaced by the Equality Authority (with an expanded remit) in 1998. In other cases the state has ceased involvement in these activities, for example Irish Shipping was abolished in 1984 and the state rescue agency Fóir Teoranta was abolished in 1989. More recently, the state sold off some of these companies, for example Telecom Éireann in 1999 and Aer Lingus in 2006. Budget 2009 announced the amalgamation, merger and combination of a number of state agencies in the implementation of thirty rationalisation decisions across eleven government departments. As a first step, the government decided to reduce the number of state bodies and agencies by forty-one, and said it would examine the scope for the further rationalisation of agencies. The Minister for Finance noted that while cost savings and economy were an important aspect of the rationalisation process, a key outcome was to deliver a more citizen-friendly system of government, with a more focused delivery of services.

As part of the *Towards 2016* social development plan, a new National Employment Rights Authority was established. Plans were announced for a new Dublin Transportation Authority (to combine the Dublin Transport Office, the Commission for Taxi Regulation, and the public transport licensing functions of the Department of Transport) and a new Sea-Fisheries Protection Authority, which is now up and running. The trend to create new single-function executive agencies in response to the demand for new services from government – rather than to upgrade local authorities and devolve responsibilities to them – typifies what Adshead (2003: 117–18) describes as a system whereby 'practical problems are often solved at the expense of democratic accountability'.

Commercial State Bodies

These bodies are sometimes called public enterprises because they operate in the marketplace, providing goods and services from whose sale they derive the greater part of their revenue. They include bodies that provide an infrastructural base for the whole economy, the undertaking of which the private sector found either unattractive or beyond its resources at the time the need for the activities arose (for example An Post and the ESB). They also include bodies to develop natural resources (Bord na Móna and Bord Gáis); bodies set up as a rescue operation by the state when a private undertaking was threatened with financial difficulties (the former Irish Life Assurance Company); bodies to provide finance for certain sectors (the former Agricultural Credit Corporation); and bodies to promote a particular industry (Horse Racing Ireland and the Irish Greyhound Board).

The basic assumption behind the establishment of the commercial state bodies is the belief that the business and entrepreneurial skills employed in the private sector may be utilised to equal effect in the service of the state. In accordance with this view, it is maintained that a business task is best performed by a body with a definition of objectives and a clear mandate, which, because of the changing political scene, government departments do not generally have; that a board of directors comprising people who have what is termed 'outside experience' bring such experience, freshness and skills to augment the civil service in the conduct of public service tasks; and that the practice results in the harnessing of the talents of persons who might wish to give public service and who might not otherwise have the opportunity of doing so. In this way, the argument runs, the best of both worlds is achieved.

Non-Commercial State Bodies

These bodies carry out a wide variety of tasks such as the promotion of Irish business (for example Enterprise Ireland), agricultural and industrial advice (Teagasc and Forfás), the provision of health services (Irish Blood Transfusion Service and Dublin Dental School and Hospital) and the regulation of certain professions (the Opticians Board and An Bord Altranais). Other areas of activity include industry (IDA Ireland), training and employment (FÁS), education (Higher Education Authority), tourism (Fáilte Ireland), culture (Arts Council) and research (Health Research Board).

These are all activities that in some other countries are carried out by government departments. The Public Services Organisation Review Group (Devlin report, 1969) noted that most of the activities of the non-commercial state-sponsored bodies are such as are, were or could be carried out within the civil service. The group referred to a tacit acceptance by ministers, officials and the public generally that functions such as the bodies carry out are best performed outside the civil service with its existing organisation and constraints. It pointed out, however, that every decision to allocate a new function to a state-sponsored body while similar functions are left in the civil service structure represented a failure to face the problems of the efficiency of the machinery of government or at least to think through the roles of the parts of that machinery. This critical reappraisal of the role of the non-commercial bodies may have been partly responsible for some of the terminations and amalgamations referred to above. The proliferation in the number of agencies in the public sector in more recent years also reflects these dynamics. MacCarthaigh (2008) notes that agencies:

. . . are created to regulate, co-ordinate, adjudicate, implement, evaluate and advise on policy in a manner that is regarded as more effective than the core Civil Service and which draws on expertise not readily available within the central bureaucracy.

The establishment of an agency is also an unrivalled method of signalling political intent, and may give policy focus to a particular issue. Some may hold that agencies are established to deflect public attention away from a particular aspect of government work; but the evidence suggests that, to the contrary, they act as magnets for media attention. In Ireland, State agencies have been an integral part of independent government.

Methods of Establishment

State agencies and state-sponsored bodies are set up in various ways:

1. As a statutory corporation, which derives its powers and authority directly from the act that sets it up. Its relationship with the sponsoring minister, its functions and powers are laid down in the act. Examples of bodies set up in this manner are Teagasc and FÁS.

2. As a public company set up pursuant to a statute and incorporated by registration under the Companies Act. In these cases, the act provides for the setting up of a company, which is subsequently established by memorandum and articles of association issued under ministerial authority. Examples are the Irish National Stud and the Housing Finance Agency.

3. As a private company incorporated by registration under the Companies Act in accordance with company law. The objects of the company and the special conditions governing its operations are contained either in the memorandum and articles of association or in administrative directions from the parent department. The Irish Museum of Modern Art is an example.

4. A corporate body set up under a statutory instrument made by a minister. For example, the Health (Corporate Bodies) Act 1961, as amended, by order issued by the Minister for Health for a body to provide health services such as the Dublin Dental School and Hospital.

5. A private company limited by guarantee and thus legally independent of ministers, but which, because of its dependence on the state for some of its finance, is sometimes regarded as being a state-sponsored body. Examples are the Institute of Public Administration and the Economic and Social Research Institute.

6. A body that has no governing legislation or articles of association, whose constitution amounts to a statement from the government or the minister concerned as to what its tasks are.

Clear criteria as to when some of the above methods should be used are not discernible. McGauran *et al.* (2005: 41) note that 'In terms of legal status there are no general statutory definitions of different styles of agencies in Ireland'. The company mould, at least in the earlier days when the commercial bodies were being set up, seems to have been preferred for the reason that the public might be encouraged to take up some of the shares. There was also the consideration that changes in direction could be more flexibly provided for without going through the elaborate procedure of an amending statute.

Prescribed Functions

The functions are normally prescribed in such a way as to enable the board and management to exercise a certain amount of discretion. Sometimes the prescription can be so broad as to lead to problems of interpretation as to what the functions really are; such problems do not, however, normally emerge into public view, being dealt with between the department and the body concerned. A broad prescription can lead to such wide diversification of activities that it raises questions about state bodies entering into competition with private firms. On other occasions the functions can be prescribed in such detail as to leave little discretion with the body and to raise the question why the sponsoring department did not itself carry them out. For example, the functions of FÁS, the body set up under the Labour Services Act 1987 to provide training and employment schemes and job services, are set out in considerable detail, amounting to about one thousand words.

Boards

Board members are all part-time, save for those bodies where the chief executive is a member. The number of directors is normally prescribed in the governing legislation and varies from board to board. In general six is about the lowest membership and ten or twelve is the norm. The government is committed to achieving a minimum of 40 per cent representation of women on state boards. In July 2002 all ministers were asked to review the gender balance composition of the state boards and committees under the aegis of their department, and to take measures to redress gender imbalances where the 40 per cent target was not reached. In January 2005 the government decided that all nominating bodies should be required to nominate both male and female options for those appointments to state boards where they are the responsible authority. All ministers were requested to put in place the necessary procedures to implement the government decision. Progress on this issue is reported to government at six-monthly intervals.

Selection

In the selection of directors, ministers have almost unlimited discretion and choice. In practice, ministers notify their colleagues informally at government meetings of the appointments they propose to make. In some cases, however, the legislation provides that certain organisations must be represented on the board. For example, in the case of FÁS, employers and unions must be represented; and in the case of Teagasc, there should be representatives of farming organisations. But even in such circumstances ministers may choose from names submitted to them. Members of the Oireachtas and of the European Parliament are debarred from board membership.

In order to meet the persistent criticism that many directors owe their appointments to their services to a political party rather than to professional competence, a scheme to regulate the selection of board members was announced in December 1986. It involved, on the one hand, the introduction of a register of suitable appointees, to be prepared in consultation with bodies such as the Irish Congress of Trade Unions and the Irish Management Institute; and, on the other, the drawing up by ministers of a range of required competences for boards under their aegis, so that these could be matched with the abilities of prospective appointees. Although such a register has been formed, the criticism persists. The *Programme for Economic and Social Progress* (1991) stated, 'The primary considerations which should apply in the appointment of directors to state companies are the experience and expertise of the individuals concerned. The chairman should be consulted prior to the appointment of directors in order to provide the minister concerned with the necessary information on the experience, talents and qualifications required for the board of the company in question.' This principle was accepted by the government. Under the Standards in Public Office Commission's rules, state appointments 'should be made on the basis of merit, taking into account the skills, qualifications and experience of the person to be appointed'.

In September 2006 Taoiseach Bertie Ahern accepted that he had appointed friends of his to state boards, insisting, 'I might have appointed somebody but I appointed them because they were friends, not because of anything they had given me.' In reply to a parliamentary question in October 2006 he stated:

> With regard to boards generally, not just recently, but for a long time the position has been that Governments have had to try hard to get people for them. These people are from organisations and professions and are known. The Government has not been partisan about appointing boards and packing them with supporters as can be seen if one looks at the range of people on the various boards. Many of the chairmen of State boards are not affiliated to Fianna Fáil or the Progressive Democrats, but they do a good job.

A bill to establish an independent merit-based system for the appointment of board chairpersons and board members was defeated at second stage in the Dáil in March 2007. In October 2008 Fine Gael frontbench spokesperson Deputy Leo Varadkar published the Public Appointments Transparency Bill. The bill seeks to increase democratic scrutiny of appointments to state boards by the Oireachtas, to enhance transparency, to make state agencies more accountable to the people and to end the practice of unqualified political candidates being appointed to the boards of state agencies. It proposes four major reforms. All ministerial appointments to state boards to be laid before the Dáil and the qualifications of the candidate to be included in the order of appointment. Chairpersons of certain state bodies to be subject to a hearing of the relevant Oireachtas committee before their nomination is ratified in the Dáil. Certain state agencies to furnish to the relevant Oireachtas committee a copy of their annual report, annual accounts, work plan and strategic plan. Chief executives and board chairpersons to be required to appear before the relevant Oireachtas committee when called upon to do so. The Labour Party has also called for the relevant minister to be questioned by the appropriate Oireachtas committee about the basis on which appointments are made.

Worker Representation

Worker representation on the boards of a number of then state bodies (including Aer Lingus, CIÉ, ESB and An Post) was provided for under the Worker Participation (State Enterprise) Acts 1977 to 1988. Under these arrangements, one-third of the seats on the boards of the designated bodies were reserved for worker representatives. The reasons for worker participation were: the entitlement of workers to participate in company decision making, the need to harness the total resources of a company, and the beneficial effect on industrial relations.

Elections among the workers employed by the bodies are held every four years under the auspices of the body concerned. The successful candidates are then appointed by the minister.

Clearly, ministers and trade unions are happy with the arrangements. It is not so clear that some chairpersons and chief executives are entirely satisfied with them. They have referred to conflicts of interest, and also to problems of confidentiality that can arise, for example when worker representatives return from a board meeting to their fellow workers (i.e. their own electorate), who may not fully appreciate the need for discretion regarding the proceedings at the meeting.

Civil Service Representation

In some cases ministers appoint senior officials in their departments to boards under their aegis. The practice is, however, neither common nor uniform. The arguments for it have not been openly advanced by ministers, but they are accepted as being the desirability of providing a direct and useful flow of information between the body concerned and the department, to the advantage of both. During the DIRT Inquiry (Committee of Public Accounts 1999) it was revealed that it had been the practice since 1983 to have a civil servant from the Department of Finance on the board of ACC Bank. Secretary General of the Department of Finance Paddy Mullarkey explained at the hearings on 23 September 1999 that the civil servant did not make reports:

> No. the civil servant would not be expected and didn't report in the normal way. That would be seen to be inappropriate. The civil servant was expected to play his ordinary role, the normal role of a board member in relation to a bank or in relation to any State company and . . . as I say, I think it would be unacceptable to a State company generally . . . for a board member for a Department to be reporting back regularly on operational matters.

The appointment of civil servants to boards is not always acceptable to some chief executives or to some of the other board members. They regard such appointments as inhibiting and interfering, and point out that they can cause conflicts of role in that civil service appointees are often called upon, as part of their departmental responsibilities, to evaluate and adjudicate on proposals from boards of which they are members. They also point to the risk of such appointments cutting across the lines of communication that should normally obtain between the chairperson of a board and the minister.

Fees

Membership of boards generally carries a fee, but, again, the practice is not uniform, nor is the amount of the fee. The Department of Finance categorises state bodies to determine the remuneration to be paid to board members. Fees, where payable, were in the range of €20,000 to €28,000 a year in 2009 for the chairperson (but there are a few exceptions where the fee is higher) and €12,000 to €17,500 for ordinary members. The chairperson of the Dublin Port Company, for example, is paid €22,000 a year. The chairperson of FÁS, for example, is paid €24,000 annually and the board members are paid a fee of €14,000 per year. Fees are not payable to civil servants for board membership, on the grounds that their work on the board is merely an extension of their work in their departments. Travelling and subsistence expenses at the highest rates applicable to the civil service are in all cases paid for attendance at meetings on the business of the board.

The Minister for Finance has overall responsibility for determining the remuneration and conditions of chairpersons, board members and chief executives of the state-sponsored bodies and state agencies under the aegis of the various civil service departments. All departments have a liaison unit or person formally linking each individual agency and the department. Some departments have established corporate governance units, which work with the relevant line divisions to administer matters in relation to these aspects in close consultation with the bodies themselves. Details of the remuneration of board members and chief executives are published in the annual reports of many bodies and can be accessed on their individual websites.

A performance-related award scheme operates in thirty-nine non-commercial state bodies. The role of the Minister for Finance and the Department of Finance is to approve the introduction of such schemes where the relevant board and parent department are of the view that the state body's remit can meet the principles laid down by the Review Body on Higher Remuneration in the Public Sector for the effective application of such schemes. Most of the schemes apply to the post of chief executive only and provide for awards up to a maximum of 20 per cent of salary.

Finance

Commercial Bodies

The commercial bodies are financed in three main ways: from the Exchequer, from internal sources, and through borrowing from the banks and other financial institutions at home and abroad. The Exchequer provides loans, share capital and subsidies. In the case of statutory corporations, the financial structure is subject to statutory control. Limits on the aggregate of loans for individual corporations are prescribed in the establishing legislation and increases over these limits require further legislation.

The sole or main shareholder in many of the commercial state-sponsored bodies is the Minister for Finance; in others it is the responsible minister. The share capital structure is prescribed in the establishing statutes and increases in that capital also require legislation.

It is government policy that the commercial state-sponsored bodies should operate, as far as possible, without Exchequer assistance, i.e. that they should make ends meet from their own resources, for example from the fares charged in the case of the transport bodies. Some of them, such as the ESB and the Voluntary Health Insurance Board, are required by law to break even, taking one year with another. Despite these aspirations and legal imperatives, however, it is not unusual that, for reasons of a social or political nature, one finds that the policies of the government make attainment of these more difficult. This happens, for example, when the government delays price increases, as it does sometimes in the case of CIÉ; or when it seeks to delay the termination of a loss-making activity, as in the case of the closure of some post offices by An Post. The board and management of An Post look after matters relating to post office closures. In reply to a parliamentary question on 27 March 2007 it was shown that 399 post offices were closed around the country between 1997 and 2007.

Some of the bodies raise a proportion of the capital they need through borrowing abroad. In some instances, the borrowing is guaranteed by the state. The incidence of guarantees is being greatly reduced in line with current government policy. Where guarantees are given, the Department of Finance must be satisfied that the money to be borrowed is to be used for properly authorised projects and that the terms of the loan are reasonable. What this means, in effect, is that no state body has the authority to incur obligations that ultimately fall upon the Exchequer unless the Minister for Finance agrees. (The collapse of the previously successful Irish Shipping in 1984 was due to its having entered a number of highly speculative, long-term, fixed-rate agreements fundamental to the future of the company, without the knowledge of the Minister for Finance. The government refused to underwrite the massive costs arising from these unauthorised agreements.)

The government is taking a tougher line on the payment of dividends to the Exchequer. In 2007 returns to the Exchequer from the seventeen state-owned companies currently operating totalled over €84 million. The ESB was the largest contributor with over €63 million. There are no central guidelines for the calculation of dividend payments and it is done on a case-by-case basis. Dividend policy from state companies varies widely and there are moves to standardise this. Commentators have suggested around 30 per cent of profits may be set as a benchmark, though allowances would be made for the particular financial positions and investment needs of the different state companies. For example, Coillte, the state forestry company was set up in 1989 as a state-owned, private limited company with the Minister for Finance as the only shareholder. It was given ownership of the state's forests, about 376,000 hectares, or 1,500m^2. It did not make a payment to the Exchequer between 1989 and 2007.

Non-Commercial Bodies

The non-commercial bodies, state agencies and public bodies employ about 16,000 people, and the number of staff mushroomed by more than 60 per cent between 2000 and 2008. These agencies depend mainly on the

Exchequer for their funds. As indicated earlier, they were not set up to trade and in very many cases are performing tasks that could be carried out by government departments. Minister of State Martin Mansergh (2008) noted, 'that annual expenditure by the State Agencies has risen from €3.7 billion in 2003 to €6.1 billion in 2008.' The normal procedure is that they get a specific sum of money, called a grant-in-aid, from their parent department. The sum is arrived at by consultation between officials of the body concerned, the parent department and the Department of Finance. The final determination is made by the government.

Accounts

All state-sponsored bodies prepare annual statements of accounts. These are certified in some cases by the Comptroller and Auditor General, and in others, mainly the commercial bodies, by auditors in the private sector. In the latter cases, the accountants responsible for certification must be approved by the Minister for Finance, who can also prescribe the format of the accounts. In all cases, the accounts must be submitted to the parent department; and, where the establishing legislation so provides, they must be submitted to the government prior to subsequent presentation to the Dáil (in effect making them available in the Oireachtas library). Kehoe (2006) notes that the financial performances of eight of the largest semi-state companies under the control of the Department of Communications, Marine and Natural Resources, including RTÉ, An Post, Bord Gáis and ESB, were to be scrutinised by a government-appointed team of external consultants.

The Mechanism of Control

Ministerial Control

Ministerial control derives mainly from the act or other document setting up the body, but also from the fact that the minister is a member of the government, which has ultimate control. The constituent document, the founding legislative instrument, in addition to prescribing the functions of the board, normally lays down that certain powers may not be exercised except with the approval of the minister, and that such reports and infor - mation as the minister requests must be made available. Ministers maintain regular contact with the chairpersons of agency boards by telephone and formal and informal meetings. Occasionally ministers will meet the full board in a structured setting. Ministers also meet with senior managers from time to time. These contacts address mattes such as the review of overall strategies, business plans, financial outlook, performance, structures, possible rationalisation, investment programmes and proposals for legislative change. Such discussions complement the ongoing talks between the department and the agency.

Individual sections within the departments concerned are responsible for carrying out the duties directly arising from the operations of the state bodies under their aegis. These duties can range from the preparation of warrants of appointment of directors to examining new proposals and answering parliamentary questions. The normal lines of communication are between the chairperson of the board and the minister, between the chief executive and the assistant secretary in charge of that work, and otherwise between officials in the body and in the department at various levels, exchanging information and making suggestions.

The degree of ministerial control depends to some extent on the attitude of individual ministers. Some are very interested in the performance of the bodies under their aegis and meet their boards frequently; some meet them only occasionally; some never meet them. On the rare occasions when boards are reluctant to accept government policy, they can earn themselves a ministerial reprimand, however, this is a power that a minister will feel able to apply only in the last resort.

Oireachtas Control

The state-sponsored bodies and state agencies are answerable to the Oireachtas in a number of ways. They are obliged to present annual reports and accounts. Even though, as with the annual reports and accounts of most companies, these may not reveal a great deal about the thinking behind a body's policies, the presentation nevertheless affords members of the Oireachtas an opportunity to have a discussion initiated by way of a motion in either House. Parliamentary questions may be asked. In answering, however, ministers seek to ensure that a body is not subjected to such degree of scrutiny as would disclose commercial information or undermine its proper managerial prerogative. Usually, therefore, ministers do not answer questions that relate solely to day-to-day matters; the conventional reply is that the minister has no function in these. There has been increasing disquiet about the accountability of state bodies, which are not directly accountable through the parliamentary question system. There have also been delays in getting replies from agencies to specific questions. Speaking in the Dáil on 26 February 2008 then Government Chief Whip, Tom Kitt, noted, 'there are valid concerns among all parliamentarians with regard to access to speedy replies from those agencies. The item is very much on our agenda for discussion. I have no doubt that my party is also concerned about the problem of getting information from the quangos and agencies we establish. A danger exists that many of these agencies do their own thing and we must address the matter of accountability.' When amending legislation in relation to a particular body is being debated, deputies and senators have wide scope for raising issues relating to the body concerned. The annual presentation by ministers of the estimates for their departments affords members of the Dáil an opportunity of commenting on the affairs of those bodies for which funds are being provided in the estimate. Individual members of the Dáil or Seanad may, at any time, table motions relating to the affairs of individual bodies or of the bodies as a whole. By and large, however, the above means of inquiring into the affairs of state bodies are not greatly availed of, that task being left mainly to the Oireachtas committees.

Oireachtas Committees

While most Oireachtas committees meet in public session and their proceedings are televised, the work of the committees has not captured the public interest or imagination. Representatives of the media and members of the public may attend. Each House decides the orders of reference, membership and powers of committees. It is the practice for committee membership to be proportionally representative of the House that sets it up. Committee reports are published and it is for the House(s) thereafter to decide on any follow-up action. With the exception of the month of August, committees meet throughout the year. The expansion in the number and range of committees in recent years has enabled the Houses to deal with an ever-increasing volume of parliamentary business, while providing members with additional opportunities to participate in all aspects of the work of parliament. As required, ministers are ex officio members of Dáil select committees when they are considering bills or estimates for public services. The orders of reference of some committees also allow for the appointment of substitute members or indeed the attendance of members of the Houses who are not formal members.

The Co-ordinating Group of Secretaries proposed that 'The process of Oireachtas reform, in particular of the Committee System, be continued in support of the change to greater openness and transparency in public administration. In this regard also, the need for greater clarity in relation to the role and remit of individual committees is essential' (Department of the Taoiseach 1996: 17). The commercial and non-commercial state agencies and bodies have had limited parliamentary scrutiny and are not directly answerable to the Dáil. MacCarthaigh (2005: 211) notes that 'a joint committee had been established in the Oireachtas in 1976 to oversee the work of commercial state-sponsored bodies, but no equivalent committee to investigate non-commercial was ever established. In fact it was not until 1999 that the Dáil debated one of the joint committee's reports'.

The Committee of Public Accounts – commonly referred to as the Public Accounts Committee (PAC) is the most powerful Dáil Committee. It is one of the longest standing committees in the Oireachtas. It is charged with overseeing government expenditure and is considerably helped in its activities by the work of the Comptroller and Auditor General, a constitutional officer of the state (see Chapter 13). In its report of December 1999, entitled *Parliamentary Inquiry into DIRT – First Report*, the PAC identified a number of weaknesses in procedures and practices and made a series of recommendations as to how matters might be improved. It was of the view that 'accountability to the Oireachtas is weakened . . . by a lack of clear boundaries between Parliament and Government'. At a meeting of the PAC on 13 July 2000, then chairperson, Deputy Jim Mitchell, noted that 'Following the DIRT inquiry it was the conclusion of this committee that all the recent scams, going back to the beef scandal, were contributed to, in part at least, by the lack of performance by the Oireachtas itself in obtaining accountability from the Government and state agencies'. He went on to comment that insufficient attention was being paid by the House itself to 'the need for accountability, proper processes, and checks and balances in the system'. Gallagher *et al.* (1997: 5) found that committees were weakly embedded in the Oireachtas infrastructure and that there was 'a lack of clarity about the overall purpose of the committee system'.

The first head of the Office of the Director of Telecommunications Regulation, Etain Doyle, initially refused to appear before a meeting of the Oireachtas Joint Committee on Public Enterprise and Transport in early 1998, but eventually appeared after taking legal advice. Deputy Dick Roche, quoted in the *Irish Independent* of 14 January 1998, described the regulator's initial reply as 'bizarre and absurd' and said that 'it seems to me that the regulator may be independent of the Minister but it is a serious misreading of her role to suggest the office is independent of the Oireachtas'.

Oireachtas committees are taking an increasingly active interest in the large numbers of state agencies, reflecting the growing role of these bodies in the public sector. The question of privilege for witnesses appearing before the committees is governed by the Committees of the Houses of the Oireachtas (Compellability, Privileges and Immunities of Witnesses) Act 1997.

The government announced that the orders of reference of Oireachtas committees would be amended to put a greater emphasis on the efficiency and effectiveness of public spending. This included a greater emphasis on annual output statements, value for money and policy reviews. Speaking in April 2008 to the Association of Chief Executives of State Agencies, the Ceann Comhairle, John O'Donoghue, said that the agencies should use the Oireachtas committees 'as a means of making their arguments and increasing awareness of their agenda. The Oireachtas Committees are a channel through which there is a real opportunity for communication. It is a channel through which understanding of the issues behind policy can be greatly enhanced. Away from the sometimes adversarial nature of the Dáil and Seanad Chambers, the committee structure allows for a more reasoned discussion of issues'. He argued that the tradition whereby state agencies focus only on reporting to their respective parent department leads to a lack of communication between the agency and the Oireachtas, which ultimately approves the budgets for non-commercial bodies.

The Ombudsman

Only the largest of the commercial bodies comes within the remit of the Ombudsman, namely An Post. On receiving a complaint about this body, the Ombudsman can investigate it at no cost to the complainant. However, the latter must have pursued the matter fully with An Post before approaching the Ombudsman. The Ombudsman and Information Commissioner, Emily O'Reilly, said in her 2007 annual report that new state bodies should automatically be required to comply with the Freedom of Information Act, adding, 'Given the number of new agencies established each year, and an emerging trend whereby existing functions are being moved to new bodies, I now consider it urgent that this matter be addressed' (Office of the Information Commissioner 2008). The Ombudsman (Amendment) Bill 2008 aims to widen the Ombudsman's remit and update the existing Ombudsman legislation. This will extend the power of the Ombudsman to investigate the hundreds of state agencies, including the Courts Service, FÁS, vocational education committees, third-level institutes of education and many other agencies whose daily actions and decisions affect large numbers of people. This is the first major expansion in the remit of the Ombudsman's office since its creation in 1984 with a remit to cover the civil service, local authorities, the public health services (with the public voluntary hospitals being added in 2007) and An Post. The Ombudsman noted that 'The agencies are subject to little or no parliamentary oversight and there has been a diminution in ministerial responsibility for, and control over, functions which were formerly part of the relevant Government department' (O'Reilly 2008). The 2008 bill also provides for increased powers for the Ombudsman; for example, where the requirement on a public body to provide information to the Ombudsman is not being met, the Ombudsman can institute legal proceedings.

The Debate on Accountability and Control

Public accountability is the hallmark of modern democratic governance. As state agencies and state-sponsored bodies have been established in the national interest, it is accepted that the government and the Oireachtas should be in a position to measure adequately whether they are carrying out efficiently the tasks assigned to them. At the same time, it is accepted that the very fact of the setting up of such bodies to carry out specific functions outside the civil service structure and without direct ministerial responsibility is an indication of an intention to give them a reasonable amount of freedom and scope for initiative. There is something of a dilemma here, and it is reflected in a general lack of definition concerning the relationship between the bodies and their departments. Tutty (1997: 83) notes, 'Adequate and effective arrangements for governance and accountability . . . are fundamental elements of a democratic system of government . . . governance is about the collection of rules, standards and norms that inform the behaviour of civil and public servants and politicians in conducting the business of the state with and on behalf of the public'.

The accountability and control of state agencies is as yet an unsolved problem, and the failure to devise a precise and comprehensive system has meant that the level of control tends to depend on such factors as the political visibility of an organisation (for example RTÉ), its geographical spread (CIÉ), its financial performance (Irish Greyhound Board) and the attitudes of individual ministers and boards.

Government policy over the years has, in broad terms, been to allow state agencies and state-sponsored bodies as much freedom as possible consistent with the achievement of the objectives for which they were established. More recently, it has been explicitly indicated that the commercial bodies must achieve commercial results within a competitive framework, without the benefit of financial help from the state. In so far as the non-commercial bodies are concerned, performance is to be measured not so much financially as by innovativeness in generating revenue, increasing industry involvement in their task, and achieving set targets and improved productivity. They can no longer rely on incremental increases in their annual grants.

The question of the appropriate nature and degree of control over agencies and state-sponsored bodies has long been debated. The debate has become more intensive in recent years because of the severe strain on the Exchequer imposed by some of the bodies in the general context of a relentless national drive for efficiency and economy. Accountability and control and the problems of performance associated with them also received considerable attention in both commercial and non-commercial bodies and agencies over the years. Among the reasons identified were the lack of clarity of objectives, roles, responsibilities and reporting relationships and confusion between social and strategic roles. The OECD 2008 report on Ireland noted that the public service 'will have to amend or revise existing accountability structures and ways of working, to allow for integrated system-wide action where this is required'. The OECD (2008b: 24) comments that 'In the context of controls on recruitment to the Civil Service, Ireland has gone down a path of agencification in order to build up needed capacity. Without putting in place the proper governance structures and performance incentives, however this has led to further fragmentation and reduced transparency'.

This concern had earlier led to the government deciding that a system of information to enable ministers to anticipate problems rather than have problems thrust upon them was necessary and, accordingly, that each commercial body should prepare a corporate plan for its activities for the five years ahead, which would be rolled over on an annual basis. It was indicated that such a plan would encourage a systematic approach to planning and would provide standards for the evaluation of performance, especially in such areas as finance, investment and employment. The plans were submitted to the parent departments, where they were evaluated in consultation with the Department of Finance. Other ameliorative measures, mainly providing for a more strictly regulated system of submission of reports and accounts, were also put in place. Difficulties in this area persisted, however.

In 1992 the Department of Finance found it necessary to issue guidelines to the state bodies for the conduct of their operations. These provided, *inter alia*, that all such bodies should have adequate internal audit arrangements; that competitive tendering should be normal practice; that the establishment of subsidiaries and participation in joint ventures should be subject to the approval of the relevant minister and the Minister for Finance; that a written code of conduct should be put in place, of which an essential element would be disclosure of interest; that chairpersons of boards were responsible for the implementation of government policy in relation to the remuneration of the chief executive; and that all chairpersons should furnish comprehensive annual reports to ministers on significant developments during the preceding year and in which they would confirm that the above-mentioned matters are being complied with.

The chief executives of the commercial bodies do not like some of these arrangements. They maintain that what they describe as the dead hand of bureaucracy is creeping more and more relentlessly into the management of the bodies. They are unhappy also about government control over remuneration, which, they say, should be left free for their boards to determine. This is a long-standing grievance. The chief executives point to what they call the illogicality of giving boards responsibility for spending millions of euro and yet not giving them responsibility for the pay of their staff. The government answer to this is that all parts of the public service must conform to its guidelines on pay, which, because of the relative size of public sector employment to total employment in the country, are vital to the economy because of the spin-off effects. It is sometimes pointed out that when control over pay was not exercised centrally, many boards were excessively generous in rewarding their staff.

The Comptroller and Auditor General (C&AG) carries out the annual audit of most non-commercial state-sponsored bodies. This is a standard financial/regularity type of audit carried out in accordance with the relevant accounting standards. The Comptroller and Auditor General (Amendment) Act 1993 extended the C&AG's powers to include examination of the economy, efficiency and management effectiveness of the non-commercial state bodies. The C&AG's reports on these bodies are considered by the Public Accounts Committee, thereby improving accountability. The commercial state bodies are audited by private sector firms. The 1993 act did not extend the powers of inspection of the C&AG to these bodies.

In the larger commercial bodies the objective is to strike the correct balance between necessary public accountability and commercial freedom. There has been a significant emphasis placed on corporate governance – the system of directing and controlling companies and agencies.

The government has sought to deal with the problem of how to give state bodies the degree of freedom required, while at the same time securing the level of accountability needed. The Department of Finance (2001) issued a mandatory *Code of Practice for the Governance of State Bodies*, which requires the boards of state bodies to ensure that a system of reporting and auditing is installed in each body so that the board can assure itself that the body is operating efficiently and effectively. The code is quite financially focused and sets out details on internal audit, procurement, disposal of assets, establishment of subsidiaries, diversification, investment appraisal, fees, reporting arrangements, corporate planning and tax compliance. This code, which dates from 2001, applies to all agencies but was drawn up with commercial agencies in mind. It is used extensively at the sub-national level in Ireland, and oversight arrangements such as external audits are a routine occurrence for local and regional organisations. MacCarthaigh (2007) reveals a complex web of inter-linkages and inter-dependencies between sub-national organisations. He also highlights the importance of local and regional organisations in the delivery and implementation of national policies. Speaking at the Institute of Public Administration's annual governance forum in 2007, Padraic White, former Managing Director of the IDA, said that codes of governance appeared to be a 'one-way street' leading out from government departments. Public bodies who complied with the requirements deserved reciprocity in timely decision making from the centre.

The state employment agency, FÁS, was under intense scrutiny in 2008 by the Oireachtas Enterprise and Employment Committee, the Public Accounts Committee, the C&AG and two separate Garda investigations. The director-general resigned from FÁS in November 2008 amid controversy over extravagant expenditure. This occurred despite the presence of a Department of Finance representative on the board of FÁS and on its internal audit committee. A code of ethics reminding staff of their responsibility to secure value for money for FÁS was introduced in July 2003. Its guiding principles are 'honesty, integrity and public accountability'. It states that employees must 'not benefit inappropriately' from their work for FÁS nor 'engage in any activity that is in conflict with these work duties'. Among the alarming examples of profligate expenditure revealed in 2008 were all-expenses-paid trips to the United States, expensive air tickets, chauffeur-driven cars, golfing at exclusive clubs and lavish entertainment. As a result, FÁS put in place more robust structures with enhanced management and control systems, including the internal audit function. Procedures and governance arrangements were further reviewed.

An Organisational Zoo

The majority of agencies in the state sector must, by virtue of their roles and objectives, collaborate with other agencies and co-ordinate their activities with a government department. Thus, the strength and vitality of the governance arrangements are critical. The tendency to set up agencies and bodies at one remove from the government is 'an abdication of respon-sibility,' then Minister for Justice Brian Lenihan said in a highly publicised speech in July 2007. He stated:

> That isn't a viable way of running a country. That is not a very fashionable point of view, but we have gone down the road a little too far – I am not talking about the Department of Justice, but right across the range of government business – of setting up agencies and bodies at one remove from the govern-ment to whom the government can then abdicate responsibility for dealing with certain matters. I subscribe to the old-fashioned point of view that we have a general election. The purpose of it is to create a majority in the Dáil who will then unite around a government and who are then accountable for running the country and the people can get rid of you and replace you with someone else if they don't like how you run the country. This tendency to establish a lot of agencies and bodies at one remove from the government is a form of abdication from governmental responsibilities and I don't agree with it.

Agency management, co-ordination and accountability is a challenge faced by many countries. Sabel and O'Donnell (2000: 102–103) state:

> The upshot, as Rhodes shows is that in Britain government agencies in fact develop a near monopoly of expertise in their policy area, notwithstanding efforts to outfit the politically responsible minister with capacities for strategic surveillance. Policy therefore emerges from innumerable small decisions, such

that 'the agency tail will wag the departmental dog.' To increase the confusion, the department, emboldened by official encouragement to assert its directive powers, often uses its oversight responsibility to meddle in the details of agency decision-making. If results disappoint the minister can play on the ambiguities in the distinction between policy (her responsibility) and management (the domain of the operating agency) to avoid accountability. Civil servants are no longer in charge; but no one else is, either. Rhodes for one concludes that 'British government has undergone a significant decrease in political accountability'.

Although there are many new agencies handling functions previously discharged by central departments, there has been no corresponding reduction in the size of government. In reply to a parliamentary question on 4 June 2008 Minister for Finance Brian Lenihan said, 'Important considerations arise in regard to the traditional control the Department of Finance has raised over establishments in the public service. It is my considered view that the Department must control the size of those establishments, because control over expenditure is an essential weapon in maintaining the control over public expenditure.' Speaking to the Association of Chief Executives of State Agencies in September 2008, Minister of State Martin Mansergh noted:

> Research by the Institute of Public Administration suggests that almost a quarter of Agencies are carrying out what many would regard as the traditional role of Departments, that of 'providing advice'. Decisions regarding the rationalisation of Agencies will take into account the role of Government Departments as the primary locus of policy formulation, evaluation and analysis. Such decisions will also support and enhance the established model of Ministerial accountability to Dáil Éireann, and to the Oireachtas as a whole, where outsourcing has sometimes led to a situation where decisions are perceived as remote from democratic scrutiny and control.

There is a risk of duplication and overlap of services provided by agencies, particularly at local level. There is a need for proper governance, accountability, greater cost control and stronger financial systems. Due to the deteriorating Exchequer position in July 2008, the government indicated that the widespread amalgamation and abolition of state agencies would form a central part of its efficiency drive. The first stage of this rationalisation process was set out in budget 2009. A major challenge facing the government in reviewing the efficiency of agencies is that nobody really knows precisely how many agencies there are, how many personnel work in each agency, what the budget for each agency is and who has the authority to spend what and where.

The OECD (2008b: 296) noted that 'no official Irish statistics are available for staff numbers in agencies today or 10 or 20 years ago' and estimated 'that currently there are over 500 non-commercial agencies in Ireland'. Many commentators put the number of agencies as high as 800. 'Agencies vary significantly in size and budget and it is unclear how much public funding they use for their own functioning, for further distribution or for investment. Neither is it known how many staff they employ' (OECD 2008b: 296–7). The OECD report, which is elsewhere quite positive and constructive of the public service generally, suggests that one of the factors driving the creation of so many agencies in the past few years in particular is to create public sector jobs and to justify increased budgets. It notes (2008b: 298) that 'Some officials have asserted in OECD interviews that the creation of agencies has been used to make increases in employment numbers and budget resources more acceptable to policy-makers and the general public by placing them outside of the core civil service and, in doing so, circumventing the effective limit on civil service numbers'. It went on to say that TDs can suggest the creation of an agency during a debate on the floor of the Dáil – something which cannot be done elsewhere. Once a decision is made to set up an agency, the report observes, there is no discussion on the agency's precise functions or authority and in many cases the agency is given very little decision-making powers, with real power retained by central government. The OECD (2008b: 300) comments that 'This situation has led to an organizational zoo where citizens, private firms and government have little clarity on how the public service operates'. In addition, the alphabet soup of agencies, creates confusion and lack of clarity between, for example, the National Economic and Social Development Office (NESDO), the National Economic and Social Council (NESC), the National Economic and Social Forum (NESF), the National Centre for Partnership and Performance (NCPP) and the Economic and Social Research Institute (ESRI).

MacCarthaigh (2008) notes:

> While immediate concern with public spending has necessarily forced attention on the manner in which the State administration is arranged, a major stimulus for questioning the use of agencies was the establishment of the HSE and the perception that it has been unable to deliver on its promise. The criticisms levelled against it – not only charges of inefficiency and unbalanced staffing but, perhaps especially, the deficits in political and public accountability that have opened up – have quickly been extended to the State agency sector in general . . .
>
> There is some irony in the fact that the HSE's creation led to one of the greatest incidents of agency mergers and abolitions in the history of the State. But it was not the only case of agency rationalisation . . . In Ireland, the focus on agencies as a collective and the belief that they are an aberration rather than a normal part of modern government deflects attention from what it is they actually do. In fact there is no evidence that their performance has been bad

. . . However, if agencies are to be merged or abolished, careful consideration should be given to the level of government to which their functions should be transferred, and to the range of functions that it may be appropriate for Government to perform. There is nothing wrong with using agencies. Given our administrative tradition, it seems likely that the State agency is here to stay. The real issue is devising the means of getting the best out of them.

Following budget 2009 considerable work was done throughout the civil service relating to data collection and analysis of the roles and respon - sibilities of agencies, together with the progressing of a number of pieces of legislation relevant to rationalisation and discussions with agencies on the implementation of these organisational changes.

The Debate on Privatisation

An issue which is debated from time to time in the media, in academia and in the Dáil is that of privatisation. Privatisation may include charging for services previously supplied by government agencies at prices not reflecting the true commercial cost; injecting private non-voting capital into the financial structures of nationalised undertakings; opening up an agency's market to competition from private sector firms; and full-scale denation- alisation, involving the sale of a majority shareholding to the private sector. It is this last concept of privatisation that has been the main focus of debate in Ireland to date. Normally, behind a debate such as this there is a clash of ideologies, a clash of views as to the role of the state in society. One view is that government is a burden on society, that all creative forces are in the marketplace and that the state is largely an obstacle to economic progress. The other view is that the state is a moral system superimposed on the disorder of nature and that the mission of government is to bring order and justice to an unjust world. The state, according to this view, has to provide social justice. It has to make up for market failure.

Irish Sugar and the Irish Life Assurance Company were privatised in 1991. In 1992 the shipping company B&I Line was sold to Irish Continental Group. In June 1999 the government sold its entire shareholding in Telecom Éireann, following full deregulation of the telecommunications market in December 1998. ICC Bank was sold to Bank of Scotland in February 2001. ACC Bank was sold to Rabobank Nederland in March 2002. Aer Rianta, the airports authority, was mentioned in the context of privatisation, but this did not happen and the State Airports Act 2004 provided the legal basis for the establishment of Dublin, Cork and Shannon Airports as independent authorities under state ownership. In 2006 the government agreed to privatise a majority stake in Aer Lingus. The state retained 25.1 per cent of the airline's shares in the initial public offering in order to protect Ireland's access to the valuable slots at Heathrow Airport. Within a week of the flotation on the Dublin and London stock exchanges, rival airline Ryanair, founded in 1985, had bought a significant percentage of the shares in Aer Lingus.

Originally opened in August 1939 as Irish Steel Ltd, the privately owned firm went into receivership in 1946. A year later, the government purchased the company's assets and nationalised the industry to secure some 240 jobs. Eventually, in 1996, the state wrote off debts of £27.5 million (€34.9 million) and sold Irish Steel to Indian company Ispat International Group for £1 (€1.27); this was on the understanding that significant investment would be made in the plant and its 330 jobs would be secured under a five-year plan. The plant closed in 2001.

The arguments in favour of privatising state bodies include:

- *Efficiency:* public sector enterprises sometimes have difficulty in measuring their efficiency since they have to satisfy conflicting social and commercial objectives. Such enterprises are inevitably constrained in their actions by political considerations. Greater speed and flexibility in decision making would be possible if there were not the need for frequent reference to government departments or to the government.
- *Funding:* public ownership would provide companies with opportunities for further development by means of funding secured in the private sector if national budgetary considerations precluded the financing of such developments by the Exchequer.
- *Wider public interest:* providing shares to the general public would increase their interest in the companies, would be to the benefit of democracy and would provide better for the interests of the consumer.
- *Improved performance:* the sale of shares to employees, sometimes by means of preferential offers, is said to increase the sense of employee involvement in the concern and to act as a stimulus to improved performance on the part of employees and, consequently, of the firm.
- *The public sector borrowing requirement:* the reduction of this requirement could help in dealing with the problem of high taxation and the national debt.

The arguments against privatisation include:

- *Uncertainty:* there is no certainty that the free market will automatically lead to the optimum economic out-turn, nor that it will lead to social equality. The only way in which these goals can be achieved is through state intervention; otherwise the profit motive will prevail.
- *Benefits for private investors:* potential purchasers in the private sector will be interested only in those state concerns that are profitable and the

state will be left with the bodies that continue to be a drain. Such private investors will reap the benefit of large amounts of taxpayers' money injected into the state sector over the years. Thus, privatisation would bring profit to the few at the expense of the community.

- *Job losses:* employment is a vital part of community interest. Its provision might not, however, be given its due importance should a state enterprise be privatised.
- *Efficiency:* there is no evidence that state bodies are any less efficient than private businesses, as witnessed by the collapse of many high-profile private enterprises.
- *Removal of constraints:* the question is asked why the state bodies were set up in the first place and whether the situation has changed. Any weakness caused by the constraints of state ownership could be remedied by dealing with such constraints, while retaining the bodies in state ownership.

Successive governments have adopted a pragmatic view on the question of the privatisation of state-sponsored bodies. What is important is that state-sponsored bodies work, that they contribute to economic activity and growth, and that they compete fairly in the open market place. In a reply to a parliamentary question on 15 February 2000, Minister for Finance Charlie McCreevy noted:

> In general terms, when the sale, in whole or in part, of commercial State bodies occurs, the burden on the Exchequer is set to diminish both from the revenue realised from the process itself and the reduced need to inject share capital into the bodies to keep them adequately capitalised. In addition, the economy, and therefore, the Exchequer, stand to benefit from the efficiencies which flow from the release of commercial State bodies from State control to compete in a fully commercial manner in the market place. However, it is not possible to quantify the exact extent of the savings to the taxpayer from the process of disposing of commercial State bodies. This would be dependent on a wide range of factors, which would include the financial position of individual bodies prior to sale, the interest shown in acquiring them, the method and timing of, and conditions applying to, sale and the circumstances pertaining to the particular sectors of the economy in which individual bodies have been operating.

State Bodies and the European Union

The Treaty of Rome, as do subsequent European treaties, sees market forces as the prime motor of a trans-national economy. It regards these forces as being capable, subject to adequate supervision, of bringing about 'harmonious development of economic activities, a continuous and balanced expansion, an increase in stability, an accelerated raising of the standard of living and closer relations between the states belonging to it' (Article 2). There is no 'community role' for public enterprise. Essentially, the EU requires both private and state commercial organisations to be bound by the same rules of competition, i.e. that there be no discrimination in favour of state bodies. It points to the fact that the state, in relation to its bodies, is generally looking for results, among which profit may not always be the major consideration, and that a state body can be in direct competition in its activities with those of other undertakings, whether public or private, in its own or other countries. The risk (as far as the EU is concerned) of distortions of competition between undertakings becomes real at this point and is highlighted by the difficulty of defining normal market behaviour.

It was against this background that the EU adopted, in 1980, a directive on the transparency, or openness, of the financial relations between member states and their public enterprises. The directive imposes on member states the obligation to supply, on request, certain information on these relations; it also defines certain types of financial relationship to which the EU considered it particularly important that transparency should be applied. Examples of these relationships are the forgoing of a normal return on public funds and the compensation for financial burdens imposed by the state. The directive was not acceptable to some member states (Ireland did not object), who unsuccessfully challenged it in the European Court of Justice.

It was in the light of this general situation that, even before the directive, Bord Bainne (the Dairy Board) had to change its status from that of a state-sponsored body to that of a co-operative. An Bord Gráin (the Grain Board), the Pigs and Bacon Commission and the Dublin and Cork District Milk Boards were forced to terminate their activities.

Conclusion

It is difficult to disagree with the following assessment given by Tom Barrington (1980: 65):

> Overall [the Irish state-sponsored body] has shown itself to be a very considerable instrument for development. It has played a big part in raising the level of management in this country. In an unstructured, unplanned sort of way, the state-sponsored bodies have contributed very effectively to the development of the country, and represent a most interesting adaptation of a form of organisation from the private business world to the needs of public administration. This has not been without its problems, and there are other problems still to be faced; but, overall, one cannot but be impressed by the record. This record, if accepted, poses major challenges, and opportunities, for the future of Irish public administration.

Lee (1989: 635) comments, 'The rapid growth in the size of the civil service since 1970, and the proliferation of institutions in the semi-state sector, not least in the knowledge industry, run up without any sense of overall direction, have now congealed into a "disorganised complexity".' Ryan (1982: 85) speaks of formidably obstructive vested interests that impede effective decision making. Speaking in 2005, then Taoiseach Bertie Ahern noted that 'A striking feature of Irish public administration has been the growth in the range and type of organisations operating in the public arena. There is no longer a single 'ship of State' – rather we have developed a fleet of different sized vessels, each capable of performing different functions and best utilised when doing so'. In order to ensure the maximum efficiency of the flotilla of the ships of state, it is necessary to clarify the roles, responsibilities and reporting relationships of state agencies and bodies, to provide a clear sense of purpose and overall direction by 'strengthening the steering capacity of central ministries' (McGauran *et al.* 2005: 59), and to reinforce mechanisms for accountability and control. The era of the rapid proliferation of state agencies has ended, and they are being slowly dismantled where possible, merged or reformed where not.

Web Resources

Code of Practice for the Governance of State Bodies at www.finance.gov.ie/
    documents/publications/other/codeofpractice.pdf
Committee of Public Management Research at www.cpmr.gov.ie
Comptroller and Auditor General at www.audgen.gov.ie
Information Commissioner at www.oic.gov.ie
Ombudsman at www.ombudsman.gov.ie

10

THE HEALTH SERVICES

The role of the state in healthcare has been evolving since the late eighteenth century, from the locally funded provision of essential basic services (mainly for the very poor) to the wide and sophisticated range of services provided on a national basis for the whole community today. The rationale for the dominant role now adopted is that health is perceived in the modern state as a basic human right, the protection of which is accepted as a valid function of the state. The objective of the health services is to provide safe, high-quality services that achieve the best possible outcome for patients. In recent years, Ireland has experienced a re-structuring of its health system with the abolition of the regional health boards and the establishment of the Health Service Executive (HSE). The health system accounts for one-quarter of all the money spent running the country and employs one-third of all public servants.

The Irish healthcare system has a unique structure. It is a mixture of a universal health service, free at the point of consumption for some services, and a fee-based private system, with direct and indirect payments, where individuals subscribe to insurance for coverage of medical expenses. While health status indicators have improved substantially, they remain relatively low compared to some other European countries, with a life expectancy figure suggesting that healthcare outcomes could be improved. Services are recognised internationally to be of high quality.

The current role of the state in relation to health services might be described as involving three aspects: regulating and setting standards for inputs to the health system; providing services (health services staff are, in the main, state employees, and many hospitals, health centres and so on are in the ownership of the state); and funding services. The dominant source of health funding is the Exchequer. The major responsibility for health policy in Ireland lies with the Minister for Health and Children and the Department of Health and Children, established as the Department of Health in 1947. This department is primarily a policy-making unit with the great bulk of publicly funded health services provided by other health agencies.

The Irish health service is a large and complex system employing a vast range of expertise and skills in over 300 grades in approximately 100 public hospitals (including 52 acute hospitals). Centres for the care of persons with a disability or with a mental illness, community health centres and general practitioners provide additional essential health services. The system encompasses a mix of public and private care, involving the same institutions and personnel, and with a degree of interaction in funding arrangements.

Over 130,000 people work on a full-time or part-time basis in the public health services. The well-qualified, committed and caring staff trained to the best international standards are one of the most important strengths of the system. In recent years the government's high level of investment in health has achieved and maintained significant increases in the number of doctors, nurses and other healthcare professionals employed in the public health services (see Table 1). The government has also invested heavily in the education and training of such personnel in order to secure a good supply of graduates to provide for the healthcare needs of the population into the future. One-third of medical and dental staff working for the HSE are from ethnic minorities, and 10 per cent of health service staff are from overseas. Expenditure on staff represents about 70 per cent of current public expenditure on the health services.

Policy Framework

Since the 1980s a fundamental reappraisal of the organisation and the strategic outlook of the health service has been considered by various reports and working groups.

Health: The Wider Dimensions (1986)

The Department of Health published a consultative document (the first in twenty years) on health policy *Health: The Wider Dimensions* in 1986, which emphasised the importance of health promotion and also recommended changes in organisation structure in the health boards. In the years preceding this publication, healthcare policy had tended to emphasise curing, which resulted in a rapid development of the acute general hospital system and a significant reliance on high technology medicine. This document recom - mended a redirection of the health services and recognised that the essential management structures had been largely neglected. It identified the need within the healthcare system for greater accountability, closer integration between the statutory and non-statutory sectors and a more structured plan - ning cycle to incorporate, *inter alia*, the monitoring of the quality of care.

The challenges and constraints in the health area are highlighted by Kelly (2007: 15), who comments that the manner of publication of *Health: The Wider Dimensions* is significant, 'Rather than a more orthodox approach

Table 1. Numbers Employed in the Public Health Service 1997–2007

Grade/category	1997	1998	1999	2000	2001	2002	2003	2004	2005	2006	2007	% change
Medical/dental	4,976	5,153	5,385	5,698	6,285	6,775	6,792	7,013	7,266	7,712	8,005	60.9
Nursing	27,346	26,611	27,044	29,177	31,429	33,395	33,766	34,313	35,248	36,737	39,006	42.6
Health and social care professionals	5,969	6,422	6,836	7,613	9,228	12,577	12,692	12,830	13,952	14,913	15,705	163.1
Management/ administration	8,844	9,480	10,599	12,366	14,714	15,690	15,766	16,157	16,699	17,262	18,043	104.0
General support staff	20,705	21,973	22,928	25,216	13,803	13,729	13,838	13,771	13,227	12,910	12,900	47.8*
Other patient and client care					14,842	13,513	13,647	14,640	15,586	16,739	17,846	* In above
Total	67,841	69,640	72,793	80,070	90,302	95,679	96,501	98,723	101,978	106,273	111,505	68.4

Source: Health Service Personnel Census

involving a Green or White Paper, either of which would have required prior Government approval, it was decided to publish the document as "a consultative statement on health policy". My recollection is that this was done in the belief that a more dilute version of the document and its proposals would have emanated from any process of detailed examination by the Department of Finance in particular.'

Commission on Health Funding (1989)

The *Report of the Commission on Health Funding* (Department of Health 1989) offered a comprehensive assessment of the Irish healthcare system and Irish health policy. The commission's terms of reference were 'To examine the financing of the health services and to make recommendations on the extent and source of the future funding required to provide an equitable comprehensive and cost effective public health service and on any changes in administration which seem desirable for that purpose.' The report's coverage extends far beyond financing to include eligibility, roles of the public and private sectors, administration and management, planning and delivery of services, the individual services and organisational structure. The commission was of the opinion that 'the solution to the problem facing the Irish health services does not lie primarily in the system of funding but rather in the way that services are planned, organised and delivered'.

The major deficits it identified in the healthcare organisational structure were:

- It confuses political and executive functions, and therefore undermines both.
- It fails to achieve a proper balance between national and local decision making.
- The decision-making process does not provide a sufficient role for information and evaluation.
- Accountability within the structure is inadequate.
- There is no evaluation of effectiveness, efficiency and quality of service.
- Insufficient integration of related services.
- There is no independent appeal system for individuals dissatisfied with decisions.
- Inadequate representation of service users.

It recommended that:

- The Department of Health should focus on policy and remove itself from the day-to-day management of individual services.

- A new agency, the Health Services Executive Authority, should be responsible for the management of the health service.
- A structure of area general managers, responsible to the authority, should be established.
- The existing health boards should be abolished and replaced by health councils to represent local interests.

Hospital Efficiency Review Group (1990)

The Hospital Efficiency Review Group, chaired by Noel Fox, focused mainly on the internal management arrangements of the acute hospitals to determine whether greater efficiencies could be achieved. It concluded that the acute hospital services could be delivered more efficiently if mechanisms could be developed to 'better co-ordinate services, more intensively use facilities and improve resource management' (Government of Ireland 1990b).

Dublin Hospital Initiative Group (1990)

The Dublin Hospital Initiative Group, chaired by David Kennedy, was critical of the existing organisational structure for delivery of health services in the eastern region. It recommended 'an integrated and comprehensive health service, based on a systematic evaluation of patients' needs, with decision-making located as close as possible to the point of delivery of service, and with a continuation and development of the voluntary contribution to health care in the region' (Government of Ireland 1990a: ix). The Kennedy group (as it became known) made recommendations for new structural arrangements, which included a regional policy board and a strengthened management executive based on an area management structure. Examining the role of the voluntary sector, the group stated its conviction that the independence and operational autonomy of the voluntary agencies should continue. It recommended that 'the best way to achieve an integrated service to patients while maintaining the contribution of the voluntary ethos would be for the funding and service role of each agency to be expressed in detail in a contract between the area unit and the agency or hospital concerned' (1990a: 24).

Shaping a Healthier Future (1994)

Shaping a Healthier Future, published in April 1994, set out the national strategy for the development of the health services. The health strategy was underpinned by three key principles: equality, quality of service and accountability. The main theme of the strategy was the reorientation of the system towards improving the effectiveness of the health and personal social services by reshaping the way that services are planned and delivered. The strategy set out the three dimensions involved in this reorientation: the services, the framework of management and organisation, and the participants and patients.

The 1994 strategy provided the health system with an action plan for the following years and gave a strategic direction to the entire system in a move from illness treatment to illness prevention. It proposed a new organisational structure for the Dublin area, which would provide for more coherent and integrated planning for all services, including hospital care, than had hitherto prevailed. In addition, there were significant developments on funding mechanisms, which were now more appropriately linked to the case-mix experience of major acute hospitals. Also, the strategy laid particular emphasis on establishing a new performance audit responsibility for the Department of Health, which would allow the agencies and the department to agree on service priorities and objectives and to measure the effectiveness of service delivery to the patient.

Following from *Shaping a Healthier Future*, several policy documents were produced, including:

- Dental Health Action Plan 1994.
- Health Promotion Strategy 1995.
- White Paper on Mental Health 1995.
- National Policy on Alcohol 1996.
- Report of the Review Group on Health Services for Persons with a Physical or Sensory Disability 1996.
- Management Development Strategy for the Health and Personal Social Services 1997.
- Plan for Women's Health 1997.
- Cancer Strategy and Cancer Action Plan 1997.
- Statement of Strategy 1997.
- Services for Persons with a Mental Handicap: An Assessment of Need 1997–2001.
- Health Promotion Strategy for Older People 1998.
- Report of the National Task Force on Suicide 1998.
- Working for Health and Well-being: Strategy Statement 1998–2001.
- Cardiovascular Health Strategy 1999.
- Best Health for Children 1999.
- National Children's Strategy 2000.
- National Health Promotion Strategy 2000–2005.
- AIDS Strategy 2000.
- National Drugs Strategy 2001–2008.

This list is indicative of the detailed examination and analysis of the various demands on the system.

Health (Amendment) (No. 3) Act 1996

The Health (Amendment) (No. 3) Act 1996 tackled some of the weaknesses in the system, significantly enhancing the role and responsibilities of the health boards. The respective roles of health boards and their chief executives were clarified, and financial accountability within the system was strengthened by a range of measures, including the requirement that each health board produce an annual service plan and publish an annual report. The act defined more clearly the remit of a health board, imposing on it an obligation in carrying out its functions to:

- Secure the most beneficial, effective and efficient use of resources.
- Co-operate with voluntary bodies providing services in its area.
- Co-ordinate its activities with other health boards, local authorities and public bodies.
- Give due consideration to the policies and objectives of ministers and of the government.

Quality and Fairness: A Health System for You (2001)

In 2001 the government launched a new health strategy, *Quality and Fairness: A Health System for You*, its blueprint for building a world-class health service. Seven years had passed since the 1994 strategy and during that time Ireland had experienced unprecedented economic growth and a significant increase in health spending. Despite this, deficiencies in the health system persisted, including long waiting lists for elective procedures, delays in accident and emergency departments, structural and capacity problems and quality issues. A participative and consultative approach was the hallmark of the development of the strategy. Lead responsibility was assigned to a steering group, chaired by the Secretary General of the Department of Health and Children, which included representatives of the department and of the health boards. The guiding principles underpinning the 2001 strategy emphasised:

- Equity and fairness.
- A more people-centred/consumer-oriented system.
- Developing integrated sets of quality services, accessed on the basis of need.
- Clear financial, professional and organisational accountability.

In addition to the agendas for service and professional development, key themes of the strategy were health structures, health promotion/population health, quality, information systems and e-health, delivery systems including human resource issues, funding and eligibility. The principles underlying the strategy informed the 121 actions throughout the text, which had the capacity to deliver the highest quality of care and support to all.

Four national goals were identified with specific action points related to them:

- Better health for everyone.
- Fair access.
- Responsive and appropriate care delivery.
- High performance.

Six frameworks for change were identified to assist in the achievement of the strategy:

- Strengthening primary care and developing a properly integrated system capable of delivering a full range of health and personal social services.
- Reforming the acute hospital system through improved access for public patients.
- Funding increased capacity and improving performance through evidence-based funding methods such as case-mix budgeting, improved accountability and stronger incentives for efficiency.
- Developing human resources and harnessing the vital contribution made by all staff working in the system.
- Organisational reform aimed at providing a responsive, adaptable health system, which meets the needs of the population at affordable cost.
- Information aimed at improving performance by supporting quality, planning and evidence-based decision making and improved access to the health system.

Value for Money Audit (2001)

Deloitte & Touche produced a separate *Value for Money Audit of the Irish Health System* in 2001. The report concluded that, although there had been significant increases in health expenditure, there had been only a modest improvement in services. The report found many gaps in services, a lack of integration between primary and secondary care, and that additional spending was being absorbed by pay and non-pay inflation and in the increased cost of demand-led schemes. The report recommended:

- Establishment of a separate agency to focus on information provision and performance measurement.
- Reviewing the Department of Health to ensure that it is adequately resourced to focus on strategic planning and to implement the reform programme.
- Reviewing the health board structure that had been in existence for over thirty years.
- Ensuring that future strategies include objectives, deliverables and funding.
- Increased investment in information systems.

Primary Care: A New Direction (2002)

A separate primary care strategy, *Primary Care: A New Direction*, was published in October 2002. It sought to shift the emphasis from the current over-reliance on acute services, such as hospitals, to one-stop-shops where patients will be able to access a team of general practitioners (GPs), nurses, physiotherapists, chiropodists, social workers and home helps. Wider networks of health and social care professionals, including community pharmacists, would also work with a number of primary care teams. Its stated aims were to provide:

- A strengthened primary care system that would play a more central role as the first, and ongoing, point of contact for people with the health system.
- An integrated, inter-disciplinary, high-quality, team-based and user-friendly set of services to the public.
- Enhanced capacity for primary care in the areas of disease prevention, rehabilitation and personal social services to complement the existing diagnosis and treatment focus.

Among the actions that would be put in place to implement this were:

- Establishment of a national primary care task force.
- Preparation of needs assessment for primary care teams.
- Production of a primary care human resource plan.
- Putting primary care teams in place.
- Development of primary care networks to support the primary care teams.
- Extension of the out-of-hours availability of primary care services.
- Introduction of an information and communications infrastructure.
- Greater integration between primary and secondary care.
- Investment in extending GP co-operatives.

Assessing the Health Service

Three reports (Prospectus report, Brennan report and Hanly report), underpinning the government's health service reform plan, were launched on 18 June 2003.

Prospectus management consultants had conducted an audit of the health services and found that there were too many public health agencies (fifty-eight in total) leading to a complex and fragmented system. The report said that there was a lack of clarity between the roles of the Department of Health and the health system, resulting in tensions between local representation and those making decisions in relation to national policy objectives and governance issues. There was a need for adequate planning processes, needs assessment, service planning and stakeholder participation. The report recommended:

- Creating a consolidated healthcare structure.
- Establishing a Health Service Executive.
- Restructuring the Department of Health and Children.
- Establishing a Health Information and Quality Authority.
- Developing supporting processes to strengthen the consolidated structure.
- Developing service planning and funding processes.
- Establishing links between service delivery and evaluation.
- Supporting integration.
- Enhancing system capability and performance.
- Strengthening governance and accountability.
- Reorganising existing structures and their functions in line with the new structure.
- Reducing the overall number of agencies, while at the same time developing and strengthening some of them.
- Strengthening the accountability and funding mechanisms for agencies.

The 2003 Commission on Financial Management and Control Systems in the Health Services, chaired by Niamh Brennan, carried out a detailed examination and review of the financial management and control systems in the Irish health service. The Brennan report found problems in the existing systems, including:

- Absence of any organisation responsible for managing the health service as a unified national system.
- Systems are not designed to develop cost-consciousness among those who make decisions to commit resources, and provide no incentives to manage costs effectively.

- Insufficient evaluation and analysis of existing programmes and related expenditure.
- Inadequate investment in information systems and management development.

It adopted four core principles in addressing the problems:

1. The health service should be managed as a national system.
2. Accountability should rest with those who have the authority to commit the expenditure.
3. All costs incurred should be capable of being allocated to individual patients.
4. Good financial management and control should not be seen solely as a finance function.

The commission made 136 recommendations including:

- The establishment of an executive to manage the Irish health service as a unitary national service.
- A range of reforms to governance and financial management, control and reporting systems to support the executive in the management of the system.
- The designation of clinical consultants and general practitioners (GPs) as the main units of financial accountability in the system.
- Substantial rationalisation of existing health agencies.
- All future consultant appointments to be on the basis of contracting the consultants to work exclusively in the public sector; more transparent arrangements for existing consultants.
- Reform of the medical card scheme to include a practice budget for each GP, monitoring of activity and referral patterns etc.
- Strengthening the process of evaluation of clinical and cost effectiveness for publicly funded drug schemes.

The report of the National Task Force on Medical Staffing, chaired by David Hanly, focused on the most controversial element of the wider reform package decided upon by the government. The Hanly report was the latest in a series of reports dealing with hospital medical staffing and the acute hospital system published over the previous three decades. The report identifies a clear and pressing need to reform existing service provision, improve working arrangements for medical staff and develop medical education and training. These reforms must take account of the facilities, volumes of activity and medical expertise needed to provide the best possible service for patients. It sets out a series of principles regarding the future organisation of acute hospital services. It emphasises the need to provide a full range of specialist services appropriate to a region and to designate suitable roles for each type of hospital, whether major, general or local. The report states that a full range of acute hospital services should be available within each region, so that patients should not have to travel far other than for specialised supra-regional or national specialty services. The report addresses the need to improve patient care, reform medical education and training, and support the continued provision of safe, high-quality acute hospital care twenty-four hours a day, seven days a week. It sets out the measures needed to comply with the European Union's working time directive by reducing the working hours of junior doctors and introducing a consultant-provided service. The Hanly report antagonised communities and local politicians because of proposals to create clusters of hospitals in twelve centres throughout the state, withdrawing specialist services from a number of smaller hospitals.

Department of Health and Children

The mission of the department is 'To improve the health and well-being of people in Ireland; to support the Minister and the Government by advising on the strategic development of the health system including policy and legislation; supporting their parliamentary, statutory and international functions; evaluating the performance of the health and social services; and working with other sectors to enhance people's health and well-being.'

In Ireland, health and healthcare are extremely sensitive political issues. For example, proposals in budget 2009 for changes in the entitlement to medical cards for people aged over seventy and the decision to defer the introduction of a life-saving cervical cancer vaccine resulted in the government losing the support of several TDs in late 2008. Former Health Minister Brian Cowen famously compared the Department of Health to Angola, implying that it is a department full of unexploded political landmines. A former secretary general Michael Kelly (2007: 23) referred to it as 'an environment beset by crisis management and negative public commentary'. One political adviser described the department to the Oireachtas Joint Committee on Health and Children on 27 April 2005 as 'a very complex Department with a range of issues arising on an hourly basis'. He continued, 'The people who worked in the Department of Health and Children *vis-à-vis* the civil service generally would have drawn a short straw given the difficulties and the complex issues they would meet on a daily basis.' The Travers report (2005: 57) notes:

> . . . the business of the Department of Health and Children is distinguishable from that of other Departments of State by the breadth, complexity, scale and public sensitivity of its activities. It funds a wide range of services beyond those funded by health ministries in other countries . . . The life and death nature of the issues with which it is concerned, the scale, the breadth and complexity of the policy agenda, the number of unpredictable events to be handled and the constant media and political attention all combine to produce an environment of immense organizational and individual work pressures in which the urgent constantly conspires to drive out the important.

This report was highly critical of the long-term systemic failure of administration on the practice of charges for long-stay care.

The Minister for Health and the Department of Health are responsible for health policy and legislation. The minister appoints the board of the Health Service Executive (HSE). The board appoints the chief executive of the HSE (except for the first one, who was appointed by the minister). The HSE manages and funds all health and social services. Introducing the Health Bill in the Dáil in November 2004, Minister for Health Mary Harney said that 'the key to the Health Bill is clarity, clarity of roles and clarity of responsibility – the Minister for Health will retain clear accountability for our health services . . . Most of all, people will have clarity about who is in charge of policy and who is in charge of the management of services'. The Health Act 2004, which legislated for the foundation of the HSE, did not specify the responsibilities of the department and the HSE. There is no reference to the role of the department and its secretary general in the act.

The Department of Health's role is to support the minister in the formulation and evaluation of policies for the health services. It also has a role in the strategic planning of health services. This is carried out in conjunction with the HSE, voluntary service providers, government departments and other stakeholders. Legislation and regulations setting the broad structure within which better health services for the nation can be developed are introduced by the minister and department and approved by the Dáil and Seanad.

The creation of the HSE as an agency has blurred the lines of accountability. The question can be asked as to who is to blame when something goes wrong in the health service. Minister Mary Harney, speaking to the Joint Oireachtas Committee on Health and Children on 22 November 2007, noted that 'Policy is a matter for the Minister and operational issues a matter for the HSE. However, there are many areas where policy and operational issues cannot be easily separated because many operational issues have policy implications and *vice versa*'.

Health Service Executive

In June 2003 the government introduced a health reform programme, which entailed:

- Major project planning and communications programmes.
- Abolition of the health boards.
- Establishment of the Health Service Executive (HSE).
- Establishment of the Health Information and Quality Authority.
- Addressing related human resource and industrial relations issues.
- Restructuring the Department of Health and Children.
- Mainstreaming a range of other health bodies and functions.
- Development of national frameworks for governance and service planning and reporting.

It was widely accepted that radical change was needed in order to help achieve national healthcare goals in an efficient, effective and sustainable manner. Clearly, there were deficiencies in the old structures in terms of service delivery. When launching the bill establishing the HSE in November 2004 Minister of Health Mary Harney described it as an 'historic piece of legislation which would provide for the most comprehensive reorganisation of our health services since 1970'. The former health boards were abolished and replaced by a single unified executive, which was charged with administering and delivering public healthcare services on a national level.

The HSE is responsible for providing health and personal social services for everyone living in Ireland. It was established on 1 January 2005, as part of the provisions of the Health Act 2004, which states in section 7 that the objective of the HSE is to provide services that improve, promote and protect the health and welfare of the public. It merged more than forty organisations and specialist agencies into one unified structure and assumed full operational responsibility for running the country's health and personal social services. It is the largest organisation in Ireland, employing over 130,000 people, with a budget of €14.9 billion and it operates twenty-four hours a day, seven days a week.

The HSE provides thousands of different services in hospitals and communities across the country through two central service 'pillars': the National Hospitals Office and the Primary, Community and Continuing Care Directorate. These services range from public health nurses treating older people in the community to carers for children with challenging behaviour; from educating people how to live healthier lives to performing highly complex brain surgery; from planning for major emergencies to controlling the spread of infectious diseases.

The establishment of the HSE represented the beginning of the largest programme of change ever undertaken in the Irish public service. Prior to its establishment, services were delivered through a complex structure of regional health boards, and a number of other different agencies and organisations. The Health Act 2004 provided for the dissolution of these bodies and the transfer of their functions to the HSE, which became the single body responsible for ensuring that everybody can access cost-effective and consistently high-quality health and personal social services. The reform of the health services by the HSE was to be achieved through a five-year transformation programme, which outlined a number of action points. Its overall vision was that patients experience a seamless service across the care journey from GPs, hospitals and community care.

Governing Body

As set out in the Health Act 2004 the board of the HSE is the governing body of the executive and is required to inform the minister of any matter that it considers requires his or her attention. The HSE submits corporate (section 29) and annual service plans (section 31) to the minister, who then lays them before the Houses of the Oireachtas, but the minister is not directly responsible for them. The result of this is that the person in charge of HSE finances and services, the Chief Executive Officer (CEO), is at arm's length from the Oireachtas and the people. Under section 20 of the act the CEO of the HSE is the accounting officer with responsibility and accountability to the government. Services must be delivered within the financial parameters set down by the government. Previously, the Secretary General of the Department of Health had been the accounting officer for health spending. The role of the accounting officer is to balance the budget and to sign and present for audit the appropriation accounts for the voted expenditure, taking personal responsibility for the regularity and propriety of the transactions for which he or she is answerable. The CEO of the HSE is answerable for the accounts, the control of assets held by the agency, the economy and efficiency in the use of the agency's resources and for the systems, practices and procedures used to evaluate the effectiveness of its operations. The concentration of responsibility in one individual differs from arrangements in the private commercial sector, where ultimate financial responsibility normally rests with the board.

National Directorates

The HSE provides health and personal social services to patients through three principal national directorates:

- *National Hospitals Office (NHO):* provides public hospital and ambulance services. It provides a strong centralised approach to the delivery of hospital services by bringing all fifty-three statutory and non-statutory acute hospitals into a single, unified structure.
- *Primary, Community and Continuing Care (PCCC) Directorate:* provides care in the community. It is based on a multi-disciplinary approach (representing a transition from hierarchical working relationships of various professionals to more self-managed collaborative working arrangements) and on the development of primary care teams. The *Towards 2016* social partnership agreement contained a target of 300 primary care teams by 2008, 400 by 2009 and 500 by 2010.
- *Population Health Directorate:* has overall responsibility for strategic planning for all aspects of the HSE to influence health, health service delivery and outcomes positively by promoting and protecting the health of the entire population and large groups.

Administrative Areas

Each of the four HSE administrative areas is responsible for the provision of health and social services in its area. They provide many of the services directly and they arrange for the provision of other services by health professionals, private health service providers, voluntary hospitals and voluntary/community organisations. All of the services provided by the NHO and the PCCC Directorates are delivered through the administrative areas. The four administrative areas cover:

- *HSE Dublin Mid-Leinster:* Dublin city south of the River Liffey, south Dublin county, Wicklow, Kildare, Longford, Westmeath, Laois and Offaly.
- *HSE Dublin North East:* Dublin city north of the River Liffey, Fingal county, Louth, Meath, Cavan and Monaghan.
- *HSE West:* Limerick, Clare, Tipperary (North Riding), Galway, Mayo, Roscommon, Donegal, Sligo and Leitrim.
- *HSE South:* Carlow, Kilkenny, Tipperary (South Riding), Waterford, Wexford, Cork and Kerry.

The main function of a HSE administrative area is to provide or arrange for the provision of health, community care and personal social services to the people in its area. Community care and personal social services can be broadly defined as those that are designed to enable people to remain living in their communities, especially when they have difficulties doing so because of illness, disability or age. Examples include home nursing services, home helps, occupational therapy and social work services. Each area is obliged to provide certain services, for example family doctor (GP) and public hospital services. There are other services that they may provide, for example home helps and other community care services. A significant part of the HSE's overall budget is allocated to those services that are obligatory.

Service Planning and Accountability

All HSE administrative areas must provide service plans that review the previous year's spending and give a detailed breakdown of how funding provided by the HSE will be spent during the year in question. These are incorporated into one overall national service plan. The department formally sets out a statement of national priorities for health, which will then be addressed by the HSE in preparing their individual service plans. The health strategy seeks to strengthen this process by providing for greater account-ability and closer monitoring of performance based on the deliverables (specific stated goals) given in the service plans.

The issue of democratic accountability throughout the health services is an important one and in the Health Act 2004 accountability at all levels of the system is part of the reform. The government was anxious to ensure proper accountability to public representatives at national and local levels. Provision is made in the act to ensure the accountability of the HSE to the Oireachtas Joint Committee on Health and Children and, under section 79, to regulate dealings between members of the Oireachtas and the HSE.

New HSE structures such as a national forum and regional health forums are in place, which further public representation and user participation. Under section 41 of the 2004 act the role of the national health consultative forum is to advise the minister on matters relating to the provision of health and personal social services. Minister Mary Harney convened the first national health consultative forum in Kilkenny in 2006. Its theme was: 'How can we achieve a collaborative partnership between policy makers, providers, users and local communities? What can we learn from other sectors?' Approximately 350 persons were appointed as national forum members under ministerial order; they included representatives from senior management, service providers, voluntary and professional bodies, patient and client groups, trade unions and other government departments.

Section 42 of the act provides specifically for the establishment of a number of regional health forums. These forums facilitate local repre - sentatives in raising issues of local concern about health services within their region with the HSE. Membership of the regional forums is based on nominations from city and county councils within the functional areas of each forum. Putting such arrangements in place ensured that the voice of local public representatives continued to be heard in the development of health services.

Each of the HSE's four administrative areas has a regional health forum, which makes representations to the HSE on the range and operation of health and personal social services in that area, and the HSE in turn provides administrative services to the forum. The four regional health fora are:

- Regional Health Forum, Dublin Mid-Leinster (40 members).
- Regional Health Forum, Dublin North East (29 members).
- Regional Health Forum, South (39 members).
- Regional Health Forum, West (40 members).

These arrangements were designed to complement and reinforce the role of the Oireachtas Joint Committee on Health and Children in reflecting the views of public representatives in the ongoing oversight of the health system. Section 43 of the act provided for the establishment of advisory panels. It is a matter for the HSE to determine the terms of reference, membership, rules and procedures for each panel. Section 44 provides that the minister may direct the HSE to establish an advisory panel for a specified purpose.

The HSE established a customer service division. A key challenge for this division was to design an effective model of consumer involvement and an open approach to service-user feedback and comment. It also has a parliamentary affairs division, which provides answers to parliamentary questions.

Evaluation

The new HSE was intended to be a more integrated, effective and accountable health service. The 2005 report of the Review Body on Higher Remuneration in the Public Sector on senior posts in the HSE found that 'the HSE is in an evolving form and a major process of change is under way. Movement from the previous structure of separate health boards to a unified organisation represents a major challenge . . . The absence of stability created difficulties for us in evaluating the posts covered by our review'.

The 2001 health strategy promised 'that no public patient will wait longer than three months for treatment following referral from an out-patient department by the end of 2004'. Figures published in the National Treatment Purchase Fund's 2008 annual report showed that there are still nearly 14,000 patients waiting for more than three months, with 1,576 public patients waiting more than one year for surgery.

The HSE services treat approximately three thousand people in the accident and emergency departments every day and approximately one thousand patients a day are admitted to hospitals – 90 per cent of these are admitted immediately and the remaining 10 per cent must wait for admission. However, many patients wait for less than six hours. In 2007 the target was to have no patients waiting for admission for more than twenty-four hours and the target for the winter is to have no patient waiting for admission for more than twelve hours; this goal was achieved in the majority of cases and it is hoped to reduce this waiting time further. This difficult and sensitive topic emerges every winter as an issue.

Plans for Further Restructuring

In 2007 the HSE commissioned McKinsey management consultants to look at the appropriate organisational structure required for the HSE. The consultants recommended the restructuring of management, the merging of the hospital and community pillars and the devolution of more decision making.

Organisational modifications to partially decentralise the health service, giving some decision-making powers back to the regions, were announced in July 2008. According to the HSE (2008c) these 'would facilitate more local responsibility and authority and strengthen area structures within the national umbrella of the HSE and they will enable more clinical involvement in the design and management of patient services which will be a key driver in the enhancement of the quality of patient services'. Minister Mary Harney explained, 'We want to make sure that the appropriate organisation structures are in place. We want to see policymaking and standard-setting carried out at national level with implementation at local level' (Wall 2008). The plan is the second major reform of the HSE , which has a yearly budget of over €14 billion, within five years.

These plans will see the creation of ten regional directors to oversee both hospital and community services in their area and will take a period of eighteen months to implement. Under the new devolved structure, regional directors will be given power to deliver an integrated healthcare service across hospitals and primary care locations in their area. The regional directors will also be given authority for the healthcare budget in their locality and they will decide on how the money should be divided up between hospital, primary care, mental health and other sectors. At national level, the department and the HSE will make healthcare policy and set national standards, while the new regional directors will implement it at local level. The number of proposed new healthcare regions to be established remains unclear, with some sources indicating that there will be four and others suggesting that it could be as many as eight.

The HSE believes that the new structures will lead to a streamlining of management levels in the organisation, which had been strongly criticised as being overly bureaucratic and too highly centralised. The HSE has been trying to transform the system, while at the same time continuing to deliver an existing level of services within the given level of resources.

The system of administering hospital and community healthcare services separately will be abolished by merging the NHO and the PCCC directorates to ensure a more streamlined and co-ordinated service. The post of national director for population health will be subsumed into a new directorate of planning. The HSE appointed a new national director for communications as well as a national clinical director to co-ordinate with new hospital clinical directors appointed under the terms of the revised consultants' contract.

This announcement was in marked contrast to the approach that accompanied the establishment of the HSE more than three years previously. The aim then was to have one unified health authority that would bring better patient services, increased efficiency and better co-ordination. While there may have been problems with the old health board system, it had at least the virtue of having formal structures of local accountability.

McAuliffe and McKenzie (2007: 8) comment:

> . . . one cannot but be struck by the near obsessive focus on structures, infrastructures and capacity in attempts to reform our health service over the past decade, from the establishment and demolition of the Eastern Regional Health Authority in a timeframe of less than five years, the huge shift from health boards to a single authority in the form of the Health Service Executive and the speculation on a further move towards a regional authority structure, to the start-stop attempts to effect a dramatic increase in medical manpower in the system.

At the 2008 *Sunday Business Post* iQuest fifth annual National Healthcare Summit, Eilish McAuliffe called for a moratorium on 'externally generated reports' (O'Meara 2008).

Health Service Governance

The policy, legislative and resource allocation frameworks are determined by the Minister for Heath and by the government, while the HSE is responsible for the management and delivery of health and personal social services on the ground. All policy issues, such as health service pay, legislation, industrial relations and priorities in services are decided by the government. While the HSE's CEO is the accounting officer for expenditure by the HSE, overall political responsibility rests with the minister. The landmark OECD 2008 report on the Irish public service examined the reconfiguration of hospitals in the health sector, taking the north east as a case study. It made the following detailed observations (2008b: 288):

While the HSE is largely involved in administering and delivering on policy, it also has a role to play in 'selling' policy changes to the population. The apparent lack of a co-ordinated approach to informing the local population, the staff in the hospitals, and the wider medical community in the primary and community areas of the intent, timeframe and purpose of the reforms, has led to confusion and hampered efforts to promote the reforms as a positive development . . . It is possible that the HSE is trying to do too much at once and is not actively looking at what it can achieve and deliver on in the short term, and to improve consumer/public confidence in the health system in Ireland generally, and in the reform programme . . . the governance and management structures that exist between the agency (HSE) and its parent Department (Health and Children) should be examined to ensure that there is a shared understanding and agreement on how the HSE is working to advance implementation of government policy.

Health Service Expenditure

In common with other Western countries, Ireland has experienced substantial increases in health expenditure in recent decades. The main reasons for this may be summarised as: technological advances, which have been expensive and complement (rather than replace) existing facilities, thereby increasing total costs; demographic factors, particularly the growing proportion of elderly people in the population, since they account for a significant part of total health spending; wage and salary increases; personnel increases due to higher demands for services and growing specialisation; expanded scope of services; the growth in coverage of services with extensions in eligibility; and the appearance or re-emergence of infectious diseases such as HIV/AIDS and tuberculosis.

In 2009 the government provided over €16 billion for expenditure on the health group of votes. This was one-quarter of government current spending and comprised €15,256 billion for the HSE, €547 million for the Office of the Minister for Children and €530 million for the Department of Health and Children. It placed Ireland very high in international terms in relation to growth in public health spending. According to the OECD, health spending in Ireland grew in real terms by an average of 9.1 per cent per year between 1999 and 2004, whilst the OECD average was 5.2 per cent. Alongside Norway, Ireland had the highest level of public capital investment in health as a proportion of national income in 2004. At 9.6 per cent of GNP, this is twice or more times the level of most OECD countries. The National Development Plan continues the high level of public investment generally and health capital development in particular.

In Ireland nearly 80 per cent of health spending in 2009 was funded by government revenues, which was above the OECD average of 73 per cent.

This compares to a figure for Ireland of 71.5 per cent in the mid-1990s. The OECD health data report for 2008, which compared health systems and government spending across thirty countries, found total health spending accounted for 7.5 per cent of Ireland's GDP (gross domestic product), almost 1.5 per cent lower than the average of 8.9 per cent across OECD countries. Cross-national comparisons of health spending are notoriously difficult. A fairer comparison for Ireland is measuring health spending as a proportion of GNP (gross national product), which brings it to 8.5 per cent. GNP is a better measure of the taxable base and of the annual flow of income available for domestic spending, due to the measurement problems for Ireland created by multi-national corporation transfer pricing. Expressing health expenditure as a proportion of GNP makes very little difference to any of the other OECD countries, but it increases Irish spending markedly. The 2008 report found that per capita health spending in Ireland is above the OECD average but it is lower than the United States, Norway, Switzerland and Luxembourg. 'Health spending per capita grew, in real terms, by an average of 8.8 per cent a year, between 2000 and 2006, the second fastest growth of all OECD countries during this period and significantly higher than the OECD average of 5 per cent a year,' the report said.

It cannot be overstated, however, that higher expenditure on health in itself does not guarantee desirable outcomes. The institutional structure of the welfare state, and the precise structure of entitlements, can have a strong influence on both economic impact and welfare outcomes. Between 1998 and 2008 health spending rose fivefold; adjusting for a larger population and inflation, health spending in 2008 was three times higher than it was in 1998. Much of the health reform agenda is about a more effective and efficient use of the available public funding. Much of Ireland's increased spending on health has gone on pay and pensions. The Travers report (2005), however, notes that 'the Irish health system is widely characterised by a chronic shortage of both finance and of systems of management and delivery which can optimize the finance available'. Kelly (2007: 16) notes that 'Not unusually, the Department [of Health] very often found itself as the unfortunate meat in a sandwich, between unions and health service employers on one side and a rigid Department of Finance on the other'.

Improved outcomes in the health sector are inevitably associated with long time-lags, so that positive outcomes, for example increased life expectancy, reduced mortality rates from various diseases and reduced morbidity rates, can only be achieved and detected after a considerable period of time has elapsed between increased investment in the policy area and the measure - ment of outcomes. Furthermore, outcomes in the health sector are the result of a large number of different variables interacting over a long period of time: good examples are health indicators that are shaped by lifestyle factors and overall levels of socio-economic development, in addition to health expenditure. Timonen (2005: xii) comments, 'Irish spending on social services needs to better reflect its position as one of the wealthiest countries in the world. The most urgent issues include more equitable access to healthcare and the high cost of primary healthcare as well as education and care services for children. In other words, while the money is being spent, the poor quality of the outcomes demands a more thorough appraisal of how the money is being spent.'

Health services are extremely labour intensive. The shortage of staff, rather than the lack of facilities, creates real bottlenecks in the system by, for example, causing the growth of waiting lists for palliative care for terminally ill patients. Absenteeism in the HSE's largest hospitals was running at 5 percent on average in late 2008. A memo to HSE staff in November 2008 identified the elimination of 'double-digit absenteeism or inappropriately high sickness levels' as a priority. However, a statistical aspect of Ireland's health system noted by the OECD (2008a: 279) is the very large number of practising nurses (15.2 per 1,000), which is twice the OECD average; 40 per cent of nurses in Ireland work part-time.

In a letter dated 10 December 2007 then Finance Minister Brian Cowen expressed his concerns to Health Minister Mary Harney about HSE financial management systems and emphasised the need to control performance to bring its spending into line with the estimates allocated by the Dáil (Brennan 2007). The HSE is changing its business code to provide cash accounting as required under public financial procedures and to improve its financial management system. This will see a move towards evidence-based practices rather than historical budgets. At present, due to lack of information, the HSE is unable to link the money it spends with its activities.

Changing demography is a significant cost driver for the HSE, with a growing elderly population and a dramatic rise in the birth rate. According to the Central Statistics Office, there were 70,620 new arrivals in 2007, which was the highest number of newborns recorded since 1982. The world's oldest working maternity hospital, the Rotunda Hospital in Dublin, recorded its busiest year in the hospital's history in 2007.

Secretary General of the Department of Health Michael Scanlan, speaking at the 2007 MacGill summer school, noted that extra investment in the health service was not the panacea and 'we need to recognize that resources are finite, regardless of how a health system is funded'. He noted the need to build confidence in the health service among the public, at political level, in the media and among staff. Constant criticism can affect staff morale, and ultimately, impact on the quality of patient care provided.

At the Public Accounts Committee on 29 June 2006, in a discussion of the report of the Comptroller and Auditor General, *Value for Money Report No. 49*

– *Waste Management in Hospitals*, an official from the Department of Finance gave that department's view on health funding, particularly on service-level agreements:

> The report states funding should be linked to service need, rather than the provider's capabilities. From the perspective of the Department of Finance, this is the lesson to be learned in this regard. We support the conclusion that service agreements are the way forward. Such agreements tend to result in a win-win situation for all the bodies involved, namely, patients, service providers, service purchasers and ultimately, the taxpayer. They will clarify the roles and responsibilities of the funder and service providers and help to enforce standards of care. They will provide the basis for monitoring, evaluation and future planning of services.

The Former Regional Health Boards

The eight health boards established under the Health Act 1970 were the statutory bodies responsible for the provision of health and personal social services in their respective geographical areas. They were also the main providers of healthcare at regional level. The boards served populations ranging from 200,000 to 1.3 million. Membership of the boards comprised elected local representatives, ministerial nominees and delegates of consumer and health professional organisations. The boards replaced a system under which health services were administered on a county basis by twenty-seven main local authorities. The boards decided and administered the practical details and working of the health service at local level and were the largest employers of staff in the health service. In order to ensure that central policy decisions were implemented in a way that was acceptable to local interests, a majority of their members were appointed by the relevant local authorities for the areas served by each board.

The 1970 legislation arose from the necessity to make the organisation and administration of the health services as efficient and economic as possible. As the state had the major financial interest in the health services and this interest was increasing, it was desirable that a new administrative framework combining national and local interests should be developed for services. It was also necessary to broaden both the geographical and the representational basis of the local bodies in charge of the health services so as to get a more balanced approach towards desirable changes such as the reorganisation of the general hospital services. Developments in professional techniques and equipment and management methods indicated that the county was too small an administrative unit to be the basis for health services and that better services could be provided on an inter-county basis. This was particularly true in relation to the hospital service.

While the system had served Ireland well, a number of reviews had identified key weaknesses in the structure of the health boards. These included a lack of clarity with regard to the respective roles and responsibilities of health boards and their chief executives; inadequate accountability within the structure; and over-involvement by the Department of Health in the detailed management of the services.

The Health Act 1970 set up the health boards and also provided for the establishment of the regional hospitals and of a central body – Comhairle na n-Ospidéal (Hospital Council), thereby creating a regional structure for healthcare. The regional health boards had responsibility for the general organisation and development but not the administration of hospital services in their areas. The central body controlled the number and type of specialist appointments in all hospitals, both the health boards' and the voluntary hospitals. The objective of these bodies was to bring about an integrated and efficient hospital system and to avoid unnecessary duplication of specialist services. The effect of a multiplicity of health boards was to discourage rational development with a national perspective – as there was a tendency for each region to have a 'flagship hospital'.

Health (Eastern Regional Health Authority) Act 1999

The Health (Eastern Regional Health Authority) Act 1999 established the Eastern Regional Health Authority (ERHA) and three new area health boards to replace the Eastern Health Board, within the county borough of Dublin and the administrative counties of South Dublin, Fingal, Dún Laoghaire-Rathdown, Kildare and Wicklow. This act also established a Health Boards' Executive, the members of which were the chief executives of the health boards, with work assigned to a designated chief executive officer who assumed lead executive responsibility. The overall work of the executive was directed by the chief executives collectively.

Health Agencies

Specialist agencies are significant partners in the health sector. Outside of the Department of Health and Children, there are a number of bodies established on a permanent basis, for example the Medical Council, Dental Council, Irish Medicines Board and Adoption Board, which provide a wide range of services and advice on their relevant area of activity. For those aspects of the work of the health services not suited to localised operation, the practice has evolved of setting up special central executive agencies, for example the Irish Blood Transfusion Service, St James's Hospital Board, Beaumont Hospital Board, National Treatment Purchase Fund and Health Research Board. The government pushed through emergency legislation in December 2007, the Health (Miscellaneous Provisions) Act 2007, to avoid a constitutional crisis and retrospectively legalise the establishment of many health bodies set up over the previous forty-six years under 1961 legislation. Special broadly based working parties and committees are also established from time to time, as required, to advise on specific aspects of the services.

The Economic and Social Research Institute's health policy and information division manages two national information systems on behalf of the HSE: the hospital in-patient enquiry scheme (HIPE) collects data on discharges from all acute hospitals nationally and the national perinatal reporting system (NPRS) collects data on all births in Ireland. The HIPE/Case-mix programme provides input and support for analysis of hospital activity data.

National Treatment Purchase Fund

The National Treatment Purchase Fund (NTPF) was set up in 2002 to take those public patients who have been waiting longest for procedures in public hospitals off waiting lists. The NTPF buys treatment in private hospitals for patients waiting more than three months for operations. It was established after the 2001 health strategy promised that no patient would have to wait more than three months for treatment by the end of 2004. The idea of the NTPF came from Norway, where hospitals were obliged by statute to refer patients to it.

The Minister for Health allocated special funding for the NTPF, allowing it to make arrangements to treat those waiting longest on public hospital waiting lists. The NTPF arranges treatment, with the permission of each patient and in a confidential manner, in private hospitals in Ireland, in Britain, or, if necessary, in other countries. Treatments available range from cardiac surgery to hip replacements to treatment for varicose veins and cataracts. Patients who opt for treatment with the NTPF receive their treatment free of charge. More than 140,000 people have been treated privately since it was established in 2002.

In May 2004 the minister announced the transfer of responsibility for the collation and publication of surgical waiting list data to the NTPF. In October 2004 the NTPF conducted an analysis of waiting list data from hospitals, which indicated that data: focused on volumes, not length of time patients are waiting; had not been validated and were not reconcilable from one period to the next; did not capture changes in patients' status, i.e. treated, temporary unavailability, no longer in need of treatment; and were not treated in a consistent manner and could be up to six months out of date. The NTPF decided in December 2004 not to publish waiting list figures, but instead opted to develop a National Patient Treatment Register, which would focus on the waiting times of individual patients rather than statistically based waiting lists. At the Public Accounts Committee in May 2008, the Chief Executive of the National Treatment Purchase Fund indicated that hundreds of patients have been waiting for more than two years to be seen by the government's private treatment fund. This is despite the NTPF's promise that no public patient should have to wait more than three months for surgery or other treatment. More than two thousand people had waited for more than twelve months. Some consultants were being paid privately by the NTPF to treat patients privately who were on their public waiting lists. The NTPF has no control over which patients are referred to it by hospitals.

Health Information and Quality Authority

In March 2005 an interim Health Information and Quality Authority (HIQA) was established. The body was formally established under the Health Act 2007. It has three main functions: developing health information; promoting and implementing quality assurance programmes nationally; and conducting health technology assessments. It also undertakes an annual review of hospital hygiene levels. HIQA drew up draft national standards for infection prevention and control in 2008. It recommended an increase in the number of clinical microbiologists and infection-control nurses employed in the state and the standards cover accountability, hand hygiene, reducing infection from medical instruments, surveillance of infections, the provision of appropriate multi-disciplinary infection-control teams, informing patients immediately of their infection status and management of outbreaks.

Community Care

The HSE has placed an emphasis on shifting appropriate activity from a hospital-based system to primary, community long-term care, rehabilitation and chronic disease management services, in line with international best practice. This involves accelerating the movement towards community care. Implementing these tasks requires the active support and co-operation of all stakeholders. The development of an integrated health system with far fewer acute hospital beds and a much-expanded primary care sector is the direction in which health policy is moving. The 2001 health strategy stated that 'primary care needs to become the central focus of the health system'. The development of primary care teams is behind the original schedule set out by the Department of Health. The absence of appropriate step-down, com - munity or convalescent care elsewhere in the system can otherwise 'block' beds and services in acute hospitals as patients lack appropriate alternative or follow-up care options.

Traditionally, hospitals and their staffs operated as totally separate entities to community and social care services (physiotherapists, public health nurses, social workers and occupational therapists). These professions in turn have operated separately from the general practitioner (GP) service. Under this system it was up to individual patients to organise access to their own individual care providers, while recounting their medical history at each occasion. Central to all integrated health systems are health professionals working in teams with a focus on improving access and delivering better value for patients and clients and strengthening the capacity to deliver a modern health service.

A report by PA Consulting in January 2008 said that the Irish health system is overly reliant on acute hospital beds with service provision configured around hospitals rather than the patient. It said that should current practice continue, the state will require over 8,000 more public patient beds by 2020. It found that there were 11,660 public patient beds and 2,461 private beds in Irish public hospitals, and a further 1,926 private patient hospital beds, which was 20 per cent less acute hospital beds per capita than the EU average.

The PA Consulting report found that the average length of stay in acute hospitals in Ireland is relatively long and that there is significant potential to reduce it. The reasons for this are the predominant Monday to Friday pattern in the hospitals and the admission of more than 50 per cent of patients before their day of surgery. The report highlighted the lack of available long-term beds in the system, particularly around Dublin. This results in patients who have completed their acute care, remaining in hospital beds. The report found that 40 per cent of all patients could potentially be treated in another more fitting setting. These alternatives include home-based patient care involving GP support, therapy, specialist nursing, community nursing and home-care packages. The report argued that the state has to make a choice between maintaining the current system or treating more patients in a community care setting.

The OECD (2008a: 286) notes:

> . . . developing primary care teams and improving the supply of GPs is needed to ensure that sufficient capacity exists at the community level to provide alternative treatment and healthcare options for those with non-acute medium to long-term care needs. For those, however, who no longer require acute hospital care, but who equally cannot yet return home or to independent living, it is important to ensure that sufficient places are available in community care facilities such as nursing home, or convalescent care/step-down facilities.

It will be a challenge to decouple in the public mind the idea that good healthcare only comes from getting into a hospital. The reasons behind the emphasis on moving people into the community, rather than providing bigger hospitals with more beds, must be clearly explained.

The Voluntary Sector

The health service also has a unique mix of public and voluntary involvement. The voluntary sector plays a vital role in the delivery of health and personal social services in Ireland. Numerous voluntary organisations serve the elderly, people with a disability, the mentally ill and many other groups by providing a very valuable service on a local and/or national basis. They include national organisations, councils and associations for specific diseases or conditions and bodies concerned in the organisation of social services. Their role involves not just the delivery of services, often on behalf of the HSE, but also participation in the process of policy development. Even the use of the term 'voluntary' is a misnomer for the most part, as these bodies are dependent for virtually all their funding on Exchequer sources.

Health Service Achievements

In recent years the population of Ireland has been growing more rapidly than at any time since the foundation of the state, and has increased by almost 16 per cent since the mid-1990s. Population ageing is a key feature that has clear implications for health service planning. The number of people over the age of sixty-five is projected to increase by about 80 per cent to over 800,000 people between 2008 and 2025. Life expectancy in Ireland is now above the EU-27 average for the first time; there has been a rapid increase, unmatched by any other EU country, since 1999. The OECD (2008a: 279) notes that 'the health of the Irish is good and improving at an exceptionally rapid pace. Ireland is the country which has had the most spectacular increase in its life expectancy'. Much of this increase is due to significant reductions in major causes of death such as circulatory disease. Ireland has the highest levels of self-perceived health of those countries in Europe that have conducted such research: 80 per cent of men and women rate their health as being good or very good. The Department of Health's 2007 survey also shows significant chronic health problems in the older age groups. Diseases of the circulatory system and cancer continue to be the major causes of death, but there has been a very significant reduction in the rate of circulatory system disease: a reduction of 38 per cent between 1997 and 2008 and a reduction of 50 per cent since the 1970s.

Since 1997 there has been close to a 50 per cent increase in hospital discharges. This can be broken down into a 13 per cent increase in total in-patients and a 130 per cent increase in day-case discharges. Improved and less invasive medical practice is largely responsible for the rapid growth in day patient activity. There has been a reduction of about 30 per cent in in-patients discharged from district/community hospitals over the period 1997 to 2008. Numbers in psychiatric hospitals have fallen by 28 per cent over the same period reflecting a policy of more appropriate community-based models of care.

There have been significant positive developments throughout the health system. The HSE annual report for 2007 shows that the volume of services delivered was, in most cases, substantially above the targets set for the year in the National Service Plan, and well above the levels provided in 2006. An air ambulance service is provided by the Air Corps on the basis of a service-level agreement prepared by the relevant agencies. This arrangement has operated successfully for a number of years and was renewed in 2007 to take account of the air ambulance capabilities of new aircraft acquired by the Air Corps. In addition, the Irish Coastguard provides air ambulance inter-hospital transfers as part of its mission tasking and also provides for emergency medical evacuation from the islands around Ireland.

A new contract for hospital consultants was agreed in 2008 after four years of negotiation. This will trigger the appointment of hundreds of additional consultants and pave the way for long-awaited reforms that envisage the introduction of a service where public patients are seen by a consultant rather than a non-consultant doctor. Appointments for out-patient and diagnostic services will be on the basis of medical need and private patients will not have any priority. Doctors will work over an expanded day and be present in hospitals for a number of hours at weekends. Another significant achievement was the enactment of the Medical Practitioner's Act 2007, which imposes key regulatory responsibilities on doctors, as well as giving a lay majority to the Medical Council. All doctors will be required to take part in regular training and assessment.

Health Service Challenges

The ambitious health reform programme is happening at a time of considerable demographic change in Ireland. The Irish population grew by 20 per cent between 1997 and 2009 and will be 15 per cent higher again by 2016, while the Irish birth rate was the highest in twenty-five years in 2007. People are living longer, the population is growing, expectations and demands are increasing and medical costs are rising. As people get older they are also more likely to suffer from chronic illness and disease.

The OECD (2008b) review of public services, looking at aspects of the health sector, listed the following headings: sequencing of reforms: primary and community care; putting primary care teams in place; supply of general practitioners (GPs); dependent care: capacity and financial supports; communication of policy objectives; governance (particularly the earlier sharing of information on delivery to the minister); performance assessment;

and capital funding. Clearly, health managers face a myriad of different and complex issues in consistently delivering services, while implementing the reform programme.

The health service has been involved in a number of high-profile controversies. These include tainted blood transfusions, questions over the legality of the payments made for nursing home care, standards of care and allegations of the abuse of elderly patients in private nursing homes, the death in transit of two patients in the north east, unnecessary surgical procedures on women in Drogheda, questions about the regulation of health professionals, breast cancer misdiagnoses and recalls, concerns over the legality of the establishment of health bodies and the continued intractability of the accident and emergency situation. These have undermined confidence in the system. The autumn 2008 decision by the Health Minister to defer the introduction of the planned national cervical cancer vaccination programme means that Ireland lags behind other EU member states in this life-saving public health initiative.

The HSE put controversial employment controls and recruitment restric-tions in place to allow hospitals and health agencies to remain within approved staffing levels and financial allocations. These included a temporary recruit-ment pause and a moratorium on promotions, 'acting-up arrangements' or the additional use of locums or agency staff. Agencies tried to replace some staff in key areas to minimise the impact on patients.

Health is a topic with the highest level of public interest. Analysis by Brandenburg and Zalinski (2007) found that in terms of content, health was the biggest story of the 2007 general election campaign, while the top three priorities were health, tax and housing. A full-scale political crisis developed over the budget 2009 decision to remove the automatic entitlement to medical cards from people aged over seventy. Minister for Community, Rural and Gaeltacht Affairs Éamon Ó Cuív made strong criticism of the HSE in October 2007 when he said in a radio interview, 'my experience day to day as a local constituency politician is that I just cannot make head nor tail of the HSE as an organisation' and that he found the HSE 'impossible' to deal with.

Accident and Emergency Departments

A report by the Irish Association of Emergency Medicine (2007) for the HSE found that at least seven hospital accident and emergency (A&E) depart-ments were unfit for purpose. The Emergency Department Task Force said that particular difficulties existed at the Mercy Hospital in Cork, Wexford General Hospital, Cavan General Hospital, Letterkenny General Hospital, Our Lady of Lourdes Hospital in Drogheda and the Mater and Beaumont Hospitals in Dublin. It concluded that the core problems in A&E services were a shortage of beds to meet patient need, variations in the availability of clinical and decision-making personnel and a significant number of hospitals working close to 100 per cent capacity. The report said that a maximum wait of six hours must be set by the HSE for patients, from arrival to A&E to either admission or discharge. It added that there should be zero tolerance for a situation in which patients must wait on trolleys. The report recommended greater access to diagnostic tests, nearly 2,500 more long-term care beds and improved chronic disease management.

Cancer Care

Between 1999 and 2008, over one hundred additional consultants and 360 additional clinical nurse specialists were appointed in key areas of cancer care. About €1 billion has been invested in cancer services nationally. Survival rates are up for breast cancer. More people overall are being treated – over 96,000 in-patient and day patients were discharged from hospital following a diagnosis of cancer in 2006, an increase of 75 per cent over 1997. Over 60,000 people were treated as day cases in 2006, an increase of 140 per cent over 1997. There have been expansions of radiotherapy facilities in St Luke's in Dublin and in Cork and Galway. Public patients are being treated in private facilities in Waterford and Cork, as capacity is expanded nationally. There is now a national cancer screening service, with BreastCheck being offered in the west and south of the country, to achieve national coverage.

The cancer care strategy provides for the eventual transfer of all modalities of treatment for all types of cancer to major multi-disciplinary hospital centres in eight locations around the country. In addition to thirteen centres being ordered to stop breast cancer surgery (Naas, Tullamore, Louglinstown, Mallow, Louth, Cavan, Navan, Nenagh, Ennis, St Michael's in Dún Laoghaire, Roscommon, Portiuncula in Ballinasloe and Mercy Hospital in Cork), a number of smaller centres will have their breast cancer services phased out as care becomes centralised in the eight major centres. The eight designated cancer centres, in which most cancer care, including breast care, will, according to the HSE, be centralised by 2009, are – Beaumont, the Mater, St James's and St Vincent's Hospitals in Dublin; Cork University Hospital; Waterford Regional Hospital; University College Hospital Galway; and Limerick Regional Hospital. An outreach cancer service will be provided for Donegal from the Galway centre. The eight centres, with two in each of the four HSE regions, will deliver diagnostic, surgical, medical and radiation oncology cancer treatment.

In August 2007 the Department of Health's Chief Medical Officer was informed by the Health Information and Quality Authority about its concerns relating to the adequacy of the management and care of ten women who had attended the breast disease services at Barrington's Hospital in Limerick within the previous four years. University College Hospital Galway decided to discontinue the gynaecology cytology service for women in the south east because it did not have enough staff due to the HSE staff freeze. In September 2007 thirteen smaller hospitals around the country were ordered to stop providing breast cancer treatment immediately, as part of a major revamp of cancer services announced by Health Minister Mary Harney and the HSE.

Another cancer crisis erupted in November 2007 after it emerged that hundreds more patients from two hospitals (Cork University Hospital and University College Hospital Galway) were to have their tests reviewed after concerns arose about the work of a pathologist who had since left the country. There were fears that up to fifteen patients in one of the hospitals could have been misdiagnosed and falsely given the all clear for cancer. Two separate inquiries were conducted.

The misdiagnosis of cancer patients at the Midland Regional Hospital in Portlaoise caused a major political controversy in late 2007. Nine women were falsely given the all clear for breast cancer following mammograms. A review of breast cancer services at the hospital by former Dublin City Manager John Fitzgerald identified major problems, including systemic weaknesses in governance, management and communication. His report, entitled *Management, Governance and Communications Issues Arising from the Review of Breast Radiology Services at Midland Regional Hospital, Portlaoise*, examined the management of all events following the HSE's decision in August 2007 to suspend breast radiology services in Portlaoise. It covered the period between August and December 2007 and was released shortly after the HSE's most senior hospital manager, John O'Brien, shocked observers at an Oireachtas health committee on 22 November by revealing that ninety-seven women were being recalled following a review of ultrasounds at the hospital. Fitzgerald found that inconsistency and lack of clarity in communications was the 'inevitable result' of the deficiency in overall management of the review of patients' breast examinations. Fitzgerald said his report did not focus on individuals because to do so 'would be unfair given the considerable pressure of work that people were under, but more importantly that by doing so I might create the erroneous impression that problems arose primarily from the action or inaction of individuals, rather than what in my view were systemic problems of governance, management and communications'. There was no suggestion of wilful neglect by staff. Communication was inconsistent, confused and sometimes contradictory.

In terms of clinical management, Dr Ann O'Doherty, among the most eminent breast radiologists in Ireland, reviewed more than three thousand mammograms from the Portlaoise hospital and found serious shortcomings in the management of cases there. The main finding of her report, *Report on a Clinical Review of Mammography Service at Midland Regional Hospital, Portlaoise for the HSE Dublin Mid-Leinster*, was that the safety, quality and standard of many aspects of the service at the hospital fell below achievable best practice for breast imaging. The time that elapsed between the original 'false negative' mammogram and the new diagnosis varied between four-and-a-half months and two years, nine months. The figure of nine mis-diagnoses out of 3,037 mammograms reviewed fell within the acceptable rates. The quality of the mammograms presented for review was patchy, mostly for technical reasons. Many of the reports issued on mammography and breast ultrasounds at the hospital were difficult to interpret.

A third report on the situation, *Report on the Circumstances Leading to the Suspension of Radiology Services at Midland Regional Hospital, Portlaoise*, was prepared by Ann Doherty of the HSE. This report, which referred to individuals by job title rather than by name, showed that the decision to suspend breast radiology services at Portlaoise was made two months after detailed concerns were raised that patients were at risk of being misdiagnosed.

Minister Mary Harney apologised to the women affected by the breast cancer controversy. She said that steps would be taken to ensure that similar events did not happen again. The CEO of the HSE, Professor Brendan Drumm, also apologised to the affected women and said that similar situations would be handled appropriately in the future.

In May 2008 it emerged that thousands of chest X-rays and scans carried out on patients in the north east were being reviewed following concerns regarding the possibility of misdiagnosis in a small number of cases. A separate external review examined a number of cases where patients who died of lung cancer had their diagnosis delayed because an abnormality on their chest X-ray may not have been spotted. Further cases of cancer misdiagnosis were revealed in Ennis Hospital in September 2008 and another investigation was launched.

On the basis of these investigations and reports it is difficult to argue against the proposed centralisation of cancer services in a small number of centres of excellence across the state. It is clear from all the evidence and expert advice that safe, specialist cancer services of the highest quality will only be delivered where there are large numbers of consultants working together on large numbers of cases, with continuing competence assurance and audits.

Professor Niall O'Higgins, former President of the College of Surgeons and author of the report that first recommended dedicated multi-disciplinary cancer centres, said in the *Sunday Tribune* of 11 November 2007:

> I really want to support the minister for having the courage to take the decision to set up designated centres and for activating the process but, yes, I am worried that there is no sign of costing or a dedicated budget having been earmarked by the HSE. The public are demanding action and that demand is becoming angry, and before long, the demand will be strident. The voice of advocacy is growing hoarse and the voice of opposition is growing harsh.

Ten years previously, the National Cancer Forum recommended that regional cancer services be subsumed into one centre of excellence per region. This thinking – later espoused by Professor Niall O'Higgins in his 2000 report of the sub-group to the National Cancer Forum on the development of symptomatic breast disease services – is now widely accepted as the best way to treat cancer. The higher the volume of procedures, the greater is the expertise of the consultant, and the better the outcome for patients.

In a debate in the Dáil on cancer services on 27 November 2007 Minister Mary Harney said:

> The issue of cancer care and health care reform is as fundamental to our society today as resolving the Northern Ireland problem was for many years. I am not naive and seeking a *carte blanche* on the health care issue but I invite the leaders of the Opposition to consider a bipartisan approach on cancer services. Our citizens deserve that we do that . . . Undiluted and unequivocal accountability and responsibility are issues I take seriously. We must be responsible for our actions or inactions. That is what political accountability is about . . . We have established a Health Service Executive to implement Government policy on health care, to be responsible for the delivery of services. I did not dream up the HSE one day. All the advance reports examining our health system advised strongly that for 4.3 million people we should have a single entity instead of effectively 11 boards.

The appointment in 2007 of a Director of the National Cancer Control Programme was a positive step. Having overseen the overhaul of cancer services in a Canadian province with a similar population size to Ireland, Professor Tom Keane brought extensive experience of the rationalisation needed to implement the cancer control strategy. In response to a parliamentary question on 2 April 2008, Minister Harney replied:

> I have recently received the report from Mr John Fitzgerald in relation to the decision to suspend breast radiology services in Portlaoise Hospital. This report has identified that the problems arose fundamentally from systemic weaknesses of governance, management and communications within the HSE

in dealing with the situation which arose in Portlaoise. I have asked the Board to consider whether the lessons arising from the systemic weaknesses of governance and management which have been identified in relation to the events at Portlaoise have wider application across the HSE. To this end, the Chairman of the Board of the HSE and I have discussed the need to optimise the HSE's operational capability by addressing issues such as:

- robust governance and management structures, processes and procedures;
- clear reporting relationships and lines of accountability;
- having permanent top level managers in key posts;
- good systems of delegation; and
- a strong sense of corporate identity which permeates all levels of the organisation.

I have asked the Board to consider these wider aspects and to let me have its assessment of the overall situation as a matter of urgency, and its proposals to address matters, as soon as possible.

While few would dispute the logic of replacing a proliferation of hospitals in a relatively small geographical area with a single, superior centre of excellence, there are concerns that the high costs of building and commissioning the new centres of excellence may lead to a delay in bringing the new centres into operation. The centralisation of cancer services has been strongly opposed by patients in areas such as Sligo.

Hospital-Acquired Infections

Another challenge facing the health system is the incidence of hospital-based infections. The results of hygiene audits of hospitals in 2005 and 2006 indicate that significant work has been carried out at hospital and national levels to improve hygiene. Almost every hospital increased its overall score following the first audit, with some of the most significant improvements being shown by those hospitals that had previously recorded 'poor' scores. The first HIQA review of hygiene in hospitals in 2007 found that nine rated 'poor' and thirty-five 'fair', with not one attaining a 'very good' rating. The December 2008 HIQA report on hygiene in fifty acute hospitals found that, while standards of hygiene had improved marginally, most hospitals had room for significant improvement. Only one hospital, Cappagh National Orthopaedic Hospital in Dublin scored a 'very good' mark for hygiene.

The Director of the State Claims Agency, Ciarán Breen, told the Public Accounts Committee on 19 June 2008 that the state is already facing 100 claims for damages for Methicillin-Resistant Staphylococcus Aureus (MRSA). This number could rise to 1,500 if there was a successful court case against the state. 'We could certainly be heading up to €0.5 billion, inclusive of costs, if these cases had to be settled,' he said.

Patient Safety

The Commission on Patient Safety and Quality Assurance, chaired by Dr Deirdre Madden of University College Cork, was established in January 2007 to develop recommendations to ensure the safety of patients within the health service. A lack of accountability and of structures designed to underpin patient safety were among the shortcomings identified by the commission's report, launched by the government in July 2008. The chief executive within each defined healthcare organisation must be ultimately accountable for patient safety and quality within that organisation. Other aspects such as paying special attention to the employment of locums and the appointment of a new complaints body to address mistakes made by individuals and multi-disciplinary teams were recommended. Legislation will be required to deal with these matters, along with the introduction of a formal licensing system for public and private hospitals and other sources of medical care.

Palliative Care

Each year almost thirty thousand people die in Ireland. These deaths are associated with older age and with chronic illness and, despite the fact that a large majority of people wish to die at home, the reality is that approximately two-thirds die in hospital and two-fifths die in acute hospitals. Research internationally has raised concerns about the quality of end-of-life care in hospitals and a consensus is emerging that care at the end of life is a valid indicator of the performance of health systems.

In Ireland, the Irish Hospice Foundation undertook a feasibility study, followed by a pilot project, to examine how a comprehensive approach could be developed to change the culture of care and organisation regarding dying, death and bereavement in hospitals. The Pilot Project (2004–2006) was undertaken at Our Lady of Lourdes Hospital in Drogheda in partnership with the HSE. It was one of three winners of the 2006 Public Service Excellence Awards selected to represent Ireland in Europe. The foundation has since established a national programme to mainstream hospice principles in hospital practice, involving over forty hospitals of which twenty are acute hospitals. It focuses on four key themes generated from the pilot project: integrated care; communication; dignity and design; and patient autonomy.

A 2008 study by the Irish Centre for Social Gerontology, jointly commissioned by the National Council on Ageing and Older People and the Irish Hospice Foundation, criticised the lack of palliative care beds and the lack of privacy for people in their last days. The Finance Act 2008 introduced tax relief to investors in private hospice facilities.

Private Health Insurance

There has been considerable debate in Ireland, as in other countries, on the appropriate public/private mix in healthcare. In Ireland, private insurance and private providers of services are integral parts of the healthcare system, with a close, complementary relationship with the public sector. Many people supplement their statutory entitlements to health services by taking out private health insurance cover. The state pays a significant part of the cost through tax relief, while much of the income of these schemes is, in turn, spent on the services of public hospitals. The state also pays private providers, such as general practitioners and pharmacists, for their services to certain categories of patient.

Under the Health Insurance Act 1994 the Minister for Health is the regulator of the private medical insurance market and ensures that it is operated within the statutory framework. This act introduced competition into the market for private health insurance, as Ireland was required to do on foot of the third EU directive on non-life insurance. The 1994 act and the 1996 Health Insurance Regulations provide the regulatory framework for the operation of the competitive private medical insurance market in Ireland. The act ended the state monopoly on the provision of health insurance. Since its establishment in 1957 this had effectively been the sole prerogative of the Voluntary Health Insurance Board (VHI). The Health Insurance Authority was established as a regulatory body for private health insurance in Ireland under the Health Insurance Acts 1994 to 2007. Its functions include: licensing private health insurers, monitoring the health insurance market, advising the minister, managing and administering the risk equalisation scheme, and providing information and assistance to consumers of the private health insurance market.

Only companies registered are permitted to carry on the business of private medical insurance in Ireland. In addition to the VHI, other insurers include Quinn Healthcare and Hibernian (who took over the clients of BUPA and Vivas respectively), St Paul's Garda Medical Aid Society, the ESB Staff Medical Provident Fund and the Prison Officers' Provident Fund.

The legislation requires insurers offering medical insurance to comply with the principles of community rating (an insurer must charge the same premium for a given level of benefits irrespective of age, sex or health status), open enrolment (an insurer is required, with certain qualifications, to provide cover to any individual under the age of sixty-five who wishes to enrol) and lifetime cover (an insurer may not, except in prescribed circumstances, refuse to renew cover once an individual has enrolled).

Insurers offering cover for hospital in-patient services are also required to provide minimum benefit (i.e. a minimum level of cover) across a range of services, including general hospitals, out-patient and maternity benefits, convalescence, psychiatric treatment, substance abuse and daycare.

Insurers were also required to participate in a risk equalisation scheme, which is an essential feature of a competitive market that operates under the principles of community rating and open enrolment. It provides for the equitable distribution of risk between insurers, thereby ensuring that insurers will not benefit from preferred risk selection ('cherry-picking'); and without it the system of community rating/open enrolment would be inherently unstable. A Supreme Court ruling in July 2008 granted BUPA its appeal aimed at preventing the introduction of the risk equalisation scheme in the private health insurance market. The court ruled the scheme was invalid because it was based on an incorrect interpretation of the phrase 'community rating' in a provision of the Health Insurance Act 1994. The risk equalisation scheme was intended to spread the claims of high-risk persons amongst all insurers in proportion to their market share, effectively meaning insurance companies with lower risk customers would compensate the VHI for its older and less profitable customer base.

The private medical insurance market plays a pivotal role in the delicate mix between public and private care in Ireland. At the end of 2007 there were in excess of 2.2 million persons (more than 50 per cent of the population) holding private health insurance, of which VHI has 70 per cent of the health insurance market.

Co-location of Public and Private Hospitals

The high-profile policy of the co-location of public and private hospitals has attracted significant attention. Following on from the 2001 health strategy, which gave a commitment to provide more public patient beds, Minister for Health Mary Harney announced plans on 14 July 2005 to have new private hospitals built on the campuses of public hospitals in order to free up 1,000 more beds for public patients. By encouraging new private hospitals to take a substantial number of private and semi-private beds out of the public hospital system, the policy hoped to create new beds for public patients in the fastest and most cost-effective way over a five-year period. The aim of the policy is to increase bed capacity for public patients in public hospitals; encourage the participation of the private sector in generating extra capacity; maximise the potential use of public hospital sites; promote efficiency among public and private sector acute hospital service providers; and offer improved quality and choice to all patients.

Minister Harney explained the rationale for co-location to the Oireachtas Joint Committee on Health and Children on 22 November 2007:

The whole purpose of co-location is to provide increased public capacity in public hospitals.

When we have the preferred health model mentioned by Professor Drumm [CEO of HSE] with more happening at community and primary level and more effective use of our current acute beds, clearly there will be issues around capacity. We need more single rooms and more isolation facilities in our public hospitals. All of these matters will be important in how we organise the acute system in the future. I see co-location as the speediest and most cost effective way of providing increased capacity on the big public hospital sites over the next five years.

Under the scheme, public hospitals will lease land to private developers to build hospitals in a bid to free up beds for public patients. There are eight hospital sites involved in the process: St James's, Tallaght, Beaumont and Connolly Hospitals in Dublin; Cork University Hospital; Limerick Regional Hospital; Sligo General Hospital; and Waterford Regional Hospital. In the case of Limerick, for instance, the private hospital will match the case-mix of the public hospital in that all specialties catered for in the public hospital will also be catered for in the co-located hospital – both medical and surgical, with the exception of national specialties.

The Irish Congress of Trade Unions, among others, has strongly criticised the policy of co-located private and public hospitals, which it regards as a euphemism for the privatisation of medicine, and fears that the real intention of the policy is to create a private internal market in the private sector of healthcare. Others believe it will damage the public hospital services and lead to the privatisation of the health services. They have warned that this will exacerbate the two-tier system, with deluxe private facilities located next to under-resourced public hospitals.

Plans are well-advanced for a new private hospital for women and children – the first of its kind in Europe – in south County Dublin, intended to take the pressure off Dublin's maternity hospitals, which have one of the highest birth rates in Europe. Tax breaks were introduced for private hospitals in the Finance Act 2003 and abolished in the April 2009 Budget.

Cross-Border Healthcare in the European Union

The European Commission tabled draft legislation in July 2008 setting out rules whereby patients who choose to receive medical treatment in another member state of the European Union would be reimbursed by their national health authority. The aim of the proposal was to provide legal clarity and more information for patients.

The proposal follows several judgments over the previous decade by the European Court of Justice confirming that individuals have the right to be reimbursed for healthcare they receive in another EU member state, subject to certain conditions. However, uncertainty over the exact way the right should be exercised and the effects that an increase in demand would have on countries' health services have prompted governments to ask for clear pan-European legislation on the issue. The proposals build on a process involving health ministries and other stakeholders that began in 2003.

These proposals would replace the arrangements established in the 1970s, when it became clear that free movement within the EU would require that people could receive healthcare in other member states. It was also recognised that people might need to be sent to another member state for treatment, but that this should be controlled by the organisations paying for the care. The number of people crossing European borders has increased exponentially. A new generation of Europeans regards national frontiers as increasingly irrelevant. Some of them have challenged what they see as unjustifiable restrictions on their right to obtain healthcare in another country and, in many cases, their arguments have been upheld by the European Court of Justice. This has resulted in a legislative framework regulating cross-border care that is full of legal precedents, but with little clarity about what those precedents mean in practice. It was not easy to resolve this complex situation, and a recent attempt to treat health services like any other service foundered when the many specificities of healthcare became clear.

The European Commission's proposals have three main strands. Firstly, the values (universality, access to good quality care, equity and solidarity) and principles (quality, safety, care based on evidence and ethics, patient involvement, redress, privacy and confidentiality) underpinning European health systems are clearly stated. These were previously agreed by Europe's health ministers in June 2006.

Second, a specific framework will be introduced for the aspects of cross-border care not already covered by existing legislation, such as that covering people who fall ill while temporarily in another EU member state. Key elements relate to people who choose to go to another member state to obtain care. If this is non-hospital care, they simply arrange it themselves. If it is hospital or other specialised care, which the European Commission will define, countries may introduce systems that require people to seek prior authorisation before obtaining care in another member state, but only if they can show that this is necessary to prevent outflow of patients from making their hospitals non-viable. Refusals must be limited to those necessary to avoid such adverse effects on their existing hospital system. Where the home country has a system of primary care gatekeeping, this will be respected. In both cases, patients will be entitled to reimbursement only up to the amount that would be paid at home and will not be allowed to make a profit. This framework also proposes a network of national contact points for patients seeking information and tidies up several other unresolved matters.

Third, mechanisms will be established to foster European collaboration on health services, such as shared facilities in border areas, common methods of technology assessment, and centres of excellence for rare conditions.

The draft EU legislation is not designed to harmonise national health systems. These continue to remain the sole responsibility of national authorities.

Conclusion

The mark of a civilised society is how it treats its sick and vulnerable citizens. Health is not everything but everything is nothing without health. The overall health of the Irish people has improved considerably since the mid-twentieth century. Life expectancy at birth in Ireland has also increased substantially and according to provisional Central Statistics Office figures is estimated at 81.5 years for Irish women and 76.7 years for Irish men in the period 2004 to 2006. In comparison with 1950, men's life expectancy had increased by thirteen years and women's by fourteen years. In comparison with 2001 to 2003, men's life expectancy had increased by 1.6 years and women's by 1.2 years. The main causes of mortality are coronary heart disease, cancer, respiratory disease and stroke. In the older age groups, the proportion of deaths from coronary heart disease is higher in men, whereas deaths from cancer are higher in women.

Health systems around the world are facing similar challenges – rising costs, demographic pressures, an increased burden of disease, new technologies and treatments. The population is beginning to age, there is a need for pandemic preparedness planning and the health services will have to provide increasingly for high-dependency groups in the population.

Successive governments have tried to meet these challenges through the improvement and development of services through the provision of additional resources to areas of special need and by striving to deliver services in an equitable and cost-efficient manner. Reform is a long and difficult process. Ireland's health transformation programme is on a larger scale than any other public service redesign programme in the history of the state. International experience shows that changes of this magnitude take a number of years to settle down and can be hard to sustain against the more short-term pressures of political or budgetary cycles. The OECD review of the Irish public service (2008b: 12) notes, 'It is clear from studying the Irish system, and in particular the health sector, that there are difficulties involved in leading system-level change, and in pursuing system-wide coherence'. The work done to date represents an important step in the incremental development and streamlining of the healthcare system. It is understandable that in the face of significant change people will express their concerns and fears and that this is manifested through resistance and indeed criticism. Delivering the health service reform programme is crucial for the health and welfare of all citizens and for future generations. There can be no doubt that the need to continue the reform of the health services, and bring it to a successful conclusion, is the most significant challenge facing government.

Web Resources

Department of Health and Children at www.dohc.ie
Economic and Social Research Institute at www.esri.ie
European Centre for Disease Prevention and Control at www.ecdc.europa.eu
Health Information and Quality Authority at www.hiqa.ie
Health Service Executive at www.hse.ie
Health Services National Partnership Forum at www.hsnpf.ie
Irish Cancer Society at www.cancer.ie
Irish College of General Practitioners at www.icgp.ie
Irish Hospice Foundation at www.hospice-foundation.ie
Irish Hospital Consultants Association at www.ihca.ie
Irish Pharmaceutical Healthcare Association at www.ipha.ie
Mental Health Commission at www.mhcirl.ie
National Cancer Screening Service at www.cancerscreening.ie
National Treatment Purchase Fund at www.ntpf.ie
World Health Organization at www.who.int

11

APPEALS AND INQUIRIES

Every day officials in government departments, regulatory bodies, state agencies and public bodies make hundreds of discretionary decisions that deprive people of entitlements and benefits or impose restrictions on them. Inevitably, many of those adversely affected by these decisions feel that they have not been treated fairly. They complain that they have not been given the reasons for a decision, that they have not been given a chance to provide their side of the story, that there has been unreasonable delay, or simply that a mistake has been made. In addition, there are occasions when the actions of public bodies appear to exceed their legal and constitutional rights.

Since public servants are not the best judges of their own conduct, it is clearly desirable that there should be independent systems of review under which the grievances of citizens against public bodies can be effectively examined and, if well founded, remedied. By this means it would be possible to ensure that the exercise of discretionary power is not abused; that natural justice obtains; that there are not wrong motives or irrelevant grounds; that decisions are not taken arbitrarily, unreasonably or erroneously; and that, in short, the activities of public bodies are controlled in the interests of the people.

A formalised system of complaints and redress is now well developed in Ireland, as in many European countries. In Ireland all executive powers are vested by parliament in individual ministers, who are accountable to parliament for their actions and those of their officials. This concept is enshrined in the Ministers and Secretaries Act 1924, which makes ministerial responsibility central to the Irish form of democracy. As a result, the idea of political rather than legal protection for citizens who have a grievance against the administration is embedded in political tradition and therefore the development of appeals bodies has been both limited and patchy; for example, Ireland did not get an Ombudsman until 1984. The High Court has, of course, always been available to complainants, but the situations in which it is employed to intervene in relations between the executive and the citizen are rare. This is largely because of its long delays and prohibitive costs, not to mention its reluctance to get involved in administrative decisions.

The need for adequate appellate institutions and procedures was stressed as far back as 1969 by the Public Services Organisation Review Group (Devlin report). In this connection, it also recommended that ministers should shed their executive functions, making them over to executive agencies, a number of which would be created in each department. These agencies would be responsible for day-to-day work, including detailed operations such as the payment of grants, issuing of licences and awarding of contracts (i.e. the type of activities frequently involving controversial decisions). Successive governments have, however, proved extremely reluctant to adopt this recommendation, thereby exemplifying the preference of politicians for the established practice of seeking political remedies.

In Ireland there are a number of informal methods as well as systems of a more formal kind for obtaining the investigation and, if appropriate, redress of grievances. The informal methods include approaches to public representatives (who may air the grievance by means of a parliamentary question), to interest groups and trade unions, and even directly to the decision-making body concerned, as well as publicity in the press and on the radio. Delaney (2001: 41) notes that 'Ireland is a small society, with a strongly political culture and it is no accident that our Duty Officer system, with its passport facility, was almost unique among European countries'. The formal systems include the courts (both domestic and European), legally established tribunals and the Ombudsman.

Access to Information

A significant development was the passing of the Freedom of Information Act 1997. It asserts the right of members of the public to obtain access to official information to the greatest extent possible consistent with the public interest and the right to privacy. It has helped public servants to be more open in their dealings with people. The act established three new statutory rights allowing each person to:

- Gain access to information relating to oneself held by public bodies.
- Have official information relating to oneself amended where it is incomplete, incorrect or misleading.
- Obtain reasons for decisions affecting oneself.

In addition, the act provided for the establishment of an independent office of Information Commissioner (see below) to review decisions relating to freedom of information made by public bodies.

The widespread publication of reports, consultation papers, reasoned decisions, annual reports and website information by public agencies has significantly increased the amount of openness and transparency in public policy. It has increased the access and availability of information on all aspects of public policy, including the criteria used to make decisions. The growth of e-government and the explosion of political and administrative information on websites mean that the Internet has become an important resource for civil and political information. Websites hosted by government departments, state agencies, public agencies, public representatives, interest groups and news organisations contain a volume of current information on policies, appeal procedures and online application forms to appeal a decision. Digital citizenship, or the ability to participate in society online, has facilitated the appeals and grievance procedures and has helped to improve community engagement. In addition, the media provides forensic analysis and detailed information on the activities of public agencies and brings the information in speeches, parliamentary questions, Dáil debates and annual reports to a much wider audience.

Another development has been the establishment of complaints sections. Many public bodies, for example the Revenue Commissioners, have set up their own complaints section. The Ombudsman has said that most public bodies should follow this lead. In addition, there has been the development of customer charters or statements of customer rights. For example, the Revenue Commissioners first published in 1989 a charter of taxpayers' rights; the Department of Health published a patient charter for users of the health services in 1992; and the Houses of the Oireachtas produced separate charters for customers, for political staff, for members and for staff.

There are a number of agencies with a legislative mandate in this area. The Director of Consumer Affairs, for example, was a statutory post established under the Consumer Information Act 1978. The post was abolished on the enactment of the Consumer Protection Act 2007, which established the National Consumer Agency (budget 2009 included proposals to amalgamate the National Consumer Agency and the Competition Authority). The Office of the Director of Corporate Enforcement was established in 2001 to improve the compliance environment for corporate activity. It primarily serves the public interest, rather than acting to remedy individual grievances in the company law area. The Equality Authority was established in 1999 to prohibit discrimination on the following nine grounds: gender; marital status; family status; sexual orientation; religion; age; disability; race; and membership of the Traveller community.

The Citizens Information Board is the statutory body that supports the provision of information, advice and advocacy on the broad range of social and civil services to the public. It has developed a three-channel approach to information service delivery that includes a nationwide network of drop-in citizens information centres, a lo-call citizens information phone service and the award-winning citizens information website (formerly Oasis). This website (www.citizensinformation.ie) receives over 200,000 visits a month and has a huge volume of information available on all aspects of living and working in Ireland, from details on the taxation system and social welfare services to information on schools, the courts and the health services. Minister of State Martin Mansergh noted in September 2008:

> The Government recognises the important role that our State Agencies play in the delivery of services and information to citizens including in some cases the vindication of rights. Our agencies are part of an extensive network of interaction between Citizens and the State. However, in some cases, the large number and diverse range of Agencies and Bodies can make it difficult for Citizens to know how to access information and services. Decisions regarding the rationalisation of Agencies will be cognisant of the relationship between Citizens and the State, the key relationship in any democratic society. One of the goals of this process is to bring about a more citizen-friendly system of government that will enhance citizens' awareness of, and access to, State services and that will provide greater transparency and accountability in the delivery of services and greater Value-for-Money.

The Department of Enterprise, Trade and Employment has built the BASIS system – Business Access to State Information and Services – to provide an effective service for business customers (see www.basis.ie). It facilitates doing business online, including paying taxes, finding a government tender and accessing information on legal, regulatory and employment issues, and contains commonly used forms from a wide range of government agencies. At the level of the economy, the Competition Authority has completed reports on the professions, including engineering, architecture, optometry, law and dental. A number of these matters have been inserted in legislation.

Regulatory Bodies

The establishment of more regulatory bodies has highlighted the need for a system of challenge, appeal and redress. Among the principal regulators are: the Competition Authority (established in 1991), the Commission for Energy Regulation (established in 1999), the Commission for Aviation Regulation (established in 2001), the Commission for Communications Regulation or ComReg (established in 2002), the Financial Services Regulator (established in 2003) and the Commission for Taxi Regulation (established in 2004). The range and functions of these commissions is evolving as the regulatory framework in Ireland and in Europe develops. For example, the regulatory capacity of the regulator for the postal sector was significantly enhanced in May 2008. The regulator, ComReg, can now seek financial sanction, by way of an application to the High Court, should An Post, the postal service operator, fail to comply with one of its directions. The Chief Executive of the Financial Regulator resigned in January 2009 following a report on Anglo Irish Bank directors' loans and the regulatory response.

The regulators have to manage the complex interaction between the political system, the civil service, operators and other stakeholders. They have to be independent in the exercise of their roles. There was some concern at the time of the creation of the regulatory bodies that they would be very powerful, taking decision-making functions away from government and the Oireachtas and imposing difficult situations for customers and operators. These fears have not been realised. Regulators have made a positive contribution to the effectiveness of the machinery of government. They are 'creatures of statute', operating within a specified framework of national and European Union law. Regulators work in a very contentious environment and have to be careful that their decisions are well founded and can be upheld by the courts if subjected to legal challenge. Regulation has followed the six core principles of necessity, effectiveness, proportionality, transparency, accountability and consistency. In 2006 Minister for Communications, Marine and Natural Resources Noel Dempsey stated, 'I believe our appeals system should be fair, accessible and effective. It should protect the rights of the individual but also ensure that Ireland's economic and social advancement is not blocked.'

The detailed enabling provisions and the interpretation of the founding legislation and regulations, which are the mandate given by the Oireachtas, are critical. The founding legislation sets out specific provisions in respect of audit by the Comptroller and Auditor General, reports on activities to the Oireachtas, and the Freedom of Information Act. When called upon, the courts have provided detailed examination of the decisions made and how they have been implemented. Appeals mechanisms have been introduced.

Regulators were set up to impose significant changes in the status quo in entrenched industries and economically significant sectors. To work effectively and quickly, they must have serious enforcement powers. Regulation by agreement, while an ideal objective, cannot always be achieved. Therefore, appeals procedures, arbitration mechanisms and complaints processes are important. Where regulators decide price levels, service charges, impose fines or penalties, determine levels of output or quality standards they have the potential to distort the market. Secretary General of the Department of the Taoiseach Dermot McCarthy (2007) noted that 'regulatory policy and practice can and should be a source of competitive advantage'. Open consultation processes are vital to know what interested parties think before deciding on key proposals and projects. It is necessary to work in partnership to ensure full industry engagement in the processes necessary for implementation, while at the same time retaining the neutrality and independence of action of the regulator. Collins (2007: 130–1) observes, 'The current regulatory framework does allow for much more transparency than used to be the case. Indeed, appeals against regulatory decisions prior to the current system were likely to be made covertly by vested interests via informal pressure on politicians or senior civil servants. Further, Ireland is well ahead of most EU Member States in addressing the appeals issue.'

The Department of the Taoiseach published a survey of business attitudes to regulation in March 2007. This comprehensive survey of over 800 companies, including small and medium-sized enterprises, was widely distributed. It identifies priorities for improving the regulatory environment for business. The findings of the survey are positive, indicating that regulation ranked in the middle of challenges faced by business, and are being implemented by the Department of Enterprise, Trade and Employment, which established a high-level group chaired by its secretary general to drive this policy. Speaking in the Dáil on 3 October 2007 Taoiseach Bertie Ahern noted:

> In general, business feels the amount of regulation is about right, although, obviously, a number of areas have been identified . . . issues that still exist are taxation, mainly for smaller companies because larger companies are on-line and do not have difficulties with the Revenue Commissioners; health and safety which, rightly or wrongly, drives business mad because they believe it is too much regulation for them; environment law; statistical returns; and employment and company law. It is recognised nationally and internationally that our economy is lightly regulated but these issues have been highlighted in business surveys . . . Therefore, before regulating, there is a discussion with the stakeholders as to whether it is necessary. Under the regulation, accountability makes it clear precisely who is responsible for whom and for what. Business people also feel strongly about an effective appeals process. One must also ask whether the regulation will give rise to anomalies and inconsistencies given the other regulations in place, and whether we are applying best practice in developing one area while relegating others.

The regulatory impact assessment process has been helpful in providing a set of guidelines to be followed prior to the introduction of legislation, statutory instruments or other action.

The social partnership programme *Towards 2016* (Department of the Taoiseach 2006) notes the need to seek views on 'the most appropriate appeals mechanisms for the key economic regulators, reflecting best international practice, as well as the specific regulatory arrangements and market structures operating in individual sectors'. Regulators cannot employ cumbersome or slow processes and procedures even if they eventually provide technically perfect decisions. In a globally competitive market, customers, operators and investors will move elsewhere. For regulatory bodies, as for all public agencies, 'justice delayed is justice denied', to quote the famous adage of William E. Gladstone, so expeditious appeals and grievance procedures are vital.

Public Representatives

By far the most frequently used of the informal remedies regarding a grievance is the approach to a politician, usually a TD, who then uses his or her influence with the minister or with others who are responsible for making decisions. Such approaches are encouraged by the politicians themselves, who do not generally regard themselves as legislators and are more at home in dealing with constituency issues. The Dáil itself has long been regarded as a watchdog against government, and the handling by TDs of individual grievances could be regarded as a natural extension of this. Furthermore, because of the Irish system of multi-seat constituencies, where members of even the same party are in competition with each other for election, there are considerable benefits to be gained from services provided for constituents. FitzGerald (2003: 92) comments on a special feature of this system:

> . . . the electorate, who vote for individual candidates rather than for parties, can choose between different members of the same party. As a result of this the chances of members losing their seats is approximately doubled, indeed trebled in the case of Fianna Fáil. For overall, approximately half of the seats lost by members of the two larger parties are lost to other members of their own group rather than to members of others parties.

For these reasons, little interest has been shown in other forms of remedy. For example, only four deputies took part in the debate on the bill to establish the office of Ombudsman, and after its enactment four years elapsed before an appointment to the vacant office was made. At an earlier stage, in 1966, Minister Charles Haughey stated, 'We don't need an Ombudsman because there is hardly anyone without a direct personal link with someone be he minister, Dáil deputy, clergyman, county or borough councillor, who will interest himself in helping a citizen to have a grievance examined and, if possible, rectified . . . the basic reason we do not need the Ombudsman is because we have so many unofficial but nevertheless effective ones.' This preference for the use of representatives is shared by the general public. As MacCarthaigh (2005: 294) explains, 'The emphasis on constituency service means that much of political life in Ireland appears to be based on personality rather than policy, on constituency issues rather than national issues, and on delivery of services and favours rather than reform of institutions that would make these personal interventions unnecessary.'

There are a number of ways in which this informal system works. By far the most widely used is that which is known as 'representations'. A politician belonging to a government party makes a request by letter on behalf of a constituent to the minister responsible. Those in the opposition parties who have previously held office write personally to the secretary general of the department, while ordinary backbenchers write to the secretary general formally or to an official whom they have got to know. Letters to the minister are, in the first instance, acknowledged by the minister personally, with an additional copy of his or her reply for the politician to send to the constituent. The original letter is then sent from the minister's private office to the appropriate section of the department for preparation of a final reply. Normally, this reply will be prepared by the official who either recommended or made the decision complained of. Thus, unless a minister takes a personal interest (which he or she usually does only when personally approached by the party member making the representations) and the decision is one of a discretionary nature, it is unlikely that it will be altered. Much of the brokerage work of TDs is little more than advice about the benefits to which people are entitled and help with access to various public services. TDs are expected by their voters to help them to sort out problems with the machinery of government. Butler and Collins (2004: 144) note:

> Various studies have revealed a strong tendency for citizens to channel not just *complaints* about public services but also non-controversial *requests* for a public service to which they are entitled as of right, through a local Teachta Dála (TD, or Member of Parliament). Matters of social welfare, housing and medical entitlements dominate the case loads of TDs, and in many cases the TD does little more than transmit the constituent's request to the department or agency concerned.

Officials are not impressed by representations, to which they are well accustomed. The matter may or may not be re-examined, depending on the issue, the nature of the examination already made, and the political standing of the person making the representations. The reply, prepared for signature by the minister on his or her personal headed paper, may, however, contain a fuller restatement of the reasons for the original decision and generally includes a soothing last sentence to the effect that 'the minister regrets that he cannot be of more assistance on this occasion'. It is then sent back to the minister's private office, where the private secretary scrutinises the letter before presenting it to the minister for signature. Again, an extra copy of the reply is sent to the politician concerned. In the vast majority of cases this ends the correspondence.

A minister receives directly all the grievances and all the requests for favours from his or her constituents, irrespective of whether they are members or supporters of the minister's party. If the subject matter relates to the work of the minister's department, the procedure is as outlined above. If it does not, the letter is transmitted over the minister's signature to whichever colleague has the responsibility, with a request for favourable consideration, and the constituent is informed accordingly. In due course a final reply is received from the investigating minister, whose investigation has been the same as that referred to above. This reply is sent by the minister to the constituent, who thus has evidence of the high level at which the request has been handled.

Occasionally, politicians, especially those who have been in the Oireachtas for some time and may have got to know many of the senior officials, inquire on the telephone about constituency affairs. This practice is not common, however, since it does not produce any written matter to show the constituent that action has been taken on his or her behalf.

The nature of the multi-seat proportional representation system requires all politicians, including ministers, to be active, and to be seen to be active, in constituency terms. Ministers continue to hold regular weekly constituency clinics, despite the pressures of ministerial office. For example, it was revealed in January 2008 that 6,200 passport applications were processed through the special passport facility for Oireachtas members. An official investigation of this fast-track process concluded that the system should be retained with the additional requirement of a declaration form. Sixty-two Oireachtas members who submitted written replies were in favour of retaining the facility. Komito (1985) suggests viewing clientelism in Ireland:

> . . . in terms of information and access. Even when only legitimate benefits are provided, politicians' interventions often achieve results which the voter cannot himself achieve. Politicians argue that, whatever the legal entitlements, the person would achieve nothing without the politician's help. Many people do not understand the bureaucratic system well enough to obtain all that they are entitled to. The politician is one expert who can be trusted to assist them through the bureaucratic maze, and provide a state service that might otherwise be denied.

Officials generally regard this elaborate and expensive representations procedure with a degree of cynicism, since it very rarely results in the reversal of an administrative decision. They complain that it has detrimental effects on their work. Since ministers demand that priority be given to representations, official resources are diverted away from dealing with the issues that the representations are intended to ameliorate. Officials who should be engaged full-time on, for example, paying grants, have to detach themselves to deal with representations about delays in the payment of the same grants. They also point out that the system distracts ministers and senior officials from the policy-making activities in which they should more properly be engaged.

A further undesirable feature of the system is the creation of an impression among the public that everything can be fixed. Collins and O'Shea (2002: 11) state that 'In Ireland, there is an expectation that politicians will act on behalf of constituents looking for favourable treatment by public servants, especially when some ambiguity or grounds for discretion can be identified. This is referred to in the Irish context as clientelism, although it is more accurately brokerage. The key distinction is that the politician is dispersing state-owned benefits rather than personal largesse'. The All-Party Oireachtas Committee on the Constitution (2002: 19) was told, 'There is an ever-growing emphasis on clientelism and intense, even vicious, intra-party competition which is wasteful of resources and leads to a culture of "gombeenism".'

Clientelism Rap
Joseph O'Connor

Well if you have a problem,
You know who's there to *solve* 'em.
Leinster House is waitin' on your S.O.S.
We've far too many *Tee*Ds
And when we're feelin' *nee*dy
We're turnin' to them frequently
To sort the mess.

We take it to the *Tee*D, *Tee*D, *Tee*D,
He might be short and *wee*dy, he might be tall.
He might be Green or Labour, she might be a Sinn Féiner,
Resplendent independently, or Fianna Fáil.

When fate has cruelly mocked us, we contact the Oireachtas
And ask the help of *Teachtaí* that we barely know.
It ain't why we elect 'em, sponsor and select 'em.
The Constitution says they're there *to run the show*.

But we take it to the *Tee*D, *Tee*D, *Tee*D,
His eyes are gettin' beady, thinkin' of our votes.
He's offerin' affection, political protection.
He thinks of the election. And he's takin' notes.

If your cousin is in prison and the cost of visitin's risen
Or you need a letter written to put pressure on the judge.
Take it to your *Tee*D, for your support he's *gree*dy.
It ain't an opportunity he's goin' to fudge.

You're gettin' represented. The system's gone demented.
Constituency rivals at each other's throats.
Plámás is flyin' from their lips, they're lobby-fodder for the whips.
They're fightin' one another for the selfsame votes.

If your granny needs free dentures, write to your back-benchers.
It's part of their adventures and they WILL NOT shirk.
Buildin' reputations 'stead of runnin' the nation,
Askin' useless questions which they then call work.

If your feelin' fairly adamant your road needs tarmadacam-ent,
You cannot get the Corpo to send out the truck.
Don't be feelin' sensitive, ring up your representative,
He won't be very tentative in sayin' YOU'RE IN LUCK.

You're rappin' with your *Tee*D, *Tee*D, *Tee*D,
Speedily agreed he'd put your case.
That's what he is *there* for, what he lost his hair for,
Why he's sayin *where*fore, keepin' pace.

Doesn't wanna legislate or contribute to dull debate,
Significant affairs of state are *such* a bore.
His mind it is directed, on gettin' re-elected.
He's paid the hefty goin' rate and much, much more.

His generous expenses he'd like to keep and hence his
Sense he wants to help you 'cos he's duty bound.
He doubtless didn't mention his controversial pension,
He's focusin' attention on appearin' sound.

In other countries' parliaments they have debates an' arguments
On things like the enlargement of
The EU – NOT
Like how we do it *here* in
The lovely land of Erin.
The Dáil ain't too endearin' and it *costs a LOT*.

'Cos

It's fulla bleedin' *Tee*Ds, claimin' freebies,
Goin' on the *tee*vee, when they may.
Off to Galway *Races*, showin' off their *faces*,
Junketin' to places far away.

It's easy to be cynical; but it sometimes seems inimical
To democratic practices, so some believe.
We don't elect a *fixer* to do a little nixer, lickin'
Envelopes he's sendin', you don't wanna receive!

But we take it to the *Tee*Dee, yes indeed he's
Writin' to the minister "with great regret."
He's gonna fight your corner, and he's gonna be a mourner
At the funeral of a voter that *he never even met.*

He's goin' to removals, seekin' our approvals,
Supermarket openings, sports events!
The stress is fairly fiery, will have him in the Priory
The pressure on his diary is quite intense.

It isn't too heart-warmin'; the system needs reformin'.
A TD's time is wasted on consumin' strife.
The better ones'd change it and want to rearrange it.
You wouldn't hardly blame them when you see their LIFE.

It's funerals and luncheons, fetes and feckin' functions.
Walkin' up to strangers in the public bar:
Holdin' out your *hand*-teh those who think you're Santa:
Constituents your meant-teh buy DRINK for.

You're treatin' them with def'rence, writin' them a ref'rence,
Hopin' for a pref'rence come Election Day.
You do a lotta boastin'. Literature your postin'.
It's no way for the faint-of-heart to earn their pay.

You're in the legislature, your family nearly hate yer,
The little time you've left for them, it ain't too warm.
Last time you saw the missus, instead of tender kisses,
You gave a manifesto and a membership form!

You're canvassin' the neighbours, gettin' photos in the papers,
Of undignified capers, it's a great mistake.
Sayin' "Look at the style o'me, look at the guile o'me,
Singin' *Baidin Fheidhlimi* at some constituent's wake."

The way it goes in Fianna Fáil, with every party in the Dáil,
We play 'em off each other and they'll get our tick.
Clientelist traditions and on-the-ground ambitions
Combine to make our politics sadly sick.

It's deeply unconventional, the system is dysfunctional,
Designed for an eventual election gain;
Not to make the nation feel participation.
It's nothing but frustration dressed as pain

What all the fuss was fought for, Wolfe Tone was hot for,
Connolly was shot for – democracyyy!
Sad that it was bound to eventually come down to
Chancers writin' letters sayin' VOTE FOR ME.

We need the system *un*blocked. Accordin' to the *Bunreacht*
TDs are there to legislate and *nothing more*.
They AREN'T there to get your grant,
They AREN'T there to help your aunt,
They AREN'T there for knockin' on the voter's door.

But we took it up with *Tee*Ds, *Tee*Ds, *Tee*Ds,
Fine Gael and *Pee*Ds/ Labour too.
They should be takin' *[pause]* an' writin' better laws an'
Leave the feckin' funerals
to me
and you.

Joseph O'Connor's *Clientelism Rap* was originally broadcast on RTÉ
Radio One's *Drivetime With Mary Wilson*, to which he contributes a
popular column every Wednesday.

Another type of public representative, the local councillor, can play a role as intermediary between the citizen and the administration at local authority level. Councillors have a certain advantage over TDs in following up individual complaints because of their proximity to the citizen, their close involvement with the administrative process and their more ready access to local offices.

Parliamentary Questions

The procedures relating to the tabling and answering of parliamentary questions have been dealt with in Chapter 3. Parliamentary questions (PQs) may be divided into two broad categories: those which relate to policy matters and those which relate to matters of day-to-day administration. It is those in the latter category with which we are concerned here, and specifically those where TDs seek to air grievances. There are five types of oral question: questions to the Taoiseach; ordinary questions; priority questions; private notice questions; and leaders' questions. 'The PQ, if used correctly, is theoretically the most potent facility at the disposal of the opposition in order to obtain information and to hold ministers (and therefore government) to account' (MacCarthaigh 2005: 115).

By far the most numerous parliamentary questions are those relating to matters such as the non-payment, inadequate payment or delay in payment of grants and allowances. These questions take a form such as: 'To ask the Minister for Social and Family Affairs the reason a person (details supplied) in County Clare was not assisted; and if she will make a statement on the matter.' By convention, the actual name of the applicant is not published. The TD conveys the question to the Dáil office, whence it is sent to the minister's office and thence to the appropriate section of the department. The main difference between the treatment of this type of complaint and that of the 'representations' is that the reply to the parliamentary question is normally seen and approved by the assistant secretary concerned before its transmission to the minister's office for presentation to the Dáil. Copies of the replies to all parliamentary questions are normally seen also by the secretary general of the department, but not necessarily for clearance. Only on rare occasions does this procedure result in any alteration of the reply at the insistence of one of these senior officials. What the procedure does ensure is that the reply will be technically correct and will be in such terms as to protect the minister from criticism by way of supplementary questions (where the question is for oral reply) or from other questions on the same issue on a subsequent occasion. Replies must arrive in the minister's private office at least twenty-four hours before they are due for answer; this rule, however, is not always adhered to, especially if there is an amount of information to be collected for the reply.

The replies to all questions that a minister has to answer orally are examined by the minister before going to the Dáil to present them. In these cases the minister will have the benefit of an accompanying note giving the background to the question, together with sufficient information to enable him or her to deal with supplementary questions. To change the nature of the reply, for example to approve some benefit already rejected, is normally within the minister's prerogative. However, this prerogative is very rarely exercised, and the minister normally accepts the judgment of the officials.

The replies to written questions are generally seen by the senior officials only, and are rarely seen by the minister. Copies of the reply are provided by the minister's private secretary to the Dáil to be passed on to the TD concerned and for subsequent publication in the record of Dáil debates. Delaney (2001: 61) comments:

> Replying to PQs [Parliamentary Questions] was an art in itself. The idea was to say as little as possible, as one Agriculture Civil Servant foolishly admitted to the Beef Tribunal. We had to protect the State from overly inquisitive TDs and there was no point in being garrulous and volunteering information. Looking over my shoulder at the green screen of prose I was preparing for a draft reply, my First Sec would say 'I don't like it already – there's too much text!' Instead, there was a great amusement taken from a Westminster PQ which got passed around. An opposition MP had asked a long and detailed question, enquiring if an overall situation would be such given various hypothetical criteria – to which the Minister replied succinctly, 'No'.

While parliamentary questions have little effect on the work of civil servants, beyond the amount of time taken up in the administrative procedure that the careful preparation of replies and notes entails, they have a greater impact in the political system. There is always a sense of urgency, since the standing orders of the Dáil provide that three clear days' notice only need be given, i.e. that deputies are entitled to, and invariably receive, answers to their written questions (by far the most numerous) on such short notice. The officials preparing the replies to parliamentary questions are obliged under their own standing departmental regulations to drop all other work and attend to parliamentary questions. Information about the problems of individual constituents can, of course, be obtained by deputies, through either a telephone call or a letter, especially now that members of the Oireachtas have secretarial assistance. However, civil servants are aware that the main reasons for questions on constituency matters are, firstly, to allow politicians to represent themselves openly as advocates of the defenceless citizen against the powerful minister and soulless bureaucrat, and, second, to provide them with written material that they can send to their constituents and to their local newspapers as evidence that they are about their constituents' business. Questions are, nevertheless, an essential element of democracy.

Parliamentary questions are not only put in order to receive information. In many cases TDs could obtain the information through normal channels of inquiry. Parliamentary questions are also put in order to give information to government, the civil service and other stakeholders about topics of current interest and concern. Walter Bagehot (1826–1877), one of the father figures of public administration, recognised this in the nineteenth century:

> There is no limit to the curiosity of parliament . . . As soon as bore A ends, bore B begins. Some inquire from a genuine love of knowledge, or from a real wish to improve what they ask about; others to see their name in the papers; others to show a watchful constituency that they are alert; others to get on and to get a place in the Government; others from an accumulation of little motives they could not themselves analyse, or because it is their habit to ask things (1993: 188–9).

Based on an analysis of how twenty parliaments in Western Europe (including Dáil Éireann) handle questioning in various forms, Wiberg (1995: 181) identifies the following different motivations for parliamentary questioning:

- To request information.
- To press for action.
- To gain personal publicity.
- To demand an explanation.
- To test ministers in controversial areas of their policies.
- To attack ministers in controversial areas of their policies.
- To dispose of a large number of heterogeneous topics rapidly and conveniently.
- To show concerns for the interests of constituents.
- To help build up a reputation in some particular matters.
- To force compromises on an unwilling government.
- To delay a headstrong government until other forces and events make their influence felt.
- To demonstrate the government's faults.
- To rally the troops within an opposition party, with only a remote intention of forcing change on the government.
- To create elements of excitement and drama.

Wiberg notes that 'One single question may be motivated for many reasons, and may simultaneously serve many ends. To reiterate: questioning is signalling. By putting questions MPs [TDs] typically signal different things to different actors. There may be many kinds of trade-offs to be taken into account here'. Clearly, this is relevant in the Dáil. During 2006, 42,538 parliamentary questions were submitted, with 5 per cent answered orally. In 2007, 33,753 questions were asked, a lower figure because it was an election year. In 2008 almost 45,000 questions were asked. Between 1996 and 2006 there was almost a 100 per cent increase in the number of questions asked.

Based on a comprehensive analysis of 9,905 parliamentary questions on foreign policy issues to Ministers for Foreign Affairs over the period 1973 to 2002, Clery (2007: 65–6) shows that they can have an influence on policy in discrete areas:

> Parliamentary questions concentrate the minds of ministers and their civil servants . . . If officials know that a particular area of work will be the subject of parliamentary attention, there will be a natural tendency to focus on that area. PQs concentrate deliberation on particular issues. In some cases a PQ will kick start a discussion, which might not otherwise have taken place or draw attention to an issue not previously on the department's radar. Without the PQ process, the same level of attention might not be paid to the same policy areas, the same research might not be done, the same discussion might not take place. The articulation of policy through a PQ is, of course, also a product in itself. The government's views have been put on the official record and become a standard against which future comments or actions will be judged.

The limited value of the parliamentary question as a means of formal parliamentary accountability, however, was recognised by Hamilton CJ at the Beef Tribunal, 'I think that if the questions that were asked in the Dáil were answered in the way that were answered here, there would be no need for this inquiry and an awful lot of money and time would have been saved' (O'Toole 1995: 241).

The value of the parliamentary question as a means of resolving grievances, however, is questionable. The majority of questions are asked by opposition TDs (government backbenchers, with more direct access to ministers, rarely need to use this procedure). Neither ministers nor civil servants are disposed to admit readily that they have been remiss in the exercise of the discretion vested in them, particularly given the adversarial manner in which question time is conducted in the Dáil. Thus, ministers tend to defend themselves against what they regard as attacks on them and their departments and to justify decisions rather than admit error, and civil servants tend to seek additional arguments to support the decisions taken, rather than to seek compromise.

Furthermore, Dáil standing orders contain a number of restrictions that greatly reduce the efficacy of the parliamentary question as a way of having decisions altered. Questions may be asked only about matters for which a minister has direct responsibility; thus, any questions raised on matters connected with the day-to-day work of local authorities, the health service and state-sponsored bodies are automatically rejected. Debates or statements at question time are prohibited, and votes are not taken on issues raised. Moreover, the Dáil has no sanctions: it cannot alter a decision or punish decision makers. The only course still open to a deputy dissatisfied with a reply is to seek the permission of the Ceann Comhairle to raise the matter again on the adjournment. Thus, unless the deputy is in a position to make a forceful and detailed case on the basis of information not hitherto disclosed, he or she is unlikely to succeed in having a decision altered.

One effect that the raising of grievances through parliamentary questions may have, however, is to ensure that similar cases are handled more sympathetically in the future. To this extent, the parliamentary question could be regarded as being better at preventing rather than remedying grievances.

The cost of parliamentary questions is an area of enduring interest to some commentators and political scientists. In reply to a parliamentary question on 22 November 1995 Minister for Finance Ruairí Quinn indicated that the figure of £64 (€81.24) per parliamentary question answered in the Dáil was calculated by applying increases in the general level of inflation to a base figure of £40 (€50.79), which emerged as the average cost of answering a parliamentary question following an extensive survey in 1982. In 2008 a parliamentary question to each minister asked the average cost of answering a parliamentary question. Minister for Finance Brian Cowen replied:

> Parliamentary questions are dealt with, as the need arises, by the staff in the sections dealing with the particular issue(s) raised in individual Parliamentary Questions. The number and level of staff and time spent on an individual answer depends on the complexity and importance of the issue raised, the form in which the information exists in the Department, and the form of the proposed response, i.e. whether written or oral. As the processing of individual parliamentary questions is undertaken as part of the normal day to day work of individual sections within the Department it is not possible to isolate the administrative costs of processing parliamentary questions from the overall administrative costs of the Department (*Dáil Debates*, 5 February 2008, Question 227, vol. 646).

Minister for Enterprise, Trade and Employment Micheál Martin replied to the same question:

> No data is kept in my Department on the cost of answering parliamentary questions. Answering parliamentary questions is an activity which is integral

to my Department's activities, and the costs are spread across a wide number of divisions and systems; there are also costs arising in the Oireachtas for which my Department would not be accountable. However, it is estimated that the staffing cost of answering a parliamentary question in my Department is not less than €200 per question. However, for complex questions requiring coordination across all Divisions in the Department and requiring also an input from all agencies under the aegis of my Department, the average is likely to be many multiples of this amount (*Dáil Debates*, 5 February 2008, Question 423, vol. 646).

Given the growth in influence of the European Union, the expanding volume of parliamentary questions in the European Parliament, both written and oral, is also becoming increasingly important. The questions are sent to the commissioners, cabinets and directorates general concerned, and the replies are transmitted back to the parliament.

Miscellaneous Informal Remedies

An informal, though very effective, means of redress is provided by the media, especially newspapers and radio. Many newspapers and some radio programmes provide facilities whereby people may bring to the public's attention instances of what they consider to be unfair treatment by public bodies. On occasion, journalists follow up the complaints directly with the bodies concerned. Otherwise the publicity itself often results in the bodies re-examining the complaint.

Another informal means is through pressure groups or trade unions, particularly in cases related to employment-linked social welfare and health entitlements. No matter how formal a relationship may appear to be, the reality is that the officers in pressure groups and unions normally have good personal relations with the officials with whom they deal on a daily basis, thus enabling matters in which either side is interested to be discussed informally.

Everyone may, of course, use the hierarchical method of appeal. They may make a written complaint about a matter of concern to them directly to the head of the organisation concerned. In general, this method is used by the more articulate and well-informed section of the community. It is perhaps as effective as any of the means described above.

The Irish Courts

The Constitution provides a right of appeal in Article 34.3.4°, 'The Courts of First Instance shall also include Courts of local and limited jurisdiction with a right of appeal as determined by law.'

While the courts have no concern with the vast majority of the administrative decisions of public bodies, since it is not their function to entertain appeals against such decisions, they are concerned to ensure that actions and decisions are within the law. The High Court is available to citizens in certain circumstances to contest decisions with which they are not satisfied. The area of judicial review is somewhat complex, and the remedies provided are frequently hedged about with restrictions as to the type of person eligible to apply and the type of body against whom the remedy will lie. It is sometimes difficult even for lawyers to determine which remedy is appropriate to the particular circumstances.

Generally speaking, individual citizens acting alone in their own interest do not seek the help of the courts. The technicality and complexity of the law can be a deterrent, as can the long delays involved, and the inaccessibility to citizens of the case law and precedents on which so many of the legal decisions depend. The uncertainty of the law, owing to the fluidity of judicial interpretation, is a further factor. But above all, perhaps, is the prohibitive cost of legal proceedings, which is well beyond the reach of ordinary citizens; even those who win their case may be left with substantial costs to pay.

Types of Appeal

There is an extensive literature on all aspects of appellate procedures conducted in the Irish courts. It is possible here only to indicate in broad terms the three most usual situations in which the courts will intervene to provide remedies.

- *Constitutional rights infringed.* Citizens may resort to the courts if they consider that an act of the Oireachtas infringes their constitutional rights. An example of this case is that of a farmer (Mr Brennan) in County Wexford who contested the constitutionality of the rating system as it applied to him. Under the Valuation Acts 1852 to 1864 his farm was valued by reference to the price of certain crops in the years 1849 to 1852. The amount of the valuation determined his liability for rates and his eligibility for certain kinds of state assistance. He pleaded that this method of valuation violated his personal and property rights under the Constitution. The court found in his favour in 1984, because the use of the 1852 valuation long after farming methods had changed was an infringement of his property rights in that he was paying more in rates than neighbours with better land. The fact that there was no other source of review of the valuation open to him was a further attack on his property rights.
- *Constitutional justice disregarded.* The second type of situation is where a public body making a decision did not observe the principles of justice provided for each citizen by the Constitution, i.e. that the decision maker

must not be biased or be seen to be biased, that an opportunity be given to the person whose case is under review to know what evidence has been given against him or her and to give his or her side of the story, and that no body should be a judge in its own case. The requirement to follow fair procedures binds ministers and officials to act in good faith and to listen carefully to both sides of the case. Court decisions suggest that when a citizen has a legitimate expectation that, for example, an application for a discretionary benefit such as a licence or a permit will not be refused without a chance to put his or her case, then that citizen is entitled to some kind of hearing. Where citizens already enjoy this benefit, the expectation is that they should not be deprived of it arbitrarily and be unheard by the decision maker. This may make the citizen's case legally and morally stronger.

- *Ultra vires.* Cases under the third situation, i.e. where public bodies have gone beyond the powers conferred on them by statute, are by far the most numerous. The body, for example, might not have observed prescribed procedures, or it might have taken extraneous matters into account in arriving at its decision. The courts have no concern with the vast majority of administrative decisions, since they assume, reasonably, that when the legislature allocates the power to make such decisions to a public body, it does not intend that the power should be taken over by the courts. On the other hand, the courts are concerned that decisions are taken within the law. Therefore, the courts are available to citizens who contest the legality of decisions taken in their cases, and a number of remedies are provided.

European Court of Human Rights

The European Court of Human Rights (ECHR) is an institution of the Council of Europe and is based in Strasbourg. The promotion and development of human rights is one of the main tasks of the Council of Europe, of which Ireland was a founder member in 1949. The Convention for the Protection of Human Rights and Fundamental Freedoms was drawn up within the Council of Europe. It was opened for signature in Rome on 4 November 1950 and entered into force in September 1953. Taking as their starting point the 1948 Universal Declaration of Human Rights, the framers of the Convention sought to pursue the aims of the Council of Europe through the maintenance and further realisation of human rights and fundamental freedoms. The Convention was to represent the first steps for the collective enforcement of certain of the rights set out in the Universal Declaration (see Appendix to this Chapter). The European Convention on Human Rights Act 2003 gives the Convention further effect in Irish law, providing for a more direct role for the Convention in Irish courts. Since 1960 there have been over twenty cases in the ECHR to which Ireland has been a party. For example, in November 2008 the ECHR intervened in the case of a Sligo-based Nigerian woman who lost her High Court bid to prevent her deportation; it asked the Irish government not to deport the woman pending the hearing of her case at the ECHR.

European Union Bodies

The task of the European Court of Justice (ECJ) in Luxembourg is to ensure observance of the law in the interpretation and application of the treaties setting up the European Union and in implementing regulations issued by the Council of Ministers or the European Commission. It guarantees the uniform interpretation and application of community law in all member states and decides on legal disputes between member states, EU institutions, companies and private individuals. The ECJ may review the legality of acts of the council or commission on the grounds of lack of competence, infringement of an essential legal requirement, infringement of a treaty or of any legal rule relating to its application, or misuse of power. A person may appeal any decision given against him or her or against other persons that is of direct and individual concern to him or her. All proceedings held before the ECJ are free of court fees. The internal working language is French, although petitioners can speak in any of the EU's official languages and declare them to be the language of the proceedings.

Another method of complaint is the petition to the European Parliament. This is a written request or complaint submitted to the parliament by any EU citizen, either individually or jointly with other citizens, and examined by the European Parliament Committee on Petitions. Petitions to the parliament often concern implementation at local or national level of European legislation. In a majority of cases, the parliament decides that it requires either further infor - mation or the commission's opinion. Petitions are forwarded to the competent commissioner and directorate general for further action. Petitions to the parliament and subsequent referrals to the commission have increased signifi- cantly in recent years. The parliamentary petitions procedure was enshrined in the Treaty on European Union (also known as the Maastricht Treaty).

The task of the European Ombudsman is to mediate between the citizens and the authorities of the EU. The European Ombudsman is authorised to receive complaints from every EU citizen. These are levelled against insufficiencies and defects in the administrative structures of the European institutions, for example unfair treatment, discrimination, unnecessary delay, abuse of power, refusal to provide information and incorrect procedures. Investigations are carried out on the ombudsman's own initiative or as a result of complaints received. The European Ombudsman is elected by the European Parliament every five years and must act in a completely independent and impartial manner.

The Lisbon Treaty, if ratified, provides that, for the first time, one million citizens from different member states will be able to request the European Commission to bring forward an initiative of interest to them in an area of EU competence.

Tribunals

A wide variety of bodies have the word 'tribunal' in their title, for example the Valuation Tribunal, Employment Appeals Tribunal, Rent Tribunal and Pensions Tribunal. Tribunals have also been set up to resolve disputes or to discipline members within the public service, for example those in An Garda Síochána, the Permanent Defence Forces and the Irish Prison Service. Most of these have been established by law and operate in the field of public law, assisting in the dirigiste and welfare aspects of the state's responsibilities. The lack of uniformity extends to nomenclature. Hogan and Gwynn-Morgan (1991) note, 'not only do the names of tribunals differ – Board, Commission, Tribunal, Officer, Registrar, Controller, Referee, Umpire – but different authorities use different titles for the entire species. Thus one finds tribunals described as: administrative tribunals; special tribunals; statutory tribunals; or even quasi-judicial tribunals.' Typical of the vague terminology that obtains in regard to tribunals are what might be termed domestic tribunals, set up by professions, organisations, clubs and so on, which may have rules for dealing, themselves, with the discipline of their own members.

The Refugee Appeals Tribunal was established on 4 October 2000 in accordance with sections 14 and 15 of the Refugee Act 1996 and decides the appeals of those asylum seekers whose applications for refugee status has not been recommended by the Office of the Refugee Applications Commissioner. It is a statutorily independent body and exercises a quasi-judicial function under the 1996 act. The tribunal consists of a chairperson and such number of ordinary members as the Minister for Justice, with the consent of the Minister for Finance, considers necessary for the expeditious dispatch of the business of the tribunal. Staff are assigned to the tribunal from the Department of Justice. It received 2,849 appeals against initial decisions taken by the Refugee Applications Commissioner in 2007.

The Solicitors Disciplinary Tribunal is an independent statutory tribunal appointed by the President of the High Court to consider complaints of misconduct against solicitors. The members of the tribunal are appointed by, and are answerable only to, the President of the High Court. The tribunal consists of twenty solicitor members and ten lay members. It sits in divisions of three, comprising two solicitor members and one lay member. Where the tribunal decides that a complaint discloses a prima facie case of misconduct by a solicitor, there will be an inquiry, with oral evidence, conducted by the tribunal in public. Evidence is given to the tribunal under oath and may be subject to cross-examination. The procedures of the tribunal are regulated by the Solicitors Acts 1954 to 2002 and by the Solicitors Disciplinary Tribunal Rules 2003.

Administrative Tribunals

A number of tribunals have been set up to which aggrieved people may bring their complaints about the discretionary decisions made by public bodies. The tribunals may be individual persons or groups of persons who have been designated by law to adjudicate in these situations. Some examples are those where an application for a social welfare allowance has been rejected or where the valuation placed on a property for rating purposes is regarded as excessive. In those cases an appeal lies to the Social Welfare Appeals Office and to the Valuation Tribunal respectively.

Appeal tribunals in Ireland cannot be said to constitute a formal system. They have been established by individual ministers on a more or less ad hoc basis over a number of years, and there are inconsistencies in their composition, their procedures and the areas in which they operate. As regards the last point, there is, for instance, provision for an appeal against assessment to income tax but not against assessment to customs duty; yet both of these functions are under the same jurisdiction, i.e. that of the Revenue Commissioners. Their total number, including bodies set up to adjudicate on issues arising between parties in the private sector, for example the Employment Appeals Tribunal or the Rights Commissioners (which do not concern us directly here), is about eighty. This number is a small fraction of those in Britain, where there are over two thousand, supervised by a General Council on Tribunals.

Common features of tribunals are:

1. Independence of the administration and the power to decide cases impartially as between the parties before them. This makes the tribunal form of remedy different from that of an internal administrative review of a decision, which may sometimes be offered by a public body and may be carried out by the official who made the decision in the first place.
2. Binding decisions reached by a person or persons who are not engaged full-time on this work and who are not judges. The members may represent opposing interests with, perhaps, some neutrals and a chairperson who is often a lawyer.

3. Flexible procedures, generally less formal than those in the courts. Tribunals can formulate their own standards and depart from these if the situation so warrants.
4. A facility to acquire considerable expertise in a particular and generally limited area.
5. Less rigid attitudes towards precedents.
6. Speed and the absence of the heavy legal costs entailed in court appearances, where counsel can spend a whole day explaining to a judge how a particular scheme is designed to operate.

The Devlin report (1969), as part of its proposal to establish executive agencies, recommended that tribunals with unlimited scope of appellate jurisdiction should be set up within every agency or for groups of agencies. There would thus be a right of appeal to a single, independent, fully trained person attached to the body by which the decision was given; in cases of particular complexity, two experts in the matter under examination might be brought on to the tribunal. This recommendation was not adopted.

The Mental Health Commission appoints review tribunals to review automatically all decisions to detain patients involuntarily or to extend the duration of such detentions under the provisions of the Mental Health Act 2001. When the commission receives a copy of an admission or a renewal order, it must refer the matter to a review tribunal; assign a legal representative to represent the patient unless the patient personally engages one; direct, in writing, a member of the panel of consultant psychiatrists to examine the patient; interview the consultant psychiatrist responsible for the patient's treatment and care; and review the patient's records in order to decide, in the interests of the patient, whether the patient is suffering from a mental disorder. The report must be presented by the consultant psychiatrist to the tribunal and to the patient's legal representative, within fourteen days.

The review tribunal must review the detention of the patient and make a decision within twenty-one days of the making of the order. If the tribunal is satisfied that the patient is suffering from a mental disorder and that the proper procedures have been followed (or, if they have not, the failure does not affect the substance of the order and does not cause an injustice), it affirms the order. If it is not satisfied, it revokes the order and directs that the patient be discharged. In order to carry out its functions, the tribunal has similar powers to a court, including the power to require the attendance of the relevant people and the production of documents. The tribunal is, of course, obliged to respect the usual requirements of natural justice, for example it must ensure that the patient has copies of the reports that are being considered by the tribunal. 2007 was the first full year of the implementation of the Mental Health Act 2001, which gives patients the right to an automatic independent review if they are admitted to a psychiatric unit against their will. Some 2,096 reviews, or mental health tribunals, were held in 2008, which resulted in 11 per cent of orders being revoked.

In some instances a tribunal comprises one person only, for example in the area of social welfare, where about 12,000 cases are dealt with every year. The Social Welfare Act 1952, which set up the system of adjudication in that area, provides for the appointment of a number of deciding officers and appeals officers. A case is decided in the first instance by a deciding officer on the basis of the information available, without an oral hearing. This decision may be appealed to an appeals officer, who operates under prescribed procedures. These include the power to take evidence on oath and to require persons to give evidence and produce documents. Appeals officers have the power to award costs and expenses and the award must be paid by the minister. It has been established by the High Court (*McLoughlin v Minister for Social Welfare* 1958 IR 5) that an appeals officer is independent of the minister in the exercise of his or her functions, which are judicial functions, and that it would be improper for the minister to give the officer instructions as to how to decide a particular case, or for the officer to accept such instructions. Thus, appeals officers are different from other civil servants, who are answerable to their ministers for actions taken in the ordinary course of administration, such actions being invariably taken in the name of the minister, who accepts both legal and political responsibility for them.

The social welfare tribunals now operate under the Social Welfare Appeals Office (see below), following the recommendation in the 1986 report of the Commission on Social Welfare, which had noted a perception that the existing appeals procedure was not independent of the workings of the department. The commission recommended also that the reasons for the rejection of appeals be given. This is also now being done and has greatly improved the system.

Another example of a one-person tribunal is the Minister for the Environment, Heritage and Local Government, who may be appealed to by an officer of a local authority against a decision such as a suspension. Similarly, the Minister for Enterprise, Trade and Employment may be appealed to by a person aggrieved by a decision of the Controller of Industrial and Commercial Property (the Patents Office) not to register a trademark.

An example of a two-person tribunal is the Office of the Appeals Commissioners, to which appeals against assessments to income tax may be made. These full-time commissioners are appointed by the Minister for Finance; one is normally a lawyer or an accountant and the other a revenue official. The appeals are held orally and are attended by the inspector who made the assessment and the aggrieved taxpayer (with or without his or her professional adviser).

The Valuation Tribunal, which was set up in 1988, has thirteen part-time members, who are lawyers and property valuers. Appeals can be made to this tribunal against the valuation placed by the Commissioner of Valuation on buildings and other fixed property as a basis for the levying of rates by local authorities. It deals with about 250 appeals a year. An Bord Pleanála, which deals with appeals against the granting of planning permissions in some cases and against the refusal of others, has six full-time members. The Levy Appeals Tribunal, set up by the Minister for Labour to determine appeals by employers against assessments to training levies imposed by FÁS, has sixteen members, four of whom – the chairperson and three deputy chairpersons – must be lawyers; the other twelve must be representatives of employer organisations and trade unions.

Tribunals of Inquiry

Tribunals of inquiry are tribunals established for the purposes of inquiring into a definite matter of urgent public importance. The Tribunals of Inquiry (Evidence) Act 1921 provides extensive powers to these bodies. They have the power to enforce the attendance and examination of witnesses and the production of documents. This is based on the unspoken, but unbroken, assumption that the public respect enjoyed by the judiciary should be drawn upon to engender confidence in the impartiality of the inquiry. A tribunal of inquiry may consist of one or more persons, sitting with or without an assessor or assessors; an assessor is not a member of the tribunal. The Tribunals of Inquiry (Evidence) (Amendment) Act 1979 updated these provisions.

There have been several occasions in recent years when the public disquiet at some event has been such that some form of inquiry has been necessary. The Law Reform Commission (2003) distinguished between three types of tribunals of inquiry: general inquiries that concern system failures; specific inquiries that consider allegations against individuals or organisations; and mixed inquiries that consider both elements.

A tribunal may make such orders as it considers necessary for the purpose of its functions and in that respect has the powers, rights and privileges that are vested in the High Court. A statement or admission by a person before a tribunal of inquiry is not admissible as evidence against that person in any criminal proceedings. An interesting insight on the impact of tribunals of inquiry on the machinery of government was provided in 1997 by Rory Brady, who subsequently became Attorney General:

. . . tribunals have taken the place of State agencies and statutory bodies in investigating alleged wrong doing by politicians. An aspect of rule by government is now being replaced by rule by tribunal. Statutory agencies such as the Revenue Commissioners and An Garda Síochána are being relegated, by this cultural change, to a secondary role.

Tribunals have, in reality, become a new political art form. It is interesting to note that in 1997 alone there were four tribunals either sitting or established and there is a further tribunal promised. Thus we had the tribunal of inquiry into the BTSB, the Dunnes Payments Tribunal, Lowry and Mr Charles J. Haughey, the planning inquiry and a promised inquiry in relation to blood given to haemophiliacs. In contrast during the entire decade of the 1980s there were only two full judicial tribunals sitting, i.e. the Kerry Babies and the Whiddy Disaster tribunals. Thus it is the very frequency with which tribunals have been established, during 1997, that requires us to look carefully at this process and its impact on our system of government.

A tribunal that has been appointed to inquire into matters of public interest pursuant to resolutions of the Oireachtas may inquire into all matters within its terms of reference, including matters that are the subject of current civil proceedings or allegations of breaches of the criminal law or matters that involve allegations attacking the good name of a citizen. For example, in the case of *Goodman International v Mr Justice Hamilton* (HC & SC 1992), the Supreme Court held that the tribunal was not conducting an administration of justice. In this case, and also in *Haughey v Moriarty* [1999] 2 IR 1, the courts can review parliamentary resolutions authorising the establishment by government of a tribunal of inquiry under the 1921 act.

Although tribunals of inquiry do not constitute courts established under the Constitution, section 2(a) of the Tribunals of Inquiry (Evidence) Act 1921 provides that a tribunal shall not refuse 'to allow the public or any portion of the public to be present at any of the proceedings of the tribunal unless in the opinion of the tribunal it is in the public interest expedient so to do for reasons connected with the subject matter of the inquiry or the nature of the evidence to be given'. In certain instances the Oireachtas has sought to give one of the parties the right to object to a public hearing. Thus, for example, section 5(17)(a) of the Hepatitis C Compensation Tribunal Act 1997 provided that 'An appeal under this section shall be heard otherwise than in public at the request of the claimant making the appeal'. In 2000 the Supreme Court ruled that tribunals are 'held in public for the purpose of allaying the public disquiet that led to their appointment' (*Murphy v Flood (No. 2)* 2 IR 298). In January 2008 the Mahon Tribunal had to erect crowd control barriers and notices warning members of the public that they would be evicted for clapping or heckling.

The Attorney General represents the public interest at tribunals of inquiry. This has proved controversial where the state or a member of the government is involved. The question has been asked as to how the Attorney General can represent both parties, and resolve the potential conflict of interest that may arise in such a situation. This problem has been resolved in recent years through the appointment of separate counsel to represent the public interest. The Attorney General delegates his or her responsibilities to act as guardian of the public interest to separate counsel for the public interest. Separate counsel for the public interest was first appointed to the Hepatitis C Tribunal in 1995.

The most well-known tribunal is the Tribunal of Inquiry into Certain Planning Matters and Payments, which was set up on 4 November 1997 and first chaired by Mr Justice Feargus Flood, who had been a High Court judge since 1991. The tribunal was to investigate certain planning matters following the making of allegations that payments of money had been made in order to procure favourable planning decisions in the north Dublin area. Mr Justice Flood defined the job of the tribunal as discovering 'who gave what to whom' in relation to a few hundred acres of land in north County Dublin, and compared it on Day 38, 14 April 1999, to 'wandering like an Arab in the Sahara'.

In July 2001 Mr Justice Flood requested the Dáil to appoint additional members to the tribunal, in effect two to sit with him and a reserve member. The composition of the tribunal was altered to three members and one reserve member by statutory instrument dated 24 October 2002. In June 2003 Mr Justice Flood resigned as a member and as chairperson of the tribunal. He was replaced by Judge Alan Mahon.

The Mahon Tribunal finally closed its doors in October 2008 after nearly 1,000 public sittings, approximately 80 million spoken words, 400 witnesses, 130,000 pages of documents and almost eleven gruelling years (Molony 2008). Following criticisms of the tribunal's cost (€300 million), length and approach, Judge Mahon gave a summary on the morning of 21 December 2007 of the tribunal's approach to Taoiseach Bertie Ahern's cross-examination. It is useful to look at his comments. He said:

> A tribunal of inquiry is inquisitorial in nature and it approaches its work – especially the taking of evidence in public – on this basis. It does not make allegations or promote any particular view or predetermine any matter. Evidence given in public hearings, including documentary evidence, can be true or false, or be partly true or be partly false. False or inaccurate evidence can be given accidentally or innocently, or more seriously can be given intentionally and designed to mislead the inquiry.
>
> It would be a useless and meaningless exercise for a tribunal to merely put every witness into the witness box and simply record his or her evidence without question or where appropriate without challenge . . .

It is the role and duty of counsel to the tribunal to probe and test the evidence of witnesses and of documentary evidence in a manner which will ensure that the tribunal will have at the end of the day the fullest possible picture of the evidence so that it will be in a position to determine the accuracy and effect of that evidence, especially in those circumstances where there is apparent conflict between the testimony of witnesses or with documentary evidence.

Cross-examination of a witness where there is a significant absence of supporting documentary evidence, which it has to be said is not an indication of anything improper, is lengthy, complex and at times tedious. In so far as any of these descriptions might be deemed to apply to the cross-examination of the Taoiseach, the tribunal is satisfied that such detailed cross-examination is necessary and appropriate if the tribunal is to be placed in a position where it can ultimately, properly and fairly adjudicate on the issues arising. In no way is Mr Ahern being treated any differently to any other witnesses in this regard.

In reply to parliamentary questions on 30 January 2008 Taoiseach Bertie Ahern stated:

The total cost to date of the McCracken tribunal is €6.56 million. As regards the Moriarty tribunal, the total cost incurred by my Department since 1997 up to 31 December 2007 was €30,466,497. For 2007, up to 31 December, the figure was €4,154,564. It is not possible at this stage to estimate the final costs. ... To the end of 2007, the total cost to the Exchequer of completed and sitting tribunals of inquiry and other public inquiries is €323.17 million, not including the third party costs that will emanate.

Lawyers' fees account for approximately 70 per cent of the costs. It has been estimated that every sitting day of the Mahon Tribunal has come at an average cost of €32,500, based on the total cost of the tribunal divided by the number of sitting days. The *Sunday Independent* of 6 July 2008 provided extracts from the briefing document to the incoming Finance Minister, Brian Lenihan, in May 2008 on the cost of the tribunals:

Completed and sitting tribunals and other public inquiries have to end of February 2008 cost €328.6m., of which €237m. derives from legal costs, including €111m. for third-party legal costs. Third-party legal costs are set to increase very significantly, as a large proportion of the costs already incurred have yet to be presented and taxed ... The Constitutional entitlement to legal representation for those whose good name or personal and property rights are at issue, combined with the necessity for a tribunal to be independent in its operations, means that it is very difficult to control costs once an inquiry is established.

Brady (1997) concludes:

The State has available to it a variety of bodies that can conduct investigations. The courts are available in which to ventilate issues of fact that have legal implications and they have very wide powers to compel disclosure of documents and evidence under the sanction of contempt of court. The Dáil and the Seanad can debate and discuss matters of public controversy. The Gardaí and the Revenue Commissioners have very wide powers of investigation including powers of search and seizure. A vigilant media can pursue and investigate a rogue politician.

However, to date such bodies appear not to have satisfied the requirements of certain situations. Notwithstanding all of these mechanisms of investigation the plain fact is that it was only through a tribunal that facts of cardinal importance relating to the BTSB [Blood Transfusion Service Board] Inquiry and the Dunnes Payments Inquiry were revealed to the public. There is a price to be paid for this. The full panoply of a judicial tribunal carries with it very large costs. While there is a public interest in public investigation there is also a public interest in containing costs. Reconciling these two interests and minimising the risk of political abuse requires some adjustment to the current law and practice of tribunals.

In July 2008 the government decided, due to the high costs of the tribunals and the major expenditure constraints facing the government, that it was essential that tribunals and inquiries concluded their business as early as possible and that legal costs were managed in the interests of the taxpayer. The government decided that no further moneys would be authorised for legal teams and staffs associated with the public hearings beyond the completion of the public hearings.

The Mahon Tribunal has been the most contentious tribunal of inquiry. The five judges of the Supreme Court decided that the three-judge tribunal had ignored changes to its terms of reference, which it had sought itself just three years before. The Supreme Court's landmark unanimous decision overturned a judgment of the High Court in December 2006. In March 2005 Mr Justice Geoghegan noted:

> A 1921 Act tribunal is, in my view, perfectly entitled to formulate a policy and indeed the efficient execution of its work requires that there be such a policy. A literal application of court procedures will often not be either necessary, desirable or efficient. A tribunal is also perfectly entitled to conduct separate hearings of separate modules and to try as far as possible to discipline counsel and the witnesses so that the evidence at any given time is confined to the evidence relevant to that module.
>
> This tribunal did not claim that it was absolutely hide-bound by its own policy or by any rules or systems which it may have devised and, quite rightly so, because whereas the tribunal undoubtedly has the latitude which I have

suggested and which may not be available to a court of law, it is always bound to ensure, as far as possible, compliance with constitutional rights and obligations and that, of course, includes the vindication of a person's good name. The tribunal relies on an understanding of confidentiality.

Mr Justice Hardiman, in a lengthy judgment, said that a full and unhampered right to cross-examine a person who makes grave allegations against another at a tribunal is an important constitutional right.

In another Supreme Court case it was held that the Mahon Tribunal had not complied with its amended terms of reference and, consequently, had no jurisdiction to hold a public hearing in relation to a political contribution made by the Fitzwilton Group in June 1989. In a Supreme Court judgment in 2007 on this case Mrs Justice Denham concluded, 'The Tribunal was established in 1997. The concept behind the establishment of a tribunal is that there be an inquiry into definite matters as a matter of urgent public importance. The fact that the Tribunal is still inquiring ten years later is the antithesis of an urgent public inquiry.'

In January 2008 the Mahon Tribunal issued a statement designed to reassure the public about the fairness of its procedures, while also appealing to witnesses not to leak confidential documents. 'The tribunal believes that it is appropriate that the public should understand the reasons for the circulation of documents in advance of public hearings. Tribunals, including this tribunal, circulate documents to interested parties in advance of the calling of evidence . . . The tribunal endeavours to restrict the number of parties to whom such documentation is circulated as far as legally permissible.' This followed criticism from then Taoiseach Bertie Ahern (and six ministers), who said that the tribunal had failed to stop the persistent disclosure of documentation relating to him and was not giving him a 'fair hearing'.

Article 15.13 of the Constitution states that members of the Oireachtas are not answerable for any utterance in the Houses of the Oireachtas to any authority, except the Houses themselves. In May 2008 the High Court found in favour of former Taoiseach Bertie Ahern that the parliamentary privilege over Dáil statements as provided for in Article 15.13 of the Constitution did not permit the Mahon Tribunal – in its report or while Mr Ahern was giving evidence to it – to draw attention to his Dáil statements about his financial affairs that may have been inconsistent with his statements outside the Dáil or in his evidence. The court ruled that the Mahon Tribunal may reproduce the Dáil statements of September and October 2006 in its report but was prohibited by Article 15.13 from suggesting that they were untrue or misleading or inspired by improper motivation. Members of the public could draw their own conclusions as to whether the statements were inaccurate and, if so, whether such inaccuracies were 'deliberate or accidental'.

Among the tribunals of inquiry that have been set up are those into or on: illegal moneylending (1970); the Whiddy Island disaster (1979); the Stardust fire (1981); the 'Kerry Babies' case (1985); the beef processing industry (1991); the Hepatitis C scandal (1997); payments to politicians by Dunnes Stores (McCracken Tribunal) (1997); payments to politicians (Moriarty Tribunal) (1997); certain planning matters and payments (Flood/Mahon Tribunals) (1997); the infection with HIV and Hepatitis C of persons with haemophilia (Lindsay Tribunal) (2002); certain Garda activities in Donegal (Morris Tribunal) (2002); and the facts and circumstances surrounding the fatal shooting of John Carthy at Abbeylara (Barr Tribunal) (2002).

Commission to Inquire into Child Abuse

The Report of the Commission to Inquire into Child Abuse was published in May 2009. It was chaired by Justice Sean Ryan, a High Court Judge, and ran into five volumes and thousands of pages. The Child Abuse Commission published a disturbing interim report in 2004. It was originally headed by Justice Mary Laffoy who resigned in 2003 over a lack of cooperation by the Department of Education. She was replaced by Justice Sean Ryan. The Commission benefited from the powers and protection of a court, including privilege and compellability of witnesses, discovery of documents, taking evidence on oath and offences for failure to cooperate or for obstruction. The May 2009 report by the Commission catalogued in harrowing detail the scale of the violent physical, emotional and sexual abuse which was meted out to thousands of vulnerable children who had been entrusted to the care of religious orders.

Commissions of Investigation

A commission of investigation provides a less expensive and speedier method of investigating matters of urgent public concern than a tribunal of inquiry. The government can set up a commission of investigation based on a proposal by a minister, with the approval of the Minister for Finance. The Houses of the Oireachtas must approve a draft of the order establishing the commission, and a statement of the reasons for establishing the commission must be laid before each House.

The Commissions of Investigation Act 2004 gives the commission the power to conduct its investigation in any manner it considers appropriate, as long as it adheres to the act and the commission's rules and procedures. It must seek and facilitate the voluntary co-operation of people whose evidence it requires, and it must conduct its proceedings in private, unless there are exceptional circumstances. A commission is entitled to compel witnesses to give evidence. It can also direct a person to provide it with any documents in the person's possession or power relating to the matter under investigation. If the person fails to comply, the commission can apply to the court to compel compliance; or it may impose a costs order against the individual for the costs incurred by all other parties arising from the delay. A commission is set up on the basis of a fixed fee to encourage completion on time.

A commission of investigation reports to a specified minister. The minister is obliged to publish the commission's final report unless the minister considers that such publication might prejudice any criminal proceedings that are in progress. In such a case, the minister may apply to the High Court for directions. Examples include:

- Commission of investigation into the Dublin and Monaghan bombings of 1974, which was established by order of the government made under the Commissions of Investigation Act 2004.
- The Dublin Archdiocese Commission of Investigation, which was established by government order in 2006 to investigate the handling of allegations or complaints of child sexual abuse made against clergy operating under the aegis of the Catholic Archdiocese of Dublin and the response to such cases, and the handling of cases where there was knowledge or concern regarding sexual abuse.
- Commission of investigation to investigate the circumstances surrounding the making of a confession by Dean Lyons (deceased) about the deaths of two women in March 1997 in Grangegorman, Dublin 7, which was established in 2006.
- Commission of investigation to investigate the death of a prisoner in Mountjoy Prison, which was established in 2007.
- Commission to investigate the management, operation and supervision of Leas Cross Nursing Home, which was established in 2007 by the Minister for Health.

Public Inquiries by the Oireachtas

The role of the Oireachtas in conducting public inquiries has been considered in several court cases. The Supreme Court has held that a resolution by both Dáil Éireann and Seanad Éireann providing for the establishment of a tribunal of inquiry into allegations of illegal activities, fraud and malpractice did not amount to a usurpation of judicial functions. The Supreme Court held that the beef tribunal did not amount to either a criminal trial or an administration of justice. The Supreme Court held that the power to initiate inquiries was an inherent power of the Houses of the Oireachtas. The court unanimously rejected the contention that a tribunal could not investigate facts within its remit merely on the ground that some of them were subject to civil litigation. Once the Houses of the Oireachtas had properly concluded that these were matters of public importance, it could investigate matters that were the subject of disputes between private persons. Furthermore, the tribunal was also entitled to inquire whether criminal acts had been committed by specific individuals. Clearly, however, under the separation of powers, the Houses of the Oireachtas cannot interfere in the administration of justice or replace the right to a trial with due process of law. In the 1999 case concerning the Moriarty Tribunal (*Haughey v Moriarty* [1999] 3 IR 1), the Supreme Court ruled that the powers of the Oireachtas are not confined to those expressed in the Constitution. A resolution of both Houses of the Oireachtas giving effect to the decision to establish a tribunal enjoyed the presumption of constitutionality. Thus, the courts could not review a decision by the Oireachtas to establish an inquiry under the Tribunals of Inquiry (Evidence) Act 1921 into matters properly described as of 'urgent public importance', nor could they entertain the submission that the Oireachtas should have availed of other forms of inquiry, such as a select committee of one or both Houses. The court cautioned that this power of inquiry should not be abused, exercised for improper motives or in breach of constitutional rights. In *Maguire v Ardagh* [2002] the Supreme Court held that the Oireachtas sub-committee inquiring into the fatal shooting of John Carthy at Abbeylara did not have the power to make findings of fact that could adversely affect the reputation of persons who were not members of the Oireachtas or that might put such citizens at risk of being found to have committed an offence.

Parliamentary Inquiries

Parliamentary inquiries have traditionally selected witnesses who are acknowledged experts, questioned them formally, minuted their evidence verbatim and produced detailed reports for consideration by policy makers. They are a feature of the machinery of government in many Western democracies and are often used to inquire into cases of tragedies, fiascos, failures, natural disasters, plane crashes or rail accidents (Bovens 2005). The work of parliamentary committees in conducting inquiries is fraught with difficulties due to concerns about the extent of committee independence, party discipline, the strength of government, logistical clashes with parliamentary plenary meetings and votes, and the potential to produce politically damaging results. There is a risk that parliamentary inquiries may lead to scapegoating rather than ascertaining the facts. They 'must only be used in specific circumstances and always with great care' (Committee of Public Accounts 1999: chapter 16).

The work of parliamentary committees in conducting inquiries in Ireland was brought to a close in November 2001, when the High Court ruled that the Oireachtas did not have the power to set up inquiries that are likely to lead to findings of fact or expressions adverse to the good name of individuals not belonging to the Dáil.

DIRT Inquiry

Perhaps the most high-profile Oireachtas committee inquiry was that undertaken by the Dáil Public Accounts Committee (PAC) in accordance with the resolution of Dáil Éireann dated 17 December 1998. The Parliamentary Inquiry into Deposit Interest Retention Tax (DIRT) was the first Oireachtas inquiry to take place in Ireland in recent times. It was historic in that the hearings were broadcast live on television by TG4, they were also carried live on the Internet and the website published the daily transcript of the proceedings. As the inquiry's first report (Committee of Public Accounts 1999) notes, 'This was the first occasion on which an Oireachtas Committee carrying out an Inquiry used extensive new powers. The principal Acts granting these powers are the Committees of the Houses of the Oireachtas (Compellability, Privileges and Immunities of Witnesses) Act [discussed in Chapter 3], and the Comptroller and Auditor General and the Committees of the Houses of the Oireachtas (Special Provisions) Act, 1998.' It concluded that 'All of these developments – the enhanced powers of the Committee of Public Accounts, examination under oath, live broadcasting and rapid publication of the proceedings – represent a major advance and modernization of the parliamentary process and parliamentary scrutiny. The Hearings therefore represent an historic moment in our parliamentary development'.

The report also said that the work of Oireachtas inquiries was inquisitorial rather than adversarial in nature, and concerned with issues of fact, in line with the jurisprudence of the Supreme Court. Clearly, Oireachtas inquiries would not be the appropriate forum to probe essentially political or policy issues. Martin (2007), based on research in thirty-one democratic assemblies, suggests that strong parliamentary committees can emerge as a structural solution to the need of each party in a coalition government to monitor the behaviour and action of ministers from other parties within the coalition.

Then Chairperson of the PAC, Deputy Jim Mitchell, and the committee conducted their work effectively and expeditiously. The first report was produced inside a year and cost less than £800,000. It suggests that Oireachtas inquiries should have clear terms of reference with concise and definite boundaries. It notes the importance for each inquiry of a specific focus, a finite nature and a specific timeframe within which evidence must be heard and reports completed. As regards future Oireachtas inquiries, the report recommends:

1. Committees
   - Each chairperson of an Oireachtas committee should be fully briefed on the modalities of parliamentary inquiries.
   - A handbook of parliamentary inquiries should be prepared by the secretariat of committees.
   - Powers of discovery for committees should be amended so that any documentary discovery made by any parliamentary inspector is automatically discovered to the committee.
2. Witnesses
   - General powers of direction of witnesses should be included in the resolution of the Oireachtas establishing a parliamentary inquiry.
   - The procedures for the taking of evidence before a parliamentary inquiry should provide for groups of witnesses to be taken.
   - All witnesses appearing before a committee to which the Compellability Act 1997 applies should be under direction.
3. Business
   - All business, including ordinary business of the Committee of Public Accounts, should be under direction.
   - All parliamentary inquiries should be conducted by a sub-committee of a manageable size.
   - Provisions should be made to have all further parliamentary inquiries and tribunals of inquiry broadcast live on television.
   - A comparative study should be undertaken by the Department of Finance and the Attorney General's office into parliamentary inquiries and tribunals of inquiry, and report back to the Oireachtas by 1 December 2000.

The final report of the DIRT Inquiry (Committee of Public Accounts 2001: 92) comments, 'The main argument for the strengthening of the Houses of the Oireachtas is that it enhances public accountability. A vigorously active and independent parliament with the powers to investigate matters of serious public importance will ensure that the systemic abuses and breakdowns of good government highlighted by this [DIRT] Inquiry, the Tribunals and other inquiries, makes it much less likely that it will happen again'.

Abbeylara Inquiry

The Joint Oireachtas Committee on Justice, Equality, Defence and Women's Rights established a sub-committee to consider the Garda Commissioner's report to the Minister for Justice following the fatal shooting of John Carthy at Abbeylara, County Longford on 20 June 2000, and submissions received therein. The High Court held that the Oireachtas had acted *ulta vires* in establishing a committee of inquiry into the Abbeylara shooting and in the process decided that the Oireachtas had no power to establish quasi-judicial tribunals. The functions of the Oireachtas are expressly designated by the Constitution. Chief among these is the law-making power itself in Article 15.2.1°. The High Court held that the sub-committee had breached fair procedures by not allowing the thirty-six gardaí involved an opportunity to cross-examine witnesses until the last day of public hearings (*Maguire v Ardagh* [2002] 1 IR 385).

The Supreme Court ruled that 'the question as to whether inquiries of this nature might be more economically and expeditiously conducted by an Oireachtas committee than by a tribunal of inquiry established under the 1921 Act was referred to during the course of the arguments, how it is answered cannot exclusively determine the issue which has to be resolved in this case'. The Supreme Court held that the Oireachtas sub-committee had 'no explicit, implicit or inherent power to conduct an inquiry'. Geoghegan J. advanced four reasons for rejecting the claim that the Oireachtas had such an inherent power:

1. It was inconsistent with the doctrine of the separation of powers enshrined in the Constitution.
2. Parliamentary inquiries had been discredited by 1921 and so it was unlikely that the draftsmen of the 1922 Constitution contemplated parliamentary inquiries leading to findings of personal culpability.
3. Having regard to the constitutional obligation to protect the good name of the citizen, there was no need to read into the Constitution an inherent power on the part of the Oireachtas to conduct investigations of the type in question in this case when the Tribunals of Inquiry Evidence Act 1921 provided machinery for an independent non-political investigation of matters of public concern.
4. Having regard to the inherent likelihood of structural bias or at least the difficulties in avoiding objective bias in any given case, there was no reason to infer that the Oireachtas had the inherent powers of inquiry claimed in this case.

Supreme Court Judge Adrian Hardiman (2004) has argued *ex obiter* that 'Anything which constitutes an "administration of justice" is within the exclusive domain of the Courts and cannot be undertaken by any other body such as a parliamentary committee (as in the Abbeylara case), the Oireachtas by the passage of legislation, or a public inquiry'. As a result of the Supreme Court judgment, the Barr Tribunal was established by resolutions passed by Dáil Éireann and Seanad Éireann on 17 and 18 April 2002 under the 1921 act to investigate the Abbeylara incident. MacCarthaigh (2005: 179) observes that 'The "Abbeylara judgement", as it is now known, has raised serious long-term difficulties for the ability of committees, and by proxy parliament, to extend their scope for providing accountability'.

CIÉ/Mini-CTC Signalling Project

In 2001 an Oireachtas sub-committee of the Joint Committee on Public Enterprise and Transport was set up so that 'The circumstances surrounding the entering into and the performance of the Iarnród Éireann mini-CTC and Knockcroghery signalling projects and the Esat/CIÉ cabling and telecommunications project and related matters be inquired into and reported on'. This inquiry was concerned with the delay in the completion of a centralised traffic control and signalling system (the mini-CTC) for more lightly used rural sections of the rail network of Iarnród Éireann and the project's apparent over-run against budget.

The result in the High Court on the Abbeylara case led this sub-committee to suspend its work indefinitely. In an interim report (2002: 6.62), the committee notes:

> Apart from retaining a formal role in electing the government and in assenting to government proposals for legislation, the two Houses of the Oireachtas are in genuine danger of being relegated to the same sort of status as one of the recent National Forums – a reasonably well paid and well staffed talking shop, whose members sound off on various of the issues of the day, without any real input into either the formulation of public policy or the scrutiny of its execution.

The Ombudsman

Ireland was behind many European countries in adopting the institution of Ombudsman. The reason for being late into this field is the preference for political remedies noted above. Discussion on the creation of the office began in the mid-1960s and received a further impetus with the publication of the Devlin report in 1969. It was not until 1975, however, that the matter began to be considered by the Oireachtas – both then and subsequently only as a result of the efforts of private members. These efforts eventually led to the introduction of a government bill, which became the Ombudsman Act 1980. The first Ombudsman was not appointed until 1984.

The 1980 act provided for the establishment of the office of the Ombudsman, the appointment to the post to be made by the President upon resolutions passed by the Dáil and Seanad. Under the act the Ombudsman has the same remuneration as a judge of the High Court, holds office for a period of six years and may be reappointed for a second and subsequent terms. The Ombudsman may act either on a complaint received or on his or her initiative as to where an investigation would be warranted. The Ombudsman may investigate the actions of any officials in any organisations within his or her remit where it appears '(a) that the action has or may have adversely affected a person . . . and (b) that the action was or may have been taken without proper authority or on irrelevant grounds; the result of negligence or carelessness; based on erroneous or incomplete information; improperly discriminatory; based on undesirable administrative practice; or otherwise contrary to fair or sound administration'. In short, the Ombudsman is responsible for ensuring decent standards of behaviour in all areas of administration in the organisations within his or her remit. Ombudsman Emily O'Reilly said in her 2007 annual report:

> The resolution of individual complaints involves lessons being learned by the public bodies involved and may lead to improvements in the way they administer schemes or carry out their day-to-day functions. This can lead to wider improvements in the case of other public bodies carrying out similar functions provided they take the time and effort to study the outcomes of cases I describe in my annual reports and apply those lessons, where appropriate.

The organisations within the Ombudsman's remit are government departments and offices, local authorities, health boards and An Post. There is provision for extending the list of organisations by ministerial order. All matters relating to public service personnel (for example their pay, promotion or transfer) are excluded from the Ombudsman's remit.

In general, complaints have to be made within twelve months of the action complained of taking place. In general also, complaints are not accepted for investigation unless the complainant has already taken up the matter unsuccessfully with the public body concerned and has already used whatever appeal facilities are available. The services are free, and no lawyers are required. The Ombudsman's staff investigate on the citizen's behalf, and all the latter needs to do is to set out the complaint in a letter.

For the purpose of an investigation the Ombudsman must be provided with all documents that he or she considers relevant. The Official Secrets Act does not apply to the supply by civil servants of documents or information to the Ombudsman. The Ombudsman may also require persons to appear for examination. Investigations are conducted in private, and an opportunity must be given to all parties concerned to comment. The Ombudsman, on finding that the action complained of has had an adverse effect on the complainant, can recommend to the organisation concerned that (1) the matter in relation to which the action in question was taken be reconsidered, (2) measures be taken to remedy the adverse effects of the action or (3) the reason for taking the action be given. The Ombudsman is empowered to require the body concerned to notify him or her within a specific time of its response to the recommendations. The Ombudsman does not, however, have the power to overturn decisions; the power of recommending is considered adequate.

There is provision for a ministerial veto on investigations. If a minister so requests in writing, the Ombudsman may not investigate an action specified in the request. The minister must provide the Ombudsman with a written statement setting out the reasons for this request. The purpose of the provision is to provide a means whereby the discretionary decisions of a minister can be exempted from the scrutiny of the Ombudsman. It was never intended that the provision would be widely used, and the Ombudsman's annual report can include references to potential abuses of the provision. In fact, no minister has to date vetoed an investigation.

To facilitate the work of the Ombudsman in dealing with government departments, each department nominates an officer in the grade of principal to act as liaison officer with the Ombudsman's office. It is this officer's duty to ensure that written or oral enquiries are directed to the appropriate section for attention, that time limits applying to requests for information are met, and that the relevant documents and files are made available for inspection as required. Much of the work of the office is done on an informal basis as a result of discussions between the investigators and the officials concerned in the various bodies. Where these discussions are not concluded to the satisfaction of the investigators, and where there is prima facie evidence of maladministration, the investigation moves to a more formal stage. The Ombudsman writes formally to the chief officer of the body concerned, enclosing a written summary of the complaint and requesting written observations thereon. Such requests are dealt with as a matter of priority, and replies are issued within two weeks of receipt. If a department does not accept that a complaint has been properly referred to it (i.e. if it is of the view that the matter is not one for the Ombudsman, or if it considers that the complaint is not appropriate to the department), the chief officer conveys this view to the Ombudsman within seven days.

Under the Civil Service Regulation (Amendment) Act 2005 the power of appointing a person to be an officer or servant of the Ombudsman is vested in the Ombudsman. However, the Minister for Finance determines the number of officers and servants appointed to the office of the Ombudsman and all such officers and servants hold office on such terms and conditions as the Minister for Finance determines.

The Ombudsman's annual report presents statistics and detailed particulars of complaints dealt with during the year and gives typical examples, together with information on general issues arising from the work of the office. The report must be laid before both Houses of the Oireachtas. The Ombudsman may also make such other reports with respect to his or her functions as he or she sees fit. The Ombudsman has issued a guide to standards of best practice for public servants, which states that 'public bodies should strive for the highest standards of administration in their dealings with the citizen, they should be dealt with properly, fairly and impartially'. The annual number of complaints from the public to the Ombudsman's office increased almost 15 per cent in 2007, the highest annual intake of valid complaints since 1999.

Writing in *The Irish Times* in July 2008 Ombudsman Emily O'Reilly noted:

> It is very difficult for any person who has been refused benefits or a service to mount a successful appeal. A decision to refuse can look convincing, particularly when it begins with the words 'it is not the policy of the [Minister, Health Service Executive, Local Authority, etc] to pay a grant/benefit to someone in your circumstances'. Many people will not think it worthwhile referring the matter to my office because of a belief that they have no entitlement to the grant/benefit in question. But those that do come to my office have at their disposal the experience of my staff and their expert knowledge of all relevant programmes.

The Ombudsman has said that each decision made by her office not only helped the individual concerned, but helped other public bodies to learn from the mistake and improve their own services.

Ombudsman (Amendment) Bill

The Minister for Finance published the Ombudsman (Amendment) Bill in 2008, which is the first major expansion of the Ombudsman's remit since the creation of the office in the 1980s. For most of that time, the remit has covered the civil service, local authorities, the public health services (with the public voluntary hospitals being added in 2007) and An Post. The bill will extend the remit to more than one hundred additional state agencies, to include bodies whose actions affect significant numbers of people and bodies set up in recent years whose functions were formerly carried out by government departments that were within the Ombudsman's remit. Examples include the colleges and universities, Courts Service, vocational education committees, FÁS, National Treatment Purchase Fund, National Roads Authority, Dublin Transportation Office and other state bodies. A public body will be legally obliged by the legislation 'consistent with its resources' to deal with people fairly and in a timely manner. In addition, the government will in future be able to expand the scope of the Ombudsman to allow other bodies to be brought under the remit, using regulation rather than the slower method of legislation.

The bill also sets out further criteria and procedures that are to apply to departments and agencies under the remit of the legislation and increases the powers of the Ombudsman in respect of access to information. The Ombudsman will be entitled to institute legal proceedings where a requirement to provide information is not met and may refer any question of law arising in an examination or an investigation to the High Court. This bill is also expected to ensure that any new regulatory offices cannot be titled as ombudsmen, reflecting the fear that the number of such agencies created to date is confusing the public.

Information Commissioner

The office of the Information Commissioner was established on 21 April 1998, the date on which the Freedom of Information (FOI) Act 1997 came into effect. The aim was to create a culture of greater openness and transparency in the civil service. The passing of the FOI act constituted a legislative development of major importance. It represented a considered and deliberate step that dramatically altered the administrative assumptions and culture of centuries. It replaced the presumption of secrecy with one of openness. It opened up the workings of government and administration to scrutiny. It let light into the offices and filing cabinets of decision-makers.

The main functions of the Information Commissioner are to:

- Review decisions made by public bodies in relation to freedom of information requests and to affirm, vary or annul these decisions; if the decision is annulled, the commissioner may make a new decision.
- Keep the operation of the FOI act under review with a view to ensuring maximum compliance.
- Foster an attitude of openness among public bodies by encouraging the voluntary publication by them of information on their activities.
- Prepare and publish commentaries on the practical operation of the FOI act.

The Freedom of Information (Amendment) Act 2003 introduced significant changes to the FOI system, the most important of which were:

- The time limit for potential release of cabinet records was increased to ten years from five years.
- Records submitted to the government, or proposed to be submitted to the government, or records of communications between ministers relating to government business were now mandatorily exempt (previously this was a discretionary exemption.
- The definition of 'government' under section 19 of the FOI act was widened to include a committee of officials and/or advisers where that committee is certified as such by the Secretary General to the Government.
- Records may now be totally excluded from the scope of FOI if the secretary general of a department certifies that they contain 'matter relating to the deliberative processes of any department of state'.
- Records relating to security, defence and international relations were now subject to a mandatory exemption.
- The FOI act will not apply to parliamentary briefing records, including records created for the purpose of briefing in relation to the answering of parliamentary questions.
- Provision was made for the introduction of 'up-front' fees.
- A right of appeal from the High Court to the Supreme Court was introduced.

The result of the 2003 amendment act was to make information less accessible than before. The introduction of a right of appeal from the High Court to the Supreme Court under section 23 of the act has resulted in two decisions being handed down to date, both of which overruled the Information Commissioner. The first case (*Sheedy v Information Commissioner and Others* IESC 35, 30 May 2005) related to reports on primary schools by Department of Education inspectors that had initially been sought under the FOI act by *The Irish Times*. The case turned on the interpretation of section 53 of the Education Act 1998, which provided that 'Notwithstanding any other enactment, the Minister may refuse access to any information which would enable the compilation of information in relation to the comparative performance of schools in respect of the academic achievement of students'. The Supreme Court held that the word 'notwithstanding' as a prepositional sentence starter unequivocally meant despite any other legislation, and underlined in the clearest possible manner the free-standing nature of the provision thereafter set out in section 53. Other similarly worded legislative provisions may operate in the same manner. The second case (*McK v Information Commissioner* IESC 2, 24 January 2006) related to access to personal information, in the form of hospital notes, by parents/guardians relating to minors. The Supreme Court overruled the Information Commissioner and found that 'The Commissioner erred in determining that release of the medical information would only be directed where there is tangible evidence that such release would actually serve the best interests of the minor'.

The Information Commissioner has a powerful role in that all records are to be given to the commissioner, who may enter the premises of public bodies. The decisions of public bodies that the commissioner may review are decisions to:

- Refuse to provide all the records requested.
- Refuse to provide a complete record.
- Refuse to provide the record in the format sought.
- Defer the granting of access to the record.
- Refuse a request to correct personal information.
- Refuse to give reasons for actions of public bodies that materially affect a person.
- Charge a fee or seek a deposit before information is released.
- Release records in the public interest relating to a third party where the records contain information that is personal, given in confidence to the public body or is commercially sensitive.
- Extend the time limit within which a request for access must be decided.

In the first decade of the FOI legislation Irish public bodies dealt with 130,000 FOI requests from members of the public, the media and business and political interests. On average 70 per cent of these requests were granted in full or in part. The office of the Information Commissioner has received 5,300 appeals, slightly more than 3 per cent of all FOI requests made between 1998 and 2007, and of these, 4,058 were valid appeals. Of the valid appeals approximately 25 per cent were decided in favour of the appellant, in approximately 40 per cent the public body's decision was affirmed, and in the remaining cases the appeal was discontinued.

When the legislation first came into operation in 1998 it applied to just sixty-seven public bodies, this number had grown to about 520 public bodies in 2008. The level of FOI requests in Ireland compares favourably with the situation in other countries. Speaking at the tenth anniversary conference of FOI, Finance Minister Brian Lenihan commented, 'FOI has been an important catalyst for change. By turning the presumption of secrecy on its head, it has fundamentally altered the nature of the engagement between the citizen and the administration. It has been a culture change for everyone involved, including members of the Government.'

Emily O'Reilly was appointed Information Commissioner with effect from 1 June 2003 by the President on the recommendation of each of the Houses of the Oireachtas. She was appointed as Ombudsman on the same day. Many other countries with freedom of information legislation have the same person serve as both Ombudsman and Information Commissioner.

Garda Síochána Ombudsman Commission

The Garda Síochána Ombudsman Commission (GSOC) is an independent statutory body. It was established under the Garda Síochána Act 2005, which involved very significant legislative changes for policing in Ireland. The commission, under the act, is required and empowered to:

- Directly and independently investigate complaints against members of An Garda Síochána.
- Investigate any matter, even where no complaint has been made, where it appears that a garda may have committed an offence or behaved in a way that would justify disciplinary proceedings.
- Investigate any practice, policy or procedure of An Garda Síochána with a view to reducing the incidence of related complaints.

Three people make up the GSOC, which provides an independent civilian oversight of policing. It deals with the public's complaints concerning gardaí fairly and efficiently so that everyone can have confidence in the complaints system. It received almost three thousand complaints in its first year of operation. Speaking at the launch of the first annual report of the commission, Mr Justice Kevin Haugh, then chairperson of the GSOC, highlighted the tensions inherent in such a role, 'We can't decline to investigate matters just because the Garda Síochána say their actions were lawful. We may conclude that at the end of an investigation. To say we should not investigate what they say is lawful is to miss the point' (Coulter 2008a).

Financial Services Ombudsman

The Financial Services Ombudsman is a statutory officer who deals independently with unresolved complaints from consumers about their individual dealings with financial service providers. It is a free service to the complainant, set up in 2004. The Financial Services Ombudsman is empowered to mediate, adjudicate, resolve and, where appropriate, make awards. Such findings are binding on both parties, subject only to appeal to the High Court. The Financial Services Ombudsman published revised guidelines following the High Court's judgment in the case of *J & E Davy trading as Davy v Financial Services Ombudsman & Others* IEHC 256 of 30 July 2008. The office of the Financial Services Ombudsman initiates a mediation procedure once it has received a complaint form and final response letter from the financial service provider involved in the case, and both parties are invited to participate in the process. If mediation is not availed of or is unsuccessful, then a formal investigation by the Financial

Services Ombudsman begins. The Financial Services Ombudsman has highlighted the sale of inappropriate financial products to the elderly by insurance companies, banks and brokers.

Ombudsman for Children

The Ombudsman for Children holds the unique, independent and statutory position of promoting the rights and welfare of children and young people. The Ombudsman for Children's office was set up by the Ombudsman for Children Act 2002 as an independent voice and catalyst for change on behalf of all children and young people in Ireland, to promote their rights and welfare and to promote a shared responsibility for developing a society where children and young people are better respected. Central to this is assisting in reviewing law, policy and practice to check compliance with human rights standards, particularly the UN Convention on the Child.

Ombudsman for the Defence Forces

The office of the Ombudsman for the Defence Forces started operations in December 2005. It was set up in response to concerns about bullying and harassment in the Defence Forces. Its purpose is to provide serving and former members with an independent and fair appeal for complaints that they believe have not been adequately addressed by internal military processes. A total of one hundred and six cases were referred to the Ombudsman for the Defence Forces in 2008; a tiny percentage in the context of the overall membership of the Defence Forces. Just over one in ten of all cases came from female members.

Data Protection Commissioner

The office of the Data Protection Commissioner was established under the Data Protection Act 1988. The Data Protection Amendment Act 2003 updated the legislation, implementing the provisions of a relevant EU directive 95/46. These acts set out the general principle that individuals should be in a position to control how data relating to them is used. 'Data controllers' – people or organisations holding information about individuals on computer or in structured manual files – must comply with certain standards in handling personal data, and individuals have certain rights.

The Data Protection Commissioner is responsible for upholding the rights of individuals as set out in the acts, and enforcing the obligations upon data controllers. The Commissioner is appointed by the government and is independent in the exercise of his or her functions. The Commissioner makes an annual report to the Oireachtas. Individuals who feel their rights are being infringed can complain to the commissioner, who will investigate the matter, and take the necessary steps to resolve it.

The commissioner also maintains a register, available for public inspection, giving general details about the data-handling practices of many important data controllers, including government departments and financial institutions. The office received 1, 031 new complaints in 2008, compared to 300 in 2005. In the words of the commissioner in the foreword to his 2007 annual report, 'Have we not succumbed to terror and submitted to extremism when we lose the liberty to live our lives without constant intrusion by the State in the name of security?'

A 2008 audit by the commissioner of the security of data at the Department of Social and Family Affairs uncovered a number of weaknesses in systems and practices and noted seven alleged breaches of data security. The department controls more personal information about Irish citizens than any other body in the state. The commissioner raised concerns about a number of issues surrounding laptop security, the use of generic passwords, and failings in the logging and auditing of employees' use of some systems. The audit team found that while there was a strong awareness at senior management level of data protection principles, there was little desire to follow this through at an operational level due to the size and diversity of the department. It raised concerns over the large number of external agencies that have access to information held by the department, the extent of information shared with these bodies, and that information being exchanged between some of these agencies was not secure.

The Department of Social and Family Affairs said it had responded in detail to the commissioner's recommendations, which covered access management, security, data sharing and data protection policies. The department acknowledged the concern over breaches of data security in recent years and assured the public that it treats any unauthorised access to or disclosure of personal data to be an extremely serious offence. All civil servants are subject to the Official Secrets Act as well as departmental data protection policies and all allegations of breaches are fully investigated. Any staff member found to have breached the department's data protection policies and procedures is subject to the highest disciplinary sanction, up to and including dismissal.

Press Ombudsman and Press Council of Ireland

The office of the Press Ombudsman, which began operating on 1 January 2008, is part of a new system of regulation for the printed media in Ireland. The system is independent of government and the industry. The job of the

Press Ombudsman is to investigate complaints that breach a code of practice, which the press industry signed up to in 2007. The key element of the code of practice is that newspapers and periodicals shall strive at all times for truth and accuracy. The Press Ombudsman aims to provide the public with a quick, fair and free method of resolving any complaints they may have in relation to newspapers and periodicals that breach the code. The public can make a complaint to the office of the Press Ombudsman about an article or about the behaviour of a journalist. The office will, in the first instance, attempt to resolve the matter by making direct contact with the editor of the publication concerned. It will outline the complaint to the publication and seek to resolve the matter by a process of conciliation. If conciliation is not possible, the Press Ombudsman will examine the case and make a decision.

The Press Ombudsman may refer significant or complex cases to the Press Council of Ireland. The Press Council has thirteen members, seven of whom, including the chairperson, are drawn from suitably qualified persons representative of a broad spectrum of Irish society. The remaining six members provide senior editorial and journalistic expertise and perspectives reflective of the press industry. The Press Council is the body that appoints the Press Ombudsman. It takes decisions in cases of significance or complexity that have been referred to it by the Press Ombudsman. It also decides on appeals from decisions of the Press Ombudsman. If the council fails to live up to its promises, the government has threatened to introduce a Privacy Act. Minister for Justice Brian Lenihan said in early 2008, 'I am bound to make it clear to you that if the media fails to show respect for the right to privacy as specified in its own code of practice, the Government will have no choice but to proceed with its privacy legislation. . . . Be warned: there are many sceptics out there. You would do well to prove them wrong at an early date.'

Social Welfare Appeals Office

The Social Welfare Appeals Office (SWAO) operates independently of the Department of Social and Family Affairs. It was set up in 1990 and its mission is to 'provide an independent, accessible and fair appeals service for entitlement to social welfare payments and to deliver that service in a prompt and courteous manner'. It is not a forum for addressing complaints about matters such as delays in dealing with applications for payment, discourtesy, failure to provide appropriate information to claimants and related complaints. It is headed by a chief appeals officer and has its own appeals officers who make the decisions. The SWAO's headquarters are at D'Olier House in Dublin and appeals in the Dublin area are held there. Appeals officers also visit other cities and large towns throughout Ireland to keep to a minimum the distance that people have to travel for an appeal hearing. The initial decision is made by a 'deciding officer' within the Department of Social and Family Affairs. Appeals should be made in writing within twenty-one days of receiving that decision. The case is referred back to the department, where it may be revised or put forward for consideration by the appeals officer. The appeal is heard *de novo* by the appeals officer.

The strengths of the SWAO are that it gives social welfare claimants a statutory right of appeal and it operates in a reasonably informal and non-legalistic manner that respects the individual's rights while not being unduly restrictive about issues such as time limits or rules for the service of documents. Individuals can present their own case – with the help of family and friends – without the need for legal advice or professional advocacy. The appeals regulations require that appeals officers give reasons for their decisions when the decision does not favour the appellant. People who have used the SWAO may pursue their case further at the Ombudsman's office and ultimately to the courts. Decisions of appeals officers are final and conclusive, subject to appeal to the High Court on a point of law.

Web Resources

Appeal Commissioners on taxation matters at www.appealcommissioners.ie
BASIS: Business Access to State Information and Services at www.basis.ie
Citizens' information at www.citizensinformation.ie
Commission for Aviation Regulation at www.aviationreg.ie
Commission for Communications Regulation at www.comreg.ie
Commission for Energy Regulation at www.cer.ie
Commission for Taxi Regulation at www.taxireg.ie
Competition Authority at www.tca.ie
Data Protection Commission at www.dataprotection.ie
European Court of Human Rights at www.echr.coe.int
European Court of Justice at www.curia.europa.eu
European Ombudsman at www.ombudsman.europa.eu
Freedom of Information at www.finance.gov.ie (under FOI)
Financial Regulator at www.financialregulator.ie
Financial Services Ombudsman at www.financialombudsman.ie
Garda Síochána Ombudsman Commission at www.gardaombudsman.ie
Information Commissioner at www.oic.gov.ie
Ombudsman at www.ombudsman.gov.ie
Ombudsman for Children at www.oco.ie
Ombudsman for the Defence Forces at www.odf.ie
Press Council at www.presscouncil.ie

Press Ombudsman at www.pressombudsman.ie
Refugee Appeals Tribunal at www.refappeal.ie
Social Welfare Appeals Office at www.socialwelfareappeals.ie
UN Universal Declaration of Human Rights at www.un.org/Overview/
rights.html
Valuation Tribunal at www.valuation-trib.ie

APPENDIX: UNIVERSAL DECLARATION OF HUMAN RIGHTS

UNIVERSAL DECLARATION OF HUMAN RIGHTS

Adopted and proclaimed by General Assembly resolution 217 A (III) of 10 December 1948

PREAMBLE

Whereas recognition of the inherent dignity and of the equal and inalienable rights of all members of the human family is the foundation of freedom, justice and peace in the world,

Whereas disregard and contempt for human rights have resulted in barbarous acts which have outraged the conscience of mankind, and the advent of a world in which human beings shall enjoy freedom of speech and belief and freedom from fear and want has been proclaimed as the highest aspiration of the common people,

Whereas it is essential, if man is not to be compelled to have recourse, as a last resort, to rebellion against tyranny and oppression, that human rights should be protected by the rule of law,

Whereas it is essential to promote the development of friendly relations between nations,

Whereas the peoples of the United Nations have in the Charter reaffirmed their faith in fundamental human rights, in the dignity and worth of the human person and in the equal rights of men and women and have determined to promote social progress and better standards of life in larger freedom,

Whereas Member States have pledged themselves to achieve, in co-operation with the United Nations, the promotion of universal respect for and observance of human rights and fundamental freedoms,

Whereas a common understanding of these rights and freedoms is of the greatest importance for the full realization of this pledge,

Now, Therefore THE GENERAL ASSEMBLY proclaims THIS UNIVERSAL DECLARATION OF HUMAN RIGHTS as a common standard of achievement for all peoples and all nations, to the end that every individual and every organ of society, keeping this Declaration constantly in mind, shall strive by teaching and education to promote respect for these rights and freedoms and by progressive measures, national and international, to secure their universal and effective recognition and observance, both among the peoples of Member States themselves and among the peoples of territories under their jurisdiction.

Article 1

All human beings are born free and equal in dignity and rights. They are endowed with reason and conscience and should act towards one another in a spirit of brotherhood.

Article 2

Everyone is entitled to all the rights and freedoms set forth in this Declaration, without distinction of any kind, such as race, colour, sex, language, religion, political or other opinion, national or social origin, property, birth or other status. Furthermore, no distinction shall be made on the basis of the political, jurisdictional or international status of the country or territory to which a person belongs, whether it be independent, trust, non-self-governing or under any other limitation of sovereignty.

Article 3

Everyone has the right to life, liberty and security of person.

Article 4

No one shall be held in slavery or servitude; slavery and the slave trade shall be prohibited in all their forms.

Article 5

No one shall be subjected to torture or to cruel, inhuman or degrading treatment or punishment.

Article 6

Everyone has the right to recognition everywhere as a person before the law.

Article 7

All are equal before the law and are entitled without any discrimination to equal protection of the law. All are entitled to equal protection against any discrimination in violation of this Declaration and against any incitement to such discrimination.

Article 8

Everyone has the right to an effective remedy by the competent national tribunals for acts violating the fundamental rights granted him by the constitution or by law.

Article 9

No one shall be subjected to arbitrary arrest, detention or exile.

Article 10

Everyone is entitled in full equality to a fair and public hearing by an independent and impartial tribunal, in the determination of his rights and obligations and of any criminal charge against him.

Article 11

(1) Everyone charged with a penal offence has the right to be presumed innocent until proved guilty according to law in a public trial at which he has had all the guarantees necessary for his defence.

(2) No one shall be held guilty of any penal offence on account of any act or omission which did not constitute a penal offence, under national or international law, at the time when it was committed. Nor shall a heavier penalty be imposed than the one that was applicable at the time the penal offence was committed.

Article 12

No one shall be subjected to arbitrary interference with his privacy, family, home or correspondence, nor to attacks upon his honour and reputation. Everyone has the right to the protection of the law against such interference or attacks.

Article 13

(1) Everyone has the right to freedom of movement and residence within the borders of each state.

(2) Everyone has the right to leave any country, including his own, and to return to his country.

Article 14

(1) Everyone has the right to seek and to enjoy in other countries asylum from persecution.

(2) This right may not be invoked in the case of prosecutions genuinely arising from non-political crimes or from acts contrary to the purposes and principles of the United Nations.

Article 15

(1) Everyone has the right to a nationality.

(2) No one shall be arbitrarily deprived of his nationality nor denied the right to change his nationality.

Article 16

(1) Men and women of full age, without any limitation due to race, nationality or religion, have the right to marry and to found a family. They are entitled to equal rights as to marriage, during marriage and at its dissolution.

(2) Marriage shall be entered into only with the free and full consent of the intending spouses.

(3) The family is the natural and fundamental group unit of society and is entitled to protection by society and the State.

Article 17

(1) Everyone has the right to own property alone as well as in association with others.

(2) No one shall be arbitrarily deprived of his property.

Article 18

Everyone has the right to freedom of thought, conscience and religion; this right includes freedom to change his religion or belief, and freedom, either alone or in community with others and in public or private, to manifest his religion or belief in teaching, practice, worship and observance.

Article 19

Everyone has the right to freedom of opinion and expression; this right includes freedom to hold opinions without interference and to seek, receive and impart information and ideas through any media and regardless of frontiers.

Article 20

(1) Everyone has the right to freedom of peaceful assembly and association.
(2) No one may be compelled to belong to an association.

Article 21

(1) Everyone has the right to take part in the government of his country, directly or through freely chosen representatives.
(2) Everyone has the right of equal access to public service in his country.
(3) The will of the people shall be the basis of the authority of government; this will shall be expressed in periodic and genuine elections which shall be by universal and equal suffrage and shall be held by secret vote or by equivalent free voting procedures.

Article 22

Everyone, as a member of society, has the right to social security and is entitled to realization, through national effort and international co-operation and in accordance with the organization and resources of each State, of the economic, social and cultural rights indispensable for his dignity and the free development of his personality.

Article 23

(1) Everyone has the right to work, to free choice of employment, to just and favourable conditions of work and to protection against unemployment.
(2) Everyone, without any discrimination, has the right to equal pay for equal work.
(3) Everyone who works has the right to just and favourable remuneration ensuring for himself and his family an existence worthy of human dignity, and supplemented, if necessary, by other means of social protection.
(4) Everyone has the right to form and to join trade unions for the protection of his interests.

Article 24

Everyone has the right to rest and leisure, including reasonable limitation of working hours and periodic holidays with pay.

Article 25

(1) Everyone has the right to a standard of living adequate for the health and well-being of himself and of his family, including food, clothing, housing and medical care and necessary social services, and the right to security in the event of unemployment, sickness, disability, widowhood, old age or other lack of livelihood in circumstances beyond his control.

(2) Motherhood and childhood are entitled to special care and assistance. All children, whether born in or out of wedlock, shall enjoy the same social protection.

Article 26

(1) Everyone has the right to education. Education shall be free, at least in the elementary and fundamental stages. Elementary education shall be compulsory. Technical and professional education shall be made generally available and higher education shall be equally accessible to all on the basis of merit.

(2) Education shall be directed to the full development of the human personality and to the strengthening of respect for human rights and fundamental freedoms. It shall promote understanding, tolerance and friendship among all nations, racial or religious groups, and shall further the activities of the United Nations for the maintenance of peace.

(3) Parents have a prior right to choose the kind of education that shall be given to their children.

Article 27

(1) Everyone has the right freely to participate in the cultural life of the community, to enjoy the arts and to share in scientific advancement and its benefits.

(2) Everyone has the right to the protection of the moral and material interests resulting from any scientific, literary or artistic production of which he is the author.

Article 28

Everyone is entitled to a social and international order in which the rights and freedoms set forth in this Declaration can be fully realized.

Article 29

(1) Everyone has duties to the community in which alone the free and full development of his personality is possible.
(2) In the exercise of his rights and freedoms, everyone shall be subject only to such limitations as are determined by law solely for the purpose of securing due recognition and respect for the rights and freedoms of others and of meeting the just requirements of morality, public order and the general welfare in a democratic society.
(3) These rights and freedoms may in no case be exercised contrary to the purposes and principles of the United Nations.

Article 30

Nothing in this Declaration may be interpreted as implying for any State, group or person any right to engage in any activity or to perform any act aimed at the destruction of any of the rights and freedoms set forth herein.

12

THE IMPACT OF THE EUROPEAN UNION

The European Union, as a supranational organisation, represents a distinct approach to international relations that is of profound significance for its member states in the economic, legal, social and political areas. The EU has developed its own system of law, which is independent of national law. It is more than an international organisation, but not quite a federation. The EU is a hybrid body, with federal and inter-governmental elements. It combines those elements in a unique way that is not replicated elsewhere.

The Treaties

The European Community dates from 1951, when the six founder members signed the Treaty of Paris to found the European Coal and Steel Community in July 1952. The Rome Treaties of 1957 established the European Economic Community (EEC) and the European Atomic Energy Community (Euratom). In 1967 the institutions serving the three communities were merged and were termed the 'European Community' (EC), from 1993 known as the European Union (EU). The EU is founded on three treaties:

1. The Treaty establishing the European Economic Community (EEC), which was signed on 25 March 1957 in Rome and came into force on 1 January 1958.
2. The Treaty establishing the European Atomic Energy Community (Euratom), which was signed in Rome along with the EEC Treaty. These two treaties are often referred to as the 'Treaties of Rome'. When the term 'Treaty of Rome' is used, however, only the EEC Treaty is meant.
3. The Treaty on European Union (TEU), which was signed in Maastricht on 7 February 1992 and came into force on 1 November 1993.

A fourth treaty, the Treaty establishing the European Coal and Steel Community (ECSC) on which the current innovative institutional structure is based, came into force on 23 July 1952 and expired on 23 July 2002.

The treaties have been amended, with the unanimous consent of all member states, to enable adjustments to the institutions to accommodate successive enlargements. Following unanimous agreement by all member states, amendments to the treaties have also provided areas of competence to be transferred from the member state to EU level. These are:

- The Single European Act (SEA), which was signed in February 1986 and came into force on 1 July 1987, amended the EEC Treaty and paved the way for completing the single market.
- The Treaty of Maastricht, which came into force on 1 November 1993, set the stage for an eventual common currency and also introduced a number of important institutional changes, notably legislative co-decision between the European Parliament and the Council.
- The Treaty of Amsterdam, which was signed on 2 October 1997 and came into force on 1 May 1999, provided, *inter alia*, for greater co-operation at EU level in justice and home affairs.
- The Treaty of Nice, which was signed on 26 February 2001 and entered into force on 1 February 2003, further amended the other treaties, streamlining the EU's institutional system so it could continue to work effectively for a union then expected to grow to twenty-seven member states.

Ireland's 2004 EU presidency produced agreement on a constitution for Europe. However, this was abandoned following its defeat in referenda held in France and the Netherlands in May and June 2005 respectively. The member states continued to work towards the development of a treaty that would enable greater efficacy in the governance of the enlarged EU. On 13 December 2007 representatives of the twenty-seven national governments signed the Treaty of Lisbon (Reform Treaty). The Irish people rejected this treaty at a referendum held in June 2008 (see below).

Ireland's Membership

Ireland became a member of the EEC on 1 January 1973, joining at the same time as Britain and Denmark. Ireland's membership of the EU affects every citizen of the state. It has had a profound impact on every aspect of Irish life, and the development of the country owes much to membership of the EU. The Irish people have historically been well disposed to and at ease with EU membership and Ireland's position in Europe. However, Kennedy and Sinnott (2007) show that while the conventional wisdom suggests Irish people tend to be very positive about the EU, the reality of Irish opinion is more nuanced. Using individual data from Eurobarometer 61 they show that opinion towards European integration is not a single entity but a complex set of opinions. Moreover, the defeat of the first Nice Treaty referendum in 2001 and the defeat of the Lisbon Treaty referendum in 2008 have confirmed this and begun to raise questions about Ireland's future in Europe.

Until 1993 neither the Dáil nor the Seanad possessed a parliamentary committee to monitor foreign policy. However, there was from the mid-1970s a Joint Oireachtas Committee on the Secondary Legislation of the European Communities with a limited remit essentially confined to scrutinising the EC regulations and directives. Limited sittings of the Dáil and Seanad precluded close scrutiny of EU policy. Supervision was limited to annual policy debates surrounding the budgetary estimates, government statements, special debates, votes on international treaties or agreements, together with parliamentary questions to the Taoiseach and the Minister for Foreign Affairs. While in the early days of Ireland's EU membership, EU integration was largely seen as a 'foreign policy' issue, that situation has changed dramatically. Nowadays the EU draws an increasingly wide range of officials in government departments, state agencies and local authorities into the policy-making and implementation process. There are few, if any, areas of the public service and the machinery of government which are untouched by EU developments on a day-to-day basis.

Ireland has drawn significant economic benefit from its membership of the EU. From the outset Irish people embraced the European project. Instantly Ireland's status as being offshore, beyond Britain, was changed and quickly the Irish were at the heart of European affairs. In addition, 'the potent effect of donning the green jersey is felt, for example, by overseas personnel in our multi-national enterprises as they seek to maximise investment and development opportunities for Ireland in the ongoing battle for projects within and across corporations' (McCarthy 2007). Since joining the EEC in 1973, membership of the EU has supported Ireland's economic development in a myriad of different ways. Economic growth has resulted in the convergence of Ireland's per capita income levels with some of the highest in the EU, a mere aspiration one generation ago. Irish per capita gross domestic product (GDP) has increased from 59 per cent of the EU average in 1973 to almost 125 per cent in 2006 (EU-15 average).

Ireland is expected to contribute an estimated €500 million annually to the EU budget by 2013, as it moves from being a net recipient of some €40 billion in support over the years. Ireland received approximately €60 billion in EU support between 1973 and 2008. During that period it also paid out some €20 billion, leaving net receipts of around €40 billion. In 2007 Ireland received some €2 billion in support from the EU budget, but contributed about €1.5 billion. The trend reflects the state's position as a wealthy nation in an enlarged EU of twenty-seven member states. By 2011 the Department of Finance estimates that the amounts by which Ireland receives and contributes to the EU budget will be roughly equal. These estimates indicate that more than 80 per cent of the money allocated from the EU budget in 2007 related to agricultural projects, reflecting the extent to which farmers continue to rely on EU funding. By 2013 Ireland will have received approximately €72 billion and is expected to have paid out approximately €31 billion.

Constitutional Implications

Accession to the EU heralded a new era in the context of the work of the government and the public service in Ireland. The shaping and execution of EU policies is now an everyday part of that work.

The Constitution had not anticipated Ireland's membership of a supra - national organisation such as the EU. It was clear during the negotiations prior to accession that several articles were incompatible with EU membership (for example Articles 5, 15.2, 28, 29.4.1° and 34 to 38). An amendment was accordingly put before the people in a referendum on 10 May 1972 and following the result Article 29.4.10° was inserted into the Irish Constitution: 'No provision of this Constitution invalidates laws enacted, acts done or measures adopted by the State necessitated by the obligations of membership of the Communities or prevents laws enacted, acts done or measures adopted by the Communities, or institutions thereof, from having the force of law in the State.' Robinson (1972) notes that this amendment is very broad and gave a large measure of constitutional immunity to EU laws, measures and acts. There was a relatively high turnout of 71 per cent, with a total of 82 per cent voting in favour of membership. Thus, at that stage, the government and public service was given a clear mandate by the people in the context of membership of the EU.

The European Communities Act 1972 provided that the treaties of the European Communities and the existing and future acts of their institutions were binding on the state and thus brought European law into the Irish legal system. Since 1973 the Rome Treaty, as amended, has become part of the Irish Constitution and the exclusive law-making power of the Oireachtas provided for in Article 15 has been removed. In *Horgan v An Taoiseach* ([2003] 2 ILRM 357 at 389) Kearns J. referred, *obiter*, to the 'strictly circumspect role which the courts adopt when called upon to exercise jurisdiction in relation to the executive's conduct of international relations generally'. As Henchy J. said in *Doyle v An Taoiseach* (1985 ILRM 135), community law 'has the paramount force and effect of constitutional provisions'.

This was exemplified by the celebrated case of *Crotty v An Taoiseach* ([1987] IESC 4; [1987] IR 713, 9 April 1987), in which the Supreme Court ruled that the Single European Act (SEA) could not be ratified by Ireland unless the Constitution was amended, since the SEA contained provisions which were in contravention of the Constitution. In this case, the plaintiff, Raymond Crotty, a private citizen, successfully prevented the state from ratifying the SEA in the absence of a referendum. Barrington J. noted in this regard:

> In so much as it is a matter which affects the whole constitutional and political structure of the society in which he lives it is a matter in which the individual citizen might have a legitimate interest which might be accepted in a court of law . . . The plaintiff clearly has *locus standi* [right to bring an action] because his contention is that what is being done [amounts to an] amendment of the Constitution which should be submitted to a referendum, and that he as a citizen has the right to be consulted in such a referendum and that his right is being infringed.

The necessary amendment was approved by the people on 26 May 1987 and allowed the state to ratify the Single European Act. This judgment made it more problematical to ratify European treaties without a referendum, especially where they expand the foreign policy competence of the institutions of the EU. This decision of the Supreme Court, which was reached by a narrow majority of three to two overruling a unanimous judgment of a three-judge High Court, has been a controversial one.

The question arises as to the extent to which individual acts of the Oireachtas, delegated legislation and administrative actions that implement EU legislation can be said to be 'necessitated' by Article 29.4.10° of the Constitution. This is particularly complex when EU legislation confers a discretion on the member states. Casey (2000: 211) notes, 'The crucial word [in Article 29.4.10°] is, obviously, "necessitated". In its overall context – especially the phrase "obligations of membership" – this conveys the idea of something imperatively required, or made mandatory, by such membership. It would not appear sufficient that Community membership makes what has been done "convenient" or "desirable".' Another constitutional amendment was required for the ratification by Ireland of the Treaty on European Union. On 18 June 1992 the Irish people voted two to one in a referendum in favour of ratification. The traditional 'necessitated obligations' formula in this article no longer sufficed where member states were increasingly empowered to take decisions that resulted from a voluntary act on their part and which decisions could not in any way be described as 'necessitated' by the obligations of membership. Accordingly, a new provision, Article 29.4.6°, was introduced by the Eighteenth Amendment to the Constitution Act 1998. This provision enables the state to exercise certain 'options and discretions' contained in the Treaty of Amsterdam, provided the prior consent of both Houses of the Oireachtas is obtained, 'The State may exercise the options or discretions provided by or under Articles 1.11, 2.5 and 2.15 of the Treaty referred to in subsection 5° of this section and the second and fourth Protocols set out in the said Treaty but any such exercise shall be subject to the prior approval of both Houses of the Oireachtas'. This referendum passed on 22 May 1998.

A referendum was held on the Nice Treaty on 7 June 2001 at which 54 per cent voted No and 46 per cent Yes in a turnout of just 35 per cent of voters. Sinnott (2002) suggests that the lack of major party involvement in the Nice I campaign contributed to a demonstrable gap in people's understanding of the issues. A second Nice referendum held on 19 October 2002, with a turnout of 50 per cent, was carried comfortably with 63 per cent voting Yes and 37 per cent voting No. This result allowed the state to ratify the Treaty of Nice and inserted a new Article 29.4.8° in the Constitution, 'The State may exercise the options or discretions provided by or under Articles 1.6, 1.9, 1.11, 1.12, 1.13 and 2.1 of the Treaty referred to in subsection 7 of this section but any such exercise shall be subject to the prior approval of both Houses of the Oireachtas.' Article 29.4.9° now provides that the state would not exercise any options for common defence pursuant to Article 1.2 of the Nice Treaty 'where the common defence would include the State'. Hogan and Whyte (2003: 519) note that:

> The combined effect of these amendments is to give constitutional authority for a significant transfer of legislative, executive and juridical sovereignty to the European Union within defined – but nonetheless capacious – parameters. Within the last decade the Union has gradually transformed itself from an economic community to an entity with an increasingly important political role . . . It is thus plain that the effects of Article 29.4.10° are, as Barrington J put it in *Crotty v An Taoiseach*, 'far reaching' since: 'The Constitution could not be invoked to invalidate any measures which the State has directed by the institutions of the [European Communities] to take arising out of the exercise of their powers nor to invalidate any regulation or any decision of the European Court which had direct effect within this State by virtue of the provisions of the Treaties'.

Following the No result in the 2008 Lisbon Treaty referendum (see below), the question was asked whether a referendum was needed to ratify the treaty in Ireland. Fanning (2008) notes:

> The legal justification commonly offered is that the Constitution requires a referendum. That proposition is itself based on a gross and widespread misunderstanding of what the Supreme Court held in 1987 in a case brought by the late Raymond Crotty challenging the Government's proposed method of ratification of the Single European Act (SEA). The Supreme Court decision in Crotty is commonly thought to bar ratification of a treaty by statute. In fact,

it does nothing of the sort. Crotty in fact authorises the ratification of future treaties by statute provided that 'such amendments do not alter the essential scope or objectives' of the existing EU.

Barrington (2008) suggested that the Oireachtas could enact a bill ratifying Lisbon on the understanding that President Mary McAleese might use her discretion to refer the bill to the Supreme Court under Article 26 for a decision as to its constitutionality. This would establish what exactly in the Lisbon Treaty required a constitutional amendment. A former adviser on European law at the Department of Foreign Affairs Charles Lysaght (2008) pointed out that the Crotty judgment in 1987 found that the original referendum decision in 1972 to join the then European Communities was an authorisation to join in amendments of treaties 'so long as such amendments did not alter the essential scope or objectives of the communities'. The government did not publish the Attorney General's opinion on the holding of this referendum, as there is a long-standing precedent that the advice of the Attorney General is not published. Clearly, however, the government is influenced by political as well as legal factors. Particularly in the context of the initial rejection of the Nice Treaty, the government might stand accused of bypassing the electorate for fear of rejection by it. There would also be some risk of a challenge to the Supreme Court.

Following the rejection of Nice I in June 2001 it took sixteen months to come up with a formula to put the Nice Treaty back before the people. Given that just 34 per cent of the electorate turned out to vote on Nice the first time around, it was argued that the low turnout merited a new referendum. The issue of neutrality was highlighted as a key reason why people rejected the treaty, enabling a targeted response on this issue to meet voters' concerns and win the argument at the second attempt. The comparatively high turnout in the 2008 Lisbon referendum (53.13 per cent), and the myriad of different reasons provided by voters who voted No, make the staging of an early re-vote much more difficult. The EU External Affairs Commissioner Benita Ferrero-Waldner, saw the issue as an Irish problem, and said that Ireland should be 'allowed to analyse and reflect' in order to 'tell us what they must do . . . It's up to them to take a decision' (Collins 2008).

European Union Law

The law-making power of the EU is extensive and unique. There are a number of fundamental principles of EU law that institutions and member states are obliged to respect. Among these are non-discrimination on the ground of nationality; subsidiarity, which implies that decisions must be made at the level at which they are most effective; and proportionality, which means that obligations imposed by a regulation must stand in reasonable proportion to the objective that the regulation is intended to achieve.

The founding treaties of the EC are the primary sources of EU law, laying down principles and rules that are binding on the member states. The legal acts of the EU are the secondary source of law. EU legal instruments have direct applicability in the member states, and in any conflict between national and EU law the latter predominates. Membership of the EU has qualified the exclusive role of the Irish courts, since the body ultimately responsible for the interpretation of the Treaty of Rome is the Court of Justice of the European Communities (ECJ). The primacy of EU law was established by the ECJ long before Ireland's entry. In two landmark cases the principle of primacy was clearly established by the court and has been accepted by all member states since that time. In the Van Gend en Loos case in 1963 the ECJ held that EC law had direct effect in national legal systems. In the case of Costa van Enel in 1964 the court held that the law stemming from the Treaty of Rome could not be overridden by national law without the legal base of the community itself being called into question.

The ECJ ensures that European law is applied uniformly in the same way in every member state and that the rule of law applies within the EU. The court has laid down rules on how the body of European law relates to the national legal system of the member states. It has assisted national courts in developing a standard approach to the interpretation of European legislation. The court has a horizontal relationship with national courts, which means that national courts may refer questions to the ECJ on how to interpret certain provisions of European law. The ECJ provides the national court with answers to its questions, and the national court then makes its ruling. The operation of the ECJ shows that EU law is 'like an incoming tide. It flows into the estuaries and up the rivers. It cannot be held back' (Lord Denning (H.P.) in *Bulmer Ltd v J. Bollinger SA* (1974) 1 ch. 401 at 418).

Membership of the EU has placed legal restrictions on what an Irish government can do in a wide range of social and economic areas. For example, the ECJ ruled on 3 July 2008 that Irish planning legislation failed to protect the environment and that the installation of wind turbines required an environmental impact assessment under EU law. On 25 July 2008 the ECJ ruled that an Irish law denying residency rights to spouses from outside the EU breached EU legislation on the free movement of citizens. Previously Ireland had required foreign spouses to have lived in another EU country to qualify for residency rights. In September 2008 the ECJ ruled that Ireland had breached an EU directive on the provision of waste water treatment plants. In November 2008 the ECJ ruled that Ireland had not fully brought into Irish law a 1985 directive requiring it to examine the ecological effects of agricultural schemes before granting planning permission for them.

The obligation to implement EU law and the resulting impact on Irish law have been of crucial significance in the operation of government and public administration in Ireland in areas as diverse as equal pay and environmental protection. For the purpose of carrying out their tasks under the treaties, there are three legally binding instruments available:

- *Regulations:* are of general application and immediate effect, and are binding in their entirety. They are directly applicable in all member states, requiring no implementing measures by the national authorities, and become part of Irish law as soon as they have been formally adopted by the Council of Ministers or the European Commission. They are the most common type of secondary legislation and generate rights and obligations for every person in the EU.
- *Directives:* are EU acts adopted by the Council of Ministers or the European Commission. They are binding on any member state to which they are addressed as to the objectives to be achieved but leave the choice of method of implementation to the member state. They indicate the reasons on which they are based, are communicated to the countries to which they are addressed, and state the date on which they come into effect. They are normally used in the harmonisation of legal provisions where the end is not specific. Directives are addressed only to the governments of member states; they create rights but do not create obligations for individuals in a member state. Directives can be implemented in Ireland in either of two ways: by primary legislation, which involves the passing of a bill by the Oireachtas; or by secondary legislation, which involves ministerial regulations. The majority of directives are implemented through this latter method.
- *Decisions:* are legally binding instruments designed to achieve administrative aims and may be directed to a member state, a corporation or an individual. They are used to fill out the framework of regulations where necessary.

In addition to regulations, directives and decisions, there are also *recommendations* and *opinions*. These are non-binding and are used in areas where the community legal base is limited. They usually contain a political message and are normally agreed by unanimity. If it is not possible to reach a unanimous agreement the text becomes a *presidency conclusion*.

Under the prospective Lisbon Treaty, qualified majority voting (QMV) becomes the standard rule for adoption of legislation, known as 'the ordinary legislative procedure', although sensitive areas such as defence and taxation will continue to require a unanimous decision in council. Under the Lisbon Treaty, twenty-two areas from the existing treaties would move from unanimity to QMV. In many cases the extensions to QMV are limited in scope, involving only aspects of a treaty article, or the further use of QMV in an article already chiefly subject to it. Areas moving from unanimity to QMV include incentive measures in the cultural field and aspects of the statute of the ECJ. Other examples are in the area of freedom, security and justice, where Ireland has a special arrangement that enables participation in measures on a case-by-case basis. There are also a number of new areas, not previously covered in the existing treaties, which will be subject to QMV. The areas from the existing treaties that will move from unanimity to QMV are:

- Article 2.36: Diplomatic and consular protection measures.
- Article 2.51: Social security for migrant workers (with an 'emergency brake' whereby if a proposal is particularly sensitive it can be referred to the European Council for a decision by consensus).
- Article 2.54: Provisions for self-employed persons.
- Article 2.70: Establishment of rules concerning transport.
- Article 2.90: Certain measures relating to the broad economic guidelines and excessive deficit procedure.
- Article 2.93: Amendment of some articles of the statute of the European System of Central Banks.
- Article 2.126: Incentive measures in the cultural field.
- Article 2.158: Aspects of the common commercial policy.
- Article 2.211: Establishment of specialised courts.
- Article 2.226: Amendment of aspects of the ECJ statute.
- Article 2.228: Appointment by the European Council of the president, vice-president and members of the European Central Bank's governing council.
- Article 2.236: Rules and general principles concerning mechanisms for control by member states of the European Commission's exercise of implementing powers (comitology).
- Article 2.273: Internal financial regulations.

The following areas are moving to qualified majority voting but Ireland is not obliged to participate and may opt in on a case-by-case basis:

- Article 2.65: Measures concerning border checks.
- Article 2.65: Measures concerning a common European asylum system.
- Article 2.65: Aspects of immigration policy.
- Article 2.67: Judicial co-operation in criminal procedural matters.
- Article 2.67: Minimum rules for criminal offences and sanctions.
- Article 2.67: Crime prevention.

- Article 2.67: Regulations concerning aspects of Eurojust's structure, operation, field of action and tasks.
- Article 2.68: Aspects of police co-operation.
- Article 2.68: Europol.

Competence

The EU relies on its founding legal documents, without which it could not function. It can act only within the limits of the powers given to it by the member states in the treaties. In other words, the EU cannot act if the power to act has not been given, or 'conferred', on it by the member states. Such conferral of powers is done only through treaty change by unanimous agreement.

EU competences vary according to the policy area. In the agriculture and the environment areas, for example, there is a well-developed community acquis, whereas in the education and culture area, the acquis is much less. The term *'acquis communautaire'* is used in EU law to refer to the total body of EU law accumulated so far. The term is French – *acquis* means 'that has been acquired' and *communautaire* means 'of the community'.

In some areas the member states have given the EU exclusive competence to act on their behalf. These areas are: customs, competition in the internal market, euro countries' monetary policy, conservation of marine biological resources and international trade.

In other areas the member states share competence with the EU. These areas are: the internal market, certain aspects of social policy, cohesion, agriculture, fisheries, environment, consumer protection, transport, trans-European networks, energy, security and justice and common safety concerns in public health.

In still other areas the EU can act only to co-ordinate or supplement action taken by the member states. These areas are: public health, industry, culture, tourism, education, youth, sport, vocational training, civil protection and administrative co-operation between national authorities.

The prospective Lisbon Treaty seeks to identify three categories of EU competence:

- *Exclusive competence:* where the EU institutions have exclusive power to legislate.
- *Shared competence:* where competence is shared between the EU and the member states, so that 'when the Union takes action in these areas, the member states may act only within the limits defined by the Union legislation'.

- *Supporting competences:* areas where the EU can support or co-ordinate action by the member states, but does not have the competence to legislate.

Lisbon Treaty (Reform Treaty)

The EU treaties must be agreed by all twenty-seven member states. From time to time, these important documents need to be revised and updated so that an evolving Europe can keep pace with the demands of a changing world. The prospective Lisbon Treaty represented the latest updating of the treaties. Ireland's 2004 EU presidency produced agreement on a constitution for Europe but, as it turned out, that document was not ratified by all member states. Two further years of negotiation produced the Lisbon Treaty, which is the product of the 2004 constitution. There is much similarity between these two agreements, but the Lisbon Treaty is presented as a series of amend - ments to the existing treaties. Those amendments lack the constitutional flavour of the 2004 agreement. The prospective Lisbon Treaty offers a blueprint for continuity and pragmatic adjustment of structures rather than the appearance of radical constitutional change. FitzGerald (2008b) comments, 'If ever there was an international treaty that bears the stamp of Irish negotiating skills, and is designed to serve Irish interests, this surely is that document'. The Lisbon Treaty has important features:

- It gives legal effect to the Charter of Fundamental Rights.
- It seeks to reinforce EU democratic accountability by extending European Parliament co-decision with the Council in almost all legislative and budgetary areas, while also giving an important new role in European affairs to national parliaments.
- It establishes the new posts of an elected President of the European Council (to replace the six-month presidency that rotates among heads of state or government of the member states) and a High Representative for Foreign Affairs and Security Policy. These posts are intended to increase efficiency by providing for greater continuity in the conduct of business and to give the EU a clearer voice in the world. It would thus replace the six-month rotating presidency for these two posts, while retaining the rotating presidency in other policy areas.
- It gives the EU new responsibilities in the areas of energy and climate change, challenges that clearly require concerted European effort.
- It makes the Council of Ministers more accountable and more transparent. It will meet in public when deciding new legislation. A freedom of information act is included and citizens will be able to

propose new legislation – a petition with one million names will force the European Commission to consider an idea.

- National competence is retained over tax, defence, foreign affairs, social security and culture. Neutrality is safeguarded under Article 3a, which says, 'in particular, national security remains the sole responsibility of each member state'. The main protection for Ireland's neutral status continues to reside in the provision carried forward from the Maastricht Treaty that the EU's security and defence policy 'shall not prejudice the specific character of the security and defence policy of certain Member States'.
- It aims to make the EU more efficient by reforming the institutions, slimming down the European Commission, capping the size of the European Parliament and producing a clearer Council voting system so that populations as well as individual states are taken account of in any contested decision.

On 13 December 2007 representatives of the twenty-seven national governments signed the Reform Treaty in the Hieronymite Monastery in Lisbon, Portugal. Former Taoiseach Bertie Ahern and Minister for Foreign Affairs Dermot Ahern signed the treaty on behalf of the Irish government. It is a tradition that international agreements bear the name of the city in which they were signed, which is why the Reform Treaty is officially known as the Lisbon Treaty. It was a complex legal document, stretching to some 272 pages, which could not be read as a stand-alone document, as much of its content is by way of amendment to earlier treaties.

Out of all the twenty-seven EU member states, Ireland was the only country that held a referendum to approve or reject the Lisbon Treaty. The Supreme Court decision in *Crotty v An Taoiseach* in 1987 exposes Irish governments to significant political and legal risks if they do not refer significant EU treaties to a referendum. Surveys revealed that a high percentage of the nation's citizens did not understand the issues at stake in the Lisbon Treaty. Following the McKenna judgment (see Chapter 4), the Referendum Commission, an impartial body, studied the issues being proposed on a pro and contra basis and offered the key arguments on both sides in plain language to assist the citizenry in understanding the issues and reaching a reasonably informed decision. The December 2007 Eurobarometer showed strong support in Ireland for the EU at 74 per cent but found that people felt left out of EU decision-making processes.

On 12 June 2008, with a turnout of 53.13 per cent, the Irish nation voted to reject the Lisbon Treaty by 53.4 per cent against and 46.6 per cent in favour. Whether this was a verdict on the Lisbon Treaty or on the unease people felt on a range of challenges facing post-Celtic Tiger Ireland was an open question. It seemed certain from the result that a streamlined EU was only one of the public's concerns ahead of the vote. Just ten of the forty-three constituencies voted in favour: five in the more middle-class parts of Dublin, two in Dublin commuter constituencies and three in more rural counties. In general, working-class constituencies and rural constituencies voted against, while more affluent urban and suburban areas were in favour. Younger people and women also voted against the treaty in higher percentages. The 2008 Lisbon Treaty campaign highlighted a disconnection between the establishment and the people. Fears about the possible impact of immigration into Ireland, rising unemployment, collapsing retail sales, declining consumer confidence, and falling house prices resulted in a concerned electorate. Other possible factors mentioned included young people being disconnected from Europe; spurious suggestions about taxation, abortion, euthanasia and conscription; the ongoing World Trade Organization talks; and other rumours of all kinds, including a standardised EU six-week school holiday period.

In September 2008 Minister for Foreign Affairs Micheál Martin published the report on the reasons underlying the result of the Lisbon Treaty referendum. The report, which was prepared by Millward Brown IMS, also gave details about public attitudes to Ireland's future role in the EU. It confirmed that people clearly had worries about issues that came up during the campaign, including worries about the possible loss of influence for Ireland, corporation tax and neutrality. The report also showed that the potential loss of an Irish commissioner, abortion, corporation tax, neutrality, conscription and workers' rights were among the main topics that gave rise to concern among voters. The survey found that people felt they did not have enough clear information in the run-up to voting day. This lack of information was the single biggest reason given for the decision to vote No or to abstain. For example, more than four in every ten people who voted against the treaty said they did so because of a lack of information, which gave rise to genuine concerns about what they were being asked to vote on. The results also show that people want Ireland to continue to be fully involved in the EU: 70 per cent agree that membership is a good thing, while a mere 8 per cent disagree. The divisive referendum campaign of 2008 had not shaken Ireland's belief in the EU.

The Standards in Public Office Commission, in its annual report for 2007, declared its frustration with the complex provisions of the Electoral Acts in this context. Figures released on advertising expenditure revealed that the spend by one anti-treaty group, Libertas, on its No campaign was greater than the total spend on the Yes campaign, which included all the main political parties. Libertas was defined as a 'third party' and not a political party. Third parties were not subject to the same financial disclosure rules as political parties under the legislation. Clearly, in the interests of democracy, all political parties and all corporate and individual activists should be subjected to full financial scrutiny. In November 2008 Libertas confirmed that it had registered in Ireland as a European political party.

International reaction to the June 2008 result was swift and blunt. On 21 June 2008 France's Europe Minister Jean-Pierre Jouyet gave a speech in Lyons blaming Ireland's No vote on American neo-conservatives, saying Europe has 'powerful enemies with deep pockets' and adding that 'the role of the American neo-conservatives in the Irish referendum was very important'. Germany's Foreign Minister Frank Walter Steinmeier suggested Ireland take a 'break' from the EU after its rejection of the Lisbon Treaty to allow other member states to continue with integration (Scally 2008), 'Ireland could exit the integration process for a time to clear the way for the Lisbon Treaty to come into force in 26 countries.' Germany's Interior Minister Wolfgang Schäuble said in an interview with the German newspaper *Welt am Sonntag*, 'Of course we have to take the Irish referendum seriously, but a few million Irish cannot decide on behalf of 495 million Europeans' (Castle and Dempsey 2008). Uffe Ellemann-Jensen (2008), former Danish Foreign Minister, commented on why it might be better for Ireland to withdraw from the EU:

> Ireland should do the rest of Europe a favour and withdraw from the European Union. That seems to be the only tenable solution to the situation created by the Irish 'No' to the Lisbon Treaty. The Irish have created a problem for themselves. They should not let it be a problem for others. It would be sad to lose the merry people of the emerald island from the EU family. But it would be even sadder if, because of the Irish 'No' all those who wish to secure the same benefits from European integration that made it possible for the Irish to prosper are left out in the cold.

'Renegotiation of the Treaty is excluded' said French President Nicolas Sarkozy (Smyth 2008) in response to suggestions that the Lisbon Treaty could be renegotiated to meet the demands of Irish voters. Produced after seven years of deliberation, the existing consensus might quickly collapse in such negotiations. Even if an agreement was reached, a new ratification process could potentially present huge difficulties – and not just in Ireland. As there are no referendums planned for any other countries, unlike what happened following the defeat of the Constitutional Treaty in Holland and France, ratification is likely to be completed in the remaining twenty-six member states. Full renegotiation of the Lisbon Treaty is not going to happen, since it would involve the reopening of a Pandora's Box and – unless Ireland changes its stance on ratification – the other member states may seek a way to go ahead with the reforms without Ireland. While an Irish No vote will be respected as determining the Irish view, other member states, quite properly, do not see the requirements of mutual respect or democracy as giving Ireland the right to tell them how to determine their mutual relations or indeed whether they should ratify the Lisbon Treaty. Ireland has the right to change its mind if it wants to, but a No vote in a further referendum – if there is one – runs the risk of leading to the rest of the member states going their own way with further integration. This could leave Ireland isolated and possibly even being asked to leave the EU or to opt for association status.

Another possibility is the other twenty-six member states continuing separately with the process on integration under the 'enhanced co-operation' provisions of the treaty. Professor of European Politics at University College Dublin, Brigid Laffan (2008b), notes, 'The existing Union is replete with 'opt-in' and 'opt-out' clauses. This would deliver Ireland into a second tier of EU engagement, something that was always regarded as against our essential interests. The other member states will make every effort to accommodate Ireland's needs and concerns but there are limits to accommodation as the needs of one will never be allowed to trump the needs of the Union.'

Failure to ratify the Lisbon Treaty meant that, at EU level, under Article 213 of the existing EC Treaty as amended at Nice, a reduction in the number of commissioners was scheduled to happen in 2009 (not 2014, as under the Lisbon Treaty). In addition, a decision to run the 2009 European Parliament elections under the Nice Treaty (which provides for a parliament of 736 members) would have meant that twelve member states had fewer MEPs than they would have had in elections under the Lisbon Treaty (which provides for a parliament of 754 members). An opinion poll by *The Irish Times*/TNS mrbi in November 2008 confirmed earlier surveys showing a clear division of opinion across social class. In the poll, people were asked how they would vote if the Lisbon Treaty was modified to allow Ireland to retain its EU commissioner, with other concerns on neutrality, abortion and taxation clarified in special declarations. This opinion poll showed that a second referendum on the Lisbon Treaty has a chance of being carried, subject to these reassurances.

The European Council meeting in December 2008 agreed that, provided the Lisbon Treaty enters into force, a decision will be taken to allow each member state to retain a commissioner. It also agreed to provide assurances to meet Irish concerns on taxation, neutrality and family, social and ethical issues. The Irish government agreed to hold a second Lisbon referendum before October 2009. Ireland's legal guarantees will be attached to the EU treaty allowing Croatia to join the EU in 2010.

The Houses of the Oireachtas and the EU

The government is kept fully aware of all developments in the EU affecting Ireland. Many important EU issues come before the full cabinet, either formally or informally, and occasionally the cabinet has set up a sub-committee to deal with a particular EU issue, for example on climate change. Since 1998 there has been a cabinet sub-committee on European affairs, which meets monthly. This is chaired by the Taoiseach, and includes the Ministers for Foreign Affairs, Agriculture and Enterprise, Trade and Employment. Other ministers attend when issues affecting their department arise.

The members of the Oireachtas are advised of such developments by the obligation on the government to report on these matters and by the existence of a joint Oireachtas committee to monitor this area. Many opportunities exist for them to discuss and debate EU policy issues. Such matters can be raised, and are raised, in both Houses of the Oireachtas, either in the form of special motions or on the adjournment. The annual debate on the estimate for the Department of Foreign Affairs, reports on meetings of the European Council and Dáil question time all provide opportunities for debate and discussion. Cromien (2000: 151) notes:

> While our political and administrative systems have been very successful in handling European matters, there has been one obvious deficiency. This is that it has proved very difficult to establish a way of appraising all the Community initiatives which are under consideration at any one time and deciding on an integrated national strategy for them, setting bargaining tactics and priorities, based on what is considered to be best for the country'.

The Oireachtas scrutiny arrangements have gone a long way to rectifying this deficiency. The Dáil and Seanad have developed more effective means of supervising the executive activities of government, particularly as regards the executive activities of the EU. There is almost unanimous agreement among member states that national parliaments should be given a greater role in the supervision of European legislation. Some member states have introduced more effective mechanisms to ensure that national parliaments are informed and consulted about developments in policy making at EU level. In addition, the Oireachtas has two parliamentary committees that scrutinise EU legislation on a continuous basis: the Joint Committee on European Scrutiny and the Joint Committee on European Affairs. The direct participation of Members of the European Parliament (MEPs) is very useful. These committees have made a significant contribution to maintaining democratic control and accountability of foreign policy in Ireland, making a valuable input to the examination of the key foreign policy and EU issues of the moment.

Members of the Houses of the Oireachtas play an international political role through their membership of bodies such as the Parliamentary Assembly of the Council of Europe, the Euro-Mediterranean Parliamentary Assembly, the Parliamentary Assembly of the Organization for Security and Cooperation in Europe, and the Parliamentary Assembly of the Western

Union. Members also maintain close working relationships with the EU institutions through their participation in the Conference of Speakers of European Union Parliaments and meetings of COSAC (Association of European Affairs Committees of EU National Parliaments and the EU Parliament), as well as other pan-European parliamentary roundtables and other contacts. An official of the Oireachtas is based in the European Parliament headquarters in Brussels and reports back on all relevant developments.

The Oireachtas Scrutiny System

The Oireachtas scrutiny system was introduced in July 2002 and subsequently put on a statutory footing by the European Union (Scrutiny) Act 2002. This act was enacted in the wake of the defeat of the first Nice referendum, amid increasing concerns about the democratic deficit associated with the enactment and transposition of EU legislation into domestic law. Speaking in a personal capacity to the Association of European Journalists on 22 November 2000, Attorney General Michael McDowell identified a 'democratic deficit' arising from the non-involvement of the Oireachtas in relation to EU law-making. He noted that 'unlike some other European member state parliaments, the Oireachtas does not, to any significant extent, claim for itself a right of input into forthcoming directives or regulations'. The 2002 act seeks to remedy these deficiencies and to promote the scrutiny in advance of proposed measures emanating from the EU. Subject to exceptions on confidentiality and urgency, the act provides that:

> Section 2(1): As soon as practicable after a proposed measure is presented by the Commission of the European Communities or initiated by a member state, as the case may be, the Minister shall cause a copy of the text concerned to be laid before each House of the Oireachtas together with a statement of the Minister outlining the content, purpose and likely implications for Ireland of the proposed measure and including such other information as he or she considers appropriate.
>
> Section 2(2): The Minister shall have regard to any recommendations made to him or her from time to time by either or both Houses of the Oireachtas or by a committee of either or both such Houses in relation to a proposed measure.

Section 2(5) of the act requires all government ministers to provide each House of the Oireachtas with a six-monthly report on progress in relation to measures, proposed measures and other relevant developments for which they have lead responsibility. These reports are submitted to the Oireachtas within four weeks of the period under review, i.e. at the end of July and the end of January each year. In this legislation, 'measure' means:

- A regulation or directive adopted under the Treaty establishing the European Community.
- A joint action adopted under Article 14 of the Treaty on European Union (TEU).
- A common position adopted under Article 15 of the TEU.
- Any other measure requiring the prior approval of both Houses of the Oireachtas pursuant to Article 29.4.6° of the Constitution.

The system requires departments to submit an information note to the Oireachtas Joint Committee on European Scrutiny in respect of any proposal for a regulation, directive or decision and for EU green and white papers. (A green paper is a discussion document and a white paper is a decision document). The committee may decide to call the relevant officials before it to give a presentation and answer questions on the proposal concerned. It may refer cases for further, more detailed scrutiny by the relevant sectoral committees of the Oireachtas, at which officials responsible for the dossier may be requested to appear. In addition, the Department of Foreign Affairs prepares a separate annual report.

Joint Committee on European Scrutiny

The growing importance of EU legislation has been recognised by the Oireachtas with the establishment of the Joint Committee on European Scrutiny, the watchdog for EU legislative action. The committee examines every item of proposed EU legislation, which can be up to 600 pieces of draft legislation in one year. It scrutinises any areas of proposed EU legislation that have serious implications for Ireland. Its detailed work covers the full spectrum of EU policy, including agriculture, fisheries, economic, finance, competition, regulation, environment, transport and external relations matters.

It is able to request the attendance of ministers and senior officials to answer questions on specific pieces of draft legislation and it invites the views of interest groups and other organisations affected by EU action. It also relies on the help of the specialised sectoral committees in examining proposals. The committee can make recommendations to the government, which is negotiating proposed EU legislation on Ireland's behalf, and alert the Oireachtas to any proposal that it believes might be detrimental to Ireland. It can also send its observations directly to the European Commission.

The committee receives all European Commission documents at the same time as national governments and the European Parliament. This gives parliaments an opportunity to influence EU policy making at a very early stage in the decision-making process. However, the work of the committee is reactive and primarily document-based with little opportunity to prioritise and select those proposals that are most relevant to Ireland.

Joint Committee on European Affairs

The Joint Committee on European Affairs examines the policies and legislative proposals that emanate from the EU including priority areas that are of special importance for Ireland. At the beginning of each year the committee draws up a work programme that sets out the main topics it will address during the coming year. An interim review of the work programme is undertaken after six months to ensure that all items listed are still relevant and are being progressed as planned and also to determine whether any further items need to be added to the work programme. The committee meets in public session on average once per week during the parliamentary calendar. Transcripts of the proceedings are available on the website after each meeting. The committee holds discussions and exchanges views with invited speakers on a wide range of subjects, including, for example, EU institutional reform, agriculture and trade policy, enlargement and the EU's relations with its immediate neighbours. It holds a monthly meeting with the Minister for Foreign Affairs or the Minister of State for European Affairs prior to each meeting of the General Affairs and External Relations Council in Brussels. In October 2007 Government Chief Whip Tom Kitt said that 'additional staffing, training and advisory supports will be put in place to assist the Joint Committee on European Affairs, to achieve and maintain the highest standards in quantity, quality and timeliness of their scrutiny and oversight of EU policymaking in Ireland and in Europe' (*Dáil Debates*, 11 October 2007, vol. 639, no. 3).

Sub-Committee on Ireland's Future in the European Union

In September 2008 Minister for Foreign Affairs Micheál Martin said that a national debate about Ireland's place in the EU would be the focus of a new parliamentary forum on Europe, which was being established with all-party support. The forum, which was a sub-committee of the Joint Committee on European Affairs called the Sub-Committee on Ireland's Future in the European Union, actively examined Ireland's position in the EU and the future direction of the union and reported to the government. The sub-committee, made up of twelve members representing the main political parties, was the first all-party committee in the history of the state to be webcast. Official figures show that the first seven meetings during October

2008 drew a total of 515 hits. The sub-committee heard evidence from 114 witnesses from more than forty different organisations.

The November 2008 report of the Oireachtas sub-committee found that Ireland's standing and influence in the EU had been diminished, which 'inhibits Ireland's ability to promote and defend its national interests at a European level'. Ireland could suffer serious economic consequences as a result of the No vote in the Lisbon Treaty referendum in June 2008. The majority report warned that other member states are likely to develop a mechanism to allow them to move forward – without Ireland – with the reforms envisaged by the treaty. The findings were endorsed by all the main parties in the Dáil, but Sinn Féin and independent Senator Ronan Mullen dissented from the main report.

The June 2008 referendum result could, the report said, damage the ability of Irish banks to raise funds in international money markets and make it more difficult to compete for foreign direct investment. The majority report said that it is for the government to devise a way of dealing with the consequences of the No vote, however, ratification by the Oireachtas would not be desirable and a solution involving Ireland leaving the EU was 'unthinkable'. It notes that 'it does appear that having a Commissioner nominated by the Government is a matter of national sensitivity. While this Commissioner would not represent the Irish Government within the Commission, he or she can act as a conduit for the Commission in understanding any sensitivities which are particular to Ireland. This serves both the Commission and Ireland'.

The report made recommendations to engage the public in EU issues including:

- Further emphasis on the use by citizens of the European Parliament's petitions committees.
- Further efforts are needed to ensure the Council of Ministers meets in public when legislating.
- European treaties should be accompanied by explanatory texts in clear and comprehensible terms.
- Strong and prominent coverage by the media of the institutions of the EU is vital to promote public understanding.
- Assuming the introduction of an Oireachtas digital television channel, the work of the Dáil on EU matters should get priority billing.
- Modern European history should be accorded a more prominent place on the school curriculum, with a greater emphasis on European studies.
- The teaching of European languages should be introduced into the primary school curriculum.
- A new body should be established to assist public understanding of the EU.

- Consideration should be given to the development of a cross-party foundation for the development of thought on EU issues.

To enhance the role of the Oireachtas in EU affairs the report recommended a series of reforms to address the 'accountability deficit in EU decisions by enhancing the role of national parliaments' to influence ministers and to hold them to account, to ensure that Oireachtas members are provided with all information available to the EU institutions and to provide a source of information and analysis for the public. Among the recommendations were:

- The introduction of a formal scrutiny reserve mechanism to provide more influence for the Oireachtas in the negotiating position of Irish ministers at council meetings.
- National parliaments should be formally consulted about the European Commission's annual policy strategy and legislative work programme before they are finalised.
- The introduction of a more structured arrangement for Oireachtas committees to meet with ministers before council meetings to consider the government's negotiating position on agenda items.
- Ministers should report back in writing to the appropriate Oireachtas committee on the outcome of the discussion and the specific decisions made.
- The Joint Committee on European Affairs should examine what measures could be put in place to enhance oversight of statutory instruments.
- Regulatory impact assessments, which have to be prepared for significant EU directives, regulations and secondary legislation, should be forwarded to Oireachtas committees when significant EU laws are being considered. The government should ensure that compliance with the Cabinet Handbook is addressed.
- The text of statutory instruments used to give effect to an EU law, or at least the heads of the instrument, should be circulated to Oireachtas members to increase transparency.
- A new panel should be constituted in the Seanad for a minimum of five senators to participate in the Oireachtas European committees, to build relations with the Irish MEPs, as well as directly with the EU institutions.
- The Oireachtas standing orders should be amended to implement these recommendations, to have more regular debates on EU legislative proposals, to enhance powers for Oireachtas committees, and to provide for participation by MEPs in debates and for informal monthly meetings by Irish MEPs and the European committees in the Oireachtas.

- The Oireachtas should establish its own EU information office.
- For a proposal to send Irish troops overseas on a peacekeeping mission, the triple lock for approval by a simple majority in the Dáil should be strengthened. Dáil Éireann should be required to have a 'super majority', where a two-thirds majority is needed for such a proposal to succeed.

The report also said that there are no legal obstacles to prevent Ireland from holding a second referendum on the Lisbon Treaty: 'No legal obstacle appears to exist to having a referendum either on precisely the same issue as that dealt with on June 12 [2008] or some variation thereof.'

Relations with the European Commission

On 1 September 2006 the European Commission began a new initiative of forwarding all draft EU legislative proposals, commission consultation documents and the commission's annual policy strategy and annual legislative and work programme directly to national parliaments upon publication. It forwards these documents to national parliaments at the same time as to the European Parliament and the Council of Ministers. In undertaking the direct transmission of documents to national parliaments, the commission invited them to provide their comments 'so as to improve the process of policy formulation'. The European Council called on the commission in 2006 to 'duly consider' comments by national parliaments – in particular with regard to the subsidiarity and proportionality principles (*Presidency Conclusions 15–16 June 2006*, 10633/1/06 REV 1, para. 37).

The aim of this initiative is to inform national parliaments promptly and fully of the European Commission's legislative and policy initiatives and to involve them purposefully in the EU decision-making process at an early stage. Commenting on this initiative, Commissioner and Vice-President Margot Wallström, responsible for relations with national parliaments, told the Joint Committee on European Affairs on 28 February 2008, 'A greater voice for parliaments is a greater voice for Europe's citizens. The Commission sends a signal to the national parliaments that we will inform them and we will listen to them. Their comments will be carefully considered.' This development has significantly increased the potential level of influence that national parliaments have on the EU policy development and legislative process. The Houses of the Oireachtas, through the Joint Committee on European Affairs and the Joint Committee on European Scrutiny, are using this opportunity to have greater input into the European decision-making process in a timely and ongoing basis by sending contributions to the commission on proposed EU legislation and policy formulation. This initiative has facilitated the Houses of the Oireachtas in contributing to European policy in the upstream stage of the commission's legislative programme.

The Government and the EU

In addition to the Taoiseach, three ministers in particular are intensively involved in EU business: Finance, Foreign Affairs and Agriculture. They are obliged frequently and regularly to attend meetings at EU headquarters in Brussels. Other ministers attend when their areas of responsibility are discussed at meetings of the Council of Ministers. Ministers with a good network of European contacts can identify problems early and build strategic alliances with like-minded colleagues. There are also opportunities for bilateral meetings with the relevant commissioner and a lot of business is done in the margins of council meetings in Brussels. Ireland has a good record in building strategic alliances.

As full members of the EU since 1973, Ireland, represented by ministers and civil servants, is involved in all the meetings that decide all the EU's policies. It is not a 'them and us' situation, but a partnership of neighbours. Like all partnerships, it works best as an open discussion and debate leading to well-founded decisions on how to tackle the real issues and challenges. Each member state faces the same challenges and through co-operation, collaboration, exchange of information and best practice great progress has been made. In agreeing on EU legislation, there is an emphasis on consensus and compromise. Like all partnerships it is based on mutual confidence, trust, personal contacts and formal, together with, informal, networks. Irish ministers and officials are particularly effective in operating and negotiating in this environment. McDonagh comments (1998: 32), 'Around the table there were many familiar faces. There always are at European Union meetings. For individuals closely involved in European negotiations, the process gets into the bloodstream like malaria. Once it's in the system, you never quite get rid of it. Figures from your past keep cropping up, often in new incarnations: in a new job, promoted or even serving a new master.'

In the context of enlargement, Eppink (2007: 327) comments, 'With a group of twenty-seven national leaders, it is much harder to develop the closer personal relationships which have worked so well in the past. Does the prime minister of Portugal know who the prime minister of Latvia is? Can the Irish premier spell the name of his Greek colleague? I fear not.' However, the enduring success of Irish diplomacy has been that it has managed to develop and maintain close personal relationships through knowing the key players, delivering on promises made and respecting the concerns and sensitivities of others. Council of Ministers meetings are regularly attended by Irish government ministers and senior officials. Ministers also meet in an informal session once during each presidency, if such a meeting is scheduled by the presidency.

Whilst the Department of Enterprise, Trade and Employment takes the lead role in the Competitiveness Council for example, given the cross-cutting nature of some of the issues involved, a number of other departments also make inputs to this council. The Department of Foreign Affairs co-ordinates, prepares and develops policy inputs to all council meetings on both horizontal and sectoral issues. In addition, the Competitiveness Council prepares a key issues paper for consideration by the Spring European Council attended by heads of state and government.

There are nine Council of Ministers configurations as follows:

- General Affairs and External Relations (including European security and defence policy and development co-operation).
- Economic and Financial Affairs (including budget).
- Justice and Home Affairs (including civil protection).
- Employment, Social Policy, Health and Consumer Affairs.
- Competitiveness (including internal market, industry and research).
- Transport, Telecommunications and Energy.
- Environment.
- Agriculture and Fisheries.
- Education, Youth and Culture.

The Minister of State for European Affairs accompanies the Minister for Foreign Affairs to the General Affairs and External Relations Council meetings. He or she also attends regular meetings with other European affairs ministers and represents Ireland at meetings and conferences of international organisations.

Ministers' and Secretaries' Group on EU Policy

Given the increasing importance of EU matters, a special committee known as the Ministers' and Secretaries' Group on EU Policy was set up in 1989. This committee is chaired by the Taoiseach. Originally it was concerned with issues relating to the internal market and structural funds, but its remit was later extended to include an examination of more general EU matters. The group is composed of the ministers and secretaries general of the key relevant departments. It co-ordinated Ireland's negotiating strategy on issues such as the intergovernmental conference and enlargement. It ensures a comprehensive and co-ordinated negotiating position on issues crucial to Ireland.

In advance of and during Ireland's 1990, 1996 and 2004 EU presidencies, overall national co-ordination of the presidency was overseen by the

Ministers' and Secretaries' Group. It specifically co-ordinates and ensures appropriate policy inputs at the highest level throughout the presidency. Its membership has included the Tánaiste, Minister for Foreign Affairs, Minister of State for European Affairs and the Ministers for Agriculture, Enterprise, Finance, Justice, and Social Affairs. Other ministers attend as and when required. The secretaries general of these departments, the permanent representative from Brussels, and other senior officials as necessary, also participate in the group.

In 2003 an Intergovernmental Conference Group was established, chaired by the Taoiseach, to advise on intergovernmental conference (IGC) issues during Ireland's presidency. The Minister for Foreign Affairs, the Minister of State for European Affairs and a number of senior officials from key departments, including the Department of the Taoiseach, attended meetings of this group.

The Public Service and the EU

The civil service has the main responsibility for the implementation in Ireland of directly applicable EU legislation. Adaptation to the demands of EU membership has been perhaps the greatest challenge faced by the Irish civil service since the foundation of the state. Not alone has participation in the EU increased the range and complexity of the issues facing Irish civil servants by the addition of a new dimension to national policy making, but membership has greatly increased the workload of the public service. Laffan (2000: 137) notes, 'membership of the EU altered the working environment of Irish diplomats and civil servants by breaking down the barrier between the internal and external, between domestic and the international'.

As more and more issues fall within the ambit of the EU, a wider range of civil and public service agencies has become involved. All government departments and state agencies have been affected to varying degrees by membership. In the civil service the impact has perhaps been greatest in the central Departments of Finance, Taoiseach and Foreign Affairs. Of the other departments that have responsibility for policy formulation and execution in specific sectors, the greatest impact has been on the Departments of Agriculture, the Environment and Enterprise. Laffan (2005: 174) notes that in some departments, for example Health, Education and Social Affairs, the national focus remains the primary area, whereas for others, for example Agriculture, Finance and Enterprise, EU policies are central to what they do.

The line government departments are all relatively autonomous of each other and tend to retain control of the Irish position on EU proposals within their own area of activity. The comparatively small size of the Irish civil service facilitates informal and loosely structured administrative arrangements for the co-ordination of EU business; this enables a less formal and less institutionalised approach that can respond quickly. The civil and public service also evaluates the impact of EU policy in Ireland across a broad range of economic and social spheres. Laffan (2000: 145) notes:

> . . . the informal and personal nature of Irish administration and the wider culture, makes the Irish system less bureaucratic and inert than the systems in other countries. The predominant mode is to allow those responsible get on with the job without embedding them in an elaborate system of committees and tortured discussions. The system is probably well adapted to the shifting sands of EU negotiations and provides the flexibility that is always necessary in negotiations.

Inter-Departmental Co-ordination

The original co-ordinating body at senior official level was known as the European Communities Committee and described accordingly in the 1973 Department of Foreign Affairs' EC co-ordination arrangements circular. It pre-dated EC membership. Until 1987 it was chaired by the Department of Foreign Affairs, and composed of assistant secretaries of the Departments of the Taoiseach, Foreign Affairs, Agriculture, Finance and other relevant departments. It was replaced in 1987 by a committee chaired by the minister of state at the Taoiseach's department with special responsibility for European affairs and for a number of years was named for the minister of state concerned – initially it was known as the 'Geoghegan-Quinn Committee' and later as the 'Kitt Committee'. The creation of a minister of state post for EU affairs is an indication of the importance of this area.

The Inter-Departmental Co-ordinating Committee on EU Affairs (ICCEUA) essentially has the same role and follows the same structure albeit with a change in nomenclature. The ICCEUA was established in 2002 and co-ordinates national policy across all government departments on EU policy matters. It ensures coherence in the Irish position and assists in the preparation of meetings of the cabinet sub-committee on European affairs. The secretariat of the ICCEUA is in the Department of the Taoiseach. The Inter-Departmental Co-ordinating Committee for the 2004 EU presidency and the Inter-Departmental Administrative Presidency Planning Group both reported to the ICCEUA.

Permanent Representation of Ireland to the EU

The Permanent Representation of Ireland to the EU (in effect, the Irish embassy to the EU) plays the central role in co-ordinating a consistent Irish position to the EU across all policy areas, and the majority of government departments have an attaché based there for this purpose. This is the nerve centre of Ireland's EU presence and is based in Brussels in the heart of the European district. It is the largest Irish overseas mission and arguably the most important. Cromien (2000: 149) notes that 'The centre of adminis-tration for many Irish civil servants has moved for at least part of each month nowadays to Brussels or Luxembourg'. The permanent representative (a senior ambassador) heads a large team of officials drawn from all government departments, who act as the eyes and ears of the domestic public administration system. These officials maintain contact with the European Commission on a daily basis, liaise with the committees of the European Parliament and service the continuous round of council meetings. Helga Schmid of the Council Secretariat told the Oireachtas Sub-Committee on Ireland's Future in the European Union on 11 November 2008:

> I note the work done by the diplomatic staff at the Irish permanent repre-sentation in Brussels. They advance and defend Ireland's interests with great skill in the policy debates we have on an almost daily basis in the various working groups, the Political and Security Committee, where I spend much time, and the Committee for Permanent Representatives. Their considered input is greatly appreciated. In consequence, Ireland has always punched above its weight.

The permanent representation is a mini-Irish civil and public service at the coalface of EU policy making. Promoting Ireland's interests is at the core of its activities. The representation has influenced policy proposals in ways favourable to Ireland and adapted quickly to the growing power of the European Parliament. Its task is to act as a channel of communication from the European Commission and the Council of Ministers and to advise the government and departments about the strategies of other member states. It co-ordinates a coherent Irish position across the entire public service. The permanent representation services the meetings of COREPER (Committee of Permanent Representatives) and of many working parties of the Council. Laffan (2008a) comments:

> Since 1973, the Irish government system has built up considerable expertise at playing the Brussels system. Although representing a small member state, Irish policy-makers have managed to navigate the multi-level politics of the European Union in a manner that has promoted Ireland's essential interests. This was achieved by a high level of prioritisation, sophisticated negotiation tactics, high-quality presidencies, not opposing for the sake of opposing and a problem-solving approach to negotiations.

The 2008 report of the Organisational Review Programme noted:

Historically Ireland's officials are valued as being effective negotiators and problem-solvers in the EU arena. However, there are some concerns now that Departments may be drifting down the scale of effectiveness at EU level . . . The change in the EU landscape – for instance, the enlargement of the EU to 27 Member States as well as the shifting focus of influence within the EU – mean that Ireland's relationships must keep in step. The management of this more complex environment brings with it an additional resource requirement, and it will be essential to manage this requirement in a more strategic manner, selecting and supporting appropriate staff and ensuring that they have the appropriate skillsets (such as negotiating and networking) as well as technical competence in relation to their functional areas. The management of the nexus between Departments and our representatives in the EU will also continue to be important. It will, in addition, be necessary to devote more energy to the European Parliament and to supporting Ireland's MEPs. One avenue, which helps give additional staff a good understanding of the operation of the EU institutions, is the placement of Irish civil servants as National Experts within the institutions, and Departments should consider a managed strategic programme of placement and where necessary suitable support of staff (Department of the Taoiseach 2008c: 74–75).

Department of Foreign Affairs

The primary function of the Department of Foreign Affairs is to advise the government on Ireland's external relations and to act as the channel of official communication with foreign governments and international organisations. Diplomacy is a political art. Forging strategic alliances and compromises is an essential component of statecraft. A cabinet decision in 1973 gave the department primary responsibility for overseeing day-to-day European co-ordination. The role of the department has been transformed by EU membership and, in addition to co-ordination, it acts as custodian of Ireland's presence in the EU system. It is as a conduit between Dublin and Brussels. It does not get involved in all the details of domestic policy; rather it maintains a strategic overview and ensures that domestic departments adequately service meetings in Brussels and that policy developments in one sector do not impinge on general policy priorities.

The Department of Foreign Affairs takes the lead substantive respon - sibility for matters relating to the Common Foreign and Security Policy; the institutional development of the EU, including treaty reform; and the political aspects of external relations issues such as enlargement. Laffan (1996: 297) comments that 'Membership of the Community has blurred the distinction between foreign and domestic affairs and has meant that the Department of Foreign Affairs is more intensely involved in domestic issues than at any stage in the Department's history'. The department integrates European business, co-ordinates an overall Irish position when several departments are involved, maintains the priorities established between the various departments and ensures that policy remains coherent. It also acts as facilitator in disagreements between other departments over areas of competence. Much of the strength of Irish public administration in response to the requirements of EU membership has resided in its use of centralisation (Laffan 2001: 88) and the Department of Foreign Affairs has facilitated this.

The department plays a pivotal role in Irish policy on European issues and in the domestic impact of European policies. It provides an overview of EU developments from a political and institutional perspective, as well as utilising the network of embassies in EU countries, and further afield, as a source of information and briefing. Ireland's diplomatic network consists of seventy-five missions abroad, and offices in Armagh and Belfast. The Minister for Foreign Affairs has the overall responsibility for providing impetus and co-ordination to the development of policy on the EU. The department administers the Communicating Europe Initiative, which promotes public awareness of the EU and provides grants to groups developing information initiatives on the EU and its impact on citizens.

Section 5 of the European Union (Scrutiny) Act 2002 requires the government to report once a year to the Oireachtas on developments in the EU over the course of the preceding calendar year. The report is compiled by the department on the basis of submissions received from all departments.

Department of the Taoiseach

The growing role of the Department of the Taoiseach reflects the importance of the European Council, which is the meeting of EU leaders and is often called the EU summit. Some four times a year the heads of state and government of the member states and the President of the European Commission assemble at a summit meeting to discuss EU co-operation. The Department of the Taoiseach takes an active interest in EU matters. It takes a strategic focus on developments at EU level and involves itself when critical national issues are on the table. It chairs ad hoc inter-departmental groups as required. In 2003, for example, the department chaired groups on the EU language regime and enlargement. In addition, it participates in a range of groups chaired by the Departments of Foreign Affairs, Finance and Enterprise, including groups on the presidency, the initiative for growth, communicating Europe, Oireachtas scrutiny and the Asia strategy.

Department of Finance

The Department of Finance played a central role in negotiating Ireland's entry into the EC, and since the beginning it has had a large involvement with

European matters. While its co-ordinating role was gradually taken over by the Department of Foreign Affairs in the late 1970s, it continues to occupy a unique and prominent position in that it must be consulted by all other departments on proposals that have expenditure implications. However, it does not have overriding authority among government departments, and although it can advise, support and persuade, it cannot order; disagreements between departments have to be resolved at cabinet level.

The Department of Finance has retained responsibility for the important major sources of funds, negotiations on the EU budget, together with control of the central economic issues such as Ireland's financial contributions, economic and monetary union, financial regulation and monetary policy, economic co-ordination and the financial aspects of agriculture policy. Since 1997 Ireland has been a founder member of the economic and monetary union and subsequent eurozone, which provides the foundation for long-term economic stability. Peter Brennan (2008: 393) notes that in the negotiations on the EU financial perspectives, 'Ireland's negotiating position was coordinated by a small group of the five departments most concerned, including Foreign Affairs, Agriculture and Food, and Enterprise, Trade and Employment, with an Assistant Secretary from the Department of Finance in the chair. This group analysed material emanating from the Commission and intelligence concerning the position of other member states.'

Departmental EU Units

Most government departments have a division or unit dedicated to dealing with EU matters. Many departments have internal cross-divisional committees that meet regularly to discuss key EU policy issues of relevance to the department. The EU affairs division or unit in departments usually provides the secretariat to the committee. At the beginning of each year the secretariat presents a key departmental EU programme document based on the purposed programme for incoming EU presidencies, for agreement by the management committee for the forthcoming year. The secretariat also provides the management committee with a mid-year report on the basis of current EU priorities, having regard to incoming presidency priorities.

The EU units monitor and report on the transposition of EU directives falling under the aegis of the department. Timely transposition of EU directives is essential for good governance and national transposition. Performance is measured twice yearly by the European Commission's Internal Market Scoreboard. Regular reports on the transposition record of each department as well as infringement cases taken against Ireland are conveyed to the Inter-Departmental Co-ordinating Committee on EU Affairs. Government departments transmit details of directives transposed by departments to the European Commission via the NEM (national execution measures) database following advertisement in *Iris Oifigiúil*. Directives are also monitored by the EU returns database, which is overseen by the Department of the Taoiseach.

Irish Regions Office

The Irish Regions Office (IRO) was established in 2000, with the support of the Department of the Environment, Heritage and Local Government, as a Brussels-based resource for the Irish members of the Committee of the Regions (CoR) and their regional authorities. CoR, based in Brussels, was established in 1994 as a consultative body to provide representatives of local and regional government with a voice at the heart of the EU. This is particularly important as much of the legislation originating in the EU is implemented by local authorities. The Minister for the Environment, Heritage and Local Government nominates the nine Irish members and nine alternates on behalf of the government. Nominations take account of geographical, gender and political considerations, with all regional authorities represented. All Irish members are elected members of their local authority and automatically become members of their regional authority.

The activities of the office have been expanded through a collaboration of the Association of Irish Regions and county and city managers to provide a wider range of services to Irish local and regional authorities. The key functions of the office include acting as a source of EU information for sub-national government in Ireland; representing the views of Irish sub-national government at EU level; providing general executive support to, and acting as a contact point for, elected representatives and officials of sub-national authorities in Ireland in relation to EU matters; and assisting local and regional authorities with the development of EU projects.

Defence Forces

The EU has the potential to play an increasing role in responding to emergency crises, in providing humanitarian relief and in supporting the maintenance of international peace and security in furtherance of the aims of the United Nations and the UN Charter. Ireland has actively participated in missions operating under a United Nations (UN) mandate and led by the EU. The ambition of the EU to be able to respond rapidly to emerging crises is, and continues to be, a key objective of the development of the European Security and Defence Policy. The tasks to be carried out under this policy (the so-called Petersberg tasks) are defined in the Amsterdam Treaty as 'humanitarian and rescue tasks, peacekeeping tasks and tasks of combat forces in crisis management, including peacemaking'. Ireland's participation was endorsed and supported in successive referendums on the Maastricht, Amsterdam and Nice Treaties. This participation in EU battlegroups is in line with Ireland's traditional policy of military neutrality and firm support for the UN. The 'triple lock' requirements of UN mandate, government and Dáil approval remain firmly in place.

Speaking at McKee Barracks, Dublin on 14 October 2004 then UN Secretary-General, Kofi Annan, specifically stressed how important strengthened EU capacities, in particular rapid-deployment capabilities, are to the UN. From 1 January 2008 Irish members of the Permanent Defence Forces (Óglaigh an hÉireann) went on standby as members of an EU battlegroup. Ireland is part of the Nordic battlegroup, which comprises Sweden, as framework nation, along with troops from Norway, Finland and Estonia. The purpose of a battlegroup is to provide a standby capability to address rapidly escalating crises or humanitarian disasters. The term 'battlegroup' itself can be misleading. It is a standard, technical military term to describe a coherent military force capable of stand-alone operations. In the case of an EU battlegroup, it means a force of approximately 1,500 personnel that can deploy at five to ten days' notice for a period of between 30 and 120 days.

Ireland's participation in the Nordic battlegroup had additional significance as 2008 marked the fiftieth anniversary of Ireland's first UN peacekeeping mission in 1958. Over the course of those fifty years Irish troops performed more than 56,000 tours of duty on fifty-eight UN peace-support operations worldwide. In 2008 over 800 members of the Permanent Defence Forces served with courage and commitment on twelve different missions in some of the world's most difficult trouble spots.

Also in January 2008 EU Foreign Ministers voted to approve a 3,700-strong UN-mandated operation in Chad. Under the overall command of Deputy Chief-of-Staff of the Irish Defence Forces, Lieutenant General Patrick Nash (Operational Commander EUFOR – EU Force – Chad and Central African Republic), who is based in Paris, its purpose is to protect over 200,000 civilians, aid workers and refugees fleeing the conflicts in neighbouring Darfur and the Central African Republic. There were troops from fourteen nations on the ground. Ireland made a significant contribution of 350 troops to the overall force, including special forces from the Army Ranger Wing that were deployed in the vanguard.

UN Security Council Resolution 1778 of 25 September 2007 was unanimously approved under chapter seven of the UN Charter and authorises 'all necessary measures' to achieve the mandated tasks. This means that the force deployed peace-enforcement troops on behalf of the EU.

Military Neutrality

The Irish people have a deep attachment to military neutrality. Ireland's stance of military neutrality has been significant for the Irish public and is embedded in national political culture. Neutrality is seen as a symbol of national identity and an expression of anti-militarism.

The essence of neutrality is not being involved in wars between other countries. A state whose neutrality is legally recognised has a right to have its integrity respected by other states. It must, in turn, perform certain neutrality duties: it must deny the use of its national territory (including airspace and territorial waters), by force if necessary, to all belligerents; it must give no support to belligerents, although normal trade can continue; and it must apply impartially the rules of neutrality under international law.

In contrast with, for example, Austrian, Swedish or Swiss neutrality, Irish neutrality is not enshrined in the Constitution, in the law or in an international agreement. However, the state 'affirms its devotion to the ideal of peace and friendly cooperation among nations founded on international justice and morality' (Article 29.1). It 'affirms its adherence to the principle of the pacific settlement of international disputes by international arbitration or judicial determination' (Article 29.2). Furthermore, the maintenance of foreign forces or bases is prohibited by Article 15.6.2°, 'No military or armed force, other than a military or armed force raised and maintained by the Oireachtas, shall be raised or maintained for any purpose whatever'. Article 28.3.1° clearly provides that 'War shall not be declared and the State shall not participate in any war save with the assent of Dáil Éireann'. Article 29.4.9° provides that 'The State shall not adopt a decision taken by the European Council to establish a common defence pursuant to Article 1.2 of the [Nice] Treaty referred to in subsection 7° of this section where that common defence would include the State'.

The Constitution Review Group (1996: 93) rejected a suggestion that the policy of military neutrality should be enshrined in the Constitution. The All-Party Oireachtas Committee on the Constitution (2003: 15) notes that 'The issue of neutrality assumed a greater importance with the defeat of the first Nice referendum on 7 June 2001 when an opinion survey taken afterwards showed that it was the principle concern of those voting against the treaty'. In the second Nice referendum, which was approved by the people, the amendment included the following provision: '9° The State shall not adopt a decision taken by the European Council to establish a common defence pursuant to Article 1.2 of the Treaty referred to in subsection 7° of this section where that common defence would include the State.'

Ireland's security concerns have been accommodated with sensitivity on the part of the other EU member states. The contours of the European

Defence and Security Policy as it has developed to date are in line with traditional Irish stances. As then EU Commissioner for External Relations, Chris Patten, said in an interview in *The Irish Times* on 18 February 2002, 'what we are speaking about in the Petersberg tasks is something that is clearly within the tradition of Irish foreign policy'. The Petersberg tasks are a list of military and security priorities incorporated within the European Security and Defence Policy signed on 19 June 1992, near Bonn, Germany. They are designed as an instrument to equip the EU to pursue more effectively its foreign policy objectives of promoting peace, stability and security, conflict prevention and resolution, humanitarian relief and human rights protection. In this context, the protections for Ireland's traditional security and defence policy stand on their own merits. The changing security environment has pushed back the case for the EU developing a traditional defence capacity.

The prospective Lisbon Treaty will have no effect on Ireland's traditional policy of military neutrality. The 2008 act for the referendum on the Lisbon Treaty retains the constitutional prohibition on participation in an EU common defence, should one ever be proposed. In addition, the treaty retains the provision that the EU's security and defence policy 'shall not prejudice the specific character of the security and defence policy of certain Member States', a formulation originally proposed by Ireland to protect its particular position. Unanimity also remains the rule for decision making on security and defence issues within the EU, including in respect of the launch of any crisis management mission.

A Solidarity Clause relates to circumstances where an EU member state is the object of a terrorist attack or the victim of a natural or man-made disaster. In responding to a request from such a member state, it would be for Ireland to determine the nature of the response it might make, in accordance with the Irish constitutional and legal framework.

The EU Presidency System

The presidency of the Council of Ministers is held by a different member state every six months, according to an agreed rotation. Although the presidency is not a formal institution of the EU, the office has grown in political importance over the years and is highly prized by the member states for the prestige it confers on the holder. It is an important role which carries fundamental responsibilities for the conduct of the EU's affairs. It fosters a sense of belonging and the urge to excel on the part of those holding office. The office has evolved from passively presiding over council meetings to providing proactive leadership in shaping the internal work programme and managing external relations. The Lisbon Treaty sought to provide greater continuity by replacing this system with an eighteen-month rotating presidency shared by three member states. The exception would be the Foreign Affairs formation in the Council of Ministers, which would be chaired by a newly created post of High Representative for Foreign Affairs and Security Policy.

The successful organisation of an EU presidency is a formidable challenge for any member state. The six-month rotating presidency is the engine that drives the EU. It sets the EU priorities, steers through a raft of new legislation and becomes the principal broker in international negotiations in many areas. The key to an effective EU presidency is the ability to separate the European interest from the national interest. The most successful EU presidencies tend not to lead from the front but rather act behind the scenes as good conciliators. Small member states tend to run good presidencies, even though they represent a greater administrative challenge in these countries. Hayes-Renshaw and Wallace (2006: 136) note that 'In recent years, some of the most effective presidencies have been exercised by small member states (for example, Denmark in the second half of 2002, and Ireland in the first half of 2004)'.

Successive Irish governments have given the EU presidency the highest political priority, with the government setting out its objectives at an early stage. Ireland has held a number of very successful EU presidencies. During Ireland's 2004 EU presidency, partnership, which goes to the heart of Ireland's approach to the EU, was reflected in its theme: 'Europeans – Working Together'. This theme embodied the shared vision of the people of Europe working collectively for common objectives. The 2004 EU presidency was the sixth held by Ireland. Since Ireland's previous presidency in 1996 there was a significant increase in the workload, notably in the areas of Common Foreign and Security Policy and Justice and Home Affairs. Ireland was also the first member state to preside over an enlarged union of twenty-five member states as ten states joined during the term. There were 230 meetings, including ministerial-level meetings, held in Ireland during the presidency (reply to a parliamentary question on 24 June 2004). There were thirty-six ministerial summit meetings held during the presidency (reply to a parliamentary question on 14 October 2004).

An inter-departmental planning group was concerned with the operational and logistical aspects of the presidency. The Centre for Management and Organisation Development in the Department of Finance did a training-needs analysis and arranged a series of specialist seminars on the EU. The Irish EU Presidency website was launched in December 2003 and proved very successful, receiving, in total, over 47 million hits (which equated to over 250,000 visits per day), most of which came from outside Ireland.

The role of the Taoiseach during a presidency is of paramount importance. During the 2004 EU presidency Taoiseach Bertie Ahern travelled twice to each of the other twenty-six capitals to get unanimous agreement on the proposed European Constitution. Norman (2005: 287) notes that 'the presidency embarked on an intense and wide-ranging series of contacts with all of the EU's existing, acceding and candidate states, as well as with the European Commission and Parliament. Some of the contacts were informal talks at the highest level'. During this presidency successful summits were also held with the United States, Russia, Canada, Japan, Switzerland and the countries of Latin America and the Caribbean. An EU–US Summit at Dromoland Castle, County Clare focused on revitalising transatlantic integration and growth. In addition, 3,000 working group meetings took place in Brussels between January and June 2004, which were chaired by Irish officials.

Agreement on the European Constitution, the formal accession of ten new member states, efforts to revitalise the European economy and the EU's external relations, particularly the strengthening of transatlantic relations, were numbered among the successes of Ireland's 2004 EU presidency – successes which would not have been possible without collaborative effort. Particular credit was accorded to the excellent negotiating skills and quiet diplomacy of then Taoiseach Bertie Ahern and his team of officials. Dur and Mateo (2008) note that the success of the Irish EU presidency on the European Constitution was due to Ireland's neutrality on the most controversial issues under negotiation, enabling it to function as an effective mediator in these negotiations.

The sixth Irish presidency of the EU in 2004 is the latest in a series of successful Irish presidencies over two decades. For a smaller member state like Ireland, the presidency provides a valuable opportunity to play a major international role not only with/on behalf of the EU and other member states but on the wider world stage.

The role of the Minister for Foreign Affairs and the part played by the Department of Foreign Affairs is of crucial importance to a successful EU presidency. In reply to a parliamentary question on 27 January 2004 the minister noted that 'In addition to the work at the Department's headquarters and the permanent representation in Brussels, our other missions abroad also have important Presidency responsibilities. Our missions in third countries, for example, will chair meetings of the EU member state representatives in their countries of accreditation and will act on behalf of the EU in relations with their host Governments' (*Dáil Debates*, 27 January 2008, vol. 578, no. 4).

Ireland will next assume the EU presidency in January 2013 when, if the new arrangements are implemented, its team members will be Lithuania and Greece.

Rural Development Groups

The government made €425 million available in 2008 in a new Rural Development Programme. The programme is operated through the Department of Community, Rural and Gaeltacht Affairs and administered through local LEADER development groups. It covers quality of life in rural areas and diversification of the rural economy. The Rural Development Programme for Ireland 2007–2013 is funded through €234 million from the EU and €191 million from the Irish taxpayer. The package was three times larger than the previous programme (2000–2006) and carried enhanced rates of aid for some capital projects, which increased from 50 per cent to 75 per cent. The package allowed local action groups to facilitate the continued development of rural communities across Ireland. The activities involved are varied and include diversification into non-agricultural activities, support for business creation, encouragement of tourism activities, basic services for the economy and rural population, village renewal and development, conservation and upgrading of the rural heritage, training and information.

Communicating about the European Union

Laffan (2005: 172) argues that the defeat in June 2001 of the first Nice Treaty referendum was a critical juncture in Ireland's management of European affairs that led to pressures on the Irish administrative and political system to adapt to the new circumstances. The National Forum on Europe was established in October 2001 to promote a national debate on the EU, on its future and on Ireland's role in it. The forum's purpose is not to advocate or promote a particular course of action. It is a politically neutral public space within which political views and analyses of all shades can be put forward on the EU, and on Ireland in the EU. Membership of the forum includes members of the Oireachtas and people nominated by parties represented in the Oireachtas; there is also provision for representatives of a whole range of other civic alliances and interest groups to take part in the work of the forum and to have a full role in its debates. There is provision for members and alternate members. The allocation of seats in the forum for its Oireachtas members takes into account the number of seats won and the percentage of first preference votes achieved in the general election; proportionately, the allocation is to the benefit of the smaller parties and groups. Irish MEPs, from north and south, have the right of attendance and participation, within agreed procedures. Speaking to a joint meeting of the Joint Committee on European Scrutiny and the Joint Committee on European Affairs on 3 July 2008, Minister for Foreign Affairs Micheál Martin noted in relation to meetings of the forum, 'I suspect the suggestion is that we have to look at alternative ways of getting people involved. It is usually the political elite who attend these meetings.' This form was closed in April 2009.

Minister Martin also noted that 'Ireland must avoid doing a crash course on Europe every time there is a referendum. There must be an ongoing communication effort as a society to become far more engaged with what is happening in Europe because it does affect us'. The EU needs to be more transparent in its day-to-day business, for example with a more open election of the President of the European Commission, by allowing citizens to see how the Council of Ministers amends EU laws and by allowing national parliaments to scrutinise all EU laws. The result of the referenda on the draft constitutional treaty in France and the Netherlands in 2005 and on the Lisbon Treaty in Ireland in 2008 showed that the European project has simply not convinced its citizens in sufficient numbers that it makes enough of a positive difference to their lives to warrant their endorsement. That has long been one of the greatest challenges for the EU. The results of these referenda show that this issue is getting bigger, not smaller. There has been much institutional introspection and the creation of an impenetrable jungle of jargon. The European Commission has been trying in recent years to improve understanding of the activities of the EU. This is seen as a means of bringing the public closer to the EU's institutions and a way of stimulating a more informed and involved debate on EU policy. Additional steps have been taken to improve access to websites and databases; the relay network of information on the EU; the listing of documents on general topics in the official journal each week; and the publication of work schedules and legislative programmes.

Early warning of the thinking of the European Commission has been one of the criteria for successfully influencing policy and subsequent decisions, whether on the content of legislation or on the acquisition of funds and contracts, and the EU institutions have introduced a greater degree of transparency relating to the legislative process. The impact of EU legislation on domestic affairs is so vast that national governments alone cannot act as gatekeepers between national and supranational politics. Therefore, influence, goodwill and the perception of each country in Brussels by its partners is of paramount importance. Ireland faces challenges in this regard. Peter Brennan (2008: 272) notes in relation to the Regional Aid Guidelines (RAGs) approved in Brussels in 1999 that 'the mood in Brussels was so anti-Ireland that no effort would have persuaded the Commission to give Ireland much leeway. It could be said that the days of giving Ireland the benefit of the doubt at EU negotiations ended with the RAGs'. More recently, and particularly following the 2008 Lisbon Treaty referendum, these challenges have increased. Catherine Day, Secretary General of the European

Commission, told the Oireachtas Sub-Committee on Ireland's Future in the European Union on 22 October 2008:

> I will give my very honest assessment of what has happened. Ireland's image in the European Union and beyond has been tarnished by the "No" vote. I can see every day that it has reduced our ability to shape and influence events in the European Union. Other European states tend to view us now only through the prism of the Lisbon treaty. Whenever Ireland raises its flag at a meeting one can see all the other member states remembering what happened in regard to the Lisbon treaty and wondering what the Irish members will say. It has had an effect. I do not believe Ireland's image has been tarnished irrevocably . . . It is a source of great personal pride to me to see just how many Irish people there are at senior levels in the Commission. We are certainly punching way above our weight. We have three directors-general. Of the 27 heads of cabinet, three are Irish . . . It is also the case that it is more difficult for Ireland to contribute positively and express concern in the many debates that take place every day in the European decision-making machinery. They have to weigh more carefully now when Ireland wants to put its hand up and say, "Well, I am sorry, we don't agree with this." Immediately, the mood in any committee meeting is that the Irish are being difficult again.

Connolly (2008) reports that MEPs have experienced a similar reaction. She notes that 'Irish MEPs and diplomats lobbying for Ireland in Europe are being cold-shouldered in the wake of the rejection of the Lisbon Treaty earlier this year, according to MEPs'. However, Foreign Minister Micheál Martin told the Oireachtas Sub-Committee on Ireland's Future in the European Union on 11 November 2008 that there was 'no question' of Ireland's EU partners putting pressure on the government and that 'There is an appreciation that the result of the referendum reflected serious and genuinely held concerns, and that it has consequences not just for Ireland, but for the EU as a whole. It is also clear that we need to communicate more effectively with the Irish people about the work the EU does on their behalf and the very real benefits this confers'. The need for continuous communication on the benefits of Europe and the syndrome of democratic deficit in the EU has a number of features, including poor public identification with Europe; lack of popular participation in decision making; limited understanding of the institutions and policies of the EU; and inadequate dissemination of information. In addition, there is a tendency to blame Brussels for unpopular measures, for example the nitrates directive, the criminalisation of fishing offences, water charges for schools, excessive form filling for farmers and the ending of domestic turf cutting, so much a part of life in the West of Ireland.

The offices of the European Parliament and of the European Commission in the member states are at the sharp end of information and communication.

They provide information and documentation to the general public about developments in the EU. They engage with all sectors of the media through regular personal interaction, advertisements, press releases and information visits. They also provide feedback to the EU institutions to enable them to produce material to meet an individual state's needs and circumstances. The opening of the European Public Information Centre as a one-stop shop for all kinds of information on Europe, the opening of Info Points about Europe around the country and the operation of a mobile information unit have brought a broad range of European information to a much wider audience. Councillor Seamus Murray (Meath County Council and the Mid-East Regional Authority) (2006) notes:

> Clearly each Irish representative in the EU has their own remit and responsibilities and that is how it should be. But that brings me to my final theme – the benefits of a more systematic approach to Irish participation in the EU. Communication is not a one-way process and must not focus only on how Brussels can reach out to citizens. It must also be about how citizens and the authorities here that represent them, can interact with and influence what happens in the EU . . .
>
> By way of example, I refer to the Scotland House model in Brussels. This is a partnership of public, private and voluntary bodies that combine to provide a central point of contact, information and analysis for Scottish interests and at the same time, provides a high profile for Scotland in Brussels and a focal point for Scottish activities in the EU capital.
>
> This is a model from which Ireland may learn.

Languages

There are twenty-three official languages in the EU: Bulgarian, Czech, Danish, Dutch, English, Estonian, Finnish, French, German, Greek, Hungarian, Irish, Italian, Latvian, Lithuanian, Maltese, Polish, Portuguese, Romanian, Slovak, Slovene, Spanish and Swedish. All legislation is published simultaneously in all the official languages (except Irish). Private citizens have the right to address the EU institutions in one of the official languages and to receive a reply in the same language.

On 24 November 2004 the Irish government tabled a proposal in Brussels seeking official and working status in the EU for the Irish language. Up to that point Irish had been accorded the status of a treaty language. (This derives from the fact that the treaties are in Irish and that, in the treaties, Irish is listed as one of the languages in which the text is authentic.) The government's proposal required the unanimous support of member states and this was given by the General Affairs and External Relations Council on 13 June 2005 after a sustained lobbying campaign by the Irish government and officials. Irish became an official and working language of the EU on 1 January 2007. Key EU regulations (those adopted jointly by the Council of Ministers and the European Parliament) are translated into Irish. The possibility of extending the range of documents to be translated into Irish will be the subject of a review to take place not later than the end of 2010. Interpretation from Irish will be provided on request at ministerial meetings and at the European Parliament. Certain other consequences will also flow from this decision, including Irish being one of the languages taken into account for the purposes of recruitment to, and promotion within, the EU institutions.

Accessing Documents

The EU's rules on openness and transparency give citizens the right of access to any official documents of the European Parliament, the Council of Ministers and the European Commission that are not classified as secret. If an EU institution receives a request to access an official document it must be dealt with within fifteen days. If the official document is not released, the institution is obliged to give reasons for its decision and the decision must be open to appeal. According to a ruling in the Court of First Instance and in the Court of Justice, the non-secret parts of an official document partially classified as secret must be released.

Conclusion

In 1946 Winston Churchill said that 'We must build a kind of United States of Europe . . . The structure of the United States of Europe will be such as to make the material strength of a single State less important. Small nations will count as much as large ones and gain their honour by a contribution to the common cause. If at first all states of Europe are not willing to join the union, we must nevertheless proceed to assemble and combine those who will and those who can'. At a meeting of the American Bar Association in the Law Society of Ireland on 21 July 2000 Mary Harney, speaking as Minister for Enterprise, Trade and Employment said, 'As Irish people our relationships with the United States and the European Union are complex. Geographically we are closer to Berlin than Boston. Spiritually we are probably a lot closer to Boston than Berlin.' The trends of internationalisation, globalisation, competition, liberalisation and harmonisation will continue to require constant reappraisal and review of the role, the functions and the procedures of public sector organisations.

Ireland has been a full participant in the process of European integration for over a generation. Its involvement has always been about more than free trade and financial transfers, important as they may be. It has benefited enormously from EU membership, and has at the same time contributed constructively to the EU's development. The period of Ireland's membership of the EU has coincided with an increase in national self-confidence, a strengthening of Irish identity and an increase in Ireland's international profile.

In Ireland the positive lessons of EU membership were rapidly absorbed, along with the experience of higher agricultural prices, a growing volume of transfers and the diversification of trade and diplomacy away from Britain. In recent years EU membership has come to be seen as part of an emancipating process for the Irish state and Irish society. Ireland has been fairly treated in terms of representation within the institutions and the benefits from common policies such as the Common Agricultural Policy and cohesion.

The decision to join with Europe was one of the defining moments in the history of modern Ireland. The Ireland that voted to join in 1972 was one of the poorest countries in western Europe. Given the unprecedented growth in the Irish economy since joining the EEC, one might have expected that the Irish people would feel that their economic future would be more secure at the heart of Europe. However, in the June 2008 referendum, economic uncertainty prompted many people to pull back from the EU, rather than embracing further integration. It would be wrong to interpret this as an anti-EU membership vote and successive Eurobarometer surveys have shown widespread support in Irish public opinion for Ireland's membership of the EU. Finding a solution to this conundrum is the biggest challenge facing the political and administrative system and its outcome is a matter of crucial economic and political significance for the people of Ireland.

An indication of the direction in which matters might move was provided by the widely respected Luxembourg Premier Jean-Claude Juncker, 'I am not in favour of a two-speed Europe. I would like the European Union to move ahead with twenty-seven member states on board in the same direction having the same ambitions – but if this [becomes] no longer possible, we don't have any choice other than a two-speed Europe' (Barrett 2008b). Ireland has opposed the concept of a two-speed EU, fearing that it will be relegated to the sidelines. At the time of writing, the latest opinion poll (*The Irish Times*/TNS mrbi 18 May 2009) on the Lisbon Treaty indicates that the electorate are increasingly likely to deliver a 'Yes' vote second time around, with 52 per cent in favour and 29 per cent against. The economic downturn has clearly encouraged the shift in public opinion. Close to 80 per cent of voters thought it better to be part of the EU in the current economic situation. The European Council in June 2009 is expected to give the necessary firm commitments on taxation, neutrality and abortion. The risk is that the long-term consequence of the double Nice and Lisbon votes is that the electorate may feel bruised and treated as recalcitrant until the 'correct' result is delivered.

As part of its EU membership Ireland has negotiated opt-out (and indeed opt-in) arrangements to EU integration in areas such as justice, police co-operation and immigration. Specific safeguards have been obtained for Irish positions in the areas of family law and defence. Clearly, EU membership is vital to Ireland's strategic national interest and the Irish people strongly favour its continuation. In this context experts have suggested that it might be timely to establish with greater certainty the aspects of EU treaties that actually have constitutional implications.

Web Resources

Council of Europe Parliamentary Assembly (PACE) at www.assembly.coe.int
Council of the European Union at http://ue.eu.int
Defence Forces at www.military.ie
Department of Community, Rural and Gaeltacht Affairs at www.pobail.ie
Department of Foreign Affairs at www.dfa.ie
European Central Bank at www.ecb.int
European Commission at www.ec.europa.eu
European Commission Representation in Ireland at www.euireland.ie
European Court of Auditors at http://eca.europa.eu
European Investment Bank at www.eib.org
European Ombudsman at www.euro-ombudsman.eu.int
European Parliament at www.europarl.europa.eu
European Parliament Office in Ireland at www.europarl.ie
European Union at www.europa.eu.int
Irish Regions Office, Brussels at www.iro.ie
Parliamentary Assembly of the Organization for Security and Co-operation in Europe (OSCE) at www.oscepa.org

13

THE MANAGEMENT OF GOVERNMENT

As a small open economy, with a reliance on open-trading markets, inward investment and information technology, Ireland has been seen, until relatively recently, as the model of a globalisation success story. Always at a crossroads culturally and through its huge migration overseas and significant immigration, Ireland has transformed itself from the 'valley of the squinting windows' to the most globalised economy in the world. The political and administrative systems played a central role in this process. As T.K. Whitaker (1973: 415), the architect of the post-1958 turn towards the outside world and foreign investment, put it at the time, 'there is really no choice for a country wishing to keep pace materially with the rest of Europe'. While globalisation has initially been kind to Ireland, there are more challenging times ahead for the political and administrative systems in driving change and managing the new realities.

People are long accustomed to hearing about the need for change in the public service. There have been frequent and increasingly persistent calls, from within and outside the public service, for public service reform. Those calls continue to grow in volume as the cost of maintaining public services increases and as greater emphasis is placed on value for money and public accountability. In Ireland, therefore, there is an ongoing programme of modernisation in the public service.

New Challenges

Growing Ireland

Ireland has the fastest-growing population in the European Union, driven mainly by high levels of immigration. From 1995 to 2005 Ireland experienced a significant population growth rate of 14.7 per cent. According to the Central Statistics Office (2008b), the overall population is estimated to have increased by more than 100,000 in the space of the year to April 2008, bringing the overall number of people living in Ireland to 4.4 million – the highest level since 1861. Ireland's population is set to increase by 52 per cent to 6.7 million by 2050, according to official forecasts compiled by the EU

(Eurostat 2008). Ireland's population is also expected to be significantly older, with one-quarter aged sixty-five or over, and one-tenth aged eighty or over. The proportion of the population aged sixty-five and over relative to those of working age will more than double by 2050, which will inevitably lead to increased pressures across various age-related expenditure categories. The pace of such rapid population growth, which far outstrips the EU average, illustrates the scale of the challenge facing the government in providing public services.

Rapid population growth has an impact on the entire range of government and public services, for example the provision of housing, access to hospitals, places in schools, adequacy of public transport, supply of electric power, traffic flow in urban settings, provision of clean water and sewage systems, number of gardaí, traffic levels at airports, coverage by fire services and the workload of the courts. Public services may be subject to congestion and the government has to ensure that rapid population growth does not lead to lower service levels in terms of quality and quantity. Congestion refers not merely to crowded roads, airports, schools and hospitals, but to maintaining the same service level for state-funded activities. Ireland's physical infrastructure remains poor despite high levels of investment. Cuffe (2008) notes, 'In a recent international survey comparing how long it takes to transport goods across a city, Dublin was placed second from the bottom at 57 minutes just ahead of Calcutta'. Transport, energy, information and communications infrastructures, upon which the economy depends, appear to lag behind those of other countries. 'Ireland has one of the lowest stocks of capital per head in the OECD' (OECD 2008b: 57). Bottlenecks in, for example, road networks, electric power and broadband may limit economic growth and lower the quality of life of citizens.

The National Development Plan (NDP) 2007–2013 is the largest and most ambitious investment programme ever undertaken in Ireland. It builds on the achievements of the previous NDP, which ran from 2000 to 2006. The NDP (Government of Ireland 2007b) provides substantial levels of investment: the government has allocated €184 billion to fund numerous projects and initiatives throughout the country to address deficits in infrastructure and to meet commitments set out in the national social partnership agreement *Towards 2016*. In planning for such large infrastructural programmes, the public service must think in a more strategic and long-term manner than heretofore. It also requires skills in areas such as project management, technical/engineering, information technology and statistical analysis. To facilitate this, the 2000–2006 NDP provided for the introduction of specialist positions in the public sector to be filled by open recruitment from the private sector where a shortage existed.

Changing Ireland

The 1990s saw the emergence of an economic transformation in Ireland with the creation of half a million new jobs. Ireland also experienced, within a short space of time, a substantial rise in immigration, mostly from other EU countries, and a smaller but significant increase in non-EU immigrants. What distinguished the situation in Ireland from other European states was the rapidity with which it experienced this social change and went from being a nation of emigration to being a recipient country with immigrants from across the globe. There has been an unprecedented rise in the number of people living in Ireland whose nationality is not Irish. People from 188 different countries were living in the state at the time of the 2006 census, and it is estimated that as many as 200 different languages are now spoken in Ireland. The percentage of people resident in Ireland, yet born outside the state, could be as high as 14.7 per cent of the population, according to the Central Statistics Office (2008a). The figures show 420,000 immigrants living in Ireland, across all cities, towns and villages. The people who migrated to Ireland were predominantly male and aged between twenty and forty. Some came in search of asylum, but most came seeking employment and helped to meet the needs of the burgeoning Irish economy. Figures in 2008 from the European Commission show that, of all the EU member states, Ireland had received the most people from Eastern Europe relative to its size, equivalent to around 5 per cent of its working age population.

The public service had to adjust rapidly to meet the needs of this changing and diverse population. For example, in May 2005 the Department of Education and Science launched inter-cultural education in the primary school guidelines to support the development of a more inclusive learning environment and to equip students to participate in a multi-cultural world. The National Consultative Committee on Racism and Interculturalism (NCCRI 2008) called for interpreting and translating services in key areas such as health, justice, education and housing. This NCCRI report states that uneven standards and a lack of regulation are undermining the capacity of state bodies to provide a coherent interpreting and translation service to migrants. It identifies people from four countries (China, Latvia, Lithuania and Poland) as likely to reflect the greatest number of people living in Ireland with low or no proficiency in English. A minister of state post with special responsibility for integration was created in 2007 to ensure that people coming to work and live in Ireland are fully integrated into Irish society, on an equal footing to people already living in Ireland. This post works across three government departments: Community, Rural and Gaeltacht Affairs; Education and Science; and Justice, Equality and Law Reform. In August 2007 Minister for Integration Conor Lenihan said that the civil service should introduce employment policies similar to those adopted by An Garda Síochána in order to increase the number of foreign nationals among its ranks. In May 2008 he launched the government's strategy paper *Migration Nation*, which outlines official policy in the area of inter-culturalism and integration. A key principle informing and underpinning this policy is a partnership approach between the government, non-governmental organisations and civil society bodies, to deepen and enhance the opportunities for integration.

The growing diverse and multi-cultural population is a challenge to the public management system. Government departments and state agencies have responded by developing integration policies that focus on customers and staff. For example, as 10 per cent of health service staff are from overseas and service users come from across the community, the Health Service Executive (HSE) has to address the needs of people from diverse ethnic and cultural backgrounds. It launched the *National Intercultural Health Strategy 2007–2012* to ensure that the healthcare and support needs of all service users would be addressed in a culturally sensitive manner. This strategy includes a national translation service, anti-racism training for health professionals and research into health outcomes for different ethnic groups. Other examples include the Director of Public Prosecutions' office, which makes its brochures available in nine languages (Arabic, French, Irish, Latvian, Lithuanian, Mandarin, Polish, Russian and Spanish). The National Employment Rights Authority (NERA) produces most of its literature in eleven languages in an attempt to cater for the large and growing immigrant proportion of the workforce. Also, ten of NERA's inspector posts are reserved for people with eastern European languages, and it employs interpreters when necessary.

Characteristics of Public Administration

In considering the efficiency and effectiveness with which public sector tasks are carried out, it is necessary in the first instance to identify the unique aspects of public administration – those features distinguishing it markedly from management in the private sector:

1. The prime purpose of public administration is to serve the public, i.e. to seek the common good.
2. The public service is not judged on a profit basis.
3. The activities of public servants are fixed by law.
4. Public authorities have coercive powers; hence there is a need to provide for consultation, objection and appeal.
5. There is limited discretion and freedom of action in public administration.

6. Public administration is carried on in a 'glass bowl' in that there is a high degree of scrutiny and transparency, with the taxpayers entitled to know how their money is being spent. The most efficient and effective management of other people's money is important.

7. Public administration has a social responsibility and has to balance achievement of the common good with the demands of vested interests. It also has to balance present necessities with future desirables.

8. A much greater number of varying viewpoints must be considered in the governmental process.

9. There is a need for a high degree of consistency in the actions of public servants.

10. Government departments work for, with and under the direction of politicians; hence public administration operates in a 'political milieu'. The way in which things are done often owes more to political factors than to bureaucratic rationality.

11. Public administration often acts to compress the various demands made upon it, for example in education and health.

12. Public administration deals with a great diversity of matters, many of which are purely governmental, that the government cannot opt out of, for example defence, prisons, social services and taxation.

13. The society-wide base of public service operations, for example health and education, increases their scale, complexity and integrative and allocative functions.

14. It is difficult to measure much of the work of the public service.

15. The concept of public accountability: under the doctrine of ministerial responsibility there is a tendency to refer matters upwards for a decision to be made at a higher level.

16. In much of what the government does it is immune from competition. Public administration does not depend on clients or customers for financial support. Some public services have an inherent tendency to expand headcount and expenditure levels.

17. The often simultaneous performance of competing functions in public administration, for example taxation and social welfare.

18. There is an organisation culture determined by socio-political aims (in contrast to the market orientation of the private sector). There is an inexorable and inevitable tendency to expand the remit of government. Politicians react to public demands to 'do something' – often by setting up a working party or a new agency.

To the list above might be added other aspects of the public service such as the fragmentation of authority and accountability, the growth of new agencies and the need for equity for all citizens. Equally, there are core values at the heart of the public service, including integrity, honesty, objectivity and political impartiality. A career in the public service is for some a real form of practical patriotism.

Ireland has 'a well-regarded Public Service that has a tradition of discretion, impartiality and flexibility' (OECD 2008b: 24). People in Ireland trust the public service. Houston and Harding (2008: 14) note that 'More than three-fourths of citizens in Austria, Ireland and the United States have a positive attitude about the commitment of the public service'. In an international comparison of seventy-eight countries, Van de Walle (2007) used data from the World Values Study to describe and compare confidence in the civil service. Of the twenty-six EU member states (Cyprus was not included) that were examined in this study, Ireland came in second place in terms of confidence in the civil service, after Luxembourg.

Public sector management is largely concerned with a network of several different quasi-autonomous organisations that interact with each other. Indeed, public service management has been described as getting things done through other organisations. Thus, an emphasis on partnership and networking is important. There has been a turn towards partnership at all institutional levels requiring a multi-player approach to problem solving. Public service organisations are increasingly developing dynamic networks of specialised organisations facing similar complex tasks at national and international levels. In addition, a recent domestic development has been the introduction of public–private partnerships as a means of delivering infrastructural projects in a timely fashion, which has tended to blur the line between both sectors.

Knowledge of the unique aspects of public administration is particularly important to the reform programme. The Organisation for Economic Co-operation and Development (OECD 2008b: 14) notes that 'Supporting and driving a renewed reform agenda and developing a broader integrated approach . . . will require significant leadership from senior management, who have a detailed understanding of the broad range of issues and challenges unique to the Public Service'. Ombudsman Emily O'Reilly noted on 11 July 2008:

> The vocabulary of public service reform is taken from the world of business. But it sometimes concerns me that, in the midst of this change, we may lose sight of some of the fundamental values which have informed our public service. These are values which, in many respects, are at odds with the values of business. They have to do with fairness, equality, integrity, and a recognition of the common good. Efficiency and cost-effectiveness are, of course, key elements which the public service must pursue, but it must never be forgotten that, unlike his or her counterpart in the private sector, the user of public services seldom has a choice of an alternative supplier.

Mintzberg (1996) points out that 'assessment of many of the most common activities in government requires soft judgement – something that hard measurement cannot provide'. He also cautions against blind acceptance of the mantra that government works best the more it mimics business. He claims that as a result of this bias, 'the private sector has become good, the public sector bad, and the co-operatively and non-owned (non-profit) sectors have become irrelevant'. Mintzberg argues that we are not merely customers of our government – we are also subjects (who have obligations), citizens (who have rights) and clients (who have complex needs) – and thus we need a wide range of management models for providing public services.

The New Public Management Approach

Private sector management models cannot be simply and directly transferred into the public sector. Private companies are essentially profit-making organisations, whereas public sector bodies aim to provide a high quality of 'service' (a much less measurable concept than 'profit'). Such differences, arising from fundamental institutional and political factors, account for the lack of success in past attempts to introduce business management practices directly into government.

Nevertheless, public service managers must ensure that the work is carried out with maximum efficiency and effectiveness. In order to achieve this, an approach termed 'new public management' seeks to apply a business sector management approach to traditional public administration and to its concerns with democracy, accountability, equity, consistency and equality. It involves, for example, specialised methods of measuring outputs and outcomes (always a problem in the public sector) using techniques such as performance indicators and cost-benefit analysis.

The productivity of the public sector is important to Ireland's economic performance. The National Economic and Social Council (NESC 2008: 166) notes, 'There are strong linkages between the productivity of the public sector and national economic performance. They hinge essentially around what the public sector does with the level of resources that government raises for it through taxation, and depend less on the actual level itself.' Thornhill (2006) identifies three main reasons why public sector productivity is important. Firstly, the public sector is a major employer. Second, the public sector is a major provider of services in the economy, particularly business services (affecting costs of inputs) and social services (affecting labour quality). Third, the public sector is a consumer of tax resources. Changes in public sector productivity can therefore have significant implications for the economy. Information on public sector productivity in Ireland is quite limited and cross-national comparisons are notoriously challenging. However, the European Central Bank (ECB) developed indicators for twenty-three industrialised countries to compare public sector performance and efficiency. The ECB (2003: 14) noted that some countries such as Greece, Portugal, Spain and Ireland managed to deliver a relative improvement in public sector performance. Only Ireland, however, succeeded in placing itself above the average of the sample of twenty-three OECD countries. The same study showed that the most efficient public sectors were those of the United States, Japan, Luxembourg, Australia, Ireland and Switzerland.

The public service, particularly the civil service, operates under numerous constraints and controls that are not present in the private sector. Constraints include social, economic, financial, legislative, political, international and accountability factors, such as the system of parliamentary questions and motions in the Dáil or Seanad. Action within the public service is subject to public accountability, enforced through the electoral system. The political process is not a limited one: all members of the public have the right of expression, and no issue, however small, can be assumed to be of no concern. Another important constraint is the perplexity and vagueness of the objectives that the civil service organisations have, many of them of a social or redistributive nature, some of them conflicting. There are motivational constraints also in that managers in the civil service are deprived of many of the incentives and sanctions normally associated with such a post, for example there is little power to hire or fire, to award bonuses or to promote. Other controls include the Constitution, the cabinet, the judiciary and legal system, the Department of Finance, the Comptroller and Auditor General, the Public Accounts Committee, pressure groups and public opinion.

In recent years there has been a greater emphasis on a 'whole-of-government' approach and 'cross-cutting initiatives' have been launched. This has led to a more coherent approach and has helped to reduce the complexity of decision making. The challenge for the public service is to work in partnership with other organisations, both public and private sector. The NESC (2008: 168) notes:

> A particular challenge and opportunity to Ireland's public service is that it continue to develop improved ways of working with the large number and wide diversity of organisations and self-employed with whom it concludes service agreements of one form or another for the delivery of public services. The modernisation of the civil service, the reform of local government and the restructuring of the health services are, justly, headline examples of how and where improved productivity has major potential to improve national economic performance.

The Public Service Excellence Awards were established by Taoiseach Bertie Ahern in 2004 and have resulted in successful projects being replicated throughout the system. They have played a central role in promoting a consistently high level of service to customers and in raising awareness of best practice in the system.

The approach to public sector reform in Ireland, as in most other European countries, has been influenced by the performance-driven ideas of 'new public management' and its main hypothesis that more market orientation in the public sector will lead to greater cost-efficiency. However, the NESC (2003: 157) notes that 'For a variety of reasons, Ireland has not adopted the New Public Management approach. This puts a greater onus on us to show that our alternative approach – based on partnership and the Strategic Management Initiative (SMI) – can do better in addressing cross-cutting problems'.

The New Public Service Approach

At the international level the new public management approach has not been unchallenged. Denhardt and Denhardt (2003) offer a synthesis of alternative ideas and favour an approach that they call 'new public service', based on the idea that 'the public administrator is not the lone arbiter of the public interest. Rather, the public administrator is seen as a key actor within a larger system of governance including citizens, groups, elected representatives, as well as other institutions . . . the role of government becomes one of assuming that the public interest predominates' (2003: 81).

Denhardt (1999) addresses five trends that confront public managers in the new millennium and two important directions that public managers will take in the future. He sees the five challenges facing the public service as:

1. An extraordinary explosion of new knowledge and technological innovations.
2. Changing institutional patterns resulting from the emergence of post-industrial economies and structures of governance.
3. The increasing integration and globalisation of business, politics, culture and environmental concerns.
4. Demographic and socio-cultural shifts towards more and more diversity and potential conflicts.
5. An erosion of confidence in traditionally structured institutions to cope with the consequences of challenges.

As a result of these trends, Denhardt envisions two dramatic changes in the way that public managers operate. The first is a shift from an internal focus of management to an external focus on citizens and citizenship. The second is a shift from the traditional, hierarchical management approach to one of shared leadership. In summary, the result is a more caring, compassionate and creative public bureaucracy, which includes external community groups. These concepts are important for the future of the public service, however, their advancement as acceptable practising values by public managers is not a new one.

According to Denhardt and Denhardt (2003: 3), 'Government shouldn't be run like a business; it should be run like a democracy. Across . . . the world, both elected and appointed public servants are acting on this principle and expressing commitment to such ideals as the public interest, the governance process and expanding democratic citizenship.' They divide their argument into seven principles:

1. Serve citizens, not customers.
2. Seek the public interest.
3. Value citizenship over entrepreneurship.
4. Think strategically, act democratically.
5. Recognise that accountability is not simple.
6. Serve rather than steer. (This involves listening to the real needs of the people and the community, not just responding in the manner that a business would do to a customer.)
7. Value people, not just productivity.

In this context, the extraordinary explosion of new knowledge and techno-logical innovations has revolutionised the way that people communicate and that organisations operate. These range from the Internet, text messaging, mobile e-mail and communication, and audio- and video-conferencing. Regarding the commitment to public service, Denhardt and Denhardt (2003: 4) note:

> We find no other reasonable explanation for the extraordinary dedication and commitment of the people who work to make the world safer and cleaner, to improve our health, to teach our children, and to unravel the host of societal maladies that confront us. Where else can we find the foundations for our efforts to facilitate citizenship and public engagement as a central part of our work? What else can keep the firefighters, the police officers, the social workers, the planners and the inspectors, the receptionists and the clerks, the managers and the analysts serving their communities and their country with energy, resolve and determination?

Perry (1996) identifies six dimensions to measure public service motivation: attraction to the making of public policy, commitment to the public interest, civic duty, social justice, self-sacrifice, and compassion. Professor Niamh Brennan, speaking in November 2008, while critical of some aspects of the Irish public service such as benchmarking and underperforming employees who did not appreciate the privileges of their positions, stressed that there were many public servants whose high level of commitment and work ethic was 'mind-boggling' for relatively small amounts of money.

Public Service Reform

Public services all over the world are being subjected to radical change and modernisation, reflecting the growing demands of society and the complexities of governing in today's global economy. Indeed, in April 1996 the United Nations Assembly discussed, for the first time ever, reform of public administration. OECD member countries have all been undergoing major change and modernisation. Some well-known examples are Australia, New Zealand, Canada and Britain, all of which have the same model of administration – the Westminster model – as Ireland.

Approaches to Public Service Reform

Any programme for reforming the Irish public service has to be based on the following four fundamental principles:

1. Reform can only be implemented successfully if there is a genuine culture change within the department or agency being reformed.
2. Reform cannot be implemented unless there is genuine and consistent support from the Taoiseach, which is recognised as such throughout the public sector.
3. Reform will not be implemented in a climate in which departments and agencies ('us') see the reformers ('them') as hostile outsiders.
4. Reform and modernisation are worthwhile objectives in themselves, and are best pursued separately from public expenditure reviews or cutbacks.

The most crucial aspect to public service reform is that the change culture is internalised within each public sector organisation and each individual public servant. The NESC (2008: 167) summarises the situation succinctly:

> It is probable that the needed improvements in productivity hinge much less on any measures that can be taken at central level – for example, changes made by the Department of Finance to budgets and recruitment levels or strategic initiatives by the Department of the Taoiseach – than on the

internalization of a commitment and responsibility to implement an outcomes-focused, coherent, user-centred approach within each line Department, public agency and third party in receipt of funds. Ensuring the requisite autonomy, accountability and capability in each case is at the heart of the challenge of raising public sector productivity. Each Department and public agency must also internalize a responsibility for the public system as a whole.

The OECD (2008b: 14) makes precisely the same point, albeit in a slightly different manner, 'Success in achieving the vision of a more integrated Public Service will require strong leadership at political and administrative levels to move from a traditional control position, to one of vision, support and direction in developing the modernisation and change agenda.' This movement from the traditional command and control approach to one of high performance teams with a focus on results is occurring gradually through the system.

Public sector reform has focused attention on how different approaches can contribute to organisational change. Traditional 'top down' approaches are unlikely to achieve the necessary change. O'Brien (2002) notes that direct participation, involving frontline staff, played a key role in ensuring acceptance of change and in creating the conditions for employees to make effective contributions to their organisation. Direct participation plays a vital role in employee development. However, it also places demands on organisations to adopt a more facilitative and supportive style of management and to put in place mechanisms that will ensure that participation becomes an integral part of the work process. The OECD (2008b: 25) notes that the expectation was that the changes introduced in the civil service would spill over and transform the rest of the public service, 'The reform process has, in fact, taken longer than expected for the Public Service as a whole and reforms have been adapted to varying degrees within the different organizational cultures of public service bodies. While substantial reforms have taken place within the Public Service, there has been limited ability to capture and replicate innovation.' Minister for Finance Brian Lenihan, replying to a parliamentary question in June 2008, said that he agreed with the OECD report that 'there is a compelling need to adopt a more citizen-centred approach. There must be an increased focus on service delivery over internal reforms and a shift in emphasis from organizational inputs to outcomes for the citizens'.

Recognising the Need for Change

A brief review of the history of public service reform in Ireland is helpful in terms of indicating the lessons from the past and identifying those elements that succeeded and those that were less successful.

The 1918 British report of the Haldane committee on the machinery of government saw the relationship between ministers and civil servants as one of mutual independence, with ministers providing authority and officials providing expertise. It stressed the notion of partnership between ministers and civil servants to meet the more complicated requirements of busier governments when substantial departments emerged after World War I. Government required investigation and thought in all departments to do its job well: 'continuous acquisition of knowledge and the prosecution of research' were needed 'to furnish a proper basis for policy'. Basically the same machinery of government existed in Ireland; as the Brennan Commission of 1936 commented, 'Under changed masters the main tasks of administration continued to be performed by the same staffs, on the same general lines of administration.'

There have been several major blueprints for public service reform in Ireland. The Devlin report (1969) presented a comprehensive plan based on two underlying principles: greater emphasis on policy making, and the need for greater integration of the public service. The recommendations can be summarised as the establishment of a Department of the Public Service and of a Public Service Advisory Council; the introduction of a policy-making core to be called the Aireacht (the senior staff closest to the aire – the minister); a unified staff structure in government departments; classifications of jobs; career development; improved personnel practices; administrative audits; and appellate procedures. Little progress was made in implementing these proposals due to concerns about the situation in Northern Ireland; entry to the European Community; the economic situation; changes of ministers and governments; and public apathy.

The White Paper *Serving the Country Better* (Government of Ireland 1985) was an important landmark in the development of the civil service and set out a blueprint for the future, together with a series of practical steps and initiatives to bring about the best possible, most cost-efficient and courteous service for the public. It focused on the introduction in all departments of management systems based on corporate planning and placed an emphasis on personal responsibility for results, costs and service. A change of emphasis from public administration towards public management was the central theme of the paper. The need for clear aims and objectives in all public services was underlined.

Both of these blueprints had one thing in common: a belief that some changes were needed. This belief was based on the need to improve the delivery of services and to manage resources better.

Accepting the Need for Change

In many respects public service reform reached a watershed in the late 1980s. The 1985 White Paper had not been widely welcomed. The debate surrounding it was overtaken by other, more immediate concerns in the 1986/1987 period. The public financial situation resulted in budgetary cuts and constraints and staff retrenchment policies. However, these events focused renewed attention on service delivery and the use and management of resources, which placed the White Paper in a different light. In fact, the questions of how well the civil service was performing and being managed became central topics of a growing internal debate in the late 1980s and early 1990s. This, in turn, gave rise to a more critical self-analysis of management practices and the perceived constraints under which civil servants at all levels were operating. It is useful to examine the concerns that eventually led to the adoption of a strategic approach. These reform pressures were focused on the performance of the machinery of government – rather than on the roles and structures of the civil service.

Internal awareness. In the 1990s management and staff at various levels in the civil and public service became increasingly aware of:

- Static/shrinking resources.
- Demands for new and improved services.
- The need to overhaul the existing system.
- Failure to identify and act on priorities.
- Lack of context for key decisions.
- The need for the increased use of information technology.
- Lack of a corporate approach.
- The use of multi-annual budgeting and the emphasis on value for money.
- The need for better financial and human resource management systems.
- Greater emphasis on departmental co-ordination.
- The significant contribution of the Institute of Public Administration in public service education, training and research.
- The solid work of the Department of the Taoiseach and the Department of Finance, particularly the Centre for Management and Organisation Development (CMOD).
- The impact of the Master's programmes in public sector analysis and in strategic management held in Trinity College, Dublin.
- Interaction with other administrative systems, particularly in the EU.

External influences. Concerns raised internally were reinforced by views being aired publicly and by events that brought the workings of the public service to the notice of the media and the public, including:

- The increasing cost of the public service.
- The need to address the complex demands of modern public administration.
- Rising public expectations.
- The emphasis on improved performance, increased accountability and better value for money.
- Recognition of the central role of the public service in economic development.
- Greater emphasis on policy formation and analysis.
- Concern with regulation.
- Emerging 'value for money' role of the Comptroller and Auditor General.

International influences. In addition, Ireland was experiencing the effects of:

- Globalisation, emphasising the contribution of the public service.
- Increased international debate and discussion on the role of government.
- Active membership of the EU, and several terms holding the EU presidency.
- The participation of civil servants at the French École Nationale d'Administration.
- The influence of the OECD in terms of public service reform.
- Ireland's terms on the United Nations (UN) Security Council in 1981/1982 (and again in 2001/2002) and the active participation of Irish soldiers and gardaí in UN peacekeeping missions (which would reach more than 59,000 individual tours of duty involving seventy-four missions in the first fifty years).

This combination of factors focused minds on developing an effective response – basically, an alternative, better way of managing and discharging the business of government, and of the civil service in particular. This response came from within the system. It recognised that earlier reform efforts had met with resistance, and that an internally driven process, with an emphasis on consultation and co-operation, was needed.

In 1988 and 1989 informal networks for assistant secretaries and principals were set up in response to calls for such fora to provide a means for discussing issues of concern to these officers. It was through these informal discussions that the debate gathered momentum and focused on finding a better way. The key element of these discussions was recognition that the civil service could do better, if the system was not imposed as a top-down approach. A strong emphasis was placed on consultation and participation to facilitate:

- The development of a framework within which direction and priorities are set.
- Balance between the short and long terms.
- More effective use of available resources.
- Continual evaluation of performance.
- A clearer sense of direction.
- Greater clarity of role.
- Greater teamwork.

In essence, the civil service actively pursued a strategic approach based on the need for better planning and management in the future.

Strategic Management Initiative

Strategic management is a process by which an organisation maintains a considered and coherent view of the likely development in its internal and external environment in the medium to long term. It develops plans designed to maximise its effectiveness and efficiency in the expected circumstances. It implements these plans and continually reviews progress and makes any necessary adjustments. A strategic approach provides a better balance, more control and a framework for making key strategic decisions. It provides a more coherent view of what the civil service should be doing and how it might go about it. It is not a panacea to all the ills in the organisation, however.

It was in this context, and the growing acceptance arising out of it that the civil service needed to manage better, that the Strategic Management Initiative (SMI) had its roots. Launched in 1994 by Taoiseach Albert Reynolds, who had a strong background in business, its main objective was to deliver an excellent service for the customer, based on a high-performance organisation. SMI entailed the setting up of the Co-ordinating Group of Secretaries (re-titled the Implementation Group of Secretaries General in 1997) to oversee its implementation. The SMI was action-oriented and results-oriented. Each department was required to produce an action-oriented statement of strategy, setting out its objectives; how it will meet its objectives; and how it will use its available resources to this end. The strategy statements identified the intended outputs, together with effective methods of measuring output attainment. Importantly, it was a matter for each department and office to devise and implement its own strategy.

The strength of the SMI process was the role of the co-ordinating/ implementation group. It acted as the interface between the political and the administrative systems. Its function was to facilitate the process; evaluate strategy statements; recommend how interacting strategies could be co-ordinated; recommend changes to enable more efficient and effective management of the civil service; and report to government. It reviewed the strategy statements and submitted a progress report to government. The government decided in 1995 to advance the process with a view to its deepening within departments and mandated the group to develop a modernisation programme. This decision was based on the perceived benefits of the SMI, which included more focus on: strategic issues and objectives; policy formation and evaluation; clients' needs and services; objectives and targets. It was noted that the SMI led to better management cohesion and commitment. The commencement of the extension of the SMI to the wider public service began in 1997.

The implementation group was chaired by the Secretary General of the Department of the Taoiseach and generally met once a month. It co-ordinated and provided leadership to the modernisation programme for the civil service. It provided impetus and direction to the reform process. The group established the Change Management Network in 2002 to assist and support the integration of the various strands of the modernisation process in departments/offices. The network, which also met monthly, provided a forum for discussion and the sharing of experience and best practice among civil servants charged with overseeing the modernisation process in their departments/offices. It also provided a channel for effective and timely dialogue between the centre and senior managers with responsibility for change management in relation to initiatives being progressed under the aegis of the implementation group.

The establishment in 1997 of the Committee for Public Management Research (CPMR) has also been very useful in enhancing the knowledge base on public management issues. It has produced over forty reports and discussion papers on all aspects of public service management and delivery. It sponsors research on issues of relevance to the development and management of the civil and wider public service. This research is undertaken by the research division of the Institute of Public Administration (IPA). The CPMR comprises researchers from the IPA, representatives from the civil service and university academics.

Strategic management has been put in place in every department and office and is becoming an integral part of the approach to the day-to-day work of the public service. The requirement for staff at all levels in the public service to be multi-skilled and flexible is fundamental to the capacity of the civil and public service to deal with the challenging new issues and areas of work created by economic, societal and technological change. In particular, these skills are necessary prerequisites for delivering services in a joined-up and integrated manner. There is an increasing focus on the nature and balance of the required skill mix, and on performance and accountability for managers at all levels. At the level of the organisation, there is a requirement that annual output statements be submitted to the Oireachtas, along with the annual estimates. This is aimed at clearly linking resources with outputs and outcomes, and demands a rigorous approach to the management of all resources across the civil service.

Delivering Better Government (DBG)

Delivering Better Government: A Programme of Change for the Irish Civil Service, the second report of the Co-ordinating Group of Secretaries, was published in May 1996. It sets out a vision for the Irish civil service and recognises that quality services are the essence of an excellent civil service. It is a series of inter-dependent elements collectively aimed at improving service delivery and the management and performance of the civil (and public) service. Its overall purpose is to enable the civil service to meet the needs of government and the public more efficiently, effectively and economically. These elements are set out within an overall vision for the civil service – a vision that builds on the civil service's strengths and core values of integrity, impartiality and equity. In addition to setting the requirement for legislative change to clarify the allocation of authority, accountability and responsibility in the system, the report identifies specific areas that need to be addressed on a service-wide basis if the objectives of the SMI are to be achieved.

Working groups were set up to address key areas. These working groups involved senior civil servants and non-civil servants in developing further the key initiatives. In addition, three frontline groups addressed customer service; training and development; and information technology. These groups comprised administrative, executive and clerical staff at various levels in the civil service. They provided an important input to the relevant working groups in relation to issues affecting frontline staff in the areas in question. The work of the various groups was overseen by an extended co-ordinating group made up of senior figures from the civil service, trade unions and private sector. This group was required to oversee the implementation of the change programme and to report regularly to government on the progress in developing the initiatives. A cross-departmental team was established to support the development of the overall programme of change and its implementation in departments. This team was based in the Department of the Taoiseach and provided advice on issues of common concern.

Appropriate structures were put in place in each department to ensure consultation with and participation by all staff. Departments nominated facilitators to provide liaison with the cross-departmental team. Some departments engaged in extensive dialogue to ensure widespread participation. Others set up in-house task forces representative of all grades. A newsletter was published to keep civil servants up to date on the development of the SMI and DBG process.

Quality Customer Service

A key aim of SMI and DBG was to bring about a clearer focus on objectives, particularly in relation to meeting the needs of the consumer of public services. The public has the right to expect the same standard of service from the public service as it does from a private sector business. Traditionally, however, the culture of the civil service had not been conspicuously customer-oriented, leading to insufficient emphasis on service delivery.

DBG proposed an approach to quality service delivery based on the following principles:

- Specification of the quality of service to be provided by departments and offices to their customers.
- Consultation with and participation by customers on a structured basis.
- Provision of quality information and advice to customers.
- Provision of reasonable choice for customers in relation to the methods of delivery of services.
- Integration of public services at local, regional and national levels.
- Introduction of a comprehensive system to measure and assess customer satisfaction.
- Introduction of complaints and redress mechanisms that operate close to the point of delivery.

DBG recommended the introduction of quality service initiatives based on these principles and under which each department would have a programme to improve the quality and delivery of its services. A quality service initiative for the civil service was launched in May 1997, emphasising the importance of detailed customer service action plans. The LoCall telephone service was introduced on a phased basis and allows people to contact government departments from anywhere in Ireland for the price of a local call. A Civil Service Quality Assurance Group was put in place. Speaking in the Dáil in April 2008 Taoiseach Bertie Ahern announced that customer satisfaction surveys will be conducted by departments on an annual basis.

Public Service Management Act 1997

The Public Service Management Act 1997, which came into effect on 1 September 1997, set out a formal structure for assigning authority and accountability within the civil service in a clear and unambiguous manner. It clarified the roles and duties of civil servants (so that each person knows what is expected of him or her, either in an individual capacity or as part of a team) and enabled them to assume responsibility for the results of their work. The reason for the introduction of this legislation was to improve the internal management of the civil service. These changes ensured greater efficiency and effectiveness on an ongoing basis in the way the civil service does its business and provides value for money.

The pace and volume of business transacted by government departments have increased enormously in recent years. The previous system had tended to concentrate too much responsibility on ministers for matters in which they had no direct or immediate involvement. The act provided a framework for formally assigning responsibility and accountability to heads of departments and in turn to other officers. It signalled, as such, a clear change in the operation of the system of government. In accordance with the Constitution, ministers retain overall responsibility for their departments, which they exercise in accordance with the framework provided in the act.

The act is a key element in advancing the strategic management process in the civil service. Each government department publishes a statement of strategy every three years or within six months of the appointment of a new minister, which is presented to the Oireachtas. These statements of strategy set out the department's key objectives and the outputs to be achieved together with the resources to be used. A typical template for a strategy statement is: the mission; the vision; the strategic plan, in terms such as the goals, the objectives, the strategies, the action plans and the projects involved; and the systems for monitoring and assessment. The production of these strategy statements and their publication on the departmental websites has been extremely helpful in increasing public understanding and insight into the work of government departments. The frequency of their production provides an evolving picture of the development of policies and changes in priorities. Each secretary general is responsible for managing, implementing and monitoring government policies and delivering outputs as determined with the minister and set out in the department's statement of strategy.

The act contains a significant change in the terms of employment of civil servants. It provides the secretary general with the responsibility for appointment, performance, discipline and dismissals of staff below the grade of principal. Furthermore, these responsibilities, with the exception of dismissal, can be delegated to other officers within the department. The previous arrangements continue in respect of staff at the grade of principal and above. Prior to the passing of this act, established civil servants could be removed from office only by the government. The operation of these powers of appointment, discipline and dismissal now vested in the secretary general is contingent on the need to ensure that systems are in place to treat all civil servants fairly and equitably, on the basis of a transparent performance management system and in accordance with natural justice.

The Civil Service Regulation (Amendment) Act 2005 was passed to allow certain provisions in the Public Service Management Act 1997 to take effect. The 1997 act established a framework in which managerial responsibility, including powers of dismissal, for certain staff was given to secretaries general and senior civil servants. However, the practical implementation of these powers was constrained by the Civil Service Regulation Act 1956, which reserved most disciplinary functions to ministers. The 2005 act removed those constraints.

Influence of Social Partnership

Further support for the implementation of SMI was set out in the social partnership agreements *Programme for Prosperity and Fairness, Sustaining Progress and Towards 2016*. The Programme for Prosperity and Fairness, which was agreed in 2000, advanced the objectives of SMI by focusing on continuous improvements in service delivery, resource management and organisational responsiveness. *Sustaining Progress*, which was agreed in 2003, provided for the continuation of the modernisation programme across the public service. A major innovation under *Sustaining Progress* was that the payment of all the general rounds of the pay agreement and the final two phases of the benchmarking increases for each sector, organisation and grade was made conditional on verification of satisfactory achievement of the provisions on co-operation with flexibility and ongoing change, satisfactory implementation of the modernisation agenda, the maintenance of stable industrial relations and the absence of industrial action. *Towards 2016*, which was agreed in 2006, contained a range of commitments on modernisation, co-operation and flexibility designed to ensure that the progress made across the public service under earlier agreements would continue, but at a faster rate. It set out a mechanism for the verification of progress at sectoral, organisational and grade level in the public service through the establishment of a performance verification group for each of the sectors – health, education, local authority, An Garda Síochána and the Defence Forces. Under the terms of *Towards 2016*, payment of each of the public service pay increases is dependent on verification of satisfactory achievement in relation to co-operation with flexibility and ongoing change, including co-operation with satisfactory implementation of the agenda for modernisation, the maintenance of stable industrial relations and the absence of industrial action.

Other Developments

Other significant public sector reform developments have included:

- The Public Service Management (Recruitment and Appointments) Act 2004 modernises the recruitment system for the civil service.
- A code of standards and behaviour published in 2004 sets standards for service delivery, behaviour at work and integrity for civil servants.
- In 2004 the civil service began to recruit a number of staff by open competition for the higher executive officer and assistant principal grades.
- An evaluation of the Performance Management and Development System (PMDS) for staff has been completed and, following negotiations with the unions, improvements have been made to ensure that human resource systems are more closely related to PMDS.
- A White Paper, *Regulating Better*, setting out the principles to inform the government's approach to regulatory policy was published in 2004. A key element of this process was the use of regulatory impact analysis (RIA) in departments. In 2005 a report on the introduction of RIA was published, along with guidelines on consultation for public sector bodies.
- The introduction of the management information framework in departments and offices to provide better and more timely financial and management information.
- Multi-annual capital budgets have been agreed to allow departments greater flexibility in managing resources.

Ongoing Evaluation

A review of SMI by PA Consultants in March 2002 found:

- Quality customer service does not seem to have benefited 'cross-cutting customers'.
- Gains from regulatory reform and management need to be more actively sold.
- There is a need for stronger, more direct leadership within each department.
- The link between financial analysis and decision making remains weak.
- The issue of performance-related pay and reward policy is unfinished business.

The report noted that 'the civil service is a more effective organisation than it was a decade ago . . . Much of this change can be attributed to SMI/DBG . . . Progress is not yet complete'.

Keogan (2003: 96) states, 'In its attempts at reforming the civil service and state agencies, the SMI tinkered with the existing system rather than looking at the system *de novo* or from a first principles basis. The various programmes of the SMI – strategy statements, quality customer service, value for money, new financial management, performance measurement, and information technology systems – have been superimposed on existing operations and structures.'

Addressing the IPA's national conference in June 2006, Taoiseach Bertie Ahern announced that the next phase of the modernisation process would focus on four areas:

1. A review of performance information provided to the Oireachtas to ensure that performance indicators are appropriate, useful and measure performance across departments and agencies.
2. A system of external review of the structures, capacities, procedures and leadership of departments and agencies, so that problem areas are identified and support can be given for future improvement. This will give assurance about their overall performance, but also target practical support and advice on areas of particular concern.
3. A new leadership initiative for the public service as a whole, which will involve not just the development of skills and competences in the traditional way, but also the organisation of career development and succession planning. This will ensure that the right people are in the right place at the right time to serve the needs of the citizens.
4. A study of how the Irish public service as a whole performs relative to its international peers, particularly those who are recognised as representing good practice in various different aspects of public administration and policy. International bodies such as the OECD could help in this process.

In its 2007 annual report the National Competitiveness Council makes a number of recommendations for the Irish public sector:

• The principles of the SMI need to be reinvigorated and applied more widely across public sector bodies, including local authorities.
• Greater client focus is required and the client base for different areas of public service provision should be clearly identified and involved, through representative groups or otherwise, in monitoring the effectiveness of services provided.

- The remuneration for key management posts should have a performance element.
- Further efforts are required to ensure the adoption of merit-based promotion in all cases and to promote the entry of talent from outside the public administration system.

The report also highlights a number of structural challenges:

- The public service has successfully brought together ad-hoc groups to devise key strategies but there has been less perceived success in developing similar groups to progress the implementation of strategies.
- Care should be taken to ensure that decentralisation does not reduce the efficiency of the public service. As the report states, 'it is also important that the policy roles of the civil service and public agencies are strengthened and not weakened through dispersion'.
- Given the substantial expansion in the number of public agencies in recent years, it is important to put in place appropriate structures to evaluate their objectives and how successful they are in achieving them.

Ireland has good quality public services and many improvements have been made in recent years. However, the agenda for change, for enhancing the efficiency of public services and the quality of services to citizens, is not a static one. It needs to be regularly reviewed and adapted as needs and demands change. A series of efficiency reviews of public services was announced in budget 2008 along with a programme of organisational reviews to examine the capability of individual departments and agencies to meet their current service delivery requirements and to deal effectively with future changes in direction and new challenges.

OECD 2008 Review

The purpose of the Organisation for Economic Co-operation and Development's 2008 review was to benchmark the public service in Ireland against other comparable countries and make recommendations regarding future directions for public service reform. There was a particular emphasis on how the various parts of the public service related to each other. At the launch in April 2008 Taoiseach Bertie Ahern said that commissioning the report 'reflects the government's desire to accelerate a process of renewal so as to deliver improved outcomes for citizens with increased efficiency'. The government encouraged a bold approach and forwarded all 936 submissions received during a major public consultation process directly to the OECD.

The OECD, which is based in Paris, was established in 1961 with Ireland as one of its twenty founding members. It is an international organisation, with thirty full members, which promotes dialogue and the exchange of good practices in public and corporate governance areas, including issues relating to the economy, policy making, human resource management, ethics and information technology. Much of the OECD's work is based on peer review and dialogue and it has extensive databases and access to key policy-makers through its network of committees and working parties.

The 2008 review was undertaken by the OECD's Public Governance and Territorial Development Directorate. It involved extensive dialogue with and questioning of Irish officials by OECD staff and international experts drawn from the governments of five countries. Four key themes were emphasised by the OECD: the capacity of the public service; performance and budgeting; governance; and service delivery. In addition to wide-ranging consultations and meetings with the public service, the OECD also used case studies in five sectoral areas – education, health, local government, agencies and An Garda Síochána – to examine in greater detail how the public service was performing.

Speaking in the Dáil on 20 May 2008 Taoiseach Brian Cowen noted:

> The OECD acknowledges that our public service is on a sound path of modernisation. It found that our relatively small Public Sector has contributed to our competitive advantage. However, it also acknowledges that there is, overall, an insufficient focus on performance that delivers outcomes in line with the needs of citizens. It correctly categorises our public service reform as overly focused on process and on procedures, inward facing, without sufficiently demonstrating that it is driven by the complex and diverse needs of citizens, or focused on making a difference to the quality of their lives.
>
> The OECD's main recommendation is that we think about the Public Service as a more integrated 'system'. An integrated Public Service means getting people within the different elements of the Irish Public Service system to work in a more consistent, co-ordinated, networked way across the traditional sectoral and organisational boundaries. This does not necessarily mean changing the structure of the Public Service, or changing the existing number of Offices or Agencies. Rather it is about ensuring that Departments, Offices, and Agencies interact with each other in new ways ensuring integrated action in policy-making, delivery and implementation.

The OECD's report, *Towards an Integrated Public Service*, is a compre - hensive analysis set out in an extensive document, running to nearly 375 pages. The report (2008b: 12) notes that Ireland's 'public service remains segmented overall, leading to sub-optimal coherence in policy development, implementation and service delivery. As public policy becomes more diverse and complex, public service organisations need to have even more interaction with each other and with stakeholders at local, national and international levels, and across these levels'. Its key findings and recommendations include:

- General government employment in Ireland is relatively low when compared to other OECD countries. It is significantly less than the level of public employment in Norway, Sweden, France, Finland and Belgium.
- Ireland has the third smallest total public expenditure as a percentage of GDP (third to Korea and Mexico), and this figure has decreased over the previous ten years. Increases in expenditure are reflective of a need to play catch-up from historically low levels. In comparison with other OECD countries therefore, Ireland has been able to deliver services with a public service that is relatively small given the size of the economy and the labour force.
- While structures and systems exist to enable co-operation and co-ordination, disconnects remain between the civil service and the broader public service, leading to sub-optimal coherence in policy development, implementation and service delivery. If the public service is to become more responsive to meeting citizens' expectations and achieving broader societal objectives, the OECD recommends thinking about the public service as a more integrated 'system'. Rather than creating one overall super-structure, consistent and co-ordinated networks of people work across the traditional sectoral and organisational boundaries.
- While Ireland has had many successes in developing internal e-government systems, co-operation across public service bodies is not widespread. The potential for citizens of ICT and e-government is not being fully realised by public sector organisations.
- As with other countries, the focus in Ireland has been on performance reporting rather than on managing for performance. The focus needs to shift from inputs and processes, to outputs and achieving outcomes. Performance measures and initiatives need to be better aligned with the overarching outcomes and high-level societal goals in order for the general public to understand the benefits of the public service.

Given the breadth of the recommendations contained in the OECD's report, the government agreed that the Implementation Group of Secretaries General would respond to government within two months with proposals for a comprehensive and integrated action plan as a response to the report. In addition, the government announced the establishment of a high-level task force, comprising both public servants and private sector members, to develop and oversee the response to the report. The government requested the task force to develop a new action plan for the public service of the twenty-first century that would examine ways in which services provided by government departments might be amalgamated and to devise a plan to make more public services available electronically. The task force reported in November 2008 (see below).

Organisational Review Programme

The Organisational Review Programme (ORP) is a public service modernisation initiative managed by the Department of the Taoiseach. It was set up to examine the capabilities of government departments in a number of key areas, focusing on their ability to deal effectively with future challenges. The ORP, commissioned by Taoiseach Bertie Ahern in 2006 as an organisational 'health check', is overseen by a committee of senior public servants and a selection of independent external members. It conducts comprehensive reviews of each government organisation in terms of current and likely future capacities in three key areas:

- *Strategy:* How effective is the organisation at developing strategy?
- *Managing delivery:* How good is the organisation at delivering services to its customers?
- *Evaluation:* Does the organisation evaluate what it does and, if so, do the findings contribute to new policies?

The template developed for the pilot phase of ORP reviews sub-divided these three areas into ten organisational attributes:

- *Strategy:*   Setting strategic direction.
                       Giving leadership.
                       Creating shared understanding.
- *Managing delivery:* Customer service and delivery.
                       Continuous improvement and innovation.
                       Managing resources (HR, ICT, financial).
                       Governance.
- *Evaluation:*   Performance measurement.
                       Customer and stakeholder feedback.
                       Input into policy and strategy.

The three departments reviewed in the first phase of the ORP were Agriculture, Enterprise and Transport. Over 6,000 online questionnaires, 55 workshops and 115 face-to-face meetings were carried out as part of the analysis, involving the staff, stakeholders and agencies of the three departments. The report on the pilot phase (Department of the Taoiseach 2008c) found that communication on 'strategic and operational priorities' between top management and staff in the Department of Transport needed to be addressed further. It noted that the Department of Enterprise, Trade and Employment will be better placed to respond to challenges if it develops its 'policy analysis, evaluation and development capacity, especially in relation to proposals from its offices and agencies'; whereas the Department of Agriculture, Fisheries and Food is 'well placed to meet future challenges' and 'is good at developing strategy and setting direction based in part on its thorough knowledge and experience of the agri-food sector'.

The government announced in 2008 that the ORP would be extended to all government departments and major offices over the following three years.

Report of the Task Force on the Public Service

The task-force's work was extensive and engaged key stakeholders. Its 47-page report, which was adopted in full by the government, provides a comprehensive analysis and insight into the challenges facing the public service reform process and sets out a challenging agenda for change. It endorsed the core message of the OECD's (2008b) evaluation, namely, that by working in new ways the Irish public service has the potential to deliver significantly improved services and outcomes. 'We believe this to be the case notwithstanding the quality outcomes and improved internal management processes recorded by the OECD in many areas of the public service. The public expects improved and expanded services while the current budgetary situation severely constrains the resources available to maintain and enhance such services' (Government of Ireland 2008c). The report was published in tandem with the *Government Statement on Transforming Public Services* (see below) and clearly provided the intellectual analysis for the decisions made. The main areas covered by the report are:

- The transformation context in terms of the growing expectations of citizens, the Irish system in comparative perspective, outcome comparisons, current economic and fiscal challenges, and partnerships for change. The purpose of the Irish public service is to achieve valued outcomes for the citizen that, when taken together, make Ireland a more 'successful' story. In this context, there is a need for a system-wide, integrated public service.
- Motivating performance at organisational, sectoral and individual levels and the extension of performance management systems for individuals to all public servants whatever their role.

- Deepening citizen engagement with an emphasis on putting the citizen first. The public service must be empowered to share and re-use the significant amount of data at its disposal.
- E-government and its potential to facilitate the policy integration, collaborative activity, enhanced citizen engagement and restructuring recommended by the OECD.
- Experience in both public and private sectors demonstrates that benefits can be realised by the adoption of shared services models under certain conditions.
- People and leadership through mobility, redeployment, flexibility, liberating the talent and reviewing staff resources. The creation of a senior public service would send a strong, highly visible signal of the government's intent to promote a cultural change within the public service.
- Strengthening the governance of the public service. Regarding the public service as a single labour market and a unified resource should allow for faster restructuring and the redirection of resources to priority areas. Networks are a suitable approach for dealing with complex issues, particularly when actors come from different organisations and sectors within the public service and when drawn from the public, private and not-for-profit sectors.
- State agencies have at times been created due to a reluctance to increase the size or direct responsibility of government departments. Such artificial drivers should not be a factor in deciding whether to abolish or retain agencies.
- An implementation strategy with political championship and leadership, a programme office and an emphasis on accountability. The task force also recommended that an annual report on the state of the public service be prepared.

Transforming Public Services

The government's public service transformation programme was announced on 26 November 2008 and includes a comprehensive range and breadth of management models. If implemented, it will represent the most fundamental reform of the public service in the history of the state. The plans include a specified period of time during which the changes are to be implemented. It remains to be seen whether this programme will move from aspiration to action, however, the government has indicated that there is a strong determination at the political level to implement these changes fully, to overcome any resistance within the system and to end the institutional inertia. Taoiseach Brian Cowen (2008b) said, 'Delivering on the trans-formation agenda represents a challenge of the highest political priority. It requires, therefore, the strongest possible political engagement and leadership. Implementation, therefore, will be driven by me, as chair of a new Cabinet Committee on Transforming Public Services.'

At the heart of these reforms is the establishment of a Special Group on Public Service Numbers and Expenditure Programmes, colloquially referred to as An Bord Snip Nua, to examine the expenditure programmes in each department and to make recommendations for reducing public service numbers so as to control public spending. Whelan (2008) states that 'The establishment of this group is actually the most significant decision included in a wider series of public sector reforms'. The group announced in 2008 is modelled on the Efficiency Audit Group (EAG) established in April 1988 to examine the workings and practices of each government department with a view to recommending improved and alternative policies and methods to reduce costs and improve efficiency. The EAG had the task of establishing whether, by more efficient or alternative work practices, costs could be reduced or a better service could be provided at the same cost. It quickly became more commonly known as An Bord Snip. Subsequently, it was decided that the role of the EAG would be extended to other parts of the public service. Speaking in the Dáil on 19 June 1990 Minister for Finance Albert Reynolds noted that 'The group [EAG] have made, and are making a valuable contribution to the process of improving the efficiency of the administration of Departments and providing better service to the public'.

The other significant element of the government's 2008 transformation programme is the decision to establish a unified public service, which would involve a breaking down of the traditional barriers between the civil service, local authorities, state agencies and health services. Taoiseach Brian Cowen (2008b) notes, 'I want all public servants to see themselves as part of a single system. I want them to work across the organisational, professional and geographical boundaries that can act as barriers to joined up planning and service delivery.' In this context, former Taoiseach Garrett FitzGerald (2008c) comments:

> The OECD has said our civil service is relatively small among developed countries. Nevertheless, in any sizeable organization, public or private, there are bound to be areas where numbers could be reduced without damaging the services. The Government's proposal to move towards creating a single public service and facilitating mobility in the system, if effectively implemented – and we have been weak in implementing such schemes – should help to resolve such issues.

The government hopes that implementation of the action plan will help to eliminate the 2008 budget deficit of €4.7 billion by 2011. Ministers were told to cut their €20 billion departmental and agencies' payroll for 2009 (approximately one-third of total current expenditure) by 4 per cent, which equates to 10,000 jobs.

Among the elements underpinning the transformation programme are:

- A statement on transforming public services.
- The report of the Task Force on the Public Service.
- The report of the Organisational Review Programme.
- Guidelines for the preparation of customer charters and customer action plans.
- Results of the civil service customer satisfaction survey 2008.

Speaking at the launch on 26 November 2008 of the *Government Statement on Transforming Public Services*, Taoiseach Brian Cowen said:

> Today, we are announcing measures to effect fundamental change and trans-formation of our public services. This sector plays a huge role in determining the progress of our nation. Our economy, our environment and the quality of life of our citizens literally from the cradle to the grave depend in substantial measure on the capacity of our public service. There has rightly been a major focus on the performance of the public sector over recent times and it is apparent that real reform is necessary to deal positively with the challenges of the 21st century.

The statement on the transformation programme outlines an integrated package of measures to deliver real change in the public service. These mutually reinforcing measures are seen by the government as providing the basis for the transformation of the Irish public service. The actions set out in the government statement are designed to:

- Achieve improved performance by organisations and individuals.
- Create flexibility in the deployment of people, assets and other resources.
- Identify the precise transformation agenda in each sector and engage and mobilise the necessary actors.
- Achieve greater efficiency, effectiveness and economy.

They are also designed to build capacity for ongoing transformation, through a focus on:

- Promoting a shared identity, ethos and vision through the joint achievement of societal goals.

- Developing leaders at every level of organisation.
- Empowering employees through mobility, shared performance data and training.
- Developing performance metrics that are meaningful to the citizen.
- Increasing organisational and individual accountability for achieving performance targets.
- Promoting long-term planning.
- Innovation, shared governance, networks and collaborative working.
- Sharing infrastructure and new technologies.

The statement contains thirteen points reflecting the priorities for change in the public service:

1. *Special Group on Public Service Numbers and Expenditure Programmes:* the objectives of this special group are to review the scope for reducing or discontinuing expenditure programmes; to analyse and make recommendations on the numbers employed in each area of the public service; and having regard to the need to identify and prioritise particular output targets and areas, the achievement of greater efficiency and economy in the delivery of all services, and the scope for rationalising and streamlining delivery of public services in the interests of consumers, to make recommendations on reallocation of staffing or expenditure resources between public service organisations and to examine and make recommendations for further rationalisation of state agencies beyond the proposals and principles set out in budget 2009. The group will submit a final report in June 2009.

2. *Better value for money in public procurement:* the government will establish a National Operations Unit (NOU) within the Office of Public Works to allow all public agencies to acquire a range of goods and services more effectively, efficiently and with better value for money. The NOU will provide professional procurement advice to the public service. Targeted and accredited procurement training and education measures will be developed. The NOU will further develop web-based solutions in this area.

3. *Value for money and policy reviews:* an evaluation perspective requires both a culture of evaluation within individual public sector organisations and external oversight to ensure that key questions in relation to what is being achieved and how costs can be driven are asked and answered. The government will develop a more focused system of value-for-money reviews to target areas of significant spending in the health, education, social welfare and justice sectors. The results of these reviews will be

published. In addition, a series of specific policy and programme reviews will be undertaken.

4. *Clear commitments and keeping promises to the public:* the public service will become more focused on performance and delivery and will be made more accountable for what it achieves through the measurement of that performance. This is only possible if there is clarity about the goals and targets to be achieved, and against which performance is to be measured. The government will specify priority outcomes for all sectors, for example education, health and local government, together with the relevant performance indicators by which achievement will be assessed. Instead of measuring performance by individual organisations alone, the government will develop performance indicators that span the efforts of groups of organisations involved in areas such as children and disability. Specific targets will be the basis on which performance of organisations is assessed and evaluated.

5. *Measure performance of people and organisations:* the government will require all public agencies (in addition to departments) to produce output statements relating resources to planned achievements. All public bodies will produce an integrated annual report (covering both input usage and output delivery) as a basis for comprehensive Oireachtas scrutiny. The system for measuring and reporting outputs will be subject to external validation.

6. *Managing for performance and challenging under-performance:* the government will strengthen, standardise and monitor the performance management system in the civil service and local government sectors to link performance ratings with achievement. The government will design, negotiate and introduce performance assessments in those areas of the public service where none exist, which will be initially targeted at tackling under-performance.

7. *Engaging and empowering the citizen:* customer satisfaction with service providers in each part of the public service will be measured systematically on an ongoing basis. All public service organisations will publish a customer charter setting out the service standards that the public can expect. All existing charters will be revised to include new commitments to improve specific services. Organisations will publish evaluations of their charters and their service delivery, which will record customer input and feedback. Local government, as the level of government closest to the citizen, will be given a leadership role in providing integrated responses to the needs of citizens through case working and other methods, while elected councils will be the focus for consultation and feedback on all services delivered at local level. A

database of all publicly funded programmes and projects will be established and maintained at county level to avoid duplication and to encourage integration. The government will examine the feasibility of putting in place a single LoCall telephone number for all public services, using call centres.

8. *Better use of information:* the government will introduce an adminis - trative burden reduction programme for citizens to reduce volume and frequency of data required from the public. Where appropriate, the public will be asked for consent to information sharing between public bodies. A consolidated inspections' programme will be developed to reduce the number of visits to businesses. The government will force public bodies to share information and will establish a central data store to allow public bodies to maximise the re-use of data, particularly around events such as births, deaths, marriages and company formations and registrations.

9. *E-government and shared services:* the government is committed to a significant expansion in the number of online services available to the individual and business user. The government will announce priority e-government projects in all sectors of the public service in early 2009 and will publish six-monthly progress reports on the implementation of these projects. It will provide relevant support to smaller public bodies and will promote the establishment of shared corporate services centres to be used by all public bodies.

10. *People and leadership:* the government will begin work immediately to identify and remove barriers to a unified public service labour market. New arrangements on redeployment and exit options will be developed. All promotions across the public service will be competitive, based on merit and clearly linked to individual performance assessments. Recruitment, promotion and training practices will be updated to take account of a new emphasis on leadership skills. A Senior Public Service to manage and deploy top public servants centrally will be designed during 2009 and introduced initially in the civil service at assistant secretary level for twelve months, before being extended to other relevant groups across the wider public service.

11. *Better management of the public service:* The government is committed to better integration of the public service. It will extend the pilot Organisational Review Programme to ensure that all government departments and major offices will be reviewed by 2011. It will specify priority targets in relation to key cross-cutting issues that require better co-ordination of the relevant departments and agencies. It will issue guidance as to the best practice management of cross-cutting issues,

including the use of networks. It will ensure that, wherever possible, service providers adopt county boundaries for the organisation, delivery and evaluation of services. A database of all public services available by county level will be published. Government departments and agencies will explore the feasibility of devolving more responsibility at local level to individual local authorities. The multi-agency county and city development boards will be strengthened to improve the co-ordination of local service delivery.

12. *State agencies:* the government believes that a more vigilant approach is now required so that the need for individual state agencies is regularly evaluated and to ensure that agencies continue to meet their intended objectives. The Special Group on Public Service Numbers and Expenditure Programmes will report to the government on the scope for further rationalisation of agencies. The government will not create any new agencies pending the development of new performance management and governance arrangements. Ministers will be required to demonstrate a clear business case for any incremental resources associated with the creation of any new agency or the conferring of new functions on an existing agency. All agencies will be required to publish output statements relating the resources allocated to them with target achievements. Departments will put in place service-level agreements that commit agencies to delivering agreed volumes and standards of service to the public. Agencies will be compelled to use shared services options.

13. *Implementation and accountability for transformation:* the implementation of this transformation agenda will be driven by the Taoiseach and the Minister for Finance. The government created, with immediate effect, a Cabinet committee, chaired by the Taoiseach and comprising the Ministers for Finance, Health, Education, Justice and the Environment, to oversee the transformation effort. A Central Programme Office, based in the Department of the Taoiseach, will support the Cabinet committee and the relevant secretaries general and public service leaders in the implementation of the programme. A steering group for the implementation and monitoring of progress will be established comprising public servants and outside members with relevant expertise. The government will publish the first annual report on the state of the public service in 2009. The government will prepare legislation to give effect to this transformation programme.

Customer Service

Public service organisations have been producing customer action plans since 1997 to assist them in improving the way they deliver services to their customers. The Customer Charter Initiative was launched in 2002 to provide customers with a clear and unambiguous statement of the level of service they can expect. This initiative also includes a framework that allows for the measurement and improvement of the quality of services provided and for this to be reported publicly. Practical guidelines for the preparation of customer charters were published in 2003 to assist public service organisations. In 2006 the government commissioned Fitzpatrick Associates to undertake a comprehensive review of the customer charter process in the civil service; this evaluation was published in 2007.

Guidelines for the Preparation of Customer Charters and Customer Action Plans (Department of the Taoiseach 2008b) contributes to this continuing commitment to the implementation of quality customer service in the Irish public service. The guidelines provide for customer charters and customer action plans for the period 2008 to 2010 to be produced as part of the same process. The timeframe mirrors that of departments' strategy statements. The various parts of the strategic planning process – strategy statements, business plans, performance management and development system, annual reports and modernisation plans – are to be used to prioritise and support customer service commitments on a continuous and mutually reinforcing basis.

A survey of civil service customer satisfaction (Department of the Taoiseach 2008a) found that the most frequently contacted civil service body was the Department of Social and Family Affairs, followed by the Office of the Revenue Commissioners. The most popular reason for the contact was to enquire about a particular service, entitlement or application. Telephone was the most common method used to contact the civil service (71 per cent), followed by calling in person (53 per cent), writing (37 per cent), Internet (16 per cent) and e-mail (15 per cent). The report found that the overall level of satisfaction (very/fairly satisfied) with the service received was 80 per cent, while the proportion of those dissatisfied (very/fairly dissatisfied) was 14 per cent. Telephone customers were less satisfied with speed and waiting times: the highest level of overall dissatisfaction expressed was for the amount of time left holding (26 per cent), and 22 per cent of respondents were dissatisfied with the speed with which the phone was answered. Of those who had accessed Irish language services, 79 per cent were satisfied with the levels of service received, while 8 per cent were dissatisfied. Of those with a first language other than Irish or English, 60 per cent were satisfied with the access to necessary services (the report notes that, because of the small sample who answered this question, this result should only be considered indicative). Finally, the report found that 'Of those who had contact with the civil service in the last 12 months, 69 per cent considered the civil service to be very efficient or fairly efficient' (2008a: 41).

E-Government

E-government is the use of information and communications technology (ICT) to improve the delivery of public services to citizens. E-government is organised more horizontally and openly than conventional government. It helps to modernise and transform how governments interact with citizens and how citizens interact with governments, as well as making new connections possible within the public sector. The reasons for e-government include:

- Expectations from citizens and customers.
- Desire to emulate best international practice and that in the private sector.
- Reductions in administrative costs.
- Delivery of new and better services.
- Ensuring regularity and probity.

The information society action plan produced in January 1999 set out a three-strand approach to online delivery of public services in Ireland:

- *Strand 1 – information services:* ensuring that all public service information is available online through the websites of departments and agencies, and at the same time as it is delivered through traditional channels.
- *Strand 2 – interactive services:* delivery of public services online, enabling complete transactions to be conducted through electronic guidelines.
- *Strand 3 – integrated services:* rearrangement of information and service delivery around user needs so that it is available in an integrated manner through a single point of contact with government.

In the context of progressing central components of this strategy, the OASIS (Online Access to State Information and Services) and BASIS (Business Access to State Information and Services) projects were initiated during 2000. Since 2000 all departments have been required to produce e-strategies for the delivery of public services online, and to report on progress with implementation in their annual reports. An analysis by PA Consulting Group (2002) found that there were significant qualitative differences across departments and offices resulting in a disparity in the tone and extent of these strategies, which ranged from vague, aspirational documents to highly detailed project plans.

There are considerable synergies between e-government and the wider government modernisation agenda. The Department of Finance (2002a) notes that the customer focus of e-government 'aligns very closely with the approach to quality customer service adopted by SMI'. This involves devolving more decision making closer to the customer, improving financial information systems and creating more effective mechanisms for addressing cross-cutting issues.

In 2002 the Department of the Taoiseach published a strategy document, *New Connections*, outlining what e-government services should be given priority and setting a timetable for their implementation. It notes that 'The growing influence of information and communication technologies (ICTs) in recent years is phenomenal. The internet is the fastest growing communications medium in history. And mobile phones have become part of our everyday lives. We are experiencing a transformation in our daily living and working conditions' (2002: 4). The strategy notes the range of measures agreed by the government in June 2001 to strengthen engagement with the information society agenda. These included a new cabinet committee on the information society, and a complementary eStrategy Group at secretary general level. The government also appointed an Information Society Commission, drawing on high-level representatives from business, the social partners and the government, and reporting directly to the Taoiseach. It provided independent expert advice to the government, and monitored Ireland's progress as an information society. These structures were being co-ordinated by an expanded information society policy unit in the Department of the Taoiseach, working in close partnership with the technology policy unit in the Department of Finance. The arrangements were designed to deliver a more coherent overall approach, at the highest level of government, to formulate and implement policy on a wide range of issues that cut across traditional departmental boundaries – between departments and agencies, and between central and local government.

In addition, the Department of the Taoiseach established an inter-departmental working group of assistant secretaries to ensure the necessary co-ordination across government departments in addressing legal and regulatory issues relevant to information society development. Reporting to the cabinet committee on the information society, this group was to ensure overall consistency, coherence and agreement on priorities; ensure that emerging bottlenecks were identified and addressed; ensure that stakeholders were aware in good time of draft legislation impacting on them; liaise as appropriate with the high-level group on regulation (which was progressing the *Better Regulation* reform agenda); and liaise as appropriate with the Information Society Commission. The monitoring arrangements to ensure the necessary momentum and progress by departments and agencies towards electronic service delivery targets were the subject of quarterly reports to the cabinet committee on the information society.

In this context, departments had co-ordinating responsibility for agencies under their aegis. The eGovernment Implementation Group, at assistant secretary level, monitored and promoted the implementation of e-government across the public sector. The remit of the group included the development of a communications strategy for the e-government process, both internally and externally. Despite this clear architecture, targeted support initiatives and monitoring arrangements, by 2008 more than half of these projects had yet to be implemented, were not finished on time or had been scrapped, and there was no overall e-government legislation in Ireland.

An earlier CPMR discussion paper (Timonen *et al.* 2003: 7) had noted:

> Considerable progress has been made in the area of e-government during the very short time that it has been on the political and public service reform agendas. However, it is clear from this study that Ireland, along with all other countries, is far from reaching the full potential benefits of e-government. It is becoming clear to decision makers in Ireland and elsewhere that: efficiency and the government modernisation goals can only be achieved through re-engineering the way government operates; greater customer focus will be helped when e-government is genuinely accessible to all; and confidence in e-government can only be achieved through clearly demonstrating that electronic service delivery is secure and prevents abuse of the system.

The annual survey by Capgemini for the European Commission on the supply of online public services of September 2007 set out twelve services for citizens that could be delivered electronically:

- Income taxes: declaration, notification of assessment.
- Job search services by labour offices.
- Social security benefits.
- Personal documents: passport and driver's licence.
- Car registration (new, used, imported cars).
- Application for building permission.
- Declaration to the police (for example in a case of theft).
- Public libraries (availability of catalogues, search tools).
- Birth and marriage certificates: request and delivery.
- Enrolment in higher education/university.
- Announcement of change of address.
- Health-related services (interactive advice on the availability of services in different hospitals; appointments for hospitals).

The survey then looked at eight services for enterprises that might be provided electronically:

- Social contributions for employees.
- Corporate tax: declaration, notification.
- VAT: declaration, notification.
- Registration of a new company.
- Submission of data to statistical offices.
- Customs declarations.
- Environment-related permits (including reporting).
- Public procurement.

For each of the twenty overall public services (twelve for citizens and eight for businesses), the sophistication stage reached is indicated with reference to the maximum stage possible for the service. This survey found Ireland ranked fifteenth in Europe for the provision of online public services, behind, for example, Austria, Estonia, Malta, Sweden and Norway. It found that just half of these twenty basic public e-government services for citizens and businesses were available in Ireland. The report concluded that Ireland was slipping in terms of the online availability of key public services from central and local government. It also found that the sophistication of online services was falling behind that of other countries. From a strong start in this area in the early 2000s, topping the poll of e-government services in EU bench-marking exercises in 2001 and 2002, the relative performance of Ireland has declined (McLindon 2002).

The Comptroller and Auditor General, in a special report on e-government in October 2007, noted that the original ambition to get services online by 2005 was 'clearly unrealistic' and found that the progress on many projects was slower than expected:

> While Ireland has some on-line transaction services that compare favourably with what has been achieved elsewhere, an EU-wide benchmark survey indicates that it has achieved the highest level of on-line service in only ten of 22 key public services for individual and business users. Overall, Ireland's position is around the average for EU member states and some states are delivering a significantly higher level of on-line service. Greater emphasis should be placed on looking at the experiences of other countries and learning from them for application to Irish public services.
>
> The management process for the administration of eGovernment projects needs to be improved. All projects should have clear, measurable business objectives, and time and cost targets. A much stronger project cost and performance measurement and reporting system is required, integrated with departmental and agency reporting systems.

Information technology has been one of the key drivers of Ireland's economic expansion. In a globalised world, Ireland is rapidly becoming a knowledge economy, reliant on the knowledge of a highly educated workforce providing services for export. Speaking to the Committee of Public Accounts in March 2008, the Comptroller and Auditor General stated:

> It is good to note that Ireland has some on-line transaction services that compare favourably with what has been achieved elsewhere. However, Ireland's overall position in international benchmarking surveys is around the average for EU member states; some states are delivering a significantly higher level of on-line service. For this reason, I state in the report that we need to keep looking at the experiences of other countries and learning from them what best might have application to Irish public services. The overall investment in e-government has been considerable . . . While broad strategic objectives were identified for e-government, measurable targets were not set for these objectives. There is a case for a stronger central function for the future development of e-government, for instance, in enforcing robust reporting and monitoring of progress against realistic cost and time targets and in identifying and prioritising projects where the benefit will be greatest in terms of quality of service and/cost-savings. In this context, potential gains in the area of so-called cross-cutting projects have yet to be fully realised. My review suggests that the momentum evident in the early years towards developing e-government appears to have faded.

The 2007 survey for the European Commission by Capgemini produces a disappointing report on Ireland's performance in this area. Among the twenty-seven EU member states, Ireland remains more a laggard than a leader. Broadband is essential to the provision of e-government, to offsetting Ireland's peripheral geographical location, to minimising isolation from the rest of the world and to bridging the digital divide. The 'digital divide' refers to the gap between individuals, households, businesses and geographic areas at different socio-economic levels with regard both to their opportunities to access ICT and to their use of the Internet for a wide variety of activities.

Responsibility for e-government moved from the Department of the Taoiseach to the Department of Finance in 2008, on the change of Taoiseach. Prior to that, the minister of state at the Department of the Taoiseach (with special responsibility as Government Chief Whip, and for the information society) provided the overall policy leadership in this area. As part of the Transforming Public Services Programme set out in 2008, the government stated that it would announce priority e-government projects in all sectors of the public service in early 2009 and would publish six-monthly progress reports on their implementation.

Regulatory Reform

Regulatory simplification has been recognised internationally as an integral part of any strategy to foster growth, competitiveness and employment. There is a need for high-quality, easily understood and efficiently implemented regulations that are in the public interest. A proactive programme of managing and improving government regulations and the regulatory process has been introduced in Ireland. The principles governing such improvements, while in each case protecting the public interest, include:

- Improving the quality, rather than quantity, of regulations.
- Eliminating unnecessary and/or inefficient regulations (including legislation).
- Simplifying necessary regulations and related procedures as much as possible.
- Lowering the cost of regulatory compliance.
- Making regulations more accessible to the public.

Each department is endeavouring to reduce red tape. It is intended that regulations be reviewed every five years on this basis. A good regulatory regime is essential to promoting a sound and socially responsible economic environment conducive to job creation and to fair competition. An OECD report on regulatory reform was published in 2001. Since then significant progress has been made in the area. A government White Paper, *Regulating Better*, was published in January 2004 in response to the OECD's report and provides the basis for work on the regulatory reform agenda. Importantly, it set out six core principles as the basis for the design, implementation and review of legislation and regulation:

- *Necessity:* Is the regulation necessary? Can we reduce red tape in this area? Are the rules and the structures that govern this area still valid?
- *Effectiveness:* Is the regulation properly targeted? Is it going to be properly complied with and enforced?
- *Proportionality:* Are we satisfied that the advantages outweigh the disadvantages of the regulation? Is there a smarter way of achieving the same goal?
- *Transparency:* Have we consulted with stakeholders prior to regulating? Is the regulation in this area clear and accessible to all? Is there good back-up explanatory material?
- *Accountability:* Is it clear under the regulation precisely who is responsible to whom and for what? Is there an effective appeals process?

- *Consistency:* Will the regulation give rise to anomalies and inconsistencies, given the other regulations that are already in place in this area? Are we applying best practice developed in one area when regulating other areas?

Adherence to these principles ensures that Ireland's regulatory framework remains flexible and responsive to the needs of businesses and citizens alike. A dedicated unit within the public service modernisation division in the Department of the Taoiseach promotes the better regulation agenda.

Financial Management

The introduction of an effective accountability framework, involving greater delegation and increased emphasis on the measurement of results, necessitates the development of better financial management systems and the adoption of a more devolved approach to expenditure management generally.

A number of important initiatives are being pursued in this area. The system of multi-annual budgeting, announced in the 1996 budget, is operating to a fixed annual cycle to produce a rolling three-year budgetary process. This is facilitating changing circumstances, both budgetary and economic, while accommodating existing and emerging priorities in public expenditure. Major programmes of expenditure are also subject to a thorough review at least once every three years.

The budgets covering administrative costs were delegated in 1991 in most cases. Departments have agreed three-year administrative budget contracts with the Department of Finance. The increased delegation of financial authority to departments is an integral part of this process. Enhanced financial management systems are being introduced. These include the incorporation of accrual accounting principles into departmental accounting procedures as necessary, as a first step in the development of financial management systems concerned with performance measurement and management.

In 2000 the EU adopted directive 2000/35/EC to protect companies from being paid after an agreed deadline for payment has expired. In Ireland the Prompt Payment of Accounts Act 1997, which applies to all public bodies and provides automatic entitlement to interest, anticipated this EU legislation.

The Value for Money and Policy Review Initiative was introduced in June 2006, replacing the former Expenditure Review Initiative (ERI). It encompassed formal reviews for the period 2006 to 2008, already agreed to be carried out under the ERI, as well as all other policy reviews. These reviews focused on significant areas of expenditure and on major policy issues. All these reviews were published and submitted to the relevant select Oireachtas committees, facilitating better engagement by the Oireachtas in the value for money agenda. The ERI was introduced in 1997 to review public expenditure systematically. It has undergone a number of reforms since then, which were designed to enhance the efficiency and effectiveness of expenditure review.

The National Development Finance Agency (NDFA) was established on 1 January 2003 in accordance with the National Development Finance Agency Act 2002. Its primary function under that act is to provide a financial advisory service to state authorities in respect of capital projects over a certain size (€30 million), under guidelines issued by the Minister for Finance. The National Development Finance Agency (Amendment) Act 2007 significantly expanded the role of the agency to include the procurement of certain public capital projects by way of public–private partnerships (PPPs). This consolidated the agency's procurement role, which began in 2005, in the education, justice and health areas. With the passing of the 2007 act the NDFA's procurement remit was extended to include a wider range of state authorities. For example, in early 2007 the NDFA commenced pre-procurement work on behalf of the Department of Arts, Sport and Tourism for the National Concert Hall and the Abbey Theatre. The areas excluded from its procurement remit are transport projects, which are already provided for in the mandates of the National Roads Authority and the Railway Procurement Agency, as well as certain local authority PPPs. However, all these projects continue to be subject to the NDFA financial advisory remit.

The rationale for the decision to assign these functions to the NDFA was the need to have a central and enduring professional expertise available to state authorities to analyse all financial aspects of infrastructure projects and, in a significant number, to act as procurement agent. Another reason was the recognition that a rapid growth in government capital projects would have to be matched by a developed institutional expertise. A third rationale was the fact that the National Treasury Management Agency was already managing a number of significant financial businesses on behalf of the state. The procurement function complements the financial advisory functions already established within the NDFA and is governed by guidelines issued by the Minister for Finance.

In view of the new procurement responsibilities assigned to the NDFA, a technical project management group was established in the agency. In the education sector, for example, the PPP programme of twenty-seven schools cost €320 million.

Speaking on RTÉ television in May 2008, John Purcell, then recently retired from the role of Comptroller and Auditor General, warned of an over-reliance on PPPs in the changed economic climate. 'With the current downturn in the public finances, capital programmes will have to be met to a greater extent by borrowing, and obviously as a surrogate for borrowing, public private partnerships can act in that way. But I think that it is wrong to see them as the panacea for all our ills and the absolutely number one solution to all the difficulties we might encounter,' he said.

Kuhry (2004) examined the performance of the public sector relative to the resources absorbed by producers active in the public sector. He finds little connection between public sector performance and the level of public and private spending. He notes (2004: 15) that 'by this measure, Finland and Denmark score the best results at moderately high costs, while Luxembourg, Austria and Ireland score average to good at low costs'.

Comptroller and Auditor General

Article 33 of the Constitution stipulates that 'there should be a Comptroller and Auditor General (C&AG) to control on behalf of the state all disbursements and to audit all accounts of monies administered by or under the authority of the Oireachtas'. There are three constitutional officers: the President, the Attorney General and the Comptroller and Auditor General, with the latter being the least well known. The Constitution requires the C&AG to report to the Dáil at stated periods as determined by law. As a constitutional officer the C&AG is appointed by the President on the nomination of the Dáil and holds office until the retiring age (sixty-five) prescribed by law. The C&AG may not be a member of the Oireachtas and may not hold any other office or paid position. The independence of the office is secured by the constitutional requirement that the C&AG cannot be removed from office except for stated misbehaviour or incapacity, and then only upon resolutions passed by both Houses of the Oireachtas. The main statutes are the Exchequer and Audit Departments Act 1866 and the Comptroller and Auditor General (Amendment) Act 1993, which extended the range and scope of the C&AG's remit. The salary of the C&AG is at the same level as a secretary general of a government department.

The main statutory functions are, first, as Comptroller General of the Exchequer, to ensure that no money is issued from the central fund by the Minister for Finance except for purposes approved by the Oireachtas; second, as Auditor General, to audit government accounts for accuracy and regularity and to carry out such examinations as he or she considers appropriate in regard to economy and efficiency in the use of resources and the effectiveness of certain management systems.

The 1993 amendment act consolidated and updated the statutory provisions in relation to the role of the C&AG and extended the C&AG's

statutory powers and remit. The provisions of the act related to the following broad changes:

- All non-commercial state bodies are now audited by the C&AG, as well as the Health Service Executive and the vocational education committees.
- In any year of account in which a body receives 50 per cent or more of its gross income directly or indirectly by way of grants from a department, it will be subject, at the C&AG's discretion, to examination by the C&AG of its books, records and accounts to establish that the public funds have been spent for the purpose for which they were provided.
- The most significant new provision relates to the value for money of public expenditure. The C&AG has discretion to conduct examinations of the economy and efficiency with which departments use their resources and the measures used by departments for appraising the effectiveness of their operations. The provisions extend the traditional non-statutory discretionary function of the C&AG of identifying and reporting in the Dáil on instances of loss, waste or uneconomic expenditure. These powers are now on a statutory basis.
- The duties of secretaries general, as accounting officers, in giving evidence before the Committee of Public Accounts are set out in statute for the first time. The act expressly prohibits an accounting officer from questioning or expressing an opinion on the merits of a governmental or ministerial policy.
- The act enables the C&AG, subject to the consent of the Minister for Finance, to charge fees in respect of any audit, examination or inspection.

The role of the C&AG was further expanded under the Comptroller and Auditor General and Committees of the Houses of the Oireachtas (Special Provisions) Act 1998, which provided for the carrying out of examinations and investigations by the C&AG into the operation of deposit interest retention tax (DIRT) by the Revenue Commissioners and the financial institutions as well as related matters. The C&AG has also become an ex officio member of the Standards in Public Office Commission and the Referendum Commission.

Public bodies are subject to value for money (VFM) reviews. The purpose of a VFM audit is to provide the Dáil with independent assurance as to the economy, efficiency and effectiveness with which a body has used its resources in discharging its functions:

- *Economy:* minimising the cost of goods, or services, having regard to appropriate quality.
- *Efficiency:* maximising the output of goods, services or other results for the resources used to produce them
- *Effectiveness:* the relationship between the intended results and the actual results of programmes and other activities.

Section 10 of the 1998 act reinforces the C&AG's right of access, as a constitutional officer of the state, to documents and information. Every effort is made at working level to meet the C&AG's requirements in this regard. If a document or a file that has been requested is deemed by the department to be of such a secret nature (for example relating to the security of the state) as to preclude its release to the C&AG's staff, the document or file in question is shown in confidence to the C&AG personally.

This act has emphasised the importance of good management in the public service. Section 9 allows the C&AG to form opinions as to how well the audited departments and other bodies are managed. The C&AG is required to satisfy himself or herself as to the adequacy of management effectiveness – the management system, procedures and practices for examining effectiveness. This involves examining the:

- Organisation of the evaluation function.
- System of reporting.
- Methodology used in effectiveness examinations.
- Use made of effectiveness evaluation reports.

It allows the C&AG to make comparisons between different bodies and operations and to draw conclusions from these comparisons. The C&AG is enabled to cite examples of effective systems and good management, which might repay study and emulation by management in other bodies. This has encouraged the development of performance management systems, including performance indicators, and mechanisms for the evaluation and review of public expenditure programmes. It is worth noting that the C&AG is precluded, under section 11(5), from questioning or expressing an opinion on the merits of policies or policy objectives in any of his or her reports.

The C&AG also carries out a number of joint audits of north/south bodies in conjunction with the Comptroller and Auditor General of the Northern Ireland Audit Office.

In summary, the revised audit, inspection and VFM functions of the C&AG are having a major impact on the public sector. Public bodies are accountable to the Dáil, through the Public Accounts Committee, for the:

- Regularity of their transactions and the accuracy of their accounts.
- Evaluation of the effectiveness of their operations.
- Economical and efficient use of their resources in discharging their statutory functions.

Freedom of Information

The Freedom of Information Act 1997 came into effect on 21 April 1998. The purpose of the act is to provide a right of access to information held by public bodies. The long title of the act, which sets out its purpose, states that it is to enable the public to obtain access to official information to the greatest extent possible consistent with the public interest and the right to privacy. The benefits of freedom of information are seen as:

- Increased openness and transparency.
- Improved decision making.
- Improved relationships with clients.
- Better records management.

Freedom of information (FOI) derives from the following broad principles:

- When government is more open to public scrutiny it becomes more accountable.
- If people are adequately informed and have access to information, there is likely to be greater appreciation of issues involved in policy decisions and stronger public ownership and acceptance of decisions made.
- Groups and individuals who are affected by government decisions should know the criteria applied in making those decisions.
- All individuals have a right:
  - to know what information is held in government records about them personally, subject to certain exemptions to protect key interests;
  - to inspect files relating to them; and
  - to have inaccurate material on file corrected.
- Citizens, as shareholders in public bodies, are entitled to examine and review the deliberation and processes of public bodies.

The act established three new statutory rights:

- A legal right for each person to access information held by public bodies.
- A legal right for each person to have official information relating to himself or herself amended where it is incomplete, incorrect or misleading.
- A legal right to obtain reasons for decisions affecting oneself.

In relation to this last point, Hogan and Morgan (1998: 574–6) state that the FOI act establishes a 'far reaching duty to give reasons', saying that, where it applies, 'the Act goes beyond the previous obligation to give reasons which have been deduced (mainly) from constitutional justice'. They explain that the act goes beyond the previous obligation in four important respects. Firstly, the requirement that reasons be required in order to facilitate a judicial review or appeal has no equivalent in the FOI act. Second, there is no restriction on the type of decision and the circumstances to which the right to a statement of reasons is attracted. Third, it may be that 'reasons will have to be given for both negative and positive acts'. Finally, they suggest that, in considering the *audi alteram partem* principle in the performance of the duty to give notice of the case against a person, section 18(1), because of the way the obligation has been formulated, is likely to require the giving of reasons when the final decision is taken. These rights are overseen by an independent Information Commissioner, who reviews decisions made by public bodies under the act.

This legislation was seen as a milestone on the road to good governance and best practice in terms of accountability. It was grounded in the belief that public bodies must be accountable to the ordinary public they are there to serve and that accountability requires openness. Connolly and O'Halpin (1999: 267) comment that the act 'represented a reversal of the presumption of frequency that has underpinned Irish government . . . It is, in practice, a far more powerful investigative instrument than a parliamentary question'.

In 2003 the government amended the FOI act. The new act introduced fees for FOI requests, ranging from €15 to €150. There has been a decline in the number of queries made since these fees were introduced. Information Commissioner Emily O'Reilly (2003) noted in relation to these FOI charges:

> I have already publicly stated that the progressive nature of these charges may dissuade many people, on grounds of cost, from exercising their rights of appeal under the Act. In fact, I have little doubt that the scale of the charges will prove a disincentive to accessing what is a right – information – and if refused, further access to an independent appeals mechanism. Already, it seems that there has been a significant reduction in the number of requests for non-personal information to government departments.

Speaking in the Dáil in December 2007 Taoiseach Bertie Ahern defended this imposition of fees for non-personal FOI requests. He said that the legislation impacted upon those 'who engaged in a trawl for non-personal information. The legislation was never designed so people could do this'. He also argued that companies and individuals 'were doing trawling exercises with a view to using the information they obtained commercially to benefit a client base'. O'Reilly (2003) succinctly stated, 'the original Freedom of Information Act may have been winded but hasn't yet been stretchered off the pitch'.

An FOI request must be made in writing to the appropriate public body. It must refer to the act and specify the records requested. The public body is obliged to give assistance to the requester. The appropriate fees must be paid. The public body must decide to release or refuse to release the record within four weeks. There is a right to an 'internal review'. There is a right to an independent review by the Information Commissioner if the individual is not satisfied. Personal records are free and there is a sliding scale of fees for non-personal records, with reduced fees for lower-income groups.

The Information Commissioner (see Chapter 11) is independent of government, reviews the decisions of public bodies, keeps the operation of the FOI act under review, and reports to the Oireachtas. All records are to be given to the commissioner, who may enter the premises of public bodies and can impose strict penalties for non-compliance.

The Information Commissioner has made a number of landmark decisions in terms of public management. In 1998 a request was made for information on the expenses paid to TDs. The Oireachtas claimed that this was personal information. The commissioner agreed that this was personal information, but held that it should be released in the public interest in terms of the accountability of public funds. Another case involved a request to the North-Eastern Health Board (NEHB) for access to the 1998 inspection report of a private nursing home. The NEHB decided to grant access to the report, but the nursing home objected to its release as it contained commercially sensitive information. The commissioner found that part of the record contained commercially sensitive information and also some personal information about the owners, however, there was a public interest in release in terms of how inspections are carried out and in terms of regulatory functions. In another case, a request was made to the Refugee Appeals Authority (RAA) for a record on a positive recommendation that it had made. The department refused on the grounds that the reasoning of the RAA would be revealed, that other applicants could thus build false cases and there would be difficulties in determining false/legitimate claims. The commissioner found that there was nothing to prevent asylum seekers sharing facts, that parts of the recommendation were very general, that the UN High Commissioner for Refugees sets out the basis for granting asylum and that staff of the RAA would be able to determine false and legitimate claims. The commissioner's binding decision (Case 000274) of December 2000 is instructive, 'sometimes a public body will have to accept the risk of some reduction in the effectiveness of its procedures in the interests of transparency and accountability'.

A fully functioning FOI act allows light to be shone on all aspects of government; it fosters a spirit of transparency, accountability and good governance.

Certain exemptions are provided in the legislation so as to protect key sensitive information of government and of public bodies. These exemptions are based on standard practice in other countries with this type of law. Most of these exemptions are not absolute and many are subject to an overall test of whether disclosure is in the public interest. Exemptions provide for the protection of certain material relating to matters such as meetings of the government; deliberations and functions of public bodies; law enforcement, defence, security and international relations; third-party information (i.e. personal, commercially sensitive and confidential information); parliamentary and court matters; economic interests of the state. However, for material to be protected under many of these exemptions, damage must be likely to be caused by the release of the information involved.

Under two exemptions, those of law enforcement (section 23) and defence, security and international relations (section 24), a minister may, in the case of exempt information that is also of sufficient sensitivity or seriousness to justify doing so, issue a certificate. Where such a certificate is issued, a review of the decision to refuse information is undertaken by members of the government, rather than the Information Commissioner. Information can be released in exceptional circumstances, notwithstanding possible damage, where the balance of public interest favours this course.

The entire activities of An Garda Síochána are precluded from FOI enquiries. Ireland is one of the few Western countries not to include its police force in transparency legislation. While transparency is not possible in all areas of garda work, for example prosecutions and criminal investigations, there are calls for areas of management, administration and decision making to be included under FOI.

Conclusion

Change is the only constant in the public service. The 1969 report of the Public Services Organisation Review Group concluded that the civil service had worked reasonably efficiently, had served different governments loyally, had operated impartially and, within the framework of its organisation and resources, had done the best it could to promote the development of the nation. The report also found that the civil service had given its advice to ministers fairly and honestly and had implemented the final decisions of the government without reservations, and that recruitment is based on merit and not favouritism. The OECD review (2008b: 14) reached a broadly similar conclusion and noted that 'Increased open recruitment will allow the public service to rapidly acquire the necessary skills and competencies that cannot be easily located or grown in the short-term among the existing cohort of generalist public servants'.

Boyle (2007) notes that in a comparative context 'Ireland tends to come out of the analysis of the quality and efficiency of public administration relatively well'. No organisation can afford to stand still or to rest on its laurels, however. The profound changes in society that were a dominant feature of the late twentieth century have continued into the twenty-first century. Central themes in the reshaping of organisational life are the necessity for flexible, responsive structures and systems based on knowledge as the most fundamental resource. 'Ireland is facing a more complex environment with increased expectations for effective service delivery; and a need for alternative solutions to developing horizontal approaches to policy and service delivery challenges' (OECD 2008b: 15).

Pressures relating to costs to the taxpayer, efficiency, the quality of management and effective deployment of people mean that virtually all public service organisations are re-examining the way they manage themselves, and are looking at what lessons can be drawn from other sectors to give them more effective ways of working. The agenda for change in the public service across Europe is a strong one and one for which the impetus is gathering pace. The aim of the change management process in the Irish public service has been to build upon the foundation of the good service that has been provided in the past. This is essential given the importance of the services provided by the civil and public service to the well-being of the individual citizen and to the coherence of society as a whole.

Improvements are also essential for economic reasons given the importance of the work of the public sector for national competitiveness and the realisation of the people's vision for Ireland in the twenty-first century. Accordingly, there have been significant changes in the public service in recent years. These have seen the development of a more open and flexible organisation operating to high standards of integrity, equity, impartiality and accountability. In a comparison of 181 economies, the World Bank's *Doing Business 2009* report, covering the period April 2007 to June 2008, found that Ireland was in seventh place for doing business in terms of the regulatory environment being conducive to the operation of business and in fifth place for starting a business.

Central to the change management process is the devolution of authority and responsibility to line managers and staff. The person closest to the point of delivery is the person in the best position to make decisions, including resource allocation. The training and development of staff with the appro -

priate skills and expertise and the emphasis on performance measurement and evaluation are integral parts of this process. New mechanisms have been created across the entire system of government to empower individuals and ensure a heightened degree of individual accountability for decisions and the use of public resources. There have been reports, recommendations, plans and task forces. There is an urgent need for action. McCarthy (2005) concludes:

> I believe that public service reform has advanced very significantly in Ireland over the last decade. We need to demonstrate more clearly than we have to date precisely what is being achieved through reforms of structures and processes in terms of the outputs and outcomes and the value which they represent. However, what may ultimately matter most is the commitment to a culture of change and reform, empowering public servants, in all the various roles which they occupy, to take the initiative to make changes that make sense. It may be that grand strategies of change, even those implemented with revolutionary zeal, ultimately express themselves in incremental rather than radical or strategic change. But beneficial opportunism and pragmatic reform can and, in my view, regularly do result in valuable gains in productivity, service quality, transparency and fairness. Reform is a challenge worth meeting.

The reform process has been successful in improving accountability and leading to better public management. McCarthy (2007) notes, 'We need less administration and more management. In securing the essential values and loyalties of the public service for the future, we should not be afraid to change our structures and processes, no matter how radical that change may appear.' It remains to be seen how much progress will be achieved with the Transforming Public Services Programme and whether it will be easier to implement public service reform during a time of significant economic challenges.

Web Resources

BASIS: Business Access to State Information and Services at www.basis.ie
Better Regulation website at www.betterregulation.ie
Central Statistics Office at www.cso.ie
Comptroller and Auditor General at www.audgen.gov.ie
École Nationale d'Administration, France at www.ena.fr
Institute of Public Administration at www.ipa.ie
National Competitiveness Council at www.competitiveness.ie
National Development Finance Agency at www.ndfa.ie
OECD Review of the Irish Public Service available at www.bettergov.ie
Office of the Minister for Integration at www.ria.gov.ie/integration
Public service modernisation at www.bettergov.ie
Revenue Commissioners at www.revenue.ie

REFERENCES

A & L Goodbody Consulting, *Rationalisation of Allowances of Members of the Oireachtas* (Dublin: A & L Goodbody Consulting, 2006)

Adshead, Maura, 'Policy Networks and Sub-national Government in Ireland' in Maura Adshead and Michelle Millar (eds.), *Public Administration and Public Policy in Ireland: Theory and Methods* (London: Routledge, 2003) 108–28

Advisory Expert Committee on Local Government Reorganisation and Reform, *Local Government Reorganisation and Reform* [Barrington report] (Dublin: Stationery Office, 1991)

Ahern, Bertie, 'What Government Expects from State Agencies', speech to the Association of Chief Executives of State Agencies (Burlington Hotel, Dublin, 17 November 2005)

Ahern, Bertie, interview with Bryan Dobson on RTÉ's *Six One News* (broadcast on RTÉ Television, Dublin, 26 September 2006)

Ahern, Bertie, 'Address by Taoiseach, Bertie Ahern, TD, OECD Review of the Irish Public Service, Launch of the OECD Report *Towards an Integrated Public Service*' (Dublin: Department of the Taoiseach, 28 April 2008)

All-Party Oireachtas Committee on the Constitution, *First Progress Report* (Dublin: Stationery Office, 1997a)

All-Party Oireachtas Committee on the Constitution, *Second Progress Report: Seanad Éireann* (Dublin: Stationery Office, 1997b)

All-Party Oireachtas Committee on the Constitution, *Third Progress Report: The President* (Dublin: Stationery Office, 1997c)

All-Party Oireachtas Committee on the Constitution, *Fourth Progress Report: The Courts and the Judiciary* (Dublin: Stationery Office, 1999)

All-Party Oireachtas Committee on the Constitution, *Fifth Progress Report: Abortion* (Dublin: Stationery Office, 2000)

All-Party Oireachtas Committee on the Constitution, *Sixth Progress Report: The Referendum* (Dublin: Stationery Office, 2001)

All-Party Oireachtas Committee on the Constitution, *Seventh Progress Report: Parliament* (Dublin: Stationery Office, 2002)

All-Party Oireachtas Committee on the Constitution, *Eighth Progress Report: Government* (Dublin: Stationery Office, 2003)

All-Party Oireachtas Committee on the Constitution, *Ninth Progress Report: Private Property* (Dublin: Stationery Office, 2004)

All-Party Oireachtas Committee on the Constitution, *Tenth Progress Report: The Family* (Dublin: Stationery Office, 2006)

Asquith, Andy and Eunan O'Halpin, 'The Changing Roles of Irish Local Authority Managers', *Administration* 45/4 (1998)

Bagehot, Walter, *The English Constitution 1867* (London: Fontana, 1993)

Banotti, Mary, *There's Something About Mary* (Dublin: Currach, 2008)

Barrett, Gavin Michael, 'Brief Reflections on the Holding of a Referendum in Ireland on the Treaty of Lisbon: A Response to Rossa Fanning' (24 April 2008a); available online at Social Science Research Network: http://ssrn.com/abstract=1125246

Barrett, Gavin Michael, 'EU Can Leave Ireland Behind', *Sunday Business Post* (6 July 2008b)

Barrington, Donal, 'Insult Was Not the Real Cause of Ó Dálaigh Resignation', *The Irish Times* (2 December 2006)

Barrington, Ruth, *Health, Medicine & Politics in Ireland 1900–1970* (Dublin: Institute of Public Administration, 1987)

Barrington, Ruth, 'Was Holding Referendum on Lisbon Treaty Really Necessary?', *The Irish Times* (11 July 2008)

Barrington, T.J., *The Irish Administrative System* (Dublin: Institute of Public Administration, 1980)

Barrington report, *Local Government Reorganisation and Reform* [Advisory Expert Committee on Local Government Reorganisation and Reform] (Dublin: Stationery Office, 1991)

Bovens, Mark, 'Public Accountability' in Ewan Ferlie, Laurence Lynne and Christopher Pollitt (eds.), *The Oxford Handbook of Public Management* (Oxford: Oxford University Press, 2005)

Boyle, Richard, *A Review of Annual Progress Reports,* Committee for Public Management and Research (CPMR) Discussion Paper 18 (Dublin: Institute of Public Administration, 2001)

Boyle, Richard, *Comparing Public Administrations* (Dublin: Institute of Public Administration, 2007)

Boyle, Richard, Peter C. Humphreys, Orla O'Donnell, Joanna O'Riordan and Virpi Timonen, *Changing Local Government: A Review of the Local Government Modernisation Programme*, Committee for Public Management Research (CPMR) Research Report 5 (Dublin: Institute of Public Administration, 2003)

Brady, Rory, 'Reflections on Tribunals of Inquiry', *Bar Review* 3/3 (1997)

Brandenburg, Heinz and Zbyszek Zalinski, 'The Media and the Campaign' in Michael Gallagher and Michael Marsh (eds.), *How Ireland Voted*

2007: The Full Story of Ireland's General Election (Basingstoke: Palgrave and Macmillan, 2007) 167–86

Brennan, Michael, 'Cowen Gave Harney No Confidence Vote, FG Claims', *Irish Independent* (18 December 2007)

Brennan, Niamh, 'Accountability and Best Practice: Lessons from the Corporate World', Mason, Hayes and Curran seminar on accountability in the public sector (Dublin, 17 November 2008)

Brennan, Peter, *Behind Closed Doors – The EU Negotiations that Shaped Modern Ireland* (Dublin: Blackhall Publishing, 2008)

Brennan Commission, *Report of Commission of Inquiry into the Civil Service 1932–35* (Dublin: Stationery Office, 1936)

Brennan report, *Report of the Commission on Financial Management and Control Systems in the Health Services* (Dublin: Department of Health and Children, 2003)

Browne, Vincent, 'Ireland's Most Influential', *Village – Politics, Media, and Current Affairs in Ireland* (15 April 2005)

Buckley, Fiona, Neil Collins and Theresa Reidy, 'Ballot Paper Photographs and Low-information Elections in Ireland', *Politics* 27/3 (2007) 174–81

Burton, Joan, 'Submission to Dublin and Cities Electoral Area Boundary Committee, 2008', available online at: www.electoralareacommittees.ie/dublin_received.htm

Business and Finance, 'Ireland Tops EU e-Government Ranking', *Business and Finance* 42 (27 June 2002)

Butler, Patrick and Neil Collins, *Political Issues in Ireland Today* (Manchester: Manchester University Press, 2004)

Byrne, Elaine, paper presented to the Annual Forum of the Chambers of Commerce in Ireland and individual submission to Local Government Reform Consultative Process (2004)

Byrne, Elaine, 'Parties Must Change Their Tune about Funding', *The Irish Times* (14 December 2007)

Byrne, Raymond and Paul McCutcheon, *The Irish Legal System,* 4th edn (Dublin: Butterworths, 2001)

Callanan, Mark, 'Local and Regional Government in Transition' in Neil Collins and Terry Cradden (eds.), *Political Issues in Ireland Today* (Manchester: Manchester University Press, 2004) 56–78

Callanan, Mark, 'Evolution and Transformation? Critical Junctures and Drivers of Change in Public Services – A Retrospective', Public Service 2022 Project, Working Paper No. 1, Draft (Dublin: Institute of Public Administration, 2006)

Callanan, Mark, *Ireland 2022, Towards One Hundred Years of Self-Government* (Dublin: Institute of Public Administration, 2007)

Callanan, Mark and Justin F. Keogan (eds.), *Local Government in Ireland: Inside Out* (Dublin: Institute of Public Administration, 2003)

Capgemini, 'The User Challenge – Benchmarking the Supply of Online Public Services', seventh annual measurement prepared for the European Commission Directorate General for Information Society and Media (September 2007)

Casey, James, *The Irish Law Officers* (Dublin: Round Hall, Sweet and Maxwell, 1996)

Casey, James, *Constitutional Law in Ireland,* 3rd edn (Dublin: Round Hall, Sweet and Maxwell, 2000)

Castle, Stephen and Judy Dempsey, 'Split Emerges in EU after Ireland Rejects Treaty', *International Herald Tribune* (15 June 2008)

Central Statistics Office (CSO), *Population and Labour Force Projections 2011–2041* (Dublin: CSO, 2008a)

Central Statistics Office, *Population and Migration Estimates* (Dublin: CSO, 2008b)

Chubb, Basil, *The Government and Politics of Ireland* (London: Oxford University Press, 1970)

Chubb, Basil, *Cabinet Government in Ireland* (Dublin: Institute of Public Administration, 1974)

Chubb, Basil, *Constitution and Constitutional Change in Ireland* (Dublin: Institute of Public Administration, 1978)

Chubb, Basil, *The Government and Politics of Ireland*, 2nd edn (London: Longman, 1982)

Chubb, Basil, *A Source Book of Irish Government* (Dublin: Institute of Public Administration, 1983)

Churchill, Winston, 'The Tragedy of Europe', speech to the Academic Youth (University of Zurich, 19 September 1946)

Clancy, Paula and Gráinne Murphy, *Outsourcing Government: Public Bodies and Accountability* (Dublin: TASC and New Island, 2006)

Clarke, Victoria Mary, 'Tea and a Nice Taste of Grace and True Nobility with the President', *Sunday Independent* (16 November 2008)

Clery, Maeve, 'The Character of Irish Parliamentary Interest in Foreign Policy', *Administration* 55/1 (2007) 63–88

Clinch, Peter, Frank Convery and Brendan Walsh, *After the Celtic Tiger: Challenges Ahead* (Dublin: O'Brien Press, 2002)

Coakley, John and Michael Gallagher (eds.), *Politics in the Republic of Ireland*, 4th edn (London: Routledge, 2004)

Coakley, John and Michael Laver, 'Options for the Future of Seanad Éireann, Report to All-Party Oireachtas Committee on the Constitution (5 December 1996)' in All-Party Oireachtas Committee on the

Constitution, *Second Progress Report: Seanad Éireann* (Dublin: Stationery Office, 1997)

Collins, Neil, *Local Government Managers at Work* (Dublin: Institute of Public Administration, 1987)

Collins, Neil, 'The Public Service and Regulatory Reform' in Neil Collins, Terry Cradden and Patrick Butler (eds.), *Modernising Irish Government – The Politics of Administrative Reform* (Dublin: Gill & Macmillan, 2007)

Collins, Neil and Terry Cradden, *Irish Politics Today* (Manchester: Manchester University Press, 1989)

Collins, Neil and Mary O'Shea, *Understanding Corruption in Irish Politics* (Cork: Cork University Press, 2000)

Collins, Neil, Terry Cradden and Patrick Butler, *Modernising Irish Government – The Politics of Administrative Reform* (Dublin: Gill & Macmillan, 2007)

Collins, Stephen, 'Legislative Route May Be the Best Way to Get around Lisbon', *The Irish Times* (19 July 2008)

Commission of Inquiry into the Civil Service, *Report of Commission of Inquiry into the Civil Service 1932–35* [Brennan Commission] (Dublin: Stationery Office, 1936)

Commission on Financial Management and Control Systems in the Health Services, *Report of the Commission on Financial Management and Control Systems in the Health Services* [Brennan report] (Dublin: Department of Health and Children, 2003)

Commission on Patient Safety and Quality Assurance, *Building a Culture of Patient Safety, Report of the Commission on Patient Safety and Quality Assurance* (Dublin: Stationery Office, 2008)

Commission on Social Welfare, *Report of the Commission on Social Welfare* (Dublin: Stationery Office, 1986)

Commission to Inquire into Child Abuse, *Report of the Commission to Inquire into Child Abuse*, Executive Summary and Volumes I to V inclusive (Dubin: Stationery Office, 2009)

Committee of Public Accounts, Sub-Committee on Certain Revenue Matters, *Parliamentary Inquiry into DIRT: First Report* (Dublin: Houses of the Oireachtas, 1999)

Committee of Public Accounts, Sub-Committee on Certain Revenue Matters, *Parliamentary Inquiry into DIRT: Final Report* (Dublin: Stationery Office, 2001)

Comptroller and Auditor General, *Report on Value for Money Examination: Consultancies in the Civil Service*, Report No. 22 (Dublin: Stationery Office, 1998)

Comptroller and Auditor General, *Value for Money Report No. 49 – Waste Management in Hospitals* (Dublin: Comptroller and Auditor General, 2005)

Comptroller and Auditor General, *eGovernment,* Special Report No. 58 (Dublin: Comptroller and Auditor General, 2007)

Connaughton, Bernadette, 'Reform of Politico-Administrative Relations in the Irish System: Clarifying or Complicating the Doctrine of Ministerial Responsibility', *Irish Political Studies* 21/3 (September 2006) 257–76

Connolly, Eileen and Eunan O'Halpin, 'The Government and Governmental System' in John Coakley and Michael Gallagher (eds.), *Politics in the Republic of Ireland*, 3rd edn (London: Routledge, 1999)

Connolly, Niamh, 'Irish MEPs out in the Cold after Lisbon Rejection', *Sunday Business Post* (16 November 2008)

Constitution Review Group, *Report of the Constitution Review Group* [Whitaker report] (Dublin: Stationery Office, 1996)

Co-ordinating Group of Secretaries, *Delivering Better Government: A Programme of Change for the Irish Civil Service. Second Report to Government of the Co-ordinating Group of Secretaries* (Dublin: Department of the Taoiseach, 1996)

Coulter, Carol, 'A Roadmap to Child Protection', *The Irish Times* (19 December 2007)

Coulter, Carol, 'Chairman Dismisses GRA Criticism', *The Irish Times* (2 May 2008a)

Coulter, Carol, 'Judge Questions Role of Victims' Statements', *The Irish Times* (19 November 2008b)

Courts Service, *Annual Report 2007* (Dublin: Courts Service, 2007)

Cowen, Brian, 'Speech by An Taoiseach, Mr Brian Cowen TD, at the Launch of the Government's Statement on Transforming Public Services, Dublin Castle' (Dublin: Department of the Taoiseach, 26 November 2008a)

Cowen, Brian, 'Public Service Must Be Reformed', *The Irish Times* (27 November 2008b)

Cromien, Sean, 'Symposium on the Privatisation of State Assets and State Commercial Companies', *Journal of the Statistical and Social Inquiry Society of Ireland* XXV/V (paper read before the society, 3 December 1987)

Cromien, Sean, 'Serving in New Spheres' in Rory O'Donnell (ed.), *Europe – The Irish Experience* (Dublin: Institute of European Affairs, 2000)

Cuffe, Ciarán, 'Does the Car Parking Space Levy Make Sense?', *The Irish Times* (24 November 2008)

Data Protection Commissioner, *2007 Annual Report* (Dublin: Brunswick Press, 2008)

De Vere White, Terence, *Kevin O'Higgins* (London: Methuen, 1948)

Decentralisation Implementation Group, 'Progress Report to the Tánaiste and Minister for Finance' (July 2007)

Decentralisation Implementation Group, 'Report to the Minister for Finance on the State Agencies Due to Relocate under the Government's Public Service Decentralisation Programme' (July 2008)

Delaney, Eamon, *An Accidental Diplomat – My Years in the Irish Foreign Service 1987–1995* (Dublin: New Island, 2001)

Deloitte & Touche, *Value for Money Audit of the Irish Health System* (Dublin: Department of Health and Children, 2001)

Deloitte & Touche, 'Final Report: Deloitte & Touche Management Consultants Review of Staffing and Grading in the Office of the Houses of the Oireachtas' (Dublin: Deloitte & Touche, 2002)

Dempsey, Noel, 'Speech at Consultation Seminar on Regulatory Appeals' (14 September 2006)

Denhardt, Janet and Robert Denhardt, *The New Public Service: Serving, Not Steering* (London: M.E. Sharpe, 2003)

Denhardt, Robert, 'The Future of Public Administration', *Public Administration and Management an Interactive Journal*, 4/2 (1999) 279–92

Department of the Environment, Heritage and Local Government, *Better Local Government – A Programme for Change* (Dublin: Stationery Office, 1996)

Department of the Environment, Heritage and Local Government, *Annual Report 2006* (Dublin: Stationery Office, 2006)

Department of Finance, *State Bodies Guidelines* (Dublin: Department of Finance, 1992)

Department of Finance, *Code of Practice for the Governance of State Bodies* (Dublin: Department of Finance, 2001)

Department of Finance, *E-Government and the Possibilities It Provides for Organisation Development* (Dublin: Centre for Management and Organisation Development, Department of Finance, 2002a)

Department of Finance, *Report of the Working Group on the Accountability of Secretaries General and Accounting Officers* [Mullarkey report] (Dublin: Department of Finance, 2002b)

Department of Finance, 'Decentralisation a Reality in over 30 Towns in 2007', press release (Dublin: Department of Finance, 8 October 2007)

Department of Finance, *Statement of Strategy 2008–2010* (Dublin: Department of Finance, 2008)

Department of Foreign Affairs, *Annual Report* (Dublin: Stationery Office, various years)

Department of Health, *Health: The Wider Dimensions* (Dublin: Stationery Office, 1986)

Department of Health, *Report of the Commission on Health Funding* (Dublin: Stationery Office, 1989)

Department of Health, *Shaping a Healthier Future: A Strategy for Effective Healthcare in the 1990s* (Dublin: Stationery Office, 1994)

Department of Health and Children, *Quality and Fairness: A Health System for You. Health Strategy* (Dublin: Stationery Office, 2001)

Department of Health and Children, *Primary Care: A New Direction* (Dublin: Stationery Office, 2002)

Department of Health and Children, *Health in Ireland: Key Trends 2007* (Dublin: Stationery Office, 2007)

Department of Justice, Equality and Law Reform, *Balance in the Criminal Law Review Group* [Chair: Dr Gerard Hogan SC] (Dublin: Department of Justice, Equality and Law Reform, 2007)

Department of the Taoiseach, *Annual Report* (Dublin: Department of the Taoiseach, various years)

Department of the Taoiseach, *Programme for Economic and Social Progress 1991–1993* (Dublin: Stationery Office, 1991)

Department of the Taoiseach, *Delivering Better Government: A Programme of Change for the Irish Civil Service. Second Report to Government of the Co-ordinating Group of Secretaries* (Dublin: Department of the Taoiseach, 1996)

Department of the Taoiseach, *Programme for Prosperity and Fairness. Social Partnership Agreement 2000–2003* (Dublin: Department of the Taoiseach, 2000)

Department of the Taoiseach, *New Connections. A Strategy to Realise the Potential of the Information Society, Government Action Plan* (Dublin: Department of the Taoiseach, 2002)

Department of the Taoiseach, *Sustaining Progress. Social Partnership Agreement 2003–2005* (Dublin: Department of the Taoiseach, 2003)

Department of the Taoiseach, *White Paper – Regulating Better* (Dublin: Department of the Taoiseach, 2004)

Department of the Taoiseach, *Towards 2016, Ten-year Framework Social Partnership Agreement 2006–2015* (Dublin: Stationery Office, 2006)

Department of the Taoiseach, 'Taoiseach Tackles National and EU Regulatory Burdens', press release (Dublin: Department of the Taoiseach, 8 March 2007)

Department of the Taoiseach, *2008 Irish Civil Service Customer Satisfaction Survey*, prepared by Ipsos MORI (Dublin: Public Services Modernisation Division, Department of the Taoiseach, 2008a)

Department of the Taoiseach, *Guidelines for the Preparation of Customer Charters and Customer Action Plans* (Dublin: Public Services Modernisation Division, Department of the Taoiseach, 2008b)

Department of the Taoiseach, *Report of the Organisational Review Programme (Pilot Phase)* (Dublin: Department of the Taoiseach, 2008c)

Depauw, Sam and Shane Martin, 'Legislative Party Discipline and Cohesion in Comparative Perspective' in Daniela Giannetti and Kenneth Benoit (eds.), *Intra-Party Politics and Coalition Governments in Parliamentary Democracies* (London: Routledge, 2008)

Desmond, Barry, *Finally and In Conclusion, A Political Memoir* (Dublin: New Island, 2000)

Devlin report, *Report of the Public Services Organisation Review Group, 1966–69* (Dublin: Stationery Office, 1969)

Director of Public Prosecutions, 'Prosecution Policy on the Giving of Reasons for Decisions', press release (Dublin: Office of the Director of Public Prosecutions, 22 October 2008)

Doherty, Ann, *Report on the Circumstances Leading to the Suspension of Radiology Services at Midland Regional Hospital, Portlaoise* (Dublin: Department of Health and Children, 2008)

Dollard, Gerard, 'Local Government Finance: The Policy Context' in Mark Callanan and Justin F. Keogan (eds.), *Local Government in Ireland: Inside Out* (Dublin: Institute of Public Administration, 2003) 325–40

Dooney, Sean, *Irish Agriculture: An Organisational Profile* (Dublin: Institute of Public Administration, 1989)

Doyle, Oran, *Constitutional Equality Law* (Dublin: Thomson Round Hall, 2004)

Drew, Eileen, Cliona Murphy, Peter Humphreys, Sue Leigh-Doyle, Joanna O'Riordan and Sandra Redmond, *Employment and Career Progression of People with a Disability in the Irish Civil Service* (Dublin: Institute of Public Administration, 2002)

Duignan, Seán, *One Spin on the Merry-Go-Round* (Dublin: Blackwater Press, 1995)

Dukes, Alan, 'I Was in Charge during Ireland's Last Recession – and Believe Me, We Do Not Want to Go Back', *Irish Mail on Sunday* (29 June 2008)

Dunlop, Frank, *Yes Taoiseach – Irish Politics from behind Closed Doors* (Dublin: Penguin, 2004)

Dur, Andreas and Gemma Mateo, 'The Irish EU Presidency and the Constitutional Treaty: Neutrality, Skills and Effective Mediation', *Irish Political Studies* 23/1 (February 2008) 59–76

Elgie, Robert and Peter Fitzgerald, 'The President and the Taoiseach' in John Coakley and Michael Gallagher (eds.), *Politics in the Republic of Ireland,* 4th edn (London: Routledge, 2004)

Elgie, Robert and John Stapleton, 'The Parliamentary Activity of the Head of Government in Ireland (1923–2000) in Comparative Perspective', *Journal of Legislative Studies* 9/1 (2003) 37–56

Ellemann-Jensen, Uffe, 'Ireland Must Go', *Today's Zaman* (16 June 2008)

Eppink, Derk-Jan, *Life of a European Mandarin* (Tielt: Lannoo, 2007)

European Central Bank, *Public Sector Efficiency: An International Comparison*, Working Paper No. 242 by Antonio Afonso, Ludger Schuknecht and Vito Tanzi (Frankfurt: European Central Bank, 2003)

European Commission, *Free Movement of Workers is Good for Europe's Economy, Employment in Europe* (Brussels: European Commission, 2008)

Eurostat, 'Ageing Characterises the Demographic Perspectives of the European Societies', *Statistics in Focus* 72 (26 August 2008)

Fanning, Ronan, *The Irish Department of Finance 1922–58* (Dublin: Institute of Public Administration, 1978)

Fanning, Rossa, 'Lisbon Vote is Not Democracy but an Exercise in Buck-Passing', *The Irish Times* (22 April 2008)

Farrell, Brian, 'A Note on the Dáil Constitution, 1919', *Irish Jurist* IV (1969) 127–38

Farrell, Brian, *Chairman or Chief? The Role of the Taoiseach in Irish Government* (Dublin: Gill & Macmillan, 1971)

Farrell, Brian, 'Coalitions and Political Institutions: The Irish Experience' in Vernon Bogdanor (ed.), *Coalition Government in Western Europe* (London: Heinemann, 1983) 248–62

Farrell, Brian, 'The Constitution and the Institutions of Government: Constitutional Theory and Political Practice' in Frank Litton (ed.), *The Constitution of Ireland 1937–87,* special issue of *Administration* 35/4 (1987)

Farrell, Brian (ed.), *De Valera's Constitution and Ours, Thomas Davis Lectures* (Dublin: Gill & Macmillan for RTÉ, 1988a)

Farrell, Brian, 'The Irish Cabinet System' in Jean Blondel and Ferdinand Müller Rommel (eds.), *Cabinets in Western Europe* (London: Macmillan, 1988b)

Farrell, Brian, 'The Government' in John Coakley and Michael Gallagher (eds.), *Politics in the Republic of Ireland,* 2nd edn (Dublin: PSAI Press, 1993)

Farrell, Brian, 'Coalitions and Political Institutions: The Irish Experience' in Vernon Bogdonar (ed.), *Coalition Government in Western Europe* (London: Heinemann, 2003)

Feeney, Peter, 'The Media in Ireland: A Distorted Vehicle for Political Communication?' in Dónal de Buitléir and Frances Ruane (eds.), *Governance and Policy in Ireland – Essays in Honour of Miriam Hederman O'Brien* (Dublin: Institute of Public Administration, 2003)

Ferriter, Diarmaid, *Judging Dev: A Reassessment of the Life and Legacy of Eamon de Valera* (Dublin: Royal Irish Academy, 2007)

Fine Gael, *A Democratic Revolution – A Thorough Overhaul of the Institutions of the State* (Dublin: Fine Gael, 2000)

Finlay, Fergus, *Mary Robinson: A President with a Purpose* (Dublin: O'Brien Press, 1990)

Finlay, Fergus, *Snakes and Ladders* (Dublin: New Island, 1998)

FitzGerald, Garret, *State-Sponsored Bodies*, 2nd edn (Dublin: Institute of Public Administration, 1963)

FitzGerald, Garret, *All in a Life* (Dublin: Gill & Macmillan, 1991)

FitzGerald, Garret, *Reflections on the Irish State* (Dublin: Irish Academic Press, 2003)

FitzGerald, Garret, *Ireland in the World – Further Reflections* (Dublin: Liberties Press, 2005)

FitzGerald, Garret, 'Why a Reformed PR System Deserves Our Vote', *The Irish Times* (16 February 2008a)

FitzGerald, Garret, 'Lisbon Treaty Bears Stamp of Irish Negotiators and Serves Our Interests', *The Irish Times* (10 May 2008b)

FitzGerald, Garret, 'Accountability Is Key to Public Service Reform', *The Irish Times* (29 November 2008c)

Fitzgerald, John, 'Being Dublin City Manager', paper presented at the conference to commemorate the seventy-fifth anniversary of the Cork City Management Act 1929 (Cork: Department of Government, University College Cork, 2004)

Fitzgerald, John, *Management, Governance and Communications Issues Arising from the Review of Breast Radiology Services at Midland Regional Hospital, Portlaoise, Report Prepared for HSE Board* (Dublin: Department of Health and Children, 2008)

Fitzpatrick Associates, *Evaluation of Customer Charters* (Dublin: Stationery Office, 2007)

Forde, Michael, *Constitutional Law of Ireland* (Cork and Dublin: Mercier Press, 1987)

Gallagher, Michael, 'Does Ireland Need a New Electoral System?', *Irish Political Studies* 2 (1987) 27–48

Gallagher, Michael, 'Referendum Campaigns in Ireland', paper presented at the eighth international SISE conference, 'Le Campagne Elettorali' (Venice, 18 to 20 December 2003)

Gallagher, Michael and Paul Mitchell, *The Politics of Electoral Systems* (Oxford: Oxford University Press, 2005)

Gallagher, Michael, Michael Laver and Michael Marsh, *The Oireachtas Committee System* (Dublin: The Policy Institute, Trinity College, 1997)

Galligan, Yvonne, 'Women in Politics' in John Coakley and Michael Gallagher (eds.), *Politics in the Republic of Ireland*, 4th edn (London: Routledge, 2004)

Garry, John, Michael Marsh and Richard Sinnott, '"Second-order" Versus "Issue-voting" Effects in EU Referendums – Evidence from the Irish Nice Treaty Referendums', *European Union Politics* 6 (2005) 201–21

Garvin, Tom, 'Article to Mark 50th Anniversary of *Bunreacht na hÉireann*', *The Irish Times* (December 1987)

Garvin, Tom, *Preventing the Future: Why Was Ireland so Poor for so Long?* (Dublin: Gill & Macmillan, 2004)

Goggin, Isolde and Gillian Lauder, *Review of the Operation of Regulatory Impact Analysis*, report for the Department of the Taoiseach (Dublin: Stationery Office, 2008)

Government of Ireland, *Report of Commission of Inquiry into the Civil Service 1932–35* [Brennan Commission] (Dublin: Stationery Office, 1936)

Government of Ireland, *Report of the Committee on the Constitution* (Dublin: Stationery Office, 1967)

Government of Ireland, *Serving the Country Better: A White Paper on the Public Service* (Dublin: Stationery Office, 1985)

Government of Ireland, *Report of the Dublin Hospital Initiative Group* [Kennedy report] (Dublin: Stationery Office, 1990a)

Government of Ireland, *The Hospital Efficiency Review Group* (Dublin: Stationery Office, 1990b)

Government of Ireland, *A Dáil for the New Millennium* (Dublin: Stationery Office, 2000)

Government of Ireland, *Dáil Éireann Standing Orders Relative to Public Business* (Dublin: Stationery Office, 2002)

Government of Ireland, *An Inquiry into Certain Matters in Relation to Procurement, as Requested by the Taoiseach* [Quigley report] (Dublin: Department of the Taoiseach, 2005)

Government of Ireland, *Seanad Éireann Standing Orders Relative to Public Business* (Dublin: Stationery Office, 2007a)

Government of Ireland, *Transforming Ireland: A Better Quality of Life for All, National Development Plan 2007–2013* (Dublin: Stationery Office, 2007b)

Government of Ireland, *Building a Culture of Patient Safety, Report of the Commission on Patient Safety and Quality Assurance* (Dublin: Stationery Office, 2008a)

Government of Ireland, *Government Statement on Transforming Public Services* (Dublin: Department of the Taoiseach, 26 November 2008b)

Government of Ireland, *Transforming Public Services: Citizen Centred, Performance Focused, Report of the Task Force on the Public Service* (Dublin: Stationery Office, 2008c)

Grist, Berna, 'Planning' in Mark Callanan and Justin F. Keogan (eds.), *Local Government in Ireland: Inside Out* (Dublin: Institute of Public Administration, 2003) 221–52

Haldane report, *Report of the Machinery of Government Committee* (London: HMSO, 1918)

Hamilton, James, 'The Article 26 Procedure from the Point of View of the Framer of Legislation' in Constitution Review Group, *Report of the Constitution Review Group* (Dublin: Stationery Office, 1996) 544–6

Hanly report, *Report of the National Task Force on Medical Staffing* (Dublin: Department of Health and Children, 2003)

Hannon, Katie, *The Naked Politician* (Dublin: Gill & Macmillan, 2004)

Haran, Paul, 'The Irish Civil Service in a Changing World' in Dónal de Buitléir and Frances Ruane (eds.), *Governance and Policy in Ireland: Essays in Honour of Miriam Hederman O'Brien* (Dublin: Institute of Public Administration, 2003) 43–58

Hardiman, Adrian, 'The Role of the Supreme Court in Our Democracy' in Joe Mulholland (ed.), *Political Choice and Democratic Freedom in Ireland* (Dublin: MacGill Summer School, 2004)

Hardiman, Niamh, 'Social Partnership, Wage Bargaining, and Growth' in Brian Nolan, Philip O'Connell and Christopher Whelan (eds.), *Bust to Boom? The Irish Experience of Growth and Inequality* (Dublin: Institute of Public Administration and Economic and Social Research Institute, 2000) 286–309

Hardiman, Niamh, 'Partnership and Politics: How Embedded is Social Partnership?', Geary Discussion Paper Series (2005), available online at: www.ucd.ie/geary/publications/2005/GearyWp200508.pdf

Haughey, Charles, 'Speech to the Solicitors' Apprentices Debating Society of Ireland 1966', delivered by T.K. Whitaker, *The Irish Times* (12 November 1966)

Hayes-Renshaw, Fiona and Helen Wallace, *The Council of Ministers* (Basingstoke: Palgrave Macmillan, 2006)

Health Information and Quality Authority (HIQA), *National Hygiene Services Quality Review 2007* (Dublin: HIQA, 2007)

Health Information and Quality Authority, *National Hygiene Services Quality Review 2008* (Dublin: HIQA, 2008)

Health Service Executive (HSE), *Annual Report and Financial Statement 2007* (Dublin: HSE, 2008a)

Health Service Executive, *National Intercultural Health Strategy 2007–2012* (Dublin: HSE, 2008b)

Health Service Executive, 'HSE Updates Staff Associations on Current Developments', press release (Dublin: HSE, 3 July 2008c)

Heffernan, Breda, 'Partners Tired of "Difficult" Irish, Says Eurocrat', *Irish Independent* (23 October 2008)

Hennessy, Peter, *Whitehall* (London: Free Press, 1989)

Hogan, Gerard, 'Unenumerated Personal Rights: Ryan's Case Re-evaluated (1990–92)', *Irish Jurist* 25–27 (1995) 95–116

Hogan, Gerard, 'De Valera's 1937 Constitution Successfully Stood Test of Time', *The Irish Times* (29 December 2007)

Hogan, Gerard and David Gwynn-Morgan, *Administrative Law in Ireland*, 2nd edn (London: Sweet and Maxwell, 1991)

Hogan, Gerard and David Gwynn Morgan, *Administrative Law in Ireland*, 3rd edn (Dublin: Round Hall, Sweet and Maxwell, 1998)

Hogan, Gerard and Gerry Whyte, *J.M. Kelly: The Irish Constitution*, 4th edn (Dublin: Butterworths, 2003)

Horgan, John, *Mary Robinson – An Independent Voice* (Dublin: O'Brien Press, 1997)

Horgan, John, *Noel Brown: Passionate Outsider* (Dublin: Gill & Macmillan, 2000)

Houses of the Oireachtas Commission, *Annual Report 2007* (Dublin: Stationery Office, 2008)

Houston, David J. and Lauren K. Harding, 'Trust in the Public Service: A Cross-National Examination', paper prepared for presentation at the sixty-sixth annual national conference of the Midwest Political Science Association (Chicago, 3 to 6 April 2008)

Hussey, Gemma, *At the Cutting Edge: Cabinet Diaries, 1982–1987* (Dublin: Gill & Macmillan, 1990)

Hussey, Gemma, *Ireland Today* (Dublin: TownHouse, 1993)

Institute of Public Administration, *Administration Yearbook & Diary* (Dublin: Institute of Public Administration, various years)

Irish Association of Emergency Medicine (IAEM), *Emergency Department Task Force Report* (Dublin: IAEM 2007)

Irish Centre for Social Gerontology, *End of Life Care for Older People in Acute and Long-Stay Care Settings in Ireland*, study jointly commissioned by the National Council on Ageing and Older People and the Irish Hospice Foundation (Galway: National University of Ireland Galway, 2008)

Irish Planning Institute, 'Sustainable Rural Housing – Consultation Draft Guidelines for Planning Authorities' (Dublin: Irish Planning Institute, April 2004)

Irish Small and Medium Enterprises Association (ISME), 'ISME Warns of Further Traffic Chaos Costing Small Firms Millions', press release (Dublin: ISME, 29 August 2008)

Jackson, Fintan, *A Comparative Consideration of the Irish Presidency* (Galway: National University of Ireland Galway, 2003)

Jaconelli, Joseph, 'Reference of Bills to the Supreme Court? A Comparative Perspective', *Irish Jurist* (1983) 322

Johnston, Mandy, interview on *Conversations with Eamon Dunphy* (broadcast on RTÉ Radio 1, Dublin, 17 May 2008)

Joint Committee on Child Protection, *Report on Child Protection* (Dublin: Houses of the Oireachtas, 2006)

Joint Committee on Health and Children, *Interim Report on the Report on Certain Issues of Management and Administration in the Department of Health & Children Associated with the Practice of Charges for Persons in Long-Stay Care in Health Board Institutions and Related Matters* (Dublin: Houses of the Oireachtas, 2005)

Joint Committee on Public Enterprise and Transport, Sub-Committee on Mini-CTC Signalling Project, 'Interim Report' (Dublin: Houses of the Oireachtas, 4 April 2002)

Keane, Ronan, 'Judges as Lawmakers – The Irish Experience', *Judicial Studies Institute Journal* 1 at 9 (2004) 4.2

Kehoe, Ian, 'RTÉ among Eight Semi-state Bodies to Face External Audits', *Sunday Business Post* (29 January 2006)

Kelly, John, *Fundamental Rights in the Irish Law and Constitution*, 2nd edn (Dublin: Figgis, 1967)

Kelly, John M., *The Irish Constitution* (Dublin: Jurist Publishing, 1984)

Kelly, Michael, 'Steering a Policy Course' in Eilish McAuliffe and Kenneth McKenzie (eds.), *The Politics of Healthcare – Achieving Real Reform* (Dublin: Liffey Press, 2007)

Kennedy, Emma, 'Revenue Staff Take to Unpaid Leave', *Sunday Business Post* (13 July 2008)

Kennedy, Fiachra and Richard Sinnott, 'Irish Public Opinion Towards European Integration', *Irish Political Studies* 22/1 (February 2007) 61–80

Kennedy report, *Report of the Dublin Hospital Initiative Group* (Dublin: Stationery Office, 1990)

Kenny, Enda, 'Fine Gael Announces Immediate Measures for Dáil Reform', press release (Dublin: Fine Gael, 8 November 2003)

Keogan, Justin F., 'Reform in Irish Local Government' in Mark Callanan and Justin F. Keogan (eds.), *Local Government in Ireland: Inside Out* (Dublin: Institute of Public Administration, 2003) 82–96

Keogh, Dermot and Andrew McCarthy, *The Making of the Irish Constitution, 1937* (Cork: Mercier Press, 2007)

Knight, Kathleen, Yvonne Galligan and Una Nic Giolla Choille, 'Equalizing Opportunities for Women in Electoral Politics in Ireland: The Views of Women Members of Parliament', *Women & Politics* 26/1 (2004) 1–20

Komito, Lee, 'Politics and Clientelism in Urban Ireland: Information, Reputation and Brokerage' (University Microfilms International 8603660, 1985), available online at www.ucd.ie/lkomito/thesis12.htm

Kuhry, Bob, *Public Sector Performance: An International Comparison of Education, Health Care, Law and Order and Public Administration in 29 Western Countries* (The Hague: Social and Cultural Planning Office, 2004)

Labour Party, *Putting Our House in Order* (Dublin: Labour Party, 2003)

Laffan, Brigid, 'Ireland' in Dietrich Rometsch and Wolfgang Wessels (eds.), *The European Union and Member States: Towards Institutional Fusion?* (Manchester: Manchester University Press, 1996)

Laffan, Brigid, 'Rapid Adaptation and Light Co-ordination' in Rory O'Donnell (ed.), *Europe – The Irish Experience* (Dublin: Institute of European Affairs, 2000)

Laffan, Brigid, *Organising for a Changing Europe: Irish Central Government and the European Union*, Blue Paper No. 7 (Dublin: The Policy Institute, Trinity College, 2001)

Laffan, Brigid, 'Ireland's Management of EU Business: The Impact of Nice' in Michael Holmes (ed.), *Ireland and the European Union: Nice, Enlargement and the Future of Europe* (Manchester: Manchester University Press, 2005)

Laffan, Brigid, 'Astute Irish Diplomats Are Expert at Playing the Brussels System', *The Irish Times* (29 May 2008a)

Laffan, Brigid, 'Treaty Rejection Will Reduce Ireland to Minority of One', *The Irish Times* (18 June 2008b)

Laver, Michael, 'The Role and Future of the Upper House in Ireland', *Journal of Legislative Studies* 8/3 (Autumn 2002) 49–66

Lavery, Don, 'My Part in Downfall of a President over the "Thundering Disgrace" Debacle', *Irish Independent* (6 January 2007)

Law Reform Commission, *Consultation Paper on Child Sexual Abuse* (Dublin: Law Reform Commission, 1989)

Law Reform Commission, *Report on Child Sexual Abuse* (Dublin: Law Reform Commission, 1990)

Law Reform Commission, *Consultation Paper on Public Inquiries Including Tribunals of Inquiry* (Dublin: The Law Reform Commission, 2003)

Law Society of Ireland, 'Society Opposes Sea Change in DPP's Reasons' Policy', *Law Society Gazette* (June 2008) 12–13

Lawlor, John and Colm McCarthy, 'Browsing Onwards: Irish Public Spending in Perspective', *Irish Banking Review* (Autumn 2003)

Lee, Joseph J., *Ireland 1912–1985* (Cambridge: Cambridge University Press, 1989)

Lehane, Darren, 'A Legal Janus: Resolving the Conflict between the Attorney General's Functions as Guardian of the Public Interest and Legal Adviser to the Government', *Irish Student Law Review* 12 (2004)

Lemass, Seán F., 'The Role of State Sponsored Bodies in the Economy', *Administration* 6/4 (1959)

Lemass, Seán, 'Lemass on Government', *Learghas* 12 (January 1968)

Lenihan [Snr], Brian, *For the Record* (Dublin: Blackwater Press, 1991)

Lenihan [Jnr], Brian, 'Speech by the Minister for Justice to the Patrick MacGill Summer School' (Glenties, County Donegal, 6 July 2007)

Lenihan [Jnr], Brian, 'Freedom of Information: The First Decade, Speech at 10th Anniversary Conference' (15 May 2008)

Lenihan, Conor, 'Lenihan Announces Integration Taskforce', press release (Dublin: Department of Community, Rural and Gaeltacht Affairs, 13 August 2007)

Litton, Frank, 'The Civil Service and a New Design for Democracy' in Frank Litton, Tony Farmar and Frank Scott-Lennon (eds.), *Ideas at Work: Essays in Honour of Geoffrey MacKechnie* (Dublin: A. & A. Farmar, 2006) 177–99

Lysaght, Charles, 'Did We Need to Hold a Referendum at all? The Government Would Have Been Better Off Taking Its Chances with Ratification', *Sunday Independent* (22 June 2008)

MacCarthaigh, Muiris, *Accountability in Irish Parliamentary Politics* (Dublin: Institute of Public Administration, 2005)

MacCarthaigh, Muiris, 'Opposition Plans for Dáil Reform', *Village Magazine* (1 February 2006)

MacCarthaigh, Muiris, *The Corporate Governance of Regional and Local Public Bodies in Ireland* (Dublin: Institute of Public Administration, 2007)

MacCarthaigh, Muiris, '"Bonfire of the Quangos" Attitude Very Misguided on Role of State Agencies', *The Irish Times* (19 September 2008)

Mair, Peter, 'Coalition Evermore? Party Politics in Ireland in the Twenty-First Century', address to University College Dublin's politics programme (Dublin Castle, 26 February 1998)

Mansergh, Martin, 'The Changing Face of the Public Service North and South', speech to the Annual Conference of the Association of Chief Executives of State Agencies (11 September 2008)

Mansergh, Nicholas, *Survey of British Commonwealth Affairs: Problems of External Policy, 1931–39* (London: Oxford Press, 1952)

Marsh, Michael, Richard Sinnott, John Garry and Fiachra Kennedy, *The Irish Voter: The Nature of Electoral Competition in the Republic of Ireland* (Manchester: Manchester University Press, 2008)

Marshall, A.H., *Local Government Administration Abroad IV* (London: HMSO, 1967)

Martin, Shane, *Explaining Variation in the Strength of Parliamentary Committees* (2007), available online at: http://webpages.dcu.ie/~martins/committees1.pdf

Martin, Shane, 'Role Orientation, Electoral Institutions and the Internal Organisation of Legislatures', paper presented at workshop on parliamentary and representative roles in modern legislatures (Rennes, 2008)

McAuliffe, Eilish and Kenneth McKenzie (eds.), *The Politics of Healthcare – Achieving Real Reform* (Dublin: Liffey Press, 2007)

McCarthy, Dermot, 'Public Service Reform in Ireland', paper presented to the Dublin Economics Workshop (Kenmare, 15 October 2005)

McCarthy, Dermot, 'Thomas Davis Lecture: Towards 2016' (broadcast on RTÉ Radio 1, Dublin, 30 November 2007)

McCarthy, Justine, *Mary McAleese: The Outsider* (Dublin: Blackwater Press, 1999)

McDonagh, Bobby, *Original Sin in a Brave New World – An Account of the Negotiation of the Treaty of Amsterdam* (Dublin: Institute of European Affairs, 1998)

McDunphy, Michael, *The President of Ireland: His Powers, Functions and Duties* (Dublin: Browne & Nolan, 1945)

McGauran, Anne-Marie, Koen Verhoest and Peter C. Humphreys, *The Corporate Governance of Agencies in Ireland: Non-commercial National Agencies*, Committee for Public Management Research (CPMR) Research Report 6 (Dublin: Institute of Public Administration, 2005)

McKinsey and Co., *Strengthening the Local Government Service*, report prepared for the Minister for Local Government (Dublin: Stationery Office, 1971)

McLindon, Andrew, 'Ireland Tops EU e-Government Rankings' (ENN, Ireland's IT Newswire, 20 June 2002)

Mercer Human Resource Consulting, *Evaluation of Performance Management and Development System* (Dublin: Mercer HR, 2004)

Millward Brown IMS, 'Post Lisbon Treaty Referendum Research Findings' (Dublin: Millward Brown IMS, 2008)

Mintzberg, Henry, 'Managing Government, Governing Management', *Harvard Business Review* (May/June 1996) 79–80

Mitchell, Paul, 'Oh What a Tangled Web: Delegation, Accountability and Executive Power in Ireland' in Kaare Strøm, Wolfgang Müller and Torbjörn Bergman (eds.), *Delegation and Accountability in Parliamentary Democracies* (Oxford: Oxford University Press, 2003) 418–44

Molony, Senan, 'Truth Comes at a High Price for the Taxpayers and Politicians', *Irish Independent* (30 October 2008)

Montesquieu, Charles de, *The Spirit of the Laws* (1749)

Morgan, David Gwynn, *The Separation of Powers in the Irish Constitution* (Dublin: Round Hall, Sweet and Maxwell, 1997)

Morgan, David Gwynn, 'Judicial Activism – Too Much of a Good Thing' in Tim Murphy and Patrick Twomey (eds.), *Ireland's Evolving Constitution 1937–1997: Collected Essays* (Oxford: Hart Publishing, 1998) 107–19

Morgan, David Gwynn, *A Judgment too Far? Judicial Activism and the Constitution* (Cork: Cork University Press, 2001)

Morgan, Donagh, 'The Programme Managers', *AHCS Newsletter* 75 (March 1995)

Mulholland, Joe (ed.), *The Challenge for Government – Priorities for the Next Five Years, Essays from the 2007 MacGill Summer School* (Dublin: Liffey Press, 2007)

Mullarkey report, *Report of the Working Group on the Accountability of Secretaries General and Accounting Officers* (Dublin: Department of Finance, 2002)

Mulreany, Michael and Tony McNamara, 'Governance Issues in the Irish Public Sector', *Administration* 55/1 (2007)

Murphy, Kevin, 'Democracy in Ireland', speech at launch of Democratic Audit by TASC – Think Tank for Action on Social Change (20 June 2005)

Murphy, Mary C., 'Reform of Dáil Éireann: The Dynamics of Parliamentary Change', *Parliamentary Affairs* 59/3 (2006) 437–53

Murphy, Tim and Patrick Twomey (eds.), *Ireland's Evolving Constitution, 1937–1997: Collected Essays* (Oxford: Hart Publishing, 1998)

Murray, Frank and Paddy Teahon, 'The Irish Political and Policy-making System and the Current Programme of Change', *Administration* 45/4 (1998) 39–58

Murray, Seamus, 'European Communication – The Role of Local and Regional Authorities', seminar on the European Commission White Paper (Brussels, 23 November 2006)

National Commission on Restorative Justice, *Interim Report* (Dublin: Department of Justice, Equality and Law Reform, 2008)

National Competitiveness Council, *Annual Competitiveness Report* (Dublin: National Competitiveness Council, 2007)

National Consultative Committee on Racism and Interculturalism (NCCRI), *Developing Quality Cost Effective Interpreting and Translating Services for Government Service Providers in Ireland,* study carried out by FGS Consulting and Dr Jacqueline Turton of the University of Essex for the Minister for Integration (Dublin: NCCRI, 2008)

National Task Force on Medical Staffing, *Report of the National Task Force on Medical Staffing* [Hanly report] (Dublin: Department of Health and Children, 2003)

National Treatment Purchase Fund, *2007 Annual Report* (Dublin: National Treatment Purchase Fund, 2008)

Nealon, Ted, *Tales from the Dáil Bar* (Dublin: Gill & Macmillan, 2008)

NESC (National Economic and Social Council), *Achieving Quality Outcomes: The Management of Public Expenditure* (Dublin: National Economic and Social Council, 2002)

NESC, *An Investment in Quality: Service, Inclusion and Enterprise* (Dublin: National Economic and Social Council, 2003)

NESC, *The Irish Economy in the Early 21st Century* (Dublin: National Economic and Social Council, 2008)

NESF (National Economic and Social Forum), *Quality Delivery of Social Services*, Forum Report No. 6 (Dublin: National Economic and Social Forum, 1995)

Norman, Peter, *The Accidental Constitution: The Making of Europe's Constitutional Treaty* (Brussels: Eurocomment, 2005)

Norris, David, 'Seanad Reform Can Benefit Oireachtas', *The Irish Times* (7 May 2009)

Ó Briain, Barra, *The Irish Constitution* (Dublin and Cork: Talbot Press, 1929)

O'Brien, Carl, 'Supreme Court Judge Criticises Media', *The Irish Times* (26 November 2007)

O'Brien, Geraldine, 'Participation as the Key to Successful Change – A Public Sector Case Study', *Leadership and Organisation Development Journal* 23/8 (2002) 442–55

Ó Cearúil, Micheál, *Bunreacht na hÉireann: A Study of the Irish Text*, for the All-Party Oireachtas Committee on the Constitution (Dublin: Stationery Office, 1999)

Ó Cearúil, Micheál, *Bunreacht na hÉireann, Two Texts or Two Constitutions?* (Dublin: The Ireland Institute, 2002)

Ó Cinnéide, Séamus, 'Democracy and the Constitution', *Administration* 46/4 (1999) 41–58

O'Connor, John, 'The Role of Planning in Sustainable Development', speech to the Environmental Protection Agency's Environment Conference (Croke Park, Dublin, 9 September 2008)

O'Connor, John, 'The Annual Report for 2007', *The Irish Times* (6 November 2008)

O'Connor, Tom, 'The Dáil Éireann Electoral System', working paper (Cork: University College Cork, 2007)

O'Dea, Willie, 'The 1am Call that Brought the News We Were Fearing', *Sunday Independent* (5 October 2008)

O'Doherty, Ann, *Report on a Clinical Review of Mammography Service at Midland Regional Hospital, Portlaoise for the HSE Dublin Mid-Leinster* (Dublin: Health Service Executive, 2008)

O'Donnell, Rory (ed.), *Europe – The Irish Experience* (Dublin: Institute of European Affairs, 2000)

O'Donnell, Rory, *The Future of Social Partnership in Ireland – A Discussion Paper Prepared for the National Competitiveness Council* (Dublin: National Competitiveness Council, 2001)

O'Donnell, Rory and Damian Thomas, 'Partnership and Policy-making' in Sean Healy and Brigid Reynolds (eds.), *Social Policy in Ireland: Principles, Practice and Problems* (Dublin: Oak Tree Press, 1998)

O'Donoghue, John, 'Greater Communication Needed between State Agencies and the Oireachtas to Strengthen Democracy, Ceann Comhairle's address to the Association of Chief Executives of State Agencies', press release (Dublin: Houses of the Oireachtas, 8 April 2008)

O'Hagan, John W., 'Government Intervention' in John W. O'Hagan (ed.), *The Economy of Ireland: Policy and Performance* (Dublin: Institute of Public Administration, 1984)

O'Halpin, Eunan, 'Partnership Programme Managers in the Reynolds/Spring Coalition 1993–94: An Assessment', DCUBS Research Papers No. 6 (1996), available online at: www.dcu.ie/dcubs/research_papers/no6.html

O'Higgins, Niall, *Report into Symptomatic Breast Cancer Services of the Sub-group to the National Cancer Forum* (Dublin: Department of Health, 2000)

O hUiginn, Padraig, *One to One* interview with Paul Cunningham (broadcast on RTÉ Television, Dublin, 30 June 2008)

O'Keeffe, John, 'Dáil Class of 2008 Are Graduates of State School', *Sunday Independent* (20 January 2008)

O'Leary, Olivia and Helen Burke, *Mary Robinson: The Authorised Biography* (London: Hodder and Stoughton, 1998)

O'Malley, Eoin, 'Ministerial Selection in Ireland: Limited Choice in a Political Village', *Irish Political Studies* 21/3 (September 2006) 319–36

O'Meara, Aileen, 'Spotlighting Health' in Eilish McAuliffe and Kenneth McKenzie (eds.), *The Politics of Healthcare – Achieving Real Reform* (Dublin: Liffey Press, 2007)

O'Meara, Aileen, 'HSE Badly in Need of Frontline Leadership', *Sunday Business Post* (15 June 2008)

Ó Muimhneacháin, Muiris, *The Functions of the Department of the Taoiseach*, 2nd edn (Dublin: Institute of Public Administration, 1969)

O'Reilly, Emily, 'Access to Information – Rights, Objectives and Challenges', address to the fifth annual conference of the Department of Government, University College Cork (Cork, 19 September 2003)

O'Reilly, Emily, 'Public Trust in the Civil Service – Room for Improvement', address by the Ombudsman and Information Commissioner at Annual Conference of Assistant Secretaries (3 March 2005)

O'Reilly, Emily, 'Maintaining the Accountability of a Fast-changing Public Service', *The Irish Times* (11 July 2008)

O'Reilly, James and Mary Redmond, *Cases and Materials on the Irish Constitution* (Dublin: Incorporated Law Society, 1980)

O'Riordan, Joanna, *A Review of the Civil Service Grading and Pay System* (Dublin: Institute of Public Administration, 2008)

O'Toole, Fintan, *Meanwhile Back at the Ranch* (London: Vintage, 1995)

O'Toole, John, 'The Role of the Irish Permanent Representation in EU Health Policymaking' in *Forming EU Healthcare Policy – A Showcase of Irish Involvement* (Dublin: Irish Nurses Organisation, 2007)

OECD (Organisation for Economic Co-operation and Development), *Regulatory Reform in Ireland* (Paris: Organisation for Economic Co-operation and Development, 2001)

OECD, 'Synthesis Report' in OECD, *Distributed Public Governance* (Paris: Organisation for Economic Co-operation and Development, 2002)

OECD, *Competitive Cities in the Global Economy* (Paris: Organisation for Economic Co-operation and Development, 2006)

OECD, *Health Data 2008: Statistics and Indicators for 30 Countries* (Paris: Organisation for Economic Co-operation and Development, 2008a)

OECD, *Ireland: Towards an Integrated Public Service* (Paris: Organisation for Economic Co-operation and Development, 2008b)

Office of the Information Commissioner, *2007 Annual Report* (Dublin: Office of the Information Commissioner, 2008)

Office of the Minister for Integration, *Migration Nation: Statement on Integration Strategy and Diversity Management* (Dublin: Stationery Office, 2008)

Office of the Ombudsman, *Nursing Home Subventions: An Investigation by the Ombudsman of Complaints Regarding Payment of Nursing Home Subventions by Health Boards* (Dublin: Office of the Ombudsman, 2001)

Office of the Ombudsman, *Annual Report of the Ombudsman 2007* (Dublin: Stationery Office, 2008)

Osborough, Niall, *Literature, Judges and the Law* (Dublin: Four Courts Press, 2007)

PA Consulting Group, *Evaluation of the Progress of the Strategic Management Initiative/Delivering Better Government Modernisation Programme* (Dublin: PA Knowledge Ltd, 2002)

PA Consulting Group, *Review of the Number of Hospital Beds Required in the Irish Health System to 2020* (Dublin: PA Consulting Group, 2008)

Perry, James L., 'Measuring Public Service Motivation: An Assessment of Construct Validity', *Journal of Public Administration Research and Theory* 6/1 (1996) 5–22

Pollitt, Christopher, Karen Bathgate, Janice Caulfield and Colin Talbot, 'Agency Fever? Analysis of an International Policy Fashion', *Journal of Comparative Policy Analysis: Research and Practice,* 3 (2001) 271–90

PricewaterhouseCoopers, *e-Cabinet Project Final Report* (Dublin: PricewaterhouseCoopers, 2001)

Prospectus, *Audit of Structures and Functions in the Health System* (Dublin: Department of Health and Children, 2003)

Public Accounts Committee [Committee of Public Accounts], Sub-Committee on Certain Revenue Matters, *Parliamentary Inquiry into DIRT: First Report* (Dublin: Houses of the Oireachtas, 1999)

Public Accounts Committee [Committee of Public Accounts], Sub-Committee on Certain Revenue Matters, *Parliamentary Inquiry into DIRT: Final Report* (Dublin: Stationery Office, 2001)

Public Service Benchmarking Body, *Report of the Public Service Benchmarking Body* (Dublin: Stationery Office, 2002)

Public Service Benchmarking Body, *Report of the Public Service Benchmarking Body* (Dublin: Stationery Office, 2007)

Public Services Organisation Review Group, *Report of the Public Services Organisation Review Group, 1966–69* [Devlin report] (Dublin: Stationery Office, 1969)

Quigley report, *An Inquiry into Certain Matters in Relation to Procurement, as Requested by the Taoiseach* (Dublin: Department of the Taoiseach, 2005)

Quinn, Ruairí, *Straight Left – A Journey in Politics* (Dublin: Hodder Headline Ireland, 2005)

Rau, Benegal N., *India's Constitution in the Making* (Bombay: Orient Longman, 1960)

Regan, Eugene, *What the Constitutional Treaty Means: For the Irish Constitution* (Dublin: Institute of European Affairs, 2005)

Review Body on Higher Remuneration in the Public Sector, *Report of the Review Body on Higher Remuneration in the Public Sector* (Dublin: Stationery Office, 1972)

Review Body on Higher Remuneration in the Public Sector, *The Levels of Remuneration Appropriate to Higher Posts in the Public Sector,* Report No. 38 (Dublin: Stationery Office, 2000)

Review Body on Higher Remuneration in the Public Sector, *Report No. 41 to the Minister for Finance on the Remuneration of Certain Posts in the Health Service Executive* (Dublin: Stationery Office, 2005)

Review Body on Higher Remuneration in the Public Sector, *Report of the Review Body on Higher Remuneration in the Public Sector* (Dublin: Stationery Office, 2007)

Robinson, Mary, *Legal and Constitutional Implications for Ireland of Adherence to the EEC Treaty*, 9 CML Rev 167 (1972)

Roche, Desmond, *Local Government in Ireland* (Dublin: Institute of Public Administration, 1982)

Russell, Meg and Mark Sandford, 'Why are Second Chambers so Difficult to Reform?', *Journal of Legislative Studies* 8/3 (Autumn 2002) 79–89

Ryan, Louden, 'Prospects for the "80s"' in Economic and Social Research Institute (ESRI), *The Economic and Social State of the Nation* (Dublin: ESRI, 1982)

Sabathil, Gerhard, Klemens Joos and Bernd Kebler, *The European Commission* (London: Kogan Page, 2008)

Sabel, Charles and Rory O'Donnell, 'Democratic Experimentalism: What to Do about Wicked Problems after Whitehall', paper delivered at the OECD conference on Devolution and Globalisation: Implications for Local Decision-makers (Glasgow, 2000)

Scally, Derek, 'Minister Suggests Ireland Take a "Break" from EU – CDU Distances Itself from Comments', *The Irish Times* (16 June 2008)

Scanlan, Michael, 'Extra Investment in the Health Service Is Not the Panacea', speech at the 2007 MacGill Summer School, Glenties, Co. Donegal (July 2007)

Scott, Dermot, 'EEC Membership and the Irish Administrative System', *Administration* 31 (1983)

Sheehy, Edward, 'City and County Management' in Mark Callanan and Justin F. Keogan (eds.), *Local Government in Ireland: Inside Out* (Dublin: Institute of Public Administration, 2003) 123–42

Sinnott, Richard, 'Cleavages, Parties and Referendums: Relationships between Representative and Direct Democracy in the Republic of Ireland', *European Journal of Political Research* 41 (2002) 811–26

Smyth, Patrick, 'EU Leaders Make It Clear Cowen's Options Are Limited', *The Irish Times* (23 June 2008)

Standards in Public Office Commission, *Annual Report 2006* (Dublin: Standards in Public Office Commission, 2007)

Standards in Public Office Commission, *Annual Report 2007* (Dublin: Standards in Public Office Commission, 2008a)

Standards in Public Office Commission, *Donation Statement Furnished by Political Parties for 2007, Report by the Standards in Public Office Commission to the Chairman of Dáil Éireann Pursuant to Section 4(1) of the Electoral Act, 1997* (Dublin: Standards in Public Office Commission, 2008b)

Stapleton, John, 'Civil Service Reform, 1969–87', *Administration* 38/4 (1991) 303–35

Sturgess, Garry and Philip Chubb, *Judging the World: Law and Politics in the World's Leading Courts* (London: Butterworth, 1988)

Sub-Committee on Ireland's Future in the European Union, *Ireland's Future in the European Union: Challenges, Issues and Options* (Dublin: Houses of the Oireachtas, 2008)

Sullivan, Eddie, 'Review of the Office of the Attorney General', report to the Taoiseach (Dublin, June 2006)

Sullivan, Eddie, 'The Workplace of the Future: Reconciling Pregnancy, Parenting & Employment', seminar (Trinity College, Dublin, 8 November 2007)

Thornhill, Don, 'Productivity Attainment in a Diverse Public Sector', presentation at Institute of Public Administration seminar on productivity in a diverse public sector (21 April 2006)

Timonen, Virpi, *Irish Social Expenditure in a Comparative International Context: Epilogue* (Dublin: Institute of Public Administration and Combat Poverty Agency, 2005)

Timonen, Virpi, Orla O'Donnell and Peter C. Humphreys, *E-Government and the Decentralisation of Service Delivery*, Committee for Public Management Research (CPMR) Discussion Paper 25 (Dublin: Institute of Public Administration, 2003)

Tormey, Bill, *A Cure for the Crisis, Irish Healthcare in Context* (Dublin: Blackwater Press, 2003)

Travers, John, 'Report on Certain Issues of Management and Administration in the Department of Health and Children associated with the Practice of Charges for Persons in Long-Stay Care in Health Board Institutions and Related Matters' [Travers report] in Joint Committee on Health and Children, *Interim Report on the Report on Certain Issues of Management and Administration in the Department of Health & Children Associated with the Practice of Charges for Persons in Long-Stay Care in Health Board Institutions and Related Matters* (Dublin: Houses of the Oireachtas, 2005)

Tutty, Michael, 'Implications of New Organisational Structures' in Richard Boyle and Tony McNamara (eds.), *Governance and Accountability: Power and Responsibility in the Public Service* (Dublin: Institute of Public Administration, 1997)

Van de Walle, Steven, 'Determinants of Confidence in the Civil Service: An International Comparison' in Kuno Schedler and Isabella Proeller (eds.), *Cultural Aspects of Public Management Reforms* (Amsterdam: Elsevier, 2007)

Wall, Martin, 'Harney Cites Efficiencies in Defence of HSE Changes', *The Irish Times* (4 July 2008)

Walsh, Brian, 'Article to Mark 50th Anniversary of *Bunreacht na hÉireann*', *The Irish Times* (December 1987)

Walsh, Brian, 'The Constitution: A View from the Bench' in Brian Farrell (ed.), *De Valera's Constitution and Ours, Thomas Davis Lectures* (Dublin: Gill & Macmillan for RTÉ, 1988)

Walsh, Edward, 'Public Service Relocation Programme: Optimising the Opportunity', keynote address to the annual delegate conference of the Association of Higher Civil and Public Servants (Dublin, 15 May 2004)

Ward, Tanya, *Justice Matters – Independence, Accountability and the Irish Judiciary* (Dublin: Irish Council for Civil Liberties, 2007)

Weeks, Liam, 'Independents in Government: A Case-study of Ireland', paper presented at workshop on new parties in government (Uppsala University, 13 to 18 April 2004)

Wheare, Kenneth C., *Modern Constitutions* (London: Oxford University Press, 1966)

Whelan, Noel, 'Bord Snip Nua Shows Government Is Getting Serious', *The Irish Times* (29 November 2008)

Whelan, Ken and Eugene Masterson, *Bertie Ahern, Taoiseach and Peacemaker* (Dublin: Blackwater Press, 1998)

Whelan, Patrick, Tom Arnold, Agnes Aylward, Mary Doyle, Bernadette Lacey, Claire Loftus, Nuala McLoughlin, Eamonn Molloy, Jennifer Payne and Melanie Pine, *Cross-Departmental Challenges – A Whole-of-Government Approach for the Twenty-First Century* (Dublin: Institute of Public Administration, 2003)

Whitaker, T.K., 'From Protection to Free Trade – The Irish Case', *Administration* 21/4 (1973)

Whitaker report, *Report of the Constitution Review Group* (Dublin: Stationery Office, 1996)

White, Padraic, 'Good Governance: Contributing to Better Performance', speech to the Institute of Public Administration's annual governance forum (Croke Park Conference Centre, Dublin, 10 December 2007)

Whyte, Gerry, *Social Inclusion and the Legal System: Public Interest Law in Ireland* (Dublin: Institute of Public Administration, 2002)

Wiberg, Matti, 'Parliamentary Questioning: Control by Communication?' in Herbert Döring (ed.), *Parliaments and Majority Rule in Western Europe* (New York: St Martin's Press, 1995) 179–222

Wilson, Richard, 'Portrait of a Profession Revisited', speech delivered on 26 March (London: Cabinet Office, 2002)

World Bank, *Doing Business 2009*; available online at: www.doingbusiness.org/EconomyRankings/

Zimmerman, Joseph F., 'The Changing Roles of the Irish Department Secretary', *Public Administration Review* 57/7 (1997) 534–42

INDEX

A&E (accident and emergency departments), 320–1
Abbeylara Inquiry, 367, 370–1
accountability, 17, 333, 468, 475
  EU, 401
  health services, 302, 304, 306–7
  ministers and departments, 17, 171–2, 333
  Oireachtas, 104–5
  state agencies, 275–85, 468
acquis communautaire, 400
administrative officers (civil service), 164–5
Adoption Board, 314
Adshead, Maura, 265
advisers to government, 58–63
Aer Lingus, 265, 270, 285–6
Aer Rianta, 285
Agricultural Credit Corporation (ACC), 259, 263, 265, 271, 285
agriculture, 249
Agriculture, Dept of, 39, 460–1
  EU and, 413, 415
Ahern, Bertie, 34, 36, 55, 80, 218
  business regulation, 338
  cabinet meetings, 7, 11
  consultancies, 179–80
  EU, 402, 426
  freedom of information fees, 482–3
  friends appointed to state agency boards, 269
  Mahon Tribunal, 361–2, 364
  Oireachtas committees, 100, 103

programme managers, 63
public administration reform, 289, 442, 452, 456, 457, 460
Taoiseach role, 21, 26, 137
Ahern, Dermot, 402
Aiken, Frank, 34, 136
Air Corps (air ambulance service), 319
Aireacht, 446
Air Transport Service, 51–2
allowances to political parties, 108
All-Party Oireachtas Committee, 98, 99, 133, 134, 137, 143, 148, 153, 156, 216, 228, 423
ambassadors, 166
  EU representation, 416–18
amenities, 248–9
Amsterdam, Treaty of, 391, 421–2
Andrews, Barry, 4
Annan, Kofi, 422
appeals and grievances, 333–9, 371–83
  courts, 351–3
  EU bodies, 353–5
  representations, 339–46
  social welfare, 381–2
  tribunals, 355–9
  see also Ombudsman
Appeals Commissioners, 358–9
appropriation account, 168–9
Áras an Uachtaráin, 138
Archives Act 1985, 11
Arts Council, 266

Asquith, Andy and O'Halpin,
    Eunan, 237
assistant secretaries (civil service),
    166, 190, 193, 448, 471
Association of Irish Regions, 421
Attorney General, 214–21, 361
audit (local government), 252
Auditor General *see* Comptroller
    and Auditor General

B&I Line, 285
backbenchers, 28–9, 48
Bagehot, Walter, 348
Barr Tribunal, 367, 370–1
Barrington, Justice, 154, 394
Barrington, Ruth, 396
Barrington, Tom, 288
Barrington report, 238, 254
Barry, Frank, 34
BASIS (Business Access to State
    Information and Services), 336,
    470
Beef Tribunal, 349, 366–7
Behan, Joe, 29
Bermingham, Joseph, 23
Better Local Government, 238–9,
    251, 255
Bhreathnach, Niamh, 36–7, 49
bills, 4–5, 80–3, 177
    money bills, 83, 147, 149, 150
    President's powers, 146, 149,
        150–5
Blaney, Neil, 23
Blood Transfusion Service Board,
    266, 314, 363
Boland, Kevin, 37
Bord Altranais, 266
Bord Bainne, 51, 288
Bord Bia, 51
Bord Gáis, 265, 274
Bord Gráin, 288
Bord na gCapall, 264

Bord na Móna, 265
Bord Pleanála, 246–8, 359
Bord Snip Nua, 463, 465, 468
borough councils, 229, 230 *see also*
    local government
Boyle, Richard, 485
Brady, Rory, 359–60, 362–3
Breen, Ciarán, 325
Brennan, Niamh, 299, 444
Brennan, Peter, 420, 428
Brennan, Seamus, 87
Brennan Commission (1936), 446
Brennan report (2003), 299–300
Browne, Noel, 37, 41
Browne, Vincent, 64
Bruton, John, 4, 23, 34
Bruton, Richard, 44
budget, 83–4, 173, 199, 329, 476
BUPA, 327, 328
Burke, Edmund, 70
Burke, Richard, 15
Burton, Joan, 231
Butler, Patrick and Collins, Neil,
    340
Byrne, Elaine, 18
Byrne, Raymond and McCutcheon,
    Paul, 80, 151

cabinet, 1, 6–15
    Cabinet Handbook, 7–8, 51, 179,
        180
    collective responsibility, 14–15
    e-cabinet, 12–13
    ethical guidelines, 7
    meetings, 6–11, 13–14, 47–8
    sub-committees, 11–12
'cabinet system', 61
Callanan, Mark, 53, 65
cancer care strategy, 321–5
Captain of the Guard, 111
career breaks, 196
Carey, Pat, 28

cars, ministerial, 58, 107
cars, presidential, 138–9
Carthy, John, 367, 370–1
Casey, James, 36, 71, 96, 122, 144–5, 150, 151, 156, 216, 394
Cathaoirleach, 67
Ceann Comhairle, 72, 75–7, 85, 86, 88, 92
Central Criminal Court, 206, 209
Central Fund (Permanent Provisions) Act 1965, 84
Central Programme Office, 468
Central Statistics Office (CSO), 71, 72
centralisation, 227–8
Centre for Management and Organisation Development (CMOD), 447
Chad, peacekeeping, 422
Change Management Network, 450
charters (customer rights), 335, 466, 469
Chief State Solicitor's Office (CSSO), 220–1, 222
Childcare Directorate, 182
Childers, Erskine, 34, 137, 155–6, 157
Child Abuse Commission, 365
Child Protection, Joint Committee on, 214
Children, Minister for, 182–3
Children, Ombudsman for, 379
Chubb, Basil, 22, 68–9
Churchill, Winston, 431
CIÉ, 270, 273, 278
    CIÉ/Mini-CTC Signalling Project, 371
Circuit Court, 207–8, 209, 221
Citizens Information Board, 335–6
City and County Management (Amendment) Act 1955, 234
city councils, 228–9, 230 *see also* local government

city development boards, 236, 256
city managers, 232–40, 241
civil service, 158–99
    career structures and grades, 161–71, 190
    code of conduct, 185–90, 455
    consultants used by, 179–81
    cross-departmental work, 181–3
    decentralisation, 196–8
    dismissal from, 194–5, 453–4
    e-cabinet system, 13
    employment conditions and pay, 190–9
    EU and, 178, 415–22
    ministerial support, 39–46, 52–3, 56–63, 110–12, 167–71, 175–6
    mission and purpose, 158–9
    party politics and, 188–9
    promotion policy, 192–4
    recruitment, 159–61, 163, 164, 169, 193
        disabled persons, 198–9
        reforms, 453–4, 455
    reform and vision of, 451–2
    state agencies and, 262–3, 266–7, 271, 468
    tasks, 171–85
    see also public administration
Civil Service Commissioners Act 1956, 62
Civil Service Quality Assurance Group, 452
Civil Service Regulations Acts 1956–2005, 59, 138, 169, 186, 194, 195, 374, 454
Clancy, Paula and Murphy, Gráinne, 260
Clarke, Frank, 72
Clarke, Victoria, 157
clerical officers (civil service), 163
Clery, Maeve, 349

clientelism, 341–5
'clinics', 49
Cluskey, Frank, 15
CMOD (Centre for Management
    and Organisation
    Development), 447
Coakley, John, 98
coalitions, 73
    role of Taoiseach, 22
code of conduct, 17–18
    civil servants, 185–90, 455
    state bodies, 281
Coillte, 273
Colley, George, 34
Collins, Edward, 23
Collins, Neil, 237, 338, 340
    and O'Shea, Mary, 342
co-location of hospitals, 328–9
Comhairle na n-Ospidéal, 314
Commercial Court, 206, 209
Commission for Public Service
    Appointments, 159–60
Commission for the Support of
    Victims of Crime, 210
Commission on Health Funding,
    293–4
Commission on Social Welfare, 358
Commission to Inquire into Child
    Abuse, 365
commissions of investigation, 365–6
Committee for Performance
    Awards, 190
Committee for Public Management
    Research (CPMR), 450, 472
Committee of Permanent
    Representatives (COREPER),
    178, 417
Committee of Privileges, 147
Committee of the Regions (CoR),
    421
Committee on Judicial Conduct and
    Ethics, 210

Committees of the Houses of the
    Oireachtas Act 1997, 101, 104,
    277, 368, 369
Communicating Europe Initiative,
    419
community care, 305–6, 316–17
Community, Rural and Gaeltacht
    Affairs, Dept of, 427
compellability, 104–5, 368
Competition Authority, 335, 336
Competitiveness Council, 414,
    456–7
complaints *see* appeals and
    grievances
Comptroller and Auditor General
    (C&AG), 478–81
    appointment of, 140
    appropriation account, 168
    functions, 478–81
    public spending audits, 277, 281
Comptroller and Auditor General
    Acts 1993–1998, 478–80
ComReg, 336–7
Conference of Speakers of
    European Union Parliaments,
    407
confidence principle, 14
confidentiality principle, 14
congestion, 435
Connaughton, Bernadette, 44
Connolly, Eileen and O'Halpin,
    Eunan, 482
Connolly, Joseph, 1
Connolly, Niamh, 429
consolidation bills, 83
constituencies, 70–2
    ministers' clinics, 49
    representations, 339–46
Constituency Commission, 71–2
Constitution of Ireland, 114–35
    amendments, 118–19, 123–5, 132
    EU, 393, 394

appeals invoking, 352–3
Comptroller and Auditor
General, 478
earlier constitutions, 114–18
EU and, 393–6, 423
government role and powers,
1–2, 9, 14
Irish language, 130–1, 132
judicial review, 126–30
judiciary, 120, 201
local government, 227–8
Oireachtas, 67, 90, 94, 118
Presidential role and powers,
118–20, 136–53
review proposals, 131–3
rights, 118, 121–2, 127–9, 352–3
social policy directive principles,
125–6, 127
supremacy of, 122
Constitution Review Group, 126,
128, 132–3, 137, 143, 147–8,
151, 153, 156, 216, 227–8, 423
consultancies, 179–81
Consumer Protection Act 2007, 335
Control of Importation, Sale and
Manufacture of Contraceptives
Bill 1974, 15
Convention for the Protection of
Human Rights, 353
Cooney, Patrick, 49
CoR (Committee of the Regions),
421
COREPER (Committee of
Permanent Representatives),
178, 417
Corish, Brendan, 34
corporate body, 267
Corporate Enforcement, Director
of, 335
corporate governance units, 272
corporation sole, 2, 35, 171, 262
corruption, 185–6, 187

COSAC (Association of European
Affairs Committees), 407
Cosgrave, Liam, 11, 15, 33, 154
Cosgrave, W.T., 22
Costello, John A., 33, 170
Coughlan, Mary, 34, 49
Coulter, Carol, 212
Council of Europe, 353
Parliamentary Assembly, 406
Council of State, 148–9
councillors, 229–40, 346
county councils, 228–9, 230 *see
also* local government
county development boards, 236,
256
county managers, 232–40, 241
courtesy visits, 50
Court of Criminal Appeal, 207, 209,
211, 224
courts, 202–14
appeals, 351–3
conduct of officials, 210
court registrars, 202–3
Courts Service, 205, 207, 278
judiciary, 200–2, 210
statistics, 209–10
Courts and Court Officers Act 1995,
200, 201
Courts Commission Working
Group, 205
Coveney, Hugh, 23
Cowen, Brian, 34, 55–6, 63, 79,
183, 190, 191, 197–8, 301, 312,
350, 458, 463, 464
CPMR (Committee for Public
Management Research), 450,
472
Creed, Donal, 23
Criminal Justice Act 1993, 211, 224
Criminal Law Act 1935, 212
Criminal Law (Sexual Offences)
Act 2006, 212

crime
    defence of honest belief, 212–14
    prosecutions, 221–4
    statistics, 209–10
    victims of crime, 210–12
    see also courts; legal system
Cromien, Sean, 406, 417
'cross-cutting initiatives', 441, 442,
    467–8
Crotty case, 122, 393–4, 395–6, 402
CSO (Central Statistics Office), 71,
    72
CSSO (Chief State Solicitor's
    Office), 220–1, 222
Cuffe, Ciarán, 435
'Current Issues Time', 89
Curtin, Brian, 202
Customer Charter Initiative, 469
Customer Service, 452, 468–9

Dáil, 67–93, 100–13
    Clerk of the Dáil, 73, 79, 89,
        108, 111
    compellability and privilege,
        104–5, 364
    debates and voting, 77–9, 87,
        88–90, 112
    declaration of interests, 107–8
    elections and convening, 72–5
        expenses, 109–10
    EU and, 405–13
    financial procedures, 83–4
    legislative bills, 4–5, 80–3, 177
    membership, 70–2
    ministers' attendance, 47
    motions, 47, 84–5
    parliamentary questions, 29, 55,
        85–6, 346–51
    President dissolving, 144–5
    reform, 87–93
    representations, 339–46
    secretarial assistance, 110–12

support services, 93
    TDs' pay and expenses, 106–7
Dairy Disposal Company (DCC),
    259
Darcy, Michael, 23
Data Protection Commissioner,
    379–80
Day, Catherine, 428–9
DBG (Delivering Better
    Government), 451–2
decentralisation, 196–8, 308, 457
declaration of interests, 107–8
Defence Act 1954, 142
Defence Forces, 142
    Ombudsman for, 379
    peacekeeping, 421–2, 424, 448
Delaney, Eamon, 26, 43, 77, 334,
    347
delegation of functions orders, 54
Delivering Better Government
    (DBG), 451–2
demographics, 318, 319, 331,
    434–5, 436
Dempsey, Noel, 337
Denham, Justice, 114–15, 128, 129,
    205, 364
Denhardt, Robert and Denhardt,
    Janet, 442–3
Denning, Lord, 397
Dental Council, 314
deputations, 49–50
Desmond, Barry, 37, 40, 49, 149
de Valera, Eamon, 33, 97–8, 118,
    119, 130, 135
    as President, 137, 138, 140, 144,
        146, 147, 148, 157
Devlin report, 3–4, 43, 266, 334,
    357, 446
DIG (Decentralisation
    Implementation Group), 197–8
digital citizenship, 335
directives (EU), 398

Director of Public Prosecutions
(DPP), 221–4
DIRT Inquiry, 368–9
Disability Act 2005, 199
disabled persons, civil service
recruitment, 198–9
District Court, 208, 209, 221
Doing Business 2009, 485
donations and gifts, 17, 110
local authority members, 257
Donegan, Patrick, 153–4
Dooge, James, 1, 96
Dooney, Sean, 39
Doyle, Etain, 277
DPP (Director of Public
Prosecutions), 221–4
Drumm, Brendan, 323, 329
Dublin, 253–4
Dublin Archdiocese Commission of
Investigation, 366
Dublin Dental School and Hospital,
266, 267
Dublin Hospital Initiative Group,
294
Dublin Port Company, 271
Dublin Transportation Authority,
265
Dukes, Alan, 37, 173–4
Dunlop, Frank, 10–11, 44

Early Years Education Policy Unit,
182
Eastern Regional Health Authority
(ERHA), 314
e-cabinet, 12–13
ECJ (European Court of Justice),
354, 397
education, 249
multiculturalism and, 436
Education Act 1998, 376
Efficiency Audit Group (EAG), 463
e-government, 470–4

Eire, 130
eISB (Irish Statute Book), 219–20
election agents, 109
elections, general, 72–5
electronic voting, 73–5
funding and expenditure, 109–10
proportional representation, 72,
91, 124, 230, 341
reform proposals, 91
register of electors, 249
elections, local government, 230–1
by-elections, 235
Electoral Acts 1997–2008, 16, 71,
72, 73, 74, 109, 257
Electoral Commission, 75
Electricity Supply Board (ESB),
259, 263, 265, 270, 272, 273,
274
electronic services for citizens,
472–3
electronic voting
Dáil debates and votes, 78, 79,
87, 88
general elections, 73–5
Elgie, Robert and Fitzgerald, Peter,
24, 144
Elgie, Robert and Stapleton, John,
20
Ellemann-Jensen, Uffe, 404
Emergency Powers Bill 1976,
153–6
emergency, state of, 147
Employment Equality Act 1998,
193
Enterprise Ireland, 266
Enterprise, Trade and Employment,
Dept of, 358, 460–1
EU and, 414, 415
Environment, Heritage and Local
Government, Minister for, 230,
358
EU and, 421

Environmental Protection Agency, 241, 248
Eppink, Derk-Jan, 413
equality *see* gender equality
Equality Authority, 265, 335
Equality Tribunal, civil service promotion, 192–3
ERI (Expenditure Review Initiative), 476–7
ERSI (Economic and Social Research Institute), 267
ESB, 259, 263, 265, 270, 272, 273, 274
ethics and standards, 16–18
  civil servants, 185–90, 455
  courts, 210
  declaration of interests (TDs and senators), 107–8
  guidelines for cabinet, 7
  local authorities, 257–8
  political parties, funding and expenditure, 109–10
  state agencies, 275–85
Ethics in Public Office Act 1995, 7, 16–17, 107, 185, 186, 217, 221
Euro-Mediterranean Parliamentary Assembly, 406
European Affairs, Minister of State for, 409, 414, 415
European Central Bank, 399, 441
European Commission, 412–13, 428–30
  Internal Market Scoreboard, 420
European Communities Act 1972, 393
European Communities Committee, 416
European Convention on Human Rights Act 2003, 353–4
European Council of Ministers, 50–1, 178, 412, 413–14, 419
  configurations, 414
  Presidency, 401, 424–6
European Court of Human Rights, 353–4
European Court of Justice (ECJ), 354, 397
European Ombudsman, 354–5
European Parliament, 354, 429–30
European Public Information Centre, 430
European Security and Defence Policy, 421, 423–4
European Union, 390–433
  Attorney General and, 218
  civil service role, 178, 415–22
  competences, 400–1
  Constitutional implications, 393–6, 423
  cross-border healthcare, 329–31
  defence and peacekeeping, 421–2, 424
  directives and regulations, 398
  information about, 427–30
  Ireland's presidency, 425–6
  law, 396–401
  Lisbon Treaty *see* Lisbon Treaty
  neutrality and, 423–4, 432
  permanent representation, 416–18
  presidency system, 401, 424–6
  regulatory activity resulting from, 263–4, 398
  scrutiny and monitoring of, 87–8, 406, 407–9, 419, 420
  Single European Act, 391, 393–4
  state bodies and, 287–8
  Treaty of Amsterdam, 391, 421–2
  Treaty of Nice, 391, 405, 433
    referendum, 395, 396, 423, 427
  Treaty of Rome, 287–8, 390, 393
  Treaty on European Union (Maastricht Treaty), 390, 391, 394–5, 408

European Union (Scrutiny) Act
   2002, 407–8, 419
eurozone, 420
executive officers (civil service),
   163–4
Expenditure Review Initiative
   (ERI), 476–7
expenses
   allowances to political parties,
      108
   councillors, 229–30
   elections expenditure, 109–10
   FÁS, 281–2
   TDs, 106–7

Fáilte Ireland, 51, 266
family, 121–2
Family Planning Bill 1979, 15
Fanning, Ronan, 174
Fanning, Rossa, 395–6
Farmleigh House, 32
Farrell, Brian, 3, 5, 20, 21, 23, 28,
   117, 134
FÁS, 266, 267, 268, 269, 271, 359
   decentralisation, 197
   expenses investigation, 281–2
Feeney, Peter, 52–3
Ferrero-Waldner, Benita, 396
Ferriter, Diarmaid, 134
files, ministerial, 45–6, 177
Finance, Dept of, 172–4
   budget, 83–4, 173, 476
   EU and, 413, 419–20
   tax revenue, 3, 173
Finance, Minister for, 2
financial management reform,
   476–78
Financial Services Ombudsman,
   378–9
Finlay, Chief Justice, 125, 201–2
Finlay, Fergus, 65, 125
Fitzgerald, Alexis, 4

FitzGerald, Garret, 4, 6, 19, 23, 34,
   64, 96, 97, 106, 126, 135, 148,
   172, 175, 181, 217, 261, 339,
   401, 463
Fitzgerald, John, 91, 253, 322, 324
flexitime, 195
Flood, Justice Feargus, 361
Flood/Mahon Tribunal, 257, 361–5
Flynn, Pádraig, 23
Fóir Teoranta, 265
Foras Forbartha, 264
Foreign Affairs, Dept of, 30, 38, 418
   EU and, 409, 413, 414, 415, 416,
      418–19, 426
   primary functions, 418
Forfás, 266
Four Courts, 203
Fox, Noel, 294
freedom of information, 11, 334–6,
   375–7, 481–4
   EU, 401–2, 431
   exemptions, 484
   fees, 482–3
   Information Commissioner, 375–7
   number of requests, 377
Freedom of Information Act 1997,
   11, 186, 224, 334, 375, 481–2
Freedom of Information
   (Amendment) Act 2003, 11,
   186, 375–6, 482

Gallagher, Michael *et al.*, 277
Garda Síochána
   ministerial cars, 58
   Ombudsman Commission, 378
   prosecutions, 221–4
Garvin, Tom, 98, 133
gender equality
   boards of state agencies, 268
   civil service, 194
   local government, 231
   Oireachtas, 106

General Affairs and External
  Relations Council, 409, 414,
  430
Geoghegan, Justice, 363
Gibbons, James, 15
gifts and donations, 17, 110
  local authority members, 257
GIS (Government Information
  Services), 31–2
globalisation, 434, 473
gombeenism, 342
Gormley, John, 75, 99–100, 256,
  258
government role and powers, 1–6
*Government Statement on
  Transforming Public Services*,
  461, 464–8
Government Supplies Agency, 219
green papers, 5
  EU, 408
grievances *see* appeals and
  grievances
Grist, Berna, 234
*Guidelines for the Preparation of
  Customer Charters*, 469

Haldane committee, 446
Hamilton, Chief Justice, 150, 202,
  215, 349
Hamilton, James, 153, 223–4
Hanly report, 300–1
Hannon, Katie, 26, 27, 58, 103
Hardiman, Justice Adrian, 204–5,
  364, 371
Hardiman, Niamh, 41–2, 184
Harney, Mary, 24, 34, 41, 106, 302,
  303, 306, 308, 312, 322, 323,
  324–5, 328–9, 431
harp symbol, 2
Haugh, Justice Kevin, 378
Haughey, Charles, 19, 21, 23, 33,
  34, 339, 360

Hayes-Renshaw, Fiona and Wallace,
  Helen, 425
Health Act 1970, 313, 314
Health Act 2004, 302, 303, 304,
  306–7
Health Act 2007, 315, 316
Health (Amendment) (No. 3) Act
  1996, 296
Health and Children, Dept of, 290,
  301–2
  children's services, 182–3
  promotion policy, 192–3
  Travers report, 46, 170–1, 176–7,
    301–2, 311
Health and Children, Joint
  Committee on, 44, 46, 61–2,
  218
Health and Children, Minister for,
  182–3, 290, 302
health boards, 313–14
Health Education Programme, 264
health forums, 306–7
Health Information and Quality
  Authority (HIQA), 316
Health Insurance Acts 1994–2007,
  327, 328
Health Insurance Authority, 327
Health Research Board, 264–5, 266,
  314
Health Service Executive (HSE),
  303–10
  criticisms of, 284, 302, 320
health services, 290–32
  administrative areas, 305–6, 314
  agencies, 314–15
  challenges, 319–26, 331–2
  children's services, 182–3
  co-location of hospitals, 328–9
  criticisms of, 170, 284, 302,
    307–8, 310, 320–6, 329
  cross-border, 329–31
  employee statistics, 292

expenditure, 310–13
governing and accountability, 302, 304, 306–7, 309–10
insurance, 327–8
multiculturalism and, 437
national directorates, 304–5
patient charter, 335
patient safety and infections, 325–6
policy framework, 291–301
voluntary sector, 318
waiting lists, 307–8, 312, 315–16
Health: The Wider Dimensions, 291–3
Henchy, Justice, 125, 127, 393
Hepatitis C Compensation Tribunal Act 1997, 360
heritage protection, 247
High Court, 205–7, 209, 212–13, 352
Divisional High Court, 206
judicial review, 126
Mahon Tribunal and, 363
Hillery, Patrick, 137, 140, 141, 145–6, 157
Hogan, Gerard, 129, 135, 212
and Gwynn-Morgan, David, 68, 355, 482
and Whyte, Gerry, 150, 152, 215, 227, 395
Holohan, Majella and Robert, 212
home working, 195
Horgan, John, 156
hospice policy, 326
Hospital Council, 314
Hospital Efficiency Review Group, 294
hospital in-patient enquiry scheme (HIPE), 315
House Business Group, 89
housing, 242–3
Housing Finance Agency, 242–3, 267

Houston, David and Harding, Lauren, 439
HSE *see* Health Service Executive
Hussey, Gemma, 9, 36
Hyde, Douglas, 137, 141, 145, 157

ICC Bank, 285
ICCEUA, 416, 420
IDA Ireland, 51, 266
immigration, 434, 436–7
Implementation Group of Secretaries General, 449
incorporeal meetings, 13–14
information *see* freedom of information
information and communications technology, 470–4
Information Commissioner, 375–7, 483
Information Society Commission, 471
inquiries, 359–71
commissions of investigation, 365–6
parliamentary inquiries, 367–71
public inquiries by Oireachtas, 366–7, 368
tribunals, 359–67
interculturalism, 436–7
Inter-Departmental Administrative Presidency Planning Group, 416
Inter-Departmental Co-ordinating Committee on European Affairs (ICCEUA), 416, 420
Intergovernmental Conference Group, 415
IPA (Institute of Public Administration), 261, 267, 450
Iris Oifigiúil, 140, 161, 201, 219
Irish Coastguard, 319
Irish Greyhound Board, 265, 279

Irish Hospice Foundation, 326
Irish language, 130–1, 132
 in courts, 214
 EU and, 430–1
Irish Life Assurance Company, 285
Irish Medicines Board, 314
Irish Planning Institute, 235
Irish Regions Office (IRO), 421
Irish Shipping, 273
Irish Statute Book, 219–20
Irish Steel, 286
Irish Sugar, 285
Irish Youth Justice Service, 182

Jaconelli, Joseph, 153
job-sharing, 195–6
Johnson, Mandy, 31
Joint Committee on European
 Affairs, 409
Joint Committee on European
 Scrutiny, 408–9
Joint Committee on the
 Constitution, 133
joint committees, 102
journal of proceedings, 79
Jouyet, Jean-Pierre, 404
Judicial Appointments Advisory
 Board, 200–1
judicial review, 126–30
Judicial Separation and Family Law
 Reform Act 1989, 82
judiciary, 200–2
 Constitution and, 120, 201
 ethics, 210
 see also courts
Juncker, Jean-Claude, 432
junior ministers, 54–6
 'super junior' ministers, 4

Keane, Chief Justice Ronan, 126,
 128, 210, 216
Keane, Tom, 324

Kearney, Justice, 212
Kearns, Justice, 393
Keating, Justin, 49
Kelly, Cyril, 202
Kelly, J.M., 215
Kelly, John, 129
Kelly, John M., 141
Kelly, Michael, 170–1, 174, 291–2,
 301, 311
Kelly, Nicky, 141
Kennedy, David (Kennedy group), 294
Kenny, Enda, 92
Kenny, Justice, 127
Keogan, Justin, 456
Keogh, Dermot and McCarthy,
 Andrew, 118
Kingsmill Moore, Justice, 125
Kitt, Tom, 87, 275, 409, 416
Komito, Lee, 341
Kuhry, Bob, 478

Laffan, Brigid, 405, 415, 416, 417,
 418–19, 427
Laffoy, Justice Mary, 365
Laver, Michael, 98
Lavery, Don, 153
law *see* legal system; legislation
Law Reform Commission, 212,
 213, 220, 359
leaders' questions, 20–1
Leas-Ceann Comhairle, 75
Lee, Joseph, 23–4, 174, 181, 289
Legal Practitioners (Irish Language)
 Act 2008, 214
legal system, 200–26
 appeals, 351–3
 courts, 202–14
 Director of Public Prosecutions
 (DPP), 221–4
 judiciary, 200–2
legislation, 4–5, 80–3
 bills, 4–5, 80–3, 177

civil service role, 177–8
EU, 396–41
Irish Statute Book, 219–20
judicial review, 126–30
primary/secondary legislation, 80
Legislation Directory, 220
Leinster House, 69–70, 112
Lemass, Seán, 15, 22–3, 33, 34, 97, 263
Lenihan, Brian (jnr), 4, 19, 99, 182, 282, 283, 362, 377, 381, 445
Lenihan, Brian (snr), 23, 34, 49, 146
Lenihan, Conor, 436–7
Levy Appeals Tribunal, 359
Libertas, 403–4
libraries, 248–9
lighting, public, 244
Limerick Marts Bill 1989, 82
Lisbon Treaty, 401–5
    categories of competence, 400–1
    neutrality and, 424, 432
    presidency system, 424–5
    Presidential powers and, 149, 396
    referendum, 395–6, 402, 428, 429
Local Elections Act 1999, 74, 257
local government, 227–58
    councillors, 229–40, 346
    elections, 230–1
        by-elections, 235
    ethics, 257–8
    finance, 249–52
    functions of, 233–6, 241–9
    managers, 232–40, 241
    meetings, 231–2
    reform, 254–8
    regional authorities and
        assemblies, 252–3
    spending, 241, 254
    staff and administration, 240–1
Local Government Act 1898, 227
Local Government Act 1991, 16, 234, 238, 252

Local Government Act 1994, 238
Local Government Act 1998, 251
Local Government Act 2000, 233
Local Government Act 2001, 131, 228, 229, 233, 234–5, 238–9, 249, 250, 257
Local Government Act 2003, 239
Local Government Fund, 250, 251
Local Government (Planning and Development) Act 1963, 246
LoCall telephone service, 452, 467
Locke, John, 226
lord mayors, 229
Lowry, Michael, 23
Lynch, Judge Dominic, 10
Lynch, Jack, 23, 33, 58, 179
Lysaght, Charles, 396

Maastricht Treaty, 390, 391, 394–5, 408
MAC (management advisory committee), 176–7
McAleese, Mary, 137, 141, 149, 156, 157, 396
McAuley, Finbar, 214
McAuliffe, Eilish and McKenzie, Kenneth, 309
MacCarthaigh, Muiris, 20, 266–7, 276, 281, 284–5, 339, 346, 371
McCarthy, Dermot, 13, 337, 392, 486
McCracken Tribunal, 362, 363, 365
McCreevy, Charlie, 42, 196, 287
McDonagh, Bobby, 413
McDonald, Dearbhail, 205
McDowell, Michael, 28, 34, 49, 407
McDunphy, Michael, 145
McElligott, James J., 130
MacEntee, Seán, 34
McGauran, Anne-Marie *et al.*, 259, 261, 268, 289
McGrath, Finian, 149

McGuinness, Justice, 212
McKenna judgment, 108, 124, 125, 402
McKinsey report, 254, 308
MacSharry, Ray, 34
Madden, Deirdre, 326
Mahon, Judge Alan, 361–2
Mahon Tribunal, 257, 361–5
Mair, Peter, 73
managers (local authorities), 232–40, 241
Mansergh, Martin, 198, 274, 283, 336
Mansergh, Nicholas, 117–18
Marshall, A.H., 236–7
Martin, Micheál, 41, 64, 91, 350–1, 403, 409, 427–8, 429
Martin, Shane, 90, 368
mayors, 229
media
    communications with, 31–2, 52–4, 64–5
    public grievances, 351
    reportage of court cases, 205
Media Monitoring Unit, 31–2
medical card controversy, 301
Medical Council, 314
Medical Practitioner's Act 2007, 319
Meehan, Catriona, 65
meetings, cabinet, 6–11, 47–8
meetings, ministers, 47–52
Mental Health Commission, 357–8
Migration Nation, 437
military neutrality, 423–4
military tribunals, 208
Minimum Notice and Terms of Employment Act 1977, 195
Ministerial and Parliamentary Offices Acts 1938–1996, 108
ministers and departments, 35–66
    accountability, 17, 171–2, 333

appointment and selection of ministers, 1, 36–7
appropriation account, 168–9
cars, 58
civil service support, 39–46, 52–3, 56–63, 110–12, 167–71, 175–6
consultancies, 179–81
cross-departmental work, 181–3
dismissal of ministers, 23
disposition of portfolios, 37–8
ethics and standards, 7, 16–18, 107–8
EU and, 413–22
    departmental EU units, 420–1
gifts and donations, 17
grievances and appeals, 340–51
internal department work, 40–6
management advisory committee, 176–7
meetings, 47–52
ministers of state, 54–6
obligations and business interests, 15–16, 107–8
overseas visits, 51–2
parliamentary questions, 29, 55, 85–6, 346–51
pay, 19, 106
private offices, 56–8, 176
public service reform, 453–4
responsibility, 35–6, 171–2
state agencies, control over, 274–5
'super junior', 4
see also civil service
Ministers' and Secretaries' Group on EU Policy, 414–15
ministers of state, 54–6
Ministries and Secretaries Act 1924, 158, 171, 192, 215, 262, 333
Ministries and Secretaries Acts 1997–2007, 2, 35, 54

Mintzberg, Henry, 440
Mitchell, Jim, 277, 368
Mitchell, Paul, 5
Molloy, Robert, 4
money bills, 83, 147, 149, 150
Moriarty Tribunal, 362, 365, 367
Morris Tribunal, 65
motor taxation, 244
Moylan, Seán, 1
MRSA infection, 325
Mullarkey, Paddy, 271
Mullarkey report, 35, 168–9
Mullen, Ronan, 410
multiculturalism, 436–7
Murphy, Kevin, 15, 35, 62, 90,
    134
Murray, Seamus, 430
museums, 248, 267

National Cancer Forum, 324
National Children and Young
    People's Strategy Unit, 182
National Children's Strategy, 183
National Commission on
    Restorative Justice, 212
National Competitiveness Council,
    414, 456–7
National Consultative Committee
    on Racism and Interculturalism
    (NCCRI), 436
National Consumer Agency, 335
National Development Finance
    Agency (NDFA), 477
National Development Plan (NDP),
    241, 243, 245, 435
national directorates (health
    services), 304–5
National Employment Rights
    Authority (NERA), 265, 437
National Forum on Europe, 427
national health consultative forum,
    306

National Hospitals Office (NHO),
    305, 309
National Intercultural Health
    Strategy, 437
National Operations Unit (NOU),
    465
national pay deals, 185
national perinatal reporting system
    (NPRS), 315
National Roads Authority, 241,
    243–4
National Task Force on Medical
    Staffing, 300–1
National Treasury Management
    Agency, 477
National Treatment Purchase Fund
    (NTPF), 315–16
National University of Ireland, 94, 95
NCCRI (National Consultative
    Committee on Racism and
    Interculturalism), 436
NDFA (National Development
    Finance Agency), 477
NDP (National Development Plan),
    241, 243, 245, 435
NESC (National Economic and
    Social Council), 184
neutrality, 423–4
New Connections, 471
New Public Management Approach,
    440–2
New Public Service Approach,
    442–4
Nice, Treaty of, 391, 405, 433
    referendum, 395, 396, 423, 427
no-confidence vote, 68
Nordic battlegroup, 422
Norman, Peter, 426
Norris, David, 113
North-Eastern Health Board
    (NEHB), 483
Northern Ireland affairs, 30

north/south implementation bodies, 262
Norton, William, 34
NOU (National Operations Unit), 465

OASIS (Online Access to State Information and Services), 470
O'Brien, Conor Cruise, 49
O'Brien, Geraldine, 445
O'Brien, John, 322
Ó Ceallaigh, Seán T., 34, 137, 157
O'Connor, John, 248
O'Connor, Joseph, 342–5
Ó Cuív, Éamon, 320
Ó Dálaigh, Cearbhall, 137, 153–4, 155, 157
Ó Dálaigh, Chief Justice, 121, 127
O'Dea, Willie, 14
O'Doherty, Ann, 323
O'Donnell, Rory, 184, 185
O'Donoghue, John, 277–8
O'Donoghue, Martin, 37, 58
O'Donovan, D.J., 170
OECD 2008 Review, 457–66, 484–5
Offences Against the State Act 1939, 207
Office of Public Works, 196
Office of the Appeals Commissioners, 358–9
Office of the Chief State Solicitor, 220–1, 222
Office of the Director of Corporate Enforcement, 335
Office of the Minister for Children (OMC), 182–3
Office of the Parliamentary Counsel, 219
Office of the Revenue Solicitor, 225–6
Official Languages Act 2003, 131

Official Secrets Act 1963, 188, 372–3, 380
O'Flaherty, Hugh, 202
O'Hagan, John W., 263
O'Higgins, Chief Justice, 127
O'Higgins, Kevin, 188
O'Higgins, Niall, 324
O hUiginn, Padraig, 167
Oireachtas, 67–9, 100–13
  committees, 100–5, 276–8
  EU and, 405–13
  gender equality, 106
  public inquiries, 366–7, 368
  see also Dáil; Seanad
Oireachtas (Allowances to Members) Act 1962, 108
Oireachtas Broadcasting Committee, 89
Oireachtas Commission, 89, 93
Oireachtas Committee, All-Party, 98, 99, 133, 134, 137, 143, 148, 153, 156, 216, 228, 423
O'Keeffe, Jim, 98, 99
O'Leary, Michael, 34
O'Malley, Des, 181
O'Malley, Eoin, 36
Ombudsman, 278, 371–5
  Children, 379
  Defence Forces, 379
  delay in establishing, 339, 371–2
  European, 354–5
  Financial Services, 378–9
  Garda Síochána, 378
  Press, 380–1
Ombudsman (Amendment) Bill 2008, 278, 374–5
OMC (Office of the Minister for Children), 182–3
O'Meara, Aileen, 64–5
Ó Muimhneacháin, Muiris, 20
Opticians Board, 266

O'Reilly, Emily, 159, 278, 372, 374, 377, 439, 482–3
Organisational Review Programme (ORP), 460–1, 467
O'Rourke, Mary, 100
overnight allowances, 106–7
overseas journeys, 50–2

PAC (Public Accounts Committee), 93, 168, 277, 281, 368–70
palliative care policy, 326
Parliamentary Assemblies (EU), 406–7
parliamentary inquiries, 367–71
Parliamentary Legal Adviser, 225
parliamentary questions, 29, 55, 85–6, 346–51
partnership, social, 183–5, 454–5
partnerships, public–private, 241–2, 439, 477–8
party meetings, 48
Patents Office, 358
Patten, Chris, 424
pay
    civil servants, 190–1
    ministers, 19
    national pay deals, 185
    President, 138
    state agency boards, 271–2
    TDs and senators, 106
PCCC (Primary, Community and Continuing Care) Directorate, 305, 309
peacekeeping, 421–2, 424, 448
Performance Management and Development System (PMDS), 455
Permanent Representation of Ireland to the EU, 416–18
Perry, James L., 443–4
personal social services, 305–6
Petersberg tasks, 421, 424

planning, 234–5, 246–8
    Flood/Mahon Tribunal, 257, 361–5
Planning and Development Act 2000, 235, 246, 247
Planning and Development (Strategic Infrastructure) Act 2006, 247
PMDS (Performance Management and Development System), 455
political parties, allowances and funding, 108, 109–10
Pollitt, Christopher *et al.*, 261
population changes, 318, 319, 331, 434–5, 436
Population Health Directorate, 305
Post, An, 265, 270, 273, 247, 278
    regulator, 336–7
PPPs (public–private partnerships), 241–2, 439, 477–8
presidency conclusion, 398
President, 136–57
    discretionary powers, 143, 144–8
    eligibility and election, 137–8
    legislative bills and, 146, 149, 150–5
    reform of Presidency, 156–7
    removal from office, 142–3
    role and functions, 136–3, 139–44, 155–7
    summary of Presidents, 137, 157
    Taoiseach and, 30, 137
Presidential Commission, 143, 149
press
    communication with, 31–2, 52–4, 64–5
    reportage of court cases, 205
Press Council of Ireland, 380
press officers, 64–5
Press Ombudsman, 380–1
Press Secretary, 31–2, 54
pressure groups, 351

Prevention of Corruption
(Amendment) Act 2001, 185–6
Primary Care: A New Direction,
298
Primary, Community and
Continuing Care (PCCC)
Directorate, 305, 309
principals (civil service), 165–6,
448
private bill, 82–3
private company, 267
private health insurance, 327–8
private member's bill, 81–2
private office, ministerial, 56–8
private secretary, 39, 56–8
privatisation, 285–7
privilege, 104–5, 364
productivity of public sector, 440–1
Programme for Economic and
Social Progress, 269
Programme for Government (1997),
233
Programme for Government (2007),
90, 253
Programme for Prosperity and
Fairness, 454
programme managers, 63–4
Prompt Payment of Accounts Act
1997, 476
proportional representation (PR),
72, 91, 124, 230, 341
proportionality, 396–7
prosecutions, 221–4
Prospectus report, 299
protocol, 30
Provisional Collection of Taxes Act
1927, 84
Public Accounts Committee (PAC),
93, 168, 277, 281, 368–70
public administration, 434–86
characteristics of, 437–40
financial management, 476–78

New Public Management
Approach, 440–2
New Public Service Approach,
442–4
reform, 444–86
regulatory reform, 475–6
Transforming Public Services
Programme, 462–8, 474, 486
see also civil service
Public Appointments Commission,
159–61, 192, 198
Public Appointments Service,
232–3
Public Appointments Transparency
Bill 2008, 270
public bill, 80–1
public company, 267
Public Offices Commission, 17
public enterprises, 265–6 *see also*
state agencies and bodies
public inquiries, 366–7, 368
public–private partnerships (PPPs),
241–2, 439, 477–8
Public Procurement Guidelines
Competitive Process, 179,
180
public relations, 31–2, 52–4, 64–5,
111
Public Relations Office, 111
public service *see* public
administration
Public Service Advisory Council,
446
Public Service Benchmarking Body,
191
Public Service, Dept of, 446
Public Service Excellence Awards,
442
Public Service Management Acts
1997–2004, 2, 35, 59, 167, 169,
172, 181, 221, 455
terms of 1997 Act, 453–4

Public Services Organisation
  Review Group, 3–4, 266, 334,
  484
Purcell, John, 477–8

qualified majority voting (QMV),
  398–9
*Quality and Fairness: A Health
  System for You*, 296–7, 307, 316
Quality Customer Service, 452
quangos, 260
Quigley report, 180–1
Quinn, Ruairí, 37, 38, 41, 66, 167,
  174, 175, 350

Rabbitte, Pat, 4, 89
racism, 436
rates, 251–2, 352, 359
recreation and amenities, 248–9
Red Cross Act 1944, 142
redeployment, 198
referendum, 119, 123, 124–5
  Lisbon Treaty, 395–6, 402, 428,
    429
  Treaty of Nice, 395, 396, 423,
    427, 433
Referendum Act 2001, 124–5
Referendum Commission, 124–5,
  402
Reform Treaty *see* Lisbon Treaty
Refugee Appeals Authority (RAA),
  483
Refugee Appeals Tribunal, 355
Regional Aid Guidelines (RAGs),
  428
regional authorities and assemblies,
  252–3
regional development, 421, 428
regional health boards, 313–14
regional health forums, 306–7
register of interests (local
  authorities), 257

Regulating Better, 455, 471, 475–6
regulations (EU), 398
regulatory bodies, 262, 263–4,
  336–9
regulatory impact analysis (RIA), 8,
  455
regulatory reform, 475–6
representations, 339–46
Republic of Ireland Act 1948, 130,
  142
restorative justice, 212
Revenue Commissioners, 3, 469
  complaints section, 335
  recruitment, 161
Revenue Solicitor, 225–6
Review Body on Higher
  Remuneration in the Public
  Sector, 216, 272, 307
Reynolds, Albert, 23, 34, 200, 463
RIA (regulatory impact analysis), 8,
  455
rights
  Constitutional, 118, 121–2,
    127–9, 352–3
  European Court of Human
    Rights, 353–4
  Universal Declaration of Human
    Rights, 353, 383–9
roads, 241, 243–4
Roads Acts 1993–2007, 243, 244
Robinson, Mary, 137, 140–1, 146,
  156, 157
Roche, Dick, 234–5, 277
role and powers of government, 1–6
Rome, Treaty of, 287–8, 390, 393
RTÉ, 64–5, 89, 274, 279
Rural Development Programme, 427
Ryan judgment, 127, 128, 129
Ryan, Justice Sean, 365

Sabel, Charles and O'Donnell,
  Rory, 282–3

St Patrick's Day, 52
sanitation, 244–5
Sarkozy, Nicolas, 404
Scanlon, Michael, 312
Schäube, Wolfgang, 404
Schmid, Helga, 417
Sea-Fisheries Protection Authority,
    265
seals of office, 37, 138
Seanad, 94–113
    compellability and privilege,
        104–5
    declaration of interests, 107–8
    functions, 96–7
    legislative bills, 82–3, 96, 102
    membership, 94–6
    money bills, 83, 147, 149, 150
    reform proposals, 96, 97–100
    secretarial assistance, 93, 110–12
    senators' pay and expenses,
        106–7
Seanad Committee on Procedure
    and Privileges, 99
Seanad Electoral Acts 1947–1960,
    95
secretary, assistant, 166, 190, 193,
    448, 471
secretary general of department, 39,
    40–1, 167–71, 172, 449
    appointment of, 193–4
    salary and employment, 190
secretary general of government, 6,
    8, 9–10, 89, 111
secretary general to President, 138
secretary, private, 39, 56–8
select committees, 101
Senior Public Service, 467
separation of powers, 200, 226
Serving the Country Better, 446–7
sewerage, 244–5
sexual offences, 212
Shannon, Geoffrey, 214

Shaping a Healthier Future, 294–5
Sheedy, Philip, 202
Sheehy, Edward, 238
Single European Act, 391, 393–4
Sinnott, Richard, 110, 391, 395
Sinnott case, 129
Small Claims Court, 208, 210
SMI (Strategic Management
    Initiative), 181, 236, 449–57
Smith, Brendan, 4
Smith, Michael, 36
Social and Family Affairs, Dept of,
    469
social partnership, 183–5, 454–5
Social Welfare Act 1952, 358
Social Welfare Appeals Office,
    381–2
Social Welfare (Consolidation) Act
    2005, 83
Social Welfare, Dept of (data
    security), 380
Solicitors Disciplinary Tribunal,
    355–6
sovereignty, 119, 124, 130
SPCs (strategic policy committees),
    239, 256
special advisers, 58–63
special committees, 102
Special Criminal Court, 207, 209
Special Group on Public Service
    Numbers and Expenditures
    Programmes, 463, 465, 468
speech-writing, 42–3, 60
Spring, Dick, 24, 34, 49
Standards in Public Office Act
    2001, 16, 17, 185, 186
Standards in Public Office
    Commission, 17–18, 59, 108,
    109–10, 186, 257, 269, 403
standing committees, 101
standing orders, 76–7, 347, 350
    EU and, 411

state agencies and bodies, 259–89
  boards and directors, 268–72
  commercial/non-commercial,
    260, 265–7
  control and accountability,
    274–85
  defining state agencies/state-
    sponsored bodies, 261–2
  finance, 272–4
  privatisation, 285–7
  reasons for establishing, 262–7
  reform, 468
State Authorities Act 2002, 241–2
Statute Book, 219–20
Statute Law (Restatement) Act
  2002, 219
Statute Law Revision Unit, 218
statutory corporation, 267
statutory instruments, 80, 219
Steinmeier, Walter, 404
Strategic Management Initiative
  (SMI), 181, 236, 449–57
strategy statements, 453
'Stronger Local Democracy –
  Options for Change', 256–7
Sub-Committee on Ireland's Future
  in the European Union, 409–12,
  429
subsidiarity, 396
Sullivan, Eddie, 217
Superintendent of the Houses, 111
Supreme Court, 205–6, 209, 212–14
  Dáil procedures, 77
  judicial review, 126–7
  Mahon Tribunal and, 363–4
  President's reference of bills,
    149, 150–5
Sustaining Progress, 184, 192, 454

Tánaiste, 24–5
  list of Tánaistí, 34
Taoiseach, 18–24, 120

dissolving the Dáil, 144–5
EU presidency, 426
list of Taoisigh, 33–4
President and, 30, 137
Taoiseach, Dept of, 25–32
  EU and, 419
Task Force on the Public Service,
  461
task forces, 260
tax, 3, 84, 173
  motor, 244
Teagasc, 264, 266, 267, 269
technical officers, 162
Telecom Éireann, 265, 285
Thornhill, Don, 440
Timonen, Virpi, 183, 312, 472
tipstaffs, 203
TLAC (Top Level Appointments
  Committee), 192–3
Tourism Ireland, 262
*Towards an Integrated Public
  Service*, 458–60
Towards 2016, 182, 183, 185, 192,
  265, 305, 338, 435
  terms and commitments of,
    454–5
town clerk, 240
town councils, 229, 230 *see also*
  local government
Transforming Public Services
  Programme, 462–8, 474, 486
transparency, 105, 109–10, 176,
  192, 260, 270, 375, 475
  see also accountability; freedom
    of information
Transport, Dept of, 460–1
transportation, 241, 243–4
travel expenses, 106–7
Travellers, housing, 242–3
Travers report, 46, 170–1, 176–7,
  301–2, 311
Treaty of Amsterdam, 391, 421–2

Treaty of Lisbon *see* Lisbon
   Treaty
Treaty of Nice, 391, 405, 433
   referendum, 395, 396, 423,
   427
Treaty of Rome, 287–8, 390, 393
Treaty on European Union
   (Maastricht Treaty), 390, 391,
   394–5, 408
tribunals, appeals and complaints,
   355–9
tribunals of inquiry, 359–67
Tribunals of Inquiry Act 1921, 359,
   360, 363, 367, 370
Tutty, Michael, 279
'twelve o'clock items', 5–6

ultra vires, 353, 370
unanimity principle, 14
Unfair Dismissals Act 1977, 195
United Nations
   Commissioner for Refugees,
      483
   peacekeeping, 421–2, 424, 448
   Universal Declaration of Human
      Rights, 353, 383–9
University of Dublin, 94, 95
urban renewal, 247, 253

Valuation Acts, 251, 352
Valuation Tribunal, 359
Value for Money and Policy Review
   Initiative (VFM), 476–7,
   479–80
*Value for Money Audit of the Irish
   Health System*, 297–8
Van de Walle, Steven, 439
Van Gend en Loos case, 397
Varadkar, Leo, 270

VHI (Voluntary Health Insurance),
   327–8
   board, 272
victims of crime, 210–12
voting *see* elections, general;
   elections, local government
voting in Dáil, 77–9, 112
   electronic, 78, 79, 87, 88

Wallström, Margot, 412
Walsh, Justice Brian, 126–7, 128,
   133, 135, 204, 216
Walsh, Edward, 197
Walsh, Joe, 36
waste collection, 248
water supply, 244
Whelan, Ken and Masterson,
   Eugene, 184
Whelan, Noel, 463
Whelehan, Harry, 200
Whip, Chief, 26–8, 219
Whitaker, T.K., 98, 132, 174, 179,
   434
White, Padraic, 281
white paper (EU), 408
White Paper on Receipts and
   Expenditure, 83
'whole-of-government' approach,
   441
Whyte, Gerry, 129, 150, 152
Wiberg, Matti, 348–9
Wilson, John, 34
women *see* gender equality
Worker Participation (State
   Enterprise) Acts 1977–1988, 270

X case, 217

Zimmerman, Joseph, 41, 168

penguin.co.uk/vintage

Publication of *The Complete Works of George Orwell* is a unique bibliographic event as well as a major step in Orwell scholarship. Meticulous textual research by Dr Peter Davison has revealed that all the current editions of Orwell have been mutilated to a greater or lesser extent. This authoritative edition incorporates all Orwell's many textual changes as well as restoring his original intention where the hands of others have intervened.

THE COMPLETE WORKS OF

GEORGE ORWELL

VOLUME EIGHT

Animal Farm

A Fairy Story

Edited by Peter Davison

SECKER & WARBURG

LONDON

2 4 6 8 10 9 7 5 3 1

First published in England in 1945
by Martin Secker & Warburg Limited
Reprinted 1945, 1946, 1949, 1950 (twice), 1951 (twice), 1952, 1953, 1955, 1959, 1961
Uniform edition first published in England in 1965
Reprinted 1971, 1977
Complete edition, Volumes 1–9 published in England in 1986–87
Reprinted 1997
Animal Farm reprinted 1992
Complete edition, Volumes 10–20 published in England in 1998
by Martin Secker & Warburg Limited
Random House, 20 Vauxhall Bridge Road, London SW1V 2SA

Random House Australia (Pty) Limited
20 Alfred Street, Milsons Point, Sydney,
New South Wales 2061, Australia

Random House New Zealand Limited
18 Poland Road, Glenfield,
Auckland 10, New Zealand

Random House South Africa (Pty) Limited
Endulini, 5A Jubilee Road, Parktown 2193, South Africa

Random House UK Limited Reg. No. 954009

A CIP catalogue record for this book
is available from the British Library

ISBN 0 436 23135 2

Typeset in Monophoto Bembo
by Northumberland Press Limited, Gateshead, Tyne and Wear

Penguin Random House is committed to a sustainable future for
our business, our readers and our planet. This book is made from
Forest Stewardship Council® certified paper.

MIX
Paper from
responsible sources
FSC® C018179
www.fsc.org

Printed and bound in Great Britain by Clays Ltd, St Ives plc

ACKNOWLEDGEMENTS

The inclusion in this volume of Orwell's adaptation for radio of *Animal Farm* shifts the project for publishing all Orwell's writings from the new editions of his nine books (the limited, original intention) to the essays, letters, reviews, broadcasts, diaries and notebooks. It is appropriate that I take this opportunity to give interim thanks, as it were, to a few of those who have helped me in the preparation of this text and its introduction and who have also been much concerned to assist me with volumes prepared and in preparation but yet to appear in print: Mark Hamilton of the Orwell Estate; Gill Furlong and Janet Percival of the Orwell Archive at University College London; Jacqueline Kavanagh, BBC Written Archives Officer, and her staff at Caversham; Mark Bryant of Secker & Warburg; my wife, Sheila, who has laboured long and painstakingly over proofs; and, above all, Ian Angus, whose generosity and whose dedication to scholarship have continually supported and encouraged me. At this half stage I thank them most warmly. In time I hope to be able to acknowledge the many others who have also given me help.

P.D.

CHAPTER I

MR JONES, of the Manor Farm, had locked the hen-houses for the night, but was too drunk to remember to shut the pop-holes. With the ring of light from his lantern dancing from side to side he lurched across the yard, kicked off his boots at the back door, drew himself a last glass of beer from the barrel in the scullery, and made his way up to bed, where Mrs Jones was already snoring.

As soon as the light in the bedroom went out there was a stirring and a fluttering all through the farm buildings. Word had gone round during the day that old Major, the prize Middle White boar, had had a strange dream on the previous night and wished to communicate it to the other animals. It had been agreed that they should all meet in the big barn as soon as Mr Jones was safely out of the way. Old Major (so he was always called, though the name under which he had been exhibited was Willingdon Beauty) was so highly regarded on the farm that everyone was quite ready to lose an hour's sleep in order to hear what he had to say.

At one end of the big barn, on a sort of raised platform, Major was already ensconced on his bed of straw, under a lantern which hung from a beam. He was twelve years old and had lately grown rather stout, but he was still a majestic-looking pig, with a wise and benevolent appearance in spite of the fact that his tushes had never been cut. Before long the other animals began to arrive and make themselves comfortable after their different fashions. First came the three dogs, Bluebell, Jessie and Pincher, and then the pigs, who settled down in the straw immediately in

I

front of the platform. The hens perched themselves on the window-sills, the pigeons fluttered up to the rafters, the sheep and cows lay down behind the pigs and began to chew the cud. The two cart-horses, Boxer and Clover, came in together, walking very slowly and setting down their vast hairy hoofs with great care lest there should be some small animal concealed in the straw. Clover was a stout motherly mare approaching middle life, who had never quite got her figure back after her fourth foal. Boxer was an enormous beast, nearly eighteen hands high, and as strong as any two ordinary horses put together. A white stripe down his nose gave him a somewhat stupid appearance, and in fact he was not of first-rate intelligence, but he was universally respected for his steadiness of character and tremendous powers of work. After the horses came Muriel, the white goat, and Benjamin the donkey. Benjamin was the oldest animal on the farm, and the worst tempered. He seldom talked, and when he did it was usually to make some cynical remark—for instance he would say that God had given him a tail to keep the flies off, but that he would sooner have had no tail and no flies. Alone among the animals on the farm he never laughed. If asked why, he would say that he saw nothing to laugh at. Nevertheless, without openly admitting it, he was devoted to Boxer; the two of them usually spent their Sundays together in the small paddock beyond the orchard, grazing side by side and never speaking.

The two horses had just lain down when a brood of ducklings which had lost their mother filed into the barn, cheeping feebly and wandering from side to side to find some place where they would not be trodden on. Clover made a sort of wall round them with her great foreleg, and the ducklings nestled down inside it and promptly fell asleep. At the last moment Mollie, the foolish, pretty white mare who drew Mr Jones's trap, came mincing daintily in,

chewing at a lump of sugar. She took a place near the front and began flirting her white mane, hoping to draw attention to the red ribbons it was plaited with. Last of all came the cat, who looked round, as usual, for the warmest place, and finally squeezed herself in between Boxer and Clover; there she purred contentedly throughout Major's speech without listening to a word of what he was saying.

All the animals were now present except Moses, the tame raven, who slept on a perch behind the back door. When Major saw that they had all made themselves comfortable and were waiting attentively he cleared his throat and began:

'Comrades, you have heard already about the strange dream that I had last night. But I will come to the dream later. I have something else to say first. I do not think, comrades, that I shall be with you for many months longer, and before I die I feel it my duty to pass on to you such wisdom as I have acquired. I have had a long life, I have had much time for thought as I lay alone in my stall, and I think I may say that I understand the nature of life on this earth as well as any animal now living. It is about this that I wish to speak to you.

'Now, comrades, what is the nature of this life of ours? Let us face it, our lives are miserable, laborious and short. We are born, we are given just so much food as will keep the breath in our bodies, and those of us who are capable of it are forced to work to the last atom of our strength; and the very instant that our usefulness has come to an end we are slaughtered with hideous cruelty. No animal in England knows the meaning of happiness or leisure after he is a year old. No animal in England is free. The life of an animal is misery and slavery: that is the plain truth.

'But is this simply part of the order of Nature? Is it because this land of ours is so poor that it cannot afford a decent life to those who dwell upon it? No, comrades, a

thousand times no! The soil of England is fertile, its climate is good, it is capable of affording food in abundance to an enormously greater number of animals than now inhabit it. This single farm of ours would support a dozen horses, twenty cows, hundreds of sheep—and all of them living in a comfort and a dignity that are now almost beyond our imagining. Why then do we continue in this miserable condition? Because nearly the whole of the produce of our labour is stolen from us by human beings. There, comrades, is the answer to all our problems. It is summed up in a single word—Man. Man is the only real enemy we have. Remove Man from the scene, and the root cause of hunger and overwork is abolished for ever.

'Man is the only creature that consumes without producing. He does not give milk, he does not lay eggs, he is too weak to pull the plough, he cannot run fast enough to catch rabbits. Yet he is lord of all the animals. He sets them to work, he gives back to them the bare minimum that will prevent them from starving, and the rest he keeps for himself. Our labour tills the soil, our dung fertilises it, and yet there is not one of us that owns more than his bare skin. You cows that I see before me, how many thousands of gallons of milk have you given during this last year? And what has happened to that milk which should have been breeding up sturdy calves? Every drop of it has gone down the throats of our enemies. And you hens, how many eggs have you laid in this last year, and how many of those eggs ever hatched into chickens? The rest have all gone to market to bring in money for Jones and his men. And you, Clover, where are those four foals you bore, who should have been the support and pleasure of your old age? Each was sold at a year old—you will never see one of them again. In return for your four confinements and all your labour in the fields, what have you ever had except your bare rations and a stall?

'And even the miserable lives we lead are not allowed to reach their natural span. For myself I do not grumble, for I am one of the lucky ones. I am twelve years old and have had over four hundred children. Such is the natural life of a pig. But no animal escapes the cruel knife in the end. You young porkers who are sitting in front of me, every one of you will scream your lives out at the block within a year. To that horror we all must come—cows, pigs, hens, sheep, everyone. Even the horses and the dogs have no better fate. You, Boxer, the very day that those great muscles of yours lose their power, Jones will sell you to the knacker, who will cut your throat and boil you down for the foxhounds. As for the dogs, when they grow old and toothless Jones ties a brick round their necks and drowns them in the nearest pond.

'Is it not crystal clear, then, comrades, that all the evils of this life of ours spring from the tyranny of human beings? Only get rid of Man, and the produce of our labour would be our own. Almost overnight we could become rich and free. What then must we do? Why, work night and day, body and soul, for the overthrow of the human race! That is my message to you, comrades: Rebellion! I do not know when that Rebellion will come, it might be in a week or in a hundred years, but I know, as surely as I see this straw beneath my feet, that sooner or later justice will be done. Fix your eyes on that, comrades, throughout the short remainder of your lives! And above all, pass on this message of mine to those who come after you, so that future generations shall carry on the struggle until it is victorious.

'And remember, comrades, your resolution must never falter. No argument must lead you astray. Never listen when they tell you that Man and the animals have a common interest, that the prosperity of the one is the prosperity of the others. It is all lies. Man serves the interests

of no creature except himself. And among us animals let there be perfect unity, perfect comradeship in the struggle. All men are enemies. All animals are comrades.'

At this moment there was a tremendous uproar. While Major was speaking four large rats had crept out of their holes and were sitting on their hindquarters, listening to him. The dogs had suddenly caught sight of them, and it was only by a swift dash for their holes that the rats saved their lives. Major raised his trotter for silence:

'Comrades,' he said, 'here is a point that must be settled. The wild creatures, such as rats and rabbits—are they our friends or our enemies? Let us put it to the vote. I propose this question to the meeting: Are rats comrades?'

The vote was taken at once, and it was agreed by an overwhelming majority that rats were comrades. There were only four dissentients, the three dogs and the cat, who was afterwards discovered to have voted on both sides. Major continued:

'I have little more to say. I merely repeat, remember always your duty of enmity towards Man and all his ways. Whatever goes upon two legs is an enemy. Whatever goes upon four legs, or has wings, is a friend. And remember also that in fighting against Man, we must not come to resemble him. Even when you have conquered him, do not adopt his vices. No animal must ever live in a house, or sleep in a bed, or wear clothes, or drink alcohol, or smoke tobacco, or touch money, or engage in trade. All the habits of Man are evil. And above all, no animal must ever tyrannise over his own kind. Weak or strong, clever or simple, we are all brothers. No animal must ever kill any other animal. All animals are equal.

'And now, comrades, I will tell you about my dream of last night. I cannot describe that dream to you. It was a dream of the earth as it will be when Man has vanished. But it reminded me of something that I had long forgotten.

Many years ago, when I was a little pig, my mother and the other sows used to sing an old song of which they knew only the tune and the first three words. I had known that tune in my infancy, but it had long since passed out of my mind. Last night, however, it came back to me in my dream. And what is more, the words of the song also came back—words, I am certain, which were sung by the animals of long ago and have been lost to memory for generations. I will sing you that song now, comrades. I am old and my voice is hoarse, but when I have taught you the tune you can sing it better for yourselves. It is called "Beasts of England".'

Old Major cleared his throat and began to sing. As he had said, his voice was hoarse, but he sang well enough, and it was a stirring tune, something between 'Clementine' and 'La Cucuracha'. The words ran:

> Beasts of England, beasts of Ireland,
> Beasts of every land and clime,
> Hearken to my joyful tidings
> Of the golden future time.
>
> Soon or late the day is coming,
> Tyrant Man shall be o'erthrown,
> And the fruitful fields of England
> Shall be trod by beasts alone.
>
> Rings shall vanish from our noses,
> And the harness from our back,
> Bit and spur shall rust forever,
> Cruel whips no more shall crack.
>
> Riches more than mind can picture,
> Wheat and barley, oats and hay,
> Clover, beans and mangel-wurzels
> Shall be ours upon that day.

7

Bright will shine the fields of England,
Purer shall its waters be,
Sweeter yet shall blow its breezes
On the day that sets us free.

For that day we all must labour,
Though we die before it break;
Cows and horses, geese and turkeys,
All must toil for freedom's sake.

Beasts of England, beasts of Ireland,
Beasts of every land and clime,
Hearken well and spread my tidings
Of the golden future time.

The singing of this song threw the animals into the wildest excitement. Almost before Major had reached the end, they had begun singing it for themselves. Even the stupidest of them had already picked up the tune and a few of the words, and as for the clever ones, such as the pigs and dogs, they had the entire song by heart within a few minutes. And then, after a few preliminary tries, the whole farm burst out into 'Beasts of England' in tremendous unison. The cows lowed it, the dogs whined it, the sheep bleated it, the horses whinnied it, the ducks quacked it. They were so delighted with the song that they sang it right through five times in succession, and might have continued singing it all night if they had not been interrupted.

Unfortunately the uproar awoke Mr Jones, who sprang out of bed, making sure that there was a fox in the yard. He seized the gun which always stood in a corner of his bedroom, and let fly a charge of Number 6 shot into the darkness. The pellets buried themselves in the wall of the barn and the meeting broke up hurriedly. Everyone fled to his own sleeping-place. The birds jumped onto their perches, the animals settled down in the straw, and the whole farm was asleep in a moment.

CHAPTER II

THREE NIGHTS LATER old Major died peacefully in his sleep. His body was buried at the foot of the orchard.

This was early in March. During the next three months there was much secret activity. Major's speech had given to the more intelligent animals on the farm a completely new outlook on life. They did not know when the Rebellion predicted by Major would take place, they had no reason for thinking that it would be within their own lifetime, but they saw clearly that it was their duty to prepare for it. The work of teaching and organising the others fell naturally upon the pigs, who were generally recognised as being the cleverest of the animals. Preeminent among the pigs were two young boars named Snowball and Napoleon, whom Mr Jones was breeding up for sale. Napoleon was a large, rather fierce-looking Berkshire boar, the only Berkshire on the farm, not much of a talker but with a reputation for getting his own way. Snowball was a more vivacious pig than Napoleon, quicker in speech and more inventive, but was not considered to have the same depth of character. All the other male pigs on the farm were porkers. The best known among them was a small fat pig named Squealer, with very round cheeks, twinkling eyes, nimble movements and a shrill voice. He was a brilliant talker, and when he was arguing some difficult point he had a way of skipping from side to side and whisking his tail which was somehow very persuasive. The others said of Squealer that he could turn black into white.

These three had elaborated old Major's teachings into a

complete system of thought, to which they gave the name of Animalism. Several nights a week, after Mr Jones was asleep, they held secret meetings in the barn and expounded the principles of Animalism to the others. At the beginning they met with much stupidity and apathy. Some of the animals talked of the duty of loyalty to Mr Jones, whom they referred to as 'Master', or made elementary remarks such as 'Mr Jones feeds us. If he were gone we should starve to death.' Others asked such questions as 'Why should we care what happens after we are dead?' or 'If this Rebellion is to happen anyway, what difference does it make whether we work for it or not?', and the pigs had great difficulty in making them see that this was contrary to the spirit of Animalism. The stupidest questions of all were asked by Mollie, the white mare. The very first question she asked Snowball was: 'Will there still be sugar after the Rebellion?'

'No,' said Snowball firmly. 'We have no means of making sugar on this farm. Besides, you do not need sugar. You will have all the oats and hay you want.'

'And shall I still be allowed to wear ribbons in my mane?' asked Mollie.

'Comrade,' said Snowball, 'those ribbons that you are so devoted to are the badge of slavery. Can you not understand that liberty is worth more than ribbons?'

Mollie agreed, but she did not sound very convinced.

The pigs had an even harder struggle to counteract the lies put about by Moses, the tame raven. Moses, who was Mr Jones's especial pet, was a spy and a tale-bearer, but he was also a clever talker. He claimed to know of the existence of a mysterious country called Sugarcandy Mountain, to which all animals went when they died. It was situated somewhere up in the sky, a little distance beyond the clouds, Moses said. In Sugarcandy Mountain it was Sunday seven days a week, clover was in season all the year round,

and lump sugar and linseed cake grew on the hedges. The
animals hated Moses because he told tales and did no work,
but some of them believed in Sugarcandy Mountain, and
the pigs had to argue very hard to persuade them that there
was no such place.

Their most faithful disciples were the two cart-horses,
Boxer and Clover. These two had great difficulty in thinking anything out for themselves, but having once accepted
the pigs as their teachers they absorbed everything that
they were told, and passed it on to the other animals by
simple arguments. They were unfailing in their attendance
at the secret meetings in the barn, and led the singing of
'Beasts of England' with which the meetings always
ended.

Now, as it turned out, the Rebellion was achieved much
earlier and more easily than anyone had expected. In past
years Mr Jones, although a hard master, had been a capable
farmer, but of late he had fallen on evil days. He had
become much disheartened after losing money in a lawsuit,
and had taken to drinking more than was good for him.
For whole days at a time he would lounge in his windsor
chair in the kitchen, reading the newspapers, drinking, and
occasionally feeding Moses on crusts of bread soaked in
beer. His men were idle and dishonest, the fields were full
of weeds, the buildings wanted roofing, the hedges were
neglected and the animals were underfed.

June came and the hay was almost ready for cutting. On
Midsummer's Eve, which was a Saturday, Mr Jones went
into Willingdon and got so drunk at the Red Lion that he
did not come back till midday on Sunday. The men had
milked the cows in the early morning and then had gone
out rabbiting, without bothering to feed the animals.
When Mr Jones got back he immediately went to sleep on
the drawing-room sofa with the *News of the World* over his
face, so that when evening came the animals were still

unfed. At last they could stand it no longer. One of the cows broke in the door of the store-shed with her horn and all the animals began to help themselves from the bins. It was just then that Mr Jones woke up. The next moment he and his four men were in the store-shed with whips in their hands, lashing out in all directions. This was more than the hungry animals could bear. With one accord, though nothing of the kind had been planned beforehand, they flung themselves upon their tormentors. Jones and his men suddenly found themselves being butted and kicked from all sides. The situation was quite out of their control. They had never seen animals behave like this before, and this sudden uprising of creatures whom they were used to thrashing and maltreating just as they chose, frightened them almost out of their wits. After only a moment or two they gave up trying to defend themselves and took to their heels. A minute later all five of them were in full flight down the cart-track that led to the main road, with the animals pursuing them in triumph.

Mrs Jones looked out of the bedroom window, saw what was happening, hurriedly flung a few possessions into a carpet bag and slipped out of the farm by another way. Moses sprang off his perch and flapped after her, croaking loudly. Meanwhile the animals had chased Jones and his men out onto the road and slammed the five-barred gate behind them. And so, almost before they knew what was happening, the Rebellion had been successfully carried through; Jones was expelled, and the Manor Farm was theirs.

For the first few minutes the animals could hardly believe in their good fortune. Their first act was to gallop in a body right round the boundaries of the farm, as though to make quite sure that no human being was hiding anywhere upon it; then they raced back to the farm buildings to wipe out the last traces of Jones's hated reign. The

harness-room at the end of the stables was broken open; the bits, the nose-rings, the dog-chains, the cruel knives with which Mr Jones had been used to castrate the pigs and lambs, were all flung down the well. The reins, the halters, the blinkers, the degrading nosebags, were thrown onto the rubbish fire which was burning in the yard. So were the whips. All the animals capered with joy when they saw the whips going up in flames. Snowball also threw onto the fire the ribbons with which the horses' manes and tails had usually been decorated on market days.

'Ribbons,' he said, 'should be considered as clothes, which are the mark of a human being. All animals should go naked.'

When Boxer heard this he fetched the small straw hat which he wore in summer to keep the flies out of his ears, and flung it onto the fire with the rest.

In a very little while the animals had destroyed everything that reminded them of Mr Jones. Napoleon then led them back to the store-shed and served out a double ration of corn to everybody, with two biscuits for each dog. Then they sang 'Beasts of England' from end to end seven times running, and after that they settled down for the night and slept as they had never slept before.

But they woke at dawn as usual, and suddenly remembering the glorious thing that had happened they all raced out into the pasture together. A little way down the pasture there was a knoll that commanded a view of most of the farm. The animals rushed to the top of it and gazed round them in the clear morning light. Yes, it was theirs— everything that they could see was theirs! In the ecstasy of that thought they gambolled round and round, they hurled themselves into the air in great leaps of excitement. They rolled in the dew, they cropped mouthfuls of the sweet summer grass, they kicked up clods of the black earth and snuffed its rich scent. Then they made a tour of inspection

of the whole farm and surveyed with speechless admiration the ploughland, the hayfield, the orchard, the pool, the spinney. It was as though they had never seen these things before, and even now they could hardly believe that it was all their own.

Then they filed back to the farm buildings and halted in silence outside the door of the farmhouse. That was theirs too, but they were frightened to go inside. After a moment, however, Snowball and Napoleon butted the door open with their shoulders and the animals entered in single file, walking with the utmost care for fear of disturbing anything. They tiptoed from room to room, afraid to speak above a whisper and gazing with a kind of awe at the unbelievable luxury, at the beds with their feather mattresses, the looking-glasses, the horsehair sofa, the Brussels carpet, the lithograph of Queen Victoria over the drawing-room mantelpiece. They were just coming down the stairs when Mollie was discovered to be missing. Going back, the others found that she had remained behind in the best bedroom. She had taken a piece of blue ribbon from Mrs Jones's dressing-table, and was holding it against her shoulder and admiring herself in the glass in a very foolish manner. The others reproached her sharply, and they went outside. Some hams hanging in the kitchen were taken out for burial, and the barrel of beer in the scullery was stove in with a kick from Boxer's hoof, otherwise nothing in the house was touched. A unanimous resolution was passed on the spot that the farmhouse should be preserved as a museum. All were agreed that no animal must ever live there.

The animals had their breakfast, and then Snowball and Napoleon called them together again.

'Comrades,' said Snowball, 'it is half-past six and we have a long day before us. Today we begin the hay harvest. But there is another matter that must be attended to first.'

The pigs now revealed that during the past three months they had taught themselves to read and write from an old spelling book which had belonged to Mr Jones's children and which had been thrown on the rubbish heap. Napoleon sent for pots of black and white paint and led the way down to the five-barred gate that gave on the main road. Then Snowball (for it was Snowball who was best at writing) took a brush between the two knuckles of his trotter, painted out MANOR FARM from the top bar of the gate and in its place painted ANIMAL FARM. This was to be the name of the farm from now onwards. After this they went back to the farm buildings, where Snowball and Napoleon sent for a ladder which they caused to be set against the end wall of the big barn. They explained that by their studies of the past three months the pigs had succeeded in reducing the principles of Animalism to seven commandments. These seven commandments would now be inscribed on the wall; they would form an unalterable law by which all the animals on Animal Farm must live for ever after. With some difficulty (for it is not easy for a pig to balance himself on a ladder) Snowball climbed up and set to work, with Squealer a few rungs below him holding the paint-pot. The commandments were written on the tarred wall in great white letters that could be read thirty yards away. They ran thus:

THE SEVEN COMMANDMENTS

1. *Whatever goes upon two legs is an enemy.*
2. *Whatever goes upon four legs, or has wings, is a friend.*
3. *No animal shall wear clothes.*
4. *No animal shall sleep in a bed.*
5. *No animal shall drink alcohol.*
6. *No animal shall kill any other animal.*
7. *All animals are equal.*

It was very neatly written, and except that 'friend' was written 'freind' and one of the S's was the wrong way round, the spelling was correct all the way through. Snow-ball read it aloud for the benefit of the others. All the animals nodded in complete agreement, and the cleverer ones at once began to learn the commandments by heart.

'Now, comrades,' cried Snowball, throwing down the paint-brush, 'to the hayfield! Let us make it a point of honour to get in the harvest more quickly than Jones and his men could do.'

But at this moment the three cows, who had seemed uneasy for some time past, set up a loud lowing. They had not been milked for twenty-four hours, and their udders were almost bursting. After a little thought the pigs sent for buckets and milked the cows fairly successfully, their trotters being well adapted to this task. Soon there were five buckets of frothing creamy milk at which many of the animals looked with considerable interest.

'What is going to happen to all that milk?' said someone.

'Jones used sometimes to mix some of it in our mash,' said one of the hens.

'Never mind the milk, comrades!' cried Napoleon, placing himself in front of the buckets. 'That will be attended to. The harvest is more important. Comrade Snowball will lead the way. I shall follow in a few minutes. Forward, comrades! The hay is waiting.'

So the animals trooped down to the hayfield to begin the harvest, and when they came back in the evening it was noticed that the milk had disappeared.

CHAPTER III

HOW THEY TOILED AND SWEATED to get the hay in! But their efforts were rewarded, for the harvest was an even bigger success than they had hoped.

Sometimes the work was hard; the implements had been designed for human beings and not for animals, and it was a great drawback that no animal was able to use any tool that involved standing on his hind legs. But the pigs were so clever that they could think of a way round every difficulty. As for the horses, they knew every inch of the field, and in fact understood the business of mowing and raking far better than Jones and his men had ever done. The pigs did not actually work, but directed and supervised the others. With their superior knowledge it was natural that they should assume the leadership. Boxer and Clover would harness themselves to the cutter or the horse-rake (no bits or reins were needed in these days, of course) and tramp steadily round and round the field with a pig walking behind and calling out 'Gee up, comrade!' or 'Whoa back, comrade!' as the case might be. And every animal down to the humblest worked at turning the hay and gathering it. Even the ducks and hens toiled to and fro all day in the sun, carrying tiny wisps of hay in their beaks. In the end they finished the harvest in two days less time than it had usually taken Jones and his men. Moreover it was the biggest harvest that the farm had ever seen. There was no wastage whatever; the hens and ducks with their sharp eyes had gathered up the very last stalk. And not an animal on the farm had stolen so much as a mouthful.

All through that summer the work of the farm went like

clockwork. The animals were happy as they had never conceived it possible to be. Every mouthful of food was an acute positive pleasure, now that it was truly their own food, produced by themselves and for themselves, not doled out to them by a grudging master. With the worthless parasitical human beings gone, there was more for everyone to eat. There was more leisure too, inexperienced though the animals were. They met with many difficulties —for instance, later in the year, when they harvested the corn, they had to tread it out in the ancient style and blow away the chaff with their breath, since the farm possessed no threshing machine—but the pigs with their cleverness and Boxer with his tremendous muscles always pulled them through. Boxer was the admiration of everybody. He had been a hard worker even in Jones's time, but now he seemed more like three horses than one; there were days when the entire work of the farm seemed to rest upon his mighty shoulders. From morning to night he was pushing and pulling, always at the spot where the work was hardest. He had made an arrangement with one of the cockerels to call him in the mornings half an hour earlier than anyone else, and would put in some volunteer labour at whatever seemed to be most needed, before the regular day's work began. His answer to every problem, every setback, was 'I will work harder!'—which he had adopted as his personal motto.

But everyone worked according to his capacity. The hens and ducks, for instance, saved five bushels of corn at the harvest by gathering up the stray grains. Nobody stole, nobody grumbled over his rations, the quarrelling and biting and jealousy which had been normal features of life in the old days had almost disappeared. Nobody shirked— or almost nobody. Mollie, it was true, was not good at getting up in the mornings, and had a way of leaving work early on the ground that there was a stone in her hoof. And

the behaviour of the cat was somewhat peculiar. It was soon noticed that when there was work to be done the cat could never be found. She would vanish for hours on end, and then reappear at meal-times, or in the evening after work was over, as though nothing had happened. But she always made such excellent excuses, and purred so affectionately, that it was impossible not to believe in her good intentions. Old Benjamin, the donkey, seemed quite unchanged since the Rebellion. He did his work in the same slow obstinate way as he had done it in Jones's time, never shirking and never volunteering for extra work either. About the Rebellion and its results he would express no opinion. When asked whether he was not happier now that Jones was gone, he would say only 'Donkeys live a long time. None of you has ever seen a dead donkey,' and the others had to be content with this cryptic answer.

On Sundays there was no work. Breakfast was an hour later than usual, and after breakfast there was a ceremony which was observed every week without fail. First came the hoisting of the flag. Snowball had found in the harness-room an old green tablecloth of Mrs Jones's and had painted on it a hoof and a horn in white. This was run up the flagstaff in the farmhouse garden every Sunday morning. The flag was green, Snowball explained, to represent the green fields of England, while the hoof and horn signified the future Republic of the Animals which would arise when the human race had been finally overthrown. After the hoisting of the flag all the animals trooped into the big barn for a general assembly which was known as the Meeting. Here the work of the coming week was planned out and resolutions were put forward and debated. It was always the pigs who put forward the resolutions. The other animals understood how to vote, but could never think of any resolutions of their own. Snowball and Napoleon were by far the most active in the debates. But

it was noticed that these two were never in agreement: whatever suggestion either of them made, the other could be counted on to oppose it. Even when it was resolved—a thing no one could object to in itself—to set aside the small paddock behind the orchard as a home of rest for animals who were past work, there was a stormy debate over the correct retiring age for each class of animal. The Meeting always ended with the singing of 'Beasts of England', and the afternoon was given up to recreation.

The pigs had set aside the harness-room as a headquarters for themselves. Here, in the evenings, they studied black-smithing, carpentering and other necessary arts from books which they had brought out of the farmhouse. Snowball also busied himself with organising the other animals into what he called Animal Committees. He was indefatigable at this. He formed the Egg Production Com-mittee for the hens, the Clean Tails League for the cows, the Wild Comrades' Re-education Committee (the object of this was to tame the rats and rabbits), the Whiter Wool Movement for the sheep, and various others, besides insti-tuting classes in reading and writing. On the whole these projects were a failure. The attempt to tame the wild creatures, for instance, broke down almost immediately. They continued to behave very much as before, and when treated with generosity simply took advantage of it. The cat joined the Re-education Committee and was very active in it for some days. She was seen one day sitting on a roof and talking to some sparrows who were just out of her reach. She was telling them that all animals were now comrades and that any sparrow who chose could come and perch on her paw; but the sparrows kept their distance.

The reading and writing classes, however, were a great success. By the autumn almost every animal on the farm was literate in some degree.

As for the pigs, they could already read and write

perfectly. The dogs learned to read fairly well, but were not interested in reading anything except the Seven Commandments. Muriel, the goat, could read somewhat better than the dogs, and sometimes used to read to the others in the evenings from scraps of newspaper which she found on the rubbish heap. Benjamin could read as well as any pig, but never exercised his faculty. So far as he knew, he said, there was nothing worth reading. Clover learnt the whole alphabet, but could not put words together. Boxer could not get beyond the letter D. He would trace out A, B, C, D in the dust with his great hoof, and then would stand staring at the letters with his ears back, sometimes shaking his forelock, trying with all his might to remember what came next and never succeeding. On several occasions, indeed, he did learn E, F, G, H, but by the time he knew them it was always discovered that he had forgotten A, B, C and D. Finally he decided to be content with the first four letters, and used to write them out once or twice every day to refresh his memory. Mollie refused to learn any but the five letters which spelt her own name. She would form these very neatly out of pieces of twig, and would then decorate them with a flower or two and walk round them admiring them.

None of the other animals on the farm could get further than the letter A. It was also found that the stupider animals such as the sheep, hens and ducks, were unable to learn the Seven Commandments by heart. After much thought Snowball declared that the Seven Commandments could in effect be reduced to a single maxim, namely: 'Four legs good, two legs bad'. This, he said, contained the essential principle of Animalism. Whoever had thoroughly grasped it would be safe from human influences. The birds at first objected, since it seemed to them that they also had two legs, but Snowball proved to them that this was not so.

'A bird's wing, comrades,' he said, 'is an organ of propulsion and not of manipulation. It should therefore be regarded as a leg. The distinguishing mark of Man is the *hand*, the instrument with which he does all his mischief.'

The birds did not understand Snowball's long words, but they accepted his explanation, and all the humbler animals set to work to learn the new maxim by heart. FOUR LEGS GOOD, TWO LEGS BAD, was inscribed on the end wall of the barn, above the Seven Commandments and in bigger letters. When they had once got it by heart the sheep developed a great liking for this maxim, and often as they lay in the field they would all start bleating 'Four legs good, two legs bad! Four legs good, two legs bad!' and keep it up for hours on end, never growing tired of it.

Napoleon took no interest in Snowball's committees. He said that the education of the young was more important than anything that could be done for those who were already grown up. It happened that Jessie and Bluebell had both whelped soon after the hay harvest, giving birth between them to nine sturdy puppies. As soon as they were weaned Napoleon took them away from their mothers, saying that he would make himself responsible for their education. He took them up into a loft which could only be reached by a ladder from the harness-room, and there kept them in such seclusion that the rest of the farm soon forgot their existence.

The mystery of where the milk went to was soon cleared up. It was mixed every day into the pigs' mash. The early apples were now ripening, and the grass of the orchard was littered with windfalls. The animals had assumed as a matter of course that these would be shared out equally; one day, however, the order went forth that all the windfalls were to be collected and brought to the harness-room for the use of the pigs. At this some of the

other animals murmured, but it was no use. All the pigs were in full agreement on this point, even Snowball and Napoleon. Squealer was sent to make the necessary explanations to the others.

'Comrades!' he cried. 'You do not imagine, I hope, that we pigs are doing this in a spirit of selfishness and privilege? Many of us actually dislike milk and apples. I dislike them myself. Our sole object in taking these things is to preserve our health. Milk and apples (this has been proved by Science, comrades) contain substances absolutely necessary to the well-being of a pig. We pigs are brainworkers. The whole management and organisation of this farm depend on us. Day and night we are watching over your welfare. It is for *your* sake that we drink that milk and eat those apples. Do you know what would happen if we pigs failed in our duty? Jones would come back! Yes, Jones would come back! Surely, comrades,' cried Squealer almost pleadingly, skipping from side to side and whisking his tail, 'surely there is no one among you who wants to see Jones come back?'

Now if there was one thing that the animals were completely certain of, it was that they did not want Jones back. When it was put to them in this light, they had no more to say. The importance of keeping the pigs in good health was all too obvious. So it was agreed without further argument that the milk and the windfall apples (and also the main crop of apples when they ripened) should be reserved for the pigs alone.

CHAPTER IV

BY THE LATE SUMMER the news of what had happened on Animal Farm had spread across half the county. Every day Snowball and Napoleon sent out flights of pigeons whose instructions were to mingle with the animals on neighbouring farms, tell them the story of the Rebellion, and teach them the tune of 'Beasts of England'.

Most of this time Mr Jones had spent sitting in the taproom of the Red Lion at Willingdon, complaining to anyone who would listen of the monstrous injustice he had suffered in being turned out of his property by a pack of good-for-nothing animals. The other farmers sympathised in principle, but they did not at first give him much help. At heart, each of them was secretly wondering whether he could not somehow turn Jones's misfortune to his own advantage. It was lucky that the owners of the two farms which adjoined Animal Farm were on permanently bad terms. One of them, which was named Foxwood, was a large, neglected, old-fashioned farm, much overgrown by woodland, with all its pastures worn out and its hedges in a disgraceful condition. Its owner, Mr Pilkington, was an easy-going gentleman-farmer who spent most of his time in fishing or hunting according to the season. The other farm, which was called Pinchfield, was smaller and better kept. Its owner was a Mr Frederick, a tough, shrewd man, perpetually involved in lawsuits and with a name for driving hard bargains. These two disliked each other so much that it was difficult for them to come to any agreement, even in defence of their own interests.

Nevertheless they were both thoroughly frightened by

24

the rebellion on Animal Farm, and very anxious to prevent their own animals from learning too much about it. At first they pretended to laugh to scorn the idea of animals managing a farm for themselves. The whole thing would be over in a fortnight, they said. They put it about that the animals on the Manor Farm (they insisted on calling it the Manor Farm; they would not tolerate the name 'Animal Farm') were perpetually fighting among themselves and were also rapidly starving to death. When time passed and the animals had evidently not starved to death, Frederick and Pilkington changed their tune and began to talk of the terrible wickedness that now flourished on Animal Farm. It was given out that the animals there practised cannibalism, tortured one another with red-hot horseshoes and had their females in common. This was what came of rebelling against the laws of Nature, Frederick and Pilkington said.

However, these stories were never fully believed. Rumours of a wonderful farm, where the human beings had been turned out and the animals managed their own affairs, continued to circulate in vague and distorted forms, and throughout that year a wave of rebelliousness ran through the countryside. Bulls which had always been tractable suddenly turned savage, sheep broke down hedges and devoured the clover, cows kicked the pail over, hunters refused their fences and shot their riders on to the other side. Above all, the tune and even the words of 'Beasts of England' were known everywhere. It had spread with astonishing speed. The human beings could not contain their rage when they heard this song, though they pretended to think it merely ridiculous. They could not understand, they said, how even animals could bring themselves to sing such contemptible rubbish. Any animal caught singing it was given a flogging on the spot. And yet the song was irrepressible. The blackbirds whistled it in the hedges, the pigeons cooed it in the elms, it got into

the din of the smithies and the tune of the church bells. And when the human beings listened to it they secretly trembled, hearing in it a prophecy of their future doom.

Early in October, when the corn was cut and stacked and some of it was already threshed, a flight of pigeons came whirling through the air and alighted in the yard of Animal Farm in the wildest excitement. Jones and all his men, with half a dozen others from Foxwood and Pinchfield, had entered the five-barred gate and were coming up the cart-track that led to the farm. They were all carrying sticks, except Jones, who was marching ahead with a gun in his hands. Obviously they were going to attempt the recapture of the farm.

This had long been expected, and all preparations had been made. Snowball, who had studied an old book of Julius Caesar's campaigns which he had found in the farmhouse, was in charge of the defensive operations. He gave his orders quickly, and in a couple of minutes every animal was at his post.

As the human beings approached the farm buildings, Snowball launched his first attack. All the pigeons, to the number of thirty-five, flew to and fro over the men's heads and dropped their dung on them from mid-air; and while the men were dealing with this, the geese, who had been hiding behind the hedge, rushed out and pecked viciously at the calves of their legs. However, this was only a light skirmishing manoeuvre, intended to create a little disorder, and the men easily drove the geese off with their sticks. Snowball now launched his second line of attack. Muriel, Benjamin, and all the sheep, with Snowball at the head of them, rushed forward and prodded and butted the men from every side, while Benjamin turned round and lashed at them with his small hoofs. But once again the men, with their sticks and their hobnailed boots, were too strong for them; and suddenly, at a squeal from Snowball, which was

the signal for retreat, all the animals turned and fled through the gateway into the yard.

The men gave a shout of triumph. They saw, as they imagined, their enemies in flight, and they rushed after them in disorder. This was just what Snowball had intended. As soon as they were well inside the yard, the three horses, the three cows and the rest of the pigs, who had been lying in ambush in the cowshed, suddenly emerged in their rear, cutting them off. Snowball now gave the signal for the charge. He himself dashed straight for Jones. Jones saw him coming, raised his gun and fired. The pellets scored bloody streaks along Snowball's back, and a sheep dropped dead. Without halting for an instant Snowball flung his fifteen stone against Jones's legs. Jones was hurled into a pile of dung and his gun flew out of his hands. But the most terrifying spectacle of all was Boxer, rearing up on his hind legs and striking out with his great iron-shod hoofs like a stallion. His very first blow took a stable-lad from Foxwood on the skull and stretched him lifeless in the mud. At the sight, several men dropped their sticks and tried to run. Panic overtook them, and the next moment all the animals together were chasing them round and round the yard. They were gored, kicked, bitten, trampled on. There was not an animal on the farm that did not take vengeance on them after his own fashion. Even the cat suddenly leapt off a roof onto a cowman's shoulders and sank her claws in his neck, at which he yelled horribly. At a moment when the opening was clear the men were glad enough to rush out of the yard and make a bolt for the main road. And so within five minutes of their invasion they were in ignominious retreat by the same way as they had come, with a flock of geese hissing after them and pecking at their calves all the way.

All the men were gone except one. Back in the yard Boxer was pawing with his hoof at the stable-lad who lay

27

face down in the mud, trying to turn him over. The boy did not stir.

'He is dead,' said Boxer sorrowfully. 'I had no intention of doing that. I forgot that I was wearing iron shoes. Who will believe that I did not do this on purpose?'

'No sentimentality, comrade!' cried Snowball, from whose wounds the blood was still dripping. 'War is war. The only good human being is a dead one.'

'I have no wish to take life, not even human life,' repeated Boxer, and his eyes were full of tears.

'Where is Mollie?' exclaimed somebody.

Mollie in fact was missing. For a moment there was great alarm; it was feared that the men might have harmed her in some way, or even carried her off with them. In the end, however, she was found hiding in her stall with her head buried among the hay in the manger. She had taken to flight as soon as the gun went off. And when the others came back from looking for her it was to find that the stable-lad, who in fact was only stunned, had already recovered and made off.

The animals had now reassembled in the wildest excitement, each recounting his own exploits in the battle at the top of his voice. An impromptu celebration of the victory was held immediately. The flag was run up and 'Beasts of England' was sung a number of times, then the sheep who had been killed was given a solemn funeral, a hawthorn bush being planted on her grave. At the graveside Snowball made a little speech, emphasising the need for all animals to be ready to die for Animal Farm if need be.

The animals decided unanimously to create a military decoration, 'Animal Hero, First Class', which was conferred there and then on Snowball and Boxer. It consisted of a brass medal (they were really some old horse-brasses which had been found in the harness-room), to be worn on Sundays and holidays. There was also 'Animal Hero,

Second Class', which was conferred posthumously on the dead sheep.

There was much discussion as to what the battle should be called. In the end it was named the Battle of the Cowshed, since that was where the ambush had been sprung. Mr Jones's gun had been found lying in the mud, and it was known that there was a supply of cartridges in the farmhouse. It was decided to set the gun up at the foot of the flagstaff, like a piece of artillery, and to fire it twice a year—once on October the twelfth, the anniversary of the Battle of the Cowshed, and once on Midsummer Day, the anniversary of the Rebellion.

CHAPTER V

As WINTER DREW ON Mollie became more and more
troublesome. She was late for work every morning and
excused herself by saying that she had overslept, and she
complained of mysterious pains, although her appetite was
excellent. On every kind of pretext she would run away
from work and go to the drinking pool, where she would
stand foolishly gazing at her own reflection in the water.
But there were also rumours of something more serious.
One day as Mollie strolled blithely into the yard, flirting
her long tail and chewing at a stalk of hay, Clover took
her aside.

'Mollie,' she said, 'I have something very serious to say
to you. This morning I saw you looking over the hedge
that divides Animal Farm from Foxwood. One of Mr
Pilkington's men was standing on the other side of the
hedge. And–I was a long way away, but I am almost
certain I saw this–he was talking to you and you were
allowing him to stroke your nose. What does that mean,
Mollie?'

'He didn't! I wasn't! It isn't true!' cried Mollie, beginning
to prance about and paw the ground.

'Mollie! Look me in the face. Do you give me your
word of honour that that man was not stroking your nose?'

'It isn't true!' repeated Mollie, but she could not look
Clover in the face, and the next moment she took to her
heels and galloped away into the field.

A thought struck Clover. Without saying anything to
the others she went to Mollie's stall and turned over the
straw with her hoof. Hidden under the straw was a little

pile of lump sugar and several bunches of ribbon of different colours.

Three days later Mollie disappeared. For some weeks nothing was known of her whereabouts, then the pigeons reported that they had seen her on the other side of Willingdon. She was between the shafts of a smart dogcart painted red and black, which was standing outside a public-house. A fat red-faced man in check breeches and gaiters, who looked like a publican, was stroking her nose and feeding her with sugar. Her coat was newly clipped and she wore a scarlet ribbon round her forelock. She appeared to be enjoying herself, so the pigeons said. None of the animals ever mentioned Mollie again.

In January there came bitterly hard weather. The earth was like iron, and nothing could be done in the fields. Many meetings were held in the big barn, and the pigs occupied themselves with planning out the work of the coming season. It had come to be accepted that the pigs, who were manifestly cleverer than the other animals, should decide all questions of farm policy, though their decisions had to be ratified by a majority vote. This arrangement would have worked well enough if it had not been for the disputes between Snowball and Napoleon. These two disagreed at every point where disagreement was possible. If one of them suggested sowing a bigger acreage with barley the other was certain to demand a bigger acreage of oats, and if one of them said that such and such a field was just right for cabbages, the other would declare that it was useless for anything except roots. Each had his own following, and there were some violent debates. At the Meetings Snowball often won over the majority by his brilliant speeches, but Napoleon was better at canvassing support for himself in between times. He was especially successful with the sheep. Of late the sheep had taken to bleating 'Four legs good, two legs bad' both in

and out of season, and they often interrupted the Meeting with this. It was noticed that they were especially liable to break into 'Four legs good, two legs bad' at crucial moments in Snowball's speeches. Snowball had made a close study of some back numbers of the *Farmer and Stockbreeder* which he had found in the farmhouse, and was full of plans for innovations and improvements. He talked learnedly about field-drains, silage and basic slag, and had worked out a complicated scheme for all the animals to drop their dung directly in the fields, at a different spot every day, to save the labour of cartage. Napoleon produced no schemes of his own, but said quietly that Snowball's would come to nothing, and seemed to be biding his time. But of all their controversies, none was so bitter as the one that took place over the windmill.

In the long pasture, not far from the farm buildings, there was a small knoll which was the highest point on the farm. After surveying the ground Snowball declared that this was just the place for a windmill, which could be made to operate a dynamo and supply the farm with electrical power. This would light the stalls and warm them in winter, and would also run a circular saw, a chaff-cutter, a mangel-slicer and an electric milking machine. The animals had never heard of anything of this kind before (for the farm was an old-fashioned one and had only the most primitive machinery), and they listened in astonishment while Snowball conjured up pictures of fantastic machines which would do their work for them while they grazed at their ease in the fields or improved their minds with reading and conversation.

Within a few weeks Snowball's plans for the windmill were fully worked out. The mechanical details came mostly from three books which had belonged to Mr Jones—*One Thousand Useful Things to Do About the House*, *Every Man His Own Bricklayer*, and *Electricity for Beginners*.

Snowball used as his study a shed which had once been used for incubators and had a smooth wooden floor, suitable for drawing on. He was closeted there for hours at a time. With his books held open by a stone, and with a piece of chalk gripped between the knuckles of his trotter, he would move rapidly to and fro, drawing in line after line and uttering little whimpers of excitement. Gradually the plans grew into a complicated mass of cranks and cog-wheels, covering more than half the floor, which the other animals found completely unintelligible but very impressive. All of them came to look at Snowball's drawings at least once a day. Even the hens and ducks came, and were at pains not to tread on the chalk marks. Only Napoleon held aloof. He had declared himself against the windmill from the start. One day, however, he arrived unexpectedly to examine the plans. He walked heavily round the shed, looked closely at every detail of the plans and snuffed at them once or twice, then stood for a little while contemplating them out of the corner of his eye; then suddenly he lifted his leg, urinated over the plans and walked out without uttering a word.

The whole farm was deeply divided on the subject of the windmill. Snowball did not deny that to build it would be a difficult business. Stone would have to be quarried and built up into walls, then the sails would have to be made and after that there would be need for dynamos and cables. (How these were to be procured Snowball did not say.) But he maintained that it could all be done in a year. And thereafter, he declared, so much labour would be saved that the animals would only need to work three days a week. Napoleon, on the other hand, argued that the great need of the moment was to increase food production, and that if they wasted time on the windmill they would all starve to death. The animals formed themselves into two factions under the slogans, 'Vote for Snowball and the three-day

week' and 'Vote for Napoleon and the full manger.' Benjamin was the only animal who did not side with either faction. He refused to believe either that food would become more plentiful or that the windmill would save work. Windmill or no windmill, he said, life would go on as it had always gone on—that is, badly.

Apart from the disputes over the windmill, there was the question of the defence of the farm. It was fully realised that though the human beings had been defeated in the Battle of the Cowshed they might make another and more determined attempt to recapture the farm and reinstate Mr Jones. They had all the more reason for doing so because the news of their defeat had spread across the countryside and made the animals on the neighbouring farms more restive than ever. As usual, Snowball and Napoleon were in disagreement. According to Napoleon, what the animals must do was to procure firearms and train themselves in the use of them. According to Snowball, they must send out more and more pigeons and stir up rebellion among the animals on the other farms. The one argued that if they could not defend themselves they were bound to be conquered, the other argued that if rebellions happened everywhere they would have no need to defend themselves. The animals listened first to Napoleon, then to Snowball, and could not make up their minds which was right; indeed they always found themselves in agreement with the one who was speaking at the moment.

At last the day came when Snowball's plans were completed. At the Meeting on the following Sunday the question of whether or not to begin work on the windmill was to be put to the vote. When the animals had assembled in the big barn, Snowball stood up and, though occasionally interrupted by bleating from the sheep, set forth his reasons for advocating the building of the windmill. Then Napoleon stood up to reply. He said very quietly that the

windmill was nonsense and that he advised nobody to vote for it, and promptly sat down again; he had spoken for barely thirty seconds, and seemed almost indifferent as to the effect he produced. At this Snowball sprang to his feet, and shouting down the sheep, who had begun bleating again, broke into a passionate appeal in favour of the windmill. Until now the animals had been about equally divided in their sympathies, but in a moment Snowball's eloquence had carried them away. In glowing sentences he painted a picture of Animal Farm as it might be when sordid labour was lifted from the animals' backs. His imagination had now run far beyond chaff-cutters and turnip-slicers. Electricity, he said, could operate threshing-machines, ploughs, harrows, rollers and reapers and binders, besides supplying every stall with its own electric light, hot and cold water and an electric heater. By the time he had finished speaking there was no doubt as to which way the vote would go. But just at this moment Napoleon stood up and, casting a peculiar sidelong look at Snowball, uttered a high-pitched whimper of a kind no one had ever heard him utter before.

At this there was a terrible baying sound outside, and nine enormous dogs wearing brass-studded collars came bounding into the barn. They dashed straight for Snow-ball, who only sprang from his place just in time to escape their snapping jaws. In a moment he was out of the door and they were after him. Too amazed and frightened to speak, all the animals crowded through the door to watch the chase. Snowball was racing across the long pasture that led to the road. He was running as only a pig can run, but the dogs were close on his heels. Suddenly he slipped and it seemed certain that they had him. Then he was up again, running faster than ever, then the dogs were gaining on him again. One of them all but closed his jaws on Snow-ball's tail, but Snowball whisked it free just in time. Then

he put on an extra spurt and, with a few inches to spare, slipped through a hole in the hedge and was seen no more.

Silent and terrified, the animals crept back into the barn. In a moment the dogs came bounding back. At first no one had been able to imagine where these creatures came from, but the problem was soon solved: they were the puppies whom Napoleon had taken away from their mothers and reared privately. Though not yet full-grown they were huge dogs, and as fierce-looking as wolves. They kept close to Napoleon. It was noticed that they wagged their tails to him in the same way as the other dogs had been used to do to Mr Jones.

Napoleon, with the dogs following him, now mounted onto the raised portion of the floor where Major had previously stood to deliver his speech. He announced that from now on the Sunday-morning Meetings would come to an end. They were unnecessary, he said, and wasted time. In future all questions relating to the working of the farm would be settled by a special committee of pigs, presided over by himself. These would meet in private and afterwards communicate their decisions to the others. The animals would still assemble on Sunday mornings to salute the flag, sing 'Beasts of England' and receive their orders for the week; but there would be no more debates.

In spite of the shock that Snowball's expulsion had given them, the animals were dismayed by this announcement. Several of them would have protested if they could have found the right arguments. Even Boxer was vaguely troubled. He set his ears back, shook his forelock several times, and tried hard to marshal his thoughts; but in the end he could not think of anything to say. Some of the pigs themselves, however, were more articulate. Four young porkers in the front row uttered shrill squeals of disapproval, and all four of them sprang to their feet and began speaking at once. But suddenly the dogs sitting

round Napoleon let out deep, menacing growls, and the pigs fell silent and sat down again. Then the sheep broke out into a tremendous bleating of 'Four legs good, two legs bad!' which went on for nearly a quarter of an hour and put an end to any chance of discussion.

Afterwards Squealer was sent round the farm to explain the new arrangement to the others.

'Comrades,' he said, 'I trust that every animal here appreciates the sacrifice that Comrade Napoleon has made in taking this extra labour upon himself. Do not imagine, comrades, that leadership is a pleasure! On the contrary, it is a deep and heavy responsibility. No one believes more firmly than Comrade Napoleon that all animals are equal. He would be only too happy to let you make your decisions for yourselves. But sometimes you might make the wrong decisions, comrades, and then where should we be? Suppose you had decided to follow Snowball, with his moonshine of windmills—Snowball, who, as we now know, was no better than a criminal?'

'He fought bravely at the Battle of the Cowshed,' said somebody.

'Bravery is not enough,' said Squealer. 'Loyalty and obedience are more important. And as to the Battle of the Cowshed, I believe the time will come when we shall find that Snowball's part in it was much exaggerated. Discipline, comrades, iron discipline! That is the watchword for today. One false step, and our enemies would be upon us. Surely, comrades, you do not want Jones back?'

Once again this argument was unanswerable. Certainly the animals did not want Jones back; if the holding of debates on Sunday mornings was liable to bring him back, then the debates must stop. Boxer, who had now had time to think things over, voiced the general feeling by saying: 'If Comrade Napoleon says it, it must be right.' And from then on he adopted the maxim, 'Napoleon is always right,'

in addition to his private motto of 'I will work harder.'

By this time the weather had broken and the spring ploughing had begun. The shed where Snowball had drawn his plans of the windmill had been shut up and it was assumed that the plans had been rubbed off the floor. Every Sunday morning at ten o'clock the animals assembled in the big barn to receive their orders for the week. The skull of old Major, now clean of flesh, had been disinterred from the orchard and set up on a stump at the foot of the flagstaff, beside the gun. After the hoisting of the flag the animals were required to file past the skull in a reverent manner before entering the barn. Nowadays they did not sit all together as they had done in the past. Napoleon, with Squealer and another pig named Minimus, who had a remarkable gift for composing songs and poems, sat on the front of the raised platform, with the nine young dogs forming a semicircle round them, and the other pigs sitting behind. The rest of the animals sat facing them in the main body of the barn. Napoleon read out the orders for the week in a gruff soldierly style, and after a single singing of 'Beasts of England' all the animals dispersed.

On the third Sunday after Snowball's expulsion, the animals were somewhat surprised to hear Napoleon announce that the windmill was to be built after all. He did not give any reason for having changed his mind, but merely warned the animals that this extra task would mean very hard work; it might even be necessary to reduce their rations. The plans, however, had all been prepared, down to the last detail. A special committee of pigs had been at work upon them for the past three weeks. The building of the windmill, with various other improvements, was expected to take two years.

That evening Squealer explained privately to the other animals that Napoleon had never in reality been opposed

to the windmill. On the contrary, it was he who had advocated it in the beginning, and the plan which Snowball had drawn on the floor of the incubator shed had actually been stolen from among Napoleon's papers. The windmill was, in fact, Napoleon's own creation. Why, then, asked somebody, had he spoken so strongly against it? Here Squealer looked very sly. That, he said, was Comrade Napoleon's cunning. He had *seemed* to oppose the windmill, simply as a manoeuvre to get rid of Snowball, who was a dangerous character and a bad influence. Now that Snowball was out of the way the plan could go forward without his interference. This, said Squealer, was something called tactics. He repeated a number of times, 'Tactics, comrades, tactics!' skipping round and whisking his tail with a merry laugh. The animals were not certain what the word meant, but Squealer spoke so persuasively, and the three dogs who happened to be with him growled so threateningly, that they accepted his explanation without further questions.

CHAPTER VI

ALL THAT YEAR the animals worked like slaves. But they were happy in their work; they grudged no effort or sacrifice, well aware that everything that they did was for the benefit of themselves and those of their kind who would come after them, and not for a pack of idle thieving human beings.

Throughout the spring and summer they worked a sixty-hour week, and in August Napoleon announced that there would be work on Sunday afternoons as well. This work was strictly voluntary, but any animal who absented himself from it would have his rations reduced by half. Even so it was found necessary to leave certain tasks undone. The harvest was a little less successful than in the previous year, and two fields which should have been sown with roots in the early summer were not sown because the ploughing had not been completed early enough. It was possible to foresee that the coming winter would be a hard one.

The windmill presented unexpected difficulties. There was a good quarry of limestone on the farm, and plenty of sand and cement had been found in one of the outhouses, so that all the materials for building were at hand. But the problem the animals could not at first solve was how to break up the stone into pieces of suitable size. There seemed no way of doing this except with picks and crowbars, which no animal could use, because no animal could stand on his hind legs. Only after weeks of vain effort did the right idea occur to somebody—namely, to utilise the force of gravity. Huge boulders, far too big to be used as they

were, were lying all over the bed of the quarry. The animals lashed ropes round these, and then all together, cows, horses, sheep, any animal that could lay hold of the rope—even the pigs sometimes joined in at critical moments—they dragged them with desperate slowness up the slope to the top of the quarry, where they were toppled over the edge, to shatter to pieces below. Transporting the stone when it was once broken was comparatively simple. The horses carried it off in cartloads, the sheep dragged single blocks, even Muriel and Benjamin yoked themselves into an old governess-cart and did their share. By late summer a sufficient store of stone had accumulated, and then the building began, under the superintendence of the pigs.

But it was a slow, laborious process. Frequently it took a whole day of exhausting effort to drag a single boulder to the top of the quarry, and sometimes when it was pushed over the edge it failed to break. Nothing could have been achieved without Boxer, whose strength seemed equal to that of all the rest of the animals put together. When the boulder began to slip and the animals cried out in despair at finding themselves dragged down the hill, it was always Boxer who strained himself against the rope and brought the boulder to a stop. To see him toiling up the slope inch by inch, his breath coming fast, the tips of his hoofs clawing at the ground and his great sides matted with sweat, filled everyone with admiration. Clover warned him sometimes to be careful not to overstrain himself, but Boxer would never listen to her. His two slogans, 'I will work harder' and 'Napoleon is always right', seemed to him a sufficient answer to all problems. He had made arrangements with the cockerel to call him three-quarters of an hour earlier in the mornings instead of half an hour. And in his spare moments, of which there were not many nowadays, he would go alone to the

quarry, collect a load of broken stone and drag it down to the site of the windmill unassisted.

The animals were not badly off throughout that summer, in spite of the hardness of their work. If they had no more food than they had had in Jones's day, at least they did not have less. The advantage of only having to feed themselves, and not having to support five extravagant human beings as well, was so great that it would have taken a lot of failures to outweigh it. And in many ways the animal method of doing things was more efficient and saved labour. Such jobs as weeding, for instance, could be done with a thoroughness impossible to human beings. And again, since no animal now stole it was unnecessary to fence off pasture from arable land, which saved a lot of labour on the upkeep of hedges and gates. Nevertheless as the summer wore on various unforeseen shortages began to make themselves felt. There was need of paraffin oil, nails, string, dog biscuits and iron for the horses' shoes, none of which could be produced on the farm. Later there would also be need for seeds and artificial manures, besides various tools and, finally, the machinery for the windmill. How these were to be procured no one was able to imagine.

One Sunday morning when the animals assembled to receive their orders Napoleon announced that he had decided upon a new policy. From now onwards Animal Farm would engage in trade with the neighbouring farms: not, of course, for any commercial purpose but simply in order to obtain certain materials which were urgently necessary. The needs of the windmill must override every-thing else, he said. He was therefore making arrangements to sell a stack of hay and part of the current year's wheat crop, and later on, if more money were needed, it would have to be made up by the sale of eggs, for which there was always a market in Willingdon. The hens, said

Napoleon, should welcome this sacrifice as their own special contribution towards the building of the windmill.

Once again the animals were conscious of a vague uneasiness. Never to have any dealings with human beings, never to engage in trade, never to make use of money—had not these been among the earliest resolutions passed at that first triumphant Meeting after Jones was expelled? All the animals remembered passing such resolutions: or at least they thought that they remembered it. The four young pigs who had protested when Napoleon abolished the Meetings raised their voices timidly, but they were promptly silenced by a tremendous growling from the dogs. Then, as usual, the sheep broke into 'Four legs good, two legs bad!' and the momentary awkwardness was smoothed over. Finally Napoleon raised his trotter for silence and announced that he had already made all the arrangements. There would be no need for any of the animals to come in contact with human beings, which would clearly be most undesirable. He intended to take the whole burden upon his own shoulders. A Mr Whymper, a solicitor living in Willingdon, had agreed to act as intermediary between Animal Farm and the outside world, and would visit the farm every Monday morning to receive his instructions. Napoleon ended his speech with his usual cry of 'Long live Animal Farm!', and after the singing of 'Beasts of England' the animals were dismissed.

Afterwards Squealer made a round of the farm and set the animals' minds at rest. He assured them that the resolution against engaging in trade and using money had never been passed, or even suggested. It was pure imagination, probably traceable in the beginning to lies circulated by Snowball. A few animals still felt faintly doubtful, but Squealer asked them shrewdly, 'Are you certain that this is not something that you have dreamed, comrades? Have

43

you any record of such a resolution? Is it written down anywhere?' And since it was certainly true that nothing of the kind existed in writing, the animals were satisfied that they had been mistaken.

Every Monday Mr Whymper visited the farm as had been arranged. He was a sly-looking little man with side whiskers, a solicitor in a very small way of business, but sharp enough to have realised earlier than anyone else that Animal Farm would need a broker and that the commissions would be worth having. The animals watched his coming and going with a kind of dread, and avoided him as much as possible. Nevertheless, the sight of Napoleon, on all fours, delivering orders to Whymper, who stood on two legs, roused their pride and partly reconciled them to the new arrangement. Their relations with the human race were now not quite the same as they had been before. The human beings did not hate Animal Farm any less now that it was prospering, indeed they hated it more than ever. Every human being held it as an article of faith that the farm would go bankrupt sooner or later, and, above all, that the windmill would be a failure. They would meet in the public-houses and prove to one another by means of diagrams that the windmill was bound to fall down, or that if it did stand up, then that it would never work. And yet, against their will, they had developed a certain respect for the efficiency with which the animals were managing their own affairs. One symptom of this was that they had begun to call Animal Farm by its proper name and ceased to pretend that it was called the Manor Farm. They had also dropped their championship of Jones, who had given up hope of getting his farm back and gone to live in another part of the county. Except through Whymper there was as yet no contact between Animal Farm and the outside world, but there were constant rumours that Napoleon was about to enter into a definite business agreement either

with Mr Pilkington of Foxwood or with Mr Frederick of Pinchfield—but never, it was noticed, with both simultaneously.

It was about this time that the pigs suddenly moved into the farmhouse and took up their residence there. Again the animals seemed to remember that a resolution against this had been passed in the early days, and again Squealer was able to convince them that this was not the case. It was absolutely necessary, he said, that the pigs, who were the brains of the farm, should have a quiet place to work in. It was also more suited to the dignity of the Leader (for of late he had taken to speaking of Napoleon under the title of 'Leader') to live in a house than in a mere sty. Nevertheless some of the animals were disturbed when they heard that the pigs not only took their meals in the kitchen and used the drawing-room as a recreation room, but also slept in the beds. Boxer passed it off as usual with 'Napoleon is always right!', but Clover, who thought she remembered a definite ruling against beds, went to the end of the barn and tried to puzzle out the Seven Commandments which were inscribed there. Finding herself unable to read more than individual letters, she fetched Muriel.

. 'Muriel,' she said, 'read me the Fourth Commandment. Does it not say something about never sleeping in a bed?'

With some difficulty Muriel spelt it out.

'It says, "No animal shall sleep in a bed *with sheets*"' she announced finally.

Curiously enough, Clover had not remembered that the Fourth Commandment mentioned sheets; but as it was there on the wall, it must have done so. And Squealer, who happened to be passing at this moment, attended by two or three dogs, was able to put the whole matter in its proper perspective.

'You have heard, then, comrades,' he said, 'that we pigs

45

now sleep in the beds of the farmhouse? And why not? You did not suppose, surely, that there was ever a ruling against *beds*? A bed merely means a place to sleep in. A pile of straw in a stall is a bed, properly regarded. The rule was against *sheets*, which are a human invention. We have removed the sheets from the farmhouse beds, and sleep between blankets. And very comfortable beds they are too! But not more comfortable than we need, I can tell you, comrades, with all the brainwork we have to do nowadays. You would not rob us of our repose, would you, comrades? You would not have us too tired to carry out our duties? Surely none of you wishes to see Jones back?'

The animals reassured him on this point immediately, and no more was said about the pigs sleeping in the farmhouse beds. And when, some days afterwards, it was announced that from now on the pigs would get up an hour later in the mornings than the other animals, no complaint was made about that either.

By the autumn the animals were tired but happy. They had had a hard year, and after the sale of part of the hay and corn the stores of food for the winter were none too plentiful, but the windmill compensated for everything. It was almost half built now. After the harvest there was a stretch of clear dry weather, and the animals toiled harder than ever, thinking it well worth while to plod to and fro all day with blocks of stone if by doing so they could raise the walls another foot. Boxer would even come out at nights and work for an hour or two on his own by the light of the harvest moon. In their spare moments the animals would walk round and round the half-finished mill, admiring the strength and perpendicularity of its walls and marvelling that they should ever have been able to build anything so imposing. Only old Benjamin refused to grow enthusiastic about the windmill, though, as usual, he would

utter nothing beyond the cryptic remark that donkeys live a long time.

November came, with raging south-west winds. Building had to stop because it was now too wet to mix the cement. Finally there came a night when the gale was so violent that the farm buildings rocked on their foundations and several tiles were blown off the roof of the barn. The hens woke up squawking with terror because they had all dreamed simultaneously of hearing a gun go off in the distance. In the morning the animals came out of their stalls to find that the flagstaff had been blown down and an elm tree at the foot of the orchard had been plucked up like a radish. They had just noticed this when a cry of despair broke from every animal's throat. A terrible sight had met their eyes. The windmill was in ruins.

With one accord they dashed down to the spot. Napoleon, who seldom moved out of a walk, raced ahead of them all. Yes, there it lay, the fruit of all their struggles, levelled to its foundations, the stones they had broken and carried so laboriously scattered all around. Unable at first to speak, they stood gazing mournfully at the litter of fallen stone. Napoleon paced to and fro in silence, occasionally snuffing at the ground. His tail had grown rigid and twitched sharply from side to side, a sign in him of intense mental activity. Suddenly he halted as though his mind were made up.

'Comrades,' he said quietly, 'do you know who is responsible for this? Do you know the enemy who has come in the night and overthrown our windmill? SNOWBALL!' he suddenly roared in a voice of thunder, 'Snowball has done this thing! In sheer malignity, thinking to set back our plans and avenge himself for his ignominious expulsion, this traitor has crept here under cover of night and destroyed our work of nearly a year. Comrades, here and now I pronounce the death sentence

upon Snowball. "Animal Hero, Second Class", and half a bushel of apples to any animal who brings him to justice. A full bushel to anyone who captures him alive!'

The animals were shocked beyond measure to learn that even Snowball could be guilty of such an action. There was a cry of indignation, and everyone began thinking out ways of catching Snowball if he should ever come back. Almost immediately the footprints of a pig were discovered in the grass at a little distance from the knoll. They could only be traced for a few yards, but appeared to lead to a hole in the hedge. Napoleon snuffed deeply at them and pronounced them to be Snowball's. He gave it as his opinion that Snowball had probably come from the direction of Foxwood Farm.

'No more delays, comrades!' cried Napoleon when the footprints had been examined. 'There is work to be done. This very morning we begin rebuilding the windmill, and we will build all through the winter, rain or shine. We will teach this miserable traitor that he cannot undo our work so easily. Remember, comrades, there must be no alteration in our plans: they shall be carried out to the day. Forward, comrades! Long live the windmill! Long live Animal Farm!'

CHAPTER VII

IT WAS A BITTER WINTER. The stormy weather was followed by sleet and snow, and then by a hard frost which did not break till well into February. The animals carried on as best they could with the rebuilding of the windmill, well knowing that the outside world was watching them and that the envious human beings would rejoice and triumph if the mill were not finished on time.

Out of spite, the human beings pretended not to believe that it was Snowball who had destroyed the windmill: they said that it had fallen down because the walls were too thin. The animals knew that this was not the case. Still, it had been decided to build the walls three feet thick this time instead of eighteen inches as before, which meant collecting much larger quantities of stone. For a long time the quarry was full of snowdrifts and nothing could be done. Some progress was made in the dry frosty weather that followed, but it was cruel work, and the animals could not feel so hopeful about it as they had felt before. They were always cold, and usually hungry as well. Only Boxer and Clover never lost heart. Squealer made excellent speeches on the joy of service and the dignity of labour, but the other animals found more inspiration in Boxer's strength and his never-failing cry of 'I will work harder!'

In January food fell short. The corn ration was drastically reduced, and it was announced that an extra potato ration would be issued to make up for it. Then it was discovered that the greater part of the potato crop had been frosted in the clamps, which had not been covered thickly enough. The potatoes had become soft and discoloured,

49

and only a few were edible. For days at a time the animals had nothing to eat but chaff and mangels. Starvation seemed to stare them in the face.

It was vitally necessary to conceal this fact from the outside world. Emboldened by the collapse of the windmill, the human beings were inventing fresh lies about Animal Farm. Once again it was being put about that all the animals were dying of famine and disease, and that they were continually fighting among themselves and had resorted to cannibalism and infanticide. Napoleon was well aware of the bad results that might follow if the real facts of the food situation were known, and he decided to make use of Mr Whymper to spread a contrary impression. Hitherto the animals had had little or no contact with Whymper on his weekly visits: now, however, a few selected animals, mostly sheep, were instructed to remark casually in his hearing that rations had been increased. In addition, Napoleon ordered the almost empty bins in the store-shed to be filled nearly to the brim with sand, which was then covered up with what remained of the grain and meal. On some suitable pretext Whymper was led through the store-shed and allowed to catch a glimpse of the bins. He was deceived, and continued to report to the outside world that there was no food shortage on Animal Farm.

Nevertheless, towards the end of January it became obvious that it would be necessary to procure some more grain from somewhere. In these days Napoleon rarely appeared in public, but spent all his time in the farmhouse, which was guarded at each door by fierce-looking dogs. When he did emerge it was in a ceremonial manner, with an escort of six dogs who closely surrounded him and growled if anyone came too near. Frequently he did not even appear on Sunday mornings, but issued his orders through one of the other pigs, usually Squealer.

One Sunday morning Squealer announced that the hens, who had just come in to lay again, must surrender their eggs. Napoleon had accepted, through Whymper, a contract for four hundred eggs a week. The price of these would pay for enough grain and meal to keep the farm going till summer came on and conditions were easier.

When the hens heard this they raised a terrible outcry. They had been warned earlier that this sacrifice might be necessary, but had not believed that it would really happen. They were just getting their clutches ready for the spring sitting, and they protested that to take the eggs away now was murder. For the first time since the expulsion of Jones there was something resembling a rebellion. Led by three young Black Minorca pullets, the hens made a determined effort to thwart Napoleon's wishes. Their method was to fly up to the rafters and there lay their eggs, which smashed to pieces on the floor. Napoleon acted swiftly and ruthlessly. He ordered the hens' rations to be stopped, and decreed that any animal giving so much as a grain of corn to a hen should be punished by death. The dogs saw to it that these orders were carried out. For five days the hens held out, then they capitulated and went back to their nesting boxes. Nine hens had died in the meantime. Their bodies were buried in the orchard, and it was given out that they had died of coccidiosis. Whymper heard nothing of this affair, and the eggs were duly delivered, a grocer's van driving up to the farm once a week to take them away.

All this while no more had been seen of Snowball. He was rumoured to be hiding on one of the neighbouring farms, either Foxwood or Pinchfield. Napoleon was by this time on slightly better terms with the other farmers than before. It happened that there was in the yard a pile of timber which had been stacked there ten years earlier when a beech spinney was cleared. It was well seasoned, and Whymper had advised Napoleon to sell it; both Mr

Pilkington and Mr Frederick were anxious to buy it. Napoleon was hesitating between the two, unable to make up his mind. It was noticed that whenever he seemed on the point of coming to an agreement with Frederick, Snowball was declared to be in hiding at Foxwood, while when he inclined towards Pilkington, Snowball was said to be at Pinchfield.

Suddenly, early in the spring, an alarming thing was discovered. Snowball was secretly frequenting the farm by night! The animals were so disturbed that they could hardly sleep in their stalls. Every night, it was said, he came creeping in under cover of darkness and performed all kinds of mischief. He stole the corn, he upset the milk-pails, he broke the eggs, he trampled the seed-beds, he gnawed the bark off the fruit trees. Whenever anything went wrong it became usual to attribute it to Snowball. If a window was broken or a drain was blocked up, someone was certain to say that Snowball had come in the night and done it, and when the key of the store-shed was lost the whole farm was convinced that Snowball had thrown it down the well. Curiously enough they went on believing this even after the mislaid key was found under a sack of meal. The cows declared unanimously that Snowball crept into their stalls and milked them in their sleep. The rats, which had been troublesome that winter, were also said to be in league with Snowball.

Napoleon decreed that their should be a full investigation into Snowball's activities. With his dogs in attendance he set out and made a careful tour of inspection of the farm buildings, the other animals following at a respectful distance. At every few steps Napoleon stopped and snuffed the ground for traces of Snowball's footsteps, which, he said, he could detect by the smell. He snuffed in every corner, in the barn, in the cowshed, in the henhouses, in the vegetable garden, and found traces of Snowball almost

everywhere. He would put his snout to the ground, give several deep sniffs and exclaim in a terrible voice, 'Snowball! He has been here! I can smell him distinctly!' and at the word 'Snowball' all the dogs let out blood-curdling growls and showed their side teeth.

The animals were thoroughly frightened. It seemed to them as though Snowball were some kind of invisible influence, pervading the air about them and menacing them with all kinds of dangers. In the evening Squealer called them together, and with an alarmed expression on his face told them that he had some serious news to report.

'Comrades!' cried Squealer, making little nervous skips, 'a most terrible thing has been discovered. Snowball has sold himself to Frederick of Pinchfield Farm, who is even now plotting to attack us and take our farm away from us! Snowball is to act as his guide when the attack begins. But there is worse than that. We had thought that Snowball's rebellion was caused simply by his vanity and ambition. But we were wrong, comrades. Do you know what the real reason was? Snowball was in league with Jones from the very start! He was Jones's secret agent all the time. It has all been proved by documents which he left behind him and which we have only just discovered. To my mind this explains a great deal, comrades. Did we not see for ourselves how he attempted–fortunately without success–to get us defeated and destroyed at the Battle of the Cowshed?'

The animals were stupefied. This was a wickedness far outdoing Snowball's destruction of the windmill. But it was some minutes before they could fully take it in. They all remembered, or thought they remembered, how they had seen Snowball charging ahead of them at the Battle of the Cowshed, how he had rallied and encouraged them at every turn, and how he had not paused for an instant even

when the pellets from Jones's gun had wounded his back. At first it was a little difficult to see how this fitted in with his being on Jones's side. Even Boxer, who seldom asked questions, was puzzled. He lay down, tucked his fore hoofs beneath him, shut his eyes, and with a hard effort managed to formulate his thoughts.

'I do not believe that,' he said. 'Snowball fought bravely at the Battle of the Cowshed. I saw him myself. Did we not give him "Animal Hero, First Class" immediately afterwards?'

'That was our mistake, comrade. For we know now—it is all written down in the secret documents that we have found—that in reality he was trying to lure us to our doom.'

'But he was wounded,' said Boxer. 'We all saw him running with blood.'

'That was part of the arrangement!' cried Squealer. 'Jones's shot only grazed him. I could show you this in his own writing, if you were able to read it. The plot was for Snowball, at the critical moment, to give the signal for flight and leave the field to the enemy. And he very nearly succeeded—I will even say, comrades, he *would* have succeeded if it had not been for our heroic Leader, Comrade Napoleon. Do you not remember how, just at the moment when Jones and his men had got inside the yard, Snowball suddenly turned and fled, and many animals followed him? And do you not remember, too, that it was just at that moment, when panic was spreading and all seemed lost, that Comrade Napoleon sprang forward with a cry of "Death to Humanity!" and sank his teeth in Jones's leg? Surely you remember *that*, comrades?' exclaimed Squealer, frisking from side to side.

Now when Squealer described the scene so graphically, it seemed to the animals that they did remember it. At any rate, they remembered that at the critical moment of the

battle Snowball had turned to flee. But Boxer was still a little uneasy.

'I do not believe that Snowball was a traitor at the beginning,' he said finally. 'What he has done since is different. But I believe that at the Battle of the Cowshed he was a good comrade.'

'Our Leader, Comrade Napoleon,' announced Squealer, speaking very slowly and firmly, 'has stated categorically— categorically, comrade—that Snowball was Jones's agent from the very beginning—yes, and from long before the Rebellion was ever thought of.'

'Ah, that is different!' said Boxer. 'If Comrade Napoleon says it, it must be right.'

'That is the true spirit, comrade!' cried Squealer, but it was noticed he cast a very ugly look at Boxer with his little twinkling eyes. He turned to go, then paused and added impressively: 'I warn every animal on this farm to keep his eyes very wide open. For we have reason to think that some of Snowball's secret agents are lurking among us at this moment!'

Four days later, in the late afternoon, Napoleon ordered all the animals to assemble in the yard. When they were all gathered together Napoleon emerged from the farm-house, wearing both his medals (for he had recently awarded himself 'Animal Hero, First Class' and 'Animal Hero, Second Class'), with his nine huge dogs frisking round him and uttering growls that sent shivers down all the animals' spines. They all cowered silently in their places, seeming to know in advance that some terrible thing was about to happen.

Napoleon stood sternly surveying his audience; then he uttered a high-pitched whimper. Immediately the dogs bounded forward, seized four of the pigs by the ear and dragged them, squealing with pain and terror, to Napoleon's feet. The pigs' ears were bleeding, the dogs had tasted

blood, and for a few moments they appeared to go quite mad. To the amazement of everybody three of them flung themselves upon Boxer. Boxer saw them coming and put out his great hoof, caught a dog in mid-air and pinned him to the ground. The dog shrieked for mercy and the other two fled with their tails between their legs. Boxer looked at Napoleon to know whether he should crush the dog to death or let it go. Napoleon appeared to change countenance, and sharply ordered Boxer to let the dog go, whereat Boxer lifted his hoof, and the dog slunk away, bruised and howling.

Presently the tumult died down. The four pigs waited, trembling, with guilt written on every line of their countenances. Napoleon now called upon them to confess their crimes. They were the same four pigs as had protested when Napoleon abolished the Sunday Meetings. Without any further prompting they confessed that they had been secretly in touch with Snowball ever since his expulsion, that they had collaborated with him in destroying the windmill, and that they had entered into an agreement with him to hand over Animal Farm to Mr Frederick. They added that Snowball had privately admitted to them that he had been Jones's secret agent for years past. When they had finished their confession the dogs promptly tore their throats out, and in a terrible voice Napoleon demanded whether any other animal had anything to confess.

The three hens who had been the ringleaders in the attempted rebellion over the eggs now came forward and stated that Snowball had appeared to them in a dream and incited them to disobey Napoleon's orders. They too were slaughtered. Then a goose came forward and confessed to having secreted six ears of corn during the last year's harvest and eaten them in the night. Then a sheep confessed to having urinated in the drinking pool—urged

to do this, so she said, by Snowball—and two other sheep confessed to having murdered an old ram, an especially devoted follower of Napoleon, by chasing him round and round a bonfire when he was suffering from a cough. They were all slain on the spot. And so the tale of confessions and executions went on, until there was a pile of corpses lying before Napoleon's feet and the air was heavy with the smell of blood, which had been unknown there since the expulsion of Jones.

When it was all over, the remaining animals, except for the pigs and dogs, crept away in a body. They were shaken and miserable. They did not know which was more shocking—the treachery of the animals who had leagued themselves with Snowball, or the cruel retribution they had just witnessed. In the old days there had often been scenes of bloodshed equally terrible, but it seemed to all of them that it was far worse now that it was happening among themselves. Since Jones had left the farm, until today, no animal had killed another animal. Not even a rat had been killed. They had made their way onto the little knoll where the half-finished windmill stood, and with one accord they all lay down as though huddling together for warmth—Clover, Muriel, Benjamin, the cows, the sheep and a whole flock of geese and hens—everyone, indeed, except the cat, who had suddenly disappeared just before Napoleon ordered the animals to assemble. For some time nobody spoke. Only Boxer remained on his feet. He fidgeted to and fro, swishing his long black tail against his sides and occasionally uttering a little whinny of surprise. Finally he said:

'I do not understand it. I would not have believed that such things could happen on our farm. It must be due to some fault in ourselves. The solution, as I see it, is to work harder. From now onwards I shall get up a full hour earlier in the mornings.'

And he moved off at his lumbering trot and made for the quarry. Having got there he collected two successive loads of stone and dragged them down to the windmill before retiring for the night.

The animals huddled about Clover, not speaking. The knoll where they were lying gave them a wide prospect across the countryside. Most of Animal Farm was within their view—the long pasture stretching down to the main road, the hayfield, the spinney, the drinking pool, the ploughed fields where the young wheat was thick and green, and the red roofs of the farm buildings with the smoke curling from the chimneys. It was a clear spring evening. The grass and the bursting hedges were gilded by the level rays of the sun. Never had the farm—and with a kind of surprise they remembered that it was their own farm, every inch of it their own property—appeared to the animals so desirable a place. As Clover looked down the hillside her eyes filled with tears. If she could have spoken her thoughts, it would have been to say that this was not what they had aimed at when they had set themselves years ago to work for the overthrow of the human race. These scenes of terror and slaughter were not what they had looked forward to on that night when old Major first stirred them to rebellion. If she herself had had any picture of the future, it had been of a society of animals set free from hunger and the whip, all equal, each working according to his capacity, the strong protecting the weak, as she had protected the lost brood of ducklings with her foreleg on the night of Major's speech. Instead—she did not know why—they had come to a time when no one dared speak his mind, when fierce, growling dogs roamed everywhere, and when you had to watch your comrades torn to pieces after confessing to shocking crimes. There was no thought of rebellion or disobedience in her mind. She knew that even as things were they were far better

off than they had been in the days of Jones, and that before all else it was needful to prevent the return of the human beings. Whatever happened she would remain faithful, work hard, carry out the orders that were given to her, and accept the leadership of Napoleon. But still, it was not for this that she and all the other animals had hoped and toiled. It was not for this that they had built the windmill and faced the pellets of Jones's gun. Such were her thoughts, though she lacked the words to express them.

At last, feeling this to be in some way a substitute for the words she was unable to find, she began to sing 'Beasts of England'. The other animals sitting round her took it up, and they sang it three times over—very tunefully, but slowly and mournfully, in a way they had never sung it before.

They had just finished singing it for the third time when Squealer, attended by two dogs, approached them with the air of having something important to say. He announced that, by a special decree of Comrade Napoleon, 'Beasts of England' had been abolished. From now onwards it was forbidden to sing it.

The animals were taken aback.

'Why?' cried Muriel.

'It is no longer needed, comrade,' said Squealer stiffly. ' "Beasts of England" was the song of the Rebellion. But the Rebellion is now completed. The execution of the traitors this afternoon was the final act. The enemy both external and internal has been defeated. In "Beasts of England" we expressed our longing for a better society in days to come. But that society has now been established. Clearly this song has no longer any purpose.'

Frightened though they were, some of the animals might possibly have protested, but at this moment the sheep set up their usual bleating of 'Four legs good, two

legs bad', which went on for several minutes and put an end to the discussion.

So 'Beasts of England' was heard no more. In its place Minimus, the poet, had composed another song which began:

Animal Farm, Animal Farm,
Never through me shalt thou come to harm!

and this was sung every Sunday morning after the hoisting of the flag. But somehow neither the words nor the tune ever seemed to the animals to come up to 'Beasts of England'.

CHAPTER VIII

A FEW DAYS LATER, when the terror caused by the executions had died down, some of the animals remembered
– or thought they remembered – that the Sixth Commandment decreed: 'No animal shall kill any other animal.' And
though no one cared to mention it in the hearing of the
pigs or the dogs, it was felt that the killings which had
taken place did not square with this. Clover asked Benjamin to read her the Sixth Commandment, and when
Benjamin, as usual, said that he refused to meddle in such
matters, she fetched Muriel. Muriel read the Commandment for her. It ran: 'No animal shall kill any other animal
without cause.' Somehow or other the last two words had
slipped out of the animals' memory. But they saw now that
the Commandment had not been violated; for clearly there
was good reason for killing the traitors who had leagued
themselves with Snowball.

Throughout that year the animals worked even harder
than they had worked in the previous year. To rebuild the
windmill, with walls twice as thick as before, and to finish
it by the appointed date, together with the regular work
of the farm, was a tremendous labour. There were times
when it seemed to the animals that they worked longer
hours and fed no better than they had done in Jones's day.
On Sunday mornings Squealer, holding down a long strip
of paper with his trotter, would read out to them lists of
figures proving that the production of every class of food-
stuff had increased by two hundred per cent, three hundred
per cent, or five hundred per cent, as the case might be. The
animals saw no reason to disbelieve him, especially as they

could no longer remember very clearly what conditions had been like before the Rebellion. All the same, there were days when they felt that they would sooner have had less figures and more food.

All orders were now issued through Squealer or one of the other pigs. Napoleon himself was not seen in public as often as once in a fortnight. When he did appear he was attended not only by his retinue of dogs but by a black cockerel who marched in front of him and acted as a kind of trumpeter, letting out a loud 'cock-a-doodle-doo' before Napoleon spoke. Even in the farmhouse, it was said, Napoleon inhabited separate apartments from the others. He took his meals alone, with two dogs to wait upon him, and always ate from the Crown Derby dinner service which had been in the glass cupboard in the drawing-room. It was also announced that the gun would be fired every year on Napoleon's birthday, as well as on the other two anniversaries.

Napoleon was now never spoken of simply as 'Napoleon'. He was always referred to in formal style as 'our Leader, Comrade Napoleon', and the pigs liked to invent for him such titles as Father of All Animals, Terror of Mankind, Protector of the Sheepfold, Ducklings' Friend, and the like. In his speeches Squealer would talk with the tears rolling down his cheeks of Napoleon's wisdom, the goodness of his heart, and the deep love he bore to all animals everywhere, even and especially the unhappy animals who still lived in ignorance and slavery on other farms. It had become usual to give Napoleon the credit for every successful achievement and every stroke of good fortune. You would often hear one hen remark to another, 'Under the guidance of our Leader, Comrade Napoleon, I have laid five eggs in six days'; or two cows, enjoying a drink at the pool, would exclaim, 'Thanks to the leadership of Comrade Napoleon, how excellent this water tastes!'

The general feeling on the farm was expressed in a poem entitled 'Comrade Napoleon', which was composed by Minimus and which ran as follows:

> *Friend of the fatherless!*
> *Fountain of happiness!*
> *Lord of the swill-bucket! Oh, how my soul is on*
> *Fire when I gaze at thy*
> *Calm and commanding eye,*
> *Like the sun in the sky,*
> *Comrade Napoleon!*
>
> *Thou art the giver of*
> *All that thy creatures love,*
> *Full belly twice a day, clean straw to roll upon;*
> *Every beast great or small*
> *Sleeps at peace in his stall,*
> *Thou watchest over all,*
> *Comrade Napoleon!*
>
> *Had I a sucking-pig,*
> *Ere he had grown as big*
> *Even as a pint bottle or as a rolling-pin,*
> *He should have learned to be*
> *Faithful and true to thee,*
> *Yes, his first squeak should be*
> *'Comrade Napoleon!'*

Napoleon approved of this poem and caused it to be inscribed on the wall of the big barn, at the opposite end from the Seven Commandments. It was surmounted by a portrait of Napoleon, in profile, executed by Squealer in white paint.

Meanwhile, through the agency of Whymper, Napoleon was engaged in complicated negotiations with Frederick and Pilkington. The pile of timber was still unsold. Of the two, Frederick was the more anxious to get

hold of it, but he would not offer a reasonable price. At the same time there were renewed rumours that Frederick and his men were plotting to attack Animal Farm and to destroy the windmill, the building of which had aroused furious jealousy in him. Snowball was known to be still skulking on Pinchfield Farm. In the middle of the summer the animals were alarmed to hear that three hens had come forward and confessed that, inspired by Snowball, they had entered into a plot to murder Napoleon. They were executed immediately, and fresh precautions for Napoleon's safety were taken. Four dogs guarded his bed at night, one at each corner, and a young pig named Pinkeye was given the task of tasting all his food before he ate it, lest it should be poisoned.

At about the same time it was given out that Napoleon had arranged to sell the pile of timber to Mr Pilkington; he was also going to enter into a regular agreement for the exchange of certain products between Animal Farm and Foxwood. The relations between Napoleon and Pilkington, though they were only conducted through Whymper, were now almost friendly. The animals distrusted Pilkington, as a human being, but greatly preferred him to Frederick, whom they both feared and hated. As the summer wore on, and the windmill neared completion, the rumours of an impending treacherous attack grew stronger and stronger. Frederick, it was said, intended to bring against them twenty men all armed with guns, and he had already bribed the magistrates and police, so that if he could once get hold of the title-deeds of Animal Farm they would ask no questions. Moreover terrible stories were leaking out from Pinchfield about the cruelties that Frederick practised upon his animals. He had flogged an old horse to death, he starved his cows, he had killed a dog by throwing it into the furnace, he amused himself in the evenings by making cocks fight with splinters of razor-

blade tied to their spurs. The animals' blood boiled with rage when they heard of these things being done to their comrades, and sometimes they clamoured to be allowed to go out in a body and attack Pinchfield Farm, drive out the humans and set the animals free. But Squealer counselled them to avoid rash actions and trust in Comrade Napoleon's strategy.

Nevertheless feeling against Frederick continued to run high. One Sunday morning Napoleon appeared in the barn and explained that he had never at any time contemplated selling the pile of timber to Frederick; he considered it beneath his dignity, he said, to have dealings with scoundrels of that description. The pigeons who were still sent out to spread tidings of the Rebellion were forbidden to set foot anywhere on Foxwood, and were also ordered to drop their former slogan of 'Death to Humanity' in favour of 'Death to Frederick'. In the late summer yet another of Snowball's machinations was laid bare. The wheat crop was full of weeds, and it was discovered that on one of his nocturnal visits Snowball had mixed weed seeds with the seed corn. A gander who had been privy to the plot had confessed his guilt to Squealer and immediately committed suicide by swallowing deadly nightshade berries. The animals now also learned that Snowball had never—as many of them had believed hitherto—received the order of 'Animal Hero, First Class'. This was merely a legend which had been spread some time after the Battle of the Cowshed by Snowball himself. So far from being decorated he had been censured for showing cowardice in the battle. Once again some of the animals heard this with a certain bewilderment, but Squealer was soon able to convince them that their memories had been at fault.

In the autumn, by a tremendous, exhausting effort—for the harvest had to be gathered at almost the same time—the windmill was finished. The machinery had still to be

installed, and Whymper was negotiating the purchase of it, but the structure was completed. In the teeth of every difficulty, in spite of inexperience, of primitive implements, of bad luck and of Snowball's treachery, the work had been finished punctually to the very day! Tired out but proud, the animals walked round and round their masterpiece, which appeared even more beautiful in their eyes than when it had been built the first time. Moreover the walls were twice as thick as before. Nothing short of explosives would lay them low this time! And when they thought of how they had laboured, what discouragements they had overcome, and the enormous difference that would be made in their lives when the sails were turning and the dynamos running—when they thought of all this their tiredness forsook them and they gambolled round and round the windmill, uttering cries of triumph. Napoleon himself, attended by his dogs and his cockerel, came down to inspect the completed work; he personally congratulated the animals on their achievement, and announced that the mill would be named Napoleon Mill.

Two days later the animals were called together for a special meeting in the barn. They were struck dumb with surprise when Napoleon announced that he had sold the pile of timber to Frederick. Tomorrow Frederick's wagons would arrive and begin carting it away. Throughout the whole period of his seeming friendship with Pilkington, Napoleon had really been in secret agreement with Frederick.

All relations with Foxwood had been broken off; insulting messages had been sent to Pilkington. The pigeons had been told to avoid Pinchfield Farm and to alter their slogan from 'Death to Frederick' to 'Death to Pilkington'. At the same time Napoleon assured the animals that the stories of an impending attack on Animal Farm were completely untrue, and that the tales about Fred-

erick's cruelty to his own animals had been greatly exaggerated. All these rumours had probably originated with
Snowball and his agents. It now appeared that Snowball
was not, after all, hiding on Pinchfield Farm, and in fact
had never been there in his life: he was living—in considerable luxury, so it was said—at Foxwood, and had in
reality been a pensioner of Pilkington for years past.

The pigs were in ecstasies over Napoleon's cunning. By
seeming to be friendly with Pilkington he had forced
Frederick to raise his price by twelve pounds. But the
superior quality of Napoleon's mind, said Squealer, was
shown in the fact that he trusted nobody, not even Frederick. Frederick had wanted to pay for the timber with
something called a cheque, which it seemed was a piece
of paper with a promise to pay written upon it. But
Napoleon was too clever for him. He had demanded
payment in real five-pound notes, which were to be
handed over before the timber was removed. Already
Frederick had paid up; and the sum he had paid was just
enough to buy the machinery for the windmill.

Meanwhile the timber was being carted away at high
speed. When it was all gone another special meeting was
held in the barn for the animals to inspect Frederick's
bank-notes. Smiling beatifically, and wearing both his
decorations, Napoleon reposed on a bed of straw on the
platform, with the money at his side, neatly piled on a china
dish from the farmhouse kitchen. The animals filed slowly
past, and each gazed his fill. And Boxer put out his nose
to sniff at the bank-notes, and the flimsy white things
stirred and rustled in his breath.

Three days later there was a terrible hullabaloo.
Whymper, his face deadly pale, came racing up the path
on his bicycle, flung it down in the yard and rushed straight
into the farmhouse. The next moment a choking roar of
rage sounded from Napoleon's apartments. The news of

what had happened sped round the farm like wildfire. The bank-notes were forgeries! Frederick had got the timber for nothing!

Napoleon called the animals together immediately and in a terrible voice pronounced the death sentence upon Frederick. When captured, he said, Frederick should be boiled alive. At the same time he warned them that after this treacherous deed the worst was to be expected. Frederick and his men might make their long-expected attack at any moment. Sentinels were placed at all the approaches to the farm. In addition, four pigeons were sent to Foxwood with a conciliatory message, which it was hoped might re-establish good relations with Pilkington.

The very next morning the attack came. The animals were at breakfast when the look-outs came racing in with the news that Frederick and his followers had already come through the five-barred gate. Boldly enough the animals sallied forth to meet them, but this time they did not have the easy victory that they had had in the Battle of the Cowshed. There were fifteen men, with half a dozen guns between them, and they opened fire as soon as they got within fifty yards. The animals could not face the terrible explosions and the stinging pellets, and in spite of the efforts of Napoleon and Boxer to rally them they were soon driven back. A number of them were already wounded. They took refuge in the farm buildings and peeped cautiously out from chinks and knot-holes. The whole of the big pasture, including the windmill, was in the hands of the enemy. For the moment even Napoleon seemed at a loss. He paced up and down without a word, his tail rigid and twitching. Wistful glances were sent in the direction of Foxwood. If Pilkington and his men would help them, the day might yet be won. But at this moment the four pigeons who had been sent out on the day before returned, one of them bearing a scrap of paper from Pil-

kington. On it was pencilled the words: 'Serves you right.'

Meanwhile Frederick and his men had halted about the windmill. The animals watched them, and a murmur of dismay went round. Two of the men had produced a crowbar and a sledge hammer. They were going to knock the windmill down.

'Impossible!' cried Napoleon. 'We have built the walls far too thick for that. They could not knock it down in a week. Courage, comrades!'

But Benjamin was watching the movements of the men intently. The two with the hammer and the crowbar were drilling a hole near the base of the windmill. Slowly, and with an air almost of amusement, Benjamin nodded his long muzzle.

'I thought so,' he said. 'Do you not see what they are doing? In another moment they are going to pack blasting powder into that hole.'

Terrified, the animals waited. It was impossible now to venture out of the shelter of the buildings. After a few minutes the men were seen to be running in all directions. Then there was a deafening roar. The pigeons swirled into the air, and all the animals, except Napoleon, flung themselves flat on their bellies and hid their faces. When they got up again a huge cloud of black smoke was hanging where the windmill had been. Slowly the breeze drifted it away. The windmill had ceased to exist!

At this sight the animals' courage returned to them. The fear and despair they had felt a moment earlier were drowned in their rage against this vile, contemptible act. A mighty cry for vengeance went up, and without waiting for further orders they charged forth in a body and made straight for the enemy. This time they did not heed the cruel pellets that swept over them like hail. It was a savage, bitter battle. The men fired again and again, and, when the animals got to close quarters, lashed out with their sticks

and their heavy boots. A cow, three sheep and two geese were killed, and nearly everyone was wounded. Even Napoleon, who was directing operations from the rear, had the tip of his tail chipped by a pellet. But the men did not go unscathed either. Three of them had their heads broken by blows from Boxer's hoofs, another was gored in the belly by a cow's horn, another had his trousers nearly torn off by Jessie and Bluebell. And when the nine dogs of Napoleon's own bodyguard, whom he had instructed to make a detour under cover of the hedge, suddenly appeared on the men's flank, baying ferociously, panic overtook them. They saw that they were in danger of being surrounded. Frederick shouted to his men to get out while the going was good, and the next moment the cowardly enemy was running for dear life. The animals chased them right down to the bottom of the field, and got in some last kicks at them as they forced their way through the thorn hedge.

They had won, but they were weary and bleeding. Slowly they began to limp back towards the farm. The sight of their dead comrades stretched upon the grass moved some of them to tears. And for a little while they halted in sorrowful silence at the place where the windmill had once stood. Yes, it was gone, almost the last trace of their labour was gone! Even the foundations were partially destroyed. And in rebuilding it they could not this time, as before, make use of the fallen stones. This time the stones had vanished too. The force of the explosion had flung them to distances of hundreds of yards. It was as though the windmill had never been.

As they approached the farm Squealer, who had unaccountably been absent during the fighting, came skipping towards them, whisking his tail and beaming with satisfaction. And the animals heard, from the direction of the farm buildings, the solemn booming of a gun.

'What is that gun firing for?' said Boxer.

'To celebrate our victory!' cried Squealer.

'What victory?' said Boxer. His knees were bleeding, he had lost a shoe and split his hoof, and a dozen pellets had lodged themselves in his hind leg.

'What victory, comrade? Have we not driven the enemy off our soil—the sacred soil of Animal Farm?'

'But they have destroyed the windmill. And we had worked on it for two years!'

'What matter? We will build another windmill. We will build six windmills if we feel like it. You do not appreciate, comrade, the mighty thing that we have done. The enemy was in occupation of this very ground that we stand upon. And now—thanks to the leadership of Comrade Napoleon—we have won every inch of it back again!'

'Then we have won back what we had before,' said Boxer.

'That is our victory,' said Squealer.

They limped into the yard. The pellets under the skin of Boxer's leg smarted painfully. He saw ahead of him the heavy labour of rebuilding the windmill from the foundations, and already in imagination he braced himself for the task. But for the first time it occurred to him that he was eleven years old and that perhaps his great muscles were not quite what they had once been.

But when the animals saw the green flag flying, and heard the gun firing again—seven times it was fired in all—and heard the speech that Napoleon made, con-gratulating them on their conduct, it did seem to them after all that they had won a great victory. The animals slain in the battle were given a solemn funeral. Boxer and Clover pulled the wagon which served as a hearse, and Napoleon himself walked at the head of the procession. Two whole days were given over to celebrations. There were songs, speeches and more firing of the gun, and a special gift of

an apple was bestowed on every animal, with two ounces of corn for each bird and three biscuits for each dog. It was announced that the battle would be called the Battle of the Windmill, and that Napoleon had created a new decoration, the Order of the Green Banner, which he had conferred upon himself. In the general rejoicings the unfortunate affair of the bank-notes was forgotten.

It was a few days later than this that the pigs came upon a case of whisky in the cellars of the farmhouse. It had been overlooked at the time when the house was first occupied. That night there came from the farmhouse the sound of loud singing, in which, to everyone's surprise, the strains of 'Beasts of England' were mixed up. At about half-past nine Napoleon, wearing an old bowler hat of Mr Jones's, was distinctly seen to emerge from the back door, gallop rapidly round the yard and disappear indoors again. But in the morning a deep silence hung over the farmhouse. Not a pig appeared to be stirring. It was nearly nine o'clock when Squealer made his appearance, walking slowly and dejectedly, his eyes dull, his tail hanging limply behind him, and with every appearance of being seriously ill. He called the animals together and told them that he had a terrible piece of news to impart. Comrade Napoleon was dying!

A cry of lamentation went up. Straw was laid down outside the doors of the farmhouse, and the animals walked on tiptoe. With tears in their eyes they asked one another what they should do if their Leader were taken away from them. A rumour went round that Snowball had after all contrived to introduce poison into Napoleon's food. At eleven o'clock Squealer came out to make another announcement. As his last act upon earth, Comrade Napoleon had pronounced a solemn decree: the drinking of alcohol was to be punished by death.

By the evening, however, Napoleon appeared to be

somewhat better, and the following morning Squealer was able to tell them that he was well on the way to recovery. By the evening of that day Napoleon was back at work, and on the next day it was learned that he had instructed Whymper to purchase in Willingdon some booklets on brewing and distilling. A week later Napoleon gave orders that the small paddock beyond the orchard, which it had previously been intended to set aside as a grazing-ground for animals who were past work, was to be ploughed up. It was given out that the pasture was exhausted and needed re-seeding: but it soon became known that Napoleon intended to sow it with barley.

About this time there occurred a strange incident which hardly anyone was able to understand. One night at about twelve o'clock there was a loud crash in the yard, and the animals rushed out of their stalls. It was a moonlit night. At the foot of the end wall of the big barn, where the Seven Commandments were written, there lay a ladder broken in two pieces. Squealer, temporarily stunned, was sprawling beside it, and near at hand there lay a lantern, a paintbrush and an overturned pot of white paint. The dogs immediately made a ring round Squealer, and escorted him back to the farmhouse as soon as he was able to walk. None of the animals could form any idea as to what this meant, except old Benjamin, who nodded his muzzle with a knowing air, and seemed to understand, but would say nothing.

But a few days later Muriel, reading over the Seven Commandments to herself, noticed that there was yet another of them which the animals had remembered wrong. They had thought that the Fifth Commandment was 'No animal shall drink alcohol', but there were two words that they had forgotten. Actually the Commandment read: 'No animal shall drink alcohol *to excess*.'

CHAPTER IX

BOXER'S SPLIT HOOF was a long time in healing. They had started the rebuilding of the windmill the day after the victory celebrations were ended. Boxer refused to take even a day off work, and made it a point of honour not to let it be seen that he was in pain. In the evenings he would admit privately to Clover that the hoof troubled him a great deal. Clover treated the hoof with poultices of herbs which she prepared by chewing them, and both she and Benjamin urged Boxer to work less hard. 'A horse's lungs do not last for ever,' she said to him. But Boxer would not listen. He had, he said, only one real ambition left—to see the windmill well under way before he reached the age for retirement.

At the beginning, when the laws of Animal Farm were first formulated, the retiring age had been fixed for horses and pigs at twelve, for cows at fourteen, for dogs at nine, for sheep at seven and for hens and geese at five. Liberal old-age pensions had been agreed upon. As yet no animal had actually retired on pension, but of late the subject had been discussed more and more. Now that the small field beyond the orchard had been set aside for barley, it was rumoured that a corner of the large pasture was to be fenced off and turned into a grazing-ground for super-annuated animals. For a horse, it was said, the pension would be five pounds of corn a day and, in winter, fifteen pounds of hay, with a carrot or possibly an apple on public holidays. Boxer's twelfth birthday was due in the late summer of the following year.

Meanwhile life was hard. The winter was as cold as the

last one had been, and food was even shorter. Once again all rations were reduced except those of the pigs and the dogs. A too-rigid equality in rations, Squealer explained, would have been contrary to the principles of Animalism. In any case he had no difficulty in proving to the other animals that they were *not* in reality short of food, whatever the appearances might be. For the time being, certainly, it had been found necessary to make a readjustment of rations (Squealer always spoke of it as a 'readjustment', never as a 'reduction'), but in comparison with the days of Jones the improvement was enormous. Reading out the figures in a shrill rapid voice, he proved to them in detail that they had more oats, more hay, more turnips than they had had in Jones's day, that they worked shorter hours, that their drinking water was of better quality, that they lived longer, that a larger proportion of their young ones survived infancy, and that they had more straw in their stalls and suffered less from fleas. The animals believed every word of it. Truth to tell, Jones and all he stood for had almost faded out of their memories. They knew that life nowadays was harsh and bare, that they were often hungry and often cold, and that they were usually working when they were not asleep. But doubtless it had been worse in the old days. They were glad to believe so. Besides, in those days they had been slaves and now they were free, and that made all the difference, as Squealer did not fail to point out.

There were many more mouths to feed now. In the autumn the four sows had all littered about simultaneously, producing thirty-one young pigs between them. The young pigs were piebald, and as Napoleon was the only boar on the farm it was possible to guess at their parentage. It was announced that later, when bricks and timber had been purchased, a schoolroom would be built in the farmhouse garden. For the time being the young pigs were given their instruction by Napoleon himself in the

farmhouse kitchen. They took their exercise in the garden, and were discouraged from playing with the other young animals. About this time, too, it was laid down as a rule that when a pig and any other animal met on the path, the other animal must stand aside: and also that all pigs, of whatever degree, were to have the privilege of wearing green ribbons on their tails on Sundays.

The farm had had a fairly successful year, but was still short of money. There were the bricks, sand and lime for the schoolroom to be purchased, and it would also be necessary to begin saving up again for the machinery for the windmill. Then there were lamp oil and candles for the house, sugar for Napoleon's own table (he forbade this to the other pigs, on the ground that it made them fat), and all the usual replacements such as tools, nails, string, coal, wire, scrap-iron and dog biscuits. A stump of hay and part of the potato crop were sold off, and the contract for eggs was increased to six hundred a week, so that that year the hens barely hatched enough chicks to keep their numbers at the same level. Rations, reduced in December, were reduced again in February, and lanterns in the stalls were forbidden to save oil. But the pigs seemed comfortable enough, and in fact were putting on weight if anything. One afternoon in late February a warm, rich, appetising scent, such as the animals had never smelt before, wafted itself across the yard from the little brew-house, which had been disused in Jones's time, and which stood beyond the kitchen. Someone said it was the smell of cooking barley. The animals sniffed the air hungrily and wondered whether a warm mash was being prepared for their supper. But no warm mash appeared, and on the following Sunday it was announced that from now onwards all barley would be reserved for the pigs. The field beyond the orchard had already been sown with barley. And the news soon leaked out that every pig was now receiving a ration

of a pint of beer daily, with half a gallon for Napoleon himself, which was always served to him in the Crown Derby soup tureen.

But if there were hardships to be borne, they were partly offset by the fact that life nowadays had a greater dignity than it had had before. There were more songs, more speeches, more processions. Napoleon had commanded that once a week there should be held something called a Spontaneous Demonstration, the object of which was to celebrate the struggles and triumphs of Animal Farm. At the appointed time the animals would leave their work and march round the precincts of the farm in military formation, with the pigs leading, then the horses, then the cows, then the sheep, and then the poultry. The dogs flanked the procession and at the head of all marched Napoleon's black cockerel. Boxer and Clover always carried between them a green banner marked with the hoof and the horn and the caption, 'Long live Comrade Napoleon!' Afterwards there were recitations of poems composed in Napoleon's honour, and a speech by Squealer giving particulars of the latest increases in the production of foodstuffs, and on occasion a shot was fired from the gun. The sheep were the greatest devotees of the Spontaneous Demonstrations, and if anyone complained (as a few animals sometimes did, when no pigs or dogs were near) that they wasted time and meant a lot of standing about in the cold, the sheep were sure to silence him with a tremendous bleating of 'Four legs good, two legs bad!' But by and large the animals enjoyed these celebrations. They found it comforting to be reminded that, after all, they were truly their own masters and that the work they did was for their own benefit. So that what with the songs, the processions, Squealer's lists of figures, the thunder of the gun, the crowing of the cockerel and the fluttering of the flag, they were able to forget that their bellies were empty, at least part of the time.

In April Animal Farm was proclaimed a Republic, and it became necessary to elect a President. There was only one candidate, Napoleon, who was elected unanimously. On the same day it was given out that fresh documents had been discovered which revealed further details about Snowball's complicity with Jones. It now appeared that Snowball had not, as the animals had previously imagined, merely attempted to lose the Battle of the Cowshed by means of a stratagem, but had been openly fighting on Jones's side. In fact it was he who had actually been the leader of the human forces, and had charged into battle with the words 'Long live Humanity!' on his lips. The wounds on Snowball's back, which a few of the animals still remembered to have seen, had been inflicted by Napoleon's teeth.

In the middle of the summer Moses the raven suddenly reappeared on the farm, after an absence of several years. He was quite unchanged, still did no work, and talked in the same strain as ever about Sugarcandy Mountain. He would perch on a stump, flap his black wings, and talk by the hour to anyone who would listen. 'Up there, comrades,' he would say solemnly, pointing to the sky with his large beak—'up there, just on the other side of that dark cloud that you can see—there it lies, Sugarcandy Mountain, that happy country where we poor animals shall rest for ever from our labours!' He even claimed to have been there on one of his higher flights, and to have seen the everlasting fields of clover and the linseed cake and lump sugar growing on the hedges. Many of the animals believed him. Their lives now, they reasoned, were hungry and laborious; was it not right and just that a better world should exist somewhere else? A thing that was difficult to determine was the attitude of the pigs towards Moses. They all declared contemptuously that his stories about Sugarcandy Mountain were lies, and yet they allowed him

to remain on the farm, not working, with an allowance of a gill of beer a day.

After his hoof had healed up Boxer worked harder than ever. Indeed all the animals worked like slaves that year. Apart from the regular work of the farm, and the rebuilding of the windmill, there was the schoolhouse for the young pigs, which was started in March. Sometimes the long hours on insufficient food were hard to bear, but Boxer never faltered. In nothing that he said or did was there any sign that his strength was not what it had been. It was only his appearance that was a little altered; his hide was less shiny than it had used to be, and his great haunches seemed to have shrunken. The others said, 'Boxer will pick up when the spring grass comes on'; but the spring grass came and Boxer grew no fatter. Sometimes on the slope leading to the top of the quarry, when he braced his muscles against the weight of some vast boulder, it seemed that nothing kept him on his feet except the will to continue. At such times his lips were seen to form the words 'I will work harder'; he had no voice left. Once again Clover and Benjamin warned him to take care of his health, but Boxer paid no attention. His twelfth birthday was approaching. He did not care what happened so long as a good store of stone was accumulated before he went on pension.

Late one evening, in the summer, a sudden rumour ran round the farm that something had happened to Boxer. He had gone out alone to drag a load of stone down to the windmill. And sure enough, the rumour was true. A few minutes later two pigeons came racing in with the news: 'Boxer has fallen! He is lying on his side and can't get up!'

About half the animals on the farm rushed out to the knoll where the windmill stood. There lay Boxer, between the shafts of the cart, his neck stretched out, unable even to raise his head. His eyes were glazed, his sides matted with

79

sweat. A thin stream of blood had trickled out of his mouth. Clover dropped to her knees at his side.

'Boxer!' she cried, 'how are you?'

'It is my lung,' said Boxer in a weak voice. 'It does not matter. I think you will be able to finish the windmill without me. There is a pretty good store of stone accumulated. I had only another month to go in any case. To tell you the truth I had been looking forward to my retirement. And perhaps, as Benjamin is growing old too, they will let him retire at the same time and be a companion to me.'

'We must get help at once,' said Clover. 'Run, somebody, and tell Squealer what has happened.'

All the other animals immediately raced back to the farmhouse to give Squealer the news. Only Clover remained, and Benjamin, who lay down at Boxer's side, and, without speaking, kept the flies off him with his long tail. After about a quarter of an hour Squealer appeared, full of sympathy and concern. He said that Comrade Napoleon had learned with the very deepest distress of this misfortune to one of the most loyal workers on the farm, and was already making arrangements to send Boxer to be treated in the hospital at Willingdon. The animals felt a little uneasy at this. Except for Mollie and Snowball no other animal had ever left the farm, and they did not like to think of their sick comrade in the hands of human beings. However, Squealer easily convinced them that the veterinary surgeon in Willingdon could treat Boxer's case more satisfactorily than could be done on the farm. And about half an hour later, when Boxer had somewhat recovered, he was with difficulty got onto his feet, and managed to limp back to his stall, where Clover and Benjamin had prepared a good bed of straw for him.

For the next two days Boxer remained in his stall. The pigs had sent out a large bottle of pink medicine which they

had found in the medicine chest in the bathroom, and Clover administered it to Boxer twice a day after meals. In the evenings she lay in his stall and talked to him, while Benjamin kept the flies off him. Boxer professed not to be sorry for what had happened. If he made a good recovery he might expect to live another three years, and he looked forward to the peaceful days that he would spend in the corner of the big pasture. It would be the first time that he had had leisure to study and improve his mind. He intended, he said, to devote the rest of his life to learning the remaining twenty-two letters of the alphabet.

However, Benjamin and Clover could only be with Boxer after working hours, and it was in the middle of the day when the van came to take him away. The animals were all at work weeding turnips under the supervision of a pig, when they were astonished to see Benjamin come galloping from the direction of the farm buildings, braying at the top of his voice. It was the first time that they had ever seen Benjamin excited—indeed, it was the first time that anyone had ever seen him gallop. 'Quick, quick!' he shouted. 'Come at once! They're taking Boxer away!' Without waiting for orders from the pig, the animals broke off work and raced back to the farm buildings. Sure enough, there in the yard was a large closed van, drawn by two horses, with lettering on its side and a sly-looking man in a low-crowned bowler hat sitting on the driver's seat. And Boxer's stall was empty.

The animals crowded round the van. 'Good-bye, Boxer!' they chorused, 'good-bye!'

'Fools! Fools!' shouted Benjamin, prancing round them and stamping the earth with his small hoofs. 'Fools! Do you not see what is written on the side of that van?'

That gave the animals pause, and there was a hush. Muriel began to spell out the words. But Benjamin pushed her aside and in the midst of a deadly silence he read:

'"Alfred Simmonds, Horse Slaughterer and Glue Boiler, Willingdon. Dealer in Hides and Bone-Meal. Kennels Supplied." Do you not understand what that means? They are taking Boxer to the knacker's!'

A cry of horror burst from all the animals. At this moment the man on the box whipped up his horses and the van moved out of the yard at a smart trot. All the animals followed, crying out at the tops of their voices. Clover forced her way to the front. The van began to gather speed. Clover tried to stir her stout limbs to a gallop, and achieved a canter. 'Boxer!' she cried. 'Boxer! Boxer! Boxer!' And just at this moment, as though he had heard the uproar outside, Boxer's face, with the white stripe down his nose, appeared at the small window at the back of the van.

'Boxer!' cried Clover in a terrible voice. 'Boxer! Get out! Get out quickly! They are taking you to your death!'

All the animals took up the cry of 'Get out, Boxer, get out!' But the van was already gathering speed and drawing away from them. It was uncertain whether Boxer had understood what Clover had said. But a moment later his face disappeared from the window and there was the sound of a tremendous drumming of hoofs inside the van. He was trying to kick his way out. The time had been when a few kicks from Boxer's hoofs would have smashed the van to matchwood. But alas! his strength had left him; and in a few moments the sound of drumming hoofs grew fainter and died away. In desperation the animals began appealing to the two horses which drew the van to stop. 'Comrades, comrades!' they shouted. 'Don't take your own brother to his death!' But the stupid brutes, too ignorant to realise what was happening, merely set back their ears and quickened their pace. Boxer's face did not reappear at the window. Too late, someone thought of racing ahead and shutting the five-barred gate; but in another moment the

van was through it and rapidly disappearing down the road. Boxer was never seen again.

Three days later it was announced that he had died in the hospital at Willingdon, in spite of receiving every attention a horse could have. Squealer came to announce the news to the others. He had, he said, been present during Boxer's last hours.

'It was the most affecting sight I have ever seen!' said Squealer, lifting his trotter and wiping away a tear. 'I was at his bedside at the very last. And at the end, almost too weak to speak, he whispered in my ear that his sole sorrow was to have passed on before the windmill was finished. "Forward, comrades!" he whispered. "Forward in the name of the Rebellion. Long live Animal Farm! Long live Comrade Napoleon! Napoleon is always right." Those were his very last words, comrades.'

Here Squealer's demeanour suddenly changed. He fell silent for a moment, and his little eyes darted suspicious glances from side to side before he proceeded.

It had come to his knowledge, he said, that a foolish and wicked rumour had been circulated at the time of Boxer's removal. Some of the animals had noticed that the van which took Boxer away was marked 'Horse Slaughterer', and had actually jumped to the conclusion that Boxer was being sent to the knacker's. It was almost unbelievable, said Squealer, that any animal could be so stupid. Surely, he cried indignantly, whisking his tail and skipping from side to side, surely they knew their beloved Leader, Comrade Napoleon, better than that? But the explanation was really very simple. The van had previously been the property of the knacker, and had been bought by the veterinary surgeon, who had not yet painted the old name out. That was how the mistake had arisen.

The animals were enormously relieved to hear this. And when Squealer went on to give further graphic details of

Boxer's death-bed, the admirable care he had received and the expensive medicines for which Napoleon had paid without a thought as to the cost, their last doubts disappeared and the sorrow that they felt for their comrade's death was tempered by the thought that at least he had died happy.

Napoleon himself appeared at the meeting on the following Sunday morning and pronounced a short oration in Boxer's honour. It had not been possible, he said, to bring back their lamented comrade's remains for interment on the farm, but he had ordered a large wreath to be made from the laurels in the farmhouse garden and sent down to be placed on Boxer's grave. And in a few days' time the pigs intended to hold a memorial banquet in Boxer's honour. Napoleon ended his speech with a reminder of Boxer's two favourite maxims, 'I will work harder' and 'Comrade Napoleon is always right'— maxims, he said, which every animal would do well to adopt as his own.

On the day appointed for the banquet a grocer's van drove up from Willingdon and delivered a large wooden crate at the farmhouse. That night there was the sound of uproarious singing, which was followed by what sounded like a violent quarrel and ended at about eleven o'clock with a tremendous crash of glass. No one stirred in the farmhouse before noon on the following day. And the word went round that from somewhere or other the pigs had acquired the money to buy themselves another case of whisky.

CHAPTER X

YEARS PASSED. The seasons came and went, the short animal lives fled by. A time came when there was no one who remembered the old days before the Rebellion, except Clover, Benjamin, Moses the raven, and a number of the pigs.

Muriel was dead, Bluebell, Jessie and Pincher were dead. Jones too was dead—he had died in an inebriates' home in another part of the county. Snowball was forgotten. Boxer was forgotten, except by the few who had known him. Clover was an old stout mare now, stiff in the joints and with a tendency to rheumy eyes. She was two years past the retiring age, but in fact no animal had ever actually retired. The talk of setting aside a corner of the pasture for superannuated animals had long since been dropped. Napoleon was now a mature boar of twenty-four stone. Squealer was so fat that he could with difficulty see out of his eyes. Only old Benjamin was much the same as ever, except for being a little greyer about the muzzle, and, since Boxer's death, more morose and taciturn than ever.

There were many more creatures on the farm now, though the increase was not so great as had been expected in earlier years. Many animals had been born to whom the Rebellion was only a dim tradition, passed on by word of mouth, and others had been bought who had never heard mention of such a thing before their arrival. The farm possessed three horses now besides Clover. They were fine upstanding beasts, willing workers and good comrades, but very stupid. None of them proved able to learn the

alphabet beyond the letter B. They accepted everything that they were told about the Rebellion and the principles of Animalism, especially from Clover, for whom they had an almost filial respect; but it was doubtful whether they understood very much of it.

The farm was more prosperous now, and better organised; it had even been enlarged by two fields which had been bought from Mr Pilkington. The windmill had been successfully completed at last, and the farm possessed a threshing machine and a hay elevator of its own, and various new buildings had been added to it. Whymper had bought himself a dogcart. The windmill, however, had not after all been used for generating electrical power. It was used for milling corn, and brought in a handsome money profit. The animals were hard at work building yet another windmill: when that one was finished, so it was said, the dynamos would be installed. But the luxuries of which Snowball had once taught the animals to dream, the stalls with electric light and hot and cold water, and the three-day week, were no longer talked about. Napoleon had denounced such ideas as contrary to the spirit of Animalism. The truest happiness, he said, lay in working hard and living frugally.

Somehow it seemed as though the farm had grown richer without making the animals themselves any richer —except, of course, for the pigs and the dogs. Perhaps this was partly because there were so many pigs and so many dogs. It was not that these creatures did not work, after their fashion. There was, as Squealer was never tired of explaining, endless work in the supervision and organisation of the farm. Much of this work was of a kind that the other animals were too ignorant to understand. For example, Squealer told them that the pigs had to expend enormous labours every day upon mysterious things called 'files', 'reports', 'minutes' and 'memoranda'. These were

large sheets of paper which had to be closely covered with writing, and as soon as they were so covered they were burnt in the furnace. This was of the highest importance for the welfare of the farm, Squealer said. But still, neither pigs nor dogs produced any food by their own labour; and there were very many of them, and their appetites were always good.

As for the others, their life, so far as they knew, was as it had always been. They were generally hungry, they slept on straw, they drank from the pool, they laboured in the fields; in winter they were troubled by the cold, and in summer by the flies. Sometimes the older ones among them racked their dim memories and tried to determine whether in the early days of the Rebellion, when Jones's expulsion was still recent, things had been better or worse than now. They could not remember. There was nothing with which they could compare their present lives: they had nothing to go upon except Squealer's lists of figures, which invariably demonstrated that everything was getting better and better. The animals found the problem insoluble; in any case they had little time for speculating on such things now. Only old Benjamin professed to remember every detail of his long life and to know that things never had been, nor ever could be, much better or much worse—hunger, hardship and disappointment being, so he said, the unalterable law of life.

And yet the animals never gave up hope. More, they never lost, even for an instant, their sense of honour and privilege in being members of Animal Farm. They were still the only farm in the whole country—in all England!—owned and operated by animals. Not one of them, not even the youngest, not even the newcomers who had been brought from farms ten or twenty miles away, ever ceased to marvel at that. And when they heard the gun booming and saw the green flag fluttering at the masthead, their

hearts swelled with imperishable pride, and the talk turned always towards the old heroic days, the expulsion of Jones, the writing of the Seven Commandments, the great battles in which the human invaders had been defeated. None of the old dreams had been abandoned. The Republic of the Animals which Major had foretold, when the green fields of England should be untrodden by human feet, was still believed in. Some day it was coming: it might not be soon, it might not be within the lifetime of any animal now living, but still it was coming. Even the tune of 'Beasts of England' was perhaps hummed secretly here and there: at any rate it was a fact that every animal on the farm knew it, though no one would have dared to sing it aloud. It might be that their lives were hard and that not all of their hopes had been fulfilled; but they were conscious that they were not as other animals. If they went hungry, it was not from feeding tyrannical human beings; if they worked hard, at least they worked for themselves. No creature among them went upon two legs. No creature called any other creature 'Master'. All animals were equal.

One day in early summer Squealer ordered the sheep to follow him and led them out to a piece of waste ground at the other end of the farm, which had become over-grown with birch saplings. The sheep spent the whole day there browsing at the leaves under Squealer's supervision. In the evening he returned to the farmhouse himself, but, as it was warm weather, told the sheep to stay where they were. It ended by their remaining there for a whole week, during which time the other animals saw nothing of them. Squealer was with them for the greater part of every day. He was, he said, teaching them to sing a new song, for which privacy was needed.

It was just after the sheep had returned, on a pleasant evening when the animals had finished work and were making their way back to the farm buildings, that the

terrified neighing of a horse sounded from the yard. Startled, the animals stopped in their tracks. It was Clover's voice. She neighed again, and all the animals broke into a gallop and rushed into the yard. Then they saw what Clover had seen.

It was a pig walking on his hind legs.

Yes, it was Squealer. A little awkwardly, as though not quite used to supporting his considerable bulk in that position, but with perfect balance, he was strolling across the yard. And a moment later, out from the door of the farmhouse came a long file of pigs, all walking on their hind legs. Some did it better than others, one or two were even a trifle unsteady and looked as though they would have liked the support of a stick, but every one of them made his way right round the yard successfully. And finally there was a tremendous baying of dogs and a shrill crowing from the black cockerel, and out came Napoleon himself, majestically upright, casting haughty glances from side to side, and with his dogs gambolling round him.

He carried a whip in his trotter.

There was a deadly silence. Amazed, terrified, huddling together, the animals watched the long line of pigs march slowly round the yard. It was as though the world had turned upside-down. Then there came a moment when the first shock had worn off and when in spite of every-thing—in spite of their terror of the dogs, and of the habit, developed through long years, of never complaining, never criticising, no matter what happened—they might have uttered some word of protest. But just at that moment, as though at a signal, all the sheep burst out into a tremendous bleating of—

'Four legs good, two legs *better*! Four legs good, two legs *better*! Four legs good, two legs *better*!'

It went on for five minutes without stopping. And by the time the sheep had quieted down the chance to utter any

protest had passed, for the pigs had marched back into the farmhouse.

Benjamin felt a nose nuzzling at his shoulder. He looked round. It was Clover. Her old eyes looked dimmer than ever. Without saying anything she tugged gently at his mane and led him round to the end of the big barn, where the Seven Commandments were written. For a minute or two they stood gazing at the tarred wall with its white lettering.

'My sight is failing,' she said finally. 'Even when I was young I could not have read what was written there. But it appears to me that that wall looks different. Are the Seven Commandments the same as they used to be, Benjamin?'

For once Benjamin consented to break his rule, and he read out to her what was written on the wall. There was nothing there now except a single Commandment. It ran:

ALL ANIMALS ARE EQUAL
BUT SOME ANIMALS ARE MORE EQUAL
THAN OTHERS.

After that it did not seem strange when next day the pigs who were supervising the work of the farm all carried whips in their trotters. It did not seem strange to learn that the pigs had bought themselves a wireless set, were arranging to install a telephone, and had taken out subscriptions to *John Bull*, *Tit-Bits* and the *Daily Mirror*. It did not seem strange when Napoleon was seen strolling in the farmhouse garden with a pipe in his mouth—no, not even when the pigs took Mr Jones's clothes out of the wardrobes and put them on, Napoleon himself appearing in a black coat, ratcatcher breeches and leather leggings, while his favourite sow appeared in the watered silk dress which Mrs Jones had been used to wear on Sundays.

A week later, in the afternoon, a number of dogcarts drove up to the farm. A deputation of neighbouring

farmers had been invited to make a tour of inspection. They were shown all over the farm, and expressed great admiration for everything they saw, especially the windmill. The animals were weeding the turnip field. They worked diligently, hardly raising their faces from the ground, and not knowing whether to be more frightened of the pigs or of the human visitors.

That evening loud laughter and bursts of singing came from the farmhouse. And suddenly, at the sound of the mingled voices, the animals were stricken with curiosity. What could be happening in there, now that for the first time animals and human beings were meeting on terms of equality? With one accord they began to creep as quietly as possible into the farmhouse garden.

At the gate they paused, half frightened to go on, but Clover led the way in. They tiptoed up to the house, and such animals as were tall enough peered in at the dining-room window. There, round the long table, sat half a dozen farmers and half a dozen of the more eminent pigs, Napoleon himself occupying the seat of honour at the head of the table. The pigs appeared completely at ease in their chairs. The company had been enjoying a game of cards, but had broken off for the moment, evidently in order to drink a toast. A large jug was circulating, and the mugs were being refilled with beer. No one noticed the wondering faces of the animals that gazed in at the window.

Mr Pilkington, of Foxwood, had stood up, his mug in his hand. In a moment, he said, he would ask the present company to drink a toast. But before doing so there were a few words that he felt it incumbent upon him to say.

It was a source of great satisfaction to him, he said—and, he was sure, to all others present—to feel that a long period of mistrust and misunderstanding had now come to an end. There had been a time—not that he, or any of the present company, had shared such sentiments—but there had been

a time when the respected proprietors of Animal Farm had been regarded, he would not say with hostility, but perhaps with a certain measure of misgiving, by their human neighbours. Unfortunate incidents had occurred, mistaken ideas had been current. It had been felt that the existence of a farm owned and operated by pigs was somehow abnormal and was liable to have an unsettling effect in the neighbourhood. Too many farmers had assumed, without due enquiry, that on such a farm a spirit of licence and indiscipline would prevail. They had been nervous about the effects upon their own animals, or even upon their human employees. But all such doubts were now dispelled. Today he and his friends had visited Animal Farm and inspected every inch of it with their own eyes, and what did they find? Not only the most up-to-date methods, but a discipline and an orderliness which should be an example to all farmers everywhere. He believed that he was right in saying that the lower animals on Animal Farm did more work and received less food than any animals in the county. Indeed he and his fellow-visitors today had observed many features which they intended to introduce on their own farms immediately.

He would end his remarks, he said, by emphasising once again the friendly feelings that subsisted, and ought to subsist, between Animal Farm and its neighbours. Between pigs and human beings there was not and there need not be any clash of interests whatever. Their struggles and their difficulties were one. Was not the labour problem the same everywhere? Here it became apparent that Mr Pilkington was about to spring some carefully-prepared witticism on the company, but for a moment he was too overcome by amusement to be able to utter it. After much choking, during which his various chins turned purple, he managed to get it out: 'If you have your lower animals to contend with,' he said, 'we have our lower classes!' This

bon mot set the table in a roar; and Mr Pilkington once again congratulated the pigs on the low rations, the long working-hours and the general absence of pampering which he had observed on Animal Farm.

And now, he said finally, he would ask the company to rise to their feet and make certain that their glasses were full. 'Gentlemen,' concluded Mr Pilkington, 'gentlemen, I give you a toast: To the prosperity of Animal Farm!'

There was enthusiastic cheering and stamping of feet. Napoleon was so gratified that he left his place and came round the table to clink his mug against Mr Pilkington's before emptying it. When the cheering had died down, Napoleon, who had remained on his feet, intimated that he too had a few words to say.

Like all of Napoleon's speeches, it was short and to the point. He too, he said, was happy that the period of misunderstanding was at an end. For a long time there had been rumours—circulated, he had reason to think, by some malignant enemy—that there was something subversive and even revolutionary in the outlook of himself and his colleagues. They had been credited with attempting to stir up rebellion among the animals on neighbouring farms. Nothing could be further from the truth! Their sole wish, now and in the past, was to live at peace and in normal business relations with their neighbours. This farm which he had the honour to control, he added, was a co-operative enterprise. The title-deeds, which were in his own possession, were owned by the pigs jointly.

He did not believe, he said, that any of the old suspicions still lingered, but certain changes had been made recently in the routine of the farm which should have the effect of promoting confidence still further. Hitherto the animals on the farm had had a rather foolish custom of addressing one another as 'Comrade'. This was to be suppressed. There had also been a very strange custom, whose origin was

unknown, of marching every Sunday morning past a boar's skull which was nailed to a post in the garden. This too would be suppressed, and the skull had already been buried. His visitors might have observed, too, the green flag which flew from the masthead. If so, they would perhaps have noted that the white hoof and horn with which it had previously been marked had now been removed. It would be a plain green flag from now onwards.

He had only one criticism, he said, to make of Mr Pilkington's excellent and neighbourly speech. Mr Pilkington had referred throughout to 'Animal Farm'. He could not of course know—for he, Napoleon, was only now for the first time announcing it—that the name 'Animal Farm' had been abolished. Henceforward the farm was to be known as 'The Manor Farm'—which, he believed, was its correct and original name.

'Gentlemen,' concluded Napoleon, 'I will give you the same toast as before, but in a different form. Fill your glasses to the brim. Gentlemen, here is my toast: To the prosperity of The Manor Farm!'

There was the same hearty cheering as before, and the mugs were emptied to the dregs. But as the animals outside gazed at the scene, it seemed to them that some strange thing was happening. What was it that had altered in the faces of the pigs? Clover's old dim eyes flitted from one face to another. Some of them had five chins, some had four, some had three. But what was it that seemed to be melting and changing? Then, the applause having come to an end, the company took up their cards and continued the game that had been interrupted, and the animals crept silently away.

But they had not gone twenty yards when they stopped short. An uproar of voices was coming from the farmhouse. They rushed back and looked through the window

again. Yes, a violent quarrel was in progress. There were shoutings, bangings on the table, sharp suspicious glances, furious denials. The source of the trouble appeared to be that Napoleon and Mr Pilkington had each played an ace of spades simultaneously.

Twelve voices were shouting in anger, and they were all alike. No question, now, what had happened to the faces of the pigs. The creatures outside looked from pig to man, and from man to pig, and from pig to man again: but already it was impossible to say which was which.

November 1943–February 1944

THE END

APPENDIX I

Orwell's Proposed Preface to Animal Farm

Space was allowed in the first edition of *Animal Farm* for a Preface by the author, as the pagination of the Proof indicates (see Textual Note). This Preface never appeared and the typescript only surfaced years later when found by Ian Angus. It was published, with an introduction by Professor Bernard Crick entitled 'How the essay came to be written', in the *Times Literary Supplement*, 15 September 1972, pp. 1837–40; reprinted with Crick's introduction in the *New York Times Magazine*, 8 October 1972, pp. 12–13, 72, 74 and 76; and in *Quest* (Bombay), 79, Nov–Dec 1972, pp. 9–14, without Crick's introduction.

Professor Crick summarises some of the background to the writing of this essay and its non-publication in his *George Orwell: A Life* (1982, pp. 461–63). As he explains, Paul Potts, in his *Dante Called You Beatrice* (1960) described how he and Orwell proposed to publish *Animal Farm* on their own account as it was at the time being refused by those publishers to whom it was offered. Potts wrote that Orwell 'talked about adding a preface to it on the freedom of the Press ... That ... was not needed as Secker & Warburg, at the last minute, accepted the book' (Potts, pp. 76–77; Crick, p. 461). Professor Crick comments:

> The essential truth of Potts' account is shown by his being the only person who had ever heard of or who could remember 'the Freedom of the Press'—a fiery preface to *Animal Farm* which Orwell did in fact write as a blast against self-censorship, but fortunately did not use. It was

lost until 1971. People either did not believe Potts or did not notice his claim ... (p. 461)

'The Freedom of the Press' is reproduced here, using the typescript as copy-text, as an Appendix, as *Animal Farm* was not prefaced by the essay when it eventually did appear.

The typescript has, in the main, been reproduced as it stands. A few errors ('hugh' for 'huge' for example) have been silently emended but such variants as 'liberal' and 'Liberal' have been left as they stand in the typescript and not smoothed out as in printed texts. Thus, the *New York Times* (and *Quest*, which reprinted the *New York Times* version) has 'tolerance of plain dishonesty', which may be correct, but the typescript has 'tolerance or plain dishonesty'. As for *Nineteen Eighty-Four*, the American version changes Orwell's 'towards' to 'toward' on three occasions (see Textual Note to *Nineteen Eighty-Four*) and, most intriguingly, omits the reference to the Rector of Stiffkey, printing 'an Anglican priest who gets into trouble ... is headline news'. (The *TLS* does include the name.) This omission may be because American readers could not be expected to know who the Rector of Stiffkey was—though a note of explanation in square brackets follows the reference to Mosley: 'Sir Oswald Mosley, the British Fascist leader'—but it may, with deep irony, be censorship.

———

THE FREEDOM OF THE PRESS

This book was first thought of, so far as the central idea goes, in 1937, but was not written down until about the end of 1943. By the time when it came to be written it was obvious that there would be great difficulty in getting it published (in spite of the present book shortage which ensures that anything describable as a book will 'sell'), and in the event it was refused by four publishers. Only one of these had any ideological motive. Two had been publishing anti-Russian books for years, and the other had no noticeable political colour. One publisher

actually started by accepting the book, but after making the preliminary arrangements he decided to consult the Ministry of Information, who appear to have warned him, or at any rate strongly advised him, against publishing it. Here is an extract from his letter:

> I mentioned the reaction I had had from an important official in the Ministry of Information with regard to *Animal Farm*. I must confess that this expression of opinion has given me seriously to think. . . . I can see now that it might be regarded as something which it was highly ill-advised to publish at the present time. If the fable were addressed generally to dictators and dictatorships at large then publication would be all right, but the fable does follow, as I see now, so completely the progress of the Russian Soviets and their two dictators, that it can apply only to Russia, to the exclusion of the other dictatorships. Another thing: it would be less offensive if the predominant caste in the fable were not pigs.[1] I think the choice of pigs as the ruling caste will no doubt give offence to many people, and particularly to anyone who is a bit touchy, as undoubtedly the Russians are.

This kind of thing is not a good symptom. Obviously it is not desirable that a government department should have any power of censorship (except security censorship, which no one objects to in war time) over books which are not officially sponsored. But the chief danger to freedom of thought and speech at this moment is not the direct interference of the MOI or any official body. If publishers and editors exert themselves to keep certain topics out of print, it is not because they are frightened of prosecution but because they are frightened of public opinion. In this country intellectual cowardice is the worst enemy a writer or journalist has to face, and that fact does not seem to me to have had the discussion it deserves.

Any fairminded person with journalistic experience will

---

[1] It is not quite clear whether this suggested modification is Mr . . . 's own idea, or originated with the Ministry of Information; but it seems to have the official ring about it. [*Author's Note*]

admit that during this war *official* censorship has not been particularly irksome. We have not been subjected to the kind of totalitarian 'co-ordination' that it might have been reasonable to expect. The press has some justified grievances, but on the whole the Government has behaved well and has been surprisingly tolerant of minority opinions. The sinister fact about literary censorship in England is that it is largely voluntary. Unpopular ideas can be silenced, and inconvenient facts kept dark, without the need for any official ban. Anyone who has lived long in a foreign country will know of instances of sensational items of news—things which on their own merits would get the big headlines—being kept right out of the British press, not because the Government intervened but because of a general tacit agreement that 'it wouldn't do' to mention that particular fact. So far as the daily newspapers go, this is easy to understand. The British press is extremely centralised, and most of it is owned by wealthy men who have every motive to be dishonest on certain important topics. But the same kind of veiled censorship also operates in books and periodicals, as well as in plays, films and radio. At any given moment there is an orthodoxy, a body of ideas which it is assumed that all right-thinking people will accept without question. It is not exactly forbidden to say this, that or the other, but it is 'not done' to say it, just as in mid-Victorian times it was 'not done' to mention trousers in the presence of a lady. Anyone who challenges the prevailing orthodoxy finds himself silenced with surprising effectiveness. A genuinely unfashionable opinion is almost never given a fair hearing, either in the popular press or in the highbrow periodicals.

At this moment what is demanded by the prevailing orthodoxy is an uncritical admiration of Soviet Russia. Everyone knows this, nearly everyone acts on it. Any serious criticism of the Soviet régime, any disclosure of facts which the Soviet government would prefer to keep hidden, is next door to unprintable. And this nation-wide conspiracy to flatter our ally takes place, curiously enough, against a background of genuine intellectual tolerance. For though you are not allowed to criticise the Soviet government, at least you are reasonably free

to criticise our own. Hardly anyone will print an attack on Stalin, but it is quite safe to attack Churchill, at any rate in books and periodicals. And throughout five years of war, during two or three of which we were fighting for national survival, countless books, pamphlets and articles advocating a compromise peace have been published without interference. More, they have been published without exciting much disapproval. So long as the prestige of the USSR is not involved, the principle of free speech has been reasonably well upheld. There are other forbidden topics, and I shall mention some of them presently, but the prevailing attitude towards the USSR is much the most serious symptom. It is, as it were, spontaneous, and is not due to the action of any pressure group.

The servility with which the greater part of the English intelligentsia have swallowed and repeated Russian propaganda from 1941 onwards would be quite astounding if it were not that they have behaved similarly on several earlier occasions. On one controversial issue after another the Russian viewpoint has been accepted without examination and then publicised with complete disregard to historical truth or intellectual decency. To name only one instance, the BBC celebrated the twenty-fifth anniversary of the Red Army without mentioning Trotsky. This was about as accurate as commemorating the battle of Trafalgar without mentioning Nelson, but it evoked no protest from the English intelligentsia. In the internal struggles in the various occupied countries, the British press has in almost all cases sided with the faction favoured by the Russians and libelled the opposing faction, sometimes suppressing material evidence in order to do so. A particularly glaring case was that of Colonel Mihailovich, the Jugoslav Chetnik leader. The Russians, who had their own Jugoslav protégé in Marshal Tito, accused Mihailovich of collaborating with the Germans. This accusation was promptly taken up by the British press: Mihailovich's supporters were given no chance of answering it, and facts contradicting it were simply kept out of print. In July of 1943 the Germans offered a reward of 100,000 gold crowns for the capture of Tito, and a similar reward for the capture of Mihailovich. The British press 'splashed' the reward

for Tito, but only one paper mentioned (in small print) the reward for Mihailovich: and the charges of collaborating with the Germans continued. Very similar things happened during the Spanish civil war. Then, too, the factions on the Republican side which the Russians were determined to crush were recklessly libelled in the English leftwing [*sic*] press, and any statement in their defence even in letter form, was refused publication. At present, not only is serious criticism of the USSR considered reprehensible, but even the fact of the existence of such criticism is kept secret in some cases. For example, shortly before his death Trotsky had written a biography of Stalin. One may assume that it was not an altogether unbiased book, but obviously it was saleable. An American publisher had arranged to issue it and the book was in print—I believe the review copies had been sent out – when the USSR entered the war. The book was immediately withdrawn. Not a word about this has ever appeared in the British press, though clearly the existence of such a book, and its suppression, was a news item worth a few paragraphs.

It is important to distinguish between the kind of censorship that the English literary intelligentsia voluntarily impose upon themselves, and the censorship that can sometimes be enforced by pressure groups. Notoriously, certain topics cannot be discussed because of 'vested interests'. The best-known case is the patent medicine racket. Again, the Catholic Church has considerable influence in the press and can silence criticism of itself to some extent. A scandal involving a Catholic priest is almost never given publicity, whereas an Anglican priest who gets into trouble (e.g. the Rector of Stiffkey) is headline news. It is very rare for anything of an anti-Catholic tendency to appear on the stage or in a film. Any actor can tell you that a play or film which attacks or makes fun of the Catholic Church is liable to be boycotted in the press and will probably be a failure. But this kind of thing is harmless, or at least it is understandable. Any large organisation will look after its own interests as best it can, and overt propaganda is not a thing to object to. One would no more expect the *Daily Worker* to publicise unfavourable facts about the USSR than one would expect

the *Catholic Herald* to denounce the Pope. But then every think-ing person knows the *Daily Worker* and the *Catholic Herald* for what they are. What is disquieting is that where the USSR and its policies are concerned one cannot expect intelligent criticism or even, in many cases, plain honesty from Liberal [*sic–and throughout as typescript*] writers and journalists who are under no direct pressure to falsify their opinions. Stalin is sacro-sanct and certain aspects of his policy must not be seriously discussed. This rule has been almost universally observed since 1941, but it had operated, to a greater extent than is sometimes realised, for ten years earlier than that. Throughout that time, criticism of the Soviet régime *from the left* could only obtain a hearing with difficulty. There was a huge output of anti-Russian literature, but nearly all of it was from the Conservative angle and manifestly dishonest, out of date and actuated by sordid motives. On the other side there was an equally huge and almost equally dishonest stream of pro-Russian propa-ganda, and what amounted to a boycott on anyone who tried to discuss all-important questions in a grown-up manner. You could, indeed, publish anti-Russian books, but to do so was to make sure of being ignored or misrepresented by nearly the whole of the highbrow press. Both publicly and privately you were warned that it was 'not done'. What you said might possibly be true, but it was 'inopportune' and 'played into the hands of' this or that reactionary interest. This attitude was usually defended on the ground that the international situation, and the urgent need for an Anglo-Russian alliance, demanded it; but it was clear that this was a rationalisation. The English intelligentsia, or a great part of it, had developed a nationalistic loyalty towards the USSR, and in their hearts they felt that to cast any doubt on the wisdom of Stalin was a kind of blas-phemy. Events in Russia and events elsewhere were to be judged by different standards. The endless executions in the purges of 1936–8 were applauded by life-long opponents of capital punish-ment, and it was considered equally proper to publicise famines when they happened in India and to conceal them when they happened in the Ukraine. And if this was true before the war, the intellectual atmosphere is certainly no better now.

But now to come back to this book of mine. The reaction towards it of most English intellectuals will be quite simple: 'It oughtn't to have been published.' Naturally, those reviewers who understand the art of denigration will not attack it on political grounds but on literary ones. They will say that it is a dull, silly book and a disgraceful waste of paper. This may well be true, but it is obviously not the whole of the story. One does not say that a book 'ought not to have been published' merely because it is a bad book. After all, acres of rubbish are printed daily and no one bothers. The English intelligentsia, or most of them, will object to this book because it traduces their Leader and (as they see it) does harm to the cause of progress. If it did the opposite they would have nothing to say against it, even if its literary faults were ten times as glaring as they are. The success of, for instance, the Left Book Club over a period of four or five years shows how willing they are to tolerate both scurrility and slipshod writing, provided that it tells them what they want to hear.

The issue involved here is quite a simple one: Is every opinion, however unpopular—however foolish, even—entitled to a hearing? Put it in that form and nearly any English intellectual will feel that he ought to say 'Yes'. But give it a concrete shape, and ask, 'How about an attack on Stalin? Is *that* entitled to a hearing?', and the answer more often than not will be 'No'. In that case the current orthodoxy happens to be challenged, and so the principle of free speech lapses. Now, when one demands liberty of speech and of the press, one is not demanding absolute liberty. There always must be, or at any rate there always will be, some degree of censorship, so long as organised societies endure. But freedom, as Rosa Luxembourg [sic] said, is 'freedom for the other fellow'. The same principle is contained in the famous words of Voltaire: 'I detest what you say; I will defend to the death your right to say it.' If the intellectual liberty which without a doubt has been one of the distinguishing marks of western civilisation means anything at all, it means that everyone shall have the right to say and to print what he believes to be the truth, provided only that it does not harm the rest of the community in some

104

quite unmistakable way. Both capitalist democracy and the western versions of Socialism have till recently taken that principle for granted. Our Government, as I have already pointed out, still makes some show of respecting it. The ordinary people in the street—partly, perhaps, because they are not sufficiently interested in ideas to be intolerant about them—still vaguely hold that 'I suppose everyone's got a right to their own opinion.' It is only, or at any rate it is chiefly, the literary and scientific intelligentsia, the very people who ought to be the guardians of liberty, who are beginning to despise it, in theory as well as in practice.

One of the peculiar phenomena of our time is the renegade Liberal. Over and above the familiar Marxist claim that 'bourgeois liberty' is an illusion, there is now a widespread tendency to argue that one can only defend democracy by totalitarian methods. If one loves democracy, the argument runs, one must crush its enemies by no matter what means. And who are its enemies? It always appears that they are not only those who attack it openly and consciously, but those who 'objectively' endanger it by spreading mistaken doctrines. In other words, defending democracy involves destroying all independence of thought. This argument was used, for instance, to justify the Russian purges. The most ardent Russophile hardly believed that all of the victims were guilty of all the things they were accused of: but by holding heretical opinions they 'objectively' harmed the régime, and therefore it was quite right not only to massacre them but to discredit them by false accusations. The same argument was used to justify the quite conscious lying that went on in the leftwing press about the Trotskyists and other Republican minorities in the Spanish civil war. And it was used again as a reason for yelping against *habeas corpus* when Mosley was released in 1943.

These people don't see that if you encourage totalitarian methods, the time may come when they will be used against you instead of for you. Make a habit of imprisoning Fascists without trial, and perhaps the process won't stop at Fascists. Soon after the suppressed *Daily Worker* had been reinstated, I was lecturing to a workingmen's college in South London.

The audience were working-class and lower-middle class in-tellectuals—the same sort of audience that one used to meet at Left Book Club branches. The lecture had touched on the freedom of the press, and at the end, to my astonishment, several questioners stood up and asked me: Did I not think that the lifting of the ban on the *Daily Worker* was a great mistake? When asked why, they said that it was a paper of doubtful loyalty and ought not to be tolerated in war time. I found myself defending the *Daily Worker*, which has gone out of its way to libel me more than once. But where had these people learned this essentially totalitarian outlook? Pretty certainly they had learned it from the Communists themselves! Tolerance and decency are deeply rooted in England, but they are not indestructible, and they have to be kept alive partly by con-scious effort. The result of preaching totalitarian doctrines is to weaken the instinct by means of which free peoples know what is or is not dangerous. The case of Mosley illustrates this. In 1940 it was perfectly right to intern Mosley, whether or not he had committed any technical crime. We were fighting for our lives and could not allow a possible quisling to go free. To keep him shut up, without trial, in 1943 was an outrage. The general failure to see this was a bad symptom, though it is true that the agitation against Mosley's release was partly factitious and partly a rationalisation of other discontents. But how much of the present slide towards Fascist ways of thought is traceable to the 'anti-Fascism' of the past ten years and the unscrupulousness it has entailed?

It is important to realise that the current Russomania is only a symptom of the general weakening of the western liberal tradition. Had the MOI chipped in and definitely vetoed the publication of this book, the bulk of the English intelligentsia would have seen nothing disquieting in this. Uncritical loyalty to the USSR happens to be the current orthodoxy, and where the supposed interests of the USSR are involved they are willing to tolerate not only censorship but the deliberate falsifi-cation of history. To name one instance. At the death of John Reed, the author of *Ten Days that Shook the World*—a first-hand account of the early days of the Russian Revolution—the copy-

right of the book passed into the hands of the British Communist Party, to whom I believe Reed had bequeathed it. Some years later the British Communists, having destroyed the original edition of the book as completely as they could, issued a garbled version from which they had eliminated mentions of Trotsky and also omitted the introduction written by Lenin. If a radical intelligentsia had still existed in Britain, this act of forgery would have been exposed and denounced in every literary paper in the country. As it was there was little or no protest. To many English intellectuals it seemed quite a natural thing to do. And this tolerance or [*sic* = of ?] plain dishonesty means much more than that admiration for Russia happens to be fashionable at this moment. Quite possibly that particular fashion will not last. For all I know, by the time this book is published my view of the Soviet régime may be the generally-accepted one. But what use would that be in itself? To exchange one orthodoxy for another is not necessarily an advance. The enemy is the gramophone mind, whether or not one agrees with the record that is being played at the moment.

I am well acquainted with all the arguments against freedom of thought and speech—the arguments which claim that it cannot exist, and the arguments which claim that it ought not to. I answer simply that they don't convince me and that our civilisation over a period of four hundred years has been founded on the opposite notice. For quite a decade past I have believed that the existing Russian régime is a mainly evil thing, and I claim the right to say so, in spite of the fact that we are allies with the USSR in a war which I want to see won. If I had to choose a text to justify myself, I should choose the line from Milton:

By the known rules of ancient liberty.

The word *ancient* emphasises the fact that intellectual freedom is a deep-rooted tradition without which our characteristic western culture could only doubtfully exist. From that tradition many of our intellectuals are visibly turning away. They have accepted the principle that a book should be published or suppressed, praised or damned, not on its merits

but according to political expediency. And others who do not actually hold this view assent to it from sheer cowardice. An example of this is the failure of the numerous and vocal English pacifists to raise their voices against the prevalent worship of Russian militarism. According to those pacifists, all violence is evil, and they have urged us at every stage of the war to give in or at least to make a compromise peace. But how many of them have ever suggested that war is also evil when it is waged by the Red Army? Apparently the Russians have a right to defend themselves, whereas for us to do [so] is a deadly sin. One can only explain this contradiction in one way: that is, by a cowardly desire to keep in with the bulk of the intelligentsia, whose patriotism is directed towards the USSR rather than towards Britain. I know that the English intelligentsia have plenty of reason for their timidity and dishonesty, indeed I know by heart the arguments by which they justify themselves. But at least let us have no more nonsense about defending liberty against Fascism. If liberty means anything at all it means the right to tell people what they do not want to hear. The common people still vaguely subscribe to that doctrine and act on it. In our country—it is not the same in all countries: it was not so in republican France, and it is not so in the USA today—it is the liberals who fear liberty and the intellectuals who want to do dirt on the intellect: it is to draw attention to that fact that I have written this preface.

APPENDIX II

Orwell's Preface to the Ukrainian Edition of Animal Farm

In March 1947 Orwell wrote a Preface especially for the Ukrainian edition of *Animal Farm*, distributed in November of that year by a Ukrainian Displaced Persons Organisation in Munich. Orwell's original text has not been traced and the version given here is a re-casting back into English from the Ukrainian translation. This is substantially the text as published in *CEJL*, iii (1968), 110, but the last two paragraphs and a footnote, omitted from that printing, are here reproduced.

———

I have been asked to write a preface to the Ukrainian translation of *Animal Farm*. I am aware that I write for readers about whom I know nothing, but also that they too have probably never had the slightest opportunity to know anything about me

In this preface they will most likely expect me to say something of how *Animal Farm* originated but first I would like to say something about myself and the experiences by which I arrived at my political position.

I was born in India in 1903. My father was an official in the English administration there, and my family was one of those ordinary middle-class families of soldiers, clergymen, government officials, teachers, lawyers, doctors, etc. I was educated at Eton, the most costly and snobbish of the English Public Schools.[1] But I had only got in there by means of

---

[1] These are not public 'national schools', but something quite the opposite: exclusive and expensive residential secondary schools, scattered far apart. Until recently they admitted almost no one but the sons of rich aristocratic families. It was the dream of *nouveau riche* bankers of the nineteenth century to push their sons into a Public School. At such schools the greatest stress is laid on sport, which forms, so to speak, a lordly, tough and gentlemanly outlook. Among these schools, Eton is particularly famous. Wellington is reported to have said that the victory of Waterloo was decided on the playing fields of Eton. It is not so very long ago that an overwhelming majority of the people who in one way or another ruled England came from the Public Schools. [*Author's Note*]

a scholarship; otherwise my father could not have afforded to send me to a school of this type.

Shortly after I left school (I wasn't quite twenty years old then) I went to Burma and joined the Indian Imperial Police. This was an armed police, a sort of *gendarmerie* very similar to the Spanish *Guardia Civil* or the *Garde Mobile* in France. I stayed five years in the service. It did not suit me and made me hate imperialism, although at that time nationalist feelings in Burma were not very marked, and relations between the English and the Burmese were not particularly unfriendly. When on leave in England in 1927, I resigned from the service and decided to become a writer: at first without any especial success. In 1928–9 I lived in Paris and wrote short stories and novels that nobody would print (I have since destroyed them all). In the following years I lived mostly from hand to mouth, and went hungry on several occasions. It was only from 1934 onwards that I was able to live on what I earned from my writing. In the meantime I sometimes lived for months on end amongst the poor and half-criminal elements who inhabit the worst parts of the poorer quarters, or take to the streets, begging and stealing. At that time I associated with them through lack of money, but later their way of life interested me very much for its own sake. I spent many months (more systematically this time) studying the conditions of the miners in the north of England. Up to 1930 I did not on the whole look upon myself as a Socialist. In fact I had as yet no clearly defined political views. I became pro-Socialist more out of disgust with the way the poorer section of the industrial workers were oppressed and neglected than out of any theoretical admiration for a planned society.

In 1936 I got married. In almost the same week the civil war broke out in Spain. My wife and I both wanted to go to Spain and fight for the Spanish Government. We were ready in six months, as soon as I had finished the book I was writing. In Spain I spent almost six months on the Aragon front until, at Huesca, a Fascist sniper shot me through the throat.

In the early stages of the war foreigners were on the whole unaware of the inner struggles between the various political

parties supporting the Government. Through a series of accidents I joined not the International Brigade like the majority of foreigners, but the POUM militia—i.e. the Spanish Trotskyists.

So in the middle of 1937, when the Communists gained control (or partial control) of the Spanish Government and began to hunt down the Trotskyists, we both found ourselves amongst the victims. We were very lucky to get out of Spain alive, and not even to have been arrested once. Many of our friends were shot, and others spent a long time in prison or simply disappeared.

These man-hunts in Spain went on at the same time as the great purges in the USSR and were a sort of supplement to them. In Spain as well as in Russia the nature of the accusations (namely, conspiracy with the Facists) was the same and as far as Spain was concerned I had every reason to believe that the accusations were false. To experience all this was a valuable object lesson: it taught me how easily totalitarian propaganda can control the opinion of enlightened people in democratic countries.

My wife and I both saw innocent people being thrown into prison merely because they were suspected of unorthodoxy. Yet on our return to England we found numerous sensible and well-informed observers believing the most fantastic accounts of conspiracy, treachery and sabotage which the press reported from the Moscow trials.

And so I understood, more clearly than ever, the negative influence of the Soviet myth upon the western Socialist movement.

And here I must pause to describe my attitude to the Soviet régime.

I have never visited Russia and my knowledge of it consists only of what can be learned by reading books and newspapers. Even if I had the power, I would not wish to interfere in Soviet domestic affairs: I would not condemn Stalin and his associates merely for their barbaric and undemocratic methods. It is quite possible that, even with the best intentions, they could not have acted otherwise under the conditions prevailing there.

But on the other hand it was of the utmost importance to me that people in western Europe should see the Soviet régime for what it really was. Since 1930 I had seen little evidence that the USSR was progressing towards anything that one could truly call Socialism. On the contrary, I was struck by clear signs of its transformation into a hierarchical society, in which the rulers have no more reason to give up their power than any other ruling class. Moreover, the workers and intelligentsia in a country like England cannot understand that the USSR of today is altogether different from what it was in 1917. It is partly that they do not want to understand (i.e. they want to believe that, somewhere, a really Socialist country does actually exist), and partly that, being accustomed to comparative freedom and moderation in public life, totalitarianism is completely incomprehensible to them.

Yet one must remember that England is not completely democratic. It is also a capitalist country with great class privileges and (even now, after a war that has tended to equalise everybody) with great differences in wealth. But nevertheless it is a country in which people have lived together for several hundred years without major conflict, in which the laws are relatively just and official news and statistics can almost invariably be believed, and, last but not least, in which to hold and to voice minority views does not involve any mortal danger. In such an atmosphere the man in the street has no real understanding of things like concentration camps, mass deportations, arrests without trial, press censorship, etc. Everything he reads about a country like the USSR is automatically translated into English terms, and he quite innocently accepts the lies of totalitarian propaganda. Up to 1939, and even later, the majority of English people were incapable of assessing the true nature of the Nazi régime in Germany, and now, with the Soviet régime, they are still to a large extent under the same sort of illusion.

This has caused great harm to the Socialist movement in England, and had serious consequences for English foreign policy. Indeed, in my opinion, nothing has contributed so much to the corruption of the original idea of Socialism as the belief

that Russia is a Socialist country and that every act of its rulers must be excused, if not imitated.

And so for the past ten years I have been convinced that the destruction of the Soviet myth was essential if we wanted a revival of the Socialist movement.

On my return from Spain I thought of exposing the Soviet myth in a story that could be easily understood by almost anyone and which could be easily translated into other languages. However, the actual details of the story did not come to me for some time until one day (I was then living in a small village) I saw a little boy, perhaps ten years old, driving a huge cart-horse along a narrow path, whipping it whenever it tried to turn. It struck me that if only such animals became aware of their strength we should have no power over them, and that men exploit animals in much the same way as the rich exploit the proletariat.

I proceeded to analyse Marx's theory from the animals' point of view. To them it was clear that the concept of a class struggle between humans was pure illusion, since whenever it was necessary to exploit animals, all humans united against them: the true struggle is between animals and humans. From this point of departure, it was not difficult to elaborate the story. I did not write it out till 1943, for I was always engaged on other work which gave me no time; and in the end I included some events, for example the Teheran Conference, which were taking place while I was writing. Thus the main outlines of the story were in my mind over a period of six years before it was actually written.

I do not wish to comment on the work; if it does not speak for itself, it is a failure. But I should like to emphasise two points: first, that although the various episodes are taken from the actual history of the Russian Revolution, they are dealt with schematically and their chronological order is changed; this was necessary for the symmetry of the story. The second point has been missed by most critics, possibly because I did not emphasise it sufficiently. A number of readers may finish the book with the impression that it ends in the complete reconciliation of the pigs and the humans. That was not my

intention; on the contrary I meant it to end on a loud note of discord, for I wrote it immediately after the Teheran Conference which everybody thought had established the best possible relations between the USSR and the West. I personally did not believe that such good relations would last long; and, as events have shown, I wasn't far wrong.

I don't know what more I need add. If anyone is interested in personal details, I should add that I am a widower with a son almost three years old, that by profession I am a writer, and that since the beginning of the war I have worked mainly as a journalist.

The periodical to which I contribute most regularly is *Tribune*, a socio-political weekly which represents, generally speaking, the left wing of the Labour Party. The following of my books might most interest the ordinary reader (should any reader of this translation find copies of them): *Burmese Days* (a story about Burma), *Homage to Catalonia* (arising from my experiences in the Spanish Civil War), and *Critical Essays* (essays mainly about contemporary popular English literature and instructive more from the sociological than from the literary point of view).

APPENDIX III

Orwell's Radio Adaptation of Animal Farm

Orwell's adaptation of *Animal Farm* as a radio play was made at the end of 1946, a year in which he had been more active in radio work than at any time since leaving the BBC's Eastern Service in 1943. From the correspondence that has survived, it would appear that he was interested in developing work in radio and he corresponded in particular with his friend of long standing, Rayner Heppenstall. Heppenstall (1911–81), author, critic, and a BBC feature-writer and producer from 1945 to 1967, had also had a short spell as a schoolteacher in 1934, the year after Orwell gave up teaching. They first met in the early summer of 1935 (see Heppenstall's memoir, *Four Absentees*, 1960, Chapter VII). From August of that year, Orwell, Heppenstall and Michael Sayers shared a flat in Kentish Town. The arrangement broke up, rather violently, when Orwell trounced Heppenstall when the latter arrived back at the flat one night, very late and very drunk. The story is dramatically recounted by Heppenstall in Chapter XI of his memoir. Nevertheless they remained on good terms. Heppenstall was to visit Orwell when he was in hospital in Aylesford, Kent, in 1938 and several times he went to see him as he lay dying in University College Hospital in 1949. On 24 August 1943, when Orwell was working for the BBC and Heppenstall was serving in the artillery, Orwell invited Heppenstall to write a 'featurised story' in the manner of Orwell's adaptations of *Crainquebille*, by Anatole France, and Ignazio Silone's *The Fox*. The 'featurised story' was a genre that seemed to have a particular appeal for Orwell and it may have influenced his radio adaptation of *Animal Farm*.

Heppenstall was invalided out of the army in April 1945 and shortly after joined the BBC. In the following year Orwell wrote for him a dramatisation of *The Voyage of the Beagle* as the second in a series called *Voyages of Discovery* which Heppenstall was producing. This was broadcast on 29 March 1946 (and Orwell's script and introduction will be included at the appropriate point in *The Complete Works*). On 22 June 1946, Orwell signed a contract with the BBC for an adaptation of *Little Red Riding Hood*, to be broadcast in *Children's Hour* on 9 July. That adaptation, the sub-title of *Animal Farm* (A Fairy Story), his earlier version of *The Emperor's New Clothes*, and references in his letters, all reveal the fascination fairy stories had for him about this time. Later that summer, as Heppenstall recalls in his memoir and as the correspondence in the BBC and Orwell Archives confirm, he and Orwell discussed the possibility of Orwell adapting Maupassant's *Boule de Suif* and making contributions to a series of imaginary conversations.* Orwell had, in fact, written such a conversation (with Swift) in his Eastern Service days and a version was published in *The Listener*, 26 November 1942. He was interested in what parliamentary candidates really thought as distinct from what they maintained in their public statements and he suggested a conversation with Lenin and a defence of Pontius Pilate, a name that made Heppenstall wince. In the event Orwell could not spare the time to contribute.

In addition to programme proposals, the two men corresponded about the possibility of Heppenstall travelling to Jura to stay with Orwell for a week or so. Heppenstall asked Orwell on 20 May if he was 'visitable'. With some enthusiasm, Orwell invited him to come to stay with him

---

* In 1948, Heppenstall was to publish a volume of eight radio scripts which he had produced and edited entitled *Imaginary Conversations*. The subjects included a painting of Aristotle's Mother, Milton, Cardinal Newman, Hamlet aboard the pirate ship, and Ophelia in the process of losing her mind; among the authors were C. V. Wedgwood, Herbert Read (twice), and V. S. Pritchett; one of those who composed special music was Elizabeth Lutyens. The book was published by Secker & Warburg.

and a date, first 14 July, then 9 July was settled upon. Orwell twice sent detailed travelling instructions and warned Heppenstall that he might have to walk the last seven miles of the journey. He also mentioned – it was a time when food was still severely rationed in Britain – that it would be helpful if he could bring some food, especially fats, sugar, tea and a pot of jam.

In the event, Heppenstall sent a telegram on Saturday 6 July saying he would not be coming. He wrote the next week giving three reasons for this late cancellation. He had to make difficult programme arrangements (something upon which he enlarges rather obscurely in his memoir, pp. 166–67); he had taken fright at the journey; and he did not relish the thought of fruitless arguments with Paul Potts (who was also staying at Barnhill with Orwell). Heppenstall's letters indicate his anxiety about the reaction he anticipated from Orwell, but Orwell took the cancellation with equanimity.

On 3 October, at almost exactly the same time that the Drama Department decided it was not interested in the proposal for a dramatisation of *Boule de Suif* (Heppenstall conveyed the information to Orwell on 4 October), G. R. Barnes (Director of Talks for the Home Service when Orwell joined the BBC), instructed the Director of Features to commission Orwell to adapt *Animal Farm* for the Third Programme. Production was entrusted to Rayner Heppenstall and all involved were enjoined to keep the proposal under their hats until the moment when the BBC chose to give the programme publicity. In his initiating memorandum, Barnes said that it would be unfortunate if details leaked out for they 'would inevitably be given the wrong interpretation'. Heppenstall wrote to Orwell on 9 October, commissioning the adaptation and offering two live broadcasts and a recorded repeat. A length of ninety minutes was suggested but if Orwell felt that this was too restricting he could propose a modification – Orwell did. On 17 November he telephoned Heppenstall and suggested that the adaptation be split into

two parts each lasting one hour with a short interval between them. Heppenstall was prepared to go along with this if it proved necessary, especially as the book divided naturally into two, but he also thought that as Orwell's writing for radio tended to be rather diffuse, it would not be difficult to cut his script to ninety minutes. And that is what happened.

Orwell was offered £105 for the first broadcast and £52.50 for each repeat. He signed the contract accepting this fee on 31 October 1946. Antony Hopkins (1921–) was commissioned to write incidental music and music for the song, 'Beasts of England'. Hopkins, Heppenstall thought, was an appropriate choice because the music was required to be satirical. Unfortunately, a search by the BBC has not located the score and Mr Hopkins does not know its whereabouts.

When Heppenstall commissioned the adaptation he suggested as complete a dramatisation as possible, 'with connecting narrative reduced to little more than statements of time and place'. On 11 December, at about the time Orwell was to have completed his script—it was due early in December—Grace Wyndham Goldie (1900–86) of the Home Service Talks Department, wrote to Orwell asking him whether he would act as an independent critic of Third Programme drama on Friday, 24 January 1947 (the week after *Animal Farm* was due to be broadcast). This was an experimental series then being inaugurated, she explained, and Orwell was chosen because in that week three plays by Bernard Shaw were to be broadcast. Two days later, Orwell declined. He might not be in London that week, he wrote, and added, 'also I am, as you perhaps know, a very poor broadcaster'. In the event, he was in London that week, but in mid-December, when he replied, he may have considered going up to Jura in the week proposed for the broadcast instead of, or in addition to, the first week of 1947, when he was in Jura.

Orwell's script runs to seventy-nine folios, including preliminary details and opening and closing announcements

(with variants for the live repeat). The script deposited in the BBC Play Library was that used by the actor who played Mr Jones, Pig 2 and Young Cock – Frank Atkinson – and it was marked up to indicate his speeches, cues and movements. The script was presumably typed by BBC typists from Orwell's original as marked up by Heppenstall for effects and music; it was certainly not the product of the typewriter Orwell was using at the time and there are differences between his idiosyncratic spellings (such as 'today') and those of the script (which has 'to-day'). The script is marked with cuts and a few additional lines have been written in as well as the audio indications (see below). The script has now been reduced to microfiche and the original destroyed so it is not possible to distinguish colours of markings and in one or two places it is not quite clear whether a new cut has been made with a very light crayon or whether the original cut has been only partially erased. It looks as if omissions were also made by pasting paper over passages of text, e.g., $2\frac{1}{2}$ lines of Scene 348 (Narrator), possibly 3 lines of Sc. 444 (Napoleon), and 10 lines of Sc. 445 (Narrator). More puzzling is a cut from the end of Sc. 5 (Narrator) to Sc. 15. Most of this would seem to have been done prior to retyping by BBC typists because there is no jump in foliation – there should be at least one and perhaps two pages between script pages 1 and 2 to accommodate the missing scenes. It looks as if these scenes were cut from Orwell's original and then, after retyping, a further cut was made during rehearsal at the foot of script page 1 and the head of script page 2. It is not possible to allocate these missing lines. If one page were cut, some 45 lines have been omitted; if two pages, some 75 lines. A further difficulty in making calculations is that three page references given in the cast list as originally typed – 24, 24 and 52 – seem to correspond to 28, 28 and 61 in the script we have. (Scene numbers have been substituted in this edition.) A reference to page 20 (for Sc. 160) *does* correspond, however.

The extant script is some 2,200 lines in length to which

15½ lines can be added to represent paste-overs; a further 45–75 lines appear to have been cut from the beginning of the script–making a total of some 2,260 to 2,290 lines. Approximately 1,710 lines were broadcast (some very short, of course), including the announcements. The script is marked as taking 81′ 50″ to broadcast (of the ninety minutes alloted) on 14 January 1947 and 82′ 25″ on 15 January. It is not possible to be too precise but the figures that can be recovered indicate a running time prior to marking up cuts of about 109 minutes. Some 490 lines are known to have been cut of which 253 were spoken by the Narrator. In other words, a little more than half the cuts affected the Narrator. There is no reason to doubt that the passages cut from the start of the programme did not also chiefly affect the Narrator, especially as he would be 'setting the scene'. In view of Heppenstall's comments about narration before the script was written and after the broadcast (see below), it is significant that the script was cut quite sharply to less than the full time allowed for the broadcast. About 150 lines more than necessary were cut.

Following the two live broadcasts, Rayner Heppenstall wrote to Orwell asking for his reactions to the broadcast and the press notices. Heppenstall said he was inclined to think that there had been too much narration–that the adaptation was not sufficiently ruthless. In the same letter he asked for further ideas for Third Programme broadcasts. Orwell replied:

Thanks for your letter. Re. Animal Farm. I had a number of people here [27B Canonbury Square, Islington, London, N1] to listen to it on the first day, and they all seemed to think it was good, and [Hugh Gordon] Porteous [literary critic and sinologist], who had not read the book, grasped what it [sic] was happening after a few minutes. I also had one or two fan letters and the press notices were good except on my native ground, ie. Tribune. As to what I thought myself, it's hard to get a detached view, because when-

ever I write anything for the air I have the impression
it has been spoiled, owing to its inevitably coming out
different to one's conception of it. I must say I don't
agree about there being too much narrator. If anything I
thought there should have been more explanation.
People are always yearning to get rid of the narrator, but
it seems to me that until certain problems have been
overcome you only get rid of the narrator at the expense of having to play a lot of stupid tricks in order to
let people know what is happening. The thing is to
make the narrator a good turn in himself. But that
means writing serious prose, which people don't, and
making the actors stick to it instead of gagging and
trying to make everything homey and naturalistic.

I can't write or promise to write anything more
at present, I am too busy. I've still got ideas about fairy
stories. I wish they would dig up and re-b'cast my
adaptation of the Emperor's New Clothes. It was done
on the Eastern and African services, but in those days
I wasn't well-connected enough to crash the Home. I
expect the discs would have been scrapped, however. I
had them illicitly re-recorded at a commercial studio,
but that lot of discs got lost. I've often pondered over
Cinderella, which of course is the tops so far as fairy
stories go but on the face of it is too visual to be
suitable for the air. But don't you think one could
make the godmother turn her into a wonderful singer
who could sing a higher note than anyone else, or
something of that kind? The best way would be if she
had a wonderful voice but could not sing in tune, like
Trilby, and the godmother cured this. One could
make it quite comic with the wicked sisters singing in
screeching voices. It might be worth talking over
some time. Give my love to Margaret.

Heppenstall took up some of Orwell's points on 29
January, being particularly anxious to convince him 'about
the business of narration'. Narration, he argued, involved
'marked change of pace', and straight reading and Orwell's
dramatic presentation didn't mix. He strongly resisted the

idea that actors would be allowed to gag in one of his productions.

Following the two live broadcasts on 14 and 15 January 1947, a recording of the first performance was broadcast on Sunday, 2 February 1947 at 6.00 p.m.

In April 1947, Orwell gave permission for a Dutch version of *Animal Farm* to be broadcast (for which he was paid £20 for the first transmission and £10 for each subsequent broadcast). Heppenstall produced a second adaptation of *Animal Farm* after Orwell's death. This was made by Peter Duval Smith and broadcast on 3 March 1952. The reason for a new adaptation, Heppenstall explained to Ian Willison, was 'a certain lameness in Orwell's version'. There seems little doubt that Heppenstall would have preferred less narration in that first broadcast and, had time allowed, it is possible Orwell might have been persuaded to recast some of his adaptation. On the other hand, Orwell clearly had a leaning towards narrative – the 'featurised story' – and even Peter Hall's very successful musical version for the National Theatre (to mark 1984), still makes significant use of narrative, the Boy-Narrator having some ten per cent of the lines.*

The cast rehearsed the play from 11.00 to 16.15 on 12 January 1947, 11.00 to 17.30 on the 13th, and from 11.00 'onwards' on the 14th. There was a further rehearsal from 14.30 to 18.00, with a playback of the first performance, prior to the second live performance, which began at 19.25. On 14 January the singers had two two-hour rehearsals and the orchestra a three-hour rehearsal.

The text reproduced here is that used by the actor, Frank Atkinson, and in addition to the parts given above, he doubled (with various others) as a sheep and a cow. His cue-light indications and his markings of which speeches are his are not reproduced, but instructions relating to

---

* *George Orwell's Animal Farm*, adapted by Peter Hall with lyrics by Adrian Mitchell and music by Richard Peaslee; first performed at the Cottesloe Theatre, London, 25 April 1984; published by Methuen, London, 1985.

playing areas are given because these enable a little of the effect of a radio broadcast to be conveyed. The terms used, and their meanings, are:

Annexe: a separate area of the recording studio with its own microphone(s) and cue lights.

Tent: a 'dead' area of the recording studio, shielded, rather like a tent, with sound-absorbing screens around and above, to give a non-reverberating effect, as if for an open space. This would also be equipped with its own microphone(s) and cue lights, and possibly concrete flagstones, a gravel tray and the like for different walking effects.

Close [Mike]: speak very close to the microphone.

Off Mike: speak with the head turned away from the microphone to give the effect of distance. As ribbon microphones would have been used, these movements could be achieved by quite a slight movement of the head and upper body.

Open [Mike]: If the audio engineer is very preoccupied, he might leave a microphone active at a time (e.g. during music off) when those around it might think it safe to talk or move about. This is an indication that the microphone is alive and silence must be kept.

Narrator's Box: cubicle from which Narrator spoke; it might be used by actors on occasion (as at Sc. 496).

The text as performed is printed in roman type with passages cut given in a smaller typeface. Directions typed in the script are reproduced in italic within *round* brackets: words written onto the script (none by Orwell) are printed in italic but within *square* brackets. Passages which may have been fresh cuts, or which may have been restored by erasure of the lines crossing them through are printed in large-face roman type within half brackets. Consequential changes have been made silently as have corrections of typing errors. One or two words cannot be deciphered. Some effects are numbered and some are not. At page turn-

overs, scene numbers are sometimes repeated and sometimes advanced. The original numbering has not been changed in order that evidence of cuts and changes should not be obscured.

I have concentrated in setting the context for this adaptation on Orwell's BBC activities in 1946. He was, however, busy in other fields. Several important essays were published in 1946 including 'The Prevention of Literature', 'The Politics of Starvation', 'Decline of the English Murder', 'Politics and the English Language', 'James Burnham and the Managerial Revolution', 'Politics vs Literature' and 'How the Poor Die'. He continued reviewing—his review of Zamyatin's *We* appeared in *Tribune* on 4 January 1946—and he had a regular column in the *Manchester Evening News* and was writing 'As I Please' for *Tribune*. *Animal Farm* was published by Harcourt, Brace in New York in August 1946, just a year after its publication by Fredric Warburg. However, believing that he had 'been doing too much hack journalism for several years past' (as he wrote to Stafford Cottman on 25 April 1946) he took a break from journalism from May to October. For much of that time he was at Barnhill on the Isle of Jura and during the summer he began writing *Nineteen Eighty-Four* (though it had been in his mind for some time). He wrote to Heppenstall on 5 September 1946: 'I am also starting another book. I have hardly done anything to it, but I want to get enough done before coming back to give me courage to go on while writing articles etc.' What he got down on paper was probably the fifty or so pages which included Goldstein's Testament, fourteen pages of which have survived (see the facsimile edition, *Nineteen Eighty-Four: The Extant Manuscript*, pp. 196–209).

For enabling this script to be published, I must express my warm thanks to the BBC and its Play Librarians, Allan Ferris, Sue McCoulough and their staff. This has only been made possible because the BBC has looked after this script—and so many other scripts and documents—for so many decades. I am also grateful for the assistance given me by

my youngest son, Hugh, of a new generation of BBC Audio Supervisors, for interpreting the markings on the script.

———

Animal Farm
Written by George Orwell, and
Produced by Rayner Heppenstall
Music Composed and Directed by Antony Hopkins

CAST*

1. Jones, Pig 2, Young Cock	Frank Atkinson
2. Mrs Jones, Molly, Pigeon 2	Marjorie Westbury
3. Farmer 1, Man, Pig 1	Deryck Guyler
4. Farmer 2, Cock, Pig 3	Charles Maunsell
5. Narrator	Ronald Simpson
6. Major, Pig 4	Raf de la Torre
7. Napoleon	Norman Shelley
8. Snowball	Andrew Churchman
9. Squealer	John Chandos
10. Boxer	Richard George
11. Clover, Pigeon 3	Betty Hardy
12. Benjamin, Dog, Owl, Pig (Sc. 231), Horse (Sc. 236, 489)	Bryan Powley
13. Muriel, Dog, Pigeon 4, Young Goat	Vivienne Chatterton
14. Young Horse, Another Man	Hugh Munro
15. Cow, Dog, Pigeon 5, Young Sheep	Gladys Spencer
16. Pigeon, Young Mare	Margot van der Burgh

1 3 4 6 12 14 15 16 double Sheep
1 3 4 6 12 14 double Cows (Sc. 160)†

* As listed in script.
† The BBC Variety Singers and an unnamed orchestra also took part.

125

1. ANNOUNCER: This is the BBC Third Programme. Tonight we present *Animal Farm* by George Orwell, adapted for broadcasting by the author. *Animal Farm* . . . a fairy story . . .

2. EFFECTS: (*Heavy boots clumping over flagstones and dying away. An owl hoots twice.*)

3. NARRATOR: Ten o'clock had struck, and the Manor Farm was just settling down for the night—or ought to have been settling down, at any rate. Mr Jones, the farmer, had made his way up to bed, a little drunk as usual. But all through the farm buildings there was a stirring and a fluttering as soon as the bedroom light went out . . .

4. EFFECTS: (*Creep in bleating of sheep and crooning of hens, pigeons, etc.*)

5. NARRATOR (*straight on*): . . . The animals were creeping out of their stalls. Word had gone round during the day that old Major, the prize Middle White boar, had had a wonderful dream last night and now wished to address the other animals on a matter of great importance. It had been agreed that they were all to meet in the big barn as soon as Mr Jones was safely asleep . . .*

15. CAST & EFFECTS: (*Rustling of straw, crooning of hens and sound of hoofs scraping and wings fluttering, etc., as each animal is mentioned.*)

16. NARRATOR: . . . At one end of the big barn, on a sort of raised platform, Major was already sitting on his bed of straw, under a lantern that hung from a beam. He was twelve years old and he had lately grown

---

* See p. 119 regarding section omitted from here to Scene 15.

rather stout, but he was still a fine figure of a pig, with a very wise, benevolent expression of face. Before long the other animals began to arrive and make themselves comfortable after their own fashion. First came the three dogs, Bluebell, Jessie and Pincher, then came the pigs, who settled down in the straw immediately in front of the platform. The hens perched themselves on the window sills, the pigeons fluttered up to the rafters, the cows and sheep lay down behind the pigs and began chewing the cud. The two cart-horses, Boxer and Clover, came in together, walking very slowly and setting down their vast hairy hoofs with great care, lest there should be any chickens or ducklings concealed in the straw. Then Mollie, the pretty white mare who drew Mr Jones's trap on market days, came mincing daintily in, chewing at a lump of sugar. She took a place near the front and began flirting her white mane, hoping to draw attention to the red ribbons it was plaited with. Then came Muriel, the goat, and last of all came Benjamin, the donkey, with his long ears and his grizzled, obstinate-looking muzzle, the oldest animal on the farm, and the worst-tempered. (*Effects out.*)

17. MAJOR:	Comrades!
18. VOICES:	Sh! He's starting.
	(*Ad lib. till* MAJOR *starts. Audience reaction through following.*)
19. MAJOR:	(*Clears his throat and grunts.*) Comrades! You have already heard, I think, about the strange dream which I had last night. But I will come to the dream presently. I have something else to say first. I do not believe, comrades, that I shall

be with you for many months more, and before I die, I feel it my duty to pass on to you such wisdom as I have acquired. I have had a long life, I have had much time for thought as I lay alone in my stall, and I think I may claim to understand the nature of life on this earth as well as any animal now living. It is about this that I wish to speak to you.

Now, comrades, what is the nature of this life of ours? Let us face it: our lives are miserable, laborious and short. We are born, we are given just so much food as will keep the breath in our bodies, and those of us who are capable of it are forced to work to the last atom of our strength; and the very instant that our usefulness comes to an end, we are slaughtered with hideous cruelty. No animal in England knows the meaning of happiness or leisure after he is a year old. No animal in England is free. The life of an animal is misery and slavery: that is the plain truth.

But is this simply part of the order of nature? Is it because this land of ours is so poor that it cannot afford a decent life to those who dwell upon it? No, comrades, a thousand times no! The soil of England is fertile, and its climate is good. This single farm of ours could support ten times the number of animals that now live upon it. Why is it, then, that we continue in this miserable condition? Who is it that steals the produce of our labour from us? Tell me, comrades, what is the worst enemy that we animals have to contend with?

20. BENJAMIN: Fleas.

128

[Laughter]

21. MAJOR: No, comrade Benjamin, no. There are worse things than fleas, believe me.

22. CLOVER: The whip.

23. MAJOR: That is nearer the mark. I will answer my own question, comrades. *Man* is our enemy. Man is the only real enemy we have. We are poor because the produce of our labour is stolen from us by human beings. *There* is the answer to all our problems. It is all summed up in a single word—Man. Remove Man from the scene, and the root cause of hunger and overwork has vanished for ever.

Man is the only animal that consumes without producing. He does not give milk, he does not lay eggs, he is too weak to pull the plough, he cannot run fast enough to catch rabbits. Yet he is lord of all the animals. Our labour tills the fields, our dung fertilises it, and yet there is not one of us that owns more than his bare skin. And even the miserable lives that we lead are not allowed to reach their natural span. No animal escapes the cruel knife in the end. Think of the slaughterhouse, comrades! Think of the butcher's shop! To that horror we all must come—cows, sheep, pigs, hens, everyone. Even the horses and the dogs are no better off. You, Boxer, the very day that those great muscles of yours lose their power, Jones will sell you to the knacker, who will cut your throat and boil you down for the fox-hounds. As for the dogs, when they grow old and toothless, Jones ties a brick round their necks and drowns them in the

nearest pond. *That* is the reward they give us for a lifetime spent in their service.

24. COW:	He's right!
25. BOXER:	I never thought of it like that before.
26. NAPOLEON:	It's Jones who robs us of everything.
27. SNOWBALL:	Jones makes us work, and Jones keeps us hungry.
28. SQUEALER:	Down with Jones!
29. SHEEP:	DOWN WITH JONES! DEATH TO JONES!
30. MAJOR:	Comrades, it is not enough to say 'Death to Jones'. 'Death to Humanity' must be our motto: 'Death to Mankind!' What then must we do? Why, work night and day, body and soul, for the overthrow of the human race! That is my message to you, comrades: Rebellion! I do not know when this Rebellion will come, it might be in a week or in a hundred years, but I know, as surely as I see this straw beneath my feet, that sooner or later justice will be done.
31. ALL:	(*Cheers.*) [*Hurray!*]
32. MAJOR:	And remember, comrades, your resolution must never falter. No argument must lead you astray. Never listen when they tell you that Man and the animals have a common interest, that the prosperity of one is the prosperity of the other. Man serves the interests of no creature except himself. Whatever goes upon two legs is an enemy. Whatever goes upon four legs, or has wings, is a friend. And remember, too, that in fighting against Man you must not come to resemble him. Even when you have conquered him, do not adopt his vices. No animal must ever

130

live in a house, or sleep in a bed, or wear clothes, or drink alcohol, or smoke tobacco, or touch money, or engage in trade. All the habits of Man are evil. And above all, no animal must ever tyrannise over his own kind. Weak or strong, clever or simple, we are all brothers. No animal must ever kill any other animal. All animals are equal.

33. SHEEP (*murmuring*): All animals are equal. All animals are equal.

34. MAJOR: And now, comrades, I will tell you about my dream of last night.. I cannot describe that dream to you. It was a dream of the earth as it will be when Man has vanished. But it reminded me of something which I had long forgotten. Many years ago, when I was a little pig, my mother and the other sows used to sing an old song of which they knew only the tune and the first three words. I had known it in my infancy, but it had long passed out of my mind. Last night, however, it came back to me in my dream: and what is more, the words also came back—words, I am certain, which were sung by the animals of long ago and have been lost to memory for generations. I will sing you that song now, comrades. I am old and my voice is hoarse, but when I have taught you the tune, you can sing it better for yourselves. It is called 'Beasts of England'.

35. ALL (*murmuring*): 'Beasts of England'. 'Beasts of England'.
MUSIC 1
36. MAJOR (*clears his throat. Singing*):

Beasts of England, beasts of Ireland,
Beasts of every land and clime,

Hearken to my joyful tidings
Of the golden future time.

Soon or late the day is coming,
Tyrant Man shall be o'erthrown,
And the fruitful fields of England
Shall be trod by beasts alone.

CHORUS: Beasts of England, etc.
MAJOR (*declaiming with* CHORUS *accompaniment*):
            Rings shall vanish from our noses,
            And the harness from our back,
            Bit and spur shall rust forever,
            Cruel whips no more shall crack.

            Bright will shine the fields of England,
            Purer shall its waters be,
            Sweeter yet shall blow its breezes,
            On that day that sets us free.

CHORUS: Beasts of England, beasts of Ireland,
            Beasts of every land and clime,
            Hearken well and spread my tidings
            Of the golden future time.
            (*Repeat refrain to gun below. Fade down
            and hold under following.*)

37. NARRATOR: The animals sang 'Beasts of England' right through
                five times in succession, and might have continued
                singing it all night if they had not been interrupted.
                Unfortunately, however, the uproar awakened Mrs
                Jones, who prodded her husband in the ribs.
                [*Annexe.*] (*Bed creaking. The Jones's
                voices should sound coarse and vulgar
                compared with those of the animals.*)

38. MRS JONES: Albert! Albert! Wake up! What are
                them animals up to? [*Snoring.*] Can't
                you 'ear that noise they're making?
                Why it's fit to waken the dead.

39. JONES (*grunts*): (*Sound of distant singing.*)
                What's come over 'em? Sounds like—

lumme, there's a fox in the yard! 'Ere! Where'd I put that gun?

(*Stumbling and furniture.*)★

Here she is.

(*Window opening. Bang. Song stops dead. Bang again. Commotion of squawking hens, fluttering of wings, shots, rattle of hoofs, etc., dying out after a few seconds.*)

MUSIC 2 ('*Beasts of England' in solemn minor.*)

42.† NARRATOR: Three nights later old Major died peacefully in his sleep. His body was buried at the foot of the orchard.

That was early in March. During the next three months there was much secret activity. In the minds of the more intelligent animals there was now but one thought—to make ready for the Rebellion which Major had foretold. The work of teaching and organising the others fell naturally upon the pigs, who were generally recognised as being the cleverest of the animals. Pre-eminent among the pigs were two young boars named Snowball and Napoleon, whom Mr Jones was rearing up for sale. Napoleon was a large, rather fierce-looking Berkshire boar, the only Berkshire on the farm, not much of a talker, but with a reputation for getting his own way. Snowball was a more vivacious pig than Napoleon, quicker in speech and more inventive, but was not considered to have the same depth of character. All the other male pigs on the farm were porkers. The best known among them was a small fat pig named Squealer, with very round cheeks, twinkling eyes, nimble movements and a shrill voice. He was a

★ Effects noise of stumbling into furniture.
† No 40 or 41.

brilliant talker, and when he was arguing some difficult point he had a way of skipping from side to side
and whisking his tail which was somehow very
persuasive.

These three had elaborated Major's
teaching into a complete system of
thought, to which they gave the name
of Animalism. Several nights a week,
after Mr Jones was asleep, they held secret
meetings in the barn and expounded the principles
of Animalism to the others.

43. COCK: But listen, Comrade Snowball. You say that it is our
duty to get rid of Mr Jones. But it is Mr Jones who
feeds us. Surely, if he were gone, we should all starve
to death?

44. COW: And you said just now, comrade—and Major said
the same—that this Rebellion of yours is completely
inevitable. But if it is going to happen anyway, what
difference does it make whether we prepare for it or
not?

45. PIG 2: Besides, what do we care what happens after we are
dead? Why not enjoy ourselves while we have the
chance?

46. SNOWBALL: Totally contrary to the spirit of
Animalism, comrades! Freedom is
knowledge of necessity. Let me
explain——

47. MOLLIE: What *I* want to know is, will there still
be sugar after the Rebellion?

48. CLOVER: Mollie, you think of nothing except
yourself!

49. NAPOLEON: No, certainly not. When we are in
control of this farm, it will have to be
self-supporting. We have no means of
making sugar here.

50. SQUEALER: Besides, don't you know sugar is bad
for your teeth?

51. MOLLIE: And shall I still be allowed to wear

ribbons in my mane?

52. SNOWBALL: Comrade, those ribbons you are so devoted to are the badge of slavery. Can you not understand that liberty is more important than ribbons?

53. MOLLIE (*doubtfully*): Yes. I suppose so.

54. BOXER: Horses do not need sugar. We can work better on oats and hay. As for the ribbons, I had not thought of it like that before, but Comrade Snowball is right. I shall never wear ribbons again.
I am not good at thinking things out for myself; but I am strong, I know how to work. The pigs are the cleverest. Let the pigs show us what to do, and we will do it.

55. SQUEALER: Very true, Boxer! Till the Rebellion is accomplished, some must lead and others must follow. We pigs will be the leaders—in a purely democratic spirit, of course, comrades!

56. ALL: Of course ... Democratic? ... What's democratic? ... Follow, eh? etc. (*General chatter—lose under following.*)

57. NARRATOR: [?]★ The only animal on the farm who refused to become excited about the Rebellion was Benjamin, the donkey. Benjamin had never been a talkative animal. He would often go for days on end without uttering a word, and when he did open his mouth it was usually to make some cynical remark—for instance, he would say that God had given him a tail to keep the flies off, but that he would sooner have had no tail and no flies.

58. CLOVER: What do *you* think about the Rebellion, Benjamin?

59. BENJAMIN: I think that donkeys live a long time.

★ Indecipherable; possibly 'Animal noise' of preceding direction.

60. BOXER [*Annexe*]: But you do believe, comrade, that the Rebellion is going to happen?

61. BENJAMIN: Everything happens sooner or later. On the other hand nothing ever changes, except names.

62. CLOVER: There is a thing that I have noticed about you, Benjamin. You are the only animal on this farm that never laughs. Why do you never laugh?

63. BENJAMIN: So far as I know, there is nothing very much to laugh at.

64. SNOWBALL: No pessimism, comrade! There will be plenty to laugh at when Jones is gone. Do you not suppose that we shall be happier when we are our own masters?

65. BENJAMIN: We shall be very much the same—not less happy, and not more happy. The conditions of life do not change. In winter there is the cold, and in summer there are the flies: there is never quite enough to eat, and there is always work. I was working before any of you were born, and I shall be working after you are all dead. Donkeys live a long time. None of you has ever seen a dead donkey.

66. BOXER: Work is not an evil. I think that when Jones is gone there will be more food, but there will not be less work. I have worked hard for Jones, and I will work twice as hard for the Rebellion. My brain is not good, but my muscles are good. Count on me.

67. CLOVER, MURIEL, COCK, PIGEON: And me! And me! And me! And me! (*Fade.*)

68. NARRATOR: Now, as it turned out, the Rebellion was achieved much earlier and more easily than anyone had expected. June came, and the hay was almost ready for

cutting. On Midsummer's Eve, which was a Saturday, Mr Jones went into Willingdon, the neighbouring market town, and got so drunk at the Red Lion that he did not come back till midday on Sunday. His men had milked the cows in the early morning and then had gone out rabbiting without even bothering to feed the animals. When Mr Jones got back he immediately went to sleep on the drawing-room sofa with the *News of the World* over his face, so that when evening came the animals were still unfed. At last they could stand it no longer.

69. ALL [*Annexe*]:	(*Fade in general complaint.*)
70. COCK:	Why should we put up with this? We work for him, and he starves us.
71. COW:	If he won't feed us, we'll feed ourselves. Let's go down to the meadow and eat the hay.
72. PIGEON:	No! I know where there's better food than that. The store shed!
73. COCK:	Come on, come on!
74. NAPOLEON:	To the store shed, everybody.
75. COCK:	Here we are. Open the door.
76. EFFECTS:	(*Thumping.*)
77. PIGEON:	It's locked.
78. PIG 2:	Break it in, somebody.
79. NAPOLEON:	One of you cows, get your horn into the crack. That's right.
80. EFFECTS:	(*Sound of door being burst open. Loud cheers.*)
81. COCK:	Look at all that food!
82. MOLLY:	Look at that pile of oats!
83. SQUEALER:	Break open those bags of meal.
84. COW:	Beans! Who likes beans!
85. PIGEON:	Here are some biscuits for the dogs.
86. COCK:	Help yourselves, everybody!

(*Sounds of eating. Continue and hold under.*)

87. NARRATOR: But just as the starving animals were in the act of helping themselves, Jones and his four men appeared in the yard with whips in their hands. (*Commotion up.*)

88. JONES [*Annexe. Close*]: *Now* what are them brutes up to? Can't turn your back one bleeding moment. By God, if they haven't broke open the store shed! Steal my corn, would they? Get your whips ready, boys. [*Off mike.*] We'll learn 'em a lesson.

89. COCK: Look out! Here comes Jones!

90. SHEEP: They've got whips! They've got whips!

91. NAPOLEON: Stand firm, comrades. We'll beat them, whips or no whips.

92. JONES [*Off mike*]: Out of it quick, you devils!

93. EFFECTS: (*Crack of a whip. Squeal of a pig.*)

94. SQUEALER: He hit me! He hit me! Run, comrades, run! Every animal for himself!

95. SNOWBALL: No! This is our chance. Forward, comrades! Forward in the name of the Rebellion! Death to Jones!
(*Confused uproar of animal noises. Shouts of* JONES *and his men and trampling.*)

96. JONES [*Close*]: What's come over 'em? Never seen 'em take on like this before. Go on, you, don't stand lookin' at 'em! Give 'em the whip!

97. A MAN (*panting*): Can't do nothin' with 'em, sir. Seems like they're—'ere! Keep off, you devil, you!

98. EFFECTS: (*Crack of a whip.*)

99. SNOWBALL: On to them, comrades! Don't let them rest.

100. MAN: 'Ere! They're comin' after us again. I'm getting out of this.

101. ANOTHER MAN: Me too.

102. JONES [Close]: Stop, you bloody cowards! [Going off.] Come back! (Gives a cry of pain.)

103. ANIMAL VOICES: They're running! They're running! The men are running away!

104. SNOWBALL: After them, comrades! Pursue them! Don't stop till we've driven them off the farm!
(Fade.)

105. NARRATOR: Jones and his men had given up all attempt to defend themselves and were in full flight down the cart-track that led to the main road. The animals chased them out on to the road and slammed the five-barred gate behind them. And so, almost before they knew what was happening, the Rebellion had been successfully carried through: Jones was expelled, and the Manor Farm was theirs.

106. COCK: (Crows twice.)
(Fade in.)

107. SQUEALER: We've won! We've beaten them!

108. NAPOLEON: The farm is ours.

109. COW: There's not a human being on it.

110. MOLLY: Mrs Jones has gone too. I was watching her.

111. SHEEP I: She slipped out by the back gate as soon as she saw Jones running away.

112. COCK: Good riddance!

113. SNOWBALL: And now, comrades, back to the farm we go, and wipe out every sign that human beings have ever lived here.

114. NARRATOR: The animals trooped back to the farm in a body, and the pigs caused the harness-room at the end of the stables to be broken open.

[ALL: *The harness-room, the harness-room.*]

115. SNOWBALL: Bring out the instruments of torture.

116. BOXER: Here are the bits!

117. EFFECTS:	(*Jingle.*)
118. SQUEALER:	The nose rings!
	(*Jingle.*)
119. PIG 2:	The castrating knives!
120. COW:	The dog chains!
121. EFFECTS:	(*Jingle.*)
122. NAPOLEON:	Fling the whole lot of them down the well!
123. ALL:	(*Cheers.*)
124. SNOWBALL:	Throw the harness on to the incinerator. Reins, blinkers, collars, halters—away they go! Here are the worst of all. The whips! On to the fire with them!
125. SHEEP:	The whips are burning! Look at the whips burning!
126. ALL:	(*Cheers.*)
127. SNOWBALL:	⌜And where are⌝ those degrading ribbons that Jones used to decorate the horses' manes with? Burn them with the rest.
128. MOLLIE:	Must we burn the ribbons—all of them?
129. SNOWBALL:	Ribbons, Mollie, should be regarded as [*are*] clothes, which are the mark of a human being. All animals should go naked.
130. ALL:	[*Murmurs.*]
	(*Cheers.*)
131. CLOVER:	And now it's all gone! Bits, spurs, whips, nose rings—everything gone. There's not a trace of Jones left. Except——
132. BENJAMIN:	Except——
133. COCK:	The farmhouse. What shall we do with the farmhouse?
134. SNOWBALL:	The farmhouse presents a somewhat complex problem. On the one hand——
135. SQUEALER:	The farmhouse is a very desirable residence, comrades. Now, if it were put to proper use——

136. CLOVER:	But no animal must ever live in it. I feel sure of that.
137. SHEEP:	No, no! We must never live in it.
138. COCK:	What did Mayor say? 'Never to live in a house.'
139. SNOWBALL: 140. ★	I have it! The farmhouse shall be pre-served as a museum. We will keep it intact, with its mirrors and its sofas and its Brussels carpets. It will be a reminder to us of the folly and luxury in which human beings lived.
141. ALL: } † 142. COW:	Agreed! Agreed! The farmhouse shall be a museum.
143. SNOWBALL:	And the farm must have a new name. 'The Manor Farm' is too human. The new name must show it for what it is: the only farm in the whole county—in the whole of England—owned and operated by animals.
144. COCK:	'The Farm of the Animals.'
145. COW:	'Beast Farm.'
146. PIGEON:	'Animal Manor.'
147. NAPOLEON:	'Animal Farm!'
148. SNOWBALL:	So be it, Napoleon. Animal Farm!
149. ALL:	ANIMAL FARM! ANIMAL FARM! (*Cheering.* MOLLY *begins 'Beasts of England', the others join in. Fade.*)

MUSIC 3

150. NARRATOR:	That night the animals slept as they had never slept before. But they woke at dawn as usual, and when they had had breakfast the pigs called them together in the yard, saying that they had an important announcement to make.

[*Cock crow twice.*]

★ At page turnovers the scene numbering was sometimes repeated or, as here, advanced.
† Brace added on typescript by hand.

141

151. ALL: *(General chatter.)*

    [MARJORIE: Half past six.]

152. SNOWBALL [*Second Mike. Yawning.*]: Comrades, it is half past six and we have a long day before us. Today we begin the hay harvest. But there is another matter that must be attended to first. I must tell you that during the past three months we pigs have taught ourselves the art of reading and writing. We have also, by very careful study, succeeded in

153.   reducing the principles of Animalism to Seven Commandments. We propose now to inscribe these Seven Commandments on the wall of the big barn. Once written, they will form the unalterable law by which every animal on this farm must live.

154. ALL: Agreed! Agreed!

155. NAPOLEON: Bring a pot of white paint and a ladder. Comrade Snowball shall write the Commandments. He is the best at writing.

            (Fade.)

156. NARRATOR: So Snowball took the brush between the knuckles of his trotter, and with some difficulty (for it is not easy for a pig to balance on the rungs of a ladder) climbed up and set to work, while Squealer held the paint-pot a few rungs below him. Soon the Commandments were written on the tarred wall in great white letters that could be read thirty yards away. When they were finished Snowball read them aloud.

            (*Chatter up and stop dead.*)

157. SNOWBALL: [*Now I'll read them out——*]

            One.   Whatever goes upon two legs is

an enemy.

Two. Whatever goes upon four legs, or has wings, is a friend.

Three. No animal shall wear clothes.

Four. No animal shall sleep in a bed.

Five. No animal shall drink alcohol.

Six. No animal shall kill any other animal. [*Never.*]

Seven. All animals are equal.

158. ALL: All animals are equal. All animals are equal.

159. SNOWBALL: And now, comrades, to the hayfield! Let us make it a point of honour to get in the harvest in shorter time than Jones and his men could do.

160. EFFECTS: (*Distressed lowing of cows*)

161. NARRATOR: At this moment the three cows, who had seemed uneasy for some time past, set up a loud lowing. [*The cows*] They had not been milked for twenty-four hours, and their udders were almost bursting. After a little thought the pigs sent for buckets and milked the cows fairly successfully, their trotters being well adapted to this task. Soon there were five buckets of frothing creamy milk at which many of the animals looked with considerable interest.

162. SQUEALER: What is going to happen to all that milk?

163. COCK: Jones used sometimes to mix some of it in the hens' mash.

164. NAPOLEON: Never mind the milk, comrades. That will be attended to. The harvest is more important. Comrade Snowball will lead the way. I will follow in a few minutes. Forward, comrades! The hay is waiting.

(Fade.)

165. NARRATOR: So the animals trooped down to the hayfield to begin the harvest, and when they came back in the evening it was noticed that the milk had disappeared.

All that day, and every day for a week to come, how they toiled and how they sweated to get the hay in! The work, with implements which had been designed for human beings, was not easy or simple. But the pigs were so clever that they could find a way round every difficulty; and as for the horses, they knew every inch of the field—indeed, they

166. understood the business of mowing and raking far better than Jones and his men had ever done. Every animal down to the humblest worked at turning the hay and gathering it in. Even the ducks and hens toiled to and fro all day in the sun, carrying tiny whisps of hay in their beaks. In the end their efforts were rewarded, for the harvest was an even bigger success than they had hoped.

(Fade in.)

167. SHEEP: We've done it! We've done it! It's all in. The last load's in.

168. COCK: And it took us two days less than it used to take Jones.

169. MURIEL: Three cheers for Snowball and Napoleon!

170. CLOVER: We'd never have done it if it hadn't been for them.

171. COCK: I say three cheers for Boxer.

172. ALL: *(Cheers.)*

173. COW: What would we do without Boxer? He's as strong as all the rest of us put together.

174. SQUEALER: It's the biggest harvest the farm has ever had.★

175. PIGEON: And not an animal stole so much as a mouthful.

★ When the text was cut, this and the next line were presumably spoken by the Narrator, 'It's' being changed to 'It was' etc.

(Half-fade.)

176. NARRATOR: All through that summer the farm ran like clockwork. There were endless problems to overcome, but The pigs with their cleverness and Boxer with his tremendous muscles were equal to anything. Boxer had been a hard worker even in Jones's time, but now he seemed more like three horses than one. From morning to night he was pushing and pulling, always at the spot where the work was hardest. His answer to every difficulty, every setback, was 'I will work harder!' Indeed, he had adopted 'I will work harder' as his personal motto. There were days when the entire work of the farm seemed to rest upon his mighty shoulders.

On Sundays there was *no* work. After breakfast the green flag which was the emblem of the farm—it was really an old tablecloth of Mrs Jones's which Snowball had found in the harness-room—was run up the flagstaff; and then the animals trooped into the big barn for a general assembly which was known as the Meeting. At the Meeting the work of the coming week was planned out and resolutions were put forward and debated. Every decision had to be ratified by a majority vote, but it was always the pigs who put forward the resolutions in the first place. Snowball and Napoleon were by far the most active in the debates. But it was noticed that these two were never in agreement: if one of them put forward a resolution, that was sufficient reason for the other to oppose it. The Meeting always [*This*] ended with the singing of 'Beasts of England', and the afternoon was given up to study and recreation.

On Sunday afternoon Snowball busied himself

with organising the other animals into what he called Animal Committees. He was indefatigable at this. Napoleon took no interest in Snowball's committees, which he said were a waste of time. The education of the young, he said, was more important than anything that could be done for those who were already grown up. It happened that [*2 of the bitches*] Jessie and Bluebell had both whelped soon after the hay harvest, giving birth between them to nine sturdy puppies. As soon as they were weaned, Napoleon took them away from their mothers, saying that he would make himself responsible for their education. [*Snowball on the other hand——*] He took them to a small loft which could only be reached by a ladder from the harness-room, and there kept them in such seclusion that the rest of the farm soon forgot their existence.

177.

Snowball also instituted classes in reading and writing. By the autumn almost every animal on the farm was literate in some degree.

178. ALL:

(*Fade in general chatter from 'writing'.*)
[*Yes, Clover, I will*] *

179. CLOVER: †

Comrade Snowball, I know the whole alphabet now, but I cannot read words. Muriel can read words. Benjamin can read quite well, but he says there is nothing worth reading. Boxer has only been able to learn A, B, C, D. And the sheep and the ducks and hens cannot get beyond B. Also, comrade, they say they have not been able to learn the Commandments by heart. Don't you think you could shorten the Commandments in

* It is not clear who speaks this part line or where it fits in the dialogue. It may be intended as a throw-away line from the 'General Chatter'.
† Speech number and 'CLOVER' appear to have been cut in error.

some way, so that everyone can learn them?

180. SNOWBALL: Let me see. I think it can be done. Ah, yes, [*Clover,*] I have it. Now listen: 'Four legs good, two legs bad.' There you have the essential principle of Animalism in six words.

181. SHEEP [*Murmur*] (*doubtfully*): Four legs good, two legs bad! Four legs good, two legs bad!

182. SNOWBALL: Excellent, comrades! Keep that maxim in mind, and you will be completely safe against human influences.

183. SHEEP: Four legs good, two legs bad! Four legs good, two legs bad! Four legs good, two legs bad! Four legs good, two legs bad!
(*Continue under following.*)

184. NARRATOR: 'Four legs good, two legs bad' was inscribed on the end wall of the barn, above the Commandments and in bigger letters. Having once got it by heart, the sheep developed a great liking for this maxim, and often as they lay in the field they would all start bleating it together, and keep it up for hours on end, never growing tired of it.

185. SHEEP: . . . Four legs good, two legs bad! Four legs good, two legs bad!
(*Fade out.*)

186. NARRATOR: Now, during most of this time, Mr Jones had been sitting in the taproom of the Red Lion in Willingdon, complaining to anyone who would listen of the monstrous injustice he had suffered in being turned out of his property by a pack of worthless animals. The other farmers did not at first give him much help, but nevertheless, the events on Animal Farm had filled all of them with uneasiness.

187. EFFECTS: (*Creep in heavy boots from 'help'.*)

MUSIC 4

188.	(*Song of a blackbird behind the voices in the following dialogue.*)
189. FARMER 1 [*Annexe*]:	That's a funny set-up over at Jones's, ain't it? Can't last, of course. All them brutes'll be starving long afore winter comes on.
190. FARMER 2:	Bound to. What I mean to say, it's agen nature, ain't it? 'Tisn't as if a pack of animals could——
191. COCK:	(*Humming 'Beasts of England' off mike.*)
192. FARMER 2:	Shut your trap, you!
193. EFFECTS:	(*Crack of a whip. Squawk. Humming stops. Blackbird continues.*)
194. FARMER 1:	I 'ad some of my lot singing it yesterday. They sung the other side of their faces after I'd got through with 'em. But look 'ere. When them animals chased Jones out, we all said as they'd be starving inside of a fortnight, didn't we? Well, they ain't starved – yet.
195. FARMER 2:	No, but it ain't winter yet.
196. FARMER 1:	Yes, but look 'ere. Supposin'——
197. MUSIC:	(*The whistling of the blackbird changes into whistling of 'Beasts of England'.*)
198. FARMER 2:	'Ere. Give us a stone. Get off, you devil, you!
199. EFFECTS:	(*Flutter of wings. Whistling stops.*)
200. FARMER 1:	It's all over the place, that tune is. But listen, now. You know and I know as this 'ere set-up at Jones's won't last for ever. Three months I'd give it. But meantime it don't do us no good. It puts ideas into the other animals' 'eads, see? If you arst me, it's time it [*this 'ere bizness*] was put a stop to. 'Twouldn't take much to do it. Jest 'alf a dozen of us go up there with cartwhips and maybe a gun or two, and then——

201. FARMER 2: Ye-es. But what I did think—this is between you and I, mind you—I did think as it mightn't be a bad idea to leave them animals in possession for a bit. S'pose Jones finds as 'e can't get 'em out, what'll 'e do? Sell the farm, and sell cheap. Can't do nothink else. And it's a nice little property, the Manor Farm is.

MUSIC 5

(*Church bells begin playing changes faintly in the distance, and continue behind the men's voices.*)

203.★ FARMER 1: Ah, there was a lot on us thought that. But then it wasn't to be expected as them animals'd make a job of it. But from what I 'ear—don't pass this on, of course—from what I 'ear, they ain't doing so bad. They got their 'ay in like Christians. Now that won't do, see? It sets a bad example. S'pose *our* animals get trying it on? What I say is, we all got to 'ang together. Arter all, we all live orf animals, don't we?

204. FARMER 2: Yes. Got to keep a firm 'and on 'em, of course.

(*Church bells now ringing somewhat louder.*)

205. FARMER 1: And to keep 'em under we got to keep 'em ignorant. Once let 'em find out as they can do without us, and then where'd we be? The sooner Jones gets 'is farm back, the better for all of us.

206. FARMER 2: Well, maybe you're right.

207. FARMER 1: That's settled, then. I'll 'ave a word with one or two others and fix a day.

★ No 202.

149

208. We won't 'alf teach those beggars a lesson. Jest let me get in among 'em with a whip, and there'll be bloody murder.

209. FARMER 2: O.K., I'll give you a hand. You comin' to church this mornin'?

210. FARMER 1: Yes. That there bell's been ringin' these ten minutes. Come on, we best step lively.

211. MUSIC: (*Church bell louder. Suddenly it changes to 'Beasts of England', plays a few bars and fades under. At 'October' crossfade bells to whirring of wings.*)

212. NARRATOR: But the animals were aware of these developments. They had their spies and sympathisers everywhere. And they were not surprised when, one day early in October, a flight of pigeons came whirling through the air and alighted in the yard of Animal Farm in the wildest excitement.

213. PIGEONS [*Annexe*]: Brrrr! Brrrr!
 (*Wings up.*)

214. ALL MALE VOICES: What's happening? What's happening?

215. PIGEON 1: Jones is coming!

216. PIGEON 2: The men are coming back! A whole lot of them.

217. PIGEON 3: Six of them, all carrying big sticks.

218. PIGEON 4: They've just come through the gate, they're coming up the cart-track now.

219. PIGEON 5: Jones is at the head of them. And he's got his gun!

220. NAPOLEON: Every animal to his post! Comrade Snowball takes command.

221. SNOWBALL: Pigs, cows, horses, into the cowshed. And lie hidden, comrades, until the order to charge. The other animals, follow me. Remember, comrades: calmness, resolution, discipline! For the

honour of Animal Farm!

222. COCK:	Here they come! Here they come!
223. EFFECTS:	(*Distant cackling of geese.*)
224. MOLLY:	The geese are pecking their legs.
225. FARMERS 1, 2 & JONES [*Off mike well*]: Get off, you devil, you!
226. COW:	It's no good, they're beating them off.
227. MOLLY:	Look, Snowball's charging them.
228. EFFECTS:	(*Distant trampling, thumping and squeals.*)
229. COCK:	Everyone's charging them. Muriel's butting them with her horns. Benjamin's lashing out at them with his hind legs.
230. COW (*approaching*): It's no good, they're too strong, they're driving us off.
231. EFFECTS:	(*Loud squeal of a pig.*)
232. SQUEALER:	The signal for retreat! Back into the yard.
233. ALL:	Back into the yard, everybody.
234. FARMER 1:	Come on boys, now we got 'em. Drive 'em up into that there corner, and then we'll give 'em what-for. 'Ere! Look out! there's a 'ole lot more of 'em coming!
235. SNOWBALL:	Charge!
236. EFFECTS:	(*Tremendous trampling of hoofs, whinnying of a horse, shouts of panic. Fade under.*)
237. NARRATOR:	At the signal for retreat the animals fled into the yard, and the human beings—seeing, as they thought, their enemies in flight—rushed after them in disorder. At this moment Snowball sprang his surprise. As soon as the men were well inside the yard, the three horses, the three cows, and the rest of the pigs, who had been lying in ambush in the cowshed, suddenly emerged in their rear, cutting them off.

(*Bring up cheering.*)

238. NARRATOR:
And so within five minutes of their invasion the human beings were in ignominious retreat by the same way as they had come, with a flock of geese hissing after them and pecking at their calves all the way.

(*Cheering up.*)

239. COCK:
They're gone!

240. SQUEALER:
We've beaten them!

241. COW:
We've beaten them again!

242. COCK:
That's the last we'll ever see of them!

243. WOMEN:
Three cheers for Boxer!

244. MEN:
Three cheers for Snowball!

245. CLOVER:
Boxer was glorious. Did you see him rearing up on his hind legs and lashing out at them with his hoofs?

246. MURIEL:
And Snowball! The way he charged straight at Jones and never stopped for an instant even when Jones raised his gun and fired!

247. PIGEON:
But Snowball's wounded. The blood's running down your back, comrade.

248. SNOWBALL:
Nothing—a scratch. The pellets only grazed me. This battle must have a name, comrades. I suggest 'The Battle of the Cowshed'.

249. ALL BUT SHEEP:
Agreed. Agreed.

250. SHEEP:
The Battle of the Cowshed! Battle of the Cowshed! Battle of the Cowshed! Battle of the Cowshed! Battle of the Cowshed! Battle of the Cowshed! Battle of the Cowshed!

(*Cheers break in, fade out.*)

251. NARRATOR:
After the Battle of the Cowshed, Jones gave up hope of getting his property back, and went to live

252.
in another part of the county. The animals were now secure in their possession of the farm. The neighbouring human beings did not hate them any less than before, but they had developed a sort of grudging respect for them, one symptom of which was that they now took to calling Animal Farm by its proper name, and stopped calling it the Manor Farm, as they had done hitherto.

When winter drew on, and the frost and snow made it impossible to do much work in the fields, there were many meetings in the big barn, and the work of the coming year was carefully planned out. It had now come to be accepted that all questions of farm policy should be decided by the pigs. The vote was still taken, but the main decisions had always been made beforehand. The other animals thought this arrangement quite a reasonable one, but just occasionally——

[?]* [*Annexe*]

253. EFFECTS:	(*Hoofs.*)
254. CLOVER:	Boxer, do you remember how the cows were milked on the day of the Rebellion?
255. BOXER:	Yes. And I remember that when we came back in the evening the milk had disappeared.
256. CLOVER:	It has disappeared every day since. Do you know what happens to it? I have just found out. It is mixed every day into the pigs' mash. No other animal gets a drop of it.
257. BOXER:	[*Clover!*] I do not think that is any concern of ours. What use is milk to a horse?
258. CLOVER:	Yes, but there are also the apples.
259.	When the orchard was picked, the apples were stored in the harness-room, and now I hear that every one of them is to be kept for the pigs. Do you think that is quite fair?
260. MOLLY:	What, keep all the apples for themselves?
261. MURIEL:	Aren't we to have any?
262. COW:	I thought they were going to be shared out equally.
263. BOXER:	Here comes Squealer.

* Prior to 'Annexe' is an illegible indication for a sound effect—possibly of birds or cows.

264. SQUEALER: What was that you were talking about, comrades? Ah, the milk and the apples? Let me put that in its right perspective for you, comrades. Now, why do you suppose we pigs are reserving the milk and the apples for ourselves? Not from any selfish motive, naturally. Our personal wishes have nothing to do with it. Our object is simply and solely to preserve our health. Milk and apples—this has been proved by Science, comrades—milk and apples contain substances absolutely necessary to the well-being of a pig. We pigs are brain-workers. The whole management and organisation of this farm depend on us. Day and night we are watching over your welfare. It is for *your* sake that we drink that milk and eat those apples. Do you know what would happen if we pigs failed in our duty even for a single day? Jones would come back!

[*Jones left this district after the Battle of the Cowshed.*]★

265. SHEEP: Jones would come back!

266. SQUEALER: Yes, [*he*] Jones would come back! Surely, comrades, surely there is no one among you who wants to see Jones come back?

[CLOVER: (*Sigh.*)]

267. SHEEP: No! Don't let Jones come back!

268. BOXER: Comrade Squealer's explanation seems to be quite satisfactory, Clover.

269. CLOVER: Yes, Squealer is very good at explaining things.

270. NARRATOR: So the pigs continued to be the real controllers of the farm, and Napoleon and Snowball were the

★ No speech heading is given for this insertion. It was probably intended for the Sheep whose line was crossed through at 265.

acknowledged leaders among the pigs. But unfortunately, as winter wore on, the rivalry between these two became more and more acute. Indeed, at every Meeting that was held——

271. EFFECTS [*Open Mike. Political Meeting reaction*]: (*From* 'acute' *bring up confused uproar of animal noises and stamping.*)

272. SNOWBALL: Silence! I will be heard! Comrade Napoleon, I call upon you to withdraw that motion.

273. NAPOLEON: Comrade Snowball, your presumption is intolerable. You are not dictator of this farm. I say the three-acre field shall be planted with cabbages.

274. SNOWBALL: ⌜And I say the soil is totally unsuitable for cabbages.⌝ It is too light for anything except turnips.

275. NAPOLEON: Cabbages!

276. SNOWBALL: Turnips!

277. SHEEP [*Murmur*]:* Four legs good, two legs bad! Four legs good, two legs bad——

278. SNOWBALL: Silence! Comrade Napoleon, if you had even the most elementary knowledge of scientific farming ——

279. NAPOLEON: I am not interested in scientific farming. I am a practical pig. And at least I know how to grow cabbages.

280. SNOWBALL: Listen. I have looked this up in the *Farmer and Stockbreeder*. I have the passage by heart. I will repeat it to you. 'On light soils——'

281. SHEEP: Four legs good, two legs bad! Four legs good, two legs bad! Four legs good, two legs bad!
(*Repeat six* † *times. Take down and hold*

* The word looks very like 'human' and is placed over the first 'legs bad' – but it is probably a repetition of the instruction at Scene 181.
† Originally 'ten' but '6' written over.

behind.)

282. CLOVER: Have you noticed that the sheep always break into [*that slogan*] when Snowball is speaking, never when Napoleon is speaking?

283. BENJAMIN: Quite a coincidence, is it not?

(*Sheep up and fade.*)

284. NARRATOR: But of all the struggles between Snowball and Napoleon, none was so bitter as the struggle over the windmill.

In the long pasture, not far from the farm buildings, there was a small knoll which was the highest point on the farm. After surveying the ground, Snowball declared that this was just the place to build a windmill, which could be made to operate a dynamo and supply the farm with electrical power.

285. (*General chatter up.*)

286. SNOWBALL: Think of it, comrades! Think what we could do if we had electricity on this farm! Every kind of labour-saving device! A circular saw! A chaff-cutter! A mangel-slicer! A milking-machine! And central heating everywhere, and Electric light in every animal's stall.

287. MOLLY: } That's wonderful!
288. MURIEL: } Oh, but it's too good to be true.
289. NAPOLEON: } It's impossible.

290. SNOWBALL: Perfectly possible, comrades. Electricity can do anything. Let me tell you that if [*we had a dynamo and a windmill on the knoll*] our methods were brought fully up to date, there is no reason why any animal on this farm should [*need*] do more than two hours' work a day. All the rest of Our time could be spent grazing in the fields or improving our minds with reading and conversation.

156

291. NAPOLEON:	Nonsense! Pay no attention to him. This is not a time to be filling our heads with dreams. We have a hard year's work ahead of us. Food, that is what matters. Before all else our output of food must be increased.
292. SNOWBALL:	I say that When we have built the windmill, food production will increase one thousand per cent.
293. NAPOLEON:	And I say that if we waste time on this windmill of yours we shall all starve to death long before it is built.
294. BOXER (Close):	I wonder. I wonder.
295. COCK:	Only twelve hours' work a week!
296. PIGEON:	It might be true.
297. MOLLY:	I've seen the plans of the windmill. Snowball has drawn them out in chalk on the floor of one of the sheds. He says it's all worked out down to the last detail.
298. BOXER:	I wonder.
299. COCK (Well back):	I say Snowball is right.
300. COW:	I shall vote for Snowball.
301. SHEEP I:	I shall vote for Napoleon.
302. COCK:	Vote for Snowball and the twelve-hour week!
303. SQUEALER:	Vote for Napoleon and the full dinner-pail!
304. SHEEP:	Vote for Napoleon. Vote for Snowball. (Three times. Fade.)
305. NARRATOR:	At the Meeting on the following Sunday the question of whether or not to begin work on the windmill came up for discussion. There was a long and stormy debate. (General murmur up.)
306. SNOWBALL:	Comrades! Think of this farm as it might be if degrading labour were lifted off our backs! Think of the machines that we can have! Threshing machines,

ploughs, harrows, reapers and binders—electricity can run every one of them. Think of your stalls with hot and cold water and electric light. Every one of you could lie in bed till ten o'clock in the morning.

307. PIG 2: ⎤ ★ It's wonderful!

308. COW: ⎟ Lie in bed till ten o'clock!

309. ALL BUT

    SHEEP: ⎦ Vote for Snowball! Vote for Snowball!

310. NAPOLEON: Lies! Don't listen to these fairy tales he is telling you. Snowball, I warn you to be silent.

311. SNOWBALL: I will not be silent. Comrades, listen to me——

312. THE SHEEP: Four legs good, two legs bad! Four legs good, two legs bad!

313. SNOWBALL: I will not be shouted down. Comrades, every animal who has the welfare of this farm at heart will vote for the windmill. Let us cast off the burden of the past. I tell you . . .

314. NAPOLEON: Snowball, for the last time I warn you to sit down.

315. SNOWBALL: I will not sit down. I——

316. NAPOLEON: Then on your own head be it!

317. EFFECTS [*In Tent*]: (*Whistles. Cast and records: tremendous baying of dogs, sounding first outside, then nearer. The baying, growing fainter as the dogs get further away, should sound behind the speeches that follow.*)

318. COCK: Where did they come from?

319. PIG 4: Look, they're going for Snowball!

320. MOLLY: They nearly had him.

321. PIGEON: He's gone, they're after him.

322. PIG 1: Come on, out through the door.

323. CLOVER: Look, Snowball's running for his life,

★ Brace added on typescript with word 'together'.

and the dogs are on his heels. There are nine of them. They're as huge as wolves.

324. COCK: They've got him!

325. COW: No!

326. PIGEON: How he's running!

327. MURIEL: But the dogs are almost on his tail.

328. SQUEALER: He's down, they've got him!

329. PIG 3: No, he's up again!

330. COCK: That one's got him by the tail.

331. MOLLY: No, he's whisked it away just in time.

332. PIG 2: Look, he's almost at the hedge.

333. COCK: He's putting on an extra spurt.

334. SQUEALER: He's gone! He's through the hole in the hedge.

335. BOXER: They didn't get him.

336. COW: Look out! The dogs are coming back.

337. EFFECTS: *(Baying louder again and out.)*

338. NARRATOR: Amazed and terrified, the animals crept back into the barn. In a moment the dogs came bounding back. At first no one had been able to imagine where these creatures came from, but the problem was soon solved. [*These are*]* the nine puppies whom Napoleon had taken from their mothers and reared privately. They were huge, savage-looking dogs, although not yet full-grown. They kept close to Napoleon. It was noticed that they wagged their tails to him in the same way as the other dogs had been used to do to Mr Jones. Napoleon took his stand on the platform at the end of the barn, alone except for the dogs, who ranged themselves behind him.

339. *(Chatter, then silence.)*

340. NAPOLEON: Let every animal sit down and listen to me. Now that the traitor has been expelled from our midst, a new chapter

---

* Originally typed as 'They were'.

	in the history of this farm can begin. I have an announcement to make to you. From today onwards the Sunday meetings will be discontinued. They are unnecessary, and a waste of time.
341. ALL:	What! No more meetings!
342. NAPOLEON:	You will still assemble here on Sunday mornings to receive the orders for the week, but there will be no more debates. All questions relating to the working of the farm will be settled by a special committee of pigs, presided over by myself. We shall meet in private and communicate our decisions to you afterwards.
343. SQUEALER:	And a very good arrangement, too! Think of all the brainwork that will save you, comrades—not having to think for yourselves any longer.
344. COCK:	No more meetings!
345. COW:	No more voting!
346. PIGEON:	Is that right?
347. CLOVER:	Is that what Major said?
	⌐(*General reaction continuing under.*)⌐
348. NARRATOR:	*Even Boxer was vaguely troubled. He set back his ears and tried hard to marshal his thoughts, but in the end he could think of nothing to say. Some of the pigs themselves, however, were more articulate. Four young porkers sitting in the front row sprang to their feet——
	(*Murmur up.*)
349. PIG 2:	Comrade Napoleon, I protest! (*Growling.*)
350. NAPOLEON:	You protest?

* Two-and-a-half lines apparently cut by pasting over before 'Even'.

351. PIG 2:	Yes. (*Growling.*) That is to say——
352. NAPOLEON:	Well?
353. PIG 2:	Comrade, this is undemocratic. (*Louder growling.*) At least, it is not precisely undemocratic, but——(*Very ferocious growling.*) Obviously, comrade, what you have done is strictly democratic, but——(*Deafening growling.*)
354. NAPOLEON:	Well! Are you still protesting?
355. PIG 2:	No, comrade. I have stopped protesting.
356. NAPOLEON:	Then the meeting is at an end. And one last word. Remember always that when there has been one Rebellion, there can never be another. That is the just rule of Rebellions. (*Murmur.*)
357. SQUEALER:	Comrades, before we part! I wish to propose a vote of thanks to Comrade Napoleon for his self-sacrifice in taking this extra labour upon himself. Remember, comrades, that it is for *our* sakes that he has chosen to bear this burden. Three cheers for our Leader, Comrade Napoleon! [*3 times*] (*Feeble cheers, merging into a louder bleating of 'Four legs good, two legs bad'.*)
358. NARRATOR:	So the Sunday meetings came to an end, and Napoleon reigned as the undisputed master of Animal Farm. The animals accepted the situation, well knowing that the pigs were wiser than themselves, and that Napoleon was the wisest of the pigs. And yet——
359. EFFECTS:	(*Hoofs.*)
360. CLOVER:	Boxer, have you heard what has happened? The pigs have moved into the farmhouse and are living there.

361. BOXER: Living in the farmhouse! Let me try to remember ... I cannot remember. Did we not pass a resolution never to live in the farmhouse? It was on the day of the Rebellion. Was that resolution written down? [*Clover?*]

362. CLOVER: No, it was not written down. But there is something else. Do you know that the pigs are not only living in the farm-house, they have also taken to sleeping in the beds? Benjamin, I want you to read one of the Commandments for me.

363. BENJAMIN: You know I never meddle in such matters.

364. CLOVER: Muriel, you can read. Come with me to the end wall of the barn. (*Hoofs.*) There. Now read me the Fourth Commandment. Does it not say something about never sleeping in a bed?

365. MURIEL: It says (*slowly*): 'No – animal – shall – sleep – in – a – bed – with – sheets.'

366. CLOVER: With *sheets*. I had forgotten about the sheets.

367. MURIEL: We must have learned it wrong.

368. CLOVER: With sheets. How strange!

369. MURIEL: Here comes Squealer. He's got three dogs with him.

370. DOGS: (*Faint growling.*)

371. SQUEALER: What was that you were saying, comrades? Ah, you have heard that we pigs are sleeping in the beds at the farm-house. And why not? You didn't sup-pose, comrades, that there was ever a ruling against *beds*? A bed merely means a place to sleep in. A pile of straw in a stall is a bed, properly regarded. We have removed the sheets from the farm-

house beds, and sleep between blankets. And very comfortable beds they are too! But not more comfortable than we need, I can tell you, with all the brainwork we have to do nowadays. You wouldn't rob us of our repose, would you, comrades? You wouldn't have us too tired to carry out our duties? Surely none of you wishes to see Jones come back?

372. MURIEL: No, no! Don't let Jones come back!

373. SQUEALER: And now, comrades, I have a glorious piece of news for you. The windmill— you all remember Comrade Napoleon's project, which Snowball attempted to obstruct—the windmill is to be built after all. Work will begin tomorrow.

374. CLOVER: Build the windmill after all! I thought Napoleon was always against it. I thought it was Snowball who wanted the windmill.

375. SQUEALER: No, no, you have remembered it wrong, Clover. It was Comrade Napoleon's idea from the very start.

376. MURIEL: But Snowball had the plans all drawn out on the floor of one of the sheds.

377. SQUEALER: Stolen! Stolen from among Comrade Napoleon's private papers. Don't forget comrades, that Snowball was a mutineer—in fact, he was hardly better than a traitor.

378. BOXER: He fought bravely at the Battle of the Cowshed, Squealer.

379. SQUEALER: Bravery is not enough, Comrade Boxer. Loyalty and obedience are more important. And as for the Battle of the Cowshed, I believe the time will come when we shall find that Snowball's part in it was very much exaggerated. But from today onwards, comrades, we

163

must have only one thought–the building of the windmill. It will be a hard task, I warn you. It may even be necessary to reduce our rations at some time during this year.

380. BOXER: No matter. Once the windmill is built there will be plenty of everything for everybody. I will work harder!

381. CLOVER: We'll all work harder.

382. MURIEL: Long live the windmill!

383. SQUEALER: Long live Comrade Napoleon!

384. CLOVER: MURIEL: BOXER: Long live Comrade Napoleon! Long live Comrade Napoleon!

(*Fade.*)

384*. NARRATOR: And how they worked, right through that year! All through the spring and summer and far into the autumn they toiled at the building of the windmill, side by side with the daily work of the farm. The hardest task was the breaking of the stone. Since the animals were unable to use picks and crowbars, the only way of doing it was to utilise the force of gravity. They lashed ropes round huge boulders, and then all together–cows, horses, sheep, any animal that could lay hold of the rope–even the pigs sometimes joined in at critical moments–they dragged them with desperate slowness to the top of the quarry, where they were toppled over the edge, to shatter to pieces below. Nothing could have been achieved without Boxer. His strength seemed equal to that of all the other animals put together. When the boulder began

★ *Bis.*

to slip and the animals cried out in despair at finding themselves dragged down the hill, it was always Boxer who strained himself against the rope and brought the boulder to a stop. It was a noble sight to see him toiling up the slope inch by inch, his breath coming fast, the tips of his hoofs clawing at the ground, and his great sides matted with sweat. In addition to his first motto of 'I will work harder', Boxer had now adopted a second: 'Napoleon is always right'. He had also made arrangements with one of the cockerels to wake him in the morning half an hour earlier than the other animals, so that he could go down to the quarry and carry away an extra load of stone unassisted.

All through that summer the animals did not fare badly. The work was hard, but they had the satisfaction of feeling that they were working for themselves. And yet from time to time things still happened, which didn't actually cause murmurings, for somehow nobody felt inclined to murmur nowadays – there were too many dogs prowling about – but——

385. EFFECTS: *(Hoofs.)*

386. CLOVER: *(Fade in.)* Boxer, have you heard that the pigs have taken to drinking alcohol?

387. BOXER: Drinking alcohol? Impossible! It is forbidden by the Commandments.

388. CLOVER [*Annexe*]: So I thought. But it seems they discovered some barrels of beer which Jones left behind in the farmhouse cellar, and now I hear every pig gets a ration of a pint of beer a day.

389. PIGEON:	And Napoleon has half a gallon. He has it out of the Crown Derby soup tureen that was in the dining-room.
390. CLOVER:	I am sure the Fifth Commandment forbids the drinking of alcohol.
391. MURIEL:	No, Clover, it does not. Do you remember that once before we found that we had learned one of the Commandments wrong? Well, there is another. Yesterday I was reading the Commandments over to myself. Now, I thought the Fifth Commandment ran: 'No animal shall drink alcohol.' But really it runs: 'No animal shall drink *to excess.*'
392. BOXER:	Ah! No animal shall drink *to excess.* But that explains everything. Who can imagine Comrade Napoleon drinking to excess?
393. CLOVER:	And I thought I had learned the Commandments so carefully. How strange that there should be two of them that I remembered wrong.
394. BENJAMIN:	You will remember a lot more of them wrong before you have finished, Clover. (*Half-fade.*)
395. NARRATOR:	By late autumn the windmill was half-built. The animals were tired but happy. Some of the ordinary work of the farm had been neglected, and the stores of food for the coming winter were none too plentiful. But the windmill made up for everything. In their spare moments the animals would walk round and round it, marvelling that they should ever have been able to build anything so imposing. Only old

	Benjamin refused to show any enthusiasm, though, as usual, he would utter nothing beyond the cryptic remark that donkeys live for a long time.
396. EFFECTS:	(*Wind and drums.*)
397. NARRATOR:	November came, with raging southwest winds. Building had to stop because it was too wet to mix the cement. Finally there came a night when the gale was so violent that the farm buildings rocked on their foundations and several tiles were blown off the roof of the barn. Towards morning . . .
398. EFFECTS:	(*Sound of masonry falling. General commotion. Hoofs, etc.*)
399. ALL [*Annexe*]:	Look! Look what's happened! The windmill! It's fallen! The windmill's down! (*A great, concerted wail. Fade and hold chatter behind.*)
400. NARRATOR:	With one accord they rushed to the spot. Napoleon, who seldom moved out of a walk, raced ahead of them. Yes, there it lay, the fruit of all their struggles, levelled to its foundations, the stones they had broken and carried so laboriously scattered all around. Unable at first to speak, they stood gazing mournfully at the litter of fallen stone. Napoleon paced to and fro in silence, occasionally snuffing at the ground. His tail had grown rigid and twitched sharply from side to side, which in his case was a sign of great mental activity. Suddenly he halted.
401. EFFECTS:	(*Hoofs, chatter, etc., up. Stop dead.*)
402. NAPOLEON:	Comrades, do you know who is responsible for this? Do you know the enemy who has come in the night and overthrown our windmill? *Snowball!*

I can smell his footprints in the grass.
Snowball has done this thing!

403. ALL: No! No!

404. PIGEON: Snowball!

405. COW: He couldn't!

406. COCK: He couldn't be so wicked!

407. NAPOLEON: Comrades, here and now I pronounce sentence of death upon Snowball. Half a bushel of apples to any animal who brings him to justice. A full bushel to anyone who captures him alive! And now, no more delays. There is work to be done. This very morning we begin rebuilding the windmill, and we will build all through the winter, rain or shine. We⋆ will teach this miserable traitor that he cannot undo our work so easily. Forward, comrades! Long live the windmill! Long live Animal Farm!

408. SHEEP: Long live the windmill! Long live Animal Farm! (*Twice. Fade.*)

409. NARRATOR: So the rebuilding of the windmill was begun. It was a bitter winter. The stormy weather was followed by sleet and snow, and then by a hard frost which did not break till well into February. The animals carried on as best they could with the difficult work, well knowing that the outside world was watching them and that the envious human beings would rejoice and triumph if the windmill were not finished on time.

(*Chatter under.*)

Suddenly, early in the spring, an alarming thing was discovered. Snowball was secretly frequenting the farm during the night.

(*Up chatter.*)

410. SQUEALER [*Annexe*]: Yes, comrades, we have the clearest

⋆ Typescript has 'He'.

168

evidence that he has been here. Almost every night he comes creeping in under cover of darkness. He steals the corn! He upsets the milk pails! He breaks the eggs! He gnaws the bark off the fruit trees! Comrade Napoleon has already made a most careful inspection of the premises, and he could smell traces of Snowball everywhere. Be on your guard, comrades. Snowball may succeed in doing a great deal more mischief before we run him to earth.

411. COW: So that was how the dairy window got broken!

412. COCK: And that was how that drain at the bottom of the field got blocked up!

413. MURIEL: And all that water came through the roof of the barn!

414. SQUEALER: Depend on it, comrades, Snowball was at the bottom of it every time. This is his attempt at revenge. But I have something much worse than that to tell you. We believed, did we not, that Snowball's rebellion was caused merely by his vanity and ambition. Well, we were wrong, comrades. Do you know what the real reason was? Snowball was in league with Jones from the very start! [*Yes, and what's more we have found out that Snowball*] Yes, he was Jones's secret agent all the time. It has all been proved by secret documents which he left behind him and which we have only just discovered. To my mind there is a great deal which this explains, comrades. Did we not all see for ourselves how he attempted – fortunately without success – to get us defeated and destroyed at the Battle of the Cowshed?

(Pause, then, 'Eh?' 'What?' 'Surely not', etc.)

169

415. BOXER [*Annexe*]: I do not believe that. Snowball fought [*Why did he fight so*] bravely at the Battle of the Cowshed? I saw him myself. He was wounded by Jones's gun. We all saw the blood running down [*Snowball's*] his back.

416. SQUEALER: All part of the arrangement, comrade! Jones's shot only grazed him. The plot was for Snowball, at the critical moment, to give the signal for flight and leave the field to the enemy. And he very nearly succeeded—I will even say that he *would* have succeeded if it had not been for our heroic Leader, Comrade Napoleon. Do you not remember how, just at the moment when Jones and his men had got inside the yard, Snowball suddenly turned and fled, and many animals followed him?

417. COW: Yes, that's true. He did run away. He gave the signal for retreat. I do remember that.

418. SQUEALER: And do you not remember, too, that it was just at that moment, when panic was spreading and all seemed lost, that our Leader, Comrade Napoleon, sprang forward with a cry of 'Death to Humanity' and sank his teeth in Jones's leg? Surely you remember *that*, comrades?

419. MURIEL: He makes it all sound so real.

420. COW: I don't remember.

421. COCK: I believe it's true.

422. MOLLY: Yes, it is true . . . I remember.

423. BOXER: I cannot believe that Snowball was a traitor at the beginning. What he has done since is different. ⌈But I believe that at the Battle of the Cowshed he was a good comrade.⌉

424. SQUEALER: Our Leader, Comrade Napoleon, has stated categorically—categorically, comrade—that Snowball was Jones's agent

from the very beginning: yes, and from long before the Rebellion was ever thought of!

425. BOXER: Ah, that is different! If Comrade Napoleon says it, it must be right. Napoleon is always right.

426. SQUEALER: That is the true spirit, comrade! And now one last word. Let me warn every animal on this farm to keep his eyes very wide open. For we have the strongest reasons for thinking that some of Snowball's secret agents are lurking among us at this very moment. (*Half-fade.*)

427. NARRATOR: A chill struck into the animals' hearts when they heard these words. Somehow they were not surprised when next day, in the late afternoon, Napoleon ordered the whole farm to assemble in the yard. When they were all gathered together ...

428. EFFECTS: (*Cast and recorded growls.*)

429. NARRATOR [*Tent*] (*straight on*): Napoleon emerged from the farmhouse with his nine huge dogs frisking round him and uttering blood-curdling growls.
(*A pause filled up by growls.*)

430. NAPOLEON: Dogs! Do−your−duty!
[*Tent. Quickly to Annexe*]★
(*Terrific baying, scuffle and squeals, dying away into whimpers.*)
(*Panting, whimpering and low, intermittent growls behind following.*)

431. NARRATOR: The dogs bounded forward, siezed four of the pigs by the ear, and dragged them squealing with pain and terror, to Napoleon's feet. The four pigs waited, trembling, with guilt written on every line of their countenances. They were the same four pigs as had protested when Napoleon

★ A written-in direction, 'Pigs 1 2 3 4 Squeal' has been crossed through.

abolished the Sunday meetings.

(*Panting of dogs and whimpering of pigs up.*)

432. NAPOLEON: Have you anything to say before justice is done?

433. A PIG (*gabbling*): I wish to confess that I am a traitor to Animal Farm and worthy of any punishment that may be visited upon me. I have been the traitor Snowball's agent and accomplice since the time of the Rebellion, and I have been secretly in touch with him ever since his expulsion. I confess also that I assisted him in destroying the windmill and that I have entered into an agreement with him to betray Animal Farm into the hands of its human enemies. I wish to add that I did not commit these treacheries from any feeling of conviction but——

434. NAPOLEON: You are forgetting something, I think.

435. THE PIG: I am sorry, comrade. I lost the place. (*Gabbling.*) I admit also that Snowball revealed to me early in our association that he had been Jones's secret agent for many years before the Rebellion and was employed by him as a spy and *agent provocateur* among the other animals. I wish to add that I did not commit these treacheries from any feeling of conviction but in return for a bucket of pig-meal secretly supplied to me by Snowball twice a week.

436. PIG 2: [*Gulp*] I too.

437. PIG 3: And I.

438. PIG 4: And I.

439. NAPOLEON: And what is the appropriate punishment for these crimes?

440. PIG 1: Death.

172

441. PIG 2 [*Fearfully*]: Death.

442. PIG 3: Death.

443. PIG 4: Death.

444. NAPOLEON: Death it shall be!
(*Tremendous baying and terrible squeals sinking into gurgles.*)★

445. NAPOLEON (*terrible voice*): Has any other animal anything to confess? ⌐(*Twice, with marked pause. Fade second time.*)⌐

445a. NARRATOR: Three hens came forward and confessed that during the previous year they had scattered weed seeds in the fields, in an attempt to damage the corn crop. It was Snowball, they said, who had incited them to do this. A goose came forward and confessed that she had attempted to poison Napoleon with deadly nightshade berries. Two sheep confessed to having murdered an old ram, an especially devoted follower of Napoleon, by chasing him round and round a bonfire when he was suffering from a cough. They were all slain on the spot. And so the tale of confessions and executions went on, until there was a pile of corpses lying before Napoleon's feet and the air was heavy with the smell of blood.†

446. EFFECTS: (*Hoofs.*)

447. CLOVER: How many were killed altogether?

448. MURIEL: I don't know. Ten—fifteen—more.

449. BOXER: Never would I have believed that such things could happen on our farm. Who could have imagined, even yesterday,

★ Three lines appear to have been excised by pasting over after this direction.

† Ten lines appear to have been excised by pasting over after 'blood'. In the typescript, 'blood' is followed by a comma.

that we had all those traitors among us?

450. CLOVER: It is the first time that blood has been shed. In the old days, in Jones's time, these slaughters used to happen; but now they are happening among ourselves. Since Jones left, until today, no animal has killed any other animal. Not even a rat was killed.

451. BOXER: I do not understand it. Somehow the fault must lie in ourselves. Is it, perhaps, because we have not worked hard enough? From today onwards I shall get up an hour earlier in the mornings.

452. CLOVER: I thought we had taken a vow never to kill one another. Muriel, come with me to the end of the barn. There. Now read me the Sixth Commandment. Does it not say that no animal shall kill any other animal?

453. MURIEL: It says (*slowly*): 'No−animal−shall− kill−any−other−animal−without− cause'.

454. CLOVER: *Without cause.* Ah, I had forgotten that. Yes, there was cause enough. What do you think of these happenings, Benjamin?

455. BENJAMIN: I think donkeys live a long time. And one reason why they live a long time is that they never talk politics.

456. BOXER: I think that if we all work harder, there will be more of everything for everybody, and then these things will not happen. I shall go down to the quarry and collect another load of stone. (*Half-fade.*)

457. NARRATOR: So Boxer moved off at his heavy, lumbering trot. But the other animals

made their way slowly to the little knoll in the pasture where the half-finished windmill stood. And there, with one accord, they all lay down—Clover, Benjamin, Muriel, the cows, the sheep, the geese and the hens—all huddling together as though for warmth. As Clover looked down the hillside her eyes filled with tears.

458. CLOVER:

I do not understand. This is not what we looked forward to on that night when Major first put the idea of rebellion into our heads. The farm is our own. As far as the eye can see, every inch of it is ours. And yet . . . No one dares to speak his mind because huge dogs are prowling everywhere, and you have to watch your comrades confess to terrible crimes and then be torn to pieces. That was not what we expected.

MUSIC 6

(CHORUS *holding sustained chords, with hint of melody of refrain.*)
I do not wish to rebel or disobey. I know the pigs are cleverer than we are. I will work hard, I will do whatever Napoleon tells me. But, no! This is not what we intended. I think—I don't know what to think——
(CLOVER *sings very slowly and tunefully.*)
Soon or late the day is coming,
Tyrant Man shall be o'erthrown,
And the fruitful fields of England
Shall be trod by beasts alone.

CHORUS:

Beasts of England, beasts of Ireland,
Beasts of every land and clime,
Hearken to my joyful tidings

Of the golden future time.

459. CLOVER (*declaiming over* CHORUS):
Rings shall vanish from our noses
And the harness from our back,
Bit and spur shall rust——
(*Breaking off as*——)

460. SQUEALER [*Annexe*]: Comrades! Silence! Silence if you please!

461. PIGEON: It's Squealer.

462. SQUEALER: Comrades, I have to inform you that by a special decree of our Leader, Comrade Napoleon, the song entitled 'Beasts of England' is abolished. From now onwards it is forbidden to sing it.

463. COCK (*murmuring*): What? 'Beasts of England' abolished!

464. COW (*murmuring*): Can't sing 'Beasts of England'! Why not?

465. MURIEL (*aloud*): *Why* is 'Beasts of England' abolished, Squealer?

466. SQUEALER (*stiffly*): It is no longer needed, comrade. 'Beasts of England' was the song of the Rebellion. But the Rebellion is now completed. The execution of the traitors this afternoon was the final act. The purpose of 'Beasts of England' was to express our longing for a better society in days to come. But that society has now been established. Obviously, therefore, the song has lost its meaning.

467. COCK, COW, MURIEL (*doubtfully*): Yes, I suppose so.

468. SQUEALER: But I am glad to tell you, comrades, that another song—a much more inspiring song, I may say—has already been composed to take the place of 'Beasts of England'. (*Clears his throat.*) It begins:

176

Animal Farm, Animal Farm,
Never through me shalt thou come to
harm!

469. COCK (*murmuring*): I don't think that's half as good as
'Beasts of England'.

470. MURIEL: It doesn't seem fair. Why shouldn't we
sing it if we want to——

471. SHEEP: Four legs good, two legs bad! Four legs good, two
legs bad! Four legs good, two legs bad!

MUSIC 7 (*Cross-fade to sad music, giving impression
of the passage of time.*)

472. NARRATOR: Three years went by.
(*Music up and concludes, not on perfect
cadence.*)
[*Open mike*] (*Hoofs.*)

473. CLOVER: Come nearer, my dear, I can't see you
very well. I'm getting rather short-
sighted lately. And who are you? Ah
yes, you're one of the new horses we
bought at the fair yesterday. My name is
Clover. We shall have to start teaching
you the rules of the farm. You've heard all
about Comrade Napoleon, of course? And the Seven
Commandments—you'll have to learn those by
heart. and the history of the Rebellion.
Have you heard of the Battle of the Cowshed?
Why, I dare say you've never even
heard of Snowball.

474. YOUNG HORSE: Who was Snowball?

475. CLOVER: Ah, he was a bad lot, was Snowball. He was
a clever pig, but he turned traitor. The
first time the men attacked Animal
Farm—that's what we call the Battle of
the Cowshed—it was Snowball who led
them on. He charged at the head of
them shouting 'Long live humanity!'
That was the time when Napoleon bit
him on the back. I remember it. We all

saw the blood running down Snow-ball's back. And Mollie—she was a bad lot, too. She ran away and went back to the human beings. She couldn't stand the life—she must have her sugar and her ribbons. But that was [*nearly two*] years ago. There aren't so many left who remember those days. Why, some of the younger ones have hardly even heard of Boxer.

476. YOUNG COCK: Tell us about Boxer.

477. YOUNG MARE: Tell us how he died. We'd like to hear about Boxer again.

479.* CLOVER: Ah, Boxer! He was the best comrade this farm ever had. But he worked too hard. In the end it was work that killed him. It happened not long after the farm was attacked for the second time. In the early days, after the Rebellion, we didn't have anything to do with the human beings on the other farms. We didn't trust them, and they hated us. But later on, by little and little we began to have business dealings with them, as we still do. Then there was a quarrel—I never had the rights of it: it was something to do with some bad five-pound notes—and a dozen men with guns came here and attacked the farm. It was terrible! It was far worse than the Battle of the Cowshed. I think we should have been beaten if it hadn't been for Comrade Napoleon. It was an hour before we could drive the men out, and while they were here— the mean, cowardly creatures†—they packed blasting powder into the foundations of our windmill, and blew

* No 478.
† 'I think . . . creatures' was first cut, then marked to be restored.

it to pieces. So we had to start building it for the third time. We're still building it, as you can see.

Well, Boxer had split his hoof in the fighting, and had been wounded by a shot, and he went back to work too soon. He would do it. I could see, and so could everyone else, that His strength hadn't come back to him. When he was pulling a heavy load he used to breathe in a way that frightened me. Time and again I said to him, 'Take care of yourself, Boxer. One of these days your lungs will burst.' But he wouldn't listen.

480. BOXER: (*Open mike, well back.*) Who cares? I am eleven years old. There is only one thing I care about, and that is to see the windmill finished before I die. I will work harder! Napoleon is always right!

481. CLOVER: And one day–I had known it would happen–the pigeons came flying in to say that Boxer had fallen on his side, down by the windmill. We all rushed down to the place, and there he lay between the shafts of the cart. He couldn't get up, and the blood was trickling out of his mouth. We managed to get him back to his stall, and that evening Squealer told us that Comrade Napoleon was arranging to send Boxer to be treated at the hospital in Willingdon.

We didn't like to think of Boxer in the hands of human beings, but Squealer proved to us that it would be the best arrangement, because the veterinary surgeon could treat him much better than we could.

Well, two days later, when we were

weeding turnips in the field, we saw Benjamin come galloping towards us, braying at the top of his voice. It was the first time anyone had seen Benjamin excited—in fact, it was the first time we had ever seen him gallop.

482. EFFECTS [*Open*]: (*Braying faded in from 'field'.*)

483. BENJAMIN: Quick, quick! Come at once! The van's here. They're taking Boxer away!

484. CLOVER: You can imagine how we all raced after Benjamin. And when we got to the yard, ⌜Sure enough,⌝ there was a big closed van, with lettering on its side and a man in a bowler hat—a nasty, sly-looking man he was—sitting on the driver's seat. And Boxer's stall was empty. Everyone began calling out 'Good-bye, Boxer, good-bye!' But Benjamin seemed terribly angry about something and was prancing round us and stamping the earth with his hoofs.

485. BENJAMIN: Fools! Fools! Don't you see what is written on the side of that van?

486. CLOVER: Now I can read letters, but not whole words. Muriel [*the goat*]—she's dead now—could read a little, and she began to spell the letters out. But Benjamin pushed her aside.

487. BENJAMIN: *I'll* read it for you. 'Alfred Simmonds, Horse-Slaughterer and Glue-Boiler. Dealer in Hides and Bone-Meal. Kennels Supplied.' Don't you understand what that means? They are taking Boxer to the knacker's!

488. COCK, MURIEL & MOLLIE: (*Cry of despair followed by*) Boxer! Boxer! Get out of the van, quickly!

489. HORSE: (*Distant whinnying. Fade.*)

490. CLOVER: But at this moment the man on the box

whipped up his horses and drove out of the yard at a good pace, and we all rushed after it shouting out at the tops of our voices. I don't know for certain whether Boxer heard, but suddenly his face, with the white stripe down his nose, appeared for a moment at the little window in the back of the van.

491. COCK: Boxer! Get out!

492. MURIEL: Use your strength. Kick the van to pieces!

493. BENJAMIN: They're taking you to your death!

494. CLOVER: ⌐I don't know whether he understood.⌐ His face disappeared, and then there was a tremendous drumming of hoofs. Once upon a time a few kicks from Boxer would have smashed the van to matchwood. But his strength had gone. Presently the sound of his hoofs grew fainter and died away. And the stupid brutes of horses that pulled the van wouldn't listen when we called out to them to stop. They only put their ears back and went faster than ever. There was nothing we could do. In another moment the van was through the gate and disappearing down the road. We never saw Boxer again.

Three days later Squealer came to tell us that Boxer had died in the hospital at Willingdon.

495. SQUEALER [Open] (almost in tears): Comrades, I have dark and heavy news for you. Our old friend and comrade, Boxer, is dead. In spite of every care a horse could receive, the most up-to-date treatments, the most expensive medicines—paid for without a thought as to the cost by our Leader, Comrade Napoleon—he passed

away yesterday afternoon. I was at his bedside to the last. Comrades, it was the most affecting sight that I have ever seen! At the end, almost too weak to speak, he whispered in my ear that his sole sorrow was to have passed on before the windmill was finished. 'Forward, comrades!' he whispered, 'Forward in the name of the Rebellion! Long live Animal Farm! Long live Comrade Napoleon! Napoleon is always right.'*

496. CLOVER [*Narrator's Box*]: Oh, what a weight it took off our minds to hear that! But perhaps a few of us still felt just a little doubtful, because of [*As for*] those words that Benjamin had read on the side of the van However, Squealer put it right at the next moment [*explained*].

497. SQUEALER: It has come to my knowledge that a most foolish and wicked rumour was circulating at the time when Boxer was taken away. It appears that some animals noticed that the van in which Boxer was removed was marked 'Horse-Slaughterer', and they actually jumped to the conclusion that Boxer was being taken to the knacker's! It is almost unbelievable that any animal could be so stupid. Surely, comrades, surely you understand our Leader, Comrade Napoleon, better than that? But there is a very simple explanation. That van used to belong to the horse-slaughterer, and it was bought from him by the veterinary surgeon. The old name has not yet been

* From 'almost too weak ...' to '... always right' has 'Repeat' written against it.

painted out. *That* is how the mistake arose—if it really was a mistake, and not a slander deliberately circulated by some evilly-disposed animal.

498. COCK: So that was how it was!

499. MOLLIE: Oh, I am so glad to hear that.

500. MURIEL: So he wasn't murdered after all.

501. PIGEON: He died in bed. And Napoleon paid for his medicine!

502. COCK: Three cheers for Comrade Napoleon! (*Cheers.*)
(*Fade.*)

503. CLOVER [*Annexe*]: So that was how Boxer died. And Comrade Napoleon called us together and made us a beautiful speech, telling us that Boxer's life should be an example to all of us. And three days later the pigs held a special banquet in the farmhouse, in honour of Boxer's memory.

504. BENJAMIN: And do you remember that somehow or other—nobody quite knew how—they had got hold of the money to buy themselves a case of whisky.

MUSIC 8 (*Continuing mood of* MUSIC 7.)

505. CLOVER: Yes, Benjamin, I remember. Still, we did have the consolation of knowing that he died happy, and that the story about his being sent to the knacker's was only a mistake. The farm never seemed quite the same after Boxer died.★
(*Music up.*)

506. NARRATOR: Years passed. The seasons came and went, the short animal lives fled by. A time came when there was no one left who remembered the old days before the Rebellion, except Clover, and Benjamin, and a number of the pigs.
(*Music concludes.*)

★ 'The farm . . . Boxer died' originally followed 'I remember'.

183

Napoleon was now a mature boar of twenty-four stone. He was seldom seen in public, and when he did appear it was not only with a bodyguard of dogs but with a black cockerel who marched in front of him, uttering shrill cock-a-doodle-doos. Squealer had grown so fat that he could hardly see out of his eyes. Clover was growing rheumy-eyed and stiff in the joints. Only old Benjamin was much as he had always been, except that he was a little greyer about the muzzle, and, since Boxer's death, more silent and bad-tempered than ever.

The farm had grown more prosperous, it had been enlarged by several fields, its machinery was more up-to-date, and the animals had multiplied. But was life happier or less happy than it had been in the early days of the Rebellion when Jones's expulsion was still recent? Often that question was asked, but there was no clear answer. There were only Squealer's speeches—and very good speeches they were—which proved by long lists of figures that everything was growing better and better. But the animals did not know, they could not remember. So far as they knew, their life was as it had always been. They were generally hungry, they slept on straw, they drank from the pool, they laboured in the fields: in winter they were troubled by the cold, and in summer by the flies. Perhaps it had once been better—they had no way of judging. Only old Benjamin professed to remember every detail of his long life and to know that things never had been, nor ever could be, much better or much worse. And yet——(*Hoofs.*)

507. CLOVER (*to herself*): I know that things haven't turned out as we once hoped they would. But, still, it has been worth it. This farm is our own, our very own. The Republic of the Animals that Major promised us—no, it hasn't happened. It may* happen in the lifetime of any animal now living. But, yes, some day it will happen. That I do believe.

508. NARRATOR: All the animals believed it. [*And yet*] none of them ever gave up hope. More, they never lost, even for an instant, their sense of honour and privilege in being members of Animal Farm. They were still the only farm in the whole county—yes, in all England!—owned and operated by animals. And on Sunday mornings when the green flag fluttered at the masthead, their hearts swelled with imperishable pride, and the talk turned always towards the old heroic days, the expulsion of Jones, the writing of the Seven Commandments, the great battles in which the human invaders had been defeated. They knew that they were not as other animals.† If they went hungry, it was not from feeding tyrannical human beings; if they worked hard, at least they worked for themselves. No creature among them went on two legs. No creature called any other creature 'Master'. All animals were equal.

One day in early summer Squealer ordered the sheep to follow him and led them out to a piece of waste ground at the other end of the farm, which had become overgrown with birch saplings. The sheep stayed there for a whole

---

* 'Not' (found in the novel) omitted from the script.
† 'They . . . other animals' originally marked to be cut but then restored.

week, browsing at the leaves, and the other animals saw nothing of them. Squealer was with them for the greater part of every day. One evening, just after the sheep had returned, the animals were on their way back from work, when——

509. CLOVER [*Tent*]: (*Frightened neighing of a horse.*)

510. BENJAMIN, YOUNG HORSE, YOUNG MARE, YOUNG GOAT, YOUNG SHEEP & YOUNG COCK: What's that? What's happening?

511. CLOVER: (*Neighing again.*)

512. BENJAMIN: It's Clover. Something's frightened her out of her wits.

513. YOUNG HORSE: Come on! She's in the yard!

(*Half-fade.*)

(*Fade in.*)

514. BENJAMIN, YOUNG GOAT, ETC.: (*Long-drawn cry of surprise and dismay.*) A-a-a-a-a-a-ah! Look! Look! Look! He's walking on his hind legs! He's walking on his hind legs!

(*Half-fade.*) [*Chatter underneath*]

515. NARRATOR: It was a pig. Yes, it was Squealer. A little awkwardly, as though not quite used to supporting his considerable bulk in that position, he was strolling across the yard. And a moment later, out from the farmhouse came a long file of pigs, all walking on their hind legs. Some of them did it better than others, one or two were even a little unsteady and looked as though they would have liked the support of a stick, but every one of them made his way right round the yard successfully. And last of all——

516. EFFECTS: (*Faint growling of dogs, and the sharp crow*

of a cockerel.) [*Crow 3 times.*]

517. VOICES [*Young Horse*] (*whispering*): It's Napoleon! Here comes Napoleon!

518. EFFECTS: (*Another crow.*)

519. VOICES [*Young Horse*] (*whispering*): He's got a whip! He's carrying a whip in his trotter! (*Growling grows fainter and fades out during next speech.*)

520. NARRATOR: Majestically upright, casting haughty glances from side to side, Napoleon marched right round the yard, with his dogs frisking after him. The animals watched, too terrified at first to speak. It was as though their world had turned upside down. And then, when the first shock had worn off——

521. VOICES: It's not right! It's not allowed! It's against the Commandments! We won't stand it! We've stood everything else, but we won't stand this! Come on, let's——

522. THE SHEEP: Four legs good, two legs *better*! Four legs good, two legs *better*! Four legs good, two legs *better*! Four legs good, two legs *better*! (*Five times.* ★ *Slow fade.*)

523. NARRATOR: The sheep kept this up for several minutes, and by the time they had quietened down, the chance to utter any protest had passed, for the pigs had marched back into the farmhouse. [*Sheep out.*]

Benjamin felt a nose nuzzling at his shoulder. He looked round. It was Clover. Without saying anything, she tugged gently at his mane and led him round to the end of the big barn,

★ The sheep were originally required to repeat their formula eight times, evidently over-lapping the narration.

where the Seven Commandments were written. The two of them stood gazing at the tarred wall with its white lettering.

524. CLOVER [*Annexe*]: My sight is failing. Even when I was young I could not have read what is written there. But it appears to me that that wall has changed. Are the Seven Commandments the same as they used to be, Benjamin?

525. BENJAMIN: No, they are not the same. There is only one Commandment written there now. Shall I read it to you?

526. CLOVER: Yes, read it, Benjamin.

527. BENJAMIN: It reads: 'All animals are equal, but some animals are more equal than others.'

528. CLOVER: 'All animals are equal, but some animals are more equal than others!' [*I see, I see.*]

529. NARRATOR (*perceptible briskening of pace*): After that it did not seem strange when next day the pigs who were supervising the work of the farm all carried whips in their trotters. It did not seem strange to hear that the pigs had bought themselves a wireless set, were arranging to install a telephone and had taken out subscriptions to *John Bull*, *Tit-Bits* and the *Daily Mirror*. It did not even seem strange when the pigs took Mr Jones's clothes out of the wardrobes and put them on, and when Napoleon was seen strolling in the farmhouse garden with a pipe in his mouth. A week later, in the afternoon, a number of dog-carts drove up to the farm. A deputation of neighbouring farmers had been invited

to make a tour of inspection. They were shown all round the farm, and expressed a great admiration for everything they saw, especially the windmill. That evening loud laughter and bursts of singing came from the farmhouse. And suddenly, at the sound of the mingled voices, the animals were stricken with curiosity. With one accord they tiptoed cautiously into the farmhouse garden and peeped in at the dining-room window.

530. YOUNG COCK [*Narrator's Mike*]: Look, look! They're all sitting round the table together.

531. YOUNG MARE (*whispering*): Six pigs and six men, all sitting side by side.

532. YOUNG HORSE: And Napoleon sitting at the head of the table.

533. YOUNG GOAT: Look how easily the pigs are sitting up in their chairs. Just like human beings!

534. YOUNG SHEEP: They've been playing cards. I suppose they've stopped for another drink.

535. YOUNG COCK: Look how easily Napoleon holds his beer mug in his trotter.

536. YOUNG HORSE: Now they're filling up the mugs again.

537. YOUNG GOAT: Look, that farmer's standing up. Sh!

538. YOUNG MARE: He's going to make a speech.
(*Fade in clapping and "'ear, 'ear!'*)

539. FARMER I: Gen'lmen and (*coughs*)—er, that's to say, Gen'lmen! In 'alf a minute— never 'aving been one for longwinded speeches, as you all know—I shall wind up my remarks an' propose a 'ealth which I believe our 'ost, Mr Napoleon, will be very pleased to 'ear. So before I get started I ask every gen'lman to make sure as 'is glass is full to the brim.

And jest in passing I should like to remark as this is the best glass of beer I've 'ad these three weeks, and a sight better than what they got at the Red Lion in Willingdon.

Now, gen'lmen, I jest want to say 'ow 'appy it makes me to see the twelve of us—now 'ow shall I put it? All sorts and conditions, as you might say—sitting round this table together, with old scores buried and forgotten. Because it ain't no used denying as there was a time when some of us—⌐not me, mind you: no one ever⌐said that of *me*—when some of us wouldn't 'ave sat down at this table, and wouldn't 'ave been invited to, neither. ⌐There was a time when this farm wasn't well thought of in the neighbour'ood.⌐ And why? Well, it was doo to what you might call a misunderstanding— a natural one, I think we got to admit. It was thought–that's to say some folks thought–as a farm run on these lines might set a kind of a bad example and start putting ideas into the other ani- mals' 'eads all over the county. It was even thought, and I won't say as the idea wasn't natural enough, that the animals on a farm like this wouldn't be kept under the way they ought to be. Because every farmer knows that animals—and when I say animals, gen'lmen, I mean the lower animals, and no reflection on our 'osts at this table—'ave got to be kept under with a firm 'and. Well, gen'lmen, 'ow 'appy we all must be to know that them ideas

was root and branch mistaken. Now this afternoon we been right round this farm and seen the 'ole works. And what do we find? Not only reg'lar up-to-date, modern-style farming, but what you might call a discipline as we'd most of us be only too glad to see pre-vailing on our own farms. We know now, if we didn't know before, as Mr Napoleon there is *not* the one to go putting ideas into the lower animals' 'eads. I believe I'm within my rights in saying that the animals on this farm do more work and get less food than on any farm in the 'ole county. And 'oo could ask better than that? I say therefore that if ever anyone—not me, mind you—'as entertained ideas 'ostile to this farm, let him put them away and regard Mr Napoleon for what 'e is— (*drumming on table*)—a public benefactor. And now, gen'lmen, I know we're all anxious to get back to that pleasant game of cards as we was enjoying jest now. I will therefore cut my remarks short and propose that toast as I spoke to you of. Are them glasses all full? Then: to the prosperity of— Hanimal—Farm!

(*Loud applause, banging of mugs on table, shouts of ''ear 'ear!', and noisy drinking.*)

(*Half-fade. Hold under.*)

540. YOUNG COCK [*Close*]: Look, Napoleon's standing up.

541. YOUNG HORSE: Now he's going to make a speech too. (*Up applause, etc.*)

542. NAPOLEON: Gentlemen, I shall not detain you for more than a very few moments. I wish merely to express my warm thanks, on

191

behalf of the farm, for the very neighbourly speech to which we have just listened, and to associate myself with the friendly sentiments that were expressed in it. No one is more happy than I am that the period of suspicion and misunderstanding should have come to an end. In the past there have been rumours—circulated, I have reason to think, by some malignant enemy— that there was something subversive and even revolutionary in the outlook of myself and my colleagues. We have even been credited with attempts to stir up rebellion among the animals on neighbouring farms. Nothing could be further from the truth! Our sole wish, now as always, is to live at peace with our neighbours. And I think you will find, gentlemen, when business relations have been fully established, that we are well able to compete with you on your own terms. (*Uneasy laughter from the human beings.*) This farm, I may add, is a co-operative enterprise. The title deeds, which are in my own possession, are owned by the pigs jointly.

And now, gentlemen, I have only one small criticism to make of that excellent speech which we heard just now. My neighbour referred all the way through to 'Animal Farm'. He could not know—for I am only now announcing the fact for the first time— that the name 'Animal Farm' has been abolished. Henceforth this farm will be known by what, I believe, was its

true and original name—the 'Manor Farm'.

(*Applause.*)

543. CLOVER (*whispering*): What's happening? Something's happening to their faces!

544. NAPOLEON: Gentlemen, I will give you the same toast as before, but in a diffent form. Fill your glasses to the brim. Gentlemen, here is my toast: to the prosperity of the Manor Farm!

(*Applause, banging on the table, shouts of ''ear! 'ear!' and noisy drinking, as before.*)

545. YOUNG HORSE: They've finished the speeches.

546. YOUNG MARE: Look, they're starting to play cards again.

547. YOUNG COCK: Look at Napoleon dealing the cards.

548. YOUNG GOAT: How neatly he does it! Just like a human being!

549. CLOVER (*whispering*): But what's happening to the faces of the pigs?

550. BENJAMIN (*whispering*): Come away. They don't want us. We're not wanted here.

551. NARRATOR: The animals crept silently away. But they had hardly gone twenty yards when suddenly——

(*Uproar of a quarrel at a little distance.*)

552. ANIMAL VOICES: What's happened? They're quarrelling! Come on back, quick!

553. NARRATOR: The animals rushed back and looked through the window again, and——

(*Uproar.*)

554. FARMER I: Set of bleeding crooks, that's what you are.

555. NAPOLEON: Are you impugning my honour?

556. FARMER I: Honour? You ain't got no bleeding honour.

557. NAPOLEON: Withdraw that insult immediately!

558. FARMER I: Don't you get trying it on with me.

'Ow come that other ace of spades
is on the table? You know as well as
I do there's only one ace in the
pack. 'Ow many more of 'em are you
keeping 'idden? Come on, turn out
them pockets and let's 'ave a look.

559. NAPOLEON: How dare you suggest inspecting my
pockets? My word should be enough
for you.

560. FARMER I: What! Me take the say-so of a bleeding
pig? Why—
(*Voices merging into quarrel, as before.
Fade out.*)

561. NARRATOR: The quarrel continued. There were
shoutings, bangings on the table, sharp
suspicious glances, furious denials. The
eyes of the animals outside flitted from
one face to another. Some of them had
five chins, some had four, some had
three. But what was it that seemed to
be melting and changing in the faces of
the pigs?

562. CLOVER (*whispering*): It started to happen when he
said 'the Manor Farm'. Tell me, Ben-
jamin, is it really happening? Or is it
only because my eyes are growing so
dim?

563. BENJAMIN (*whispering*): No, Clover, there is nothing
wrong with your eyes. It is happening.

564. NARRATOR: Twelve voices were shouting in anger,
and they were all alike. No question,
now, what had happened to the faces
of the pigs. The creatures outside
looked from pig to man, and from man
to pig, and from pig to man again: but
already it was impossible to say which
was which.
(*'Beasts of England' to conclude.*)

565. ANNOUNCER: You have been listening to George Orwell's *Animal Farm: A Fairy Story*, in a version for broadcasting made by the author. The pigs, Major, Napoleon, Snowball and Squealer were played respectively by Raf de la Torre, Norman Shelley, Andrew Churchman and John Chandos; the horses, Clover, Molly and Boxer by Betty Hardy, Marjorie Westbury and Richard George; Benjamin the donkey by Bryan Powley. The farmer in the concluding sequence was Deryck Guyler; the Narrator, Ronald Simpson. Also taking part were Frank Atkinson, Margot van der Burgh, Vivienne Chatterton, Charles Maunsell, Hugh Munro, Gladys Spencer, the BBC Variety Chorus;★

The music was composed and directed by Antony Hopkins, and the production was by Rayner Heppenstall.

On January 14th only: There will be a second performance of *Animal Farm* in the Third Programme tomorrow evening at 7.25 p.m.†

★ There is a two-line gap after 'Chorus;'—possibly for details of the orchestra. They have not survived.

† There were slightly different opening and closing announcements when the adaptation was repeated live on 15 January 1947 and when a recording of the first broadcast was played on 2 February 1947.

TEXTUAL NOTE

The number of verbal corrections to be made to restore *Animal Farm* to what Orwell wrote is small; to these must be added a correction of one certain error and a hint at another. By far the trickiest problem to resolve is that of punctuation. That only arises, paradoxically, because Orwell's typescript, as marked up for setting by the printer, survives and, indirectly, because we can contrast the way *Nineteen Eighty-Four* was punctuated by Orwell from that typescript, and the re-punctuation he appears to have accepted by the American publisher or printer. The contrast is revealing, especially for the way it illuminates the rhetorical style Orwell adopted, consciously or not, for his punctuation of *Nineteen Eighty-Four*. A 'Uniform' edition should not, of course, make uniform what should be distinctively different. Thus, in this edition, Orwell's punctuation has been allowed to make its presence felt.

In addition to a complete typescript (which Orwell produced), marked up for the printer, there is a set of marked proofs, one hand appearing therein looking like Orwell's; these are both in the Orwell Archive, University College London. This typescript provides the copy-text for this edition. It has been collated with the proof; the first English edition of August 1945 (Secker & Warburg); its reprint of later in that same month; the first American edition, 1946 (Harcourt, Brace); the first cheap edition, 1949; and, as a specimen of the current hard-back edition, that printed in 1977. The Penguin reprints, particularly the first, of 1951, and the Modern Classics of 1963, have been consulted (see 8/27 below). Current editions in the United States are published by Harcourt Brace Jovanovich and in England by Secker & Warburg.

The text of the first edition was to begin on p. 13 (as the proof shows), not p. 9, as in the first edition, as it appears Orwell was to provide a Preface. The typescript of this, entitled 'The

Freedom of the Press', was only discovered years later (by Ian Angus). This was then published in the *Times Literary Supplement* on 15 September 1972 and is reproduced here as Appendix I. Orwell also wrote a Preface especially for the Ukrainian translation, published in November 1947. That exists only in Ukrainian translation and for English readers has been translated back into English. It was published as the final item of the third volume of *The Collected Essays, Journalism and Letters* in 1968 and appears as Appendix II in this volume. Later Orwell was to adapt *Animal Farm* for radio and his script, reproduced here for the first time, appears as Appendix III.

All editions of *Animal Farm* reproduce the punctuation of whoever prepared the text for the printer. This person—quite probably Roger Senhouse—made a little over two hundred changes in punctuation in addition to correcting errors (e.g. missing final quotation marks and full-points, which are not noted here). Most are additional commas; quite a number are changes from colon to semi-colon.

This presents the editor with a difficult problem. Orwell saw these changes in proof and very occasionally changed punctuation altered in preparing the typescript; he cannot have but noticed some changes (e.g. the uses of dashes—see 13/29); he was well at the time, as he was not when proof-reading *Nineteen Eighty-Four*, and he respected the work of Roger Senhouse. We know that Orwell was prepared to take advice. On the other hand, as the American edition of *Nineteen Eighty-Four* shows, he would accept a style of punctuation completely at variance with his own and that of the English edition. Personal experience as an editor and as one edited indicates to me that styling of this kind is often accepted by authors as if it were simply a matter of having to go along with the publisher's 'house style': indeed, that argument is often put by publishers.

After much thought, I have decided to revert to the way that Orwell punctuated his own work as revealed by the typescript, noting such changes as seem essential or proper. The result makes possible a very interesting comparison of Orwell's styles for *Animal Farm* and *Nineteen Eighty-Four*, suggesting differences in 'authorial voice'. Thus, for this text alone of those

for the nine books, the Textual Note is mainly concerned with what at first sight seem trivia. However, it is important that significant variations in punctuation should be noted in this context. (I have not listed the correction of errors.) The same can apply to capitalisation: see especially 11/21 and 15/17.

The readings given first are those in this edition; TS = Orwell's typescript; Pr = Proof; 1 = first English edition (1945); 2 = reprint of first English edition; US = first American edition (1946); 77 = 1977 edition from the Secker & Warburg Uniform series. For further details about presentation (including regularisation effected silently) see General Introduction, Volume I, pp. xix–xxiii.

Title-page: US *omits* A Fairy Story
Publication details: Pr *has* February 1945; 1 *has* May 1945;
2 *has* First Published August 1945 | Reprinted 1945–
*and so later editions. Ian Willison states that publication
date was actually 17 August 1945 and that the delay was
caused by the prevailing shortage of paper* (Bibliography,
p. 46).

2/9   fourth] sixth TS; *changed in* Pr *to* fourth (*and similarly* 4/30, 33)

3/5   herself] himself TS; *altered to* herself *in pencil*

3/16   comrades] Comrades TS; *the word is capitalised in Ch I
(with exceptions at* 6/13, 15) *but is regularly given a lower
case 'c' thereafter except when used as a title (e.g.* 37/9,
13)

3/33   Nature] nature TS, *all edns; but* 'N' *implied, as at*
25/16 *in* TS

5/22   Rebellion!] ~. TS, *all edns*

8/27   making] TS *and all edns except Penguin from Modern
Classics series onwards (e.g. 1963 edn) have* making *which
Penguin emends to* feeling. *This emendation has no authority
but gives more obvious sense (as would the omission of*
making), *which* making *seems not to. However Orwell
uses* to make *idiomatically elsewhere. Thus,* Homage
to Catalonia 60/19: I made sure I was hit by a bullet

and Down and Out 86/35: I made sure it was *for the simpler* I was sure

8/32   onto] on to TS *and all edns; Orwell's 'rule'—see General Introduction—requires* onto

10/11   anyway] any way TS

11/21   windsor] TS; Windsor *all edns; the use of the capital here (the standard form in this context) may imply a greater royal association than Orwell indicated in his typescript; contrast* 15/17.

12/13   used] using TS; *altered in pencil (by a compositor?) to* used

13/24   woke] awoke 77

13/29   theirs ——] ~, TS; *Orwell could scarcely have not noticed this change and had he objected to it would surely have marked the proof—but, of course, it is a clear improvement which he might well have appreciated; so also* 29/10, 32/34, 34/6, 57/13, 58/29–30 *and* 78/23.

14/2   hayfield] *this will suffice to explain the problem of hyphenation, to which attention is not otherwise drawn. In TS the word is typed by Orwell as* hayfield, hay-field, *and* hay field (14/2, 16/8 *and* 16/27 *of this edition). Where Orwell shows a clear and sustained preference (as for* today *over* to-day) *his practice has been followed; otherwise I have rationalised using, where listed, F. Howard Collins's* Authors' & Printers' Dictionary, Oxford, *ninth edition, eleventh impression, 1946.*

15/6   on] on to 1, 2, US *etc.* TS *and* Pr *simply have* gave on—*which is Orwell's idiom and is used in* The Road to Wigan Pier *and* Coming Up for Air

15/17   seven commandments] Seven Commandments 1 *and all edns.* TS *uses lower case in this chapter for these two words except for the display caps at* 15/26 *(which do not distinguish between small and large caps). From the next chapter onwards, each word is given an initial capital letter. This could have been an oversight on Orwell's part in Ch II, but it may have been intended to—and certainly does—distinguish between the original, naive, conception and the establishment of the* commandments *as*

sacrosanct, prior to their manipulation and distortion.
The change was made in preparing TS for the printer on
the traditional house-style basis, as indicated in a marginal
note, 'caps later in copy'. Reversion to what Orwell typed
allows the reader to judge for himself or herself.

16/16   to] for TS, Pr; Pr *amended to* to

17/4   hard;] ~, TS *but not marked up for change;* Pr *etc have*
        semi-colon. An amendment seems desirable.

17/23   days] days' *all edns*

20/5   animals] the animals 77

21/12   his] *om.* 77

21/20   five] six Pr *etc; Orwell was correct in TS: there are five*
        different letters to be learnt

25/35   the pigeons] and pigeons 77

26/23   dropped their dung on] TS, Pr; muted upon 1 *etc.*
        Changed as considered improper by publisher.

28/13   alarm;] ~, TS; *altered in TS to semi-colon; a desirable*
        emendation

31/35   bad'ₐ] ~, TS, Pr; *marked for omission in* Pr *(by*
        Orwell?)—similarly 32/3

32/9   the] *om.* 77

34/5   Windmill] Windmills 77

34/22   rebellions] rebellion 77

37/33   feeling] feelings 77

39/12   his] this 77

40/2   work;] ~, TS—*an acceptable emendation*

41/2   ropes] rope 77

43/21   own] *om.* 77

43/26   Farm!',] ~ₐ TS; *comma added in* Pr

43/27   England'ₐ] ~, TS; *comma deleted in* Pr

44/32   county] country 77

45/27   *sheets",'] sheets'?"* TS; ? *emended in pencil in TS to*
        comma

51/35   it;] ~, TS; TS *not marked up for change but* Pr *has*
        semi-colon

53/25   mindₐ] ~, TS; *deleted in* Pr

54/24   how,] ~ₐ TS

57/2-3 an especially devoted follower of Napoleon] *an*

addition, typed in later between the lines, to TS; TS is
a carbon copy whereas the addition is top-copy typing.

59/8   pellets] bullets TS *etc.*; *Jones has a shotgun—see*
27/12, 54/1, 68/23, 71/4, 19; probably an authorial
slip.

59/20   that,] ~ ˄ TS; *added in* Pr
Napoleon,] ~ ˄ TS; *added in* TS

60/3   heard] heard of 77

64/9   to] of TS, *altered in pencil to* to

64/23–24   As the] As 77

64/33, 34   death, . . . cows, . . . furnace,] TS *as here but at first*
all three were marked up as semi-colons when text was
prepared for press and were so set; then Pr *marked for*
reversion to commas

66/18   work;] ~: TS; *marked up as semi-colon*

68/33   yet] *om.* 77

69/22   except Napoleon] Napoleon included TS, Pr;
Orwell in a letter to Senhouse, 17.3.45, said:

> . . . when the windmill is blown up, I wrote 'all the
> animals including Napoleon flung themselves on
> their faces.' I would like to alter it to 'all the animals
> except Napoleon.' If the book has been printed it's
> not worth bothering about, but I just thought the
> alteration would be fair to J[oseph] S[talin], as he
> did stay in Moscow during the German advance.

> (*CEJL*, iii, 98)

71/15   again!] ~? 77

71/34   celebrations] celebration TS; 's' *added in* Pr

72/5   the] *om.* TS; The *added to* Pr; 1 *etc have* the

74/10   for ever] forever TS

75/3   too-rigid] TS; *hyphen marked out when text*
prepared for press and so all edns

76/27   in] *this should, I think, be* since *but the* TS *is perfectly*
plain and it does make sense

77/23   Demonstrations] Demonstration Pr, 1, US *etc*

79/14   grass] *om.* Pr, 1, US *etc*

79/19   words ˄] *comma added to* TS *in pencil*

79/32   out] *om.* 77

81/1   had] had had TS; *error corr in pencil*

81/19   ever] *om.* 77

82/4   knacker's] *apostrophe added to* TS (*which is already present in* TS *at* 83/25)

82/26   him;] ~: TS

84/26   day. And] TS; *changed in pencil in* TS *to* day, and

87/24   been, ... be,] ~ ∧ ... ~ ∧ TS; *first comma added in preparing* TS *but second marked for deletion and omitted from* 1, *etc*

87/25   hardship∧] *comma added to* TS *but marked for omission in* Pr—*but not omitted and so appearing in* 1 *etc*

89/34   for] *om.* 77

90/5   anything∧] *at least some copies of* 1 *seem to show a comma here followed by a full-point (e.g. that owned by Ian Angus);* 2 *reprints only the comma—but there is no punctuation here in* TS *as typed, the comma being a pencilled addition*

92/9   licence] license TS

93/27   own] *later typed addition to* TS (*compare* 57/2–3)

93/28   jointly.] *originally followed in* TS *by:* The lower animals could be regarded as their employees. *These words were then marked (in ink) to form a separate paragraph on their own; and then crossed out in ink. Does not appear in* Pr.

94/20   To] TS *originally* to *but* 't' *made* 'T' *in pencil*

94/21   The] the TS, Pr, 1 *etc;* US *has* The, *as here, as line* 16 *above, where* TS *also has* The

95/9   again:] TS *colon changed to semi-colon in pencil*

95/11   November 1943–February 1944.] *does not appear in* TS; *added to* Pr *in ink*

95/12   THE END] *as* TS (*and as frequently if not invariably in Orwell's books); om from* Pr *and all edns.*

PETER DAVISON
Albany, London